Beginning Python®: Using Python 2.6 and Python 3.1

Part I: Dipping Your Toe into Python

Part II: Python Language and the Standard Library

Part III: Putting Python to Work

Continues

Part IV: Appendices

Beginning
Python®

Beginning
Python®

Using Python 2.6 and Python 3.1

James Payne

WILEY

Wiley Publishing, Inc.

Beginning Python®: Using Python 2.6 and Python 3.1

Published by
Wiley Publishing, Inc.
10475 Crosspoint Boulevard
Indianapolis, IN 46256
www.wiley.com

ISBN: 978-0-470-41463-7

Manufactured in the United States of America

10 9 8 7 6 5 4 3 2

For general information on our other products and services please contact our Customer Care Department within the United States at (877) 762-2974, outside the United States at (317) 572-3993 or fax (317) 572-4002.

Wiley also publishes its books in a variety of electronic formats. Some content that appears in print may not be available in electronic books.

Library of Congress Control Number: 2009936814

To my patient and loving wife, Whitney, who believed in me before I did. And to my parents, Ronnie and Sharon Payne, who raised me to believe I could do anything I put my mind to, even when I told them I wanted to be Santa Claus. For my brother, Ron, who read my work even when it was bad, Dorjan, Eric, Clem, and Nick because they know things about me and will tell them if I don't include them.

About the Author

James Payne (Margate, FL) is Editor-in-Chief of Developer Shed, Inc. and has been writing and programming since the age of seven years old. Proficient in many languages, he has written over 400 articles covering practically every major programming language. As a contractor, he develops proprietary software for the financial industry using Python and likes to dabble in Django in his spare time.

Credits

Executive Editor
Carol Long

Project Editor
Ed Connor

Technical Editor
Chris McAvoy

Production Editors
Amy Weintraub and Tim Tate

Copy Editor
Kim Cofer

Editorial Director
Robyn B. Siesky

Editorial Manager
Mary Beth Wakefield

Marketing Manager
David Mayhew

Production Manager
Tim Tate

Vice President and Executive Group Publisher
Richard Swadley

Vice President and Executive Publisher
Barry Pruett

Associate Publisher
Jim Minatel

Project Coordinator, Cover
Lynsey Stanford

Proofreaders
Scott Klemp and Kristy Eldredge, Word One

Indexer
Ron Strauss

Cover Image
© istockphoto.com/Frank_U

Acknowledgments

I would like to acknowledge the gang at Developer Shed: Jack and Jay Kim, whose constant hatred is an inspiration, Charles Fagundes, who made me an editor and not just a writer, Keith Lee, who provided coding support, and a special thanks to Jenny Ruggieri, who got me the job that got me this book. Lastly, I'd like to thank all of the people that worked on the previous editions of this book for laying the groundwork, and the Editors Carol Long, Jenny Watson, Ed Connor, and Chris McAvoy who helped me meet deadlines no matter how much I didn't want to.

I would also like to acknowledge Guido Von Rossum, without whom there would be no language to write about.

Contents

Contents

Contents

Contents

Contents

Contents

Chapter 18: Numerical Programming 367

Chapter 19: An Introduction to Django 387

Contents

Introduction

Welcome to Python 3.1!

I've been working with Python for about ten years now, and every new version has caused me to fall in love with the language all over again. Version 3.1 is no different. If you are new to Python, rest easy — I'll guide you every step of the way. If, on the other hand, you are an old Python hand exploring the new version, the book is structured so that you can learn the new information you need, without wasting time on already-known information.

I wanted to write this book because I love Python. I love it! And I want to share my love with you. And, maybe you'll grow to love it as I do.

Who This Book Is For

If you're computer-literate, and want to learn a fun programming language to better control your computer, this book is for you.

If you are a system administrator who wants to learn a great language to help you better manage and configure systems and networks, this book is for you.

If you already know Python, but are wondering what cool new features are available in version 3.1, this book is for you.

In summary, this book is for anyone interested in exploring Python programming with the newest and most full-featured, easy-to-use version, 3.1.

What This Book Covers

This book is designed to cover Python 3.1. Python 3.1, released in 2009, is the latest major revision of the Python programming language. Since Python is a cross-platform language, the content and examples in the book are applicable in any platform (unless specified otherwise). When there is a choice to be made as to platform independence, the examples will be as cross-platform as possible.

In addition, since Python 3.1 is relatively new, not all supporting libraries have been updated to work in Python 3.x. In those instances where this is the case and it is felt that the theory still needs to be expounded upon, Python 2.6 will be used in lieu of version 3.1.

How This Book Is Structured

As might be expected from a "Beginning" book, the book begins with an introduction to the language. From there, you'll move through the core of the language, then move on to more advanced and specialized topics. The book is divided up into four parts.

Part I — Dipping Your Toe into Python

The first part will allow you to, as the title suggests, dip your toe in.

Programming Basics and Strings

First you'll be introduced to Python. This chapter will explore what Python is, and why it is so useful and powerful. Also explored will be Python's history from its early development to the newest version, which is the focus of this book. You'll also learn about the scope of Python's reach, and all the different areas of application development in which Python plays a part. Finally, you'll learn to work with your first data type — strings.

Numbers and Operators

This chapter will guide you through the basics of working with numbers and operators. You will learn the different types of numbers, how to perform simple — and complex — equations, and work with the various operators. You will also learn about order of precedence and formatting numbers.

Variables — Names for Values

Ultimately, programming languages help you to manage different types of information — in other words, data. An understanding of data types and how they are represented in Python is essential to programming in Python. This chapter will help you to understand the best ways to represent different data types in Python.

Part II — Python Language and the Standard Library

Of course, the core piece of knowledge you need to use a language is to know the language itself, and familiarize yourself with its syntax and modules. This part will start small, with data types and variables, and gradually introduce additional concepts until you have all the information you need to develop fully functional Python programs.

You'll want to read through these chapters sequentially — each chapter builds on the information presented in the previous chapter.

Making Decisions

Ultimately, there will come a point when your program must make a decision — do I take this path or that path? And what happens when I take that path? In this chapter, you will learn how to compare data, such as deciding if one value is greater than another, and use repetition to repeat repetitive tasks.

Functions

This chapter will help you to expand on your Python knowledge by introducing you to functional programming. Functions allow you to take advantage of powerful concepts like parameter passing and code reuse. You'll learn how to use functions to make your code more efficient and flexible.

Classes and Objects

Here you will be shown what objects are and learn to create classes. You will learn how to define them, create objects in your classes, write methods, and discuss the scope of your objects.

Organizing Programs

When your programs get larger, you'll want to divide them up into separate components. This chapter will discuss Python modules. You'll also explore packages, which are nothing but collections of modules.

Files and Directories

An important part of everyday programming is learning to work with files and directories. This chapter focuses on creating, modifying, and working with files in general. In addition, you will learn how to obtain data from files and how to interact with the various directories.

Other Features of the Language

Here you will learn about some of the other features the language has to offer, including how to make decisions with lists, string substitutions with dictionaries, and some of the featured modules.

Building a Module

Modules help you save time by allowing you to reuse snippets of code. It also ensures fewer errors, as the module you use will have been tested and used many times before. Here, we will learn to create our own modules, as well as import and work with pre-existing modules — something that makes Python particularly powerful.

Text Processing

There are so many things you can do with text in programming and in essence, text is the key to effectively communicating with your user. After all, without it, the only thing you are left with is images. In this chapter you learn to process text in a variety of ways, including: working with regular expressions, searching for files, and searching for files of a particular type.

Part III — Putting Python to Work

So, now that you know what Python is, and how to work with the language, what's next, you ask? This final part explores many of the programming topics you'll likely encounter or want to explore. These can be looked at sequentially, or in any order you like . . . these chapters are independent of each other.

Testing

There is only one way to ensure your program works before it is in the hands of the user, and that is by testing your program. Here, you will learn not only the concepts behind properly testing your programs, but the tools and frameworks available to you.

Writing a GUI with Python

Thus far in the book, all the programs work through the command line. In this chapter, you'll be introduced to the concept of GUI programming. You'll also walk through creating a few GUI programs with Tkinter, the most popular GUI toolkit used by Python programmers.

Accessing Databases

Databases store information that your program can use for an infinite amount of reasons. It also acts as a place for you to store information, and later retrieve that information for a given task. In this chapter you learn about the different types of databases and how to work with them.

Using Python for XML

XML is a powerful tool for processing data on the Internet. Here, you will learn the basics of XML including the difference between schema and DTD, basic syntax, how to create and validate your own XML, and more advanced topics such as using lxml.

Network Programming

Now that the Internet has wormed its way into our everyday lives, and has become more of a necessity than a privilege, learning to programmatically send e-mails and allow users to communicate across the web is essential. In this chapter, you will learn how to do just that.

Extension Programming with C

This chapter delves into programming with the C language, including working with C frameworks and modules, the basics of C, and passing parameters from Python to C, and then returning value back to Python.

Numerical Programming

Numbers were touched on briefly in the beginning of this book; now it is time to delve more deeply below the surface. Here you will learn all there is to know about integers and floating point numbers, as well as complex numbers, arrays, and working with built-in math functions and modules.

An Introduction to Django

Django is a web application framework written in Python, which utilizes the model-view-architecture pattern. Originally created for managing news websites, Django has become popular for its ease of use, allowing programmers to create complex websites in a simple fashion, including database-focused sites. Here we will learn the basics of Django.

Web Applications and Web Services

Here you will learn the foundations of working with web applications and web services. You will learn about the REST architecture, as well as how to work with HTTP Requests and Responses.

Integrating Java with Python

In this chapter you learn the basics of Java, building a strong foundation before you delve blending the two languages together. You will learn the various modules that allow you to work with Java in Python and how to create simple, yet effective applications.

Part IV: Appendices

In the back of the book, there are some useful appendices to further your knowledge and fun with Python:

- ❑ Answers to the Exercises
- ❑ Online Resources — where do you go from here?
- ❑ What's New in Python 3.1
- ❑ Glossary of terms

What You Need to Use This Book

There are some minimal requirements to use the material in this book. The following are recommendations, as Python itself runs on many different platforms. However, the first chapters assume that you have access to a GUI such as is available in Windows, Mac OS X, or the X Window system on UNIX and Linux. Naturally, some chapters, such as the GUI chapter, require the GUI as well, and chapters involving networking will make much more sense if a network connection is in place.

Following are the suggested minimum requirements:

- ❑ A PC running Linux, a BSD UNIX, or Windows running at 500MHz or faster, or a G3 or later Macintosh running Mac OS X version 10.2 or later
- ❑ 256MB of memory (at a minimum)
- ❑ A graphical user interface native to the platform you are on
- ❑ Necessary access to the computer you are on so that you may install required software
- ❑ Network access to a TCP/IP network such as the Internet or a campus network
- ❑ Internet access to download required software

Conventions

To help you get the most from the text and keep track of what's happening, we've used a number of conventions throughout the book.

Examples that you can download and try out for yourself generally appear in a box like this:

> **Example title**
>
> This section gives a brief overview of the example.
>
> **Source**
>
> This section includes the source code:
>
> ```
> Source code
> Source code
> Source code
> ```
>
> **Output**
>
> This section lists the output:
>
> ```
> Example output
> Example output
> Example output
> ```

Try It Out

The *Try It Out* is an exercise you should work through, following the text in the book.

1. They usually consist of a set of steps.

2. Each step has a number.

3. Follow the steps through with your copy of the database.

How It Works

After each *Try It Out*, the code you've typed will be explained in detail.

> **Boxes like this one hold important, not-to-be forgotten information that is directly relevant to the surrounding text.**

Notes, tips, hints, tricks, and asides to the current discussion are offset and placed in italics like this.

As for styles in the text:

❏ We highlight new terms and important words when we introduce them.

❏ We show keyboard strokes like this: Ctrl+A.

❑ We show file names, URLs, and code within the text like so: `persistence.properties`.

❑ We present code in two different ways:

```
We use a monofont type with no highlighting for most code examples.
We use bold highlighting to emphasize code that's particularly important
in the present context.
```

Source Code

As you work through the examples in this book, you may choose either to type in all the code manually or to use the source code files that accompany the book. All of the source code used in this book is available for download at `http://www.wrox.com`. Once at the site, simply locate the book's title (either by using the Search box or by using one of the title lists) and click the Download Code link on the book's detail page to obtain all the source code for the book.

Because many books have similar titles, you may find it easiest to search by ISBN; this book's ISBN is 978-0-470-41463-7.

Once you download the code, just decompress it with your favorite compression tool. Alternately, you can go to the main Wrox code download page at `http://www.wrox.com/dynamic/books/download.aspx` to see the code available for this book and all other Wrox books.

Errata

We make every effort to ensure that there are no errors in the text or in the code. However, no one is perfect, and mistakes do occur. If you find an error in one of our books, like a spelling mistake or faulty piece of code, we would be very grateful for your feedback. By sending in errata, you may save another reader hours of frustration and at the same time you will be helping us provide even higher quality information.

To find the errata page for this book, go to `http://www.wrox.com` and locate the title using the Search box or one of the title lists. Then, on the book details page, click the Errata link. On this page you can view all errata that has been submitted for this book and posted by Wrox editors. A complete book list including links to each book's errata is also available at `www.wrox.com/misc-pages/booklist.shtml`.

If you don't spot "your" error on the Errata page, go to `www.wrox.com/contact/techsupport.shtml` and complete the form there to send us the error you have found. We'll check the information and, if appropriate, post a message to the book's errata page and fix the problem in subsequent editions of the book.

p2p.wrox.com

For author and peer discussion, join the P2P forums at `p2p.wrox.com`. The forums are a Web-based system for you to post messages relating to Wrox books and related technologies and interact with other readers and technology users. The forums offer a subscription feature to e-mail you topics of interest of your choosing when new posts are made to the forums. Wrox authors, editors, other industry experts, and your fellow readers are present on these forums.

At p2p.wrox.com you will find a number of different forums that will help you not only as you read this book, but also as you develop your own applications. To join the forums, just follow these steps:

1. Go to p2p.wrox.com and click the Register link.

2. Read the terms of use and click Agree.

3. Complete the required information to join as well as any optional information you wish to provide and click Submit.

4. You will receive an e-mail with information describing how to verify your account and complete the joining process.

   You can read messages in the forums without joining P2P, but in order to post your own messages, you must join.

Once you join, you can post new messages and respond to messages other users post. You can read messages at any time on the Web. If you would like to have new messages from a particular forum e-mailed to you, click the Subscribe to this Forum icon by the forum name in the forum listing.

For more information about how to use the Wrox P2P, be sure to read the P2P FAQs for answers to questions about how the forum software works as well as many common questions specific to P2P and Wrox books. To read the FAQs, click the FAQ link on any P2P page.

Part I
Dipping Your Toe into Python

Programming Basics
and Strings

This chapter is a gentle introduction to the practice of programming in Python. Python is a very rich language with many features, so it is important to learn to walk before you learn to run. Chapters 1 through 3 provide a basic introduction to common programming ideas, explained in easily digestible paragraphs with simple examples.

If you are already an experienced programmer interested in Python, you may want to read this chapter quickly and take note of the examples, but until Chapter 3 you will be reading material with which you've probably already gained some familiarity in another language.

If you are a novice programmer, by the end of this chapter you will learn the following:

❑   Some guiding principles for programming

❑   Directions for your first interactions with a programming language — Python.

The exercises at the end of the chapter provide hands-on experience with the basic information that you have learned.

How Programming is Different from Using a Computer

The first thing you need to understand about computers when you're programming is that you control the computer. Sometimes the computer doesn't do what you expect, but even when it doesn't do what you want the first time, it should do the same thing the second and third time — until you take charge and change the program.

The trend in personal computers has been away from reliability and toward software being built on top of other, unreliable, software. The results that you live with might have you believing that computers are malicious and arbitrary beasts, existing to taunt you with unbearable amounts of extra work and various harassments while you're already trying to accomplish something. However, after you've learned how to program, you gain an understanding of how this situation has come to pass, and perhaps you'll find that you can do better than some of the programmers whose software you've used.

Note that programming in a language like Python, an *interpreted* language, means that you are not going to need to know a whole lot about computer hardware, memory, or long sequences of 0s and 1s. You are going to write in text form like you are used to reading and writing but in a different and simpler language. Python is the language, and like English or any other language(s) you speak, it makes sense to other people who already speak the language. Learning a programming language can be even easier, however, because programming languages aren't intended for discussions, debates, phone calls, plays, movies, or any kind of casual interaction. They're intended for giving instructions and ensuring that those instructions are followed. Computers have been fashioned into incredibly flexible tools that have found a use in almost every business and task that people have found themselves doing, but they are still built from fundamentally understandable and controllable pieces.

Programming is Consistency

In spite of the complexity involved in covering all of the disciplines into which computers have crept, the basic computer is still relatively simple in principle. The internal mechanisms that define how a computer works haven't changed a lot since the 1950s when transistors were first used in computers.

In all that time, this core simplicity has meant that computers can, and should, be held to a high standard of consistency. What this means to you, as the programmer, is that anytime you tell a computer to metaphorically jump, you must tell it how high and where to land, and it will perform that jump — over and over again for as long as you specify. The program should not arbitrarily stop working or change how it works without you facilitating the change.

Programming is Control

Programming a computer is very different from creating a program, as the word applies to people in real life. In real life, you ask people to do things, and sometimes you have to struggle mightily to ensure that your wishes are carried out — for example, if you plan a party for 30 people and assign two of them to bring the chips and dip and they bring the drinks instead, it is out of your control.

With computers that problem doesn't exist. The computer does exactly what you tell it to do. As you can imagine, this means that you must pay some attention to detail to ensure that the computer does just what you want it to do.

One of the goals of Python is to program in *blocks* that enable you to think about larger and larger projects by building each project as pieces that behave in well-understood ways. This is a key goal of a programming style known as *object-oriented programming*. The guiding principle of this style is that you can create reliable pieces that still work when you piece them together, that are understandable, and that are useful. This gives you, the programmer, control over how the parts of your programs run, while enabling you to extend your program as the problems you're solving evolve.

Programming Copes with Change

Programs are run on computers that handle real-world problems; and in the real world, plans and circumstances frequently change. Because of these shifting circumstances, programmers rarely get the opportunity to create perfectly crafted, useful, and flexible programs. Usually, you can achieve only two of these goals. The changes that you will have to deal with should give you some perspective and lead you to program cautiously. With sufficient caution, you can create programs that know when they're being asked to exceed their capabilities, and they can fail gracefully by notifying their users that they've stopped. In the best cases, you can create programs that explain what failed and why. Python offers especially useful features that enable you to describe what conditions may have occurred that prevented your program from working.

What All That Means Together

Taken together, these beginning principles mean that you're going to be introduced to programming as a way of telling a computer what tasks you want it to do, in an environment where you are in control. You will be aware that sometimes accidents can happen and that these mistakes can be accommodated through mechanisms that offer you some discretion regarding how these conditions will be handled, including recovering from problems and continuing to work.

The First Steps

The absolute first step you need to take before you can begin programming in Python is to download and install Python version 3.1. Navigate to `www.python.org/download` and choose the newest version of Python. You will be taken to a page with instructions on how to download the appropriate version for your computer. For instance, if you are running Windows, it may say Windows x86 MSI Installer (3.0).

> Programs are written in a form called *source code*. Source code contains the instructions that the language follows, and when the source code is read and processed, the instructions that you've put in there become the actions that the computer takes.

Just as authors and editors have specialized tools for writing for magazines, books, or online publications, programmers also need specialized tools. As a starting Python programmer, the right tool for the job is the Python IDLE GUI (graphical user interface).

Once the download is finished, double-click it to run the program. Your best bet is to accept the default prompts Python offers you. This process may take a few minutes, depending on your system.

After setup is complete, you will want to test to make sure it is installed properly. Click the Windows Start menu and go to All Programs. You will see Python 3.0 in the menu. Choose IDLE (Python GUI) and wait for the program to load.

Once IDLE launches, type in "Test, test, testing" and press the Enter key. If Python is running correctly, it should return the value

```
'Test, test, testing'
```

in blue letters and with single quotes (I'll get more into this soon). Congratulations — you have successfully installed Python and are well on your way to becoming a programming guru.

Installing Python 3.1 on Non-Windows Systems

If you are the proud owner of a Mac and are running Mac OS X, you are in luck; it comes with Python installed. Unfortunately, it may not be the most up-to-date version. For security and compatibility purposes, I would suggest logging on to www.python.org/download/mac. Check to see that your Mac OS X version is the right version for the Python you are installing.

If you have a Linux computer, you may also already have Python installed, but again, it may be an earlier version. I would once more suggest you go to the Python website to find the latest version (and of course, the one appropriate to your system). The website www.python.org/download should have instructions on how to download the right version for your computer.

Using the Python Shell

Before starting to write programs, you'll need to learn how to experiment with the Python shell. For now, you can think of the Python shell as a way to peer within running Python code. It places you inside of a running instance of Python, into which you can feed programming code; at the same time, Python will do what you have asked it to do and will show you a little bit how it responds to its environment. Because running programs often have a *context* — things that you as the programmer have tailored to your needs — it is an advantage to have the shell because it lets you experiment with the context you have created.

Now that you have installed Python version 3.1, you can begin to experiment with the shell's basic behavior. For starters, type in some text:

```
>>>"Hello World. You will never see this."
```

Note that typing the previous sentence into the shell didn't actually do anything; nothing was changed in the Python environment. Instead, the sentence was evaluated by Python, to determine what, if anything, you wanted Python to do. In this case, you merely wanted it to read the text.

Although Python didn't technically do anything with your words, it did give some indication that it read them. Python indicated this by displaying the text you entered (known as a *string*) in quotes. A *string* is a data type, and each data type is displayed differently by Python. As you progress through this book, you will see the different ways Python displays each one.

Beginning to Use Python — Strings

At this point, you should feel free to experiment with using the shell's basic behavior. Type some text, in quotes; for starters, you could type the following:

```
>>> "This text really won't do anything"
"This text really won't do anything"
```

You should notice one thing immediately: After you entered a quote ("), the Python shell changed the color of everything up to the quote that completed the sentence. Of course, the preceding text is absolutely true. It did nothing: It didn't change your Python environment; it was merely *evaluated* by the running Python instance, in case it did determine that in fact you'd told it to do something. In this case, you've asked it only to read the text you wrote, but doing this doesn't constitute a change to the environment.

However, you can see that Python indicated that it saw what you entered. It showed you the text you entered, and it displayed it in the manner it will always display a string — in quotes. As you learn about other *data types*, you'll find that Python has a way of displaying each one differently.

What is a String?

A *string* is one of several data types that exist within the Python language. A data type, as the name implies, is a category that a particular type of data fits into. Every type of data you enter into a computer is segregated into one of these data types, whether they be numbers or letters, as is the case in this scenario. Giving data a type allows the computer to determine how to handle the data. For instance, if you want the program to show the mathematical equation 1+1 on a screen, you have to tell it that it is text. Otherwise, the program will interpret the data as a mathematical equation and evaluate it accordingly.

You'll get more into the different data types and how important it is to define them in a later chapter. For now however, know that a string is a data type that consists of any character, be it a letter, number, symbol, or punctuation mark. Therefore, the following are all examples of strings:

"Hello, how are you?"

"1+1"

"I ate 4 bananas"

"!@#$%^&*()"

Why the Quotes?

When you type a string into Python, you do so by preceding it with quotes. Whether these quotes are single ('), double("), or triple(""") depends on what you are trying to accomplish. For the most part, you will use single quotes, because it requires less effort (you do not need to hold down the Shift key to create them). Note, however, that they are interchangeable with the double and even triple quotes.

Try typing in some strings. After you type in each sentence, press the Enter key to allow Python to evaluate your statement.

Entering Strings with Different Quotes

Enter the following strings, keeping in mind the type of quotes (single or double) and the ends of lines (use the Enter key when you see that the end of a line has been reached):

```
>>> "This is a string using a double quote"
'This a string using a double quote'
>>> 'This is a string with a single quote'
'This is a string with a single quote'
>>> """This string has three quotes
look at what it can do!"""
'This string has three quotes\nlook at what it can do!'
>>>
```

In the preceding examples, although the sentences may look different to the human eye, the computer is interpreting them all the same way: that is, as a string. There is a true purpose to having three different quoting methods, which is described next.

Why Three Types of Quotes?

The reasoning behind having three types of quotes is fairly simple. Let's say that you want to use a contraction in your sentence, as I have just done. If you type a sentence such as "I can't believe it's not butter" into the shell, nothing much happens, but when you actually try to get the program to *use* that string in any way, you will get an error message. To show you what I mean, the following section introduces you to the print() function.

Using the print() Function

A function in Python (and every other programming language) is a tool developers use to save time and make their programs more efficient. Instead of writing the same code over and over again, they store it in a function, and then call upon that function when they need it. Don't worry too much about functions at the moment; they are covered in greater detail later on. For now, it is enough to know what the term means and how it relates to programming.

The print() function is used whenever you want to print text to the screen. Try the following example in your Python shell:

```
>>> print("Hello World!")
```

When you press Enter, you should see the following:

```
Hello World!
```

You will want to note several things here. First, as you were entering in the print() function, a pop-up as shown in Figure 1-1 appeared, showing you the various options available to you within the function:

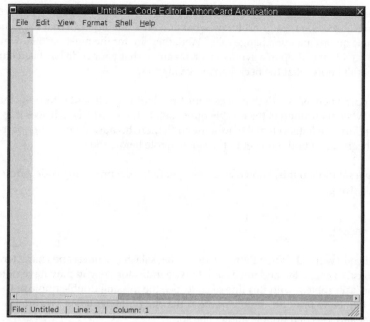

Figure 1-1

Second, the text once more appeared in blue on the next line, but this time without quotation marks around it. This is because unlike in the previous examples, Python actually *did* something with the data.

Congratulations, you just wrote your first program!

Understanding Different Quotes

Now that you know how to use the print() function, you can begin to work with the different types of quotes discussed earlier in this chapter. Try the examples from earlier:

```
>>> print('This is a string using a single quote!')
This is a string using a single quote!
>>>print("This is a string using a double quote!")
This is a string using a double quote!
>>>print("""This string has three quotes!
Look at what it can do!""")
This string has three quotes
Look at what it can do!
```

In this example, you see that the single quote (') and double quote (") are interchangeable *in those instances.* However, when you want to work with a contraction, such as *don't*, or if you want to quote someone quoting something, observe what happens:

```
>>>print("I said, "Don't do it")
```

When you press Enter to execute the function, you will get the error message: `SyntaxError: invalid syntax (<pyshell#10>, line 1)`. I know what you are thinking — "What happened? I thought double and single quotes are interchangeable." Well, they are for the most part. However, when you try to mix them, it can often end up in a syntax error, meaning that your code has been entered incorrectly, and Python doesn't know what the heck you are trying to say.

What really happens here is that Python sees your first double quote and interprets that as the beginning of your string. When it encounters the double quote before the word *Don't*, it sees it as the end of the string. Therefore, the letters *on* make no sense to Python, because they are not part of the string. The string doesn't begin again until you get to the single quote before the *t*.

There is a simple solution to this, known as an escape. Retry the preceding code, adding an escape character to this string:

```
>>>print("I said, \"Don't do it")
I said, "Don't do it
```

This time, your code worked. When Python saw the backslash (\), or escape character, it knew to treat the double quote as a character, and not as a data type indicator. As you may have noticed, however, there is still one last problem with this line of code. See the missing double quote at the end of your results? To get Python to print the double quote at the end of the sentence, you simply add another escape character and a second double quote, like so:

```
>>>print("I said, \"Don't do it\"")
I said, "Don't do it"
```

Finally, let's take a moment to discuss the triple quote. You briefly saw its usage earlier. In that example, you saw that the triple quote allows you to write some text on multiple lines, without being processed until you close it with another triple quote. This technique is useful if you have a large amount of data that you do not wish to print on one line, or if you want to create line breaks within your code. Here, in the next example, you write a poem using this method:

```
>>>print("""Roses are red
Violets are blue
I just printed multiples lines
And you did too!""")
Roses are red
Violets are blue
I just printed multiple lines
And you did too!
```

There is another way to print text on multiple lines using the newline (\n) escape character, which is the most common of all the escape characters. I'll show it to you here briefly, and come back to discuss it in more depth in a later chapter. Try this code out:

```
>>>print("Roses are red \n Violets are blue \n
I just printed multiple
lines \n And you did too!")
Roses are red
Violets are blue
I just printed multiple lines
And you did too!
```

As you can see, the results are the same. Which you use is up to you, but the newline escape is probably more efficient and easier to read.

Putting Two Strings Together

There comes a time in every programmer's life when they have to combine two or more strings together. This is known as *concatenation*. For example, let's say that you have a database consisting of employees' first and last names. You may, at some point, wish to print these out as one whole record, instead of as two. In Python, each of these items can be treated as one, as shown here:

```
>>>"John"
'John'
>>>"Everyman"
'Everyman'
```

Try It Out   Using + to Combine Strings

You can use several different methods to join distinct strings together. The first is by using the mathematical approach:

```
>>> "John" + "Everyman"
'JohnEveryman'
```

You could also just skip the + symbol altogether and do it this way:

```
>>>"John" "Everyman"
JohnEveryman
```

As you can see from these examples, both strings were combined; however, Python read the statement literally, and as such, there is no space between the two strings (remember: Python now views them as one string, not two!). So how do you fix this? You can fix it in two simple ways. The first involves adding a space after the first string, in this manner:

```
>>>"John " "Everyman"
John Everyman
```

I do not recommend this approach, however, because it can be difficult to ascertain that you added a space to the end of *John* if you ever need to read the code later in the future, say, when you are bleary-eyed and its four in the morning. The other approach is to simply use a separator, like so:

```
>>>"John" + " " + "Everyman"
John Everyman
```

Other reasons exist why you should use this method instead of simply typing in a space that have to do with database storage, but that is covered Chapter 14. Note that you can make any separator you like:

```
>>>"John" + "." + "Everyman"
John.Everyman
```

Joining Strings with the Print() Function

By default, the `print()` function is a considerate fellow that inserts the space for you when you print more than one string in a sentence. As you will see, there is no need to use a space separator. Instead, you just separate every string with a comma (,):

```
>>>Print("John" , "Everyman")
John Everyman
```

Putting Strings Together in Different Ways

Another way to specify strings is to use a *format specifier*. It works by putting in a special sequence of characters that Python will interpret as a placeholder for a value that will be provided by you. This may initially seem like it's too complex to be useful, but format specifiers also enable you to control what the displayed information looks like, as well as a number of other useful tricks.

Try It Out   Using a Format Specifier to Populate a String

In the simplest case, you can do the same thing with your friend, John Q.:

```
>>> "John Q. %s" % ("Public")
'John Q. Public'
```

How It Works

The `%s` is known as a format specifier, specifically for strings. As the discussion on data types continues throughout this book, you take a look at several more, each specific to its given data type. Every specifier acts as a placeholder for that type in the string; and after the string, the `%` sign outside of the string indicates that after it, all of the values to be inserted into the format specifier will be presented there to be used in the string.

You may notice the parentheses. This tells the string that it should expect to see a sequence that contains the values to be used by the string to populate its format specifiers.

A simpler way to think of it is to imagine that the `%s` is a storage bin that holds the value in the parentheses. If you want to do more than one value, you would simply add another format specifier, in this manner:

```
>>>"John %s%s" % ("Every" , "Man")
John Everyman
```

These sequences are an integral part of programming in Python, and as such, they are covered in greater detail later in this book. For now, just know that every format specification in a string has to have an element that matches it in the sequence that is provided to it. Each item in the sequence are strings that must be separated by commas.

So why do they call it a format specifier if you store data in it? The reason is that it has multiple functions; being a container is only one of them. The following example shows you how to not only store data with the format specifier, but specify how that data will be displayed as well.

Try It Out	More String Formatting

In this example, you tell the format specifier how many characters to expect. Try the following code and watch what happens:

```
>>> "%s %s %10s" % ("John" , "Every", "Man")
'John Every        Man'
>>> "%-5s %s %10s" % ("John" , "Every", "Man")
John  Every        Man
```

How It Works

In the first line of code, the word *Man* appears far away from the other words; this is because in your last format specifier, you added a 10, so it is expecting a string with ten characters. When it does not find ten (it only finds three . . . M-a-n) it pads space in between with seven spaces.

In the second line of code you entered, you will notice that the word *Every* is spaced differently. This occurs for the same reason as before — only this time, it occurred to the left, instead of the right. Whenever you right a negative (–) in your format specifier, the format occurs to the left of the word. If there is just a number with no negative, it occurs to the right.

Summary

In this chapter you learned how to install Python, and how to work with the Python GUI (IDLE), which is a program written in Python for the express purpose of editing Python programs. In addition to editing files, this "shell" allows you to experiment with simple programming statements in the Python language.

Among the things you learned to do within the shell are the basics of handling strings, including string concatenation, as well as how to format strings with format specifiers, and even storing strings within that same %s format specifier. In addition, you learned to work with multiple styles of quotes, including the single, double, and triple, and found out what the \n newline escape character was for.

Finally, you learned your very first function, print(), and wrote your first program, the Hello World standby, which is a time-honored tradition among programmers; it's similar to learning "Smoke on the Water" if you play guitar — it's the first thing you'll ever learn.

The key things to take away from this chapter are:

❑   Programming is consistency. All programs are created with a specific use in mind, and your user will expect the program not only to live up to that usage, but to work in exactly the same manner each and every time. If the user clicks a button and a print dialog box pops up, this button should always work in this manner.

❑   Programming is control. As a programmer, you control the actions your application can and cannot take. Even aspects of the program that seem random to the casual observer are, in fact, controlled by the parameters that you create.

❑   Programming copes with changes. Through repeated tests, you can ensure that your program responds appropriately to the user, even when they ask the program to do something you did not develop it to do.

❑   Strings are a data type, or simply put, a category of data. These strings allow you to interact with the user in a plethora of ways, such as printing text to the window, accepting text from the user, and so forth. A string can consist of any letter, number, or special character.

❑   The `print()` function allows you to print text to the user's screen. It follows the syntax: `print("Here is some text")`.

Exercises

1.   In the Python shell, type the string, `"Rock a by baby,\n\ton the tree top,\t\when the wind blows\n\t\t\t the cradle will drop."` Feel free to experiment with the number of `\n` and `\t` escape sequences to see how this affects what gets displayed on your screen. You can even try changing their placement. What do you think you are likely to see?

2.   In the Python shell, use the same string indicated in Exercise 1, but this time, display it using the `print()` function. Once more, try differing the number of `\n` and `\t` escape sequences. How do you think it will differ?

Numbers and Operators

From our first breath of air, we are raised to use numbers. As a baby, we use them for estimating distance as we begin to crawl and, eventually, stand. As time progresses, we branch out and use them on a more conscious level, such as when we purchase a beverage or calculate our monthly budget. Whether you are one year old or 90, to some degree you are familiar with numbers. Indeed, numbers are such a familiar concept that you probably don't notice the many different ways in which you use them depending on their context.

In this chapter, you are re-introduced to numbers and some of the ways in which Python works with them, including basic arithmetic and special string format specifiers for its different types of numbers.

In this chapter you learn:

❑ To be familiar with the different basic categories of numbers that Python uses.

❑ To be familiar with the methods for using those numbers.

❑ The displaying and mixing the various number types.

Different Kinds of Numbers

If you have ever used a spreadsheet, you've noticed that the spreadsheet doesn't just look at numbers as *numbers* but as different kinds of numbers. Depending on how you've formatted a cell, the spreadsheet will have different ways of displaying the numbers. For instance, when you deal with money, your spreadsheet will show one dollar as 1.00. However, if you're keeping track of the miles you've traveled in your car, you'd probably only record the miles you've traveled in tenths of a mile, such as 10.2. When you name a price you're willing to pay for a new house you probably only think to the nearest thousand dollars. At the large end of numbers, your electricity bills are sent to you with meter readings that come in at kilowatt hours, which are each one thousand watts per hour.

What this means in terms of Python is that, when you want to use numbers, you sometimes need to be aware that not all numbers relate to each other (as you see with imaginary numbers in this chapter), and sometimes you'll have to be careful about what kind of number you have and what you're trying to do with it. However, in general, you will use numbers in two ways: The first way will be to tell Python to repeat a certain action, and the second way will be to represent things that exist in the real world (that is, in your program, which is trying to model something in the real world). You will rarely have to think of numbers as anything besides simple numbers when you are counting things inside of Python. However, when you move on to trying to solve problems that exist in the real world — things that deal with money, science, cars, electricity, or anything else — you'll find yourself more aware about how you use numbers.

Numbers in Python

Python offers three different kinds of numbers with which you can work: *integers*, *floating-point numbers* (or *floats*), and *imaginary numbers*.

In previous versions of the language, Python had a different way of handling larger numbers. If a number ranged from –2,147,483,648 to +2,147,483,647, it was deemed an integer. Anything larger was promoted to a long. All that has changed, and the two types have now merged. Now, integers are described as a whole number, either positive or negative.

To determine the class of a number, you can use a special function that is built into Python, called `type`. When you use `type`, Python will tell you what kind of data you're looking at. Let's try this with a few examples.

Try It Out   **Using Type with Different Numbers**

In the Python shell, you can enter different numbers and see what `type` tells you about how Python sees them:

```
>>> type(1)
<class 'int'>
>>> type(2000)
<class 'int'>
>>> type(999999999999)
<class 'int'>
>>> type(1.0)
<class 'float'>
```

How It Works

Although in everyday life 1.0 is the same number as 1, Python will automatically perceive 1.0 as being a float; without the .0, the number 1 would be dealt with as the integer number one (which you probably learned as a whole number in grade school), which is a different kind of number.

In essence, the special distinction between a float and an integer is that a float has a component that is a fraction of 1. Numbers such as 1.01, 2.34, 0.02324, and any other number that contains a fractional component is treated as a floating-point number (except for imaginary numbers, which have rules of their own). This is the type that you would want to use for dealing with money or with things dealt with in partial quantities, like gasoline or pairs of socks. (There's always a stray single sock in the drawers, right?)

> ### A Word to the Wise: Numbers can be Tricky
>
> Experts in engineering, financial, and other fields who deal with very large and very small numbers (small with a lot of decimal places) need even more accuracy and consistency than what built-in types like floats offer. If you're going to explore these disciplines within programming, you should use the available *modules*, a concept introduced in Chapter 7, which are written to handle the types of issues pertinent to the field in which you're interested. At the very least, using modules that are written to handle high-precision floating-point values in a manner that is specifically different than the default behavior is worth investigating if you have the need for them.

The last type of number that Python offers is oriented toward engineers and mathematicians. It's the *imaginary number*, and you may remember it from school; it's defined as the square root of –1. Despite being named imaginary, it does have a lot of practical uses in modeling real-world engineering situations, as well as in other disciplines like physics and pure math. The imaginary number is built into Python so that it's easily usable by user communities who frequently need to solve their problems with computers. Having this built-in type enables Python to help them do that. If you happen to be one of those people, you will be happy to learn that you're not alone, and Python is there for you.

Try It Out   Creating an Imaginary Number

The imaginary number behaves very much like a float, except that it cannot be mixed with a float. When you see an imaginary number, it will have the letter *j* trailing it:

```
>>> 12j
12j
```

How It Works

When you use the letter j next to a number and outside the context of a string (that is, not enclosed in quotes), Python knows that you've asked it to treat the number you've just entered as an imaginary number. When any letter appears outside of a string, it has to have a special meaning, such as this modifier, which specifies the type of number, or a named variables (which you see in Chapter 3), or another special name. Otherwise, the appearance of a letter by itself will cause an error!

You can combine imaginary and nonimaginary numbers to create complex numbers:

```
>>> 12j + 1
(1+12j)
>>> 12j + 1.01
(1.01+12j)
>>> type (12j + 1)
<class 'complex'>
```

You can see that when you try to mix imaginary numbers and other numbers, they are not added (or subtracted, multiplied, or divided); they're kept separate, in a way that creates a complex number. Complex numbers have a real part and an imaginary part, but an explanation of how they are used is beyond the scope of this chapter, although if you're someone who needs to use them, the complex number module (that word again!) is something that you can explore once you've gotten through Chapter 6. The module's name is cmath, for complex math. Complex numbers are discussed further in Chapter 19.

Program Files

By now you should be fairly comfortable using the Python shell and writing different lines of code within it. You've used it for all of the examples thus far, but now you are going to use it in a different manner. Instead of simply typing in single lines of code that disappear once you close the GUI, you are now going to create and save actual files that you can open and use again.

For the remainder of this chapter, you are encouraged to use the Python shell along with Notepad to create your very own files.

Try It Out   By Typing the Following Text in Notepad

Enter the following into Notepad:

```
print("This is a basic string")
print("We learned to join two strings using " + "the plus operation")
```

Now that you have added some code to your editor, try and save it. First, go to File, then Save As (see Figure 2-1).

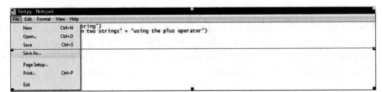

Figure 2-1

A pop-up menu appears, prompting you for a name and directory in which to save your file. Python files use the extension .py, so always be sure to add it to the end of your file name, otherwise Notepad will save it as its default type, .txt. Give it the name Test.py. Next, navigate to the directory where Python is installed. Normally, this will be something along the lines of C:/Python31/. Click the Save button and you are all set.

After you've selected a file name and saved the file, you can reopen it. To run the Test.py program, choose File ⇨ Open from the Python shell, and choose the file you want to run (in this case, Test.py).

The Python editor will now open. Click Run, choose Run Module (see Figure 2-2), and watch in amazement as your first program runs!

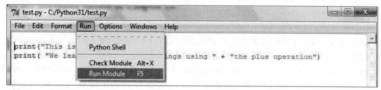

Figure 2-2

You will notice a few things. First, when you initially opened the Test.py file, Python took the liberty of highlighting your code in different colors. This makes functions and data types (and many other programming tidbits) easier to recognize. For instance, the print() function is in purple, whereas the string that comprises its value is green.

When you run this module, you no longer see the code, but its result instead, written out in blue text on your screen:

```
This is a basic string
We learned to join two strings using the plus operator
```

Do this a few more times with different strings, saving them in different files. Each one of these sessions is now available for you, and you can refer to them later.

Using the Different Types

Except for the basic integer, the other number types can grow to an unwieldy number of digits to look at and make sense of. Therefore, very often when these numbers are generated, you will see them in a format that is similar to scientific notation. Python will let you input numbers in this format as well, so it's a two-way street. There are many snags to using very large integers and floats. The topic is quite detailed and not necessarily pertinent to learning Python. If you want to know more about floating-point numbers in general, and what they really mean to a computer, the paper at http://docs.sun.com/source/806-3568/ncg_goldberg.html is a very good reference, although the explanation will only make sense to someone with prior experience with computers and numbers. Don't let that stop you from looking, though. It may be something you want to know about at some point in the future.

More commonly, you will be using integers and floats. It wouldn't be unusual to acquire a number from somewhere such as the date, the time, or information about someone's age or the time of day. After that data, in the form of a number, is acquired, you'll have to display it.

The usual method of doing this is to incorporate numbers into *strings*. You can use the format specifier method that was used in Chapter 1. It may make intuitive sense to you that you should also be able to use the + method for including a number in a string, but in fact this does not work, because deep down they are different types, and the + operator is intended for use only with two things of the same type: two strings, two numbers, or two other objects and types that you will encounter later. The definite exceptions are that floats and integers can be added together. Otherwise, you should expect that different types won't be combined with the + operation.

You are likely wondering why a string format specifier can be used to include a number, when a + can't. The reason is that the + operation relies on information contained in the actual items being added. Almost everything you use in Python can be thought of as an object with properties, and all of the properties combined define the object. One important property of every object is its type, and for now the important thing to understand about a type is that certain naturally understood things like the + operation work only when you perform them with two objects of compatible types. In most cases, besides numbers, compatible types should be thought of as the same type.

If you do want to use the + operation with numbers and strings (and doing this is usually a matter of style that you can decide for yourself), you can use a built-in function called str *that will transform, if possible, numbers into a string. It enables you to do things such as add strings and numbers into a single string. You can use* str *with most objects because most objects have a way of displaying themselves as strings. However, for the sake of consistency, you'll use string format specifiers for now.*

Try It Out   Including Different Numbers in Strings

When you combined two strings in the first chapter by using a format specifier, you used the format specifier %s, which means "a string." Because numbers and strings have different types, you will use a different specifier that will enable your numbers to be included in a string:

```
>>> "Including an integer works with %%d like this: %d" % 10
'Including an integer works with %d like this: 10'
>>> "An integer converted to a float with %%f: %f" % 5
'An integer converted to a float with %f: 5.000000'
>>> "A normal float with %%f: %f" % 1.2345
'A normal float with %f: 1.234500'
>>> "A really large number with %%E: %E" % 6.789E10
'A really large number with %E: 6.789000E+10'
>>> "Controlling the number of decimal places shown: %.02f" % 25.101010101
'Controlling the number of decimal places shown: 25.10'
```

If you're wondering where you can use format specifiers, note that the last example looks very similar to the way we print monetary values, and, in fact, any program that deals with dollars and cents will need to have at least this much capability to deal with numbers and strings.

How It Works

Anytime you are providing a format specifier to a string, there may be options that you can use to control how that specifier displays the value associated with it. You've already seen this with the %s specifier in Chapter 1, where you could control how many characters were displayed. With numeric specifiers are also conventions regarding how the numbers of a particular type should be displayed. These conventions result in what you see when you use any of the numeric format specifiers.

Try It Out   Escaping the % Sign in Strings

One other trick was shown before. If you want to print the literal string %d in your program, you achieve that in Python strings by using two % signs together. This is needed only when you also have valid format specifiers that you want Python to substitute for you in the same string:

```
>>> print("The %% behaves differently when combined with other letters, like
this: %%d %%s %%f %d" % 10)
The % behaves differently when combined with other letters, like this: %d %s
%f 10
```

How It Works

Note that Python pays attention to the combinations of letters and will behave correctly in a string that has both format specifiers as well as a double percent sign.

Basic Math

It's more common than not that you'll have to use the numbers in your program in basic arithmetic. Addition, subtraction, division, and multiplication are all built in. Addition and subtraction are performed by the + and – symbols.

Try It Out   Doing Basic Math

You can enter basic arithmetic at the Python shell prompt and use it like a calculator. Like a calculator, Python will accept a set of operations, and when you press the Enter key, it will evaluate everything you've typed and give you your answer:

```
>>> 5 + 300
305
>>> 399 + 3020 + 1 + 3456
6876
>>> 300 - 59994 + 20
-59674
>>> 4023 - 22.46
4000.54
```

How It Works

Simple math looks about how you'd expect it to look. In addition to + and –, multiplication is performed by the asterisk, *, and division is performed by the forward slash, /. Multiplication and division may not be as straightforward as you'd expect in Python, because of the distinction between floating-point numbers and whole numbers.

In previous versions of Python, as numbers became larger, they would be promoted from int to long. However, in Python 3.1, these two types have merged and there is no longer a need for such promotion. Observe the following numbers and how Python promotes numbers once they become a certain size:

```
>>> 2000403030 * 392381727
784921595607432810
>>> 2000403030 * 3923817273929
7849215963933911604870
>>> 2e304 * 3923817273929
inf
>>> 2e34 * 3923817273929
7.8476345478579995e+46
```

Note that although Python can deal with some very large numbers, the results of some operations will exceed what Python can accommodate. The shorthand for infinity, `inf`, is what Python will return when a result is larger than what it can handle.

Before Python 3.1, division was a bit more interesting. Without help, Python would not coax one kind of number into another through division. Only when you had at least one number that was a floating-point component — that is, a period followed by a number — would floating-point answers be displayed. If two numbers that were normal integers or longs (in either case, lacking a component that specifies a value less than one, even if that is `.0`) were divided, the remainder would be discarded. This has since been fixed, and now Python will still display the decimals, unless told otherwise. Observe the following:

```
>>> 44 / 11
4.0
>>> 5.0/2.5
2.0
>>> 324/101
3.2079207920792081
>>> 324.5/102.9
3.1535471331389697
```

As you can see, if you divide an integer by another integer, it still shows as a floating point, even if there is no remainder. Likewise, dividing an integer by a floating point returns a floating-point number. Note, however, that even though the integer is displayed as a float in the preceding examples of 4.0 and 2.0, it is still, for all intents and purposes, an integer. However, the result of 324/101 is converted to a float.

Try It Out   Using the Modulus Operation

There is one other basic operation of Python that you should be aware of: the remainder, or modulus operation. A new addition to Python is the ability to view the entire result of a piece of division (as you saw in the equation 324/101). Previously, if you wanted to know the remainder you had to use the modulus operator, because Python would show only the whole number portion of the answer. For 324/101, Python would have displayed 3. In some instances, believe it or not, you still need only the remainder portion of a division result. To find this part of the answer, you have to use the modulus operator, which is the `%`. Don't let this confuse you! The `%` means modulus only when it is used on numbers. When you are using strings, it retains its meaning as the format specifier. When something has different meanings in different contexts, it is called *overloading*, and it is very useful; but don't get caught by surprise when something behaves differently by design.

```
>>> 5 / 3
1.6666666666666667
>>> 5 % 3
2
```

How It Works

The preceding code indicates that 5 divided by 3 is 1.6666666666666667, and in the second example you learn that when you divide 5/3, you have a remainder of 2. One very useful task the modulus operator is used for is to discover whether one thing can be evenly divided by another, such as determining whether the items in one sequence will fit into another evenly (you learn more about sequences in Chapter 3). Here are some more examples that you can try out:

```
>>> 123 % 44
35
>>> 334 % 13
9
>>> 652 % 4
0
```

Some Surprises

You need to be careful when you are dealing with common floating-point values, such as money. Some things in Python are puzzling. For one thing, if you manipulate certain numbers with seemingly straightforward math, you may still receive answers that have extra values trailing them, such as the following:

```
>>> 4023 - 22.4
4000.5999999999999
```

The trailing nines could worry you, but they merely reflect the very high precision that Python offers. However, when you print or perform math, this special feature actually results in precise answers.

Try It Out   **Printing the Results**

Try actually printing the results, so that the preceding math with the unusual-looking results has its results displayed to a user, as it would from inside of a program:

```
>>> print("%f" % (4023 - 22.4))
4000.600000
```

How It Works

You may remember the earlier discussion regarding floating-point division, and how in Python 3.0, the entire equation is written out. Before, when you did the equation 5/3, you got the result 1.6666666666666667. But you might not want to display such a long string to the user. To truncate the answer, you can do so with the %f format specifier.

%f Format Specifier

Try out the following code and observe the different ways Python handles floating-point mathematics and then how you can manipulate the results with formatting:

```
>>> print("%f" % (5/3))
1.666667
>>> print("%.2f" % (5/3))
1.67
>>> print("%f" % (415 * 20.2))
8383.000000
>>> print("%0.f" % (415 * 20.2))
8383
```

Floating-point numbers can be confusing. A complete discussion of floating-point numbers is beyond the scope of this book, but if you are experienced with computers and numbers and want to know more about floating-point numbers, read the paper at http://docs.sun.com/source/806-3568/ncg_goldberg.html. The explanation offered there should help round out this discussion.

Using Numbers

As you can see from the previous example, you can display numbers with the print() function by including the numbers into strings, for instance by using a format specifier. The important point is that you must determine how to display your numbers so that they mean what you intend them to mean, and that depends on knowing your application.

Order of Evaluation

When doing math, you may find yourself looking at an expression like 4*3+1/4–12. The puzzle you're confronted with is determining how you're going to *evaluate* this sort of expression and whether the way *you* would evaluate it is the same way that Python would evaluate it. The safest way to do this is to always enclose your mathematical expressions in parentheses, which will make it clear which math operations will be evaluated first.

Python evaluates these basic arithmetic operations as follows: Multiplication and division operations happen before addition and subtraction, but even this can become confusing.

Using Math Operations

When you're thinking about a particular set of mathematical operations, it can seem straightforward when you write it down (or type it in). When you look at it later, however, it can become confusing. Try these examples, and imagine them without the parentheses:

```
>>> (24 * 8)
192
>>> (24 * (8 + 3))
```

```
264
>>> (24 * (8 + 3 + 7.0))
432.0
>>> (24 * (8 + 3 + 7.0 + 9))
648.0
>>> (24 * (8 + 3 + 7.0 + 9))/19
34.10526315789474
>>> (24 * (8 + 3 + 7 + 9))/19
34.10526315789474
>>> (24 * (8 + 3 + 7 + 9))%19
2
```

Notice in the examples here how the presence of any floating-point numbers changes the entire equation to using floating-point numbers, and how removing any floating-point numbers causes Python to evaluate everything as integers, unless the result is a float.

How It Works

The examples are grouped in something that resembles the normal order of evaluation, but the parentheses ensure that you can be certain which groups of arithmetic operations will be evaluated first. The innermost (the most contained) are evaluated first, and the outermost last. Within a set of parentheses, the normal order takes place.

Number Formats

When you prepare strings to contain a number, you have a lot of flexibility. The following Try It Out shows some examples.

For displaying money, use a format specifier indicating that you want to limit the number of decimal places to two.

Try It Out   Using Number Formats

Try this, for example. Here, you print a number as though you were printing a dollar amount:

```
>>> print("$%.02f" % 30.0)
$30.00
```

You can use a similar format to express values less than a cent, such as when small items are listed for sale individually. When you have more digits than you will print, notice what Python does:

```
>>> print("$%.03f" % 30.00123)
$30.001
>>> print("$%.03f" % 30.00163)
$30.002
>>> print("%.03f" % 30.1777)
30.178
>>> print("%.03f" % 30.1113)
30.111
```

How It Works

As you can see, when you specify a format requiring more accuracy than you have asked Python to display, it will not just cut off the number. It will do the mathematically proper rounding for you as well.

Mistakes Will Happen

While you are entering these examples, you may make a mistake. Obviously, there is nothing that Python can do to help you if you enter a different number; you will get a different answer than the one in this book. However, for mistakes such as entering a letter as a format specifier that doesn't mean anything to Python or not providing enough numbers in a sequence you're providing to a string's format specifiers, Python tries to give you as much information as possible to indicate what's happened so that you can fix it.

Try It Out   Making Mistakes

To understand what's going on when a mistake happens, here are some examples you can try. Their full meanings are covered later, starting in Chapter 4, but in the meantime, you should know this:

```
>>> print("%.03f" % (30.1113, 12))
Traceback (most recent call last):
  File "<input>", line 1, in ?
TypeError: not all arguments converted during string formatting
```

How It Works

In the preceding code, there are more elements in the sequence (three in all) than there are format specifiers in the string (just two), so Python helps you out with a message. What's less than helpful is that this mistake would cause a running program to stop running, so this is normally an error condition, or an *exception*. The term *arguments* here refers to the format specifiers but is generally used to mean parameters that are required in order for some object to work. When you call a function that expects a certain number of values to be specified, each one of those anticipated values is called an argument.

This is something that programmers take for granted; this specialized technical language may not make sense immediately, but it will begin to feel right when you get used to it. Through the first ten chapters of this book, arguments will be referred to as *parameters* to make them less puzzling, because no one is arguing, just setting the conditions that are being used at a particular point in time. When you are programming, though, the terms are interchangeable.

Here is another potential mistake:

```
>>> print("%.03f, %f %d" % (30.1113, 12))
Traceback (most recent call last):
  File "<input>", line 1, in ?
TypeError: not enough arguments for format string
```

Now that you know what Python means by an argument, it makes sense. You have a format specifier and you don't have a value in the accompanying sequence that matches it; thus, there aren't enough parameters.

If you try to perform addition with a string and a number, you will also get an error:

```
>>> "This is a string" + 4
Traceback (most recent call last):
  File "<pyshell#13>", line 1, in <module>
TypeError: Can't convert 'int' object to str implicitly
```

This should make sense because you've already read about how you can and can't do this. However, here is definite proof: Python is telling you clearly that it can't do what it has been asked to do, so now it's up to you to resolve the situation. (Hint: You can use the `str` function.)

```
>>> "This is a string""" + str(4)
'This is a string4'
```

Some Unusual Cases

Python offers one other feature with its numbers that is worth knowing about so that you understand it when you encounter it. The normal counting system that we use is called *base 10*, or *radix 10*. It includes numbers from 0 to 9. Numbers above that just involve combining 0 through 9. However, computers commonly represent the binary numbers they actually deal with in *base 8*, called *octal*, and *base 16*, also called *hexadecimal*. These systems are often used to give programmers an easier way to understand bytes of data, which often come in one and two chunks of 8 bits.

In addition, neither octal nor hexadecimal can be displayed as negative numbers. Numbers described in this way are said to be *unsigned*, as opposed to being *signed*. The sign that is different is the + or – sign. Normally, numbers are assumed to be positive, but if a number is a *signed type*, it can be negative as well. If a number is unsigned, it has to be positive; and if you ask for the display of a negative number but in a signed format string, you'll get unusual answers.

Try It Out   **Formatting Numbers as Octal and Hexadecimal**

```
>>> print('Octal uses the letter "o" lowercase. %d %o' % (10,10))
Octal uses the letter "o" lowercase. 10 12
```

It may seem like a mistake that the second number printed is 12 when you've provided the string with a 10. However, octal only has 8 numbers (0 to 7), so from 0 to 10 in octal is 0, 1, 2, 3, 4, 5, 6, 7, 8, 10, 11.

```
>>> print('Hex uses the letter "x" or "X". %d %x %X' % (10, 10, 10))
Hex uses the letter "x" or "X". 10 a A
```

Here is another case that needs explaining. Hexadecimal uses numbers from 0 to 15, but because you run out of numbers at 9, hex utilizes the letters a–f; and the letters are lowercase if you used the format specifier %x and are capitalized if you used %X. Therefore, the numbers 0 to 20 in decimal are as follows in hex: 0, 1, 2, 3, 4, 5, 6, 7, 8, 9, a, b, c, d, e, f, 10, 11, 12, 13.

Summary

This chapter introduced you to numbers in Python, although it doesn't cover everything available. You've seen and used three kinds of built-in numbers that Python knows about: integers, floats, and imaginary numbers. You have learned how to use string format specifiers to allow you to include numbers in your strings, and you've formatted those numbers in strings with different styles.

An important thing to remember is that the format, or how the number is displayed in a string, doesn't change the value of the number. Floats remain floats even when they are printed as integers, and vice versa.

You've performed the major built-in arithmetic operations: addition, subtraction, multiplication, division, and modulus. You have learned that if integers are mixed with a float, the result is a float, or if two integers are divided, they may also return a float, where appropriate. If arithmetic is done with an integer or a float combined with an imaginary number, the result will be a *complex number* that separates the real component and the imaginary component. You've also learned about the type function, which enables you to determine what type of number you actually have.

Lastly, you generally use numbers in base 10, or radix 10. Computers in general, and Python in particular, can easily translate numbers to base 8, or octal, and base 16, or hexadecimal.

The key things to take away from this chapter are:

❑ There are three types of numbers in Python. Those are: integers, which are whole numbers (both negative and positive; floating-point numbers, which are any number with a decimal value; and imaginary number, which is the square-root of 1, and is used in the world of engineering and physics.

❑ The + operator, when used on strings, concatenates two or more strings together. For instance, if you write print ("Hello," + " how are you?"), the result will be one sentence: "Hello, how are you?"

❑ To convert a number to a string, you can use the str function.

❑ Dividing two integers can sometimes result in a floating-point number (i.e.; 3/2). Dividing an integer by a floating-point decimal will always result in a floating-point number.

❑ The modulus operator (%) is used to return the remainder in a division. For instance, 5 % 2 will return 1.

❑ Using parentheses in your calculations helps to ensure the proper order of evaluation.

Exercises

Do the following first three exercises in Notepad and save the results in a file called `ch2_exercises.py`. You can run it from within Python by opening the file and choosing Run Module.

1. In the Python shell, multiply 5 and 10. Try this with other numbers as well.

2. Print every number from 6 through 14 in base 8.

3. Print every number from 9 through 19 in base 16.

4. Try to elicit other errors from the Python interpreter — for instance, by deliberately misspelling `print` as `pinrt`. Notice how as you work on a file in the Python shell, it will display `print` differently than it does `pinrt`.

Variables — Names for Values

In the previous two chapters, you learned how Python views strings, integers, floats, and imaginary numbers and how they can be created and displayed. This chapter presents more examples that demonstrate how these data types can be used.

In this chapter you learn:

❑ To use names to store the types you already know as well as other basic types to which you will be introduced.

❑ How to work with different types of objects that you haven't learned about yet. *Variables* and new, different types — specifically, you will become better acquainted with *lists*, *tuples*, and *dictionaries*.

❑ What a *reference* is and have some experience in using references.

❑ To get the most out of this chapter, you should type the examples yourself and alter them to see what happens.

Referring to Data — Using Names for Data

It's difficult to always write strings and numbers explicitly throughout a program because it forces you to remember everything. The exacting memory that computers have enable them to remember far more details than people can, and taking advantage of that capability is a huge part of programming. However, to make using data more flexible and easy, you want to give the data names that can be used to refer to them.

These names are commonly called *variables*, which indicates that the data to which they refer can vary (it can be changed), while the name remains the same. You'll see them referred to as *names* as well, because that is what you are presented with by Python.

```
>>> first_string = "This is a string"
>>> second_string = "This is another string"
>>> first_number = 4
>>> second_number = 5
>>> print ("The first variables are %s, %s, %d, %d" % (first_string,
second_string, first_number, second_number))
The first variables are This is a string, This is another string, 4, 5
```

How It Works

You can see that you can associate a name with a value — either a string or an integer — by using the equals (=) sign. The name that you use doesn't relate to the data to which it points in any direct sense (that is, if you name it "number," that doesn't actually have to mean that it holds a number).

```
>>> first_string = 245
>>> second_number = "This isn't a number"
>>> print(first_string)
245
>>> print(second_number)
"This isn't a number"
```

Notice that you did not need to use quotations when you just wanted to print out the value inside of a variable. Had you put quotations around the variable inside the `print()` function, it would have printed out the name of the variable, instead of its contents, seeing it as a string and not an actual variable. The benefit of being able to name your data is that you can decide to give it a name that means something. It is always worthwhile to give your data a name that reminds you of what it contains or how you will use it in your program. If you were to inventory the lightbulbs in your home, you might want a piece of your program to contain a count of the lightbulbs in your closets and another piece to contain a count of those actually in use:

```
>>> lightbulbs_in_closet = 10
>>> lightbulbs_in_lamps = 12
```

As lightbulbs are used, they can be moved from the closet into the lamps, and a name can be given to the number of lightbulbs that have been thrown out this year, so that at the end of the year you have an idea of what 'you've bought, what you have, and what 'you've used; and when you want to know what you still have, you have only to refer to `lightbulbs_in_closet` or `lightbulbs_in_lamps`.

When you have names that relate to the value stored in them, 'you've created an informal index that enables you to look up and remember where you put the information that you want so that it can be easily used in your program.

Changing Data Through Names

If your data is a number or a string, you can change it by using the operations you already know you can do with them.

Altering Named Values

Every operation you've learned for numbers and strings can be used with a variable name so that you can treat them exactly as if they were the numbers they referenced:

```
>>> proverb = "A penny saved"
>>> proverb = proverb + " is a penny earned"
>>> print(proverb)
A penny saved is a penny earned
>>> pennies_saved = 0
>>> pennies_saved = pennies_saved + 1
>>> print(pennies_saved)
1
print(pennies_saved + 1)
2
```

How It Works

Whenever you combine named values on the right-hand side of an equals sign, the names will be operated on as though you had presented Python with the values referenced by the names, even if the same name is on the left-hand side of the equals sign. When Python encounters a situation like that, it will first evaluate and find the result of the operations on the right side and then assign the result to the name on the left side. That way, there's no confusion about how the name can exist on both sides — Python will do the right thing.

Copying Data

The name that you give data is only a name. It's how you refer to the data that you're trying to access. This means that more than one name can refer to the same data:

```
>>> pennies_saved=1
>>> pennies_earned = pennies_saved
>>> print(pennies_earned)
1
```

When you use the = sign again, you are referring your name to a new value that you've created, and the old value will still be pointed to by the other name:

```
>>> pennies_saved = pennies_saved + 1
>>> print(pennies_saved)
2
>>> print(pennies_earned)
1
```

Names You Can't Use and Some Rules

Python uses a few names as special built-in words that it *reserves* for special use to prevent ambiguity. The following words are reserved by Python and can't be used as the names for data:

```
and, as, assert, break, class, continue, def, del, elif, else,
except, exec,False,  finally, for, from, global, if, import, in,
is, lambda, not, None, or, pass, print, raise, return, try, True,
while, with, yield
```

In addition, the names for data cannot begin with numbers or most non-alphabet characters (such as commas, plus or minus signs, slashes, and so on), with the exception of the underscore character. The underscore is allowed and even has a special meaning in some cases (specifically with classes and modules, which you see in Chapter 6 and later).

You will see a number of these special reserved words in the remaining discussion in this chapter. They're important when you are using Python to do various tasks.

Using More Built-in Types

Beside strings and numbers, Python provides four other important basic types: tuples, lists, sets, and dictionaries. These four types have a lot in common because they all allow you to group more than one item of data together under one name. Each one also gives you the capability to search through them because of that grouping. These groupings are indicated by the presence of enclosing parentheses (), square brackets [], and curly braces {}.

> When you write a program, or read someone else's program, it is important to pay attention to the type of enclosing braces when you see groupings of elements. The differences among {}, [], and () are important.

Tuples — Unchanging Sequences of Data

In Chapters 1 and 2, you saw *tuples* (rhymes with supple) being used when you wanted to assign values to match more than one format specifier in a string. *Tuples* are a sequence of values, each one accessible individually, and a tuple is a basic type in Python. You can recognize tuples when they are created because they're surrounded by parentheses:

```
>>> print("A %s %s %s %s" % ("string", "filled", "by a", "tuple"))
A string filled by a tuple
```

Try It Out   **Creating and Using a Tuple**

Tuples contain references to data such as strings and numbers. However, even though they refer to data, they can be given names just like any other kind of data:

```
>>> filler = ("string", "filled", "by a", "tuple")
>>> print("A %s %s %s %s" % ("string", "filled", "by a", "tuple"))
A string filled by a tuple
```

Note that you can also print out the values in the tuple by simply calling upon it in the print() function. Try the following code and observe the results:

```
>>> filler = ("string", "filled", "by a", "tuple")
>>> print(filler)
('string', 'filled', 'by a ', 'tuple')
```

As you can see, the four parts that made up the tuple were returned. This technique is useful if you ever want to see the individual parts that make up your tuple.

How It Works

You can see in the example that `filler` is treated exactly as though its data — the tuple with strings — were present and being used by the string to fill in its format specifiers because the tuple was treated exactly as though you had typed in a sequence to satisfy the format specification.

You can access a single value inside of a tuple. The value referred to by each *element* can be accessed directly by using the *dereference* feature of the language. With tuples, you dereference the value by placing square brackets after the name of the tuple, counting from zero to the element that you're accessing. Therefore, the first element is 0, the second element is 1, the third element is 2, and so on until you reach the last element in the tuple:

```
>>> a = ("first", "second", "third")
>>> print("The first element of the tuple is %s" % a[0])
The first element of the tuple is first
>>> print("The second element of the tuple is %s" % a[1])
The second element of the tuple is second
>>> print("The third element of the tuple is %s" % a[2])
The third element of the tuple is third
```

A tuple keeps track of how many elements it contains, and it can tell you when you ask it by using the built-in function `len`:

```
>>> print("%d" % len(a))
3
```

This returns the number of elements in the tuple (in this case 3), so you need to remember that the `len` function starts counting at 1, but when you access your tuple, because tuples are counted starting from zero, you must stop accessing at one less than the number returned by `len`:

```
>>> print(a[len(a) - 1])
Third
```

You can also have one element of a tuple refer to an entirely different tuple. In other words, you can create layers of tuples:

```
>>> b = (a, "b's second element")
>>>print(b)
(('first', 'second', 'third'), "b's second element")
```

Now you can access the elements of the tuple a by adding another set of brackets after the first one, and the method for accessing the second element is no different from accessing the first — you just add another set of square brackets.

Try It Out   Accessing a Tuple Through Another Tuple

Re-create the a and b tuples so that you can look at how this works. When you have these layers of sequences, they are sometimes referred to as *multidimensional* because there are two layers that can be visualized as going down and across, like a two-dimensional grid for graph paper or a spreadsheet. Adding another one can be thought of as being three-dimensional, like a stack of blocks. Beyond that, though, visualizing this can give you a headache, and it's better to look at it as layers of data.

```
>>> a = ("first", "second", "third")
>>> b = (a, "b's second element")
>>> print("%s" %b[1])
b's second element
>>> print("%s" % b[0][0])
first
>>> print("%s" % b[0][1])
second
>>> print("%s" % b[0][2])
third
```

How It Works

In each case, the code works exactly as though you had followed the reference in the first element of the tuple named b and then followed the references for each value in the second layer tuple (what originally came from the tuple a). It's as though you had done the following:

```
>>> a = ("first", "second", "third")
>>> b = (a, "b's second element")
>>> layer2 = b[0]
>>> print(layer2[0])
'first'
>>> print(layer2[1])
'second'
>>> print(layer2[2])
'third'
```

Note that tuples have one oddity when they are created. To create a tuple with one element, you absolutely have to follow that one element with a comma:

```
>>> single_element_tuple = ("the sole element",)
```

Doing otherwise will result in the creation of a string, and that could be confusing when you try to access it later.

A tuple can have any kind of data in it, but after you've created one it can't be changed. It is *immutable*, and in Python this is true for a few types (for instance, strings are immutable after they are created; and operations on them that look like they change them actually create new strings).

Tuples are immutable because they are supposed to be used for ordered groups of things that will not be changed while you're using them. Trying to change anything in them will cause Python to complain with an error, similar to the errors you were shown at the end of Chapter 2:

```
>>> a[1] = 3
Traceback (most recent call last):
  File "<stdin>", line 1, in ?
TypeError: object does not support item assignment
>>> print("%s" % a[1])
second
```

You can see that the error Python returns when you try to assign a value to an element in the tuple is a *TypeError,* which means that this type doesn't support the operation you asked it to do (that's what the equals sign does — it asks the tuple to perform an action). In this case, you were trying to get the second element in a to refer to an integer, the number 3, but that's not going to happen. Instead, a remains unchanged.

An unrelated error will happen if you try to refer to an element in a tuple that doesn't exist. If you try to refer to the fourth element in a, you will get an error (remember that because tuples start counting their elements at zero, the fourth element would be referenced using the number three):

```
>>> a[3]
Traceback (most recent call last):
  File "<pyshell#27>", line 1, in <module>
    a[3]
IndexError: tuple index out of range
```

Note that this is an *IndexError* and that the explanation of the error is provided (although it doesn't tell you the index value that was out of range, you do know that you tried to access an element using an index value that doesn't exist in the tuple). To fix this in a program, you would have to find out what value you were trying to access and how many elements were in the tuple. Python makes finding these errors relatively simple compared to many other languages that will fail silently.

Lists — Changeable Sequences of Data

Lists, like tuples, are sequences that contain elements referenced starting at zero. Lists are created by using square brackets:

```
>>> breakfast = [ "coffee", "tea", "toast", "egg" ]
```

Try It Out   **Viewing the Elements of a List**

The individual elements of a list can be accessed in the same way as tuples. Like tuples, the elements in a list are referenced starting at 0 and are accessed in the same order from 0 until the end:

```
>>> count = 0
>>> print("Today's breakfast is %s" % breakfast[count])
Today's breakfast is coffee
>>> count = 1
>>> print("Today's breakfast is %s" % breakfast[count])
Today's breakfast is tea
>>> count = 2
>>> print("Today's breakfast is %s" % breakfast[count])
Today's breakfast is toast
>>> count = 3
>>> print("Today's breakfast is %s" % breakfast[count])
Today's breakfast is egg
```

How It Works

When you are accessing more than one element of a list, one after the other, it is essential to use a name to hold the value of the numbered position where you are in the list. In simple examples like this, you should do it to get used to the practice, but in practice, you will always do this. Most often, this is done in a loop to view every element in a sequence (see Chapter 4 for more about loops).

Here, you're manually doing the work of increasing the value referred to by count to go through each element in the breakfast list to pull out the special for four days of the week. Because you're increasing the count, whatever number is referred to by count is the element number in the breakfast list that is accessed.

The primary difference in using a list versus using a tuple is that a list can be modified after it has been created. The list can be changed at any time:

```
>>> breakfast[count] = "sausages"
>>> print("Today's breakfast is %s" % breakfast[count])
Today's breakfast is sausages
```

You don't just have to change elements that already exist in the list, you can also add elements to the list as you need them. You can add elements at the end by using the append method that is built in to the list type. Using append enables you to append exactly one item to the end of a list:

```
>>> breakfast.append("waffles")
>>> count = 4
>>> print ("Today's breakfast is %s" % breakfast[count])
Today's breakfast is waffles
```

If you want to add more than one item to the end of a list — for instance, the contents of a tuple or of another list — you can use the *extend* method to append the contents of a list all at once. The list isn't included as one item in one slot; each element is copied from one list to the other:

```
>>> breakfast.extend(["juice", "decaf", "oatmeal"])
>>> print(breakfast)
['coffee', 'tea', 'toast', 'egg', 'waffle', 'juice', 'decaf', 'oatmeal']
```

As with tuples, you can't ask for an element beyond the end of a list, but the error message is slightly different from a tuple because the error will tell you that it's a list index that's out of range, instead of a tuple index that's out of range:

```
>>> count = 8
>>> print("Today's breakfast is %s" % breakfast[count])
Traceback (most recent call last):
  File "<pyshell#18>", line 1, in <module>
    print("Today's breakfast is %s" % breakfast[count])
IndexError: list index out of range
```

The length of an array can also be determined by using the `len` function. Just like tuples, lengths start at one, whereas the first element of a list starts at zero. It's important to always remember this.

Dictionaries — Groupings of Data Indexed by Name

A *dictionary* is similar to lists and tuples. It's another type of container for a group of data. However, whereas tuples and lists are indexed by their numeric order, dictionaries are indexed by *names* that you choose. These names can be letters, numbers, strings, or symbols — whatever suits you.

Try It Out   Making a Dictionary

Dictionaries are created using the curly braces. To start with, you can create the simplest dictionary, which is an empty dictionary, and populate it using names and values that you specify one per line:

```
>>> menus_specials = {}
>>> menus_specials["breakfast"] = "Canadian ham"
>>> menus_specials["lunch"] = "tuna surprise"
>>> menus_specials["dinner"] = "Cheeseburger Deluxe"
```

How It Works

When you first assign to `menus_specials`, you're creating an empty dictionary with the curly braces. Once the dictionary is defined and referenced by the name, you may start to use this style of specifying the name that you want to be the index as the value inside of the square brackets, and the values that will be referenced through that index are on the right side of the equals sign. Because they're indexed by names that you choose, you can use this form to assign indexes and values to the contents of any dictionary that's already been defined.

When you're using dictionaries, the indexes and values have special names. Index names in dictionaries are called *keys*, and the values are called, well, *values*. To create a fully specified (or you can think of it as a completely formed) dictionary — one with *keys* and *values* assigned at the outset — you have to specify each key and its corresponding value, separated by a colon, between the curly braces. For example, a different day's specials could be defined all at once:

```
>>> menu_specials = {"breakfast" : "sausage and eggs",
... "lunch" : "split pea soup and garlic bread",
... "dinner": "2 hot dogs and onion rings"}
```

To print out all of the keys and values in a dictionary, simply place the name of the dictionary in the parameters of the print() function, as shown in the following code. To access any of the values, you use square brackets with the name of the key enclosed in the brackets. If the key is a string, the key has to be enclosed in quotes. If the key is a number (you can use numbers, too, making a dictionary look a lot like a list or a tuple), you need only the bare number.

```
>>>print(menu_specials)
{'lunch': 'split pea soup and garlic bread', 'breakfast': 'sausage and eggs',
'dinner': '2 hot dogs and onion rings'}
>>> print("%s" % menu_specials["breakfast"])
sausage and eggs
>>> print("%s" % menu_specials["lunch"])
split pea soup and garlic bread
>>> print("%s" % menu_specials["dinner"])
2 hot dogs and onion rings
```

If a key that is a string is accidentally not enclosed in quotes when you try to use it within square brackets, Python will try to treat it as a name that should be dereferenced to find the key. In most cases, this will raise an exception — a NameError — unless it happens to find a name that is the same as the string, in which case you will probably get an IndexError from the dictionary instead!

Try It Out   Getting the Keys from a Dictionary

Dictionaries can tell you what all of their keys are, or what all of their values are, if you know how to ask them. The keys method will ask the dictionary to return all of its keys to you as a view so that you can examine them for the key (or keys) you are looking for, and the values method will return all of the values as a view.

```
>>> hungry=menu_specials.keys()
>>>print(list(hungry))
lunch
breakfast
dinner
>>>starving=menu_specials.value()
>>>print(list(starving))
split pea soup and garlic bread
sausage and eggs
2 hot dogs and onion rings
```

How It Works

Both the keys and values methods return views, which you can assign and use like any normal view. When you have the items in a view from the keys method, you can use the items in the view, which are keys, to get their matching values from that dictionary. Note that while a particular key will lead you to a value, you cannot start with a value and reliably find the key associated with it. You try to find the key when you know only a value; you need to exhaustively test all the possible keys to find a matching value, and even then, two different keys can have the same values associated with them.

In addition, the way that dictionaries work is that each key is different (you can't have two keys that are exactly the same), but you can have multiple duplicate values:

```
>>>menu={"breakfast" : "spam", "lunch" : "spam", "dinner": "Spam with a side
of Spam"}
>>>print(menu)
{'lunch': 'spam', 'breakfast': 'spam', 'dinner': 'Spam with a side of Spam'}
>>> menu.get("lunch")
'spam'
>>> menu.get("breakfast")
'spam'
```

As you can see, Python has no problem allowing you to see multiple values in different keys. However, watch what happens when you try the following code, whose purpose is to try and create *keys* with the *same* name:

```
>>> menu2 = {"breakfast" : "spam", "breakfast" : "ham", "dinner": "Spam with
a side of Spam:"}
>>>menu2.get("breakfast")
'ham'
```

What happened here? Although you did not get an error, there is still a mistake in your code. When you typed in the second key named `"breakfast"`, Python replaced the value in the first key with the same name, and replaced the value of the second key with the same name.

Treating a String Like a List

Python offers an interesting feature of strings. Sometimes, it is useful to be able to treat a string as though it were a list of individual characters. It's not uncommon to have extraneous characters at the end of a string. People may not recognize these, but computers will get hung up on them. It's also common to only need to look at the first character of a string to know what you want to do with it. For instance, if you had a list of last names and first names, you could view the first letter of each by using the same syntax that you would for a list. This method of looking at strings is called *slicing* and is one of the fun things about Python:

```
>>> last_names = [ "Douglass", "Jefferson", "Williams", "Frank", "Thomas" ]
>>> print("%s" % last_names[0])
Douglass
>>> print("%s" % last_names[0][0])
D
>>> print("%s" % last_names[1])
Jefferson
>>> print("%s" % last_names[1][0])
J
>>> print("%s" % last_names[2])
Williams
>>> print("%s" % last_names[2][0])
W
```

(continued)

(continued)

```
>>> print("%s" % last_names[3])
Frank
>>> print("%s" % last_names[3][0])
F
>>> print("%s" % last_names[4])
Thomas
>>> print("%s" % last_names[4][0])
T
```

For example, you can use the letter positioning of strings to arrange them into groups in a dictionary based on the first letter of the last name. You don't need to do anything complicated; you can just check to see which letter the string containing the name starts with and file it under that:

```
>>> by_letter = {}
>>> by_letter[last_names[0][0]] = last_names[0]
>>> by_letter[last_names[1][0]] = last_names[1]
>>> by_letter[last_names[2][0]] = last_names[2]
>>> by_letter[last_names[3][0]] = last_names[3]
>>> by_letter[last_names[4][0]] = last_names[4]
```

The by_letter dictionary will, thanks to string slicing, only contain the first letter from each of the last names. Therefore, by_letter is a dictionary indexed by the first letter of each last name. You could also make each key in by_letter reference a list instead and use the append method of that list to create a list of names beginning with that letter (if, of course, you wanted to have a dictionary that indexed a larger group of names, where each one did not begin with a different letter).

Remember that, like tuples, strings are *immutable*. When you are slicing strings, you are actually creating new strings that are copies of sections of the original string.

String Slicing is Very Useful

If you're new to programming, string slicing may seem like an unusual feature at first. Programmers who have used a lower-level language like C or C++ would have learned how to program viewing strings as special lists (and in Python you can also slice lists, as you'll see later), so for them this is natural. For you, it will be a very convenient tool once you've learned how to control repetition over lists in Chapter 4.

Special Types

Python has a handful of special types. You've seen them all, but they bear mentioning on their own: None, True, and False are all special built-in values that are useful at different times.

None is special because there is only one None. It's a name that no matter how many times you use it, it doesn't match any other object, just itself. When you use functions that don't have anything to return to you — that is, when the function doesn't have anything to respond with — it will return None.

True and False are special representations of the numbers 1 and 0. This prevents a lot of the confusion that is common in other programming languages where the truth value of a statement is arbitrary. For instance, in a UNIX shell (shell is both how you interact with the system, as well as a programming language), 0 is true and anything else is false. With C and Perl, 0 is false and anything else is true. However, in all of these cases, there are no built-in names to distinguish these values. Python makes this easier by explicitly naming the values. The names *True* and *False* can be used in elementary comparisons, which you'll see a lot; and in Chapter 4, you learn how these comparisons can dramatically affect your programs — in fact, they enable you to make decisions within your program.

```
>>> True
True
>>> False
False
>>> True == 1
True
>>> True == 0
False
>>> False == 1
False
>>> False == 0
True
>>> False > 0
False
>>>False < 1
True
```

Other Common Sequence Properties

The two types of sequences are tuples and lists; and as you've seen, in some cases strings can be accessed as though they were sequences as well. Strings make sense because you can view the letters in a string as a sequence.

Even though dictionaries represent a group of data, they are not sequences, because they do not have a specific ordering from beginning to end, which is a feature of sequences.

Referencing the Last Elements

All of the sequence types provide you with some shortcuts to make their use more convenient. You often need to know the contents of the final element of a sequence, and you can get that information in two ways. One way is to get the number of elements in the list and then use that number to directly access the value there:

```
>>> last_names = [ "Douglass", "Jefferson", "Williams", "Frank", "Thomas" ]
>>> len(last_names)
5
>>> last_element = len(last_names) - 1
>>> print("%s" % last_names[last_element])
Thomas
```

However, that method takes two steps; and as a programmer, typing it repeatedly in a program can be time-consuming. Fortunately, Python provides a shortcut that enables you to access the last element of a sequence by using the number –1, and the next-to-last element with –2, letting you reverse the order of the list by using negative numbers from –1 to the number that is the negative length of the list (–5 in the case of the last_names list).

```
>>> print("%s" % last_names[-1])
Thomas
>>> print("%s" % last_names[-2])
Frank
>>> print("%s" % last_names[-3])
Williams
```

Ranges of Sequences

You can take sections of a sequence and extract a piece from it, making a copy that you can use separately. The term for creating these groupings is called *slicing* (the same term used for this practice when you did it with strings). Whenever a slice is created from a *list* or a *tuple,* the resulting slice is the same type as the type from which it was created, and you've already seen this with strings. For example, a slice that you make from a *list* is a *list,* a slice you make from a *tuple* is a *tuple,* and the slice from a *string* is a *string.*

Try It Out   **Slicing Sequences**

You've already sliced strings, so try using the same idea to slice tuples, lists, and strings and see what the results are side-by-side:

```
>>> slice_me = ("The", "next", "time", "we", "meet", "drinks", "are", "on", "me")
>>> sliced_tuple = slice_me[5:9]
>>> print(sliced_tuple)
('drinks', 'are', 'on', 'me')
>>> slice_this_list = ["The", "next", "time", "we", "meet", "drinks",
"are", "on", "me"]
>>> sliced_list = slice_this_list[5:9]
>>> print(sliced_list)
['drinks', 'are', 'on', 'me']
>>> slice_this_string = "The next time we meet, drinks are on me"
>>> sliced_string = slice_this_string[5:9]
>>> print(sliced_string)
'ext '
```

How It Works

In each case, using the colon to specify a slice of the sequence instructs Python to create a new sequence that contains just those elements.

Growing Lists by Appending Sequences

Suppose you have two lists that you want to join together. You haven't been shown a purposely built way to do that yet. You can't use append to take one sequence and add it to another. Instead, you will find that you have layered a sequence into your list:

```
>>> living_room = ("rug", "table", "chair", "TV", "dustbin", "shelf")
>>> apartment = []
>>> apartment.append(living_room)
>>> apartment
[('rug', 'table', 'chair', 'TV', 'dustbin', 'shelf')]
```

This is probably not what you want if you were intending to create a list from the contents of the tuple living_room that could be used to create a list of all the items in the apartment.

To copy all of the elements of a sequence, instead of using append, you can use the extend method of lists and tuples, which takes each element of the sequence you give it and inserts those elements into the list from which it is called:

```
>>> apartment = []
>>> apartment.extend(living_room)
>>> apartment
['rug', 'table', 'chair', 'TV', 'dustbin', 'shelf']
```

Using Lists to Temporarily Store Data

You'll often want to acquire data from another source, such as a user entering data or another computer whose information you need. To do that, it is best to put this data in a list so that it can be processed later in the same order in which it arrived.

However, after you've processed the data, you no longer need it to be in the list, because you won't need it again. Temporal (time-specific) information such as stock tickers, weather reports, or news headlines would be in this category.

To keep your lists from becoming unwieldy, a method called pop enables you to remove a specific reference to data from the list after you're done with it. When you've removed the reference, the position it occupied will be filled with whatever the next element was, and the list will be reduced by as many elements as you've popped.

Try It Out   Popping Elements from a List

You need to tell pop which element it is acting on. If you tell it to work on element 0, it will pop the first item in its list, passing pop a parameter of 1 will tell it to use the item at position 1 (the second element in the list), and so on. The element pop acts on is the same number that you'd use to access the list's elements using square brackets (remember that the first value in a list is 0):

```
>>> todays_temperatures = [23, 32, 33, 31]
>>> todays_temperatures.append(29)
>>> todays_temperatures
[23, 32, 33, 31, 29]
```

```
>>> morning = todays_temperatures.pop(0)
>>> print("This mornings temperature was %.02f" % morning)
This mornings temperature was 23.00
>>> late_morning = todays_temperatures.pop(0)
>>> print("Todays late morning temperature was %.02f" % late_morning)
Todays late morning temperature was 32.00
>>> noon = todays_temperatures.pop(0)
>>> print("Todays noon temperature was %.02f" % noon)
Todays noon temperature was 33.00
>>> todays_temperatures
[31, 29]
```

How It Works

When a value is popped, if the action is on the right-hand side of an equals sign, you can assign the element that was removed to a value on the left-hand side, or just use that value in cases where it would be appropriate. If you don't assign the popped value or otherwise use it, it will be discarded from the list.

You can also avoid the use of an intermediate name, by just using pop to populate, say, a string format, because pop will return the specified element in the list, which can be used just as though you'd specified a number or a name that referenced a number:

```
>>> print("Afternoon temperature was %.02f" % todays_temperatures.pop(0))
Afternoon temperature was 31.00
>>> todays_temperatures
[29]
```

If you don't tell pop to use a specific element (0 in the examples) from the list it's invoked from, it will remove the last element of the list, not the first as shown here.

Working with Sets

Sets are similar to dictionaries in Python, except that they consist of only keys with no associated values. Essentially, they are a collection of data with no duplicates. They are very useful when it comes to removing duplicate data from data collections.

Sets come in two types: *mutable* and *immutable frozensets*. The difference between the two is that with a mutable set, you can add, remove, or change its elements, while the elements of an immutable frozenset cannot be changed after they have been initially set.

Try It Out   Removing Duplicates

Here, you assign some values and remove the duplicates by assigning them to a set:

```
>>> alphabet = ['a','b', 'b', 'c', 'a', 'd', 'e']
>>> print(alphabet)
['a', 'b', 'b', 'c', 'a', 'd', 'e']
>>> alph2 = set(alphabet)
{'a', 'c', 'b', 'e', 'd'}
```

How It Works

The example works by taking the data collection, `alphabet`, and converting it to a set. Because sets do not allow duplicate values, the extra `'b'` and `'a'` characters are removed. It was then assigned to `alph2`, and printed to show the results.

Summary

In this chapter, you learned how to manipulate many core types that Python offers. These types are *tuples*, *lists*, *dictionaries*, *sets*, and three special types: None, True, and False. You've also learned a special way that strings can be treated like a sequence. The other sequence types are tuples and lists.

A *tuple* is a sequence of data that's indexed in a fixed numeric order, starting at zero. The references in the tuple can't be changed after the tuple is created, nor can it have elements added or deleted. However, if a tuple contains a data type that has changeable elements, such as a list, the elements of that data type are not prevented from changing. Tuples are useful when the data in the sequence is better off not changing, such as when you want to explicitly prevent data from being accidentally changed.

A *list* is another type of sequence, which is similar to a tuple except that its elements can be modified. The length of the list can be modified to accommodate elements being added using the `append` method, and the length can be reduced by using the `pop` method. If you have a sequence whose data you want to append to a list, you can append it all at once with the `extend` method of a list.

Dictionaries are yet another kind of indexed grouping of data. However, whereas lists and tuples are indexed by numbers, dictionaries are indexed by values that you choose. To explore the indexes, which are called *keys*, you can invoke the `keys` method. To explore the data that is referred to, called the *values*, you can use the `values` method. Both of these methods return lists.

Sets are a collection of items (0 or more), that contain no duplicates. In theory, they are similar to dictionaries, except that they only have keys, and no values associated with those keys. One use for sets is to remove any duplicates from a collection of data. They are also good at mimicking finite mathematical sets.

Other data types are `True`, `False`, and `None`. `True` and `False` are a special way of looking at 1 and 0, but when you want to test whether something is true or false, explicitly using the names `True` and `False` is always the right thing to do. `None` is a special value that is built into Python that only equals itself, and it is what you receive from functions that otherwise would not return any value (such as `True`, `False`, a string, or other values).

The key things to take away from this chapter are:

❑ Variables are names for data that let you refer to the data.

❑ You create a variable by using the syntax: variablename = "Some value".

❑ You can copy the value in one variable by assigning it to another: variablename = copyofvariablename.

❏   Tuples store more than piece of data and are unchangeable.

❏   Lists are also sequences of data, yet unlike tuples, you can change their value.

❏   A dictionary is similar to lists and tuples. It's another type of container for a group of data. However, whereas tuples and lists are indexed by their numeric order, dictionaries are indexed by names that you choose. These names can be letters, numbers, strings, or symbols — whatever suits you.

Exercises

Perform all of the following in the Python shell:

1.   Create a list called `dairy_section` with four elements from the dairy section of a supermarket.

2.   Print a string with the first and last elements of the `dairy_section` list.

3.   Create a tuple called `milk_expiration` with three elements: the month, day, and year of the expiration date on the nearest carton of milk.

4.   Print the values in the `milk_expiration` tuple in a string that reads "This milk carton will expire on 12/10/2009."

5.   Create an empty dictionary called `milk_carton`. Add the following key/value pairs. You can make up the values or use a real milk carton:

❏   `expiration_date`: Set it to the `milk_expiration` tuple.

❏   `fl_oz`: Set it to the size of the milk carton on which you are basing this.

❏   `Cost`: Set this to the cost of the carton of milk.

❏   `brand_name`: Set this to the name of the brand of milk you're using.

6.   Print out the values of all of the elements of the `milk_carton` using the values in the dictionary, and not, for instance, using the data in the `milk_expiration` tuple.

7.   Show how to calculate the cost of six cartons of milk based on the cost of `milk_carton`.

8.   Create a list called cheeses. List all of the cheeses you can think of. Append this list to the `dairy_section` list, and look at the contents of `dairy_section`. Then remove the list of cheeses from the array.

9.   How do you count the number of cheeses in the cheese list?

10.   Print out the first five letters of the name of your first cheese.

Part II
Python Language and the Standard Library

Making Decisions

So far, you have only seen how to manipulate data directly or through names to which the data is bound. Now that you have the basic understanding of how those data types can be manipulated manually, you can begin to exercise your knowledge of data types and use your data to make decisions.

In this chapter, you learn about how Python makes decisions using True and False and how to make more complex decisions based on whether a condition is True or False.

In this chapter you learn:

- ❑ How to create situations in which you can repeat the same actions using loops that give you the capability to automate stepping through lists, tuples, and dictionaries.

- ❑ How to use lists or tuples with dictionaries cooperatively to explore the contents of a dictionary.

- ❑ How to use exception handling to write your programs to cope with problematic situations that you can handle within the program.

Comparing Values — Are They the Same?

You saw True and False in Chapter 3, but you weren't introduced to how they can be used. True and False are the results of comparing values, asking questions, and performing other actions. However, anything that can be given a value and a name can be compared with the set of comparison operations that return True and False.

Try It Out   Comparing Values for Sameness

Testing for equality is done with two equal signs — remember that the single equal sign will bind data to a name, which is different from what you want to do here, which is elicit a `True` or `False`:

```
>>> 1 == 1
True
>>> 1 == 2
False
```

How It Works

When you use the equality comparison, Python compares the values on both sides. If the numbers are different, `False` will be the result. If the numbers are the same, `True` will be the result.

If you have different types of numbers, Python will still be able to compare them and give you the correct answer:

```
>>> 1.23 == 1
False
>>> 1.0 == 1
True
```

You can also use the double equals to test whether strings have the same contents, and you can even restrict this test to ranges within the strings (remember from the last chapter that slices create copies of the part of the strings they reference, so you're really comparing two strings that represent just the range that a slice covers):

```
>>> a = "Mackintosh apples"
>>> b = "Black Berries"
>>> c = "Golden Delicious apples"
>>> a == b
False
>>> b == c
False
>>> a[-len("apples"):-1] == c[-len("apples"):-1]
True
```

Sequences can be compared in Python with the double equals as well. Python considers two sequences to be equal when every element in the same position is the same in each list. Therefore, if you have three items each in two sequences and they contain the same data but in a different order, they are *not* equal:

```
>>> apples = ["Mackintosh", "Golden Delicious", "Fuji", "Mitsu"]
>>> apple_trees = ["Golden Delicious", "Fuji", "Mitsu", "Mackintosh"]
>>> apples == apple_trees
False
>>> apple_trees = ["Mackintosh", "Golden Delicious", "Fuji", "Mitsu"]
>>> apples == apple_trees
True
```

In addition, dictionaries can be compared. Like lists, every key and value (paired, together) in one dictionary has to have a key and value in the other dictionary in which the key in the first is equal to the key in the second, and the value in the first is equal to the value in the second:

```
>>> tuesday_breakfast_sold = {"pancakes":10, "french toast": 4, "bagels":32,
"omelets":12, "eggs and sausages":13}
>>> wednesday_breakfast_sold = {"pancakes":8, "french toast": 5, "bagels":22,
"omelets":16, "eggs and sausages":22}
>>> tuesday_breakfast_sold == wednesday_breakfast_sold
False
>>> thursday_breakfast_sold = {"pancakes":10, "french toast": 4, "bagels":32,
"omelets":12, "eggs and sausages":13}
>>> tuesday_breakfast_sold == thursday_breakfast_sold
True
```

Doing the Opposite — Not Equal

There is an opposite operation to the equality comparison. If you use the exclamation and equals together, you are asking Python for a comparison between any two values that are not equal (by the same set of rules of equality that you saw for the double equal signs) to result in a `True` value.

Try It Out   Comparing Values for Difference

Try out the following examples to see how Python evaluates these comparisons:

```
>>> 3 == 3
True
>>> 3 != 3
False
>>> 5 != 4
True
```

How It Works

Every pair of numbers that would generate a `True` result when they're compared using the `==` will now generate a `False`, and any two numbers that would have generated a `False` when compared using `==` will now result in `True`.

These rules hold true for all of the more complex types, like sequences and dictionaries:

```
>>> tuesday_breakfast_sold != wednesday_breakfast_sold
True
>>> tuesday_breakfast_sold != thursday_breakfast_sold
False
```

Like numbers, any situation that would be `True` with `==` will be `False` with `!=` with these types.

Comparing Values — Which One Is More?

Equality isn't the only way to find out what you want to know. Sometimes you will want to know whether a quantity of something is greater than that of another, or whether a value is less than some other value. Python has *greater than* and *less than* operations that can be invoked with the > and < characters, respectively. These are the same symbols you are familiar with from math books, and the question is always asking whether the value on the *left* is greater than (>) or less than (<) the value on the *right*.

Try It Out	Comparing Greater Than and Less Than

```
>>> 5 < 3
False
>>> 10 > 2
True
```

How It Works

The number on the left is compared to the number on the right. You can compare letters, too. A few conditions exist where this might not do what you expect, such as trying to compare letters to numbers. (The question just doesn't come up in many cases, so what you expect and what Python expects is probably not the same.) The values of the letters in the alphabet run roughly this way: A capital "A" is the lowest letter. "B" is the next, followed by "C" and so on until "Z". This is followed by the lowercase letters, with "a" being the lowest lowercase letter and "z" the highest. However, "a" is *higher* than "Z":

```
>>> "a" > "b"
False
>>> "A" > "b"
False
>>> "A" > "a"
False
>>> "b" > "A"
True
>>> "Z" > "a"
False
```

If you want to compare two strings that are longer than a single character, Python will look at each letter until it finds one that's different. When that happens, the outcome will depend on that one difference. If the strings are completely different, the first letter will decide the outcome:

```
>>> "Zebra" > "aardvark"
False
>>> "Zebra" > "Zebrb"
False
>>> "Zebra" < "Zebrb"
True
```

You can avoid the problem of trying to compare two words that are similar but have differences in capitalization by using a special method of strings called `lower`, which acts on its string and returns a new string with all lowercase letters. There is also a corresponding `upper` method. These are available for *every* string in Python:

```
>>> "Pumpkin" == "pumpkin"
False
>>> "Pumpkin".lower() == "pumpkin".lower()
True
>>> "Pumpkin".lower()
'pumpkin'
>>> "Pumpkin".upper() == "pumpkin".upper()
True
>>> "pumpkin".upper()
'PUMPKIN'
```

Note that you could have also written the preceding code in the following manner:

```
>>> "Pumpkin".lower() == "pumpkin"
True
```

Because `"pumpkin"` is already lowercase, there is no real need to change it, though doing so may be safer. For instance, if someone types in a string incorrectly, capitalizing one of the letters in one of the strings, converting them both would solve any errors. Observe the following:

```
>>> "Pumpkin".lower() == "puMpkin"
False
>>> "Pumpkin".lower() == "puMpkin".lower()
True
```

When you have a string referenced by a name, you can still access all of the methods that strings normally have:

```
>>> gourd = "Calabash"
>>> gourd
'Calabash'
>>> gourd.lower()
'calabash'
>>> gourd.upper()
'CALABASH'
```

More Than or Equal, Less Than or Equal

There is a useful variation on *greater than* and *less than*. It's common to think of things in terms of *greater than or equal to* or *less than or equal to*. You can use a simple shorthand to do that. Join the two symbols in a way that makes sense when you look at it:

```
>>> 1 > 1
False
>>> 1 >= 2
False
>>> 10 < 10
False
>>> 10 <= 10
True
```

Reversing True and False

When you are creating situations and comparing their outcomes, sometimes you want to know whether something is true, and sometimes you want to know whether something is *not* true. Sensibly enough, Python has an operation to create the opposite situation — the word *not* provides the opposite of the truth value that follows it.

Try It Out   **Reversing the Outcome of a Test**

```
>>> not True
False
>>> not 5
False
>>> not 0
True
>>> Not True
SyntaxError: invalid syntax (<pyshell#30>, line 1)
```

Note the error in the last line of code. Be sure not to capitalize the `not` operator, or you will receive an error message similar to the one shown here.

How It Works

The `not` operation applies to any test that results in a `True` or `False`. However, remember from Chapter 3 that anything that's not zero will be seen as `True`, so you can use `not` in many situations where you wouldn't expect it or where it doesn't necessarily make sense:

```
>>> not 5 > 2
False
>>> not "A" < 3
True
>>> not "A" < "z"
False
```

Looking for the Results of More Than One Comparison

You can also combine the results of more than one operation, which enables your programs to make more complex decisions by evaluating the truth values of more than one operation.

One kind of combination is the and operation, which says "if the operation, value, or object on my *left* evaluates to being `True`, move to my *right* and evaluate that. If it doesn't evaluate to `True`, just stop and say `False` — don't do any more."

```
>>> True and True
True
>>> False and True
False
>>> True and False
False
>>> False and False
False
```

The other kind of combining operation is the or operator. Using the or tells Python to evaluate the expression on the *left*, and if it is False, Python will evaluate the expression on the right. If it is True, Python will stop evaluation of any more expressions:

```
>>> True or True
True
>>> True or False
True
>>> False or True
True
>>> False or False
False
```

You may also want to place sequences of these together based on actions you want to happen. In these cases, evaluation starts with the leftmost and or or and continues following the previous rules — in other words, until a False value is evaluated for and, or until a True value is evaluated for or.

How to Get Decisions Made

Python has a very simple way of letting you make decisions. The reserved word for decision making is if, and it is followed by a test for the truth of a condition, and the test is ended with a colon, so you'll see it referred to here as if ... :. It can be used with anything that evaluates to True or False to say "if something is true, do what follows":

```
>>> if 1 > 2:
...     print("No it is not!")
...
>>> if 2 > 1:
...     print("Yes it is!")
...
Yes, it is!
```

Only when the statements to be evaluated between the if and the colon evaluate to True will the indented statements below be visited by Python to be evaluated. The indentation indicates that the code that follows it is a part of the program but is executed only if the right conditions occur. For the if ... : statement, the proper condition is when the comparison being made evaluates to True.

You have just seen one of the most distinctive visual aspects of Python and the one that most people remark on when they encounter Python.

When you see the colon in Python programs, it's an indication that Python is entering a part of its program that is partially isolated from the rest of the program. At this point, indentation becomes important. The indentation is how Python knows that a particular block of code is separate from the code around it. The number of spaces used is important, and a Python-oriented programming editor will always carefully help you maintain the proper indentation for the code that is being written. The number of spaces is relevant, so it is important to use the editor to determine your indentation and not change the number of spaces manually.

You will see more keywords paired with the colon; and in all cases, you need to pay attention to the indentation. Python will warn you with an error if your program has changes in indentation that it doesn't understand.

You can place `if ... :` statements within the indentation of other `if ... :` statements to perform more complex decisions than what can be achieved with `and` and `or` because using `if ... :` enables you to perform any series of statements that you may need before evaluating the indented `if ... :` statement.

Try It Out   Placing Tests within Tests

Try the following example, in which one `if ...:` appears within another:

```
>>> omelet_ingredients = {"egg":2, "mushroom":5, "pepper":1, "cheese":1,
"milk":1}
>>> fridge_contents = {"egg":10, "mushroom":20, "pepper":3, "cheese":2,
"tomato":4, "milk":15}
>>> have_ingredients = [False]
>>> if fridge_contents["egg"] > omelet_ingredients["egg"]:
...       have_ingredients[0] = True
... have_ingredients.append("egg")
...
>>> print(have_ingredients)
[True, 'egg']
>>> if fridge_contents["mushroom"] > omelet_ingredients["mushroom"]:
...       if have_ingredients[0] == False:
...             have_ingredients[0] = True
...       have_ingredients.append("mushroom")
...
>>> print(have_ingredients)
[True, 'egg', 'mushroom']
```

How It Works

After a condition is tested with an `if ...:` and there is an additional level of indentation, Python will continue to evaluate the rest of the code that you've placed in the indentation. If the first `if ...:` isn't true, none of the code below it will be evaluated — it would be skipped entirely.

However, if the first `if ...:` statement is true, the second one at the same level will be evaluated. The outcome of a comparison only determines whether the indented code beneath it will be run. Code at the same level, or above, won't be stopped without something special happening, such as an error or another condition that would prevent the program from continuing to run.

As you can see from the `print()` functions, when Python checked to see if you had more eggs and mushrooms in your fridge than the omelet recipe called for, it appended those two items to your `have_ingredients` variable.

To complete the example, you could enter the rest of this (if you want to make a computer representation of an omelet):

```
>>> if fridge_contents["pepper"] > omelet_ingredients["pepper"]:
...     if have_ingredients[0] == True:
...         have_ingredients[0] = False
...     have_ingredients.append("pepper")
...
>>> if fridge_contents["cheese"] > omelet_ingredients["cheese"]:
...     if have_ingredients[0] == False:
...         have_ingredients[0] = True
...     have_ingredients.append("cheese")
...
>>> if fridge_contents["milk"] > omelet_ingredients["milk"]:
...     if have_ingredients[0] == True:
...         have_ingredients[0] = False
...     have_ingredients.append("milk")
...
>>> if have_ingredients[0] == True :
...     print("I have the ingredients to make an omelet!")
...
I have the ingredients to make an omelet!
```

You can create a chain of tests beginning with `if ...:` using `elif ...:`. `elif ...:` enables a variety of conditions to be tested for but only if a prior condition wasn't met. If you use a series of `if ...:` statements they will all be executed. If you use an `if ...:` followed by an `elif ...:`, the `elif ...:` will be evaluated only if the `if ...:` results in a `False` value:

```
>>> milk_price = 1.50
>>> if milk_price < 1.25:
...     print("Buy two cartons of milk, they're on sale")
... elif milk_price < 2.00:
...     print("Buy one carton of milk, prices are normal")
... elif milk_price > 2.00:
...     print("Go somewhere else!  Milk costs too much here")
...
Buy one carton of milk, prices are normal
```

There is also a *fall-through* statement that you can insert to handle those cases where none of the prior tests resulted in a `True` value: the `else:` statement. If none of the `if ... :` or `elif ... :` statements have test conditions that evaluate to `True`, the `else:` clause is invoked:

```
>>> OJ_price = 2.50
>>> if OJ_price < 1.25:
...     print("Get one, I'm thirsty.")
... elif OJ_price <= 2.00:
...     print("Ummm... sure, but I'll drink it slowly.")
... else:
...     print("I don't have enough money.  Never mind.")
...
I don't have enough money.  Never mind.
```

Repetition

You have seen how many times every element in a sequence, or every element in a dictionary, needs to be examined and compared. Doing this manually is impossibly boring and error prone for a person, even a fast touch-typist. In addition, if you enter these things in manually, you'll be caught off guard when the inevitable typo happens, or when something that you're evaluating is changed elsewhere, and your manually entered code can't easily accommodate that change.

To perform repetitive tasks, Python offers two kinds of repetition operations. Both are similar — in fact, they're almost identical — but each one lets you think about what you're doing differently so each one should have its place in your skill set.

How to Do Something — Again and Again

The two operations that enable you to initiate and control repetitive tasks are the `while` and `for` operations. The `while` operation tests for one truth condition, so it will be referred to as `while ... :`. The `for` operation uses each value from within a list, so it will be referred to as `for ... in ... :`.

The `while ... :` operation will first check for its test condition (the `...` between the `while` and the `:`) and if it's `True`, it will evaluate the statements in its indented block a first time. After it reaches the end of its indented block, which can include other indented blocks, it will once again evaluate its test condition to see whether it is still `True`. If it is, it will repeat its actions again; however, if it is `False`, Python leaves the indented section and continues to evaluate the rest of the program after the `while ... :` section. If names are used in the test condition, then between the first repetition and the next (and the next, and so on), the value referred to by the name could have changed and on and on until there is some reason to stop.

Try It Out   **Using a *while* Loop**

```
>>> i = 10
>>>while i > 0:
print("Lift off in:")
print(i)
i=i - 1

Lift off in:
10
Lift off in:
9
Lift off in:
8
Lift off in:
7
Lift off in:
6
Lift off in:
5
Lift off in:
4
Lift off in:
3
Lift off in:
2
Lift off in:
1
```

How It Works

In the preceding code, you create a variable named i and assign it the value of 10 (note that the variable could have any legal name). Next, you create a *while loop* that states "While the value of i is greater than 0, do this." You then have Python print the sentence Lift off in: followed by the current value of i. Finally, you deduct –1 from i each time through the loop, causing the sequence to occur over and over until the value of i is equal to 0.

Doing this the other way, with the for ... in ... : form of repetition, is, as shown before, very similar to the while ... : form, but it saves you a couple of steps. In the first part, the for ..., you once more assign a variable name (again you use i, a common practice, because it is short for index). In the second part, the in ... : part, you provide a sequence, such as a list, tuple, or in this course, a *range*, which takes each element and assigns the value of the element to the name you provided in the first part:

```
>>> for i in range(10, 0, -1):
print("T-minus: ")
print(i)
...
T-minus:
10
T-minus:
9
T-minus:
8
```

```
T-minus:
7
T-minus:
6
T-minus:
5
T-minus:
4
T-minus:
3
T-minus:
2
T-minus:
1
```

As you can see, this works in a very similar method to your `while` loop, giving you just about the same results (it would have returned the same exact results had I not changed the text to be printed). This version of the `for` loop is a bit more complicated. For an easier version, try this code:

```
>>>for i in range(10):
print(i)
...
1
2
3
4
5
6
7
8
9
```

Here, you simply tell the `for` loop to *iterate* or repeat the process until i is equal to ten. Because you are working with range, it automatically adds one to your variable, causing the program to run once and loop nine more times.

Stopping the Repetition

The common term *infinite loop* refers to a sequence of code that will repeat forever. A simple example just sets up a `while ... :` statement that tests against something that is always going to result in `True`. For instance, just using `True` will always work. You should not type in the following code, because it's the kind of thing that's better to see than to have to do yourself:

```
>>> while True:
...     print ("You're going to get bored with this quickly")
...
You're going to get bored with this quickly
You're going to get bored with this quickly
You're going to get bored with this quickly
You're going to get bored with this quickly
You're going to get bored with this quickly
```

The preceding code continues forever, or until you break out of it. Inconvenient as it seems at first glance to have something that repeats forever, sometimes you may want this — for instance, repeating code is useful in a program that waits for the user to type something in, and when the user is done, returns to waiting.

However, sometimes you will want to know that if certain conditions are met, such as the right time of day, when the water has run out, when there are no more eggs to be made into omelets, and so on, that the repetition can be broken out of even when there is no explicit test in the top of the `while ... :` or when the list that's being used in the `for ... in ... :` doesn't have an end.

Infinite loops can be exited by using the `break` statement. When you try this out, make sure your indentation matches what's on the page:

```
>>>age=0
>>> while True:
how_old=input("Enter your age: ")
if how_old=="No":
    print("Don't be ashamed of your age!")
    break
num=int(how_old)
age=age+num
print("Your age is :")
print(age)
print("That is old!")
...
Enter your age: 1
Your age is :
1
That is old!
Enter your age: 2
Your age is :
3
That is old!
Enter your age: -3
Your age is :
0
That is old!
Enter your age: 50
Your age is :
50
That is old!
Enter your age: No
Don't be ashamed of your age!
>>>
```

In the preceding program, `while`, as you may recall, is always equal to `True`; therefore, the statement `while True` will always loop if left to its own devices. To solve this, you prompt the user for some info; in this case, their age. So long as they enter in a number, the program will add it to their age, giving them a total age and making it appear that they are getting older (unless they are savvy and enter in a negative number, in which case they will get younger!). If they enter only numbers, the program will run forever. However, if they ever enter in the string, `No`, the program will print `Don't be ashamed of your age!` and break out of the loop.

Note the position of the print statement and the break; if you place the print after the break instead of before, it will execute every time the program loops, instead of just when you break out of the loop. So be careful where you place your statements!

If you use break, it will only take you out of the most recent loop — if you have a while ... : loop that contains a for ... in ... : loop indented within it, a break within the for ... in ... : will not break out of the while ... :.

Both while ... : and for ... in ... : loops can have an else: statement at the end of the loop, but it will be run only if the loop doesn't end due to a break statement. In this case, else: could be better named something like done or on_completion, but else: is a convenient name because you've already seen it, and it's not hard to remember.

Try It Out   Using *else* While Repeating

```
>>> for food in ("pate", "cheese", "crackers", "yogurt"):
...       if food == "yogurt":
...                break
... else:
...       print("There is no yogurt!")
...
>>> for food in ("pate", "cheese", "crackers"):
...       if food == "yogurt":
...                break
... else:
...       print("There is no yogurt!")
...
There is no yogurt!
```

How It Works

In each example, there is a test to determine whether there is any yogurt. If there is, the while ... : is terminated by using a break. However, in the second loop, there is no yogurt in the list, so when the loop terminates after reaching the end of the list, the else: condition is invoked.

There is one other commonly used feature for loops: the continue statement. When continue is used, you're telling Python that you do not want the loop to be terminated, but that you want to skip the rest of the current repetition of the loop, and if you're in a for ... in ...: loop, re-evaluate the conditions and the list for the next round.

Try It Out   Using *continue* to Keep Repeating

```
>>> for food in ("pate", "cheese", "rotten apples", "crackers", "whip cream",
"tomato soup"):
...       if food[0:6] == "rotten":
...            continue
...       print("Hey you can %s" % food)
...
```

```
Hey, you can eat pate
Hey, you can eat cheese
Hey, you can eat crackers
Hey, you can eat whip cream
Hey, you can eat tomato soup
```

How It Works

Because you've used an `if ... :` test to determine whether the first part of each item in the `food` list contains the string `"rotten"`, the `"rotten apples"` element will be skipped by the `continue`, whereas everything else is printed as safe to eat.

Handling Errors

You have seen examples of how Python reports errors in Chapter 2 and Chapter 3. Those errors usually contain a lot of information pertaining to what failed and how:

```
>>> fridge_contents = {"egg":8, "mushroom":20, "pepper":3, "cheese":2,
"tomato":4, "milk":13}
>>> if fridge_contents["orange juice"] > 3:
...     print("Sure, let's have some juice!")
...
Traceback (most recent call last):
  File "<pyshell#3>", line 1, in <module>
    if fridge_contents["orange juice"] > 3:
KeyError: 'orange juice'
```

Oops. There is no orange juice in the fridge right now, but it would be nice to be able to learn this without having to crash out of the program.

You have already learned one way to find out about the keys that are present in a dictionary, by using the *keys* method of the dictionary and then searching through the list of keys to determine whether the key you want is present. However, there's no reason not to take a shortcut. The last line of the error shown in the preceding code is:

```
KeyError: 'orange juice'
```

This says that the error Python encountered was an error with the key in the `fridge_contents` dictionary. You can use the error that Python has told you about to brace the program against that particular class of error. You do this with the special word `try:` telling Python to prepare for an error.

Trying Things Out

A `try:` statement sets up a situation in which an `except:` statement can follow it. Each `except:` statement handles the error, which is formally named an *exception* that was just `raised` when Python evaluated the code within the `try:` statement instead of failing. To start with, use `except:` to handle one type of error — for instance, the `KeyError` that you get when trying to check the fridge.

Multiple kinds of exceptions exist, and each one's name reflects the problem that's occurred and, when possible, the condition under which it can happen. Because dictionaries have keys and values, the `KeyError` indicates that the key that was requested from a dictionary isn't present. Similarly, a `TypeError` indicates that while Python was expecting one type of data (such as a string or an integer), another type was provided that can't do what's needed.

In addition, when an exception occurs, the message that you would have otherwise seen when the program stops (when you run interactively) can be accessed.

When you've learned more, you'll be able to define your own types of exceptions for conditions that require it.

You have only one line in which to handle the error, which may seem restrictive, but in Chapter 5 you learn how to write your own functions so you can handle errors with more flexibility.

```
>>> fridge_contents = {"egg":8, "mushroom":20, "pepper":3, "cheese":2,
"tomato":4, "milk":13}
>>> try:
...     if fridge_contents["orange juice"] > 3:
...         print("Sure, let's have some juice!")
... except KeyError:
...     print("Awww, there is no juice. Let's go shopping!")
...
Aww, there's no juice.  Lets go shopping
```

You may find that you need to print more information about the error itself, and this is the information that you have access to.

Try It Out   Creating an Exception with Its Explanation

```
>>> fridge_contents = {"egg":8, "mushroom":20, "pepper":3, "cheese":2,
"tomato":4, "milk":13}
>>> try:
...     if fridge_contents["orange juice"] > 3:
...         print("Sure, let's have some juice")
... except (KeyError)as error:
...     print("Woah!  There is no %s" % error)
...
Woah!  There is no 'orange juice'
```

How It Works

Because there is no key in the `fridge_contents` dictionary for `"orange juice"`, a `KeyError` is raised by Python to let you know that no such key is available. In addition, you specified the name *error*, which Python will use to reference a string that contains any information about the error that Python can offer. We achieve this by using the as keyword to assign the value of the KeyError to error. In this case, the string relates to the key that was requested but not present in the `fridge_contents` dictionary (which is, again, `"orange juice"`).

There may be times when you handle more than one type of error in exactly the same way; and in those cases, you can use a tuple with all of those *exception* types described:

```
>>> fridge_contents = {"egg":8, "mushroom":20, "pepper":3, "cheese":2,
"tomato":4, "milk":13}
>>> try:
...     if fridge_contents["orange juice"] > 3:
...         print("Sure, let's have some juice")
... except (KeyError, TypeError)as error:
...     print("Woah!  There is no %s" % error)
...
Woah!  There is no 'orange juice'
```

If you have an exception that you need to handle, but you want to handle it by not doing anything (for cases in which failure isn't actually a big deal), Python will let you skip that case by using the special word pass:

```
>>> fridge_contents = {"egg":8, "mushroom":20, "pepper":3, "cheese":2,
"tomato":4, "milk":13}
>>> try:
...     if fridge_contents["orange juice"] > 3:
...         print("Sure, let's have some juice")
... except (KeyError) as error:
...     print("Woah!  There is no %s" % error)
... except (TypeError):
...     pass
...
Woah!  There is no 'orange juice'
```

There is also an else: clause that can be put at the end of the try: block of code. This will only be run when there are no errors to be caught. Like before, else may not be the obvious choice for a name that could better be described as "in case it all works" or "all_clear" or something like that. By now, however, you can see how else: has become a flexible catch-all that means "in case something happens" although it's not consistent. In any case, it's there for you to use.

Summary

In this chapter, you learned about the methods for making decisions that Python offers. Any operation that results in True or False can be used by if ... : statements to determine whether a program will evaluate an indented block of code.

You have seen for the first time the important role that indentation plays in Python programs. Even in the interactive Python shell the number of spaces in the indentation matters.

You now have the knowledge to use sequence and dictionary elements in repetition loops. By using repetitions, you can perform operations on every element in a list and make decisions about the values of each list element.

The two types of repeating loops that Python offers you are the while ... : loop and the for ... in ... : loop. They perform similar jobs, continuing until a condition causes them to finish. The difference between the two lies in the conditions that will permit them to evaluate their indented block of code. The while ... : loop only tests for True or False in its test case, while the for ... in ... : loop will take a sequence you provide in the in ... : section, and each element from first to last in the sequence will be assigned to the value provided in the for ... section.

Both types of repeating loops can be exited before their test conditions are met by using the break operation. The break operation will cause the loop that is being evaluated to stop without further evaluations of any more code in the loop's code block. However, if a break operation is performed, the optional else: condition for a loop will not be run. In addition to break is the continue operation, which will skip the rest of the current loop but return to the top of the loop and evaluate the next test case.

You also learned about one other kind of decision making, which is handling the exceptions that Python uses to report errors. These exceptions are how any error is reported. If they are not accommodated, these errors will result in your program stopping at the point at which the error occurred. However, if you enclose code that may cause an error in a code block indented beneath a try: you can specify how to prevent the program from exiting, even going so far as handling the error and continuing with the program. The errors that you anticipate encountering will be specified in the except ... : clause, where the first value provided defines the type of the error (or types if a tuple of error types is provided); and, optionally, the word as followed by a name used to refer to data containing information about the error, can be provided.

The key things to take away from this chapter are:

❑ You can test for equality using two equal signs (==). If the answer is True, True will be returned. If False, False will be returned. Double equals can also be used to determine if two variables hold the same data.

❑ If you need to know if two values are not equal, you can use the not equal operator (!=). In this instance, True means that the values compared are not equal and False means that the compared values are equal.

❑ To compare if a value is greater or less than another value, you can use the greater than (>) and less than (<) operators, respectively. If you need to know if a value is equal to or greater/lesser than, you would use the greater- than-or-equal-to operator (>=) or the less-than-or-equal-to operator (<=).

❑ If you need a program to make a decision based on if a value is true or false, you can use the if statement, which simply states, if this is true, do that. To have your program do something if one value is true, and something else if it is not, you can use if...elif.

❑ Sometimes you will need to loop through a certain action a number of times. Using the while loop, you can repeat or iterate the action for as long as the while condition equals true, or literally speaking, while this is true, do this.

❑ If you need to loop through an action a set number of times, you can do so using the for loop, which uses a loop counter to tell how many times to repeat a given action.

❑ A try: statement sets up a situation in which an except: statement can follow it. Each except: statement handles the error, which is formally named an exception that was just raised when Python evaluated the code within the try: statement instead of failing.

Exercises

Perform all of the following in the codeEditor Python shell:

1. Using a series of `if ... :` statements, evaluate whether the numbers from 0 through 4 are `True` or `False` by creating five separate tests.

2. Create a test using a single `if ... :` statement that will tell you whether a value is between 0 and 9 inclusively (that is, the number can be 0 or 9 as well as all of the numbers in between, not just 1–8) and print a message if it's a success. Test it.

3. Using `if ... :`, `elif,...:` and `else:`, create a test for whether a value referred to by a name is in the first two elements of a sequence. Use the `if ... :` to test for the first element of the list; use `elif ... :` to test the second value referenced in the sequence; and use the `else:` clause to print a message indicating whether the element being searched for is not in the list.

4. Create a dictionary containing foods in an imaginary refrigerator, using the name `fridge`. The name of the food will be the key, and the corresponding value of each food item should be a string that describes the food. Then create a name that refers to a string containing the name of a food. Call the name `food_sought`. Modify the test from Exercise 3 to be a simple `if ... :` test (no `elif ... :` or `else:` will be needed here) for each key and value in the refrigerator using a `for ... in ... :` loop to test every key contained in the fridge. If a match is found, print a message that contains the key and the value and then use break to leave the loop. Use an `else ... :` statement at the end of the for loop to print a message for cases in which the element wasn't found.

5. Modify Exercise 3 to use a `while ... :` loop by creating a separate list called `fridge_list` that will contain the values given by `fridge.keys`. As well, use a variable named, `current_key` that will refer to the value of the current element in the loop that will be obtained by the method `fridge_list.pop`. Remember to place `fridge_list.pop` as the last line of the `while ... :` loop so that the repetition will end normally. Use the same `else:` statement at the end of the while loop as the one used at the end of Exercise 3.

6. Query the fridge dictionary created in Exercise 3 for a key that is not present, and elicit an error. In cases like this, the `KeyError` can be used as a shortcut to determining whether or not the value you want is in the list. Modify the solution to Exercise 3 so that instead of using a `for ... in ... :` a `try:` block is used.

Functions

Up until this point, any time you wanted to accomplish a task, you needed to type out entire programs to do the job. If you needed to do the same work again, you could type the entire program again or place it in a loop. However, loops are most useful when you are repeating the same thing, but writing the same loop repeatedly in different parts of your program with slightly modified values in each one is not a sane way to live your life.

Python has *functions* that enable you to gather sections of code into more convenient groupings that can be called on when you have a need for them.

In this chapter you learn:

❑ How to create and use your own functions.

❑ You are given guidelines to help facilitate your thinking about how to create and structure your programs to use functions.

❑ How to write your functions so that you can later interrogate them for information about how they behave and what you intend for them to do.

Putting Your Program into Its Own File

As the examples in this book get longer, typing the entire code block begins to be a burden. A single mistake causes you to retype in the entire block of code you are working on. Long before you've gotten to the point where you have more than, say, 40 lines of code to type, you are unlikely to want to have to do it more than once.

You are probably already aware that programmers write programs that are saved as source code into files that can be opened, edited, and run without a great deal of work.

To reach this far more convenient state of affairs, from here on out you should type the programs you are using into Python Code Editor, and save the examples from the book into a single folder from which you can reference them and run them. One suggestion for naming the folder could be "Learning Python," and then you could name the programs according to the chapters in which they appear.

You can do two things to make your programs easy to run. The first line of all of your Python files should look like this:

```
#!/usr/bin/env python 3.1
```

This enables UNIX and Linux systems to run the script if you follow the instructions in the appendix at the end of the book. A second important thing to do is to name all of your Python files with names that end in .py. On Windows systems, this will provide the operating system with the information that it needs to launch the file as a Python file and to not just treat it as a text file. For instance, if you put all of the examples from the chapters you've read so far into their own files, you may have a folder with the following files:

```
chapter_1.py
chapter_2.py
chapter_3.py
chapter_4.py
chapter_5.py
```

After you save your first program into a file, you'll notice that codeEditor has begun to emphasize certain parts of the file by displaying them in a few different colors and styles. You'll notice a pattern — some of the built-in functions and reserved words are treated one way, whereas strings get a different treatment and a few keywords are treated yet another way. However, most of the text in your files will still be plain black and white, as shown in Figure 5-1.

```
* chapter_5.py - Code Editor PythonCard Application *

File  Edit  View  Format  Shell  Help

 1 def make_food(ingredients_needed, food_name):
 2     """make_food(ingredients_needed, food_name)
 3     Takes the ingredients from ingredients_needed and makes food_name"""
 4     for ingredient in ingredients_needed.keys():
 5         print "Adding %d of %s to make a %s" % (ingredients_needed[ingredient], ingred
 6     print "Made %s" % food_name
 7     return food_name
 8
 9 def make_omlette(omlette_type):
10     """This will make an omlette.  You can either pass in a dictionary
11     that contains all of the ingredients for your omlette, or provide
12     a string to select a type of omlette this function already knows
13     about"""
14     if type(omlette_type) == type({}):
15         print "omlette_type is a dictionary with ingredients"
16         return make_food(omlette_type, "omlette")
17     elif type(omlette_type) == type(""):
18         omlette_ingredients = get_omlette_ingredients(omlette_type)
19         return make_food(omlette_ingredients, omlette_type)
20     else:
21         print "I don't think I can make this kind of omlette: %s" % omlette_type
22     def get_omlette_ingredients(omlette_name):
23         """This contains a dictionary of omlette names that can be produced,
24 and their ingredients"""
25         # All of our omlettes need eggs and milk
26         ingredients = {"eggs":2, "milk":1}
27         if omlette_name == "cheese":
28             ingredients["cheddar"] = 2
29         elif omlette_name == "western":
30             ingredients["jack_cheese"] = 2
31             ingredients["ham"]         = 1
32             ingredients["pepper"]      = 1

File: /home/spacey/chapter_5.py  |  Line: 1  |  Column: 1
```

Figure 5-1

Using these files enables you to type any example only once. After an example has been typed in and saved, you can run it with python -i <filename>. The -i tells python to read your program file, and then lets you continue to interact with Python, instead of exiting immediately, which is what it normally would do. Within codeEditor, you can do this automatically by selecting Run with Interpreter from the File menu.

Try It Out   **Run a Program with Python -i**

To show how you can take advantage of running python -i or Run with Interpreter, enter the following code into a file called ch5-demo.py:

```
#!/usr/bin/env python 3.1
    a = 10
b = 20

print("A added to B is %d" % (a + b))
```

Now when you invoke Python with the -i option, you will be in a Python interactive session that looks like the following:

```
A added to B is 30
>>>
```

How It Works

The code you entered into your ch5-demo.py file has all been evaluated now, and you can continue to interact with the values of a and b, as well as expand upon it, just as though 'you'd entered them by hand. This will save you time as the examples get longer. Now that you know all of this, some things are demonstrated in the shell first, but that you can save yourself to be run later. Other things are shown as code within a file that needs to be saved and run. You'll be seeing programs in files because either the material being covered doesn't demonstrate an idea that is best shown off by forcing you to do the extra work of typing in the same thing over and over, or of having you interact with it. Or it's simply too long to subject you to entering over and over each time you want to test it.

Functions: Grouping Code under a Name

Most modern programming languages provide you with the capability to group code together under a name; and whenever you use that name, all of the code that was grouped together is invoked and evaluated without having to be retyped every time.

To create a named function that will contain your code, you use the word def, which you can think of as *defining* a functional block of code.

Try It Out   **Defining a Function**

Try saving the following in your file for Chapter 5, ch5.py.def in_fridge():

```
try:
    count = fridge[wanted_food]
except KeyError:
    count = 0
return count
```

How It Works

When you invoke ch5.py (press F5 while in Code Editor) with just the in_fridge function defined, you won't see any output. However, the function will be defined, and it can be invoked from the interactive Python session that you've created.

To take advantage of the in_fridge function, though, you have to ensure that there is a dictionary called *fridge* with food names in it. In addition, you have to have a string in the name wanted_food. This string is how you can ask, using in_fridge, whether that food is available. Therefore, from the interactive session, you can do this to use the function:

```
>>> fridge = {'apples':10, 'oranges':3, 'milk':2}
>>> wanted_food = 'apples'
>>> in_fridge()
10
>>> wanted_food = 'oranges'
>>> in_fridge()
3
>>> wanted_food = 'milk'
>>> in_fridge()
2
```

This is more than just useful — it makes sense and it saves you work. This grouping of blocks of code under the cover of a single name means that you can now simplify your code, which in turn enables you to get more done more quickly. You can type less and worry less about making a mistake as well.

Functions are a core part of any modern programming language, and they are a key part of getting problems solved using Python.

Functions can be thought of as a question and answer process when you write them. When they are invoked, a question is often being asked of them: "How many?" "What time?" "Does this exist?" "Can this be changed?" and more. In response, functions will often return an answer — a value that will contain an answer, such as True, a sequence, a dictionary, or another type of data. In the absence of any of these, the answer returned is the special value None.

Even when a function is mainly being asked to just get something simple done, there is usually an implied question that you should know to look for. When a function has completed its task, the questions "Did it work?" or "How did it work out?" are usually part of how you invoke the function.

Choosing a Name

One of the first guidelines to writing functions well is that you should name your functions to reflect their purpose. They should indicate what you want them to do. Examples of this that come with Python that you have seen are print, type, and len.

When you decide on a name, you should think about how it will be invoked in the program. It is always good to name a function so that when it's called, it will be read naturally by yourself and others later. It is very common to forget the specifics of what you put into a function within a couple of weeks, so the name becomes the touchstone that you use to recall what it's doing when you return to use it again later.

Describing a Function in the Function

After you've chosen a name for your function, you should also add a description of the function. Python enables you to do this in a way that is simple and makes sense.

If you place a string as the first thing in a function, without referencing a name to the string, Python will store it in the function so you can reference it later. This is commonly called a *docstring*, which is short for *documentation string*.

Documentation in the context of a function is anything written that describes the part of the program (the function, in this case) that you're looking at. It's famously rare to find computer software that is well documented. However, the simplicity of the docstring feature in Python makes it so that, generally, much more information is available inside Python programs than in programs written in other languages that lack this friendly and helpful convention.

The text inside the docstring doesn't necessarily have to obey the indentation rules that the rest of the source code does, because it's only a string. Even though it may visually interrupt the indentation, it's important to remember that, when you've finished typing in your docstring, the remainder of your functions must still be correctly indented.

```python
def in_fridge ():
  """This is a function to see if the fridge has a food.
fridge has to be a dictionary defined outside of the function.
the food to be searched for is in the string wanted_food"""
    try:
        count = fridge[wanted_food]
    except KeyError:
        count = 0
    return count
```

The docstring is referenced through a name that is part of the function, almost as though the function were a dictionary. This name is __doc__, and it's found by following the function name with a period and the name __doc__. Note that there are two underscores (_) preceding and following doc.

Displaying __doc__

You should now exit the interactive session that you entered in the last example and re-invoke ch5.py, because it now has the docstring added to in_fridge. After you've done that, you can do the following:

```
>>> print("%s" % in_fridge.__doc__)
This is a function to see if the fridge has a food.
fridge has to be a dictionary defined outside of the function.
the food to be searched for is in the string wanted_food
```

How It Works

Functions, like other types you've seen, have properties that can be used by following the name of the function with a period and the name of the property. __doc__ is a string like any other and can be easily printed for your reference while you're in an interactive session.

The function has other information too (a set of information that it maintains that can be viewed with the built-in function dir).

dir shows you all of the properties of the object in which you're interested, such as a function, including things that Python uses internally:

```
>>> dir()
['__annotations__', '__call__', '__class__', '__closure__', '__code__',
'__defaults__', '__delattr__', '__dict__', '__doc__', '__eq__', '__format__',
'__ge__', '__get__', '__getattribute__', '__globals__', '__gt__', '__hash__',
'__init__', '__kwdefaults__', '__le__', '__lt__', '__module__', '__name__',
'__ne__', '__new__', '__reduce__', '__reduce_ex__', '__repr__',
__setattr__','__sizeof__', '__str__', '__subclasshook__']
```

Any of these properties can be accessed using the same notation that you used for getting the data referenced by in_fridge.__doc__, but normally you don't need to use most of these attributes directly, although it is a good exercise to explore these elements with the type built-in function to see how Python describes them.

The Same Name in Two Different Places

One special property of a function is that it's the first example you've seen of how the names that refer to values can be compartmentalized. What this means is that if you have a name outside of a function, that name refers to a particular value — whether it's a string, a number, a dictionary, a sequence, or a function. All of these share the same space.

For example, if you create a name for a string and then on the next line create a dictionary and reference it to the same name, the string would no longer be referenced by that name, only the dictionary:

```
>>> fridge = "Chilly Ice Makers"
>>> print(fridge)
Chilly Ice Makers
>>> fridge = {'apples':10, 'oranges':3, 'milk':2}
>>> print("%s" %  fridge)
{'apples': 10, 'oranges': 3, 'milk': 2}
```

This makes sense; however, this changes within a function when it's being used. The function creates a new space in which names can be reused and re-created without affecting the same names if they exist in other spaces in your program. This enables you to write functions without worrying about having to micromanage whether somewhere, in another function, a name that you are using is already being used.

Therefore, when you are writing a function, your function has its names, and another function has its own names, and they are separate. Even when a name in both functions contains all of the same letters, because they're each in separate functions they are completely separate entities that will reference separate values.

At the same time, if a function is going to be used in a known situation, where you have ensured that a name it needs to use will be defined and have the right data already referenced, it is able to access this *global* data by using that already-defined name. Python's ability to do this comes from separating the visibility of a name into separate conceptual areas. Each one of these areas is called a *scope*.

Scope defines how available any name is to another part of the program. The scope of a name that's used inside of a function can be thought of as being on a vertical scale. The names that are visible everywhere are at the *top* level and they are referred to in Python as being *global*. Names in any particular function are a level below that — a scope that is *local* to each function. Functions do not share these with other functions at the same level; they each have their own scope.

Any name in the top-level scope can be reused in a lower-level scope without affecting the data referred to by the top-level name:

```
>>> special_sauce = ['ketchup', 'mayonnaise', 'french dressing']
>>> def make_new_sauce():
... """This function makes a new special sauce all its own"""
...     special_sauce = ["mustard", "yogurt"]
...     return special_sauce
...
```

At this point, there is a special sauce in the top-level scope, and another that is used in the function make_new_sauce. When they are run, you can see that the name in the global scope is not changed:

```
>>> print("%s" % special_sauce)
['ketchup', 'mayonnaise', 'french dressing']
>>> new_sauce = make_new_sauce()
>>> print(special_sauce)
['ketchup', 'mayonnaise', 'french dressing']
>>> print(new_sauce)
['mustard', 'yogurt']
```

Remember that different functions can easily use the same name for a variable defined inside the function — a name that will make sense in both functions, but reference different values, without conflicting with each other.

Making Notes to Yourself

Python has an additional feature of the language to help you to keep track of your program. Everything that you type into a program, even if it doesn't change how the program behaves (like *docstrings*) up to this point, has been processed by Python. Even unused strings will cause Python to create the string just in case you were going to use it.

In addition to unneeded strings, every programming language gives you the capability to place comments within your code that don't have any effect whatsoever on the program. They are not there for Python to read but for *you* to read.

If at any point a line has the # character and it's not in a string, Python will ignore everything that follows it. It will only begin to evaluate statements by continuing on the next line and reading the remainder of the program from there.

Try It Out **Experimenting with Comments**

If you test out comments interactively you can see how they're different from strings when Python reads them:

```
>>> "This is a string"
'This is a string'
>>> # This is a comment
>>>
>>> "This is a string" # with a comment at the end
'This is a string'
    >>> print("# Here is a pound sign within a string, being treated as a
string!")
    # Here is a pound sign within a string, being treated as a string!
```

How It Works

When a comment appears by itself, Python ignores it and returns with the prompt asking for your next request, trying to prompt you to enter a statement that it can evaluate. When a comment appears on a line with something that can be evaluated, even just a string, Python knows that you have already given your instructions to it.

Normally, comments will appear in program files. It's unlikely you'll ever bother entering comments as annotations in your interactive sessions, but that's how you'll want to use them in your program files.

In addition, when you want to test changes in a program, it's very useful to use comments to disable a line (or more than one line) of code that is causing problems by placing a comment in front of it. Be careful, though. A comment does affect the indentation that Python pays strict attention to. You need to be careful to place comments that are within functions at the proper indentation level, because if you don't, Python will treat the comment as though it has closed out that function, if ...: block, or other cause of indentation, and that's almost certainly not what you want!

Keeping comments at the same indentation level also makes reading the comment much easier because it is obvious to which part of the code the comment applies.

Asking a Function to Use a Value You Provide

In the in_fridge example, the values used by the function were in the global scope. The function in_fridge only operated on already defined values whose names were already visible to the whole program. This works only when you have a very small program.

When you move to larger programs consisting of hundreds, thousands, or more lines of code (the length of a program is often measured in terms of the numbers of lines it contains), you usually can't count on the global availability of a particular name — it may be changed, based on decisions made by other people and without your involvement! Instead, you can specify that a function will, every time it is invoked, require that it be given the values that you want it to work with.

These values are the specifications or *parameters* that the function will use to do its job. When the function is invoked, these *parameters* can be names that reference data, or they can be static data such as a number like 5 or a string. In all cases, the actual data will enter the scope of the called function instead of being global.

> **With many of the examples in the book, those that progress by offering different and improved versions of themselves can be added to the same file unless you are instructed to explicitly change the function you are working on.**
>
> **You don't always need to remove the prior revision of a function, because the next version will simply "bump" it. This gives you the opportunity to look at the changes that are being made to the function by comparing the old to the new.**
>
> **As long as the most recent version is at the bottom of the file when you load it, that version will be used.**
>
> **This can be a useful practice when you're writing your own programs as well. There's little as painful as fiddling with a piece of code that was working and then not remembering how to return it to a working state.**

Notice that, in the following code, def — the definition of the function — has now changed so that it specifies that the function will expect two parameters by naming them in the tuple that follows the function name. Those parameters will enter and remain in the scope of the in_fridge function, and they'll be seen as the names some_fridge and desired_item.

```
def in_fridge(some_fridge, desired_item):
    """This is a function to see if the fridge has a food.
    fridge has to be a dictionary defined outside of the function.
    the food to be searched for is in the string wanted_food"""
    try:
        count = some_fridge[desired_item]
    except KeyError:
        count = 0
    return count
```

When you invoke a function with parameters, you specify the values for the parameters by placing the values or the names you want to use between the parentheses in the invocation of the in_fridge function, separated by commas. You've already done this with functions like len.

Try It Out   Invoking a Function with Parameters

Once again, you should re-invoke an interactive Python session by running python -i ch5.py or use Run with Interpreter so that you will have an interactive session with the new in_fridge function defined:

```
>>> fridge = {'apples':10, 'oranges':3, 'milk':2}
>>> wanted_food = "oranges"
>>> in_fridge(fridge, wanted_food)
3
```

How It Works

The fridge dictionary and the wanted_food string are given as parameters to the new in_fridge function. After the scope of the function is entered, the dictionary referenced by fridge is now referenced by the name some_fridge. At the same time, the string "oranges", referenced by wanted_food, is associated with the name desired_item upon entering the scope of the in_fridge function. After this setup is done, the function has the information it needs to do its job.

To further demonstrate how this works, you can use unnamed values — data that isn't referenced from names:

```
>>> in_fridge({'cookies':10, 'broccoli':3, 'milk':2}, "cookies")
10
```

These values are brought into the scope of the in_fridge function and assigned by the definition of the function to the names that are used inside of the functions. The proof of this is that there is no longer a global top-level name to be referenced from within the function.

Checking Your Parameters

The parameters that you intend to be used could be expecting different types than what they are given when the function is called. For example, you could write a function that expects to be given a dictionary but by accident is instead given a list, and your function will run until an operation unique to a dictionary is accessed. Then the program will exit because an exception will be generated. This is different from some other languages, which try to ensure that the type of each parameter is known, and can be checked to be correct.

Python does not check to see what kind of data it's associating to the names in a function. In most cases this isn't a problem because an operation on the provided data will be specific to a type, and then fail to work properly if the type of data that the name references is not correct.

For instance, if in_fridge is given a number instead of a dictionary, Python, when trying to access the number as though it were a dictionary, will raise an error that the except: will not catch. A TypeError will be generated indicating that the type Python tried to operate on isn't capable of doing what Python expected:

```
>>> in_fridge(4, "cookies")
Traceback (most recent call last):
  File "<stdin>", line 1, in ?
  File "<stdin>", line 7, in in_fridge
TypeError: unsubscriptable object
```

In this case, you've been shown a number being given to a function where you know that the function expects to operate on a dictionary. No matter what, a number does not have a property where a name can be used as the key to find a value. A number doesn't have keys and it doesn't have values. The idea is that in any context, finding 4("cookies") can't be done in Python, and so an exception is raised.

The term *unsubscriptable* is how Python indicates that it can't find a way to follow a key to a value the way it needs to with a dictionary. *Subscripting* is the term for describing when you access an element in a list or a tuple as well as a dictionary, so you can encounter this error in any of those contexts.

This behavior — not requiring you to specifically define what type you expect, and allowing you to flexibly decide how you want to treat it — can be used to your advantage. It enables you to write a single function that handles any kind of input that you want. You can write a single function that can take more than one type as its parameter and then decide how the function should behave based on the type it is given. Which approach you take depends on what you need to do in your own program.

To determine the type of some data, remember that you can use the type built-in function, which was introduced in Chapter 2. Using the output of this, you can verify the type of variable in the beginning of your functions:

```
def make_omelet(omelet_type):
    """This will make an omelet.  You can either pass in a dictionary
    that contains all of the ingredients for your omelet, or provide
    a string to select a type of omelet this function already knows
    about"""
    if type(omelet_type) == type({}):
        print("omelet_type is a dictionary with ingredients")
        return make_food(omelet_type, "omelet")
```

```
        elif type(omelet_type) == type(""):
            omelet_ingredients = get_omelet_ingredients(omelet_type)
            return make_food(omelet_ingredients, omelet_type)
        else:
            print("I don't think I can make this kind of omelet: %s" %
omelet_type)
```

By itself, this definition of make_omelet won't work because it relies on a few functions that you haven't written yet. You will sometimes do this as you program — create names for functions that need to be written later. You'll see these functions later in this chapter, at which point this code will become fully usable.

Try It Out   **Determining More Types with the `type` Function**

The following should be entered after loading your ch5.py file with python -i or the Run with Interpreter command:

```
>>> fridge = {'apples':10, 'oranges':3, 'milk':2}
>>> type(fridge)
<class 'dict'>
>>> type({})
<class 'dict'>
>>> type("Omelet")
<class 'str'>
>>> type("")
<class 'str'>
```

How It Works

The first thing to note here is that the type function returns the class of an object. You can use this class object in tests — it can be compared to another class object. Note that in Python, classes and types are just different words for the same thing — that is, they define the data type of variables and values.

Try It Out   **Using Strings to Compare Types**

There is one other feature you can use here. You have seen that for the print function, many objects in Python can be represented as strings. This is because many objects have a built-in capability to convert themselves into strings for the times when that's needed.

For example, an alternative way of writing the preceding comparison could be as follows:

```
>>> fridge = {'apples':10, 'oranges':3, 'milk':2}
>>> str(type(fridge))
"<class 'dict'>"
>>> if str(type(fridge))=="<class 'dict'>":
...     print("They match!")
...
They match!
```

How It Works

Because you can find out ahead of time what the string representation of a type object looks like, you can use that string to compare to a type object that has been rendered into a string by the `str` function.

Setting a Default Value for a Parameter — Just in Case

There is one more trick available to you to ensure that your functions will be easier to use. Every parameter to a function needs to have a value. If values aren't assigned to the names of all of the required parameters, a function will raise an error — or worse, it could somehow return data that is wrong.

To avoid this condition, Python enables you to create functions with default values that will be assigned to the parameter's name if the function is invoked without that parameter being explicitly provided in its invocation. You've already seen this behavior — for instance, with the `pop` method of lists, which can either be told to work on a particular element in a list, or if no value is given, will automatically use the last element.

You can do this in your own functions by using the *assignment* operator (the = sign) in the parameter list when you define them. For instance, if you wanted a variation on `make_omelet` that will make a cheese omelet by default, you have only to change its definition and nothing else.

Try It Out   Setting a Default Parameter

Cut and paste the entire `make_omelet` function. Then, by changing only the definition in your new copy of the function to the following, you'll get the behavior of having a cheese omelet by default:

```
def make_omelet2(omelet_type = "cheese"):
```

How It Works

This definition doesn't change the way that any of the remaining code in the function behaves. It sets up `omelet_type` only if it hasn't been defined when the `make_omelet2` function is invoked.

This still enables you to specify an omelet by using a dictionary or a different kind of omelet! However, if `make_omelet` is defined this way, you can call it without any particular kind of omelet being specified; and instead of bailing out on you; the function will make you a cheese omelet.

Doing this same thing to `make_omelet` is the first step toward writing a `make_omelet` function that will be able to behave in a friendly and obvious way. Remember, though, that you still need to write other functions! The goal is to have output like the following:

```
>>> make_omelet()
Adding 2 of eggs to make a cheese
Adding 2 of cheddar to make a cheese
Adding 1 of milk to make a cheese
Made cheese
'cheese'
```

```
>>> make_omelet("western")
Adding 1 of pepper to make a western
Adding 1 of ham to make a western
Adding 1 of onion to make a western
Adding 2 of eggs to make a western
Adding 2 of jack_cheese to make a western
Adding 1 of milk to make a western
Made western
'western'
```

If you write a function with more than one parameter and you want to have both required and optional parameters, you have to place the optionals at the end of your list of parameters. This is because once you've specified that a parameter is optional; it may or may not be there. From the first optional parameter, Python can't guarantee the presence of the remaining parameters — those to the right of your optional parameters. In other words, every parameter after the first default parameter becomes optional. This happens automatically, so be careful and be aware of this when you use this feature.

Calling Functions from within Other Functions

Functions declared within the top level, or global scope, can be used from within other functions and from within the functions inside of other functions. The names in the global scope can be used from everywhere, because the most useful functions need to be available for use within other functions.

In order to have a make_omelet function work the way you saw earlier, it should rely on other functions to be available, so they can be used by make_omelet.

This is how it should work: First, a function acts like sort of a cookbook. It will be given a string that names a type of omelet and return a dictionary that contains all of the ingredients and their quantities. This function will be called get_omelet_ingredients, and it needs one parameter — the name of the omelet:

```
def get_omelet_ingredients(omelet_name):
    """This contains a dictionary of omelet names that can be produced,
and their ingredients"""
    # All of our omelets need eggs and milk
    ingredients = {"eggs":2, "milk":1}
    if omelet_name == "cheese":
        ingredients["cheddar"] = 2
    elif omelet_name == "western":
        ingredients["jack_cheese"] = 2
        ingredients["ham"]         = 1
        ingredients["pepper"]      = 1
        ingredients["onion"]       = 1
    elif omelet_name == "greek":
```

```
        ingredients["feta_cheese"] = 2
        ingredients["spinach"]     = 2
    else:
        print("That's not on the menu, sorry!")
        return None
    return ingredients
```

The second function you need to make omelets is a function called `make_food` that takes two parameters. The first is a list of ingredients needed — exactly what came from the `get_omelet_ingredients` function. The second is the name of the food, which should be the type of omelet:

```
def make_food(ingredients_needed, food_name):
    """make_food(ingredients_needed, food_name)
    Takes the ingredients from ingredients_needed and makes food_name"""
    for ingredient in ingredients_needed.keys():
        print("Adding %d of %s to make a %s" %
(ingredients_needed[ingredient], ingredient, food_name))
    print("Made %s" % food_name)
    return food_name
```

At this point, all of the pieces are in place to use the `make_omelet` function. It needs to call on the `get_omelet_ingredients` and the `make_food` functions to do its job. Each function provides some part of the process of making an omelet. The `get_omelet_ingredients` function provides the specific instructions for specific kinds of omelets, and the `make_food` function provides the information needed to know that any kind of food can, if you look at it one way (a very simplistic way for the sake of demonstration!), be represented as the result of just mixing the right quantities of a number of ingredients.

Try It Out   Invoking the Completed Function

Now that you have all of the functions in place for `make_omelet` to work, invoke your `ch5.py` file with `python -i` or the Run with Interpreter command, and then try out the following code in the shell:

```
>>> omelet_type = make_omelet("cheese")
Adding 2 of eggs to make a cheese
Adding 2 of cheddar to make a cheese
Adding 1 of milk to make a cheese
Made cheese
>>> print omelet_type
cheese
>>> omelet_type = make_omelet({"eggs":2, "jack_cheese":2, "milk":1,
"mushrooms":2})
omelet_type is a dictionary with ingredients
Adding 2 of jack_cheese to make a omelet
Adding 2 of mushrooms to make a omelet
Adding 2 of eggs to make a omelet
Adding 1 of milk to make a omelet
Made omelet
>>> print omelet_type
Omelet
```

How It Works

Now that all of the functions are in place and can be called, one from another, `make_omelet` can be used by only specifying the name of the omelet that you want to make.

Functions Inside of Functions

While it's unlikely that you'll be modeling any omelet-making in your professional or amateur career, the same process of designing partial simulations of real-world situations is likely, so this section provides some ideas about how you could refine the solution you already have.

You may decide that a particular function's work is too much to define in one place and want to break it down into smaller, distinct pieces. To do this, you can place functions inside of other functions and have them invoked from within that function. This allows for more sense to be made of the complex function. For instance, `get_omelet_ingredients` could be contained entirely inside the `make_omelet` function and not be available to the rest of the program.

Limiting the visibility of this function would make sense, because the usefulness of the function is limited to making omelets. If you were writing a program that had instructions for making other kinds of food as well, the ingredients for omelets wouldn't be of any use for making these other types of food, even similar foods like scrambled eggs or soufflés. Each new food would need its own functions to do the same thing, with one function for each type of food. However, the `make_food` function would still make sense on its own and could be used for any kind of food.

Defining a function within another function looks exactly like defining it at the top level. The only difference is that it is indented at the same level as the other code in the function in which it's contained. In this case, all of the code looks exactly the same:

```
def make_omelet(omelet_type):
    """This will make an omelet.  You can either pass in a dictionary
    that contains all of the ingredients for your omelet, or provide
    a string to select a type of omelet this function already knows
    about"""
    def get_omelet_ingredients(omelet_name):
        """This contains a dictionary of omelet names that can be produced,
and their ingredients"""
        ingredients = {"eggs":2, "milk":1}
        if omelet_name == "cheese":
            ingredients["cheddar"] = 2
        elif omelet_name == "western":
            ingredients["jack_cheese"] = 2

ingredients["ham"]        = 1
            ingredients["pepper"]      = 1
            ingredients["onion"]       = 1
        elif omelet_name == "greek":
            ingredients["feta_cheese"] = 2
        else:
            print("That's not on the menu, sorry!")
```

```
        return None
    return ingredients
if type(omelet_type) == type({}):
    print("omelet_type is a dictionary with ingredients")
    return make_food(omelet_type, "omelet")
elif type(omelet_type) == type(""):
    omelet_ingredients = get_omelet_ingredients(omelet_type)
    return make_food(omelet_ingredients, omelet_type)
else:
    print("I don't think I can make this kind of omelet: %s" %
omelet_type)
```

It is important to define a function before it is used. If an attempt is made to invoke a function before it's defined, Python won't be aware of its existence at the point in the program where you're trying to invoke it, and so it can't be used! Of course, this will result in an error and an exception being raised. So, define your functions at the beginning of your files so you can use them toward the end.

Flagging an Error on Your Own Terms

If you need to indicate that a particular error has occurred, you may want to use one of the errors you've already encountered to indicate, through the function that's being called, what has gone wrong.

There is a counterpart to the try: and except: special words: the raise ... command. A good time to use the raise ... command might be when you've written a function that expects multiple parameters but one is of the wrong type.

You can check the parameters that are passed in and use raise ... to indicate that the wrong type was given. When you use raise ..., you provide a message that an except ... : clause can capture for display — an explanation of the error.

The following code changes the end of the make_omelet function by replacing a printed error, which is suitable for being read by a person running the program, with a raise ... statement that makes it possible for a problem to be either handled by functions or printed so that a user can read it:

```
if type(omelet_type) == type({}):
    print("omelet_type is a dictionary with ingredients")
    return make_food(omelet_type, "omelet")
elif type(omelet_type) == type(""):
    omelet_ingredients = get_omelet_ingredients(omelet_type)
    return make_food(omelet_ingredients, omelet_type)
else:
    raise TypeError("No such omelet type: %s" % omelet_type)
```

After making this change, make_omelet can give you precise information about this kind of error when it's encountered, and it still provides information for a user.

Layers of Functions

Now that you've an idea of what functions are and how they work, it's useful to think about them in terms of how they are called and how Python keeps track of these layers of invocations.

When your program calls a function, or a function calls a function, Python creates a list inside of itself that is called the *stack* or sometimes the *call stack*. When you invoke a function (or *call* on, which is why it can be called a *call stack*), Python will stop for a moment, take note of where it is when the function was called, and then stash that information in its internal list. It'll then enter the function and execute it, as you've seen. For example, the following code illustrates how Python keeps track of how it enters and leaves functions:

```
[{'top_level': 'line 1'}, {'make_omelet': 'line 64'}, {'make food': 'line
120'}]
```

At the top, Python keeps track starting at line 1. Then, as the function `make_omelet` is called at line 64, it keeps track of that. Then, from inside of `make_omelet`, `make_food` is called. When the `make_food` function finishes, Python determines that it was on line 64, and it returns to line 64 to continue. The line numbers in the example are made up, but you get the idea.

The list is called a stack because of the way in which a function is entered. You can think of a function as being on the top of a stack until it is exited, when it is taken off, and the stack is shortened by one.

How to Read Deeper Errors

When an error does happen in a program and an uncaught error is raised, you might find yourself looking at a more complex error than what you've seen before. For example, imagine that you've passed a dictionary that contains a list instead of a number. This will cause an error that looks like the following:

```
>>> make_omelet({"a":1, "b":2, "j":["c", "d", "e"]})
omelet_type is a dictionary with ingredients
Adding 1 of a to make a omelet
Adding 2 of b to make a omelet
Traceback (most recent call last):
  File "<stdin>", line 1, in ?
  File "ch5.py", line 96, in make_omelet
    return make_food(omelet_type, "omelet")
  File "ch5.py", line 45, in make_food
    Print("Adding %d of %s to make a %s" % (ingredients_needed[ingredient],
ingredient, food_name))
TypeError: int argument required
```

After you've entered a function from a file, Python will do its best to show you where in the stack you are (which means how many layers there are when the error occurs and at what line in the file each layer in the stack was called from) so that you can open the problem file to determine what happened.

As you create deeper stacks (which you can think of as longer lists) by calling more functions or using functions that call other functions, you gain experience in using the *stack trace*. (This is the common name for the output that Python gives you when you raise an error or when an exception is otherwise raised.)

With the preceding stack trace, which is three levels deep, you can see that in line 45, when `make_food` is called, there was a problem with the type of an argument. You could now go back and fix this.

If you thought that this problem would happen a lot, you could compensate for it by enclosing calls to `make_food` in a `try ...:` block so that TypeErrors can always be prevented from stopping the program. However, it's even better if you handle them in the function where they will occur.

In the case of something like a blatantly incorrect type or member of a dictionary, it's usually not necessary to do any more than what Python does on its own, which is to raise a TypeError. How you want to handle any specific situation is up to you, however.

The stack trace is the readable form of the stack, which you can examine to see where the problem happened. It shows everything that is known at the point in time when a problem occurred, and it is produced by Python whenever an exception has been raised.

Summary

This chapter introduced you to functions. Functions are a way of grouping a number of statements in Python into a single name that can be invoked any time that it's needed. When a function is defined, it can be created so that when it's invoked it will be given parameters to specify the values on which it should operate.

The names of the parameters for a function are defined along with the function by enclosing them in parentheses after the function is named. When no parameters are used, the parentheses are still present, but they will be empty.

As functions are invoked, they each create a scope of their own whereby they have access to all of the names that are present in the global scope of the program, as well as names that have been assigned and created inside of the function. If a name that is present in the global scope is assigned in the scope of a particular function, it will not change value when referenced by the global name but will instead only be changed within the function.

If a function is defined within another function, it can access all of the names of the function in which it was defined, as well as names that are in the global scope. Remember that this visibility depends on where the function is defined and not where it was called.

Functions can be called from within other functions. Doing this can make understanding programs easier. Functions enable you to reduce repetitive typing by making common tasks achievable with a brief name.

Functions that are defined with parameters are invoked with values — each value provided will be assigned, in the function, to the name inside the function's parameter list. The first parameter passed to a function will be assigned to the first name, the second to the second, and so on. When functions are passed parameters, each one can be either mandatory or optional. Optional parameters must be placed after mandatory parameters when the function is defined, and they can be given a default value.

You can use the `raise ... :` feature to signal errors that can be received and handled by `except ... :`. This enables you to provide feedback from your functions by providing both the type of error and a string that describes the error so it can be handled.

You have also learned about the *stack*. When an error condition is raised with `raise ... :`, or by another error in the program, the location of the error is described not just by naming the function where the error occurred, but also by naming any and all intervening functions that were invoked and specifying on what line in which file that invocation happened. Therefore, if the same function is useful enough that you use it in different places and it only has problems in one of them, you can narrow the source of the problem by following the stack trace that is produced.

The key things to take away from this chapter are:

❑   You can run a program with Python -i (or Run with Interpreter), allowing you to create longer programs instead of writing them directly into the Shell.

❑   You can save time by saving snippets of code as a function, making them reuseable in your current — and future — programs.

❑   Documentation strings begin with three quotes (""") and allow you to define the purpose of your functions, and leave comments for yourself and future programmers.

❑   You can display the documentation in your function by using __doc__.

❑   By using `dir()` you can see every property in an object.

❑   Comments are added to your code with a # symbol. Python ignores everything following this sign on the same line. Comments allow you to leave notes regarding your code in the event that you need to revisit it again several months later, or in the event that another programmer needs to read — and quickly understand — your code.

❑   The `type()` function tells you the class of an object.

Exercises

1. Write a function called `do_plus` that accepts two parameters and adds them together with the "+" operation.

2. Add *type checking* to confirm that the type of the parameters is either an integer or a string. If the parameters aren't good, `raise` a TypeError.

3. This one is a lot of work, so feel free to take it in pieces. In Chapter 4, a loop was written to make an omelet. It did everything from looking up ingredients to removing them from the fridge and making the omelet. Using this loop as a model, alter the `make_omelet` function by making a function called `make_omelet_q3`. It should change `make_omelet` in the following ways to get it to more closely resemble a real kitchen:

    a. The fridge should be passed into the new `make_omelet` as its first parameter. The fridge's type should be checked to ensure it is a dictionary.

    b. Add a function to check the fridge and subtract the ingredients to be used. Call this function `remove_from_fridge`. This function should first check to see if enough ingredients are in the fridge to make the omelet, and only after it has checked that should it remove those items to make the omelet. Use the error type LookupError as the type of error to raise.

c. The items removed from the fridge should be placed into a dictionary and returned by the `remove_from_fridge` function to be assigned to a name that will be passed to `make_food`. After all, you don't want to remove food if it's not going to be used.

d. Rather than a cheese omelet, choose a different default omelet to make. Add the ingredients for this omelet to the `get_omelet_ingredients` function.

4. Alter `make_omelet` to raise a TypeError error in the `get_omelet_ingredients` function if a salmonella omelet is ordered. Try ordering a salmonella omelet and follow the resulting stack trace.

Classes and Objects

So far, you have been introduced to most of the building blocks of programming. You have used data; you have referenced that data to names (the names are more commonly called *variables* when programmers talk); and you have used that data in loops and functions. The use of these three elements is the foundation of programming and problem-solving with computers. Named variables enable you to store values, reference them, and manipulate them. Repeating loops enable you to evaluate every possible element in a list, or every other element, or every third element, and so on. Finally, functions enable you to combine bunches of code into a name that you can invoke whenever and wherever you need it.

In this chapter you learn:

❏   How Python combines functions and data so that they are accessed using a single *object's* name.

❏   How and why classes and objects are used and how they make programs easier to write and use in a variety of circumstances.

Thinking About Programming

At this point, you've only been given a rudimentary introduction to Python. To create a description of an *object* in Python right now, you have just enough knowledge to achieve two views. One is of the data, which comes and goes as needed, except for parts that live in the top level, or global scope. The other view is of functions, which have no persistent data of their own. They interact only with data that you give them.

What is an Object?

In Python, every piece of data you see or come into contact with is represented by an object. Each of these objects has three components: an identity, a type, and a value. The identity represents the location of the object being held in your memory (and therefore is unchangeable), while its type tells us what types of data and values it can have. The value, meanwhile, can be changed in an object, but only if it is set as a mutable type; if it is set as immutable, then it may not change.

A simpler explanation might be to consider some of the things we have already seen (and will see soon). Integers, strings, lists, and so forth are all nothing more than objects. Now, it is all well and good to have all of these floating around within your program, but wouldn't it make more sense to have the ones that work closely together in one spot? That is where classes come in. A class allows you to define and encapsulate a group of objects into one convenient space.

Objects You Already Know

The next tool you learn will enable you to think of entire *objects* that contain both data and functions. You've already seen these when you used *strings*. A string is not just the text that it contains. As you've learned, *methods* are associated with strings, which enable them to be more than just the text, offering such features as allowing you to make the entire string uppercase or lowercase. To recap what you've already learned, a string is mainly the text that you've input:

```
>>> omelet_type = "Cheese"
```

In addition to the data that you've worked with the most, the text `"Cheese"`, the *string* is an object that has *methods*, or behaviors that are well known. Examples of methods that every string has are `lower`, which will return the string it contains as all lowercase, and `upper`, which will return the string as an entirely uppercase string:

```
>>> omelet_type.lower()
'cheese'
>>> omelet_type.upper()
'CHEESE'
```

Also available are methods built into *tuple*, *list*, and *dictionary* objects, like the `keys` method of dictionaries, which you've already used:

```
>>> fridge = {"cheese":1, "tomato":2, "milk":4}
>>> for x in fridge.keys():
        print(x)
  ['tomato', 'cheese', 'milk']
```

When you want to find out more about what is available in an object, Python exposes everything that exists in an object when you use the `dir` function:

```
dir(fridge)
['__class__', '__contains__', '__delattr__', '__delitem__', '__doc__',
'__eq__', '__format__', '__ge__', '__getattribute__', '__getitem__',
'__gt__', '__hash__', '__init__', '__iter__', '__le__', '__len__',
'__lt__', '__ne__', '__new__', '__reduce__', '__reduce_ex__', '__repr__'
'__setattr__', '__setitem__', '__sizeof__', '__str__', '__subclasshook__',
'clear', 'copy', 'fromkeys', 'get', 'items', 'keys', 'pop', 'popitem',
'setdefault', 'update', 'values']
```

Every bit of data, every method, and, in short, every name in a *string* or any other *object* in Python can be exposed with the dir function. dir lists all of the available names in the *object* it is examining in alphabetical order, which tends to group those names beginning with underscores first. By convention, these names refer to items considered to be internal pieces of the object and should be treated as though they are invisible. In other words, you shouldn't use them, but Python leaves that decision up to you — there's no reason not to look at these items interactively to learn from them:

```
>>> type(omelet_type.__len__)
<class 'method-wrapper'
```

This is interesting. Because this is a method, it can be invoked to see what it does:

```
>>> omelet_type.__len__()
6
```

This returns the same value as the len built-in function. When a function is built into an *object*, it's called a *method* of that object.

In fact, the method __len__ is how the len function works: It asks an object how long it is by asking this built-in method. This enables the designer of an object to define how the length is determined and to have the built-in function len behave correctly for any object that defines a __len__ method.

The other names beginning with an underscore also have special meanings. You can explore these in the Python shell. The Python shell will help you explore the normal methods of a string object, or any other method, by displaying possible names within the object that you are trying to call on, but it will not display internal names that begin with an underscore. You can determine those with the dir function yourself if you decide to do this.

Looking Ahead: How You Want to Use Objects

When you have an object, you want to be able to use it naturally. For instance, once you've defined it, the Omelet class could produce objects that behave in a way that would feel natural when you read the source code. You're going to try to make something that can do this (you see how to do this in the next section):

```
>>> o1 = Omelet()
>>> o1.show_kind()
'cheese'
```

You'd also want to have a refrigerator that can be used as an object instead of just as a dictionary. It may be nice for you to do things like be able to think of using it like a real fridge, whereby you can add food, remove food, check for foods, add or remove more than one thing at a time, and so on.

In other words, when you create an object that models something from the real world, you can form your program's objects and classes so they help the pieces of the program work in a way that someone familiar with the real-life object will recognize and be able to understand.

Defining a Class

When you are considering how even small programs of a few hundred lines of Python code is working, you will often realize that the programs are keeping track of data in groups — when one thing is accessed, it affects other things that need to go along with it. Almost as often, you'll realize that you have whole lists of this interdependent data — lists in which the first element in list1 is matched to the first element in list2 and list3, and so on. Sometimes this can and should be solved by combining the lists creatively. Python employs the concept of creating an entire *class* of code that acts as a placeholder. When a class is invoked, it creates an object bound to a name.

How Code Can Be Made into an Object

After you have an object bound to a name, using that name provides you with access to all of the data and functions you've defined. When you are writing code for a class, you start by declaring that class. You do this with the `class` keyword.

Try It Out · Defining a Class

The definition of a class is simple and mainly involves the use of the special word `class` along with a name. The style is similar to the definition of a function, except that you do not follow a simple class definition with a tuple containing terms. (Doing that defines a class to inherit from, which you see in Chapter 10.)

```
class Fridge:
    """This class implements a fridge where ingredients can be
    added and removed individually, or in groups."""
```

How It Works

From here on out, everything indented will be available through the objects created inside of this class. You've already seen this with functions in Chapter 5, and similar rules apply to classes. Note that you have the option for the built-in *docstring* with classes, as you do with functions. They behave the same way and are very useful for providing an easy way to get information about the class.

You should try creating the `Fridge` class as shown in the preceding example. Note that a capital "F" was used for this. It's a common convention for Python programmers to begin their class names with a capital letter; and when a class name has more than one word, it's also a common convention to run the words together, but to have each word begin with a capital letter to make it easier to read. For instance, a class that is modeling a fridge and a freezer together could be called `FridgeAndFreezer`.

Try It Out · Creating an Object from Your Class

Try typing the `Fridge` class into your ch6.py file (or a similar file for the examples here) and then invoke that file with *python -i* or the Run with Interpreter command, as you did in Chapter 5.

You can create a single object that is a Fridge by invoking it with the open and close parentheses:

```
>>> f = Fridge()
```

How It Works

At this point, you don't have anything complicated defined yet. `Fridge` is basically empty, so this is your starting point. However, even without anything else, you should notice that you created an empty class that is usable. It does almost nothing, but in some situations you need very little. For instance, you can now treat this nearly empty object you've created like a special kind of dictionary. You can do this by adding names to your class interactively while you're testing. This can help you develop an idea of how you'd like it to work:

```
>>> f.items = {}
>>> f.items["mystery meat"] = 1
```

In addition, as you see demonstrated in Chapter 10, exceptions are actually classes, and sometimes all you need is an empty class to make an effective exception. You should only use this sort of direct access to a class when you have a simple, undefined class like this. When you have a more developed class, accessing the names inside of its scope can interfere with how the class was written, so it can cause a lot of trouble.

The best way to start writing a class is to decide what you want it to do. For this, a Python-based model of refrigerator behaviors, `Fridge`, is the first thing, and it should be basic. While you're thinking about it, focus on what you will need a particular `Fridge` object to do for your own purposes. You want enough behaviors available that this object can be used to make food, yet you don't want to worry about aspects of real-life refrigerators that won't be included in a simplified example, such as temperature, the freezer, defrosting, and electricity — all of these are unnecessary details that would only complicate your purpose here. For now, just add to the docstring for the `Fridge` class to define the behaviors that you will be building soon.

First, you will want to have a way of stocking your `Fridge`. You're going to do this in a couple of ways: adding one type of a single item at a time and adding an entire dictionary at the same time so that it's easy to initialize. Or simulating occasions when a refrigerator is filled, such as after you've come back from a shopping trip.

Second, you'll want to have a way to take things out of the `Fridge`. You want to have the capability to do all of the same things when removing items as you do when you add: get a single item or get a whole bunch of things out of the `Fridge`.

You'll want to write a couple of other things into this object to make this selective model of a `Fridge`: a function that will determine whether a particular item is available in the `Fridge` and another one that will check an entire dictionary worth of ingredients. These enable you to prepare to begin cooking.

These are all of the things that you would need to have in order to use a `Fridge` to store ingredients and to get them out when you want to cook but only for this limited purpose of modeling, of course. In other words, these will work as a model of this specific situation, while glossing over every possible scenario.

The methods that an object makes available for use are called its *interface* because these methods are how the program outside of the object makes use of the object. They're what make the object usable.

The interface is everything you make available from the object. With Python, this usually means that all of the methods and any other names that don't begin with one or more underscores are your interfaces; however, it's a good practice to distinguish which functions you expect to have called by explicitly stating what methods can be used, and how they're used, in the class's docstring:

```
class Fridge:
    """This class implements a fridge where ingredients can be
    added and removed individually, or in groups.
    The fridge will retain a count of every ingredient added or removed,
    and will raise an error if a sufficient quantity of an ingredient
    isn't present.
    Methods:
    has(food_name [, quantity]) - checks if the string food_name is in the
fridge.  Quantity will be set to 1 if you don't specify a number.
    has_various(foods) - checks if enough of every food in the dictionary is in
the fridge
    add_one(food_name) - adds a single food_name to the fridge
    add_many(food_dict) - adds a whole dictionary filled with food
    get_one(food_name) - takes out a single food_name from the fridge
    get_many(food_dict) - takes out a whole dictionary worth of food.
    get_ingredients(food) - If passed an object that has the __ingredients__
        method, get_many will invoke this to get the list of ingredients.
    """

    def __init__(self, items={}):
        """Optionally pass in an initial dictionary of items"""
        if type(items) != type({}):
            raise TypeError("Fridge requires a dictionary but was given %s" %
type(items))
        self.items = items
        return
```

Take a moment to look at the __init__ and (self) part of the code above. These are two very important features of classes. When Python creates your object, the __init__ method is what passes the object its first parameter. The (self) portion is actually a variable used to represent the instance of the object.

In addition, documenting the methods you expect to be used is a good practice when you sit down to write a class — in effect, it is your outline for what you need to do to consider the class complete, and this can go hand-in-hand with testing your program as you write it. (See Chapter 12 for more about how to do this.)

When you write your interface methods, you'll notice that, a lot of the time, simpler methods will share a lot of common features, like "get one thing" or "get two things" or "get some large number of things," but to make them simple to call, you'll want to keep all of these variations. At first, this will seem as though it means that you need to duplicate a lot of the source code for each of these functions. However, instead of retyping the common components of your interface methods, you can save a lot of work by writing methods that are for internal use only.

These *private methods* can perform actions common to some or all of your interface methods. You'd want to do this when the private methods are more complex, or contain details that a user may not need to know in order to use them. By doing this, you can prevent confusion when your class is called, while making it easier for you to write. At its best, this is a clear win-win situation.

For the Fridge class, and in many classes you'll write, it's common to have a method that can operate on a group of data, and another method that works with just a single element. Whenever you have this situation, you can save your effort by making the method that works on a single item simply invoke the method that works on any number of items. In fact, sometimes it's useful to have this method be considered *private*, or not a part of the interface. This way it can be used or not used and changed without affecting how the class is used, because any changes you make will not be seen *outside* an object, only *inside*.

For your `Fridge` class, you can minimize your work by creating an *internal* method called __add_multi that will take two parameters — the name of the item and the quantity of items — and have it add those to the *items* dictionary that each object has.

Try It Out   Writing an Internal Method

When you add this to your file for this chapter, remember to ensure that you have the right indentation for this to appear under your `Fridge` class, not alone at the top level. The class declaration is shown here to make this clear:

```
class Fridge:
    # the docstring and intervening portions of the class would be here, and
    # __add_multi should go afterwards.
    def __add_multi(self, food_name, quantity):
        """
        __add_multi(food_name, quantity) - adds more than one of a
        food item. Returns the number of items added

        This should only be used internally, after the type checking has been
        done
        """
        if (not food_name in self.items):
            self.items[food_name] = 0

        self.items[food_name] = self.items[food_name] + quantity
```

How It Works

Now you have a way of adding any number of single food items to a `Fridge` object. However, this is an internal method that doesn't confirm whether the type that it is being given — either for `food_name` or `quantity` — is valid. You should use your interface functions to do this checking because, being a conscientious programmer, you will always ensure that you only pass the right values into your private methods. OK, just kidding. It's always a good idea to check everywhere you can. For this example, you're not going to check here, though, because you're only going to use __add_multi in a foolproof way.

Now that you have the generally useful method __add_multi for your `Fridge` class, the add_one and the add_many methods can both be written to use it instead of you having to write similar functions two times. This will save you work.

| Try It Out | Writing Interface Methods |

To make this faster, you can avoid typing in the docstrings for now. They are here so that you understand better what the actual code is doing in case you have any questions.

Like before, these need to be indented beneath the `Fridge` class definition. Anything that seems to begin at the start of a line is actually a continuation from the line before and should all be entered on one line:

```
def add_one(self, food_name):
    """
    add_one(food_name) - adds a single food_name to the fridge
    returns True
    Raises a TypeError if food_name is not a string.
    """
    if type(food_name) != type(""):
        raise TypeError, "add_one requires a string, given a %s" % type
(food_name)
    else:
        self.__add_multi(food_name, 1)

    return True

def add_many(self, food_dict):
    """
    add_many(food_dict) - adds a whole dictionary filled with food as
keys and
        quantities as values.
    returns a dictionary with the removed food.
    raises a TypeError if food_dict is not a dictionary
    returns False if there is not enough food in the fridge.
    """

    if type(food_dict) != type({}):
        raise TypeError("add_many requires a dictionary, got a %s" %
food_dict)

    for item in food_dict.keys():
        self.__add_multi(item, food_dict[item])
    return
```

How It Works

`add_one` and `add_many` each serve similar purposes, and each one has the code to ensure that it is being used appropriately. At the same time, they both use __add_multi to actually do the heavy lifting. Now, if anything changes regarding how your class works inside of __add_multi, you will save time because it will change how both of these methods behave.

Now that you've written all of this, you have enough code written to put items into a `Fridge` object, but no way of taking items out. You can just directly access the `object.items` dictionary, but that is never a good idea except when testing. Of course, you're testing now, so why not do that?

```
>>> f = Fridge({"eggs":6, "milk":4, "cheese":3})
>>> f.items
{'cheese': 3, 'eggs': 6, 'milk': 4}
>>> f.add_one("grape")
True
>>> f.items
{'cheese': 3, 'eggs': 6, 'grape': 1, 'milk': 4}
>>> f.add_many({"mushroom":5, "tomato":3})
>>> f.items
{'tomato': 3, 'cheese': 3, 'grape': 1, 'mushroom': 5, 'eggs': 6, 'milk': 4}
>>>
```

So far, everything works! This is the simple part. The second thing you'll want to add are the methods that enable you to determine whether something is in the Fridge.

It is important to write code that gives you a way to confirm that something is present because it can be used by the methods that remove items, get_one and get_many and get_ingredients, so that they ensure that they can check if enough of the items wanted are present. That's exactly what the has and has_various methods are for:

```
def has(self, food_name, quantity=1):
    """
    has(food_name, [quantity]) - checks if the string food_name is in the
fridge.  Quantity defaults to 1
    Returns True if there is enough, False otherwise.
    """

    return self.has_various({food_name:quantity})

def has_various(self, foods):
    """
    has_various(foods) determines if the dictionary food_name
        has enough of every element to satisfy a request.
    returns True if there's enough, False if there's not or if an element
does
    not exist.
    """

    try:
        for food in foods.keys():
            if self.items[food] < foods[food]:
                return False
        return True
    except KeyError:
        return False
```

After has and has_various are in place, you can use a Fridge object in tests, and when you read the code, it will almost make sense when you read your code out loud.

Using More Methods

You can now invoke your ch6.py file with `python -i` or the Run with Interpreter command so that you can use everything you've added to the Fridge class. If you get errors instead of the >>> prompt, pay attention to the exception raised and try to fix any indentation, spelling, or other basic errors identified.

The class should be usable like this now:

```
>>> f = Fridge({"eggs":6, "milk":4, "cheese":3})
>>> if f.has("cheese", 2):
...     print("It's time to make an omelet!")
...
It's time to make an omelet!
```

How It Works

Now that you've defined new methods, the f object can use them. When you re-created f with the eggs, milk, and cheese you made the object out of the new Fridge class, so it has the new methods you've added available to it.

Finally, it's time for the methods to get items from the Fridge. Here you can do the same thing you did for the methods to add to the Fridge, focusing on a single method that will take care of the hard stuff and letting the interface methods rely on this hard-working guy:

```
def __get_multi(self, food_name, quantity):
    """
    _get_multi(food_name, quantity) - removes more than one of a
    food item. Returns the number of items removed
    returns False if there isn't enough food_name in the fridge.
    This should only be used internally, after the type checking has been
    done
    """

    try:
        if (self.items[food_name] is None):
            return False;

        if (quantity > self.items[food_name]):
            return False;
        self.items[food_name] = self.items[food_name] - quantity
    except KeyError:
        return False
    return quantity
```

After this has been defined, you can create the remaining methods that the Fridge class's docstring has specified. They each use __get_multi so that they can remove items from the Fridge with a minimal amount of extra coding on your part:

```
def get_one(self, food_name):
    """
    get_one(food_name) - takes out a single food_name from the fridge
    returns a dictionary with the food:1 as a result, or False if there
wasn't
    enough in the fridge.
    """
```

```
        if type(food_name) != type(""):
            raise TypeError("get_one requires a string, given a %s" %
type(food_name))
        else:
            result = self.__get_multi(food_name, 1)
        return result

    def get_many(self, food_dict):
        """
        get_many(food_dict) - takes out a whole dictionary worth of food.
        returns a dictionary with all of the ingredients
        returns False if there are not enough ingredients or if a dictionary
        isn't provided.
        """

        if self.has_various(food_dict):
            foods_removed = {}
            for item in food_dict.keys():
                foods_removed[item] = self.__get_multi(item, food_dict[item])
            return foods_removed

    def get_ingredients(self, food):
        """
        get_ingredients(food) - If passed an object that has the __ingredients__
            method, get_many will invoke this to get the list of ingredients.
        """
        try:
            ingredients = self.get_many(food.__ingredients__())
        except AttributeError:
            return False

        if ingredients != False:
            return ingredients
```

You've now written a completely usable class for a refrigerator. Remember that there are many directions in which you can take this. Although you may be making omelets that use the Fridge class now, you can also use it for other projects — to model the product flow of a business, for example, such as a deli that has ten refrigerators with different products in each one.

When you do find an opportunity to repurpose a class that you've written (or a class that you've used), you can take advantage of the opportunity that is presented by adding features to support new needs without sacrificing what it already does.

For instance, an application that needs to take into account several refrigerators may result in a need for each Fridge object to have extra attributes, such as a name for it (like "dairy fridge"), its position in the store, its preferred temperature setting, and its dimensions. You can add these to the class, along with methods to get and set these values, while still keeping it completely usable for the omelet examples in this book. This is how interfaces help you. As long as the interfaces to the Fridge class you've already written here aren't changed, or at least as long as they behave the same, you can otherwise modify anything. This capability to keep interfaces behaving the same is called their *stability*.

Objects and Their Scope

As you saw in Chapter 5, functions create their own space, a scope, for the names that they use. While the function is being invoked, the name and value are present, and any changes made to the name persist for as long as the function is in use. However, after the function has finished running and is invoked again, any work that was done in any prior invocations is lost, and the function has to start again.

With objects, the values inside of them can be stored and attached to *self* on the inside of the object (*self* in this case is a name that refers to the object itself, and it's also the same as what is referenced by a name on the outside of the object, such as *f*). As long as the object is referenced by a name that is still active, all of the values contained in it will be available as well. If an object is created in a function and isn't returned by that function to be referenced to a name in a longer-lived scope, it will be available for as long as the single invocation of the function in which it was called, in the same way as any other data in the function.

Multiple objects are often created in tandem so that they can be used together. For instance, now that you've implemented all of the features you need to have a workable `Fridge` in your program, you need to have an `Omelet` object that works with it.

Try It Out   Creating Another Class

You've already created a class — a `Fridge`. Using the same format, create an `Omelet` class that you can use:

```
class Omelet:
    """This class creates an omelet object.  An omelet can be in one of
    two states: ingredients, or cooked.
    An omelet object has the following interfaces:
    get_kind() - returns a string with the type of omelet
    set_kind(kind) - sets the omelet to be the type named
    set_new_kind(kind, ingredients) - lets you create an omelet
    mix() - gets called after all the ingredients are gathered from the fridge
    cook() - cooks the omelet
    """
    def __init__(self, kind="cheese"):
        """ __init__(self, kind="cheese")
        This initializes the Omelet class to default to a cheese omelet.
        Other methods
        """
        self.set_kind(kind)
        return
```

How It Works

You now have a class whose intent is clearly spelled out. You've seen most of these behaviors in functions that you saw in Chapter 5, but now you have a structure within which you can combine all of these behaviors.

This class will have interface methods that enable the `omelet` to use a `Fridge` object cooperatively, and it will still offer the capability to create customized omelets as it could in Chapter 5.

Remember that all of the following code has to be indented one level beneath the `Omelet` class to be used:

```
def __ingredients__(self):
    """Internal method to be called on by a fridge or other objects
    that need to act on ingredients.
    """
    return self.needed_ingredients

def get_kind(self):
    return self.kind

def set_kind(self, kind):
    possible_ingredients = self.__known_kinds(kind)
    if possible_ingredients == False:
        return False
    else:
        self.kind = kind
        self.needed_ingredients = possible_ingredients

def set_new_kind(self, name, ingredients):
    self.kind = name
    self.needed_ingredients = ingredients
    return

def __known_kinds(self, kind):
    if kind == "cheese":
        return {"eggs":2, "milk":1, "cheese":1}
    elif kind == "mushroom":
        return {"eggs":2, "milk":1, "cheese":1, "mushroom":2}
    elif kind == "onion":
        return {"eggs":2, "milk":1, "cheese":1, "onion":1}
    else:
        return False

def get_ingredients(self, fridge):
    self.from_fridge = fridge.get_ingredients(self)

def mix(self):
    for ingredient in self.from_fridge.keys():
        print("Mixing %d %s for the %s omelet" %
self.from_fridge[ingredient], ingredient, self.kind))
        self.mixed = True

def make(self):
    if self.mixed == True:
        print("Cooking the %s omelet!" % self.kind)
        self.cooked = True
```

Now you have an `Omelet` class that can create `Omelet` objects. The `Omelet` class has the same features as the process for making omelets in Chapters 4 and 5, but using it is much easier because everything is combined and the presentation of the `Omelet` is confined to a few purposefully simpler interfaces.

Now that you have your two classes, you can make an omelet after loading everything with `python -i` or the Run with Interpreter command:

```
>>> o = Omelet("cheese")
>>> f = Fridge({"cheese":5, "milk":4, "eggs":12})
>>> o.get_ingredients(f)
>>> o.mix()
Mixing 1 cheese for the cheese omelet
Mixing 2 eggs for the cheese omelet
Mixing 1 milk for the cheese omelet
>>> o.make()
Cooking the cheese omelet!
```

This isn't any easier or harder to use than making a single omelet in Chapter 5 was. However, the benefit of using objects becomes obvious when you have many things to work with at the same time — for instance, many omelets being made at the same time:

```
>>> f = Fridge({"cheese":5, "milk":4, "eggs":12, "mushroom":6, "onion":6})
>>> o = Omelet("cheese")
>>> m = Omelet("mushroom")
>>> c = Omelet("onion")
>>> o.get_ingredients(f)
>>> o.mix()
Mixing 1 cheese for the cheese omelet
Mixing 2 eggs for the cheese omelet
Mixing 1 milk for the cheese omelet
>>> m.get_ingredients(f)
>>> m.mix()
Mixing 1 cheese for the mushroom omelet
Mixing 2 eggs for the mushroom omelet
Mixing 1 milk for the mushroom omelet
Mixing 2 mushroom for the mushroom omelet
>>> c.get_ingredients(f)
>>> c.mix()
Mixing 1 cheese for the onion omelet
Mixing 2 eggs for the onion omelet
Mixing 1 milk for the onion omelet
Mixing 1 onion for the onion omelet
>>> o.make()
Cooking the cheese omelet!
>>> m.make()
Cooking the mushroom omelet!
>>> c.make()
Cooking the onion omelet!
```

Take a moment to compare this to how you'd do the same thing using the functions from Chapter 5, and you'll realize why so much programming is done in this style — and why this kind of programming, called *object-oriented programming*, is used to make larger systems.

As long as the `Fridge` has the ingredients needed, making different kinds of omelets is very, very easy now — it involves only invoking the class to create a new object and then just calling three methods for each `Omelet` object. Of course, you could reduce it to one. That will be an exercise question.

Summary

In this chapter, you've been introduced to how Python provides you with the tools to program with *classes* and *objects*. These are the basic concepts behind what is called *object-oriented programming*.

When they are used inside a *class*, functions are referred to as *methods* because now every one has a special name called *self* that, when that method is invoked as part of an object, contains all of the data and methods of the object.

A class is invoked to create an *object* by using the class's name followed by parentheses, (). Initial parameters can be given at this time and whether or not parameters are given, the newly created *object* will invoke the method __init__. Like normal functions, methods in classes (including __init__) can accept parameters, including optional and default parameters.

The process of creating a class includes deciding what methods should be created to provide all of the functionality that you want in your class. Two general kinds of methods were described: *public interfaces* that should be invoked on the *outside* of the objects and *private methods* that should be called only by methods *inside* of the object. The *interfaces* should be made to change as little as possible, whereas the *internal* methods may change without affecting how the class can be used. This is especially important to remember when using a class written by someone else. Python expects any name within the scope of an object beginning with two underscores to be *private*, so this convention should be used by you as well. Other names are generally considered public.

The key points to take away from this chapter are:

❑ To specify how you expect the class to be used you should create a docstring for the class by entering a string on the first line after the class's definition. In that docstring, it is best to always provide the names of the methods that you expect to be used, and their purpose. It's not a bad idea to include an explanation of the class as a whole, too.

❑ All of the names that are defined in a class (both data and methods) are distinct in each object that is created. When a method is invoked in one object and that changes data in that object, other types of the same object are not affected. Examples of this that are built into Python are *strings*, which are objects that include special methods that help with common tasks when you are using text.

❑ To make objects easier to use, it's common to provide multiple interfaces that behave similarly. This can save you a lot of work by finding ways for these interfaces to call a single internal method that is more complex or accepts more parameters than the interfaces. This gives you two distinct advantages. First, it makes the code that calls on these methods easier to read because the names of the parameters don't need to be remembered by the programmer — the name of the method provides needed information to the programmer. Second, if you need to change the internal method that its related interfaces call on, you can change how all of them behave by just changing the internal method. This is especially useful when fixing problems because a single fix will correct how all of the interfaces work as well. In addition, the method that provides this support to other methods can itself be a public interface. There's no strict rule about whether or not a hard-working method like this should be private and internal. It's really up to you.

❑ One goal of writing objects is to duplicate as little code as possible, while providing as many features as possible. Creating a class that can use objects can save a lot of code writing because they are usually manipulated more conveniently than when functions and data are kept separated, because methods within the same class can count on the methods and data that they use being present. Groups of classes can be written so that they have interdependent behaviors, enabling you to model groups of things that work together. You learn how to structure these interdependent and cooperative classes in Chapter 7.

❑ Last, you've seen how codeEditor's Python shell helps you explore your objects by showing you all of the interface names once you type a period. This is much easier than typing dir to get the same information because of the more convenient and easier-to-use manner in which codeEditor displays the information.

Exercises

Each of the following exercises builds on the exercises that preceded it:

1. Add an option to the Omelet class's mix method to turn off the creation messages by adding a parameter that defaults to True, indicating that the "mixing . . . " messages should be printed.

2. Create a method in class Omelet that uses the new mix method from Exercise 1. Called quick_cook, it should take three parameters: the kind of omelet, the quantity wanted, and the Fridge that they'll come from. The quick_cook method should do everything required instead of requiring three method calls, but it should use all of the existing methods to accomplish this, including the modified mix method with the mix messages turned off.

3. For each of the methods in the Omelet class that do not have a docstring, create one. In each docstring, make sure you include the name of the method, the parameters that the method takes, what the method does, what value or values it returns upon success, and what it returns when it encounters an error (or what exceptions it raises, if any).

4. View the docstrings that you've created by creating an Omelet object.

5. Create a Recipe class that can be called by the Omelet class to get ingredients. The Recipe class should have the ingredient lists of the same omelets that are already included in the Omelet class. You can include other foods if you like. The Recipe class should include methods to retrieve a recipe, get(recipe_name), a method to add a recipe as well as name it, and create(recipe_name, ingredients), where the ingredients are a dictionary with the same format as the one already used in the Fridge and Omelet classes.

6. Alter the __init__ method of Omelet so that it accepts a Recipe class. To do this, you can do the following:

   a. Create a name, self.recipe, that each Omelet object will have.

   b. The only part of the Omelet class that stores recipes is the internal method __known_kinds. Alter __known_kinds to use the recipes by calling self.recipe.get() with the kind of omelet that's desired.

   c. Alter the set_new_kind method so that it places the new recipe into self.recipe and then calls set_kind to set the current omelet to the kind just added to the recipe.

   d. In addition, modify __known_kinds to use the recipe method's get method to find out the ingredients of an omelet.

7. Try using all of the new classes and methods to determine whether you understand them.

Organizing Programs

In Chapter 6, you began using Python's features to create separate *classes* that can be used to create entirely self-contained *objects*. Classes and the objects that are created from them are tools that enable you to gather data and functions into a contained space so that they can be viewed as part of a larger entity.

So far, the definitions of classes have all been in a single file and were not run in the way you normally think of programs being run. Instead, they were invoked interactively so that you could use them as you would from within another program. However, if you wanted to use the classes you've written with what you know so far, you would make the same file that defined the classes the program. That means putting all of the classes at the beginning of the file, and the important decision-making code at the end. The end is where it takes the most time to find the code that you're going to want to find the most often.

Another cautionary note needs to be sounded. Classes are very useful, but not all problems should be solved by creating a class. Sometimes the work of designing them is overkill, and other times what you really need are functions that don't require the long life span that data and methods can have in objects.

To make Python more useful, therefore, it offers you the great feature of enabling you to create *modules* that create a named scope for functions and data, but which are simpler than classes and objects. Modules give you a tool to separate your program into distinctly named pieces, without using classes to do it. In fact, classes can be defined within a module.

As an extension of this, you can also divide these modules into different files; Python calls this feature a *package*. Packages enable you to divide your programs among several files and even into separate directories to help you organize your programs.

So far, you have only been introduced to intrinsic pieces of the Python language — things that deal with how Python itself works. Python is also very flexible, and though it comes with a small core set of features, these are expanded in a variety of modules. To extend Python to use features provided by the operating system, there is a module called os. To extend Python to have networking features, Python provides modules that offer both low-level networking (such as sockets) and higher-level protocols (such as http, ftp, and so on). Many modules come with Python, but because it is very easy to write modules, a variety of additional modules are available from third parties, both commercial and free.

In this chapter you learn:

❑ How to write simple modules for your own use or to share.

❑ Some of the bundled Python modules.

❑ The concept of importing modules.

❑ How to use packages to contain useful functions and names, separately from the global scope.

❑ You also find out more about how scope can be used to your advantage for tasks such as testing your packages.

Modules

Modules present a whole group of functions, methods, or data that should relate to a common theme. Such a theme might be networking components (see Chapter 16), performing more complicated work with strings and text (see Chapter 12), dealing with graphical user interfaces (see Chapter 13), and other services.

After you've learned how to program in a language, you often find that you need to work with components that the language doesn't initially bundle. Python, by itself, is no different. At its core, it is a very small and simple language that doesn't offer many special features. However, because of its simplicity, it is easy to use as a platform that can be extended with additional functions and objects that can be used by anyone.

Importing a Module So That You Can Use It

To make a module usable, two things need to be available. First, the module itself has to be installed on the system. For the most part, you'll find that a lot of the basic things you want to do, such as reading and writing files (more on this in Chapter 8) and other fundamental important things that differ between platforms, are available as bundled modules with Python — that is, they are free and universally available with the language.

The simplest way to begin using a module is with the import keyword:

```
import sys
```

This will import the module named `sys` that contains services Python offers that mostly involve system-specific items. This means that it relates to things that involve how the system works, how a particular installation of Python is installed, or how the program you've written was invoked from the command line.

To start looking at modules, you're also going to begin to write in a style that facilitates running the file you're working on by itself, as a standalone program. To that end, create a file called `ch7.py` and type the following:

```
#!/usr/bin/env python3.1
# Chapter 7 module demonstration
import sys
```

The first line is for users of Linux and other UNIX systems (or Python under a UNIX-based environment like Cygwin). This is a way to get the `python3.1` binary to run in case other Python interpreters are on the system. See the website for this book for more information on running Python. For Windows and Macintosh systems, the file extension should provide information that the operating system needs to launch the Python interpreter, whether it's `python`, `python3.1`, or some other name when it's installed on your system (although some configuration may be needed). See the website for more information on this, too.

Making a Module from Pre-existing Code

To create a module, all you need to do is choose a name for your module and open a file with that name and the extension .py in your editor. For example, to create a `Foods` module, you only have to create a file called `Foods.py`. When that's finished, you can import it using the name "Foods" without the .py at the end. That's it! You've imported a simple module.

Try It Out   Creating a Module

Take your file with all of the source code from Chapter 6 and copy it to a file called `Foods.py`. When you've done this, open the Python shell so you can `import` the `Foods` module:

```
>>> import Foods
>>> dir(Foods)
['Fridge', 'Omelet', 'Recipe', '__builtins__', '__doc__', '__file__', '__name__']
>>>
```

How It Works

You now have access to the `Fridge` class, the `Omelet` class and, from the previous exercises, the `Recipe` class. Together, you have a file that is a module that contains all of these classes, and they'll be able to work together. However, you'll now access them through the name `Foods.Fridge`, `Foods.Omelet`, and `Foods.Recipe`, and they remain fully usable, albeit with some new rules.

Be aware that this is the first time you're getting the examples in the book to be run directly with your computer! By default, Python keeps a list of directories in which it will look for modules to load. This list contains several directories, though the exact locations of all of them will depend on how your running Python interpreter was installed. Therefore, if you're trying to import the Foods module but the shell has started itself in a directory other than the one in which you've saved the Foods.py file, you're going to receive an error (but you can fix this by changing to the right directory).

This path, or list of directories that Python should search through, is stored in the *sys* module, in a variable named path. To access this name, you will need to import the sys module. Until you do that, the sys.path won't be available to you:

```
>>> import sys
>>> print(sys.path)
'C:/Python31/Chapter 6', 'C:\\Python30\\Lib\\idlelib',
'C:\\Windows\\system32\\python31.zip', 'C:\\Python31\\DLLs',
'C:\\Python31\\lib', 'C:\\Python31\\lib\\plat-win',
'C:\\Python31', 'C:\\Python31\\lib\\site-packages']
```

You can see that sys.path is a normal list, and if you want to add directories that will be checked for your modules, because you want them somewhere that isn't already in sys.path, you can alter it by using the usual methods — either the append method to add one directory, or the extend method to add any number of directories.

When you've imported the Foods module, you can use Code Editor's feature of interactively helping you by popping up a list of all of the names in the scope of the module while you're typing in a name. Every time you come to a period, if the name you've just typed in has names associated with you, Code Editor will allow you to select from the interfaces that the name provides. This will help you explore the module you've just created but is even more useful with larger, more complex modules!

You can now run through examples from the prior chapters, but now you access your classes through the Foods module. For instance, you can invoke Foods.Fridge, but not just Fridge by itself. If you want to access Fridge alone, you'll see how to do this soon.

Try It Out   **Exploring Your New Module**

Code Editor provides you with a special feature in the Python shell that will interact with you as you type. You may have noticed already that when you finish typing the name of something such as a class or a module, when you type a period at the end of the name, within the shell a menu of names that exist in the scope of the module or object is shown to you. Figure 7-1 shows what this looks like, so you can do the same for yourself.

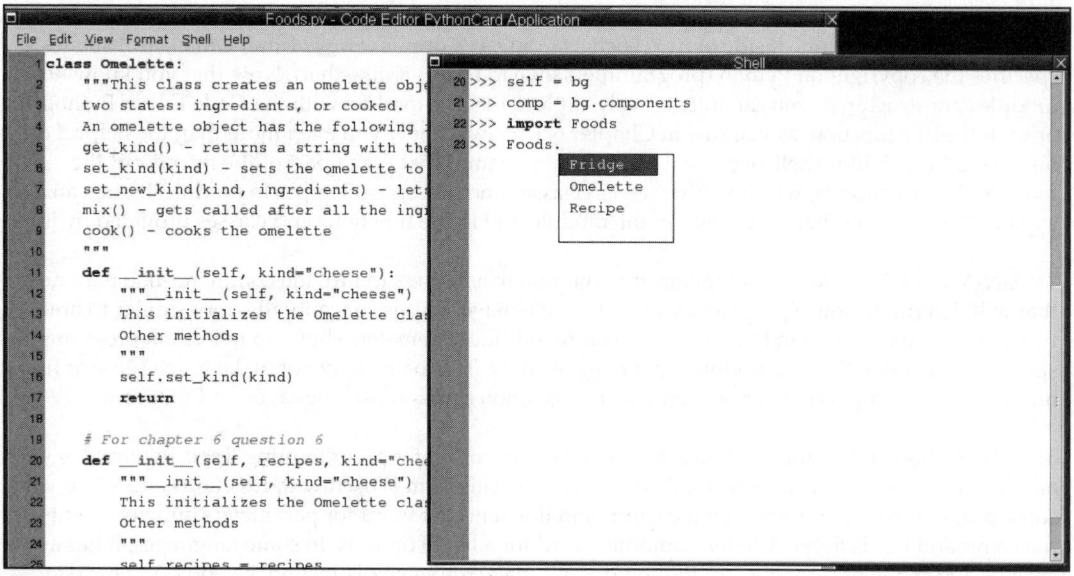

Figure 7-1

How It Works

As you type in Code Editor's Python shell, it evaluates what you are typing as you type. When it notices that you've typed certain characters, it takes actions on them. You notice this when strings take on a different color once you type in any kind of quote, or when words that are special to Python are given colors. Whenever the shell sees that you're typing a period, it knows that what you're typing will be looking inside a module or an object, so it queries that object behind the scenes and shows you the results so you can work with it.

Using Modules — Starting with the Command Line

So far, you've started by using import with a module name by itself. When a module is imported this way, all of the names it contains are put into a scope that is named for the module — that is, the name that was used in the import statement.

For example, in the case of sys, everything available is referred to by using the name sys, followed by a period, and then the name inside of sys, such as sys.path or sys.copyright, which, as it suggests, specifies the copyright on Python (programmers love to be clever like that). Now that you know how modules are structured, you can interactively explore the sys module with the Code Editor Python shell, or with the dir function, as you saw in Chapter 6. (dir will show you even more than the helpful dialog box in the Code Editor shell, because it shows *private* names that aren't part of the *interface* of the module. These concepts, which you've seen in classes and objects, still apply to modules!) You can also explore the *docstrings* that are present in the module and in the functions and classes provided by it.

On UNIX and UNIX-like environments, it's common to ask users to provide command-line parameters that will determine how a program as a whole will behave. This is conceptually very similar to how functions use parameters in Python. These command-line parameters show up in Python programs as a special name inside the sys module. That name is argv. This name may not make much sense at first, but it's an important term to know because it is common across most languages and platforms.

argv is an abbreviation for the term *argument vector*. In computer programming lingo, *argument* is another word for what you've seen called a *parameter*. This term is used with functions and when you run a program with parameters on the command line (another word for parameters and arguments on the command line is *flags*). A *vector* is another word for a list of options. In some languages, it has a very specific and different meaning, but Python doesn't make the same distinction, so you don't have to worry about it.

If you translate argv back through those definitions, you'll see that it simply means the parameters that were on the command line, accessible as a list! It's hard to convert that information into a short and comprehensible word that makes sense in English (or any other nonprogramming language that the author has heard of), so the term argv persists.

To print out the parameters from the command line, you just have to use sys.argv as you would with any other list:

```
>>>import sys
>>>print("This was given the command line parameters: %s" % sys.argv)
```

To make running this the same procedure on any platform, you can launch this from Code Editor. Select File ⇨ Run Options and then put anything you want in the Other argv field. You've used this facility before, starting in Chapter 5, but taking advantage of the Run Options dialog box's capability to let you set the command line that your program will start with is something new.

For testing programs that are changing and that aren't meant to be used interactively, you are generally better off using python -i or Run with Interpreter; this way, you can try running your program repeatedly, starting the program from the beginning each time. Figure 7-2 shows a pop-up showing optional command-line options.

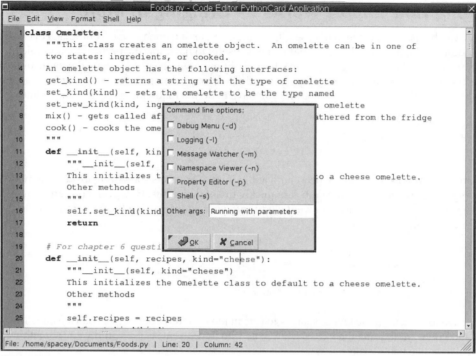

Figure 7-2

Try It Out   Printing sys.argv

Now, anytime you run this program using the Run with Interpreter option from your File menu, you will get a printed representation of the list that becomes the sys.argv. For example, if the command-line arguments provided in the Other argv field were "test 123 test," your program will print something like the following (which was run on Windows; a UNIX shell would have a very different looking sys.path):

```
This was given the command line parameters: ['D:\\Documents\\Chapter7.py',
'test', '123', 'test']
```

How It Works

The first element of the sys.argv list will always be the name of the program, and anything else will become the elements of the sys.argv list, starting at the number one in the list.

Classes that live within a module are accessed in the same way as any other name. For modules that provide classes that you use, the invocation is what you'd expect — just the addition of the parentheses to the fully spelled out path, such as calling Foods.Recipe().

Changing How Import Works — Bringing in More

`Import` can be used alone; when it's used that way, it creates a named scope from which everything in the module can be referenced. Sometimes it can be useful to have specific parts of the module brought into your program's top-level global scope, though. Eliminating the need to type the name of the module before the function or class you have to access reduces a lot of typing and makes your code a lot more straightforward. With your `Foods` module, you have to do the following to get an onion Omelet:

```
import Foods
r = Foods.Recipe()
onion_ingredients = Foods.Omelet(r, "onion")
```

You can see by this example that when you want to invoke or access something inside of a module, it means spelling out the entire path. You can quickly tire of doing this. However, you can change this behavior by bringing the names you want closer into your code by using the `from` modifier to the `import` command:

```
from Foods import Omelet
from Foods import Recipe
r = Recipe()
onion_ingredients = Omelet(r, "onion")
```

If you have to descend more levels, such as to (the made up food) `Foods.Recipes.Breads.Muffins.Bran` and you want to bring the names from `Bran` into the current scope, you'd write something similar. It would look like you'd expect:

```
from Foods.Recipes.Breads.Muffins import Bran
```

Packages

After you have a module built and in its own file, it's not uncommon to find that a single file runs headlong into organizational issues. Mainly, the issue is that an individual class becomes more useful on its own and may gain far more code than all of the rest of the classes in the module. This would be a good reason to move it to its own file, but that would break code that already uses the module! However, there is a solution.

To provide a structure for doing this, Python provides the organizational idea of *packages*. Packages use the structure of the directories (another name for folders) that every operating system uses to give you a methodology for making many files in the same directory look like a single module when they're used together.

You can start by simply making the directory. Let's break up the `Foods` module. First, you need to use a new name — `Foods.py` already exists, and it would be confusing to keep working with the module by calling it "Foods." Therefore, to work around that, start working on a new package, and call this new one the `Kitchen` package (this name is also general enough to leave you a lot of room for your imagination to work with later if you'd like to).

Simply enough, create a `Kitchen` directory. Then create a file in `Kitchen` called `__init__.py` (this name has to be the same name as the method in a class that you've seen already, and note that it has two underscores before and after the name). This file is the hint that tells Python that this is a package directory, and not just a directory with Python files in it. This is important because it ensures that you know you're responsible for maintaining this and controlling its behavior. This file has a lot of control over how the package is going to be used, because unlike a module, when a package is imported, every file in the directory isn't immediately imported and evaluated. Instead, the `__init__.py` file is evaluated, and here you can specify which files are used and how they're used!

Try It Out   Making the Files in the Kitchen Class

To make your three already written classes a part of the `Kitchen` package, create four files underneath the `Kitchen` directory and place the appropriate classes into each of the files named after a class name. Remember that under all versions of Windows, anywhere you see a forward slash (/) you should use a backslash (\) because that's what Windows uses to separate directories. In other words, create the `Kitchen/Fridge.py` file inside the `Kitchen` directory, and you'll put only the `Fridge` class in it.

Make one file for each of the classes, as well as making for the `__init__.py` file:

❑   `Kitchen/Fridge.py` — All of the code and comments for the `Fridge` class should go in here, starting from where your `ch6.py` says `class Fridge:`.

❑   `Kitchen/Omelet.py` — All of the code and comments for the `Omelet` class should go here. Use the revision of the `Omelet` class that you have as the solution to the exercises from Chapter 6.

❑   `Kitchen/Recipe.py` — All of the code and comments for the `Recipe` class should go here.

❑   `Kitchen/__init__.py` (remember to use two underscores before and after the filename) — Nothing has to go in this file.

How It Works

You have a class in each file and `__init__.py` created, so you can now import the `Kitchen` package. However, when you import `Kitchen`, Python evaluates only `__init__.py`. This is a very important detail, because without putting some further code in `__init__.py`, you'll never get to see your code. Currently, nothing is actually imported if you do what you'd assume you should do by default, which is `import Kitchen`!

To make all of your classes available when you've imported `Kitchen`, you need to put explicit `import` statements in `__init__.py`:

```
from Fridge import Fridge
from Recipe import Recipe
from Omelet import Omelet
```

After you've added these lines to __init__.py, you have all of these classes available when you've imported the Kitchen package:

```
>>> import Kitchen
>>> r = Kitchen.Recipe()
>>> r.recipes
{'cheese': {'cheese': 1, 'eggs': 2, 'milk': 1}, 'onion':
{'cheese': 1, 'eggs': 2, 'milk': 1, 'onion': 1}, 'mushroom':
{'cheese': 1, 'eggs': 2, 'milk': 1, 'mushroom': 2}}
```

By itself, this doesn't buy you much yet because this is only a very small project, but for any project that begins to grow, this facility is very important and can make development among multiple developers far easier by letting the natural assignment of functions and classes be divided into files, enabling each programmer to work on his or her own group of files in the package.

Modules and Packages

Now that modules and packages have been defined, you will continue to see how to use them — mostly interchangeably. You'll generally have your attention drawn to where packages behave differently from a single module. Because the module has been named Foods and the package has been named Kitchen, you won't be confused when you're shown something that deals with a package instead of a module. Just remember: Kitchen references are highlighting packages; Foods references are highlighting modules.

Bringing Everything into the Current Scope

Note a special feature of modules: Sometimes you may want to have the entire contents of a module available without having to explicitly specify each name that is available from it. To do this, Python provides a special character, the asterisk, which can be used with the from ... import ... statement. It's important to understand that you can *only* import using the * when you are importing into the global scope:

```
from Foods import *
```

This would bring Omelet into your current scope, as well as everything else at the top of the recipe module. In other words, now you no longer have type Foods.Omelet(), just Omelet(), and you need to do this only once, instead of one time for each name you want to make local.

Packages can be made to work in a similar fashion, but underneath, they actually work differently. For packages, you need to specify the names you want to be provided when from ... import *, and these need to be stated explicitly. You can make the three modules in the Kitchen package available by using the __all__ list in __init__.py. Any names that appear in the __all__ list will be exported by the * but *only* those names.

The elements that are present in the __all__ list are the names of functions, classes, or data that will be automatically imported into the global scope of the program that is asked to import *.

You can expect users of modules and packages you write to automatically use the `from ... import *` syntax within their programs. To work with packages, you must specify a list of names that will be exported! However, if you have a large module, you can also create an __all__ list at the top of your module file, and it will also have the effect of restricting the names in the module in the same way as it would in a package.

Try It Out   **Exporting Modules from a Package**

The __all__ list exists because using `from ... import *` is common. You will use (at first) and write (later) packages that have many layers, functions, data names, and individual modules that a user shouldn't see — they're not part of your public interface. Because you need to be careful about overwhelming users with a lot of things they don't need, the __all__ list enforces your interface decisions.

```
__all__ = ['Fridge', 'Recipe', 'Omelet']
```

How It Works

Now these names will come into the global space of your program when you invoke them with `from Kitchen import *`. It's important to know that if your __init__.py looked like this:

```
from Fridge import Fridge
from Omelet import Omelet
__all__ = ['Omelet', 'Recipe', 'Fridge']
```

With the `from Recipe import Recipe` statement eliminated, you would have to invoke `Recipe.Recipe()` to create a new recipe object after calling `from Kitchen import *`.

Re-importing Modules and Packages

Programming involves a lot of trial and error. You will often realize that you've made a mistake in the work you've done in your module while you're in the shell interactively. Because you may have done a lot of typing to get your shell set up perfectly for your test before your problem module was loaded, you'd like to be able to fix your module and have Python re-load it so that you can save yourself the work of having to set up your session again. So far, you haven't been shown how to do this, but you can.

The first thing you need to know to do this is that it's normal for a common module to be required by multiple other modules and effectively be called up multiple times in the same program. When this happens, instead of going through the extra time it would take to re-load, re-evaluate, and re-compile the module each time (see the sidebar Compiling and .pyc Files), Python stashes away the name of the module, and where it came from, in a special dictionary of all the modules that have been imported so far, called `sys.modules`. In fact, when you use the Python shell from within Code Editor, it's already loaded *sys* and many other modules for you, so any time you've called it in your own, you've had this happen!

Compiling and .pyc Files

If you've looked at your ch5.py, ch6.py, or any other Python files that you've worked on so far, you'll notice that after you run them, a file with almost the same name appears — the difference is that it ends in .pyc. This is a special file that Python writes out that contains a form of your program that can be loaded and run faster than the plaintext source code. If you make changes to the .py file, the next time it is invoked (that is, by double-clicking it, running python -i, or using the Run or Run with Interpreter menu options in Code Editor), Python will re-create the .pyc file from the newer, changed source code that you've updated.

Try It Out   **Examining sys.modules**

If you look at the list returned by sys.modules.keys, you'll see the name of every module that's loaded. Even if you start a Python shell outside of Code Editor, you'll find that after you've imported sys and can look at sys.modules, many modules are loaded by the system without your knowledge. Each operating system and installation will have slight variations on the exact contents of the dictionary, but it will usually look something like this:

```
>>> list(sys.modules.keys())
['heapq', 'tkinter.filedialog', 'functools', 'random', '_bisect',
'idlelib.macosxSupport', 'ctypes._endian', 'builtins', 'struct',
'tempfile', 'imp', 'collections', 'idlelib.MultiCall',
'tkinter.simpledialog', 'zipimport', 'string', 'encodings.utf_8',
'_bytesio', 'tkinter.constants', 'bisect', 'signal',
'idlelib.IOBinding', 'pydoc', 'threading', 'token', 'tkinter._fix',
'dis', 'locale', 'idlelib.TreeWidget', 'idlelib.rpc', 'encodings',
'idlelib.RemoteDebugger', 'abc', '_thread', '_tkinter', 'bdb', 're',
'idlelib.RemoteObjectBrowser', 'ntpath', 'math', 'idlelib.Debugger',
'inspect', '_ctypes', 'ctypes', 'codecs', '_functools', '_locale',
'idlelib.AutoComplete', 'tkinter', 'socket', 'traceback', '_stringio',
'queue', 'itertools', 'opcode', '_pickle', 'idlelib.StackViewer',
'idlelib.CallTipWindow', 'os', 'marshal', '__future__',
'idlelib.AutoCompleteWindow', '_collections', '_sre', 'operator',
'array', 'select', '_heapq', 'idlelib.ZoomHeight', 'pkgutil',
'errno', '_socket', 'binascii', 'sre_constants', 'encodings.latin_1',
'os.path', 'tokenize', '_warnings', 'idlelib.HyperParser',
'encodings.cp1252', '_struct', 'unicodedata', 'keyword',
'tkinter.commondialog', 'tkinter.messagebox', 'stringprep',
'encodings.aliases', 'fnmatch', 'sre_parse', 'pickle', '_fileio',
'reprlib', 'sre_compile', 'socketserver', '_random', 'site', 'io',
'__main__', 'copyreg', 'configparser', '_weakrefset', '_abcoll',
'_codecs', 'nt', 'idlelib.PyParse', 'genericpath', 'stat', 'warnings',
'sys', 'idlelib.CallTips', 'idlelib.configHandler', 'types',
'idlelib.ScrolledList', '_weakref', 'idlelib.ObjectBrowser',
'idlelib', 'tkinter.dialog', 'linecache', 'encodings.idna',
'time', 'idlelib.WindowList', 'idlelib.run']
```

How It Works

Depending on the operating system and when you call it, the `sys.modules` dictionary shows you all of the modules that have been called. For modules that you haven't explicitly imported, you can assume that they are automatically called in by Python to handle things like the operating system or other mechanisms that Python doesn't force you to deal with directly. The preceding sample is from a Linux system, and certain things are obviously OS-related — `posix` and `posixpath`, for example, if you have worked with UNIX — whereas some other things are not.

You can take this opportunity to look at the values associated with any keys that interest you. You'll see that some modules are listed as *built-in* and some are listed as being from a file, and when this is the case, the entire path to the module file is listed in the information that the module provides to you. Don't worry if the list of modules that comes up in your Python shell looks very different from the preceding example. After you've loaded the `Foods` module, it will be present in the `sys.modules` dictionary, and when it's there, Python will not re-evaluate the `Foods.py` module, even if you've changed it! To fix this in an interactive session, you can simply remove the record of the `Foods` module from the `sys.modules` dictionary and then import the module again. Because Python no longer has a record in `sys.modules` it will do as you ask instead of trying to save effort as it did before you removed the reference:

```
>>> import Kitchen
>>> 'kitchen' in sys.modules
True
>>> sys.modules['Kitchen']
<module 'Kitchen' from 'Kitchen\__init__.py'>
>>> sys.modules.pop('Kitchen')
<module 'Kitchen' from 'Kitchen\__init__.py'>
>>> sys.modules['Kitchen']
Traceback (most recent call last):
  File "<input>", line 1, in ?
KeyError: 'Kitchen'
```

However, now that you know how this works under the hood, you also need to know that you have a simplified way of doing the same thing. Python provides a built-in function called `reload` that reloads the module you specified as though you'd done the manual labor you've just seen:

```
import Kitchen
reload(Kitchen)
<module 'Kitchen' from 'Kitchen\__init__.pyc'>
```

Note that this doesn't change any objects that already exist. They're still potentially tied to the old definition, which you could have changed in the module you've just reloaded! If you altered the `Recipe` and the `Omelet` classes, you'd need to re-invoke the classes and use them to re-create new versions of all objects of these types, but you already know how to initialize objects:

```
>>> r = Omelet.Recipe()
>>> o = Omelet.Omelet(r, 'onion')
```

Basics of Testing Your Modules and Packages

There is a very interesting side effect of the scope that is created for modules. Within your program is always a special name, __name__, that tells you what the scope you're running in is called. For instance, if the value of __name__ were checked from within the Foods module, it would return the string 'Foods'.

One special reserved name, the name of the top-level global scope, is __main__. If you have a module that's normally never used directly, you can stick some code at the end that has one purpose in life — verifying that your module works! This is a great opportunity to make your testing easy.

You'll have many occasions when you see a module with the following code at the end:

```
if __name__ == '__main__':
```

You can use this statement at the end of your modules; and from this point on, you can have tests that will ensure that classes are made, that functions will return the values that you expect, or any other tests you can think of. It's very common as you program to have situations in which something that once worked suddenly breaks. It's always a great idea to place tests for these situations in your packages so that you never forget that they can happen, and you can be ahead of the game! There is a lot more information about testing in Chapter 12.

Summary

In the previous chapters, you learned how to write code at the interactive Python shell, as well as put code into individual files that can be run. In this chapter, you've been shown ways of organizing your programs into modules and packages.

Modules are distinct names that Python uses to keep a scope for local names. Within a module, a name can be used directly; however, from outside of a particular module (for instance, in the global top-level scope whose name is actually __main__), the names within a module can be accessed by first specifying the name of the module where the name you want to use is defined, followed by a period, followed by the name you're looking for. An example of this is sys.path. This enables you to use the same name in different modules for different purposes, without being confusing.

To use a module, it must be brought into your program with the import statement. Import will find a file with the name of the module you want to use, with the extension .py, and make it available. It does this by examining each of the directories in the list sys.path until it finds the file.

You will often want specific parts of a module to be available with less typing than the entire specification would require — the long form would be the name of the module, any intermediate modules (separated with periods), and then the name you actually want. In such cases, you can use the construct from ... import ... to just import names that you will be frequently using. When a module is imported, it is evaluated, and any code that is not inside of a function or a class will be evaluated.

When you have a lot of code to write, you can use a *package* to group your code into a structure that is provided by the underlying file system of your operation system. This structure begins with a directory (the same thing as a folder), which will be the name of the package when it is imported into your program. What makes a directory into a package is the presence of a file called __init__.py. This file will be read and parsed, and it can contain any code that could be useful to the entire package, such as data that should be available to all parts of the package, like version information, locations of important files, and so on, as well as import statements that could be required to bring in modules that will be needed in order for other parts of the package to work correctly.

When you have a package, the files in that package will not be automatically exported when a programmer requests it by using from ... import *, even if those files are modules that have been imported inside of __init__.py. With a package, the names that will be exported by default to this request have to be specified in a list called __all__.

The key things to take away from this chapter are:

❏   You can import modules using the import keyword.

❏   Argv is short for argument vector and refers to parameters that are on the command line. These parameters are accessible as a list by using sys.argv.

❏   Packages use the structure of the directories (another name for folders) that every operating system uses to give you a methodology for making many files in the same directory look like a single module when they're used together.

❏   To make the entire contents of a module available, use from modulename import *.

Exercises

Moving code to modules and packages is straightforward and doesn't necessarily require any changes to the code to work, which is part of the ease of using Python.

In these exercises, the focus is on testing your modules, because testing is essentially writing small programs for an automated task.

1.   Write a test for the Foods.Recipe module that creates a recipe object with a list of foods, and then verifies that the keys and values provided are all present and match up. Write the test so that it is run only when Recipe.py is called directly, and not when it is imported.

2.   Write a test for the Foods.Fridge module that will add items to the Fridge, and exercise all of its interfaces except get_ingredients, which requires an Omelet object.

3.   Experiment with these tests. Run them directly from the command line. If you've typed them correctly, no errors should come up. Try introducing errors to elicit error messages from your tests.

Files and Directories

In this chapter, you'll get to know some of the types and functions that Python provides for writing and reading files and accessing the contents of directories. These functions are important, because almost all nontrivial programs use files to read input or store output.

Python provides a rich collection of input/output functions; this chapter covers those that are most widely used. First, you'll use file objects, the most basic implementation of input/output in Python. Then you'll learn about functions for manipulating paths, retrieving information about files, and accessing directory contents.

In this chapter you learn:

❏ Some of the types and functions that Python provides for writing and reading files and accessing the contents of directories. These functions are important, because almost all nontrivial programs use files to read input or store output.

❏ About Python's rich collection of input/output functions; this chapter covers those that are most widely used.

❏ To use `file` objects, the most basic implementation of input/output in Python.

❏ About functions for manipulating paths, retrieving information about files, and accessing directory contents.

File Objects

In this chapter, most of the examples use Windows path names. If you are working on a different platform, replace the example paths with paths appropriate for your system.

If you do use Windows, however, remember that a backslash is a special character in a Python string, so you must escape (that is, double up) any backslash in a path. For instance, the path `C:\Windows\Temp` is represented by the Python string `"C:\\Windows\\Temp"`. If you prefer, you can instead disable special treatment of backslashes in a string by placing an r before the opening quotes, so this same path may be written r"C:\Windows\Temp".

You'll use a string object to hold the path name for a sample file you create and access. If you're using Windows, enter the following (you can choose another path if you want):

```
>>> path = "C:\\sample.txt"
```

If you're using Linux, enter the following (or choose a path of your own):

```
>>> path = "/tmp/sample.txt"
```

Writing Text Files

Start by creating a file with some simple text. To create a new file on your system, create a file object, and tell Python you want to write to it. A file object represents a connection to a file, not the file itself, but if you open a file for writing that doesn't exist, Python creates the file automatically. Enter the following:

```
>>> def make_text_file():
    a=open('test.txt',"w")
    a.write("This is how you create a new text file")
    a.close()
```

You start off by creating a new function called make_text_file(). You then tell Python to open a file named test.txt. Because Python does not find this file, it creates it for you. (Note: if the file did exist, Python would have deleted it and created a new one, so be careful when using this technique! In a moment, you learn to check to see if a file exists *prior* to creating one.) The "w" argument tells Python that you intend to write to the file; without it, Python would assume you intend to read from the file and would raise an exception when it found that the file didn't exist. Next, you add a line of text to the file, namely: "This is how you create a new text file".

Take a moment to navigate to your Python directory, which should be located somewhere such as C://Python31. You will notice that a new file named test.txt has been created. If you double-click it, you will see the text you added in the preceding example. Congratulations, you have created your first file!

Now that you have created a file with the preceding technique, create a program that first checks to see if the file name exists; if so, it will give you an error message; if not, it will create the file. Type in the following code:

```
>>> import os
>>> def make_another_file():
    if os.path.isfile('test.txt'):
        print("You are trying to create a file that already exists!")
    else:
        f=open('test.txt',"w")
        f.write("This is how you create a new text file")
...
>>> make_another_file()
"You are trying to create a file that already exists!"
```

When opening a file, and with all the other file-manipulation functions discussed in this chapter, you can specify either a *relative path* (a path relative to the current directory, the directory in which your program or Python was run) or an *absolute path* (a path starting at the root of the drive or file system). For example, /tmp/sample.txt is an absolute path, whereas just sample.txt, without the specification of what directory is above it, is a relative path.

Appending Text to a File

Appending text to a file is a pretty simple to do. Instead of using the write method ("w"), you use append instead ("a"). By doing so, you ensure that the data in the existing file is not overwritten, but instead, any new text is appended to the end of the file. Try out the following code:

Try It Out   **Appending Text to a File**

```
>>> def add_some_text():
        a=open('test.txt',"a")
        a.write("Here is some additional text!")
...
>>> add_some_text()
```

How It Works

In the example, you created a function called add_some_text(). You then used the open method to open your file, test.txt, telling Python you wanted to append to your file (this is the "a" argument). Next, you write some new text to the file. When you call the function later on, it adds the line "Here is some additional text!"

To see the results, go to the directory where Python is installed and open up the test.txt file. You should see the new text appended to the end of the file.

Note that write doesn't add line breaks automatically; you must add one yourself with the escape sequence \n wherever you want a line break in the file. The same goes for spaces. If you do not add a space, tab, or line break, the next time you add some text to the file; it will be crammed up against the previous text.

If you use write again, the text is appended to what you wrote before. If the string you pass is more than one line long, more than one line is added to the file:

```
>>> def even_more_text():
a=open('test.txt',"a")
a.write("""
here is
more
text""")
...
>>> even_more_text()
```

You've used a multi-line, triple-quoted string here. Until you close the triple quotes, Python prompts you to continue the string with " . . .". In a multi-line string, Python adds line breaks between lines. Go ahead and open the test.txt file again and see the changes first hand.

Reading Text Files

Reading from a file is similar. First, open the file by creating a `file` object. This time, use `"r"` to tell Python you intend to read from the file. It's the default, so you can omit the second argument altogether if you want.

```
a=open("test.txt","r")
```

Make sure you use the path to the file you created earlier, or use the path to some other file you want to read. If the file doesn't exist, Python will raise an exception.

You can read a line from the file using the `readline` method. The first time you call this method on a `file` object, it will return the first line of text in the file:

```
>>> a.readline()
'This is how you create a new text file\n'
```

Notice that `readline` includes the newline character at the end of the string it returns. To read the contents of the file one line at a time, call `readline` repeatedly.

You can also read the rest of the file all at once with the `read` method. This method returns any text in the file that you haven't read yet. (If you call `read` as soon as you open a file, it will return the entire contents of the file, as one long string.)

```
>>> f=open("test.txt","r")
>>> text=a.read()
>>> print(text)
This is how you create a new text file
Here is some additional text
here is
more
text
```

Because you've used `print` to print the text, Python shows newline characters as actual line breaks, instead of as `\n`.

When you're done reading the file, close the file by deleting the `file` object and closing the file:

```
>>> del a
>>> a.close()
```

It's convenient to have Python break a text file into lines, but it's nice to be able to get all the lines at one time — for instance, to use in a loop. The `readlines` method does exactly that: It returns the remaining lines in the file as a list of strings. Suppose, for instance, that you want to print out the length of each line in a file. This function will do that:

```
def print_line_lengths():
    a=open("test.txt","r")
    text=a.readlines()
    for line in text:
        print(len(line))
```

Try It Out   Printing the Lengths of Lines in the Sample File

Using the function `print_line_lengths`, you can examine the file you just created, displaying the length of each line:

```
>>> print_line_lengths()
38
28
7
4
4
```

How It Works

Each line is read as a string. Each line, as it's read, has its length displayed by using the string as an argument to the `len` function. Remember that the newline character is included in each line, so what looks like an empty line has a length of one.

File Exceptions

Because your Python program does not have exclusive control of the computer's file system, it must be prepared to handle unexpected errors when accessing files. When Python encounters a problem performing a file operation, it raises an `IOError` exception. (Exceptions are described in Chapter 4.) The string representation of the exception will describe the problem.

Many circumstances exist in which you can get an `IOError`, including the following:

❏ If you attempt to open a file for reading that does not exist

❏ If you attempt to create a file in a directory that does not exist

❏ If you attempt to open a file for which you do not have read access

❏ If you attempt to create a file in a directory for which you do not have write access

❏ If your computer encounters a disk error (or network error, if you are accessing a file on a network disk)

If you want your program to react gracefully when errors occur, you must handle these exceptions. What to do when you receive an exception depends on what your program does. In some cases, you may want to try a different file, perhaps after printing a warning message. In other cases, you may have to ask the user what to do next or simply exit if recovery is not possible.

Paths and Directories

The file systems on Windows, Linux, UNIX, and Mac OS/X have a lot in common but differ in some of their rules, conventions, and capabilities. For example, Windows uses a backslash to separate directory names in a path, whereas Linux and UNIX (and Mac OS/X is a type of UNIX) use a forward slash. In addition, Windows uses drive letters, whereas the others don't. These differences can be a major irritation if you are writing a program that will run on different platforms. Python makes your life easier by hiding some of the annoying details of path and directory manipulation in the os module. Using os will not solve all of your portability problems, however; some functions in os are not available on all platforms. This section describes only those functions that are.

Even if you intend to use your programs only on a single platform and anticipate being able to avoid most of these issues, if your program is useful you never know if someone will try to run it on another platform someday. So it's better to tap the os module, because it provides many useful services. Don't forget to import os first so you can use it.

Exceptions in os

The functions in the os module raise OSError exceptions on failure. If you want your program to behave nicely when things go wrong, you must handle this exception. As with IOError, the string representation of the exception will provide a description of the problem.

Paths

The os module contains another module, os.path, which provides functions for manipulating paths. Because paths are strings, you could use ordinary string manipulation to assemble and disassemble file paths. Your code would not be as easily portable, however, and would probably not handle special cases that os.path knows about. Use os.path to manipulate paths, and your programs will be better for it.

To assemble directory names into a path, use os.path.join. Python uses the path separator appropriate for your operating system. Don't forget to import the os.path module before you use it. For example, on Windows, enter the following:

```
>>> import os.path
>>> os.path.join("snakes", "Python")
'snakes\\Python'
```

On Linux, however, using the same parameters to os.path.join gives you the following, different, result:

```
>>> import os.path
>>> os.path.join("snakes", "Python")
'snakes/Python'
```

You can specify more than two components as well.

The inverse function is os.path.split, which splits off the last component of a path. It returns a tuple of two items: the path of the parent directory and the last path component. Here's an example:

```
>>> os.path.split("C:\\Program Files\\Python30\\Lib")
('C:\\Program Files\\Python30', 'Lib')
```

On UNIX or Linux, it would look like this:

```
>>> os.path.split("/usr/bin/python")
('/usr/bin', 'python')
```

Automatic unpacking of sequences comes in handy here. What happens is that when os.path.split returns a tuple, the tuple can be broken up into the elements on the left-hand side of the equals sign:

```
>>> parent_path, name = os.path.split("C:\\Program Files\\Python30\\Lib")
>>> print(parent_path)
C:\Program Files\Python30
>>> print(name)
Lib
```

Although os.path.split only splits off the last path component, sometimes you might want to split a path completely into directory names. Writing a function to do this is not difficult; what you want to do is call os.path.split on the path, and then call os.path.split on the parent directory path, and so forth, until you get all the way to the root directory. An elegant way to do this is with a *recursive function*, which is a function that calls itself. It might look like this:

```
def split_fully(path):
    parent_path, name = os.path.split(path)
    if name == "":
        return (parent_path, )
    else:
        return split_fully(parent_path) + (name, )
```

The key line is the last line, where the function calls itself to split the parent path into components. The last component of the path, name, is then attached to the end of the fully split parent path. The lines in the middle of split_fully prevent the function from calling itself infinitely. When os.path.split can't split a path any further, it returns an empty string for the second component; split_fully notices this and returns the parent path without calling itself again.

A function can call itself safely because Python keeps track of the arguments and local variables in each running instance of the function, even if one is called from another. In this case, when split_fully calls itself, the outer (first) instance doesn't lose its value of name even though the inner (second) instance assigns a different value to it, because each has its own copy of the variable name. When the inner instance returns, the outer instance continues with the same variable values it had when it made the recursive call.

When you write a recursive function, make sure that it never calls itself infinitely, which would be bad because it would never return. (Actually, Python would run out of space in which to keep track of all the calls, and would raise an exception.) The function split_fully won't call itself infinitely, because eventually path is short enough that name is an empty string, and the function returns without calling itself again.

Notice in this function the two uses of single-element tuples, which *must* include a comma in the parentheses. Without the comma, Python would interpret the parentheses as ordinary grouping parentheses, as in a mathematical expression: (name,) is a tuple with one element; (name) is the same as name.

Here's the function in action:

```
>>> split_fully("C:\\Program Files\\Python31\\Lib")
('C:\\', 'Program Files', 'Python31', 'Lib')
```

After you have the name of a file, you can split off its extension with os.path.splitext:

```
>>> os.path.splitext("image.jpg")
('image', '.jpg')
```

The call to splitext returns a two-element tuple, so you can extract just the extension as shown here:

```
>>> parts = os.path.splitext("image.jpg")
>>> extension = parts[1]
```

You don't actually need the variable parts at all. You can extract the second component, the extension, directly from the return value of splitext:

```
>>> extension = os.path.splitext("image.jpg")[1]
```

Also handy is os.path.normpath, which normalizes or "cleans up" a path:

```
>>> print(os.path.normpath(r"C:\\Program Files\Perl\..\Python30"))
C:\Program Files\Python30
```

Notice how the "..." was eliminated by backing up one directory component, and the double separator was fixed. Similar to this is os.path.abspath, which converts a *relative path* (a path relative to the current directory) to an *absolute path* (a path starting at the root of the drive or file system):

```
>>> print(os.path.abspath("other_stuff"))
C:\Program Files\Python30\other_stuff
```

Your output will depend on your current directory when you call abspath. As you may have noticed, this works even though you don't have an actual file or directory named other_stuff in your Python directory. None of the path manipulation functions in os.path check whether the path you are manipulating actually exists.

If you want to know whether a path actually does exist, use os.path.exists. It simply returns True or False:

```
>>> os.path.exists("C:\\Windows")
True
>>> os.path.exists("C:\\Windows\\reptiles")
False
```

Of course, if you're not using Windows, or your Windows is installed in another directory (like C:\WinNT), both of these will return False!

Directory Contents

Now you know how to construct arbitrary paths and take them apart. But how can you find out what's actually on your disk? The os.listdir module tells you, by returning a list of the name entries in a directory — the files, subdirectories, and so on that it contains.

Try It Out	Getting the Contents of a Directory

The following code gets a list of entries in a directory. In Windows, you can list the contents of your Python installation directory:

```
>>> os.listdir("C:\\Python31")
['Chapter 5', 'Chapter 6', 'Chapter 7', 'DLLs', 'Doc', 'ham', 'include',
'Lib', 'libs', 'LICENSE.txt', 'maybe', 'NEWS.txt', 'python.exe', 'pythonw.exe',
'README.txt', 'tcl', 'Test', 'Test.py', 'test.txt', 'test2.txt', 'test6.txt',
'tester.py', 'test.txt', 'Tools', 'w9xpopen.exe']
```

Note that your results may differ, depending upon the files in your directory.

In other operating systems, or if you installed Python in a different directory, substitute some other path. You can use "." to list your current directory. Of course, you will get back a different list of names if you list a different directory.

In any case, you should note a few important things here. First, the results are names of directory entries, not full paths. If you need the full path to an entry, you must construct it yourself, with os.path.join. Second, names of files and directories are mixed together, and there is no way to distinguish the two from the result of os.listdir. Finally, notice that the results do not include '.' and '..', the two special directory names that represent the same directory and its parent.

Write a function that lists the contents of a directory but prints full paths instead of just file and directory names, and prints only one entry per line:

```
def print_dir(dir_path):
    for name in os.listdir(dir_path):
        print(os.path.join(dir_path, name))
```

This function loops over the list returned by os.listdir and calls os.path.join on each entry to construct the full path before printing it. Try it like this:

```
>>> print_dir("C:\\Python30")
C:\Python31\DLLs
C:\Python31\Doc
C:\Python31\ham
C:\Python31\include
C:\Python31\Lib
C:\Python31\libs
C:\Python31\LICENSE.txt...
```

There is no guarantee that the list of entries returned by os.listdir will be sorted in any particular way: The order can be anything. You may prefer to have the entries in some specific order to suit your application. Because it's just a list of strings, you can sort it yourself using the sorted function. By default, this produces a case-sensitive alphabetical sort:

```
>>> sorted(os.listdir("C:\\Python31"))
['DLLs', 'Doc', 'LICENSE.txt', 'Lib', 'NEWS.txt', 'README.txt',
'Removepywin32.exe', 'Scripts', 'Tools', 'include', 'libs', 'py.ico',
'pyc.ico', 'python.exe', 'pythonw.exe', 'pywin32-wininst.log', 'tcl',
'w9xpopen.exe']
```

Try It Out   **Listing the Contents of Your Desktop or Home Directory**

Use print_dir_by_ext to list the contents of your desktop or home directory. On Windows, your desktop is a folder, whose path is typically C:\\Documents and Settings\\username\\Desktop, where username is your account name. On GNU/Linux or UNIX, your home directory's path is typically /home/username. Is the output what you expected?

Obtaining Information about Files

You can easily determine whether a path refers to a file or to a directory. If it's a file, os.path.isfile will return True; if it's a directory, os.path.isdir will return True. Both return False if the path does not exist at all:

```
>>> os.path.isfile("C:\\Windows")
False
>>> os.path.isdir("C:\\Windows")
True
```

> ### Other Types of Directory Entries
>
> On some platforms, a directory may contain additional types of entries, such as symbolic links, sockets, and devices. The semantics of these are specific to the platform and too complicated to cover here. Nonetheless, the os module provides some support for examining these; consult the module documentation for details for your platform.

Recursive Directory Listings

You can combine os.path.isdir with os.listdir to do something very useful: process subdirectories recursively. For instance, you can list the contents of a directory, its subdirectories, their subdirectories, and so on. To do this, it's again useful to write a recursive function. This time, when the function finds a subdirectory, it calls itself to list the contents of that subdirectory:

```
def print_tree(dir_path):
    for name in os.listdir(dir_path):
        full_path = os.path.join(dir_path, name)
        print(full_path)
        if os.path.isdir(full_path):
            print_tree(full_path)
```

You'll notice the similarity to the function `print_dir` you wrote previously. This function, however, constructs the full path to each entry as `full_path`, because it's needed both for printing out and for consideration as a subdirectory. The last two lines check whether it is a subdirectory, and if so, the function calls itself to list the subdirectory's contents before continuing. If you try this function, make sure that you don't call it for a large directory tree; otherwise, you'll have to wait a while as it prints out the full path of every single subdirectory and file in the tree.

Other functions in `os.path` provide information about a file. For instance, `os.path.getsize` returns the size, in bytes, of a file without having to open and scan it. Use `os.path.getmtime` to obtain the time when the file was last modified. The return value is the number of seconds between the start of the year 1970 and when the file was last modified — not a format users prefer for dates! You have to call another function, `time.ctime`, to convert the result to an easily understood format (don't forget to import the `time` module first). Here's an example that outputs when your Python installation directory was last modified, which is probably the date and time you installed Python on your computer:

```
>>> import time
>>> mod_time = os.path.getmtime("C:\\Python30")
>>> print(time.ctime(mod_time))
Thu Mar 15 01:36:26 2009
```

Now you know how to modify `print_dir` to print the contents of a directory, including the size and modification time of each file. In the interest of brevity, the version that follows prints only the names of entries, not their full paths:

```
def print_dir_info(dir_path):
    for name in os.listdir(dir_path):
        full_path = os.path.join(dir_path, name)
        file_size = os.path.getsize(full_path)
        mod_time = time.ctime(os.path.getmtime(full_path))
        print("%-32s: %8d bytes, modified %s" % (name, file_size, mod_time))
```

The last statement uses Python's built-in string formatting that you saw in Chapters 1 and 2 to produce neatly aligned output. If there's other file information you would like to print, browse the documentation for the `os.path` module to learn how to obtain it.

Renaming, Moving, Copying, and Removing Files

The `shutil` module contains functions for operating on files. You can use the function `shutil.move` to rename a file:

```
>>> import shutil
>>> shutil.move("server.log", "server.log.backup")
```

Alternatively, you can use it to move a file to another directory:

```
>>> shutil.move("old mail.txt", "C:\\data\\archive\\")
```

You might have noticed that os also contains a function for renaming or moving files, os.rename. You should generally use shutil.move instead, because with os.rename, you may not specify a directory name as the destination and on some systems os.rename cannot move a file to another disk or file system.

The shutil module also provides the copy function to copy a file to a new name or directory. You can simply use the following:

```
>>> shutil.copy("important.dat", "C:\\backups")
```

Deleting a file is easiest of all. Just call os.remove:

```
>>> os.remove("junk.dat")
```

If you're an old-school UNIX hacker (or want to pass yourself off as one), you may prefer os.unlink, which does the same thing.

File Permissions

File permissions work differently on different platforms, and explaining them is beyond the scope of this book. However, if you need to change the permissions of a file or directory, you can use the os.chmod function. It works in the same way as the UNIX or Linux chmod system call. See the documentation for the os module for details.

Example: Rotating Files

In this example, you tackle a more difficult real-world file management task. Suppose that you need to keep old versions of a file around. For instance, system administrators will keep old versions of system log files. Often, older versions of a file are named with a numerical suffix — for instance, web.log.1, web.log.2, and so on — in which a larger number indicates an older version. To make room for a new version of the file, the old versions are *rotated*: The current version of web.log becomes version web.log.1, web.log.1 becomes web.log.2, and so on.

This is clearly tedious to do by hand, but Python can make quick work of it. You have a few tricky points to consider, however. First, the current version of the file is named differently than old versions; whereas old versions have a numerical suffix, the current version does not. One way to get around this is to treat the current version as version zero. A short function, make_version_path, constructs the right path for both current and old versions.

The other subtle point is that you must make sure to rename the oldest version *first*. For instance, if you rename web.log.1 to web.log.2 before renaming web.log.2, the latter will be overwritten and its contents lost before you get to it, which isn't what you want. Once again, a recursive function will save you. The function can call itself to rotate the next-older version of the log file before it gets overwritten:

```python
import os
import shutil

def make_version_path(path, version):
    if version == 0:
        # No suffix for version 0, the current version.
        return path
    else:
        # Append a suffix to indicate the older version.
        return path + "." + str(version)

def rotate(path, version=0):
    # Construct the name of the version we're rotating.
    old_path = make_version_path(path, version)
    if not os.path.exists(old_path):
        # It doesn't exist, so complain.
        raise IOError("'%s' doesn't exist" % path)
    # Construct the new version name for this file.
    new_path = make_version_path(path, version + 1)
    # Is there already a version with this name?
    if os.path.exists(new_path):
        # Yes.  Rotate it out of the way first!
        rotate(path, version + 1)
    # Now we can rename the version safely.
    shutil.move(old_path, new_path)
```

Take a few minutes to study this code and the comments. The `rotate` function uses a technique common in recursive functions: a second argument for handing recursive cases — in this case, the version number of the file being rotated. The argument has a default value, zero, which indicates the current version of the file. When you call the function (as opposed to when the function is calling itself) you don't specify a value for this argument. For example, you can just call `rotate("web.log")`.

You may have noticed that the function checks to make sure that the file being rotated actually exists and raises an exception if it doesn't. But suppose you want to rotate a system log file that may or may not exist. One way to handle this is to create an empty log file whenever it's missing. Remember that when you open a file that doesn't exist for writing, Python creates the file automatically. If you don't actually write anything to the new file, it will be empty. Here's a function that rotates a log file that may or may not exist, creating it first if it doesn't. It uses the `rotate` function you wrote previously.

```python
def rotate_log_file(path):
    if not os.path.exists(path):
        # The file is missing, so create it.
        new_file = file(path, "w")
        # Close the new file immediately, which leaves it empty.
        del new_file
    # Now rotate it.
    rotate(path)
```

Creating and Removing Directories

Creating an empty directory is even easier than creating a file. Just call `os.mkdir`. The parent directory must exist, however. The following will raise an exception if the parent directory `C:\photos\zoo` does not exist:

```
>>> os.mkdir("C:\\photos\\zoo\\snakes")
```

You can create the parent directory itself using `os.mkdir`, but the easy way out is instead to use `os.makedirs`, which creates missing parent directories. For example, the following will create `C:\photos` and `C:\photos\zoo`, if necessary:

```
>>> os.makedirs("C:\\photos\\zoo\\snakes")
```

Remove a directory with `os.rmdir`. This works only for empty directories; if the directory is not empty, you'll have to remove its contents first:

```
>>> os.rmdir("C:\\photos\\zoo\\snakes")
```

This removes only the `snakes` subdirectory.

There is a way to remove a directory even when it contains other files and subdirectories. The function `shutil.rmtree` does this. Be careful, however; if you make a programming or typing mistake and pass the wrong path to this function, you could delete a whole bunch of files before you even know what's going on! For instance, this will delete your entire photo collection — zoo, snakes, and all:

```
>>> shutil.rmtree("C:\\photos")
```

Globbing

If you have used the command prompt on Windows, or a shell command line on GNU/Linux, UNIX, or Mac OS X, you probably have encountered wildcard patterns before. These are the special characters, such as `*` and `?`, which you use to match many files with similar names. For example, you may have used the pattern `P*` to match all files that start with *P*, or `*.txt` to match all files with the extension `.txt`.

Globbing is hackers' jargon for expanding wildcards in file name patterns. Python provides a function `glob`, in the module also named `glob`, which implements globbing of directory contents. The `glob.glob` function takes a glob pattern and returns a list of matching file names or paths, similar to `os.listdir`.

Globbing and Case-sensitivity

On Windows, the pattern `M*` matches file names that begin with both *M* and *m*, because file names and, therefore, file name globbing, are case-insensitive. On most other operating systems, globbing is case-sensitive.

For example, try the following command to list entries in your `C:\Program Files` directory that start with *M*:

```
>>> import glob
>>> glob.glob("C:\\Program Files\\M*")
['C:\\Program Files\\Messenger', 'C:\\Program Files\\Microsoft Office',
'C:\\Program Files\\Mozilla Firefox']
```

Your computer's output will vary depending on what software you have installed. Observe that `glob.glob` returns paths containing drive letters and directory names if the pattern includes them, unlike `os.listdir`, which only returns the names in the specified directory.

The following table lists the wildcards you can use in glob patterns. These wildcards are not necessarily the same as those available in the command shell of your operating system, but Python's `glob` module uses the same syntax on all platforms. Note that the syntax for glob patterns resembles but is *not* the same as the syntax for regular expressions.

Wildcard	Matches	Example
*	Any zero or more characters	`*.m*` matches names whose extensions begin with *m*.
?	Any one character	`???` matches names exactly three characters long.
[...]	Any one character listed in the brackets	`[AEIOU]*` matches names that begin with capital vowels.
[!...]	Any one character *not* listed in the brackets	`*[!s]` matches names that don't end with an *s*.

You can also use a range of characters in square brackets. For example, `[m-p]` matches any one of the letters *m*, *n*, *o*, or *p*, and `[!0-9]` matches any character other than a digit.

Globbing is a handy way of selecting a group of similar files for a file operation. For instance, deleting all backup files with the extension `.bak` in the directory `C:\source\` is as easy as these two lines:

```
>>> for path in glob.glob("C:\\source\\*.bak"):
...     os.remove(path)
```

Globbing is considerably more powerful than `os.listdir`, because you can specify wildcards in directory and subdirectory names. For patterns like this, `glob.glob` can return paths in more than one directory. For instance, the following code returns all files with the extension `.txt` in subdirectories of the current directory:

```
>>> glob.glob("*\\*.txt")
```

Summary

In this chapter, you learned how to write data to and read data from files on your disk. Using a `file` object, you can now write strings to a file, and read back the contents of a file, line-by-line or all at once. You can use these techniques to read input into your program, to generate output files, or to store intermediate results.

You also learned about paths, which specify the location of a file on your disk, and how to manipulate them. Using `os.listdir` or `glob`, you can find out what's on your disk.

The key points to take away from this chapter are:

❑ A file object represents a connection to a file, not the file itself, but if you open a file for writing that doesn't exist, Python creates the file automatically.

❑ To append to a file, use append instead of write. This ensures that the data in the file is not overwritten.

❑ To read from a file, use "r", as in the following: a=open("`test.txt`","r")

❑ The readline method returns the first line of text in a file.

❑ When you are finished reading a file, be sure to delete the file object and explicitly close the file.

❑ The `os.path` module, located in the os module, provides functions for manipulating paths.

❑ The `os.listdir` module tells you the files, subdirectories, and contents in a directory.

❑ Globbing is hackers' jargon for expanding wildcards in filename patterns. Python provides a function glob, in the module also named glob, which implements globbing of directory contents. The glob.glob function takes a glob pattern and returns a list of matching filenames or paths, similar to `os.listdir`.

Exercises

1. Create another version of the (nonrecursive) `print_dir` function that lists all subdirectory names first, followed by names of files in the directory. Names of subdirectories should be alphabetized, as should file names. (For extra credit, write your function in such a way that it calls `os.listdir` only one time. Python can manipulate strings faster than it can execute `os.listdir`.)

2. Modify the `rotate` function to keep only a fixed number of old versions of the file. The number of versions should be specified in an additional parameter. Excess old versions above this number should be deleted.

Other Features of the Language

In this chapter you are introduced to some other aspects of Python that are less frequently used, as well as modules that are very commonly used. Each section describes at least one way that the feature is typically used and then offers example code.

In previous chapters you looked at some common functions, and even learned to create your own. Part of the charm of Python is its breadth of built-in functions and modules that cater to both broad and obscure problems. Before learning to build your own module, you look at some of the ones Python offers to get a better understanding of their usage.

In this chapter you learn:

❑   To work with the `lambda` and `filter` functions.

❑   To use `map` to avoid loops.

❑   To string substitutions.

❑   The `getopt` module.

Lambda and Filter: Short Anonymous Functions

Sometimes you need a very simple function invocation — something that is not generally useful or that is so specific that its use needs to be completely different if it is invoked in another location in your code. For these occasions, there is a special operation: `lambda`. Lambda is not a function itself but a special word that tells Python to create a function and use it in place, rather than reference it from a name.

To demonstrate `lambda` being used, the following example uses `filter`, which is a function that enables you to take a list and remove elements based on criteria you define within a function you write. Normal functions can be used, but in simple cases, such as where you want only odd numbers (or odd-numbered elements, or strings beginning with something, and so on), a fully defined function could be overkill.

```
# use lambda with filter
filter_me = [1, 2, 3, 4, 6,7 ,8, 11, 12, 14, 15, 19, 22]
# This will only return true for even numbers (because x%2 is 0, or False,
# for odd numbers)
result = filter(lambda x: x%2 == 0, filter_me)
print(*result)
```

The functions that lambda creates are called *anonymous* functions because of their lack of a name. However, you can use the result of the lambda statement to bind the name to a function yourself. That name will be available only in the scope in which the name was created, like any other name:

```
# use lambda with filter, but bind it to a name
filter_me = [1, 2, 3, 4, 6,7 ,8, 11, 12, 14, 15, 19, 22]
# This will only return true for even numbers (because x%2 is 0, or False,
# for odd numbers)
func = lambda x: x%2 == 0
result = filter(func, filter_me)
print(*result)
```

Lambda can only be a simple function, and it can't contain statements, such as creating a name for a variable. Inside a lambda, you can only perform a limited set of operations, such as testing for equality, multiplying numbers, or using other already existing functions in a specific manner. You can't do things like use if ... : elsif ... : else: constructs or even create new names for variables! You can only use the parameters passed into the lambda function. You can, however, do slightly more than perform simple declarative statements by using the and and or operations. However, you should still keep in mind that lambda is for very limited uses.

The main use for lambda is with the built-in functions map and filter. Used with lambda, these functions provide compact ways to perform some great operations while avoiding the need for loops. You've already seen filter in action, which could be a difficult loop to write.

Map: Short-Circuiting Loops

One common place to use anonymous functions is when the map function is called. Map is a special function for cases when you need to do a specific action on every element of a list. It enables you to accomplish this without having to write the loop.

Try It Out   **Using Map**

Try this basic test:

```
# Now map gets to be run in the simple case
map_me = [ 'a', 'b', 'c', 'd', 'e', 'f', 'g' ]
result = map(lambda x: "The letter is %s" % x, map_me)
print(*result)
```

How It Works

Just like being in a loop, every element in the list will be visited. In the previous version of Python, a list would also be returned; however, in Python 3.1 an iterator is now returned instead. This is how it will look:

```
>>> print(*result)
The letter is a The letter is b The letter is c The letter is d
The letter is e The letter is f The letter is g
```

Some special things are worth knowing about map. If you pass in a list of lists (or tuples — any kind of sequence can be given to map), your function needs to expect that list. Each sequence in the main list should have the same number of elements:

```
# use map with a list of lists, to re-order the output.
map_me_again = [[1, 2, 3], [4, 5, 6], [7, 8, 9]]
result = map(lambda list: [ list[1], list[0], list[2]], map_me_again)
print(*result)
```

This results in a list of lists, where everything has been shuffled around:

```
>>> print(*result)
[2, 1, 3] [5, 4, 6] [8, 7, 9]
```

You can see that map always returns an iterator. Map can be given the name of a non-anonymous function if you like, and it operates in the same way.

Decisions within Lists — List Comprehension

The oddly named *list comprehension* feature entered the language in Python 2.0. It enables you to write miniature loops and decisions within the list dereferencing operators (the square brackets) to define parameters that will be used to restrict the range of elements being accessed.

For instance, to create a list that prints just the positive numbers in a list, you can use list comprehension:

```
# First, just print even numbers
everything = [1, 2, 3, 4, 5, 6, 7, 8, 9, 10, 11, 12 ]
print([ x for x in everything if x%2 == 0])
```

This can be a nice and compact way of providing a portion of a list to a loop — but with only the pertinent parts of the list, based on what you want in your program at the moment, being presented to your loop.

List comprehension provides you with the same functionality as filter or map combined with lambda, but it is a form that gives you more decision-making power because it can include loops and conditionals, whereas lambda only enables you to perform one simple expression.

In most cases, list comprehension will also run faster than the alternative.

Generating Iterators for Loops

Python has a special feature that enables you to create iterators — the `range` function:

```
f = range (10, 20)
print(*f)
```

This code produces an obvious-looking result:

```
>>> print(*f)
10 11 12 13 14 15 16 17 18 19
```

By itself, this doesn't seem profound, but it is essential for situations when you need to use a `for` loop that will continue for a specific number of iterations, and that isn't based on an existing list; and this number may not be determined at the time when the program was written, but it becomes known only when the program is already running.

If `range` is given only a single number, it will count from zero to that number. The number can be positive or negative:

```
for number in range(10):
    print("Number is now %d" % number)
```

This produces the obvious output, which is what you want:

```
Number is now 0
Number is now 1
Number is now 2
Number is now 3
Number is now 4
Number is now 5
Number is now 6
Number is now 7
Number is now 8
Number is now 9
```

In addition, if you only want, for example, every other number or every third number, you can use an even more optional third parameter, called the `step`, that describes what the interval will be between each number that `range` creates:

```
for number in range(5, 55, 4):
    print("Number from 5 to 55, by fours: %d" % number)
```

This results in the selective list of numbers that you specified:

```
Number from 5 to 55, by fours: 5
Number from 5 to 55, by fours: 9
Number from 5 to 55, by fours: 13
Number from 5 to 55, by fours: 17
Number from 5 to 55, by fours: 21
Number from 5 to 55, by fours: 25
Number from 5 to 55, by fours: 29
```

```
Number from 5 to 55, by fours: 33
Number from 5 to 55, by fours: 37
Number from 5 to 55, by fours: 41
Number from 5 to 55, by fours: 45
Number from 5 to 55, by fours: 49
Number from 5 to 55, by fours: 53
```

In previous versions of Python, a program could be handling huge numbers of elements — perhaps hundreds of thousands, or even millions, in which case `range` would create an array with every element that you've asked for — example, from zero to the number of all the possible systems on the Internet. When this many things need to be examined, each element uses a bit of computer memory, which can eventually take up all of the memory on a system. To avoid any problems with this sort of a really large list, Python had a special built-in class called `xrange` that created fewer elements in memory. In Python 3.1, `range` was changed so that it no longer created a list, but instead an iterator, essentially making it perform in the exact manner that `xrange` behaved. `Xrange` has since been removed from the language.

Try It Out   Examining a range Iterator

Interestingly, note that `range` returns an iterator object that behaves like a list. Note that this object has no public interfaces — just private methods that look like a subset of what most lists and tuples have:

```
>>> xr = range(0,10)
>>> dir(xr)
['__class__', '__delattr__', '__doc__', '__eq__', '__format__', '__ge__',
'__getattribute__', '__getitem__', '__gt__', '__hash__', '__init__', '__iter_
_',
'__le__', '__len__', '__lt__', '__ne__', '__new__', '__reduce__', '__reduce_
ex__',
'__repr__', '__reversed__', '__setattr__', '__sizeof__', '__str__',
'__subclasshook__']
```

Tying to call it directly doesn't result in a list; it results in a representation of how it was called:

```
>>> xr
range(0, 10)
```

You can, however, still access it by using the same dereferencing operation (the square brackets) that you can with lists, sequences, and dictionaries:

```
>>> xr[0]
0
>>> xr[1]
1
```

How It Works

`Range` produces an object that doesn't have any public methods. The only methods it has are built-in methods that enable it to act as a very simple sequence. Internally, when you use the square brackets to access a list, tuple, or a dictionary, you are telling python to invoke the __getitem__ method of that list, tuple, or dictionary. A `range` object has this private method, so it can act as a sequence and be dereferenced this way.

When you call a `range` object, it doesn't produce a list. Instead it tells you how it was created so you know what the parameters were, in case you wanted to know about the numbers it is generating.

The point is that even though it behaves like a sequence, it is different; and that's kind of cool.

Special String Substitution Using Dictionaries

One syntax you haven't been shown yet is a special syntax for using dictionaries to populate string substitutions. This can come up when you want a configurable way to print out strings — such as a formatted report or something similar.

Try It Out   String Formatting with Dictionaries

When you are doing this, you want to take individual named elements from a known set of elements, such as what you have in a dictionary, and print them out in the order that you have specified, which can be defined outside of the program itself:

```
person = {"name": "James", "camera": "nikon", "handedness": "lefty",
"baseball_team": "angels", "instrument": "guitar"}

print("%(name)s, %(camera)s, %(baseball_team)s" % person)
```

The output of this code looks like this:

```
>>> print("%(name)s, %(camera)s, %(baseball_team)s" % person)
James, nikon, angels
```

How It Works

Note that the information in the parentheses is the name of the key whose value will be substituted from the dictionary into the string. However, to use this properly, you still need to specify the type of the data being inserted after the closing parenthesis so that the string substitution knows what to do. Here, all the types were strings, but you could use the i for int, j for imaginary, l for long, and all the other format specifiers you've learned. To see different formats being used with this new format, try the following example. Notice that `person` should appear on the same line as the `print` statement — it's not on the next line; it's just the end of a long line:

```
person["height"] = 1.6
person["weight"] = 80
print("%(name)s, %(camera)s, %(baseball_team)s, %(height)2.2f,
%(weight)2.2f" % person)
```

This gives you the following terse output:

```
>>> print("%(name)s, %(camera)s, %(baseball_team)s, %(height)2.2f,
%(weight)2.2f" % person)
James, nikon, angels, 1.60, 80.00
```

These examples work with almost the same syntax that you learned in the first three chapters.

Added back in Python 2.4, another form of string substitution is located within the *String* module, which uses a new syntax for substitution grammar. This form was created to enable you to give users — for example, of a program you've written — a format that may make more sense to them at first glance:

```
import string
person = {"name": "James", "camera": "nikon", "handedness": "lefty",
"baseball_team": "angels", "instrument": "guitar"}
person["height"] = 1.6
person["weight"] = 80
t = string.Template("$name is $height m high and $weight kilos")
print(t.substitute(person))
```

This produces output that's no better or worse than the first way, except that you can't control the format information anymore:

```
print t.substitute(person)
James is 1.6 m high and 80 kilos
```

Think about using this feature when you are asking users to describe what information they want from a set of data. This can be used as an easily supported way for someone else to specify the data they want without saddling you with the need to rewrite your program. You just need to ask them to specify the `template`, and you can supply the string they've given you to the `string.Template` class to create a `template` object that will perform the desired substitution.

Featured Modules

Starting in Chapter 7, you saw modules used to add functionality to Python. In Chapter 8, you learned how interaction with the operating system and its files is achieved through modules that provide interfaces to how the system works with the `os` module.

In this section, you see examples of some other common modules that will help you to start building your own programs.

Getopt — Getting Options from the Command Line

On UNIX systems, the most common way to specify the behavior of a program when it runs is to add parameters to the command line of a program. Even when a program is not run from the command line but is instead run using `fork` and `exec` (more on this later in this chapter), a command line is constructed when it is invoked. This makes it a universal way of controlling the behavior of your programs.

You may have seen, for instance, that many programs can be run so that they provide you with some basic information about how they should be run. Python enables you to do this with -h:

```
$ python -h
usage: python30 [option] ... [-c cmd | -m mod | file | -] [arg] ...
Options and arguments (and corresponding environment variables):
-c cmd : program passed in as string (terminates option list)
-d     : debug output from parser (also PYTHONDEBUG=x)
-E     : ignore environment variables (such as PYTHONPATH)
[ etc. ]
```

In the past, different conventions were available on different UNIX platforms to specify these options, but this has largely resulted in two forms of options being used by most projects: the short form, such as the help-message producing option to Python, and a long form, such as --help for help.

To accept these sorts of options makes sense. Ideally, you'd like to offer a short and a long form of commands that are common, and allow each one to optionally take a specification. So if you wanted to write a program that had a configuration file that the user could specify, you may want one option like -c short for experienced users, but provide a longer option too, like --config-file. In either case, you'd want them to be the same function in your program to save you time, but you'd like to give users the freedom to use these options however they want to use them.

The getopt module provides two functions to make this standard convention easy to use: getopt .getopt and getopt.gnu_getopt. They are both basically the same. The basic getopt only works until the first non-option is encountered — nothing else is checked.

For getopt to be useful, you have to know what options you want to be useful. Normally, it's considered the least you can do for your users to write programs that provide them with information about how to run the program, such as how Python prints information with the -h option.

In addition, it's often very useful to have a configuration file. Using these ideas as a starting point, you could start your new programs so that -h and --help both produce a minimal message about how your program is used, and using -c or --config-file=file would enable you to specify a configuration file that is different from the default configuration:

```
import sys
import getopt
# Remember, the first thing in the sys.argv list is the name of the command
# You don't need that.
cmdline_params = sys.argv[1:]

opts, args = getopt.getopt(cmdline_params, 'hc:', ['help', 'config='])

for option, parameter in opts:

    if option == '-h' or option == '--help':
        print("This program can be run with either -h or --help for this
message,")
        print("or with -c or --config=<file> to specify a different
configuration file")
```

```
if option in ('-c', '--config'): # this means the same as the above
    print("Using configuration file %s" % parameter)
```

When long options are used and require a parameter (like --config in the preceding example), the equal sign must connect the option and the value of the parameter. However, when short options are used, one or more space or tab characters can separate the option from its corresponding value. This distinction is to duplicate the behavior of the options on older UNIX machines that persist to the modern day. They persist because so many people expect that behavior. What can you do?

The preceding code snippet, if run in a program with the parameters -c test -h --config=secondtest, produces the following output:

```
[('-c', 'test'), ('-h', ''), ('--config', 'secondtest')] []
Using configuration file test
This program can be run with either -h or --help for this message,
or with -c or --config=<file> to specify a different configuration file

Using configuration file secondtest
```

Note how the second instance of the configuration file is accepted silently; and when it is reached, the same code that sets the config file is revisited so that the second instance is used.

The second list, the args data, is an empty list because all of the options provided to the program on the command line were valid options, or valid parameters to options. If you inserted other strings in the middle of your options, the normal getopt would behave differently. If the parameters used were instead -c test useless_information_here -h --config=secondtest, the output would say a lot less, and the args array would have a lot more in it.

```
[('-c', 'test')] ['useless_information_here', '-h', '--config=secondtest']
Using configuration file test
```

The gnu_getopt lets you mix and match on the command line so that non-options can appear anywhere in the midst of the options, with more options parsed afterward instead of stopping there:

```
opts, args = getopt.gnu_getopt(cmdline_params, 'hc:', ['help', 'config='])

for option, parameter in opts:

    if option == '-h' or option == '--help':
        print("This program can be run with either -h or --help for this
message,")
        print("or with -c or --config=<file> to specify a different
configuration file")

    if option in ('-c', '--config'): # this means the same as the above
        print("Using configuration file %s" % parameter)
```

The important point to note is that if you use something that doesn't meet the criteria for an option (by beginning with a – or a +, or following an option that takes a parameter), the two behave differently. Using the options `-c test useless_information_here -h --config=secondtest`, the `gnu_getopt` function provides the following output, with the odd duck being the only part of the command line left in the `args` array:

```
[('-c', 'test'), ('-h', ''), ('--config', 'secondtest')]
['useless_information_here']
Using configuration file test
This program can be run with either -h or --help for this message,
or with -c or --config=<file> to specify a different configuration file

Using configuration file secondtest
```

Using More Than One Process

In UNIX and UNIX-like operating systems, the main way of performing certain kinds of subtasks is to create a new process running a new program. On UNIX systems, this is done using a system call that is available in Python by using `os.fork`. This actually tells the computer to copy everything about the currently running program into a newly created program that is separate, but almost entirely identical. The only difference is that the return value for `os.fork` is zero in the newly created process (the *child*), and is the process ID (PID) of the newly created process in the original process (the *parent*). This can be difficult to understand, and the only way to really get it is to use it a few times and to read some other material on `fork` and `exec` that's available online. (Or talk to your nearest UNIX guru.)

Based on the one critical difference, a parent and child can perform different functions. The parent can wait for an event while the child processes, or vice versa. The code to do this is simple and common, but it works only on UNIX and UNIX-like systems:

```python
import os
pid = os.fork()
if pid == 0: # This is the child
    print("this is the child")
else:
    print("the child is pid %d" % pid)
```

One of the most common things to do after an `os.fork` call is to call `os.execl` immediately afterward to run another program. `os.execl` is an instruction to replace the running program with a new program, so the calling program goes away, and a new program appears in its place (in case you didn't already know this, UNIX systems use the `fork` and `exec` method to run all programs):

```python
import os
pid = os.fork()
# fork and exec together
print("second test")
if pid == 0: # This is the child
    print("this is the child")
    print("I'm going to exec another program now")
    os.execl('/bin/cat', 'cat', '/etc/motd')
else:
    print("the child is pid %d" % pid)
    os.wait()
```

The os.wait function instructs Python that you want the parent to not do anything until the child process returns. It is very useful to know how this works because it works well only under UNIX and UNIX-like platforms such as Linux. Windows also has a mechanism for starting up new processes.

To make the common task of starting a new program easier, Python offers a single family of functions that combines os.fork and os.exec on UNIX-like systems, and enables you to do something similar on Windows platforms. When you want to just start up a new program, you can use the os.spawn family of functions. They are a *family* because they are named similarly, but each one has slightly different behaviors.

On UNIX-like systems, the os.spawn family contains spawnl, spawnle, spawnlp, spawnlpe, spawnv, spawnve, spawnvp, and spawnvpe. On Windows systems, the spawn family contains only spawnl, spawnle, spawnv, and spawnve.

In each case, the letters after the word spawn mean something specific. The v means that a list (a vector is what the v actually stands for) will be passed in as the parameters. This allows a command to be run with very different commands from one instance to the next without needing to alter the program at all. The l variation just requires a simple list of parameters.

The e occurrences require that a dictionary containing names and values that will be used as the *environment* for the newly created program will be passed in instead of using the current environment.

The *p* occurrence uses the value of the PATH key in the environment dictionary to find the program. The p variants are available only on UNIX-like platforms. The least of what this means is that on Windows your programs must have a completely qualified path to be usable by the os.spawn calls, or you have to search the path yourself:

```python
import os, sys
if sys.platform == 'win32':
    print("Running on a windows platform")
    command = "C:\\winnt\\system32\\cmd.exe"
    params = []

if sys.platform == 'linux2':
    print("Running on a Linux system, identified by %s" % sys.platform)
    command = '/bin/uname'
    params = ['uname', '-a']

print("Running %s" % command)
os.spawnv(os.P_WAIT, command, params)
```

Of course, this example will only work on a limited range of systems. You can use the contents of sys.platform on your own computer and for something besides linux2 in case you are on another UNIX system such as Solaris, Mac OS X, AIX, or others.

When you do this, you can either wait for the process to return (that is, until it finishes and exits) or you can tell Python that you'd prefer to allow the program to run on its own, and that you will confirm that it completed successfully later. This is done with the os.P_ family of values. Depending on which one you set, you will be given a different behavior when an os.spawn function returns.

If you need only the most basic invocation of a new command, sometimes the easiest way to do this is to use the os.system function. If you are running a program and just want to wait for it to finish, you can use this function very simply:

```
# Now system
if sys.platform == 'win32':
    print("Running on a windows platform")
    command = "cmd.exe"

if sys.platform == 'linux2':
    print("Running Linux")
    command = "uname -a"

os.system(command)
```

This can be much simpler because it uses the facilities that the operating system provides, and that users expect normally, to search for the program you want to run, and it defaults to waiting for the child process to finish.

Threads — Doing Many Things in the Same Process

Creating a new process using fork or spawn can sometimes be too much effort and not provide enough benefit. Specifically, regarding the too much effort, when a program grows to be large, fork has to copy everything in the program to the new program and the system must have enough resources to handle that. Another downside for fork is that sometimes when you need your program to do many things at the same time, some things may need to wait while others need to proceed. When this happens, you want to have all of the different components communicating their needs to other parts of the program.

Using multiple processes, this becomes very difficult. These processes share many things because the child was originally created using the data in the parent. However, they are separate entities — completely separate. Because of this, it can be very tricky to make two processes work together cooperatively.

So, to make some complex situations where subprocesses are not appropriate workable, the concept of threads is available.

Many cooperative *threads* of program execution are able to exist at the same time in the same program. Each one has potentially different objects, with different state, but they can all communicate, while also being able to run semi-independently of one another.

This means that in many situations, using threads is much more convenient than using a separate process. Note that the following example uses *subclassing*, which is covered in Chapter 10. To see how this works, try running it with a fairly large parameter, say two million (2000000):

```
import math
from threading import Thread
import time

class SquareRootCalculator:
```

```
"""This class spawns a separate thread to calculate a bunch of square
roots, and checks in it once a second until it finishes."""

    def __init__(self, target):
        """Turn on the calculator thread and, while waiting for it to
        finish, periodically monitor its progress."""
        self.results = []
        counter = self.CalculatorThread(self, target)
        print("Turning on the calculator thread...")
        counter.start()
        while len(self.results) < target:
            print("%d square roots calculated so far." % len(self.results))
            time.sleep(1)
        print("Calculated %s square root(s); the last one is sqrt(%d)=%f" %
                (target, len(self.results), self.results[-1]))

    class CalculatorThread(Thread):
        """A separate thread which actually does the calculations."""

        def __init__(self, controller, target):
            """Set up this thread, including making it a daemon thread
            so that the script can end without waiting for this thread to
            finish."""
            Thread.__init__(self)
            self.controller = controller
            self.target = target
            self.setDaemon(True)

        def run(self):
            """Calculate square roots for all numbers between 1 and the
target,
            inclusive."""
            for i in range(1, self.target+1):
                self.controller.results.append(math.sqrt(i))

if __name__ == '__main__':
    import sys
    limit = None
    if len(sys.argv) > 1:
        limit = sys.argv[1]
        try:
            limit = int(limit)
        except ValueError:
            print("Usage: %s [number of square roots to calculate]"
                    % sys.argv[0])
    SquareRootCalculator(limit)
```

For many situations, such as network servers (see Chapter 16) or graphical user interfaces (see Chapter 13), threads make much more sense because they require less work from you as the programmer, and fewer resources from the system.

Note how separate threads can access each other's names and data easily. This makes it very easy to keep track of what different threads are doing, which is an important convenience.

Summary

In this chapter, you were introduced to some of the many available functions and modules that Python offers. These features build on the material you've already learned and most of them are expanded on in the remaining chapters in the book.

You learned how to use some basic features that enable what is usually called a functional style of programming, which in Python is offered through the functions `lambda` and `map`. Lambda enables you to write a simple function without having to declare it elsewhere. These functions are called *anonymous* because they can be written and run without ever having to be bound to a name. Map operates on lists, and when used on a simple list will run a function on each element from beginning to end. It has some more complex behaviors, too, which occur when lists within lists, or more than one list, is provided to `map`.

The key things to take away from this chapter are:

❑   List comprehension is the capability to run a limited amount of code — a simple loop, for instance — within the square brackets that dereference a sequence, so that only those elements that meet the criteria within the brackets will be returned. This enables you to easily and quickly access specific members of a sequence.

❑   The `range` operation enables you to generate iterators that are commonly used in `for` loops because they can provide you with numeric lists starting at any number, and ending at any number.

❑   In addition to simple string substitution, you can provide a string with format specifiers that reference the name of keys in dictionaries by using a special syntax. This form enables you to continue to use the format specifier options, such as how many spaces you want reserved for the substitution or how many decimal points should be used.

❑   An alternative form for simple key-name-based string formatting is provided in the `string.Template` module that was added to Python 2.4. It provides a slightly simpler format that is more appropriate (or at least easier to explain) when you allow your users to specify templates. Generating form letters is one example of how this could be used.

❑   `Getopt` enables you to specify options on the command line that lets you offer your users options that determine the behavior of your programs when they're run.

❑   You now know how to create more processes when needed, and how to create threads for use in more complex programs that need to do many things in parallel. You learn more about using threads in Chapters 13 and 16.

❑   The features and modules presented here give you an idea of the different directions in which Python can be extended and used, and how easy it is to use these extensions. In Chapter 10, you see most of the concepts you've used already tied into an example working program.

Exercises

Chapter 9 is a grab-bag of different features. At this point, the best exercise is to test all of the sample code, looking at the output produced and trying to picture how the various ideas introduced here could be used to solve problems that you'd like to solve or would have liked to solve in the past.

Building a Module

As you saw in Chapter 7, modules provide a convenient way to share Python code between applications. A module is a very simple construct, and in Python, a module is merely a file of Python statements. The module might define functions and classes, and it can contain simple executable code that's not inside a function or class. And, best yet, a module might contain documentation about how to use the code in the module.

Python comes with a library of hundreds of modules that you can call in your scripts. You can also create your own modules to share code among your scripts. This chapter shows you how to create a module, step by step. This includes the following:

- ❑ Exploring the internals of modules
- ❑ Creating a module that contains only functions
- ❑ Defining classes in a module
- ❑ Extending classes with subclasses
- ❑ Defining exceptions to report error conditions
- ❑ Documenting your modules
- ❑ Testing your modules
- ❑ Running modules as programs
- ❑ Installing modules

The first step is to examine what modules really are and how they work.

Exploring Modules

A module is just a Python source file. The module can contain variables, classes, functions, and any other element available in your Python scripts.

You can get a better understanding of modules by using the `dir` function. Pass the name of some Python element, such as a module, and `dir` will tell you all of the attributes of that element. For example, to see the attributes of __builtins__, which contain built-in functions, classes, and variables, use the following:

```
dir(__builtins__)
```

For example:

```
>>> dir(__builtins__)
['ArithmeticError', 'AssertionError', 'AttributeError', 'BaseException',
'BufferError', 'BytesWarning', 'DeprecationWarning', 'EOFError',
'Ellipsis', 'EnvironmentError', 'Exception', 'False', 'FloatingPointError',
'FutureWarning', 'GeneratorExit', 'IOError', 'ImportError', 'ImportWarning',
'IndentationError', 'IndexError', 'KeyError',
'KeyboardInterrupt','LookupError', 'MemoryError',
'NameError', 'None', 'NotImplemented', 'NotImplementedError',
'OSError', 'OverflowError','PendingDeprecationWarning',
'ReferenceError', 'RuntimeError', 'RuntimeWarning', 'StopIteration',
'SyntaxError', 'SyntaxWarning','SystemError', 'SystemExit',
'TabError', 'True', 'TypeError', 'UnboundLocalError',
'UnicodeDecodeError', 'UnicodeEncodeError', 'UnicodeError',
'UnicodeTranslateError', 'UnicodeWarning', 'UserWarning',
'ValueError', 'Warning', 'WindowsError', 'ZeroDivisionError',
'__build_class__', '__debug__', '__doc__', '__import__',
'__name__', '__package__', 'abs', 'all', 'any', 'ascii', 'bin',
'bool', 'bytearray', 'bytes', 'chr', 'classmethod', 'compile',
'complex', 'copyright', 'credits', 'delattr', 'dict', 'dir', 'divmod',
'enumerate', 'eval', 'exec', 'exit', 'filter', 'float', 'format',
'frozenset', 'getattr', 'globals', 'hasattr', 'hash', 'help', 'hex',
'id', 'input', 'int', 'isinstance', 'issubclass', 'iter',
'len', 'license', 'list', 'locals', 'map', 'max', 'memoryview', 'min',
'next', 'object', 'oct', 'open', 'ord', 'pow', 'print', 'property', 'quit',
'range', 'repr', 'reversed', 'round', 'set', 'setattr', 'slice', 'sorted',
'staticmethod', 'str', 'sum', 'super', 'tuple', 'type',
'vars', 'zip']
```

For a language with as many features as Python, it has surprisingly few built-in elements. You can run the `dir` function on modules you import as well. For example:

```
>>> import sys
>>> dir(sys)
['__displayhook__', '__doc__', '__excepthook__', '__name__', '__package__',
'__stderr__', '__stdin__', '__stdout__', '_clear_type_cache',
'_current_frames', '_getframe', 'api_version', 'argv',
'builtin_module_names', 'byteorder', 'call_tracing', 'callstats',
'copyright', 'displayhook','dllhandle', 'dont_write_bytecode',
'exc_info', 'excepthook', 'exec_prefix', 'executable','exit', 'flags',
'float_info', 'getcheckinterval','getdefaultencoding',
'getfilesystemencoding', 'getprofile', 'getrecursionlimit', 'getrefcount',
'getsizeof', 'gettrace', 'getwindowsversion', 'hexversion',
'intern', 'maxsize', 'maxunicode', 'meta_path', 'modules', 'path',
'path_hooks', 'path_importer_cache', 'platform', 'prefix',
'setcheckinterval','setfilesystemencoding', 'setprofile',
```

```
'setrecursionlimit','settrace', 'stderr', 'stdin', 'stdout',
'subversion',
'version', 'version_info', 'warnoptions', 'winver']
```

Use `dir` to help examine modules, including the modules you create.

Importing Modules

Before using a module, you need to import it. The standard syntax for importing follows:

```
import module
```

You can use this syntax with modules that come with Python or with modules you create. You can also use the following alternative syntax:

```
from module import item
```

The alternative syntax enables you to specifically import just a class or function if that is all you need.

If a module has changed, you can reload the new definition of the module using the `imp.reload` function. The syntax is as follows:

```
import module
import imp
imp.reload(module)
```

Replace `module` with the module you want to reload.

With `imp.reload`, always use parentheses. With `import`, do not use parentheses.

Finding Modules

To import a module, the Python interpreter needs to find the module. With a module, the Python interpreter first looks for a file named `module.py`, where `module` is the name of the module you pass to the `import` statement. On finding a module, the Python interpreter will compile the module into a `.pyc` file. When you next import the module, the Python interpreter can load the pre-compiled module, speeding your Python scripts.

When you place an `import` statement in your scripts, the Python interpreter has to be able to find the module. The key point is that the Python interpreter only looks in a certain number of directories for your module. If you enter a name the Python interpreter cannot find, it will display an error, as shown in the following example:

```
>>> import foo
Traceback (most recent call last):
  File "<pyshell#12>", line 1, in <module>
    import foo
ImportError: No module named foo
```

The Python interpreter looks in the directories that are part of the module search path. These directories are listed in the sys.path variable from the sys module.

To list where the Python interpreter looks for modules, print out the value of the sys.path variable in the Python interpreter. For example:

```
>>> import sys
>>> print(sys.path)
['C:\\Python31\\Lib\\idlelib', 'C:\\Windows\\system32\\python3`.zip',
'C:\\Python31\\DLLs', 'C:\\Python31\\lib',
'C:\\Python31\\lib\\plat-win', 'C:\\Python31',
'C:\\Python31\\lib\\site-packages']
```

Digging through Modules

Because Python is an open-source package, you can get the source code to the Python interpreter as well as all modules. In fact, even with a binary distribution of Python, you'll find the source code for modules written in Python.

Start by looking in all the directories listed in the sys.path variable for files with names ending in .py. These are Python modules. Some modules contain functions, and others contain classes and functions. For example, the following module, Parser, defines a class in the Python 3.0 distribution:

```
"""A parser of RFC 2822 and MIME email messages."""
__all__ = ['Parser', 'HeaderParser']
import warnings
from io import StringIO
from email.feedparser import FeedParser
from email.message import Message
class Parser:
    def __init__(self, *args, **kws):
        """Parser of RFC 2822 and MIME email messages.
        Creates an in-memory object tree representing the email message, which
        can then be manipulated and turned over to a Generator to return the
        textual representation of the message.
        The string must be formatted as a block of RFC 2822 headers and header
        continuation lines, optionally preceded by a `Unix-from' header.  The
        header block is terminated either by the end of the string or by a
        blank line.
        _class is the class to instantiate for new message objects when they
        must be created.  This class must have a constructor that can take
        zero arguments.  Default is Message.Message.
        """
        if len(args) >= 1:
            if '_class' in kws:
                raise TypeError("Multiple values for keyword arg '_class'")
            kws['_class'] = args[0]
        if len(args) == 2:
            if 'strict' in kws:
                raise TypeError("Multiple values for keyword arg 'strict'")
```

```
                kws['strict'] = args[1]
        if len(args) > 2:
            raise TypeError('Too many arguments')
        if '_class' in kws:
            self._class = kws['_class']
            del kws['_class']
        else:
            self._class = Message
        if 'strict' in kws:
            warnings.warn("'strict' argument is deprecated (and ignored)",
                          DeprecationWarning, 2)
            del kws['strict']
        if kws:
            raise TypeError('Unexpected keyword arguments')
    def parse(self, fp, headersonly=False):
        """Create a message structure from the data in a file.
        Reads all the data from the file and returns the root of the message
        structure.  Optional headersonly is a flag specifying whether to stop
        parsing after reading the headers or not.  The default is False,
        meaning it parses the entire contents of the file.
        """
        feedparser = FeedParser(self._class)
        if headersonly:
            feedparser._set_headersonly()
        while True:
            data = fp.read(8192)
            if not data:
                break
            feedparser.feed(data)
        return feedparser.close()

    def parsestr(self, text, headersonly=False):
        """Create a message structure from a string.

        Returns the root of the message structure.  Optional headersonly is a
        flag specifying whether to stop parsing after reading the headers or
        not.  The default is False, meaning it parses the entire contents of
        the file.
        """
        return self.parse(StringIO(text), headersonly=headersonly)
class HeaderParser(Parser):
    def parse(self, fp, headersonly=True):
        return Parser.parse(self, fp, True)

    def parsestr(self, text, headersonly=True):
        return Parser.parsestr(self, text, True)
```

The majority of this small module is made up of documentation that instructs users how to use the module. Documentation is important.

When you look through the standard Python modules, you can get a feel for how modules are put together. It also helps when you want to create your own modules.

Creating Modules and Packages

Creating modules is easier than you might think. A module is merely a Python source file. In fact, any time you've created a Python file, you have already been creating modules without even knowing it.

The following example will help you get started creating modules.

Try It Out   **Creating a Module with Functions**

Enter the following Python code and name the file `food.py`:

```
def favoriteFood():
    print("the only food worth eating is an omelet.")
```

This is your module. You then can import the module using the Python interpreter. For example:

```
>>> import food
>>> dir(food)
['__builtins__', '__doc__', '__file__', '__name__', '__package__',
'favoriteFood']
```

How It Works

Python uses a very simple definition for a module. You can use any Python source file as a module, as shown in this short example. The `dir` function lists the items defined in the module, including the function `favoriteFood`.

Once imported, you can execute the code in the module with a command like the following:

```
>>> food.favoriteFood()
The only food worth eating is an omelet.
```

If you don't use the module name prefix, `food` in this case, you will get an error, as shown in the following example:

```
>>> favoriteFood()
Traceback (most recent call last):
  File "<pyshell#22>", line 1, in <module>
    favoriteFood()
NameError: name 'favoriteFood' is not defined
```

Using the alternative syntax for imports can eliminate this problem:

```
>>> from food import favoriteFood
>>> favoriteFood()
The only food worth eating is an omelet.
>>>
```

Congratulations! You are now a certified module creator.

Working with Classes

Most modules define a set of related functions or classes. A class, as introduced in Chapter 6, holds data as well as the methods that operate on that data. Python is a little looser than most programming languages, such as Java, C++, or C#, in that Python lets you break rules enforced in other languages. For example, Python, by default, lets you access data inside a class. This does violate some of the concepts of object-oriented programming but with good reason: Python aims first and foremost to be practical.

Defining Object-Oriented Programming

Computer geeks argue endlessly over what is truly object-oriented programming (OOP). Most experts, however, agree on the following three concepts:

❑   Encapsulation

❑   Inheritance

❑   Polymorphism

Encapsulation is the idea that a class can hide the internal details and data necessary to perform a certain task. A class holds the necessary data, and you are not supposed to see that data under normal circumstances. Furthermore, a class provides a number of methods to operate on that data. These methods can hide the internal details, such as network protocols, disk access, and so on. Encapsulation is a technique to simplify your programs. At each step in creating your program, you can write code that concentrates on a single task. Encapsulation hides the complexity.

Inheritance means that a class can inherit, or gain access to, data and methods defined in a parent class. This just follows common sense in classifying a problem domain. For example, a rectangle and a circle are both shapes. In this case, the base class would be Shapes. The Rectangle class would then inherit from Shapes, as would the Circle class. Inheritance enables you to treat objects of both the Rectangle and Circle classes as children and members of the Shape class, meaning you can write more generic code in the base class, and become more specific in the children. (The terms *children* and *child class*, and *membership in a class*, are similar and can be used interchangeably here.) For the most part, the base class should be general and the subclasses specialized. Inheritance is often called *specialization*.

Polymorphism means that subclasses can override methods for more specialized behavior. For example, a rectangle and a circle are both shapes. You may define a set of common operations, such as move and draw, that should apply to all shapes. However, the draw method for a Circle will obviously be different than the draw method for a Rectangle. Polymorphism enables you to name both methods draw and then call these methods as if the Circle and the Rectangle were both Shapes, which they are, at least in this example.

Creating Classes

As described in Chapter 6, creating classes is easy. (In fact, most things in Python are pleasantly easy.) The following example shows a simple class that represents a meal.

Creating a Meal Class

The following code defines the `Meal` class. The full source file appears in the section "Creating a Whole Module."

```python
class Meal:
    '''Holds the food and drink used in a meal.
    In true object-oriented tradition, this class
    includes setter methods for the food and drink.

    Call printIt to pretty-print the values.
    '''

    def __init__(self, food='omelet', drink='coffee'):
        '''Initialize to default values.'''
        self.name = 'generic meal'
        self.food = food
        self.drink = drink

    def printIt(self, prefix=''):
        '''Print the data nicely.'''
        print(prefix,'A fine',self.name,'with',self.food,'and',self.drink)

    # Setter for the food.
    def setFood(self, food='omelet'):
        self.food = food

    # Setter for the drink.
    def setDrink(self, drink='coffee'):
        self.drink = drink

    # Setter for the name.
    def setName(self, name=''):
        self.name = name
```

How It Works

Each instance of the `Meal` class holds three data values: the name of the meal, the food, and the drink. By default, the `Meal` class sets the name to `generic meal`, the drink to `coffee`, and the food to an `omelet`.

As with gin and tonics, omelets are not just for breakfast anymore.

The `__init__` method initializes the data for the `Meal`. The `printIt` method prints out the internal data in a friendly manner. Finally, to support developers used to stricter programming languages, the `Meal` class defines a set of methods called *setters*. These setter methods, such as `setFood` and `setDrink`, set data into the class.

These methods are not necessary in Python, because you can set the data directly.

See Chapter 6 for more information about classes.

Extending Existing Classes

After you have defined a class, you can extend it by defining subclasses. For example, you can create a `Breakfast` class that represents the first meal of the day:

```
class Breakfast(Meal):
    '''Holds the food and drink for breakfast.'''

    def __init__(self):
        '''Initialize with an omelet and coffee.'''
        Meal.__init__(self, 'omelet', 'coffee')
        self.setName('breakfast')
```

The `Breakfast` class extends the `Meal` class as shown by the class definition:

```
class Breakfast(Meal):
```

Another subclass would naturally be `Lunch`:

```
class Lunch(Meal):
    '''Holds the food and drink for lunch.'''

    def __init__(self):
        '''Initialize with a sandwich and a gin and tonic.'''
        Meal.__init__(self, 'sandwich', 'gin and tonic')
        self.setName('midday meal')

    # Override setFood().
    def setFood(self, food='sandwich'):
        if food != 'sandwich' and food != 'omelet':
            raise AngryChefException
            Meal.setFood(self, food)
```

With the `Lunch` class, you can see some use for the setter methods. In the `Lunch` class, the `setFood` method allows only two values for the food: a *sandwich* and an *omelet*. Nothing else is allowed or you will make the chef angry.

The `Dinner` class also overrides a method — in this case, the `printIt` method:

```
class Dinner(Meal):
    '''Holds the food and drink for dinner.'''

    def __init__(self):
        '''Initialize with steak and merlot.'''
        Meal.__init__(self, 'steak', 'merlot')
        self.setName('dinner')

    def printIt(self, prefix=''):
        '''Print even more nicely.'''
        print(prefix,'A gourmet',self.name,'with',self.food,'and',self.drink)
```

Normally, you would place all these classes into a module. See the section "Creating a Whole Module" for an example of a complete module.

Finishing Your Modules

After defining the classes and functions that you want for your module, the next step is to finish the module to make it better fit into the conventions expected by Python users and the Python interpreter.

Finishing your module can include a lot of things, but at the very least you need to do the following:

❑   Define the errors and exceptions that apply to your module.

❑   Define which items in the module you want to export. This defines the public API for the module.

❑   Document your module.

❑   Test your module.

❑   Provide a fallback function in case your module is executed as a program.

The following sections describe how to finish up your modules.

Defining Module-Specific Errors

Python defines a few standard exception classes, such as IOError and NotImplementedError. If those classes apply, by all means use them. Otherwise, you may need to define exceptions for specific issues that may arise when using your module. For example, a networking module may need to define a set of exceptions relating to network errors.

For the food-related theme used in the example module, you can define an AngryChefException. To make this more generic, and perhaps allow reuse in other modules, the AngryChefException is defined as a subclass of the more general SensitiveArtistException, representing issues raised by touchy artsy types.

In most cases, your exception classes will not need to define any methods or initialize any data. The base Exception class provides enough. For most exceptions, the mere presence of the exception indicates the problem.

This is not always true. For example, an XML-parsing exception should probably contain the line number where the error occurred, as well as a description of the problem.

You can define the exceptions for the `meal` module as follows:

```
class SensitiveArtistException(Exception):
    pass

class AngryChefException(SensitiveArtistException):
    pass
```

This is just an example, of course. In your modules, define exception classes as needed. In addition to exceptions, you should carefully decide what to export from your module.

Choosing What to Export

When you use the `from` form of importing a module, you can specify which items in the module to import. For example, the following statement imports the `AngryChefException` from the module `meal`:

```
from meal import AngryChefException
```

To import all public items from a module, you can use the following format:

```
from module_name import *
```

For example:

```
from meal import *
```

The asterisk, or star (`*`), tells the Python interpreter to import all public items from the module. What exactly is public? You, as the module designer, can choose to define whichever items you want to be exported as public.

The Python interpreter uses two methods to determine what should be considered public:

❑   If you have defined the variable __all__ in your module, the interpreter uses __all__ to determine what should be public.

❑   If you have not defined the variable __all__, the interpreter imports everything except items with names that begin with an underscore, _, so `printIt` would be considered public, but `_printIt` would not.

See Chapter 7 for more information about modules and the `import` statement.

As a best practice, always define __all__ in your modules. This provides you with explicit control over what other Python scripts can import. To do this, simply create a sequence of text strings with the names of each item you want to export from your module. For example, in the `meal` module, you can define __all__ in the following manner:

```
__all__ = ['Meal', 'AngryChefException', 'makeBreakfast',
    'makeLunch', 'makeDinner', 'Breakfast', 'Lunch', 'Dinner']
```

Each name in this sequence names a class or function to export from the module.

Choosing what to export is important. When you create a module, you are creating an API to perform some presumably useful function. The API you export from a module then defines what users of your module can do. You want to export enough for users of the module to get their work done, but you don't have to export everything. You may want to exclude items for a number of reasons, including the following:

❑ Items you are likely to change should remain private until you have settled on the API for those items. This gives you the freedom to make changes inside the module without impacting users of the module.

❑ Modules can oftentimes hide, on purpose, complicated code. For example, an e-mail module can hide the gory details of SMTP, POP3, and IMAP network e-mail protocols. Your e-mail module could present an API that enables users to send messages, see which messages are available, download messages, and so on.

Hiding the gory details of how your code is implemented is called encapsulation. Impress your friends with lines like "making the change you are asking for would violate the rules of encapsulation . . ."

Always define, explicitly, what you want to export from a module. You should also always document your modules.

Documenting Your Modules

It is vitally important that you document your modules. If not, no one, not even you, will know what your modules do. Think ahead six months. Will you remember everything that went into your modules? Probably not. The solution is simple: document your modules.

Python defines a few easy conventions for documenting your modules. Follow these conventions and your modules will enable users to view the documentation in the standard way. At its most basic, for each item you want to document, write a text string that describes the item. Enclose this text string in three quotes, and place it immediately inside the item.

For example, to document a method or function, use the following code as a guide:

```
def makeLunch():
    ''' Creates a Breakfast object.'''
    return Lunch()
```

The line in triple quotes shows the documentation. The documentation that appears right after the function is defined with the `def` statement.

Document a class similarly:

```
class Meal:
    '''Holds the food and drink used in a meal.
    In true object-oriented tradition, this class
    includes setter methods for the food and drink.

    Call printIt to pretty-print the values.
    '''
```

Place the documentation on the line after the `class` statement.

Exceptions are classes, too. Document them as well:

```
class SensitiveArtistException(Exception):
    '''Exception raised by an overly-sensitive artist.

    Base class for artistic types.'''
    Pass
```

Note that even though this class adds no new functionality, you should describe the purpose of each exception or class.

In addition, document the module itself. Start your module with the special three-quoted text string, as shown here:

```
"""
Module for making meals in Python.

Import this module and then call
makeBreakfast(), makeDinner() or makeLunch().

"""
```

Place this documentation on the first line of the text file that contains the module. For modules, start with one line that summarizes the purpose of the module. Separate this line from the remaining lines of the documentation, using a blank line as shown previously. The Python `help` function will extract the one-line summary and treat it specially. (See the following Try It Out example for more details about how to call the `help` function.)

Usually, one or two lines per class, method, or function should suffice. In general, your documentation should tell the user the following:

❏ How to call the function or method, including what parameters are necessary and what type of data will be returned. Describe default values for parameters.

❏ What a given class was designed for, or its purpose. Include how to use objects of the class.

❏ Any conditions that must exist prior to calling a function or method.

❏ Any side effects or other parts of the system that will change as a result of the class. For example, a method to erase all of the files on a disk should be documented as to what it does.

❏ Exceptions that may be raised and under what reasons these exceptions will be raised.

Note that some people go way overboard in writing documentation. Too much documentation doesn't help, but don't use this as an excuse to do nothing. Too much documentation is far better than none at all.

A good rule of thumb comes from enlightened self-interest. Ask yourself what you would like to see in someone else's module and document to that standard.

You can view the documentation you write using the `help` function, as shown in the following example.

Launch the Python interpreter in interactive mode and then run the `import` and `help` commands as shown in the following code:

```
>>> import meal
>>> help(meal)
Help on module meal:
NAME
    meal - Module for making meals in Python.
FILE
    c:\python30\meal.py
DESCRIPTION
    Import this module and then call
    makeBreakfast(), makeDinner() or makeLunch().
CLASSES
    builtins.object
        Meal
            Breakfast
            Dinner
            Lunch
    SensitiveArtistException(builtins.Exception)
        AngryChefException

    class AngryChefException(SensitiveArtistException)
     |  Exception that indicates the chef is unhappy.
     |
     |  Method resolution order:
     |      AngryChefException
     |      SensitiveArtistException
     |      builtins.Exception
     |      builtins.BaseException
     |      builtins.object
     |
     |  Data descriptors inherited from SensitiveArtistException:
     |
     |  __weakref__
     |      list of weak references to the object (if defined)
     |
     |  ----------------------------------------------------------------
     |  Methods inherited from builtins.Exception:
     |
     |  __init__(...)
     |      x.__init__(...) initializes x; see x.__class__.__doc__ for signature
     |
     |  ----------------------------------------------------------------
```

```
|   Data and other attributes inherited from builtins.Exception:
|
|   __new__ = <built-in method __new__ of type object at 0x1E1BCCC8>
|       T.__new__(S, ...) -> a new object with type S, a subtype of T
|
|   ----------------------------------------------------------------------
|   Methods inherited from builtins.BaseException:
|
|   __delattr__(...)
|       x.__delattr__('name') <==> del x.name
|
|   __getattribute__(...)
|       x.__getattribute__('name') <==> x.name
|
|   __reduce__(...)
|
|   __repr__(...)
|       x.__repr__() <==> repr(x)
|
|   __setattr__(...)
|       x.__setattr__('name', value) <==> x.name = value
|
|   __setstate__(...)
|
|   __str__(...)
|       x.__str__() <==> str(x)
|
|   with_traceback(...)
|       Exception.with_traceback(tb) --
|       set self.__traceback__ to tb and return self.
|
|   ----------------------------------------------------------------------
|   Data descriptors inherited from builtins.BaseException:
|
|   __cause__
|       exception cause
|
|   __context__
|       exception context
|
|   __dict__
|
|   __traceback__
|
|   args

class Breakfast(Meal)
|   Holds the food and drink for breakfast.
|
```

```
|    Method resolution order:
|        Breakfast
|        Meal
|        builtins.object
|
|    Methods defined here:
|
|    __init__(self)
|        Initialize with an omelet and coffee.
|
|    ----------------------------------------------------------------
|    Methods inherited from Meal:
|
|    printIt(self, prefix='')
|        Print the data nicely.
|
|    setDrink(self, drink='coffee')
|        # Setter for the drink.
|
|    setFood(self, food='omelet')
|        # Setter for the food.
|
|    setName(self, name='')
|        # Setter for the name.
|
|    ----------------------------------------------------------------
|    Data descriptors inherited from Meal:
|
|    __dict__
|        dictionary for instance variables (if defined)
|
|    __weakref__
|        list of weak references to the object (if defined)
|
class Dinner(Meal)
|    Holds the food and drink for dinner.
|
|    Method resolution order:
|        Dinner
|        Meal
|        builtins.object
|
|    Methods defined here:
|
|    __init__(self)
|        Initialize with steak and merlot.
|
|    printIt(self, prefix='')
|        Print even more nicely.
|
|    ----------------------------------------------------------------
|    Methods inherited from Meal:
|
```

```
 |   setDrink(self, drink='coffee')
 |       # Setter for the drink.
 |
 |   setFood(self, food='omelet')
 |       # Setter for the food.
 |
 |   setName(self, name='')
 |       # Setter for the name.
 |
 |   ----------------------------------------------------------------------
 |   Data descriptors inherited from Meal:
 |
 |   __dict__
 |       dictionary for instance variables (if defined)
 |
 |   __weakref__
 |       list of weak references to the object (if defined)

class Lunch(Meal)
 |   Holds the food and drink for lunch.
 |
 |   Method resolution order:
 |       Lunch
 |       Meal
 |       builtins.object
 |
 |   Methods defined here:
 |
 |   __init__(self)
 |       Initialize with a sandwich and a gin and tonic.
 |
 |   setFood(self, food='sandwich')
 |       # Override setFood().
 |
 |   ----------------------------------------------------------------------
 |   Methods inherited from Meal:
 |
 |   printIt(self, prefix='')
 |       Print the data nicely.
 |
 |   setDrink(self, drink='coffee')
 |       # Setter for the drink.
 |
 |   setName(self, name='')
 |       # Setter for the name.
 |
 |   ----------------------------------------------------------------------
 |   Data descriptors inherited from Meal:
 |
```

```
   |   __dict__
   |       dictionary for instance variables (if defined)
   |
   |   __weakref__
   |       list of weak references to the object (if defined)

class Meal(builtins.object)
   |   Holds the food and drink used in a meal.
   |   In true object-oriented tradition, this class
   |   includes setter methods for the food and drink.
   |
   |   Call printIt to pretty-print the values.
   |
   |   Methods defined here:
   |
   |   __init__(self, food='omelet', drink='coffee')
   |       Initialize to default values.
   |
   |   printIt(self, prefix='')
   |       Print the data nicely.
   |
   |   setDrink(self, drink='coffee')
   |       # Setter for the drink.
   |
   |   setFood(self, food='omelet')
   |       # Setter for the food.
   |
   |   setName(self, name='')
   |       # Setter for the name.
   |
   |   ----------------------------------------------------------------------
   |   Data descriptors defined here:
   |
   |   __dict__
   |       dictionary for instance variables (if defined)
   |
   |   __weakref__
   |       list of weak references to the object (if defined)
FUNCTIONS
    makeBreakfast()
        Creates a Breakfast object.

    makeDinner()
        Creates a Breakfast object.
    makeLunch()
        Creates a Breakfast object.
DATA
    __all__ = ['Meal', 'AngryChefException', 'makeBreakfast', 'makeLunch',...
```

How It Works

The help function is your friend. It can show you the documentation for your modules, as well as the documentation on any Python module.

You must import a module prior to calling the help *function to read the module's documentation.*

The `help` function first prints the documentation for the module:

```
Help on module meal:

NAME
    meal - Module for making meals in Python.

FILE
    c:\python30\meal.py

DESCRIPTION
    Import this module and then call
    makeBreakfast(), makeDinner() or makeLunch().
```

Note how the `help` function separates the first summary line of the module documentation from the rest of the documentation. The following shows the original string that documents this module:

```
"""
Module for making meals in Python.

Import this module and then call
makeBreakfast(), makeDinner() or makeLunch().

"""
```

The `help` function pulls out the first line for the NAME section of the documentation and the rest for the DESCRIPTION section.

The `help` function summarizes the classes next and then shows the documentation for each class:

```
CLASSES
    exceptions.Exception
        AngryChefException
        SensitiveArtistException
    Meal
        Breakfast
        Dinner
        Lunch
```

Each class is shown indented based on inheritance. In this example, the summary shows that the `Breakfast` class inherits from the `Meal` class.

For each function and method, the `help` function prints out the documentation:

```
 |  printIt(self, prefix='')
 |      Print the data nicely.
```

However, if you just have comments near a function or method definition, the `help` function will try to associate a comment with the function or method. This doesn't always work, however, because the `help` function alphabetizes the methods and functions. For example:

```
 |
 |  setDrink(self, drink='coffee')
 |      # Setter for the name.
 |
 |  setFood(self, food='omelet')
```

```
    |        # Setter for the drink.
    |
    |    setName(self, name='')
    |        # Setter for the name.
```

Note how the comments are associated with the wrong methods. Here is the original code:

```
# Setter for the food.
def setFood(self, food='omelet'):
    self.food = food

# Setter for the drink.
def setDrink(self, drink='coffee'):
    self.drink = drink

# Setter for the name.
def setName(self, name=''):
    self.name = name
```

The lesson here is to follow the Python conventions for documenting methods. To fix this error, change the comments that appear above each method into a Python documentation string. Move the Python documentation string down to the line immediately following the corresponding def command.

As you develop your module, you can call the help function repeatedly to see how changes in the code change the documentation. If you have changed the Python source file for your module, however, you need to reload the module prior to calling help. The reload function takes a module, as does help. The syntax follows:

```
import imp
imp.reload(module)
help(module)
```

For example, to reload the module meal, use the following code:

```
>>>import imp
>>> imp.reload(meal)
<module 'meal' from 'C:\Python30\meal.py'>
```

Just as documentation is important, so is testing. The more you can test your modules, the better your modules will fit into Python applications. You'll know that the functionality of the modules works prior to using those modules in a program.

Testing Your Module

Testing is hard. Testing is yucky. That's why testing is often skipped. Even so, testing your module can verify that it works. More important, creating tests enables you to make changes to your module and then verify that the functionality still works.

Any self-respecting module should include a test function that exercises the functionality in the module. Your tests should create instances of the classes defined in the module, and call methods on those instances.

For example, the following method provides a test of the `meal` module: (Note that this will not work if you run it yet; you'll need to add the Dinner class, which is defined later in this chapter.)

```python
def test():
    '''Test function.'''

    print('Module meal test.')

    # Generic no arguments.
    print('Testing Meal class.')
    m = Meal()

    m.printIt("\t")


    m = Meal('green eggs and ham', 'tea')
    m.printIt("\t")

    # Test breakfast
    print('Testing Breakfast class.')
    b = Breakfast()
    b.printIt("\t")

    b.setName('breaking of the fast')
    b.printIt("\t")


    # Test dinner
    print('Testing Dinner class.')
    d = Dinner()
    d.printIt("\t")


    # Test lunch
    print('Testing Lunch class.')
    l = Lunch()
    l.printIt("\t")

    print('Calling Lunch.setFood().')
    try:
        l.setFood('hotdog')
    except AngryChefException:
        print("\t",'The chef is angry. Pick an omelet.')
```

Make your test functions part of your modules, so the tests are always available. You learn more about testing in Python in Chapter 12.

Testing is never finished. You can always add more tests. Just do what you can.

Running a Module as a Program

Normally, modules aren't intended to be run on their own. Instead, other Python scripts import items from a module and then use those items. However, because a module can be any file of Python code, you can indeed run a module.

Because modules aren't meant to be run on their own, Python defines a convention for modules. When a module is run on its own, it should execute the module tests. This provides a simple means to test your modules: Just run the module as a Python script.

To help with this convention, Python provides a handy idiom to detect whether your module is run as a program. Using the test function shown previously, you can use the following code to execute your module tests:

```
if __name__ == '__main__':
    test()
```

If you look at the source code for the standard Python modules, you'll find this idiom used repeatedly.

The next example runs the meal module, created in the section "Creating a Whole Module."

Try It Out   Running a Module

You can run a module, such as the meal module, as a program by using a command like the following:

```
$ python meal.py
Module meal test.
Testing Meal class.
        A fine generic meal with omelet and coffee
        A fine generic meal with green eggs and ham and tea
Testing Breakfast class.
        A fine breakfast with omelet and coffee
        A fine breaking of the fast with omelet and coffee
Testing Dinner class.
        A gourmet dinner with steak and merlot
Testing Lunch class.
        A fine midday meal with sandwich and gin and tonic
Calling Lunch.setFood().
        The chef is angry. Pick an omelet.
```

How It Works

This example runs a module as a Python program. Using the idiom to detect this situation, the module merely runs the test function. The output you see is the output of the tests.

Note how the output runs an instance of each class defined in the module, as well as tests the raising of the AngryChefException.

If you follow all of the guidelines in this section, your modules will meet the expectations of other Python developers. Moreover, your modules will work better in your scripts. You can see all of this in action in the next section, which shows a complete Python module.

Creating a Whole Module

The sections in this chapter so far show the elements you need to include in the modules you create. The following example shows a complete module using the techniques described so far.

The meal module doesn't do much. It supposedly models a domain that includes food and drink over three daily meals.

Obviously, this module doesn't support Hobbits, who require more than three meals a day.

The code in this module is purposely short. The intent is not to perform a useful task but instead to show how to put together a module.

Try It Out　　Finishing a Module

Enter the following code and name the file meal.py:

```
"""
Module for making meals in Python.
Import this module and then call
makeBreakfast(), makeDinner() or makeLunch().
"""
__all__ = ['Meal','AngryChefException', 'makeBreakfast',
    'makeLunch', 'makeDinner', 'Breakfast', 'Lunch', 'Dinner']
# Helper functions.
def makeBreakfast():
    ''' Creates a Breakfast object.'''
    return Breakfast()
def makeLunch():
    ''' Creates a Breakfast object.'''
    return Lunch()
def makeDinner():
    ''' Creates a Breakfast object.'''
    return Dinner()
# Exception classes.
class SensitiveArtistException(Exception):
    '''Exception raised by an overly-sensitive artist.
    Base class for artistic types.'''
    pass
class AngryChefException(SensitiveArtistException):
    '''Exception that indicates the chef is unhappy.'''
    pass
class Meal:
    '''Holds the food and drink used in a meal.
    In true object-oriented tradition, this class
    includes setter methods for the food and drink.

    Call printIt to pretty-print the values.
    '''
    def __init__(self, food='omelet', drink='coffee'):
        '''Initialize to default values.'''
        self.name = 'generic meal'
```

```
            self.food = food
            self.drink = drink
        def printIt(self, prefix=''):
            '''Print the data nicely.'''
            print(prefix,'A fine',self.name,'with',self.food,'and',self.drink)
        # Setter for the food.
        def setFood(self, food='omelet'):
            self.food = food
        # Setter for the drink.
        def setDrink(self, drink='coffee'):
            self.drink = drink
        # Setter for the name.
        def setName(self, name=''):
            self.name = name
class Breakfast(Meal):
    '''Holds the food and drink for breakfast.'''
    def __init__(self):
        '''Initialize with an omelet and coffee.'''
        Meal.__init__(self, 'omelet', 'coffee')
        self.setName('breakfast')
class Lunch(Meal):
    '''Holds the food and drink for lunch.'''
    def __init__(self):
        '''Initialize with a sandwich and a gin and tonic.'''
        Meal.__init__(self, 'sandwich', 'gin and tonic')
        self.setName('midday meal')
    # Override setFood().
    def setFood(self, food='sandwich'):
        if food != 'sandwich' and food != 'omelet':
            raise AngryChefException
        Meal.setFood(self, food)
class Dinner(Meal):
    '''Holds the food and drink for dinner.'''
    def __init__(self):
        '''Initialize with steak and merlot.'''
        Meal.__init__(self, 'steak', 'merlot')
        self.setName('dinner')
    def printIt(self, prefix=''):
        '''Print even more nicely.'''
        print(prefix,'A gourmet',self.name,'with',self.food,'and',self.drink)
def test():
    '''Test function.'''
    print('Module meal test.')
    # Generic no arguments.
    print('Testing Meal class.')
    m = Meal()
    m.printIt("\t")
    m = Meal('green eggs and ham', 'tea')
    m.printIt("\t")
    # Test breakfast
    print('Testing Breakfast class.')
    b = Breakfast()
    b.printIt("\t")

    b.setName('breaking of the fast')
```

```
        b.printIt("\t")
        # Test dinner
        print('Testing Dinner class.')
        d = Dinner()
        d.printIt("\t")
        # Test lunch
        print('Testing Lunch class.')
        l = Lunch()
        l.printIt("\t")
        print('Calling Lunch.setFood().')
        try:
            l.setFood('hotdog')
        except AngryChefException:
            print("\t",'The chef is angry. Pick an omelet.')
# Run test if this module is run as a program.
if __name__ == '__main__':
    test()
```

How It Works

The `meal` module follows the techniques shown in this chapter for creating a complete module, with testing, documentation, exceptions, classes, and functions. Note how the tests are about as long as the rest of the code. You'll commonly find this to be the case.

After you've built a module, you can import the module into other Python scripts. For example, the following script calls on classes and functions in the `meal` module:

```
import meal

print('Making a Breakfast')
breakfast = meal.makeBreakfast()

breakfast.printIt("\t")

print('Making a Lunch')
lunch = meal.makeLunch()

try:
    lunch.setFood('pancakes')
except meal.AngryChefException:
    print("\t",'Cannot make a lunch of pancakes.')
    print("\t",'The chef is angry. Pick an omelet.')
```

This example uses the normal form for importing a module:

```
import meal
```

When you run this script, you'll see output like the following:

```
Making a Breakfast
        A fine breakfast with omelet and coffee
Making a Lunch
        Cannot make a lunch of pancakes.
        The chef is angry. Pick an omelet.
```

The next script shows an alternate means to import the module:

```
from meal import *
```

The full script follows:

```
from meal import *

print('Making a Breakfast')
breakfast = makeBreakfast()

breakfast.printIt("\t")

print('Making a Lunch')
lunch = makeLunch()

try:
    lunch.setFood('pancakes')
except AngryChefException:
    print("\t",'Cannot make a lunch of pancakes.')
    print("\t",'The chef is angry. Pick an omelet.')
```

Note how with this import form, you can call the `makeLunch` and `makeBreakfast` functions without using the module name, `meal`, as a prefix on the call.

The output of this script should look familiar.

```
Making a Breakfast
        A fine breakfast with omelet and coffee
Making a Lunch
        Cannot make a lunch of pancakes.
        The chef is angry. Pick an omelet.
```

Be very careful with the names you use for variables. The example module has a name of `meal`. This means you don't want to use that name in any other context, such as for a variable. If you do, you will effectively overwrite the definition of `meal` as a module. The following example shows the pitfall to this approach.

Try It Out   **Smashing Imports**

Enter the following script and name the file `mealproblem.py`:

```
import meal

print('Making a Breakfast')
meal = meal.makeBreakfast()

meal.printIt("\t")

print('Making a Lunch')
lunch = meal.makeLunch()
```

```
try:
    lunch.setFood('pancakes')
except meal.AngryChefException:
    print("\t",'Cannot make a lunch of pancakes.')
    print("\t",'The chef is angry. Pick an omelet.')
```

When you run this script, you'll see the following error:

```
Making a Breakfast
        A fine breakfast with omelet and coffee
Making a Lunch
Traceback (most recent call last):
  File "C:\Python30\mealproblem.py", line 9, in <module>
    lunch = meal.makeLunch()
AttributeError: 'Breakfast' object has no attribute 'makeLunch'
```

How It Works

This script uses meal as a module as well as meal as an instance of the class Breakfast. The following lines are the culprit:

```
import meal
meal = meal.makeBreakfast()
```

When you run this code, the name meal is now a variable, an instance of the class Breakfast. This changes the interpretation of the following line:

```
lunch = meal.makeLunch()
```

The intent of this line is to call the function makeLunch in the module meal. However, because meal is now an object, the Python interpreter tries to call the makeLunch method on the object, an instance of the Breakfast class. Because the Breakfast class has no method named makeLunch, the Python interpreter raises an error.

The syntax for using modules and calling functions in modules looks very much like the syntax for calling methods on an object. Be careful.

After building your module and testing it, the next step is to install it.

Installing Your Modules

The Python interpreter looks for modules in the directories listed in the sys.path variable. The sys.path variable includes the current directory, so you can always use modules available locally. If you want to use a module you've written in multiple scripts, or on multiple systems, however, you need to install it into one of the directories listed in the sys.path variable.

In most cases, you'll want to place your Python modules in the `site-packages` directory. Look in the `sys.path` listing and find a directory name ending in `site-packages`. This is a directory for packages installed at a site that are not part of the Python standard library of packages.

In addition to modules, you can create packages of modules, a set of related modules that install into the same directory structure. See the Python documentation at `http://docs.python.org` *for more on this subject.*

You can install your modules using one of three mechanisms:

❑   You can do everything by hand and manually create an installation script or program.

❑   You can create an installer specific to your operating system, such as MSI files on Windows, an RPM file on Linux, or a DMG file on Mac OS X.

❑   You can use the handy Python `distutils` package, short for distribution utilities, to create a Python-based installer.

To use the Python `distutils`, you need to create a setup script, named `setup.py`. A minimal setup script can include the following:

```
from distutils.core import setup

setup(name='NameOfModule',
      version='1.0',
      py_modules=['NameOfModule'],
      )
```

You need to include the name of the module twice. Replace `NameOfModule` with the name of your module, such as `meal` in the examples in this chapter.

Name the script `setup.py`.

After you have created the `setup.py` script, you can create a distribution of your module using the following command:

```
python setup.py sdist
```

The argument `sdist` is short for software distribution. You can try this out with the following example.

Try It Out   Creating an Installable Package

Enter the following script and name the file `setup.py`:

```
from distutils.core import setup

setup(name='meal',
      version='1.0',
      py_modules=['meal'],
      )
Run the following command to create a Python module distribution:
```

```
$ python setup.py sdist
running sdist
warning: sdist: missing required meta-data: url
warning: sdist: missing meta-data: either (author and author_email) or
(maintainer and maintainer_email) must be supplied
warning: sdist: manifest template 'MANIFEST.in' does not exist (using default
file list)
warning: sdist: standard file not found: should have one of README, README.txt
writing manifest file 'MANIFEST'
creating meal-1.0
making hard links in meal-1.0...
hard linking meal.py -> meal-1.0
hard linking setup.py -> meal-1.0
creating dist
tar -cf dist/meal-1.0.tar meal-1.0
gzip -f9 dist/meal-1.0.tar
removing 'meal-1.0' (and everything under it)
```

How It Works

Notice all the complaints. The setup.py script was clearly not complete. It included enough to create the distribution, but not enough to satisfy the Python conventions. When the setup.py script completes, you should see the following files in the current directory:

```
$ ls
MANIFEST          dist/            meal.py          setup.py
```

The setup.py script created the dist directory and the MANIFEST file. The dist directory contains one file, a compressed version of your module:

```
$ ls dist
meal-1.0.tar.gz
```

You now have a one-file distribution of your module, which is kind of silly because the module itself was just one file. The advantage of distutils is that your module will be properly installed.

You can then take the meal-1.0.tar.gz file to another system and install the module. First, uncompress and expand the bundle. On Linux, UNIX, and Mac OS X, use the following commands:

```
$ gunzip meal-1.0.tar.gz
$ tar xvf meal-1.0.tar
meal-1.0/
meal-1.0/meal.py
meal-1.0/PKG-INFO
meal-1.0/setup.py
```

On Windows, use a compression program such as WinZip, which can handle the .tar.gz files.

You can install the module after it is expanded with the following command:

```
python setup.py install
```

For example:

```
$ python setup.py install
running install
running build
running build_py
creating build
creating build/lib
copying meal.py -> build/lib
running install_lib
copying build/lib/meal.py -> /System/Library/Frameworks/Python.framework/
Versions/30/lib/python30/site-packages
byte-compiling /System/Library/Frameworks/Python.framework/Versions/30/lib/
python30/site-packages/meal.py to meal.pyc
```

The neat thing about the `distutils` is that it works for just about any Python module. The installation command is the same, so you just need to know one command to install Python modules on any system.

Another neat thing is that the installation creates documentation on your module that is viewable with the `pydoc` command. For example, the following shows the first page of documentation on the `meal` module:

```
$ pydoc meal
Help on module meal:

NAME
    meal - Module for making meals in Python.

FILE
    /Users/ericfj/writing/python/inst2/meal-1.0/meal.py

DESCRIPTION
    Import this module and then call
    makeBreakfast(), makeDinner() or makeLunch().

CLASSES
    exceptions.Exception
        SensitiveArtistException
            AngryChefException
    Meal
        Breakfast
        Dinner
        Lunch

    class AngryChefException(SensitiveArtistException)
     |  Exception that indicates the chef is unhappy.
```

Summary

This chapter pulls together concepts from the earlier chapters to delve into how to create modules by example. If you follow the techniques described in this chapter, your modules will fit in with other modules and follow the import Python conventions.

A module is simply a Python source file that you choose to treat as a module. Simple as that sounds, you need to follow a few conventions when creating a module:

❑ Document the module and all classes, methods, and functions in the module.

❑ Test the module and include at least one test function.

❑ Define which items in the module to export — which classes, functions, and so on.

❑ Create any exception classes you need for the issues that can arise when using the module.

❑ Handle the situation in which the module itself is executed as a Python script.

Inside your modules, you'll likely define classes, which Python makes exceedingly easy.

While developing your module, you can use the `help` and `reload` functions to display documentation on your module (or any other module for that matter) and reload the changed module, respectively.

After you have created a module, you can create a distributable bundle of the module using the `distutils`. To do this, you need to create a `setup.py` script.

Chapter 11 describes regular expressions, an important concept used for finding relevant information in a sea of data.

The key things to take away from this chapter are:

❑ Modules are Python source files. Like functions, modules are pieces of code that are reusable and save programmers coding time. They also make your programs less error prone, as modules are typically used over and over and have been thoroughly tested.

❑ You can use the `dir()` function to view attributes of modules, such as functions, classes, and variables.

❑ To use a module in a program, you must import it using import. You can also import a class or function from a module by using the code from module import item.

❑ Python looks for module files in specific places. To see where Python searches, import sys and use the print(sys.path) function to view the directories.

❑ Object-oriented programming consists of encapsulation, inheritance, and polymorphism.

❑ Use triple quotes (`'''`) to document objects in your modules. The first set of triple quotes begins the comment; the second set ends the comment.

❑ To print the documentation in a module, you can use the `help()` function (i.e., help(modulename)).

❑ You should always make test functions in your module in case you need them at a later date.

Exercises

1. How can you get access to the functionality provided by a module?

2. How can you control which items from your modules are considered public? (Public items are available to other Python scripts.)

3. How can you view documentation on a module?

4. How can you find out what modules are installed on a system?

5. What kind of Python commands can you place in a module?

Text Processing

There is a whole range of applications for which scripting languages like Python are perfectly suited; and in fact scripting languages were arguably invented specifically for these applications, which involve the simple search and processing of various files in the directory tree. Taken together, these applications are often called *text processing*. Python is a great scripting tool for both writing quick text processing scripts and then scaling them up into more generally useful code later, using its clean object-oriented coding style.

In this chapter you learn:

❑   Some of the typical reasons you need text processing scripts

❑   A few simple scripts for quick system administration tasks

❑   How to navigate around in the directory structure in a platform-independent way, so your scripts will work fine on Linux, Windows, or even the Mac

❑   How to create regular expressions to compare the files found by the os and os.path modules

❑   How to use successive refinement to keep enhancing your Python scripts to winnow through the data found

Text processing scripts are one of the most useful tools in the toolbox of anybody who seriously works with computer systems, and Python is a great way to do text processing. You're going to like this chapter.

Why Text Processing Is So Useful

In general, the whole idea behind text processing is simply *finding things*. There are, of course, situations in which data are organized in a structured way; these are called *databases* and that's not what this chapter is about. Databases carefully index and store data in such a way that if you know what you're looking for, you can retrieve it quickly. However, in some data sources, the information is not at all orderly and neat, such as directory structures with hundreds or thousands of files, or logs of events from system processes consisting of thousands or hundreds of thousands of lines, or even e-mail archives with months of exchanges between people.

When data of that nature needs to be searched for something, or processed in some way, text processing is in its element. Of course, there's no reason not to combine text processing with other data-access methods; you might find yourself writing scripts rather often that run through thousands of lines of log output and do occasional RDBMS lookups (Relational DataBase Management Systems — you learn about these in Chapter 14) on some of the data they run across. This is a natural way to work.

Ultimately, this kind of script can very often get used for years as part of a back-end data processing system. If the script is written in a language like Perl, it can sometimes be quite opaque when some poor soul is assigned five years later to "fix it." Fortunately, this is a book about Python programming, and so the scripts written here can easily be turned into reusable object classes — later, you look at an illustrative example.

The two main tools in your text processing belt are directory navigation, and an arcane technology called *regular expressions*. Directory navigation is one area in which different operating systems can really wreak havoc on simple programs, because the three major operating system families (UNIX, Windows, and the Mac) all organize their directories differently; and, most painfully, they use different characters to separate subdirectory names. Python is ready for this, though — a series of cross-platform tools are available for the manipulation of directories and paths that, when used consistently, can eliminate this hassle entirely. You saw these in Chapter 8, and you see more uses of these tools here.

A regular expression is a way of specifying a very simple text parser, which then can be applied relatively inexpensively (which means that it will be fast) to any number of lines of text. Regular expressions crop up in a lot of places, and you've likely seen them before. If this is your first exposure to them, however, you'll be pretty pleased with what they can do. In the scope of this chapter, you're just going to scratch the surface of full-scale regular expression power, but even this will give your scripts a lot of functionality.

You first look at some of the reasons you might want to write text processing scripts, and then you do some experimentation with your new knowledge. The most common reasons to use regular expressions include the following:

❑   Searching for files

❑   Extracting useful data from program logs, such as a web server log

❑   Searching through your e-mail

The following sections introduce these uses.

Searching for Files

Searching for files, or doing something with some files, is a mainstay of text processing. For example, suppose that you spent a few months ripping your entire CD collection to MP3 files, without really paying attention to how you were organizing the hundreds of files you were tossing into some arbitrarily made-up set of directories. This wouldn't be a problem if you didn't wait a couple of months before thinking about organizing your files into directories according to artist — and only then realized that the directory structure you ended up with was hopelessly confused.

Text processing to the rescue! Write a Python script that scans the hopelessly nonsensical directory structure and then divide each file name into parts that *might* be an artist's name. Then take that potential name and try to look it up in a music database. The result is that you could rearrange hundreds of files into directories by, if not the name of the artist, certainly some pretty good guesses, which will get you close to having a sensible structure. From there, you would be able to explore manually and end up actually having an organized music library.

This is a one-time use of a text processing script, but you can easily imagine other scenarios in which you might use a similarly useful script on a regular basis, such as when you are handling data from a client or from a data source that you don't control. Of course, if you need to do this kind of sorting often, you can easily use Python to come up with some organized tool classes that perform these tasks to avoid having to duplicate your effort each time.

> *Whenever you face a task like this, a task that requires a lot of manual work manipulating data on your computer, think Python. Writing a script or two could save you hours and hours of tedious work.*

A second but similar situation results as a fallout of today's large hard disks. Many users store files willy-nilly on their hard disk, but never seem to have the time to organize them. A worse situation occurs when you face a hard disk full of files and you need to extract some information you know is there on your computer, but you're not sure where exactly. You are not alone. Apple, Google, Microsoft, and others all have desktop search techniques that help you search through the data in the files you have collected to help you to extract useful information.

Think of Python as a desktop search on steroids, because you can create scripts with a much finer control over the search, as well as perform operations on the files found.

Clipping Logs

Another common text-processing task that comes up in system administration is the need to sift through log files for various information. Scripts that filter logs can be spur-of-the-moment affairs meant to answer specific questions (such as "When did that e-mail get sent?" or "When was the last time my program log one specific message?"), or they might be permanent parts of a data processing system that evolves over time to manage ongoing tasks. These could be a part of a system administration and performance-monitoring system, for instance. Scripts that regularly filter logs for particular subsets of the information are often said to be *clipping logs* — the idea being that, just as you clip polygons to fit on the screen, you can also clip logs to fit into whatever view of the system you need.

However you decide to use them, after you gain some basic familiarity with the techniques used, these scripts become almost second nature. This is an application where regular expressions are used a lot, for two reasons: First, it's very common to use a UNIX shell command like `grep` to do first-level log clipping; second, if you do it in Python, you'll probably be using regular expressions to split the line into usable fields before doing more work with it. In any one clipping task, you may very well be using both techniques.

After a short introduction to traversing the file system and creating regular expressions, you look at a couple of scripts for text processing in the following sections.

Sifting through Mail

The final text processing task is one that you've probably found useful (or if you haven't, you've badly wanted it): the processing of mailbox files to find something that can't be found by your normal Inbox search feature. The most common reason you need something more powerful for this is that the mailbox file is either archived, so that you can access the file, but not read it with your mail reader easily, or it has been saved on a server where you've got no working mail client installed. Rather than go through the hassle of moving it into your Inbox tree and treating it like an active folder, you might find it simpler just to write a script to scan it for whatever you need.

However, you can also easily imagine a situation in which your search script might want to get data from an outside source, such as a web page or perhaps some other data source, like a database (see Chapter 14 for more about databases), to cross-reference your data, or do some other task during the search that can't be done with a plain vanilla mail client. In that case, text processing combined with any other technique can be an incredibly useful way to find information that may not be easy to find any other way.

Navigating the File System with the os Module

The os module and its submodule os.path are one of the most helpful things about using Python for a lot of day-to-day tasks that you have to perform on a lot of different systems. If you often need to write scripts and programs on either Windows or UNIX that would still work on the other operating system, you know from Chapter 8 that Python takes care of much of the work of hiding the differences between how things work on Windows and UNIX.

In this chapter, we're going to completely ignore a lot of what the os module can do (ranging from process control to getting system information) and just focus on some of the functions useful for working with files and directories. Some things you've been introduced to already, and others are new.

One of the difficult and annoying points about writing cross-platform scripts is the fact that directory names are separated by backslashes (\) under Windows, but forward slashes (/) under UNIX. Even breaking a full path down into its components is irritatingly complicated if you want your code to work under both operating systems.

Furthermore, Python, like many other programming languages, makes special use of the backslash character to indicate special text, such as \n for a newline. This complicates your scripts that create file paths on Windows.

With Python's os.path module, however, you get some handy functions that will split and join path names for you automatically with the right characters, and they'll work correctly on any OS that Python is running on (including the Mac.) You can call a single function to iterate through the directory structure and call another function of your choosing on each file it finds in the hierarchy. You see a lot of that function in the examples that follow, but first look at an overview of some of the useful functions in the os and os.path modules that you'll be using.

Function Name, as Called	Description
os.getcwd()	Returns the current directory. You can think of this function as the basic coordinate of directory functions in whatever language.
os.listdir(*directory*)	Returns a list of the names of files and subdirectories stored in the named *directory*. You can then run os.stat() on the individual files — for example, to determine which are files and which are subdirectories.
os.stat(*path*)	Returns a tuple of numbers, which give you everything you could possibly need to know about a file (or directory). These numbers are taken from the structure returned by the ANSI C function of the same name, and they have the following meanings (some are dummy values under Windows, but they're in the same places!):
	st_mode: permissions on the file
	st_ino: inode number (UNIX)
	st_dev: device number
	st_nlink: link number (UNIX)
	st_uid: userid of owner
	st_gid: groupid of owner
	st_size: size of the file
	st_atime: time of last access
	st_mtime: time of last modification
	st_ctime: time of creation
os.path.split(*path*)	Splits the path into its component names appropriately for the current operating system. Returns a tuple, not a list. This always surprises me.
os.path.join(*components*)	Joins name components into a path appropriate to the current operating system.

Function Name, as Called	Description
`os.path.normcase(path)`	Normalizes the case of a path. Under UNIX, this has no effect because file names are case-sensitive; but under Windows, where the OS will silently ignore case when comparing file names, it's useful to run `normcase` on a path before comparing it to another path so that if one has capital letters, but the other doesn't, Python will be able to compare the two the same way that the operation system would — that is, they'd be the same regardless of capitalizations in the path names, as long as that's the only difference. Under Windows, the function returns a path in all lowercase and converts any forward slashes into backslashes.
`os.walk(top, topdown=True, onerror=None, followlinks=False)`	This is a brilliant function that iterates down through a directory tree from top-down or bottom-up. For each directory, it creates a 3-tuple consisting of *dirpath, dirnames, and filenames*. The dirpath portion is a string that holds the path of your directory. Dirnames is a list of subdirectories from dirpath, which exclude '.' and '..'. Lastly, filenames is a listing of every non-directory file in dirpath.

There are more functions where those came from, but these are the ones used in the example code that follows. You will likely use these functions far more than any others in these modules. You can find many other useful functions in the Python module documentation for `os` and `os.path`.

Try It Out   Listing Files and Playing with Paths

The best way to get to know functions in Python is to try them out in the interpreter. Try some of the preceding functions to see what the responses will look like.

1. From the Python interpreter, import the `os` and `os.path` modules:

    ```
    >>> import os, os.path
    ```

2. First, see where you are in the file system. This example is being done under Windows, so your mileage will vary:

    ```
    >>> os.getcwd()
    'C:\\Python31'
    ```

3. If you want to do something with this programmatically, you'll probably want to break it down into the directory path, as a tuple (use `join` to put the pieces back together):

```
>>> os.path.split (os.getcwd())
('C:\\', 'Python31')
```

4. To find out some interesting things about the directory, or any file, use `os.stat`:

```
>>> os.stat('.')
nt.stat_result(st_mode=16895, st_ino=0, st_dev=0, st_nlink=0,
st_uid=0, st_gid=0, st_size=8192, st_atime=1239767131,
st_mtime=1239767131, st_ctime=1234912369)
```

Note that the directory named '.' is shorthand for the current directory.

5. If you actually want to list the files in the directory, do this:

```
>>> os.listdir('.')
['.javaws', '.limewire', 'Application Data', 'Cookies',
'Desktop', 'Favorites', 'gsview32.ini', 'Local Settings',
'My Documents', 'myfile.txt', 'NetHood', 'NTUSER.DAT',
'ntuser.dat.LOG', 'ntuser.ini', 'PrintHood', 'PUTTY.RND',
'Recent', 'SendTo', 'Start Menu', 'Templates', 'UserData', 'WINDOWS']
```

How It Works

Most of that was perfectly straightforward and easy to understand, but let's look at a couple of points before going on and writing a complete script or two.

First, you can easily see how you might construct an iterating script using `listdir`, `split`, and `stat` — but you don't have to, because `os.path` provides the `walk` function to do just that, as you see later. The `walk` function not only saves you the time and effort of writing and debugging an iterative algorithm where you search everything in your own way, but it also runs a bit faster because it's a built into Python, but written in C, which can make things easier in cases like this. You probably will seldom want to write iterators in Python when you've already got something built in that does the same job.

Second, note that the output of the `stat` call, which comes from a system call, is pretty opaque. The tuple it returns corresponds to the structure returned from the POSIX C library function of the same name, and its component values are described in the preceding table; and, of course, in the Python documentation. The `stat` function really does tell you nearly anything you might want to know about a file or directory, so it's a valuable function to understand for when you'll need it, even though it's a bit daunting at first glance.

Try It Out	**Searching for Files of a Particular Type**

If you have worked with any other programming languages, you'll like how easy searching for files is with Python. Whether or not you've done this before in another language, you'll notice how the example script is extremely short for this type of work. The following example uses the os and os. path modules to search for PDF files in the directory — which means the current directory — wherever you are when you call the function. On a UNIX or Linux system, you could use the command line and, for example, the UNIX `find` command. However, if you don't do this too often that would mean that each time you wanted to look for files, you'd need to figure out the command-line syntax for find yet again. (Because of how much find does, that can be difficult — and that difficulty is compounded by how it expects you to be familiar already with how it works!) Also, another advantage to doing this in Python is that by using Python to search for files you can refine your script to do special things based on what you find, and as you discover new uses for your program, you can add new features to it to find files in ways that you find you need. For instance, as you search for files you may see far too many results to look at. You can refine your Python script to further winnow the results to find just what you need.

This is a great opportunity to show off the nifty os.walk function, so that's the basis of this script. This function is great because it will do all the heavy lifting of file system iteration for you, leaving you to write a simple function to do something with whatever it finds along the way:

1. Using your favorite text editor, open a script called scan_pdf.py in the directory you want to scan for PDFs and enter the following code:

```
import os, os.path
import re

def print_pdf (root, dirs, files):
    for file in files:
        path = os.path.join (root, file)
        path = os.path.normcase (path)
        if re.search (r".*\.pdf", path):
            print (path)

for root, dirs, files in os.walk('.'):
```

2. Run it. Obviously, the following output will not match yours. For the best results, add a bunch of files that end in .pdf to this directory!

```
$ python scan_pdf.py
.\95-04.pdf
.\non-disclosure agreement 051702.pdf
.\word pro - dokument in lotus word pro 9 dokument45.pdf
.\101translations\2003121803\2003121803.pdf
.\101translations\2004101810\scan.pdf
.\bluemangos\purchase order - michael roberts smb-pt134.pdf
.\bluemangos\smb_pt134.pdf
.\businessteam.hu\aok.pdf
.\businessteam.hu\chn14300-2.pdf
.\businessteam.hu\diplom_bardelmeier.pdf
.\businessteam.hu\doktor_bardelmeier.pdf
.\businessteam.hu\finanzamt_1.pdf
.\businessteam.hu\zollbescheinigung.pdf
.\businessteam.hu\monday\s3.pdf
.\businessteam.hu\monday\s4.pdf
.\businessteam.hu\monday\s5.pdf
.\gerard\done\tg82-20nc-md-04.07.pdf
```

```
.\gerard\polytronic\iau-reglement_2005.pdf
.\gerard\polytronic\tg82-20bes user manual\tg82-20bes-md-27.05.pdf
.\glossa\neumag\de_993_ba_s5.pdf
.\glossa\pepperl+fuchs\5626eng3con\vocab - 3522a_recom_flsd.pdf
.\glossa\pepperl+fuchs\5769eng4\5769eng4 - td4726_8400 d-e - 16.02.04.pdf
```

How It Works

This is a nice little script, isn't it? Python does all the work, and you get a list of the PDFs in your directories, including their location and their full names — even with spaces, which can be difficult to deal with under UNIX and Linux.

A little extra work with the paths has been done so that it's easier to see what's where: a call to `os.path.join` builds the full (relative) path name of each PDF from the starting directory and a call to `os.path.normcase` makes sure that all the file names are lowercase under Windows. Under UNIX, `normcase` would have no effect, because case is significant under UNIX, so you don't want to change the capitalization (and it doesn't change it), but under Windows, it makes it easier to see whether the file name ends in `.pdf` if you have them all appear in lowercase.

Note the use of a very simple regular expression to check the ending of the file name. You could also have used `os.path.splitext` to get a tuple with the file's base name and its extension, and compared that to `pdf`, which arguably would have been cleaner. However, because this script is effectively laid out as a filter, starting it out with a regular expression, also called *regexp*, comparison from the beginning makes sense. Doing it this way means that if you decide later to restrict the output in some way, like adding more filters based on needs you find you have, you can just add more regexp comparisons and have nice, easy-to-understand code in the text expression. This is more a question of taste than anything else. (It was also a good excuse to work in a first look at regular expressions and to demonstrate that they're really not too hard to understand.)

If you haven't seen it before, the form `r"<string constant>"` simply tells Python that the string constant should suppress all special processing for backslash values. Thus, whereas `"\n"` is a string one character in length containing a newline, `r"\n"` is a string two characters in length, containing a backslash character followed by the letter `'n'`. Because regular expressions tend to contain a lot of backslashes, it's very convenient to be able to suppress their special meaning with this switch.

Try It Out　　**Refining a Search**

As it turned out, there were few enough PDF files (about 100) in the example search results that you should be able to find the files you were looking for simply by looking through the list; but very often when doing a search of this kind you first look at the results you get on the first pass and then use that knowledge to zero in on what you ultimately need. The process of zeroing in involves trying out the script, and then as you see that it could be returning better results, making successive changes to your scripts to better find the information you want.

To get a flavor of that kind of successive or iterative programming, assume that instead of just showing all the PDFs, you also want to exclude all PDFs with a space in the name. For example, because the files you were looking for were downloaded from websites, they in fact wouldn't have spaces, whereas many of the files you received in e-mail messages were attachments from someone's file system and therefore often did. Therefore, this refinement is a very likely one that you'll have an opportunity to use:

1. Using your favorite text editor again, open `scan_pdf.py` and change it to look like the following (the changed portions are in italics; or, if you skipped the last example, just enter the entire code as follows):

```python
import os, os.path
import re

def print_pdf (arg, dir, files):
    for file in files:
        path = os.path.join (dir, file)
        path = os.path.normcase (path)
        if not re.search (r".*\.pdf", path): continue
        if re.search (r" ", path): continue

        print (path)


for root, dirs, files in os.walk ('.'):
```

2. Now run the modified script — and again, this output will not match yours:

```
$ python scan_pdf.py
.\95-04.pdf
.\101translations\2003121803\2003121803.pdf
.\101translations\2004101810\scan.pdf
.\bluemangos\smb_pt134.pdf
.\businessteam.hu\aok.pdf
.\businessteam.hu\chn14300-2.pdf
.\businessteam.hu\diplom_bardelmeier.pdf
.\businessteam.hu\doktor_bardelmeier.pdf
.\businessteam.hu\finanzamt_1.pdf
.\businessteam.hu\zollbescheinigung.pdf
.\businessteam.hu\monday\s3.pdf
.\businessteam.hu\monday\s4.pdf
.\businessteam.hu\monday\s5.pdf
.\gerard\done\tg82-20nc-md-04.07.pdf
.\gerard\polytronic\iau-reglement_2005.pdf
.\glossa\neumag\de_993_ba_s5.pdf
```

How It Works

There's a stylistic change in this code — one that works well when doing these quick text-processing-oriented filter scripts. Look at the `print_pdf` function in the code — first build and normalize the path name and then run tests on it to ensure that it's the one you want. After a test fails, it will use `continue` to skip to the next file in the list. This technique enables a whole series of tests to be performed one after another, while keeping the code easy to read.

Working with Regular Expressions and the re Module

Perhaps the most powerful tool in the text processing toolbox is the *regular expression*. Though matching on simple strings or substrings is useful, they're limited. Regular expressions pack a lot of punch into a few characters, but they're so powerful that it really pays to get to know them. The basic regular expression syntax is used identically in several programming languages, and you can find at least one book written solely on their use and thousands of pages in other books (like this one).

As mentioned previously, a regular expression defines a simple parser that matches strings within a text. Regular expressions work essentially in the same way as wildcards when you use them to specify multiple files on a command line, in that the wildcard enables you to define a string that matches many different possible file names. In case you didn't know what they were, characters like * and ? are wildcards that, when you use them with commands such as `dir` on Windows or `ls` on UNIX, will let you select more than one file, but possiblly fewer files than every file (as does `dir win*`, which will print only files in your directory on Windows that start with the letters w, i, and n and are followed by anything — that's why the * is called a wildcard). Two major differences exist between a regular expression and a simple wildcard:

❏ A regular expression can match multiple times anywhere in a longer string.

❏ Regular expressions are much, much more complicated and much richer than simple wildcards, as you will see.

The main thing to note when starting to learn about regular expressions is this: A string always matches itself. Therefore, for instance, the pattern `'xxx'` will always match itself in `'abcxxxabc'`. Everything else is just icing on the cake; the core of what we're doing is just finding strings in other strings.

You can add special characters to make the patterns match more interesting things. The most commonly used one is the general wildcard `'.'` (a period or *dot*). The dot matches any one character in a string; so, for instance, `'x.x'` will match the strings `'xxx'` or `'xyx'` or even `'x.x'`.

The last example raises a fundamental point in dealing with regular expressions. What if you really only want to find something with a dot in it, like `'x.x'`? Actually, specifying `'x.x'` as a pattern won't work; it will also match `'x!x'` and `'xqx'`. Instead, regular expressions enable you to *escape* special characters by adding a backslash in front of them. Therefore, to match `'x.x'` and *only* `'x.x'`, you would use the pattern `'x\.x'`, which takes away the special meaning of the period as with an escaped character.

However, here you run into a problem with Python's normal processing of strings. Python also uses the backslash for escape sequences, because `'\n'` specifies a carriage return and `'\t'` is a tab character. To avoid running afoul of this normal processing, regular expressions are usually specified as *raw strings*, which as you've seen is a fancy way of saying that you tack an `'r'` onto the front of the string constant, and then Python treats them specially.

So after all that verbiage, how do you really match `'x.x'`? Simple: You specify the pattern `r"x\.x"`. Fortunately, if you've gotten this far, you've already made it through the hardest part of coming to grips with regular expressions in Python. The rest is easy.

Before you get too far into specifying the many special characters used by regular expressions, first look at the function used to match strings, and then do some learning by example, by typing a few regular expressions right into the interpreter.

Try It Out   Fun with Regular Expressions

This exercise uses some functional programming tools that you may have seen before but perhaps not had an opportunity to use yet. The idea is to be able to apply a regular expression to a bunch of different strings to determine which ones it matches and which ones it doesn't. To do this in one line of typing, you can use the `filter` function, but because `filter` applies a function of one argument to each member of its input list, and `re.match` and `re.search` take two arguments, you're forced to use either a function definition or an anonymous lambda form (as in this example). Don't think too hard about it (you can return to Chapter 9 to see how this works again), because it will be obvious what it's doing:

1. Start the Python interpreter and import the `re` module:

    ```
    $ python
    >>> import re
    ```

2. Now define a list of interesting-looking strings to filter with various regular expressions:

    ```
    >>> s = ('xxx', 'abcxxxabc', 'xyx', 'abc', 'x.x', 'axa', 'axxxxa', 'axxya')
    ```

3. Do the simplest of all regular expressions first:

    ```
    >>> a=filter ((lambda s: re.match(r"xxx", s)), s)
     >>>print(*a)
    xxx
    ```

4. Hey, wait! Why didn't that find 'axxxxa', too? Even though you normally talk about matches inside the string, in Python the `re.match` function looks for matches only at the start of its input. To find strings anywhere in the input, use `re.search` (which spells the word research, so it's cooler and easy to remember anyway):

    ```
    >>> b=filter ((lambda s: re.search(r"xxx", s)), s)
     >>>print(*b)
    xxx, abcxxxabc, axxxxa
    ```

5. OK, look for that period:

    ```
    >>>c=filter ((lambda s: re.search(r"x.x", s)), s)
     >>>print(*c)
    xxx, abcxxxabc, xyx, x.x, axxxxa
    ```

6. Here's how you match *only* the period (by escaping the special character):

    ```
    >>> d=filter ((lambda s: re.search(r"x\.x", s)), s)
     >>>print(*d)
    x.x
    ```

7. You also can search for any number of *x*'s by using the asterisk, which can match a series of whatever character is in front of it:

```
>>> e=filter ((lambda s: re.search(r"x.*x", s)), s)
 >>>print(*e)
xxx, abcxxxabc, xyx, x.x, axxxxa, axxya
```

8. Wait a minute! How did 'x.*x' match 'axxya' if there was nothing between the two *x*'s? The secret is that the asterisk is tricky — it matches *zero or more* occurrences of a character between two *x*'s. If you really want to make sure something is between the *x*'s, use a plus instead, which matches *one or more* characters:

```
>>>f=filter ((lambda s: re.search(r"x.+x", s)), s)
 >>>print(*f)
xxx, abcxxxabc, xyx, x.x, axxxxa
```

9. Now you know how to match anything with, say, a 'c' in it:

```
>>> g=filter ((lambda s: re.search(r"c+", s)), s)
 >>>print(*g)
abcxxxabc, abc
```

10. Here's where things get really interesting: How would you match anything *without* a 'c'? Regular expressions use square brackets to denote special sets of characters to match, and if there's a caret at the beginning of the list, it means all characters that don't appear in the set, so your first idea might be to try this:

```
>>>h=filter ((lambda s: re.search(r"[^c]*", s)), s)
 >>>print(*h)
xxx, abcxxxabc, xyx, abc, x.x, axa, axxxxa, axxya
```

11. That matched the whole list. Why? Because it matches anything that has a character that isn't a `'c'`, you negated the wrong thing. To make this clearer, you can filter a list with more *c*'s in it:

```
>>>h=filter ((lambda s: re.search(r"[^c]*", s)), ('c', 'cc', 'ccx'))
 >>>print(*h)
c, cc, ccx
```

Note that older versions of Python may return a different tuple, ('ccx',).

12. To really match anything without a 'c' in it, you have to use the ^ and $ special characters to refer to the beginning and end of the string and then tell re that you want strings composed only of non-*c* characters from beginning to end:

```
>>>i=filter ((lambda s: re.search(r"^[^c]*$", s)), s)
 >>>print(*i)
xxx, xyx, x.x, axa, axxxxa, axxya
```

As you can see from the last example, getting `re` to understand what you mean can sometimes require a little effort. It's often best to try out new regular expressions on a bunch of data you understand and then check the results carefully to ensure that you're getting what you intended; otherwise, you can get some real surprises later!

Use the techniques shown here in the following example. You can usually run the Python interpreter in interactive mode, and test your regular expression with sample data until it matches what you want.

Try It Out   **Adding Tests**

The example `scan_pdf.py` scripts shown so far provide a nicely formatted framework for testing files. As mentioned previously, the `os.walk` function provides the heavy lifting. The `print_pdf` function you write performs the tests — in this case, looking for PDF files.

Clocking in at less than 20 lines of code, these examples show the true power of Python. Following the structure of the `print_pdf` function, you can easily add tests to refine the search, as shown in the following example:

1. Using your favorite text editor again, open `scan_pdf.py` and change it to look like the following. The changed portions are in italics (or, if you skipped the last example, just enter the entire code that follows):

```python
import os, os.path
import re

def print_pdf (arg, dir, files):
    for file in files:
        path = os.path.join (dir, file)
        path = os.path.normcase (path)
        if not re.search (r".*\.pdf", path): continue
        if re.search (r".\.hu", path): continue

        print(path)

for root, dirs, files in os.walk('.'):
```

2. Now run the modified script — and again, this output will not match yours:

```
C:\projects\translation>python scan_pdf.py

.\businessteam.hu\aok.pdf
.\businessteam.hu\chn14300-2.pdf
.\businessteam.hu\diplom_bardelmeier.pdf
.\businessteam.hu\doktor_bardelmeier.pdf
.\businessteam.hu\finanzamt_1.pdf
```

```
.\businessteam.hu\zollbescheinigung.pdf
.\businessteam.hu\monday\s3.pdf
.\businessteam.hu\monday\s4.pdf
.\businessteam.hu\monday\s5.pdf

...
```

How It Works

This example follows the structure set up in the previous examples and adds another test. You can add test after test to create the script that best meets your needs.

In this example, the test looks only for file names (which include the full paths) with an *.hu* in the name. The assumption here is that files with an *.hu* in the name (or in a directory with *.hu* in the name) are translations from Hungarian (*hu* is the two-letter country code for Hungary). Therefore, this example shows how to narrow the search to files translated from Hungarian. (In real life, you will obviously require different search criteria. Just add the tests you need.)

You can continue refining your script to create a generalized search utility in Python. Chapter 12 goes into this in more depth.

Summary

Text processing scripts are generally short, useful, reusable programs, which are either written for one-time and occasional use, or used as components of a larger data-processing system. The chief tools for the text processing programmer are directory structure navigation and regular expressions, both of which were examined in brief in this chapter.

Python is handy for this style of programming because it offers a balance where it is easy to use for simple, one-time tasks, and it's also structured enough to ease the maintenance of code that gets reused over time.

The specific techniques shown in this chapter include the following:

- ❑ Use the `os.walk` function to traverse the file system.
- ❑ Place the search criteria in the function you write and pass it to the `os.walk` function.
- ❑ Regular expressions work well to perform the tests on each file found by the `os.walk` function.
- ❑ Try out regular expressions in the Python interpreter interactively to ensure they work.

Chapter 12 covers an important concept: testing. Testing enables you not only to ensure that your scripts work, but that the scripts still work when you make a change.

Exercises

1. Modify the `scan_pdf.py` script to start at the root, or topmost, directory. On Windows, this should be the topmost directory of the current disk (C:, D:, and so on). Doing this on a network share can be slow, so don't be surprised if your G: drive takes a lot more time when it comes from a file server). On UNIX and Linux, this should be the topmost directory (the root directory, /).

2. Modify the `scan_pdy.py` script to match only PDF files with the text *boobah* in the file name.

3. Modify the `scan_pdf.py` script to exclude all files with the text *boobah* in the file name.

Part III
Putting Python to Work

Testing

Like visits to the dentist, thorough testing of any program is something that you should be doing if you want to avoid the pain of having to trace a problem that you thought you'd taken care of. This lesson is one that normally takes a programmer many years to learn, and to be honest, you're still going to be working on it for many years. However, the one thing that is of the utmost importance is that testing must be organized; and to be the most effective, you must start writing your programs knowing that it will be tested as you go along, and plan around having the time to write and confirm your test cases.

Fortunately, Python offers an excellent facility for organizing your testing called *PyUnit*. It is a Python port of the Java JUnit package, so if you've worked with JUnit you're already on firm ground when testing in Python — but if not, don't worry.

In this chapter you learn:

- ❑ The concept and use of assertions
- ❑ The basic concepts of unit testing and test suites
- ❑ A few simple example tests to show you how to organize a test suite
- ❑ Thorough testing of the search utility from Chapter 11

The beauty of PyUnit is that you can set up testing early in the software development life cycle, and you can run it as often as needed while you're working. By doing this, you can catch errors early on, before they're painful to rework — let alone before anybody else sees them. You can also set up test cases before you write code, so that as you write, you can be sure that your results match what you expect! Define your test cases before you even start coding, and you'll never find yourself fixing a bug only to discover that your changes have spiraled out of control and cost you days of work.

Note that PyUnit is not the only framework available for testing your Python programs. There are literally dozens of others out there. At the time of this writing, the vast majority of those have not been updated to work with Python 3.1, but they are definitely worth a look once they get updated.

Assertions

An *assertion* in Python is in practice similar to an assertion in day-to-day language. When you speak and you make an assertion, you have said something that isn't necessarily proven but that you believe to be true. Of course, if you are trying to make a point, and the assertion you made is incorrect, your entire argument falls apart.

In Python, an assertion is a similar concept. Assertions are statements that can be made within the code while you are developing it that you can use to test the validity of your code, but if the statement doesn't turn out to be true, an `AssertionError` is raised, and the program will be stopped if the error isn't caught (in general, they shouldn't be caught, because `AssertionErrors` should be taken as a warning that you didn't think something through correctly!)

Assertions enable you to think of your code in a series of testable cases. That way, you can make sure that while you develop, you can make tests along the lines of "this value is not None" or "this object is a String" or "this number is greater than zero." All of these statements are useful while developing to catch errors in terms of how you think about the program.

Try It Out   Using Assert

Creating a set of simple cases, you can see how the assert language feature works:

```
# Demonstrate the use of assert()
large = 1000
string = "This is a string"
float = 1.0
broken_int = "This should have been an int"

assert large > 500
assert type(string) == type("")
assert type(float) != type(1)
assert type(broken_int) == type(4)
```

Try running the preceding with *python -i*.

How It Works

The output from this simple test case looks like this:

```
Traceback (most recent call last):
  File "<pyshell#8>", line 1, in <module>
    assert type(broken_init)==type(4)
NameError: name 'broken_init' is not defined
```

You can see from this stack trace that this simply raises the error. `assert` is implemented very simply. If a special internal variable called __debug__ is `True`, assertions are checked; and if any assertion doesn't succeed, an `AssertionError` is raised. Because `assert` is actually a combination of an *if* statement that, when there's a problem, will *raise* an exception, you are allowed to specify a custom message, just as you would with *raise*. You should experiment by replacing the last assertion with this code and running it:

```
try:
    assert type(broken_int)==type(4),"broken_int is broken"
except AssertionError: print("Handle the error here.)
```

The variable __debug__, which activates assert, is special; it's immutable after Python has started up, so in order to turn it off you need to specify the -O (a dash, followed by the capital letter *O*) parameter to Python. -O tells Python to *optimize* code, which among other things for Python means that it removes assert tests, because it knows that they'll cause the program to slow down (not a lot, but optimization like this is concerned with getting every little bit of performance). -O is intended to be used when a program is deployed, so it removes assertions that are considered to be development-time features.

As you can see, assertions are useful. If you even think that you may have made a mistake and want to catch it later in your development cycle, you can put in an assertion to catch yourself, and move on and get other work done until that code is tested. When your code is tested, it can tell you what's going wrong if an assertion fails instead of leaving you to wonder what happened. Moreover, when you deploy and use the -O flag, your assertion won't slow down the program.

Assert lacks a couple of things by itself. First, assert doesn't provide you with a structure in which to run your tests. You have to create a structure, and that means that until you learn what you want from tests, you're liable to make tests that do more to get in your way than confirm that your code is correct.

Second, assertions just stop the program and they provide only an exception. It would be more useful to have a system that would give you summaries, so you can name your tests, add tests, remove tests, and compile many tests into a package that let you summarize whether or not your program tests out. These ideas and more make up the concepts of *unit tests* and *test suites*.

Test Cases and Test Suites

Unit testing revolves around the *test case*, which is the smallest building block of testable code for any circumstances that you're testing. When you're using PyUnit, a test case is a simple object with at least one test method that runs code; and when it's done, it then compares the results of the test against various assertions that you've made about the results.

> **PyUnit is the name of the package as named by its authors, but the module you import is called the more generic-sounding name** unittest.

Each test case is subclassed from the TestCase class, which is a good, memorable name for it. The simplest test cases you can write just override the runTest method of TestCase and enable you to define a basic test, but you can also define several different test methods within a single test case class, which can enable you to define things that are common to a number of tests, such as setup and cleanup procedures.

A series of test cases run together for a particular project is called a *test suite*. You can find some simple tools for organizing test suites, but they all share the concept of running a bunch of test cases together and recording what passed, what failed, and how, so you can know where you stand.

Because the simplest possible test suite consists of exactly one test case, and you've already had the simplest possible test case described to you, in the following Try It Out you write a quick testing example so you can see how all this fits together. In addition, just so you *really* don't have anything to distract you, you test arithmetic, which has no external requirements on the system, the file system, or, really, anything.

Try It Out   Testing Addition

1. Use your favorite editor to create a file named `test1.py` in a directory named `ch12`. Using your programming editor, edit your file to have the following code:

```python
import unittest

class ArithTest (unittest.TestCase):
    def runTest (self):
        """ Test addition and succeed. """
        self.failUnless (1+1==2, 'one plus one fails!')
        self.failIf (1+1 != 2, 'one plus one fails again!')
        self.failUnlessEqual (1+1, 2, 'more trouble with one plus one!')

def suite():
    suite = unittest.TestSuite()
    suite.addTest (ArithTest())
    return suite


if __name__ == '__main__':
    runner = unittest.TextTestRunner()
    test_suite = suite()
    runner.run (test_suite)
```

2. Now run the code using *python*:

```
.
----------------------------------------------------------------------
Ran 1 tests in 0.026s
```

How It Works

In step 1, after you've imported `unittest` (the module that contains the PyUnit framework), you define the class `ArithTest`, which is a subclass of the class from unittest, `TestCase`. `ArithTest` has only defined the `runTest` method, which performs the actual testing. Note how the `runTest` method has its docstring defined. It is at least as important to document your tests as it is to document your code. Lastly, a series of three assertions takes place in `runTest`.

TestCase classes beginning with `fail`, such as `failUnless`, `failIf`, and `failUnlessEqual`, come in additional varieties to simplify setting up the conditions for your tests. When you're programming, you'll likely find yourself resistant to writing tests (they can be very distracting; sometimes they are boring; and they are rarely something other people notice, which makes it harder to motivate yourself to write them). PyUnit tries to make things as easy as possible for you.

After the unit test is defined in `ArithTest`, you may like to define the suite itself in a callable function, as recommended by the PyUnit developer, Steve Purcell, in the modules documentation. This enables you to simply define what you're doing (testing) and where (in the function you name). Therefore, after the definition of `ArithTest`, you have created the `suite` function, which simply instantiates a vanilla, unmodified test suite. It adds your single unit test to it and returns it. Keep in mind that the `suite` function only invokes the `TestCase` class in order to make an object that can be returned. The actual test is performed by the returned `TestCase` object.

As you learned in Chapter 6, only when this is being run as the main program will Python invoke the `TextTestRunner` class to create the `runner` object. The `runner` object has a method called `run` that expects to have an object of the `unittests.TestSuite` class. The `suite` function creates one such object, so `test_suite` is assigned a reference to the `TestSuite` object. When that's finished, the `runner.run` method is called, which uses the `suite` in `test_suite` to test the unit tests defined in `test_suite`.

The actual output in this case is dull, but in that good way you'll learn to appreciate because it means everything has succeeded. The single period tells you that it has successfully run one unit test. If, instead of the period, you see an `F`, it means that a test has failed. In either case, PyUnit finishes off a run with a report. Note that arithmetic is run very, very fast.

Now, see what failure looks like.

Try It Out   Testing Faulty Addition

1. Use your favorite text editor to add a second set of tests to `test1.py`. These will be based on the first example. Add the following to your file:

```
class ArithTestFail (unittest.TestCase):
    def runTest (self):
        """ Test addition and fail. """
        self.failUnless (1+1==2, 'one plus one fails!')
        self.failIf (1+1 != 2, 'one plus one fails again!')
        self.failUnlessEqual (1+1, 2, 'more trouble with one plus one!')
        self.failIfEqual (1+1, 2, 'expected failure here')
        self.failIfEqual (1+1, 2, 'second failure')

def suite_2():
    suite = unittest.TestSuite()
    suite.addTest (ArithTest())
    suite.addTest (ArithTestFail())
    return suite
```

You also need to change the `if` statement that sets off the tests, and you need to make sure that it appears at the end of your file so that it can see both classes:

```
if __name__ == '__main__':
    runner = unittest.TextTestRunner()
    test_suite = suite_2()
    runner.run (test_suite)
```

2. Now run the newly modified file (after you've saved it). You'll get a very different result with the second set of tests. In fact, it'll be very different from the prior test:

```
.F
======================================================================
FAIL: Test addition and fail.
----------------------------------------------------------------------
Traceback (most recent call last):
  File "C:\Python30\ch12\test1.py", line 22, in runTest
    self.failIfEqual(1+1,2, 'expected failure here')
AssertionError: expected failure here


----------------------------------------------------------------------
Ran 2 tests in 0.062s

FAILED (failures=1)
>>>
```

How It Works

Here, you've kept your successful test from the first example and added a second test that you know will fail. The result is that you now have a period from the first test, followed by an "F" for "Failed" from the second test, all in the first line of output from the test run.

After the tests are run, the results report is printed out so you can examine exactly what happened. The successful test still produces no output at all in the report, which makes sense: Imagine you have a hundred tests but only two fail — you would have to slog through a lot more output to find the failures than you do this way. It may seem like looking on the negative side of things, but you'll get used to it.

Because there was a failed test, the stack trace from the failed test is displayed. In addition, a couple of different messages result from the `runTest` method. The first thing you should look at is the FAIL message. It actually uses the docstring from your `runTest` method and prints it at the top, so you can reference the test that failed. Therefore, the first lesson to take away from this is that you should document your tests in the docstring! Second, you'll notice that the message you specified in the `runTest` for the specific test that failed is displayed along with the exception that PyUnit generated.

The report wraps up by listing the number of test cases actually run and a count of the failed test cases.

Test Fixtures

Well, this is all well and good, but real-world tests usually involve some work to set up your tests before they're run (creating files, creating an appropriate directory structure, generally making sure everything is in shape, and other things that may need to be done to ensure that the right things are being tested). In addition, cleanup also often needs to be done at the end of your tests.

In PyUnit, the environment in which a test case runs is called the *test fixture*, and the base `TestCase` class defines two methods: `setUp`, which is called before a test is run, and `tearDown`, which is called after the test case has completed. These are present to deal with anything involved in creating or cleaning up the test fixture.

> **You should know that if `setUp` fails, `tearDown` isn't called. However, `tearDown` *is* called even if the test case itself fails.**

Remember that when you set up tests, the initial state of each test shouldn't rely on a prior test having succeeded or failed. Each test case should create a pristine test fixture for itself. If you don't ensure this, you're going to get inconsistent test results that will only make your life more difficult.

To save time when you run similar tests repeatedly on an identically configured test fixture, subclass the `TestCase` class to define the setup and cleanup methods. This will give you a single class that you can use as a starting point. Once you've done that, subclass *your* class to define each test case. You can alternatively define several test case methods within your unit case class, and then instantiate test case objects for each method. Both of these are demonstrated in the next example.

Try It Out   **Working with Test**

1. Use your favorite text editor to add a new file `test2.py`. Make it look like the following example. Note that this example builds on the previous examples.

```
import unittest
class ArithTestSuper (unittest.TestCase):
    def setUp (self):
        print("Setting up ArithTest cases")
    def tearDown (self):
        print("Cleaning up ArithTest cases")
class ArithTest (ArithTestSuper):
    def runTest (self):
        """ Test addition and succeed. """
        print("Running ArithTest")
        self.failUnless (1+1==2, 'one plus one fails!')
        self.failIf (1+1 != 2, 'one plus one fails again!')
        self.failUnlessEqual (1+1, 2, 'more trouble with one plus one!')

class ArithTestFail (ArithTestSuper):
    def runTest (self):
```

```
            """ Test addition and fail. """
            print("Running ArithTestFail")
            self.failUnless (1+1==2, 'one plus one fails!')
            self.failIf (1+1 != 2, 'one plus one fails again!')
            self.failUnlessEqual (1+1, 2, 'more trouble with one plus one!')
            self.failIfEqual (1+1, 2, 'expected failure here')
            self.failIfEqual (1+1, 2, 'second failure')

    class ArithTest2 (unittest.TestCase):
        def setUp (self):
            print("Setting up ArithTest2 cases")
        def tearDown (self):
            print("Cleaning up ArithTest2 cases")
        def runArithTest (self):
            """ Test addition and succeed, in one class. """
            print("Running ArithTest in ArithTest2")
            self.failUnless (1+1==2, 'one plus one fails!')
            self.failIf (1+1 != 2, 'one plus one fails again!')
            self.failUnlessEqual (1+1, 2, 'more trouble with one plus one!')

        def runArithTestFail (self):
            """ Test addition and fail, in one class. """
            print("Running ArithTestFail in ArithTest2")
            self.failUnless (1+1==2, 'one plus one fails!')
            self.failIf (1+1 != 2, 'one plus one fails again!')
            self.failUnlessEqual (1+1, 2, 'more trouble with one plus one!')
            self.failIfEqual (1+1, 2, 'expected failure here')
            self.failIfEqual (1+1, 2, 'second failure')

    def suite():
        suite = unittest.TestSuite()
        # First style:
        suite.addTest (ArithTest())
        suite.addTest (ArithTestFail())
        # Second style:
        suite.addTest (ArithTest2("runArithTest"))
        suite.addTest (ArithTest2("runArithTestFail"))

        return suite
    if __name__ == '__main__':
        runner = unittest.TextTestRunner()
        test_suite = suite()
        runner.run (test_suite)
```

2. Run the code:

```
Setting up ArithTest cases
Running ArithTest
Cleaning up ArithTest cases
.Setting up ArithTest cases
```

```
Running ArithTestFail
FCleaning up ArithTest cases
Setting up ArithTest2 cases
Running ArithTest in ArithTest2
Cleaning up ArithTest2 cases
.Setting up ArithTest2 cases
Running ArithTestFail in ArithTest2
FCleaning up ArithTest2 cases


======================================================================
FAIL: Test addition and fail.
----------------------------------------------------------------------
Traceback (most recent call last):
  File "C:/Python31/test2.py", line 25, in runTest
    self.failIfEqual (1+1, 2, 'expected failure here')
AssertionError: expected failure here


======================================================================
FAIL: Test addition and fail, in one class.
----------------------------------------------------------------------
Traceback (most recent call last):
  File "C:/Python31/test2.py", line 48, in runArithTestFail
    self.failIfEqual (1+1, 2, 'expected failure here')
AssertionError: expected failure here


----------------------------------------------------------------------
Ran 4 tests in 0.396s

FAILED (failures=2)
>>>
```

How It Works

Take a look at this code before moving along. The first thing to note about this is that you're doing the same tests as before. One test is made to succeed and the other one is made to fail, but you're doing two sets, each of which implements multiple unit test cases with a test fixture, but in two different styles.

Which style you use is completely up to you; it really depends on what you consider readable and maintainable.

The first set of classes in the code (ArithTestSuper, ArithTest, and ArithTestFail) are essentially the same tests as shown in the second set of examples in test1.py, but this time a class has been created called ArithTestSuper. ArithTestSuper implements a setUp and tearDown method. They don't do much but they do demonstrate where you'd put in your own conditions. Each of the unit test classes are subclassed from your new ArithTestSuper class, so now they will perform the same setup of the test fixture. If you needed to make a change to the test fixture, you can now modify it in ArithTestSuper's classes, and have it take effect in all of its subclasses.

The actual test cases, ArithTest and ArithTestFail, are the same as in the previous example, except that you've added print calls to them as well.

The final test case class, `ArithTest2`, does exactly the same thing as the prior three classes that you've already defined. The only difference is that it combines the test fixture methods with the test case methods, and it doesn't override `runTest`. Instead `ArithTest2` defines two test case methods: `runArithTest` and `runArithTestFail`. These are then invoked explicitly when you created test case instances during the test run, as you can see from the changed definition of `suite`.

Once this is actually run, you can see one change immediately: Because your setup, test, and cleanup functions all write to `stdout`, you can see the order in which everything is called. Note that the cleanup functions are indeed called even after a failed test. Finally, note that the tracebacks for the failed tests have been gathered up and displayed together at the end of the report.

Putting It All Together with Extreme Programming

A good way to see how all of this fits together is to use a test suite during the development of an extended coding project. This strategy underlies the XP (Extreme Programming) methodology, which is a popular trend in programming: First, you plan the code; then you write the test cases as a framework; and only then do you write the actual code. Whenever you finish a coding task, you rerun the test suite to see how closely you approach the design goals as embodied in the test suite. (Of course, you are also debugging the test suite at the same time, and that's fine!) This technique is a great way to find your programming errors early in the process, so that bugs in low-level code can be fixed and the code made stable before you even start on higher-level work, and it's extremely easy to set up in Python using PyUnit, as you see in the next example.

This example includes a realistic use of text fixtures as well, creating a test directory with a few files in it and then cleaning up the test directory after the test case is finished. It also demonstrates the convention of naming all test case methods with `test` followed by the name, such as `testMyFunction`, to enable the `unittest.main` procedure to recognize and run them automatically.

Implementing a Search Utility in Python

The first step in this programming methodology, as with any, is to define your objectives — in this case, a general-purpose, reusable search function that you can use in your own work. Obviously, it would be a waste of time to anticipate all possible text-processing functionality in a single search utility program, but certain search tasks tend to recur a lot. Therefore, if you wanted to implement a general-purpose search utility, how would you go about it? The UNIX `find` command is a good place to look for useful functionality — it enables you not only to iterate through the directory tree and perform actions on each file found, but also to specify certain directories to skip, to specify rather complex logic combinations on the command line, and a number of other things, such as searching by file modification date and size.

On the other hand, the `find` command doesn't include any searching on the content of files (the standard way to do this under UNIX is to call `grep` from within `find`) and it has a lot of features involving the invocation of post-processing programs that we don't really need for a general-purpose Python search utility.

What you might need when searching for files in Python could include the following:

❑ Return values you can use easily in Python: A tuple including the full path, the file name, the extension, and the size of the file is a good start.

❑ Specification of a regular expression for the file name to search for and a regular expression for the content (if no content search is specified, the files shouldn't be opened, to save overhead).

❑ Optional specifications of additional search terms: The size of the file, its age, last modification, and so on are all useful.

A truly general search utility might include a function to be called with the parameters of the file, so that more advanced logic can be specified. The UNIX find command enables very general logic combinations on the command line, but frankly, let's face it — complex logic on the command line is hard to understand. This is the kind of thing that really works better in a real programming language like Python, so you could include an optional logic function for narrowing searches as well.

In general, it's a good idea to approach this kind of task by focusing first on the core functionality, adding more capability after the initial code is already in good shape. That's how the following example is structured — first you start with a basic search framework that encapsulates the functionality you covered in the examples for the os and re modules, and then you add more functionality once that first part is complete. This kind of incremental approach to software development can help keep you from getting bogged down in details before you have anything at all to work with, and the functionality of something like this general-purpose utility is complicated enough that it would be easy to lose the thread.

Because this is an illustration of the XP methodology as well, you'll follow that methodology and first write the code to call the find utility, build that code into a test suite, and only then will you write the find utility. Here, of course, you're cheating a little. Ordinarily, you would be changing the test suite as you go, but in this case, the test suite is already guaranteed to work with the final version of the tested code. Nonetheless, you can use this example for yourself.

Try It Out   Writing a Test Suite

1.   Use your favorite text editor to create the file test_find.py. Enter the following code:

```
import unittest
import find
import os, os.path

def filename(ret):
    return ret[1]

class FindTest (unittest.TestCase):
    def setUp (self):
        os.mkdir ("_test")
        os.mkdir (os.path.join("_test", "subdir"))
        f = open (os.path.join("_test", "file1.txt"), "w")
        f.write ("""first line
second line
third line
```

```
fourth line""")
        f.close()

        f = open (os.path.join("_test", "file2.py"), "w")
        f.write ("""This is a test file.
It has many words in it.
This is the final line.""")
        f.close()

    def tearDown (self):
        os.unlink (os.path.join ("_test", "file1.txt"))
        os.unlink (os.path.join ("_test", "file2.py"))
        os.rmdir (os.path.join ("_test", "subdir"))
        os.rmdir ("_test")

    def test_01_SearchAll (self):
        """ 1: Test searching for all files. """
        res = find.find (r".*", start="_test")
        self.failUnless (map(filename,res) == ['file1.txt', 'file2.py'],
                        'wrong results')

    def test_02_SearchFileName (self):
        """ 2: Test searching for specific file by regexp. """
        res = find.find (r"file", start="_test")
        self.failUnless (map(filename,res) == ['file1.txt', 'file2.py'],
                        'wrong results')
        res = find.find (r"py$", start="_test")
        self.failUnless (map(filename,res) == ['file2.py'],
                        'Python file search incorrect')

    def test_03_SearchByContent (self):
        """ 3: Test searching by content. """
        res = find.find (start="_test", content="first")
        self.failUnless (map(filename,res) == ['file1.txt'],
                        "didn't find file1.txt")
        res = find.find (where="py$", start="_test", content="line")
        self.failUnless (map(filename,res) == ['file2.py'],
                        "didn't find file2.py")
        res = find.find (where="py$", start="_test", content="second")
        self.failUnless (len(res) == 0,
                        "found something that didn't exist")

    def test_04_SearchByExtension (self):
        """ 4: Test searching by file extension. """
        res = find.find (start="_test", ext='py')
        self.failUnless (map(filename,res) == ['file2.py'],
                        "didn't find file2.py")
        res = find.find (start="_test", ext='txt')
        self.failUnless (map(filename,res) == ['file1.txt'],
                        "didn't find file1.txt")

    def test_05_SearchByLogic (self):
        """ 5: Test searching using a logical combination callback. """
        res = find.find (start="_test", logic=lambda x: (x['size'] < 50))
```

```
            self.failUnless (map(filename,res) == ['file1.txt'],
                            "failed to find by size")

if __name__ == '__main__':
    unittest.main()
```

2. Now create another code file named `find.py` — note that this is only the skeleton of the actual `find` utility and will fail miserably. That's okay; in testing and in extreme programming, failure is good because it tells you what you still need to do:

```
import os, os.path
import re
from stat import *

def find (where='.*', content=None, start='.', ext=None, logic=None):
    return ([])
```

3. Run the `test_find.py` test suite from the command line. An excerpt is shown here:

```
C:\projects\articles\python_book\ch12_testing>python test_find.py
FFFFF
======================================================================
FAIL: 1: Test searching for all files.
----------------------------------------------------------------------

[a lot more information]

Ran 5 tests in 0.421s

FAILED (failures=5)
```

How It Works

The first three lines of the testing suite import the PyUnit module, the `find` module to be tested (which hasn't actually been written yet), and the `os` and `os.path` modules for file and directory manipulation when setting up and tearing down the test fixtures. Following this, there's a simple helper function to extract the file name from the search results, to make it simpler to check the results for correctness.

After that, the test suite itself starts. All test cases in this example are instances of the base class `FindTest`. The `FindTest` class starts out with `setUp` and `tearDown` methods to define the test fixtures used in the test cases, followed by five test cases.

The test fixture in all test cases consists of a testing directory; a subdirectory under that main directory to ensure that subdirectories aren't treated as files when scanning; and two test files with `.txt` and `.py` extensions. The contents of the test files are pretty arbitrary, but they contain different words so that the test suite can include tests to distinguish between them using a content search.

The test cases themselves are named with both a sequential number and a descriptive name, and each starts with the characters "test." This allows the `unittest.main` function to autodetect them when running the test suite. The sequential numbers ensure that the tests will be run in the proper order defined, because a simple character sort is used to order them when testing. Each docstring then cites the test number, followed by a simple description of the type of test. All of this enables the results of failed tests to be understood quickly and easily, so that you can trace exactly where the error occurred.

Finally, after the test cases are defined, there are exactly two lines of code to detect that the script is being run directly instead of being called as a module, and if it is being run, to create a default test runner using `unittest.main` in that case. The `unittest.main` call then finds all of the test cases, sorts them by the sequential number, and runs them in order.

The second file is the skeleton of the `find` utility itself. Beyond determining what it has to do and how it's called, you haven't done anything at all yet to write the code itself, so that's your next task.

Try It Out   A General-Purpose Search Framework

1. Using your favorite text editor, open `find.py` and change it to look like this:

```python
import os, os.path
import re
from stat import *

def find (where='.*', content=None, start='.', ext=None, logic=None):
    context = {}
    context['where'] = where
    context['content'] = content
    context['return'] = []

    os.walk (start, find_file, context)

    return context['return']

def find_file (context, dir, files):
    for file in files:
        # Find out things about this file.
        path = os.path.join (dir, file)
        path = os.path.normcase (path)
        try:
            ext = os.path.splitext (file)[1][1:]
        except:
            ext = ''
        stat = os.stat(path)
        size = stat[ST_SIZE]

        # Don't treat directories like files
        if S_ISDIR(stat[ST_MODE]): continue

        # Do filtration based on the original parameters of find()
        if not re.search (context['where'], file): continue

        # Do content filtration last, to avoid it as much as possible
        if context['content']:
            f = open (path, 'r')
            match = 0
            for l in f.readlines():
                if re.search(context['content'], l):
```

```
            match = 1
            break
      f.close()
      if not match: continue

   # Build the return value for any files that passed the filtration tests.
   file_return = (path, file, ext, size)
   context['return'].append (file_return)
```

2. Now, for example, to find Python files containing "find," you can start Python and do the following:

```
>>> import find
>>> find.find(r"py$", content='find')
[('.\\find.py', 'find.py', 'py', 1297), ('.\\test_find.py',
'test_find.py', 'py', 1696)]
```

How It Works

This example is really doing the same thing as the first example in the last chapter on text processing, except that instead of a task-specific `print_pdf` function, there is a more general `find_file` function to scan the files in each directory. Because this code is more complex than the other example scripts, you can see that having a testing framework available in advance will help you immensely in debugging the initial versions. This first version satisfies the first three test cases of the test suite.

Because the `find_file` function is doing most of the filtration work, it obviously needs access to the search parameters. In addition, because it also needs a place to keep the list of hits it is building during the search, a dictionary structure is a good choice for its argument, because a dictionary is mutable and can contain any number of named values. Therefore, the first thing the main `find` function does is to build that dictionary and put the search parameters into it. It then calls `os.walk` to do the work of iterating through the directory structure, just as in the PDF search code example at the beginning of this chapter. Once the walk is done, it returns the return value (the list of files found and information about them), which was built during the search.

During the search, `os.walk` calls `find_file` on each directory it finds, passing the dictionary argument built at the start of the search, the name of the current directory, and a list of all the files in the directory. The first thing the `find_file` function does, then, is to scan that list of files and determine some basic information for each one by running `os.stat` on it. If the "file" is actually a subdirectory, the function moves on; because all of the search parameters apply to file names, not to points in the directory tree (and because the content search will result in an error unless a file is being opened!), the function skips the subdirectories using the information gleaned from the `os.stat` call.

When that's finished, the function applies the search parameters stored in the dictionary argument to eliminate whatever files it can. If a content parameter is specified, it opens and reads each file, but otherwise no manipulation of the file itself is done.

If a file has passed all the search parameter tests (there are only two in this initial version), an entry is built for it and appended to the hit list; this entry consists of the full path name of the file relative to the starting point of the search, the file name itself, its extension, and its size. Naturally, you could return any set of values for files you find useful, but these are a good basic set that you could use to build a directory-like listing of hits, or use to perform some sort of task on the files.

A More Powerful Python Search

Remember that this is an illustration of an incremental programming approach, so the first example was a good place to stop and give an explanation, but there are plenty of other search parameters it would be nice to include in this general search utility, and of course there are still two unit cases to go in the test suite you wrote at the outset. Because Python gives you a keyword parameter mechanism, it's very simple to add new named parameters to your function definition and toss them into the search context dictionary, and then use them in `find_file` as needed, without making individual calls to the `find` function unwieldy.

The next example shows you how easy it is to add a search parameter for the file's extension, and throws in a logic combination callback just for good measure. You can add more search parameters at your leisure; the following code just shows you how to get started on your own extensions (one of the exercises for the chapter asks you to add search parameters for the date on which the file was last modified, for instance).

Though the file extension parameter, as a single simple value, is easy to conceive and implement — it's really just a matter of adding the parameter to the search context and adding a filter test in `find_file` — planning a logic combination callback parameter requires a little thought. The usual strategy for specification of a callback is to define a set of parameters — say, the file name, size, and modification date — and then pass those values in on each call to the callback. If you add a new search parameter, you're faced with a choice — you can arbitrarily specify that the new parameter can't be included in logical combinations, you can change the callback specification and invalidate all existing callbacks for use with the new code, or you can define multiple categories of logic callbacks, each with a different set of parameters. None of these alternatives is terribly satisfying, and yet they're decisions that have to be made all the time.

In Python, however, the dictionary structure provides you with a convenient way to circumvent this problem. If you define a dictionary parameter that passes named values for use in logic combinations, unused parameters are simply ignored. Thus, older callbacks can still be used with newer code that defines more search parameters, without any changes to code you've already got being necessary. In the updated search code found in the next Try It Out, the callback function is defined to be a function that takes a dictionary and returns a flag — a true filter function. You can see how it's used in the example section and in the next chapter, in test case 5 in the search test suite.

Adding a logical combination callback also makes it simple to work with numerical parameters such as the file size or the modification date. It's unlikely that a caller will search on the exact size of a file; instead, one usually searches for files larger or smaller than a given value, or in a given size range — in other words, most searches on numerical values are already logical combinations. Therefore, the logical combination callback should also get the size and dates for the file, so that a filter function can already be written to search on them. Fortunately, this is simple — the results of `os.stat` are already available to copy into the dictionary.

Extending the Search Framework

1. Again using your favorite text editor, open the file `find.py` from the last example and modify
    it so that it matches the following code:

```python
import os, os.path
import re
from stat import *

def find (where='.*', content=None, start='.', ext=None, logic=None):
    context = {}
    context['where'] = where
    context['content'] = content
    context['return'] = []
    context['ext'] = ext
    context['logic'] = logic

    for root, dirs, files in os.walk(start):
        find_file(context, root, files)

    return context['return']

def find_file (context, dir, files):
    for file in files:
        # Find out things about this file.
        path = os.path.join (dir, file)
        path = os.path.normcase (path)
        stat = os.stat(path)
        size = stat[ST_SIZE]
        try:
            ext = os.path.splitext (file)[1][1:]
        except:
            ext = ''

        # Don't treat directories like files
        if S_ISDIR(stat[ST_MODE]): continue

        # Do filtration based on passed logic
        if context['logic'] and not context['logic'](locals()): continue

        # Do filtration based on extension
        if context['ext'] and ext != context['ext']: continue

        # Do filtration based on the original parameters of find()
        if not re.search (context['where'], file): continue

        # Do content filtration last, to avoid it as much as possible
        if context['content']:
            f = open (path, 'r')
            match = 0
            for l in f.readlines():
                if re.search(context['content'], l):
                    match = 1
                    break
```

```
            f.close()
            if not match: continue

        # Build the return value for any files that passed the filtration tests.
        file_return = (path, file, ext, size)
        context['return'].append (file_return)
```

2. Now to find files larger than 1,000 bytes and older than yesterday:

```
>>> import find
>>> find.find(r"py$", content='find')
[('.\\find.py', 'find.py', 'py', 1297), ('.\\test_find.py',
'test_find.py', 'py', 1696)]
```

3. You can also run the `test_find.py` test suite from the command line:

```
C:\projects\python_book\ch11_regexp>python test_find.py
.....
---------------------------------------------------------------------
Ran 5 tests in 0.370s
```

During development, this run was not quite so smooth!

Formal Testing in the Software Life Cycle

The result of the test suite shown in the preceding example is clean and stable code in a somewhat involved programming example, and well-defined test cases that are documented as working correctly. This is a quick and easy process in the case of a software "product" that is some 30 lines long, although it can be astounding how many programming errors can be made in only 30 lines!

In a real-life software life cycle, of course, you will have thousands of lines of code. In projects of realistic magnitude like this, nobody can hope to define all possible test cases before releasing the code. It's true that formal testing during the development phase will dramatically improve both your code and your confidence in it, but there will still be errors in it when it goes out the door.

During the maintenance phase of the software life cycle, bug reports are filed after the target code is placed in production. If you're taking an integrated testing approach to your development process, you can see that it's logical to think of bug reports as highlighting *errors in your test cases* as well as errors in the code itself. Therefore, the first thing you should do with a bug report is to use it to modify an existing test case, or to define a new test case from scratch, and only then should you start to modify the target code itself.

By doing this, you accomplish several things. First, you're giving the reported bugs a formal definition. This enables you to agree with other people regarding what bugs are actually being fixed, and it enables further discussion to take place as to whether the bugs have really been understood correctly. Second, by defining test fixtures and test cases, you are ensuring that the bugs can be duplicated at will. As I'm sure you know if you've ever need to reproduce elusive bugs, this alone can save you a lot of lost sleep. Finally, the third result of this approach might be the most significant: If you never make a change to code that isn't covered by a test case, you will always know that later changes aren't going to break fixes already in place. The result is happier users and a more relaxed you. And you'll owe it all to unit testing.

Summary

Testing is a discipline best addressed at the very outset of the development life cycle. In general, you will know that you've got a firm grip on the problem you're solving when you understand it enough to write tests for it.

The most basic kind of test is an assertion. Assertions are conditions that you've placed inside of your program confirming that conditions that should exist do in fact exist. They are for use while you're developing a program to ensure that conditions you expect are met.

Assertions will be turned off if Python is run with the -o option. The -o indicates that you want Python to run in a higher performance mode, which would usually also be the normal way to run a program in production. This means that using assert is not something that you should rely on to catch errors in a running system.

PyUnit is the default way of doing comprehensive testing in Python, and it makes it very easy to manage the testing process. PyUnit is implemented in the unittest module.

When you use PyUnit to create your own tests, PyUnit provides you with functions and methods to test for specific conditions based on questions such as "is value A greater than value B," giving you a number of methods in the TestCase class that fail when the conditions reflected by their names fail. The names of these methods all begin with "fail" and can be used to set up most of the conditions for which you will ever need to test.

The TestCase class should be subclassed — it's the run method that is called on to run the tests, and this method needs to be customized to your tests. In addition, the test fixture, or the environment in which the tests should be run, can be set up before each test if the TestCase's setUp and tearDown methods are overridden, and code is specified for them.

You've seen two approaches to setting up a test framework for yourself. One subclasses a customized class, and another uses separate functions to implement the same features but without the need to subclass. You should use both and find out which ones work for your way of doing things. These tests do not have to live in the same file as your modules or programs; they should be kept separate so they don't bloat your code.

As you go through the remainder of this book, try to think about writing tests for the functions and classes that you see, and perhaps write tests as you go along. It's good exercise; better than having exercises here.

The key things to take away from this chapter are:

❑ Assertions are statements made within your code that allow you to test the validity of the code. If the test fails, an `AssertionError` is raised. You can use assert to create your tests.

❑ PyUnit is the name of the package as named by its authors, but the module you import is called the more generic-sounding name unittest.

❑ A test suite is a series of test cases run together for a particular project.

❑ In PyUnit, the environment in which a test case runs is called the test fixture, and the base `TestCase` class defines two methods: `setUp`, which is called before a test is run; and `tearDown`, which is called after the test case has completed. These are present to deal with anything involved in creating or cleaning up the test fixture.

In the following chapter, we will discuss GUI (graphical user interface) programming, and learn to make simple, interactive programs.

Writing a GUI with Python

Python plays a big role behind the scenes in some of the world's largest and most important server-side applications, but Python has also made a big impact on end-user applications. Writing a GUI is an expensive and painful project in C, C++, or even Java or C#, but it can be done quickly and easily in Python. Even if you only write simple Python scripts, being able to whip up a GUI can be a force multiplier that makes your script usable by less technical people, compounding its value. Python, being cross-platform and truly object oriented, has advantages that Visual Basic programmers would love to have in their rapid application development toolbox.

Python enables you to lay out GUIs one component at a time, like other programming languages. However, these days, no real programmer is writing GUI code by hand. If that's what you're used to, get ready to embrace all the rapid application development magic of Delphi with the power of a real language in Python. Of course, this kind of power is also available in other stacks, such as C#.

In this chapter you learn the basics of GUI programming in Python. A comprehensive guide to creating GUI applications would easily fill another book; what is contained herein merely scratches the surface. However, it should be enough to get you well on your way to writing elegant, interactive, and user-friendly applications.

In this chapter you learn to:

❏   Create widgets such as labels and command, radio, and checkbox buttons

❏   Lay out your graphical user interface

❏   Modify the look of your widgets and customize their appearance

❏   Create custom dialog boxes

❏   Understand packing order

❏   Insert functions in your widgets

GUI Programming Toolkits for Python

There is wide support for writing GUIs with Python with many different toolkits: You can find a dozen options at www.python.org/moin/GuiProgramming to try out. These toolkits, binary modules for Python that interface with native GUI code written in C/C++, all have different APIs and offer different feature sets. Only one comes with Python by default, the venerable TK GUI toolkit. It's always possible that if you're just using Windows, you'll install win32all and use the Win32 API directly. The truly brave will write their entire GUI in pyGame and add sound to every slider.

Other options are wxPython, PyQT, and pyGTK. These differ in many ways, but one important way is the license. The PyQT web page shows this problem of how it could restrict the decisions you can make if you are trying to create certain classes of applications or libraries. You can see this in the following paragraph:

> "PyQt is licensed under the GNU GPL (for UNIX/Linux and MacOS/X), under the QT Non-commercial License (for use with the QT v2.3.0 non-commercial version for Windows), under the QT Educational License (for use with the educational edition of QT for Windows), and under a commercial license (for Windows, UNIX/Linux and MacOS/X). . . ."

They go on to state:

> "When deploying commercial PyQt applications it is necessary to discourage users from accessing the underlying PyQt modules for themselves. A user that used the modules shipped with your application to develop new applications would themselves be considered a developer and would need their own commercial QT and PyQt licenses."

> "One solution to this problem is the VendorID package. This enables you to build Python extension modules that can only be imported by a digitally signed custom interpreter. The package enables you to create such an interpreter with your application embedded within it. The result is an interpreter that can only run your application, and PyQt modules that can only be imported by that interpreter. You can use the package to similarly restrict access to any extension module."

As you can see, unless there is a very good reason, you'll probably want to skip the whole QT toolset for this section of the license alone. No one in their right mind wants to deal with that kind of confusing licensing landscape. The QT people would claim that the advantages of their toolkit overwhelm the cost of licensing for the few people who use Windows. If you agree, tread warily into their licensing minefield. Most people simply discount it.

One open-source option is wxPython. WxPython is based on wxWidgets, a portable (Windows, Linux, Mac OS X) graphics toolkit with a long history and a tradition of looking and running just like native code. You can find the best information on wxPython on the really nice wiki at http://wiki .wxpython.org/index.cgi/FrontPage.

Beginners to GUI creation may feel overwhelmed by wxPython. Although there is good user support in mailing lists and professional organizations, the wxPython library is intimidating. Nevertheless, it's a good option for people willing to climb the learning curve. At the time of this writing, not all of these programs support 3.1, though most promise to.

With this in mind, for the rest of this chapter you will be working with Tkinter. Tkinter is Python's standard GUI package and comes installed with Python. It is perhaps the most used GUI Programming kit and is portable across virtually every platform. For more information on this venerable standby, feel free to visit http://tkinter.unpythonic.net/wiki/. You can also visit its home page at http://wiki.python.org/moin/TkInter.

Tkinter Introduction

GUIs are not as simple as they look. Once you've understood the basic concepts, however, you'll find them understandable, and proper program design will help you navigate around the major roadblocks.

Not all Tkinter applications have to be complex. Your application may be a simple dialog box that you've written to automate a business process you often do. The same things that made large applications like CANVAS, Dashboard, and PythonCAD quick and easy to write make simple applications nearly trivial. Tkinter itself has been used to make many popular programs, including most famously, IDLE itself.

Creating GUI Widgets with Tkinter

The first thing to understand is that most GUI frameworks, including Tkinter, are based on a *widget* model. A widget is a component of a GUI — buttons, labels, and text boxes are all widgets. Most widgets have graphical representations on screen, but some widgets, such as tables and boxes, exist only to contain other widgets and arrange them on the screen. A GUI is constructed out of an arrangement of widgets. In the following section, you create a simple GUI by defining some widgets and placing them inside each other.

Try It Out	Writing a Simple Tkinter Program

With Tkinter already in place, you're ready to write a real GUI application. This script, MyFirstGUI, creates a GUI of a simple window and a label. The label on the window displays a message:

```
import tkinter
from tkinter import *
widget = Label(None, text='This is my first Gui!!')      # create a label
widget.pack( )
widget.mainloop( )
```

Run this program and you'll see the "This is my first Gui!!" label in the window, as shown in Figure 13-1.

Figure 13-1

How It Works

The first thing to do is to import the Tkinter module. Next, you could either import Label from Tkinter, or simply import all (*) from Tkinter, as you did in the example. After that, you create an object for each widget (in this case, Label). The Label is then arranged in the parent window. Finally, the widget is displayed.

One problem with this script is that unlike most GUI applications, this one doesn't actually do anything. The reason for this is simple: The script as it is doesn't handle any GUI events. Don't worry; you fix this later in the chapter.

Resizing the Widget

You may or may not have noticed a few things about the window you created. For starters, it had a built-in minimize and maximize button, along with an "X" button to close the window. In addition, the user could stretch out the window. Go ahead and grab the right side of the window and pull it to the right a few inches. You will note that the label stays in the center near the top. This is a good thing.

Now, grab the bottom of the window and stretch it out. See the problem? No matter how far down you stretch the window, the label stays at the top. Ideally, when the user changes the size or shape of a window, you want the widget(s) inside to behave appropriately. With this in mind, modify your code so that the label centers when the window is resized:

```python
import tkinter
from tkinter import *
Label(text='My first GUI!').pack(expand=YES, fill=BOTH)
mainloop( )
```

When you run this program, try resizing the window; you'll see the "My first GUI!" label stay centered no matter what the window looks like, as shown in Figure 13-2.

Figure 13-2

In this example, you imported all from Tkinter once more, and then created a label with some text. Next, you assign the values Yes *to expand, and* Both *to fill. This tells Python to expand the widget when the parent window is expanded. By default, this option is turned off.*

Configuring Widget Options

You've seen one method to assign not only text to your label, but also how to configure some of the widget's options, such as expand and fill. Though the method you used was convenient in this instance, you may find yourself wanting to create your widgets first, and then configuring their options later on.

Try It Out   Configuring Your Widget

In this example you create the same parent window and the same label. However, instead of setting your options at the same time you create them, you are going to wait and do them after they have already been created:

```
import tkinter
from tkinter import *
root = Tk( )

widget = Label(root)
widget.config(text='My first GUI!')
widget.pack(side=TOP, expand=YES, fill=BOTH)
root.mainloop()
```

In this example, you called upon the configure method to achieve the same result as the previous example. If you wanted to, you could change the appearance of the widget later in the program. For instance, maybe the user wishes to change the way the window looks. You could insert a button that would trigger the configure method, which in turn would change your widget's options.

Putting the Widgets to Work

So far you've seen how to make a basic label, and how to format your widgets. But for a program to be successful, it not only has to look good; it has to actually do something. The next few examples not only teach you how to add more than one widget to your GUI, but teach you to apply actions to those widgets. Even more importantly, you learn to make the program respond to the user's actions.

You have learned how to create one type of widget so far — the label. In this example, you learn to create a button. Try typing the following code into a file called MyFirstButton.py:

```
import sys
from tkinter import *
widget = Button(None, text='Click Me', command=sys.exit)
widget.pack( )
widget.mainloop( )
```

This code is short and sweet and you may have noticed it looks very similar to the previous code. However, you will want to note that in addition to changing the widget type, you also added a new option, `command`. The value you added to command — `sys.exit` — tells Python to literally exit the system when the user clicks the button widget.

But what if you want to offer the user some option other than simply exiting the program? To do that, you have to add a second widget to your window. Create a new file and call it `MultipleWidget.py`:

```python
from tkinter import *

def result( ):
    print('The sum of 2+2 is ',2+2)

win = Frame()
win.pack( )
Label(win,  text='Click Add to get the sum or Quit to Exit').pack(side=TOP)
Button(win, text='Add', command=result).pack(side=LEFT)
Button(win, text='Quit',  command=win.quit).pack(side=RIGHT)

win.mainloop( )
```

This code introduces several new concepts we have yet to cover. First, you create a user-defined function, `result()`, and assign it the task of printing some text and returning the sum of 2+2. Next, you create three widgets. The first, a Label, holds some text, and has been giving the `side=TOP` option. Next, you create a button to call your user-defined function, which you place on the left side of the window. Lastly, you create a right-sided button and assign `win.quit` to `command`.

If the user clicks the Add button, it prints the text, "The sum of 2+2 is 4" to stdout. If the user clicks the Quit button, it closes the window.

One other thing to notice here is that for the first time we have introduced the use of the frame widget.

Creating Layouts

When creating a GUI, it is important to consider the hierarchy of your widgets. This hierarchy is commonly referred to as parent-child. In the preceding example, you created a number of widgets. The first widget is the top-level window, which acts as a parent. Next, you have a widget called win, which has a child of its own — a frame widget. The win widget, at this point, is a child of the top-level window.

Next, you have a label and two buttons, all of which are children of your frame widget. A frame widget is a widget whose purpose is to hold other widgets, and thus allow the programmer the flexibility to create a layout determining where on the window each widget should appear. As you get further into GUI programming, you will work with many different frame widgets, each occupying a specific spot on the top-level window, with each frame having its on set of widgets. These widgets that belong to each frame, being children of their respective frame, will be limited to the space provided them by their parent frame.

For example, if you have two frames of the same size, each taking up half of the window, and assign a button widget to each frame, the button assigned to the left frame will only be able to be placed within the left-hand side of the window. Likewise, the button assigned to the frame on the right side will be constrained to that section. If you were to pack the button in the left frame to the right, it would appear to the user to be in the center of the top-level window.

Packing Order

Another important aspect of layout is known as packing order. When you create each widget, and pack them, they are given all of the space for their region. For instance, if you pack a button on the LEFT, it will occupy all of the left-hand space. When you create a second widget and pack it to the left as well, the initial button is shrunk, but still holds the left-most space. This process continues, with each button shrinking to provide room for the other widgets. However, the buttons never move from their original space. The first button packed to the left will always be the left-most; likewise, the second button packed to the left will always be the second closest to the left.

Though this may sound confusing, simply rearranging your previous code should shed some light on the matter:

```
from tkinter import *

def result( ):
    print('The sum of 2+2 is ',2+2)

win = Frame()
win.pack( )
Button(win, text='Add', command=result).pack(side=LEFT)
Label(win,  text='Click Add to get the sum or Quit to Exit').pack(side=TOP)
Button(win, text='Quit',  command=win.quit).pack(side=RIGHT)

win.mainloop( )
```

Figure 13-3 shows how the program originally looked, before you modified your code.

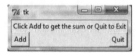

Figure 13-3

And Figure 13-4 is how it looks with the modified code.

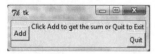

Figure 13-4

Controlling Widget Appearances

Form and function are key to creating a well-rounded GUI. Thus far, you have learned to add some code to your interfaces, and learned the basics of layout (there is much more to learn, but it is beyond the scope of this chapter). In this section, you take your program one step further and learn to control the actual appearance of your widgets.

Try It Out   Configuring Your Widget

Up to this point, you have used the default look for your widgets, which is pretty drab. To keep your user's attention and create programs that are visually appealing, you have to tweak the look of your widgets. Try out the following code:

```
import tkinter
from tkinter import *
root = Tk( )
labelfont = ('times', 24, 'italic')        # setting the family, size, and
                                             style
widget = Label(root, text='Eat At JOES')   # setting label text
widget.config(bg='black', fg='red')        # setting the back and foreground
                                             colors
widget.pack(expand=YES, fill=BOTH)
root.mainloop( )
```

Run this application and observe the result. Though the program does not actually do anything, the design does draw the eye's attention.

The following table is a list of the different ways that you can customize a widget:

Attribute	Description
Border, relief	Border sets the border width (for example: bd=1).
	Relief is used to determine the border style (for example: relief=raised).
Color	bg sets the background color, and fg sets the foreground. You can use simple color names or use hex form color codes.
Cursor	Sets the type of cursor that appears when the widget is hovered over. (for example: cursor=cross).
Font	Allows you to set the font family, size, and style (for example: Times, 24, italic bold underline).
Padding	Allows you to set extra space around a widget.
Pack expand and fill	As shown in previous examples.
State	Sets the state of the object (for example: state=DISABLED).
Size	Height and width settings control the size of the widget, allowing you to make it larger than the Tkinter Geometry Manager sets it to.

Radio Buttons and Checkboxes

So far you have worked with the following widgets: the top-level window, frames, labels, and buttons. These are all powerful widgets, but sometimes you may want to give your users more options. That is where radio buttons and checkboxes come into play.

Aside from appearance, radio buttons and checkboxes differ in one significant way: radio buttons offer users a list of options, but allow them to select only one; checkboxes offer users many options, and lets them choose as many as they want.

Creating Radio Buttons

Create a new file called MyRadio.py and include the following code in it:

```python
import tkinter
from tkinter import *
state = ''
buttons = []

def choose(i):
    global state
    state = i
    for btn in buttons:
        btn.deselect( )
    buttons[i].select( )

root = Tk( )
for i in range(4):
    radio = Radiobutton(root, text=str(i),
                            value=str(i), command=(lambda i=i: choose(i)) )
    radio.pack(side=BOTTOM)
    buttons.append(radio)
root.mainloop( )
print("You chose the following number: ",state)
```

This program creates a series of buttons ranging from 0–3 (four total), with the number 1, 2, and 3 highlighted by default. The user can then choose any of the buttons. Once a button is chosen, any other button's state becomes False, meaning that it is no longer selected. When the users close out of the program, they are given a statement showing which number they chose.

You can do something similar with checkboxes. In this instance however, you simply return whether the value of each checkbox is true or false:

```python
from tkinter import *
states = []
def check(i):
    states[i] = not states[i]

root = Tk( )
```

```
for i in range(4):
    test = Checkbutton(root, text=str(i), command=(lambda i=i: check(i)) )
    test.pack(side=TOP)
    states.append(0)
root.mainloop( )
print(states)
```

If you run this program and check off boxes 2 and 3, then close the window, your result should be:

```
>>>
[0, True, True, 0]
```

Dialog Boxes

Sometimes you want to give the user a piece of additional information. You are no doubt familiar with dialog boxes. They pop up anytime there is an error, or a program wants to confirm something, such as if you really want to uninstall a program, or if you want to display sensitive information.

Tkinter offers up two types of dialog boxes — modal and nonmodal. Modal dialog boxes wait for some action from the user before going away, and pause the progress of the program. Nonmodal dialog boxes do not interrupt the flow of the program.

Try It Out   **Creating a Custom Dialog Box**

You can use several methods to create dialog boxes. In this Try It Out, you create a custom dialog box using Toplevel. Create a new file called MyPopUp.py and enter in the following text:

```
import sys
from tkinter import *
popupper = (len(sys.argv) > 1)

def dialog( ):
    win = Toplevel( )
    Label(win,  text='Do You Always Do What You Are Told?').pack( )
    Button(win, text='Now click this one', command=win.destroy).pack( )
    if popupper:
        win.focus_set( )
        win.grab_set( )
        win.wait_window( )
    print('You better obey me...')

root = Tk( )
Button(root, text='Click Me', command=dialog).pack( )
root.mainloop( )
```

When you run this program, you first get a pop up, stating simply: "Click Me." When you do, two things occur; first, some text is written to stdout (specifically, "You better obey me . . ."). Second, another pop-up window appears, taking focus and asking for you to click it as well. When you do, it closes itself, and the original pop-up window takes back focus.

This is just the tip of the iceberg when it comes to creating dialog boxes. Aside from warnings, error messages, and confirmations, dialog boxes can also be used to load files (think about using the open command in most applications), pick a color from a color wheel, and much, much more.

Other Widget Types

This chapter has covered many of the widget types so far, but many are still left to explore. A full guide to these is beyond the scope of this chapter, and indeed, this book, but at the very least you should be aware of their existence. The following table lists the different widget classes available to you, and offers an explanation of each one.

Widget Class	Description
BitMapImage	A widget object that allows you to showcase bitmap images on top of other widgets.
Button	A "clickable" button.
Canvas	An object for displaying graphics, which can include circles, lines, images, text, and so forth.
Checkbutton	A button widget that has two states; True and False. It is used to offer users multiple choices.
Entry	A text entry field consisting of one line.
Frame	A container that holds other widgets.
Label	A widget where you can write text or a "label."
Listbox	A box that holds a selection of data.
Menu	A set of options.
Menubutton	A menu that shows another menu of options and submenus.
Message	Like a label, only for multiple lines.
PhotoImage	The same as BitMapImage, only for full color images.
Radiobutton	A button with a True/False state, used in multiple-choice situations.
Scale	A widget that slides up and down and allows the user to choose options in that manner.
Scrollbar	A widget that allows you to scroll other widgets.
Text	A browse/edit widget that works on multiple lines.
Toplevel, Tk	A new window.

Summary

There's no limit to the things you can do with your GUI using Tkinter. You can take screenshots, display graphics, handle complex information sets in large windows, draw on a blank canvas, or simply pop up quick GUIs for custom command-line utilities, exposing them to less technically oriented users.

There are, of course, personal styles to every programming project. Many people have developed tools that enable automated application development. Python's bevy of introspection and OO (object-oriented) features enables you to dynamically handle all sorts of changes in your GUI. As you become more familiar with Tkinter, you'll find these sorts of techniques to be extremely natural.

Even if you don't use Tkinter, understanding how Tkinter works will be a valuable asset in your programming toolbox. Furthermore, there's always the possibility that you have a spare 15 minutes and want to write a custom GUI chat client for your friends.

Exercises

1. Experiment with different layouts using different pack orders.
2. Practice modifying the look of your widgets by changing every property.

Accessing Databases

Just about every large enterprise system uses a database for storing data. For example, Amazon.com, the online retailer, needs a database to store information on each product for sale. For Python to prove capable of handling these types of enterprise applications, the language must be able to access databases.

Luckily, Python provides a database API (Application Programming Interface — how you program for the database), which is a generic API that enables you to access most databases, in spite of the databases' different native APIs. The database, or DB, API doesn't define all aspects of working with databases, so some minor differences exist. For the most part, though, you can access databases such as Oracle or MySQL from your Python scripts without worrying too much about the details of the specific databases.

Having a generic database API is very useful because you may need to switch databases or have your application work with multiple databases, and you won't want to recode major parts of your program to allow this. Normally, you can do all of this in Python without a lot of programming changes.

Even if you aren't writing the next amazon.com online site, databases provide a convenient means to persist data for longer than the program is running (so that you don't lose the data that a user has entered if you want to restart your program), query for items, and modify your data in a safe manner.

This chapter covers the two main database systems supported by Python: dbm persistent dictionaries and relational databases with the DB API. In addition, this chapter describes how to set up a database, in case you don't have one handy.

In this chapter you learn:

- ❏ Using the dbm libraries to create persistent dictionaries
- ❏ About relational databases

❑   Setting up the Sqlite database

❑   Setting up the MySQL database

❑   Working with the Python DB API

❑   Creating connections

❑   Accessing data with cursors

❑   Connecting to databases

❑   Querying and modifying data

❑   Working with transactions

❑   Handling errors

❑   Using other database tools

In many cases, you don't require a full-blown relational database. In such cases, creating a persistent dictionary using dbm files is enough.

Working with DBM Persistent Dictionaries

A persistent dictionary acts exactly like you'd expect. You can store name/value pairs in the dictionary, which are saved to a disk, and so their data will endure between various times that your program is run. So if you save data to a dictionary that's backed by a dbm, the next time you start your program you can read the value stored under a given key again, once you've loaded the dbm file. These dictionaries work like normal Python dictionaries, which are covered in Chapter 3. The main difference is that the data is written to and read from disk.

An additional difference is that the keys and the values must both be strings.

DBM, short for *database manager*, acts as a generic name for a number of C language libraries originally created on UNIX systems. These libraries sport names such as *dbm, gdbm, ndbm, sdbm,* and so on. These names correspond closely to the available modules in Python that provide the requisite functionality.

Choosing a DBM Module

Python supports a number of dbm modules. Each dbm module supports a similar interface and uses a particular C library to store the data to disk. The main difference lies in the underlying binary format of the data files on disk. Each dbm module, unfortunately, creates incompatible files. That is, if you create a dbm persistent dictionary with one dbm module, you must use the same module to read the data. None of the other modules will work with that data file.

The following table lists the dbm modules.

Module	Description
dbm	Chooses the best dbm module
dbm.dumb	Uses a simple, but portable, implementation of the dbm library
dbm.gnu	Uses the GNU dbm library

All of these libraries exist because of the history of the dbm library. Originally, this library was available only on commercial versions of UNIX. Free versions of UNIX, and later Linux, Windows, and so on, could not use the dbm library. This led to the creation of alternative libraries, such as the Berkeley UNIX library and the GNU gdbm library.

With all the incompatible file formats, this plethora of libraries can be a real pain. The dbm module, though, offers a handy alternative to choosing a specific dbm module. With the dbm module, you can let it choose for you. In general, the dbm module will choose the best implementation available on your system when creating a new persistent dictionary. When reading a file, the dbm module uses the function whichdb to make an informed guess as to which library created the data file.

Unless you need a specific advanced feature of one of the dbm libraries, use the dbm module.

Creating Persistent Dictionaries

All of the dbm modules support an open function to create a new dbm object. Once opened, you can store data in the dictionary, read data, close the dbm object (and the associated data file or files), remove items, and test for the existence of a key in the dictionary.

To open a dbm persistent dictionary, use the open function on the module you choose. For example, you can create a persistent dictionary with the dbm module.

Try It Out   Creating a Persistent Dictionary

Enter the following code and name your file dbmcreate.py:

```
import dbm

db = dbm.open('websites', 'c')

# Add an item.
db['www.python.org'] = 'Python home page'

print(db['www.python.org'])

# Close and save to disk.
db.close()
```

When you run this script, you'll see output like the following:

```
$ python dbmcreate.py
b 'Python home page'
```

How It Works

This example uses the recommended dbm module.

The `open` function requires the name of the dictionary to create. This name gets translated into the name of the data file or files that may already be on the disk. (The dbm module may — though not always — create more than one file, usually a file for the data and one for the index of the keys.) The name of the dictionary is treated as a base file name, including the path. Usually, the underlying dbm library will append a suffix such as `.dat` for data. You can find the file yourself by looking for the file named `websites`, most likely in your current working directory.

You should also pass the optional flag. The following table lists the available flags.

Flag	Usage
C	Opens the data file for reading and writing, creating the file if needed.
N	Opens the file for reading and writing, but always creates a new empty file. If one already exists, it will be overwritten and its contents lost.
W	Opens the file for reading and writing, but if the file doesn't exist it will not be created.

You can also pass another optional parameter, the mode. The mode holds a set of UNIX file permissions. See Chapter 8 for more on opening files.

> The `open` method of the dbm modules returns a new **dbm** object, which you can then use to store and retrieve data.
>
> After you open a persistent dictionary, you can write values as you normally would with Python dictionaries, as shown in the following example:
>
> ```
> db['www.python.org'] = 'Python home page'
> ```
>
> Both the key and the value must be strings and can't be other objects, like numbers or **python** objects. Remember, however, that if you want to save an object, you can serialize it using the `pickle` module, as you saw in Chapter 8.
>
> The `close` method closes the file or files and saves the data to disk.

Accessing Persistent Dictionaries

With the dbm modules, you can treat the object you get back from the open function as a dictionary object. Get and set values using code like the following:

```
db['key'] = 'value'
value = db['key']
```

Remember that the key and the value must both be text strings.

You can delete a value in the dictionary using del:

```
del db['key']
```

The keys method returns a list of all the keys, in the same way it would with a normal dictionary:

```
for key in db.keys():
    # do something...
```

The keys method may take a long time to execute if there are a huge number of keys in the file. In addition, this method may require a lot of memory to store the potentially large list that it would create with a large file.

You can use the following script as a guide for how to program with dbm persistent dictionaries.

Try It Out   Accessing Persistent Dictionaries

Enter the following script and name the file dbmaccess.py:

```
import dbm

# Open existing file.
db = dbm.open('websites', 'w')

# Add another item.
db['www.wrox.com'] = 'Wrox home page'

# Verify the previous item remains.
if db['www.python.org'] != None:
    print('Found www.python.org')
else:
    print('Error: Missing item')

# Iterate over the keys. May be slow.
# May use a lot of memory.
for key in db.keys():
    print("Key =",key," value =",db[key])

del db['www.wrox.com']
print("After deleting www.wrox.com, we have:")

for key in db.keys():
```

```
    print("Key =",key," value =",db[key])

# Close and save to disk.
db.close()
```

When you run this script, you'll see output similar to the following:

```
$ python dbmaccess.py
Type of dbmfile = dbhash
Found www.python.org
Key = www.wrox.com   value = Wrox home page
Key = www.python.org   value = Python home page
After deleting www.wrox.com, we have:
Key = www.python.org   value = Python home page
```

How It Works

This script works with a small database of website URLs and descriptions. You need to first run the dbmcreate.py example, shown previously. That example creates the dbm file and stores data in the file. The dbmaccess.py script then opens the preexisting dbm file.

The dbmaccess.py script opens the persistent dictionary websites in read/write mode. The call to the open function will generate an error if the necessary data file or files do not exist on disk in the current directory.

From the previous example, dbmcreate.py, there should be one value in the dictionary, under the key www.python.org. This example adds the Wrox website, www.wrox.com, as another key.

The script verifies that the www.python.org key exists in the dictionary, using the following code:

```
if db['www.python.org'] != None:
    print('Found www.python.org')
else:
    print('Error: Missing item')
```

Next, the script prints out all of the keys and values in the dictionary:

```
for key in db.keys():
    print("Key =",key," value =",db[key])
```

Note that there should be only these two entries.

After printing out all of the entries, the script removes one using del:

```
del db['www.wrox.com']
```

The script then prints all of the keys and values again, which should result in just one entry, as shown in the output.

Finally, the close method closes the dictionary, which involves saving all the changes to disk, so the next time the file is opened it will be in the state you left it.

As you can see, the API for working with persistent dictionaries is incredibly simple because it works like files and like dictionaries, which you're already familiar with.

Deciding When to Use DBM and When to Use a Relational Database

The dbm modules work when your data needs can be stored as key/value pairs. You can store more complicated data within key/value pairs with some imagination — for instance, by creating formatted strings that use a comma or some other character to delimit items in the strings, both on the key and the value part of the dictionary. This can be useful, but it can also be very difficult to maintain, and it can restrict you because your data is stored in an inflexible manner. Another way that you can be limited is technical: Note that some dbm libraries limit the amount of space you can use for the values (sometimes to a maximum of 1024 bytes, which is very, very little).

You can use the following guidelines to help determine which of these two types of data storage is appropriate for your needs:

- ❏   If your data needs are simple, use a dbm persistent dictionary.

- ❏   If you plan to store only a small amount of data, use a dbm persistent dictionary.

- ❏   If you require support for *transactions*, use a relational database. (Transactions are when more than one thing happens at once — they let you keep your data from getting changed in one place but not in another; you get to define what happens concurrently with transactions.)

- ❏   If you require complex data structures or multiple tables of linked data, use a relational database.

- ❏   If you need to interface to an existing system, use that system, obviously. Chances are good this type of system will be a relational database.

Unlike the simple dbm modules, relational databases provide a far richer and more complex API.

On a side note, I should mention that there is a third type of database you can work with, though it is beyond the scope of this chapter. That third type is known as an ORM or object-relational database, and it allows for the conversion of data between type systems that are incompatible in relational databases.

Python has several options available if you wish to work with an ORM, such as SQL Object, SQLAlchemy, and even the Django ORM. For more information, visit the Python Wiki at `http://wiki .python.org/moin/HigherLevelDatabaseProgramming`.

Working with Relational Databases

Relational databases have been around for decades so they are a mature and well-known technology. People who work with relational databases know what they are supposed to do, and how they are supposed to work, so relational databases are the technology of choice for complex data storage.

In a relational database, data is stored in tables that can be viewed as two-dimensional data structures. The columns, or vertical part of the two-dimensional matrix, are all of the same type of data; like strings, numbers, dates, and so on. Each horizontal component of the table is made up of rows, also called records. Each row in turn is made up of columns. Typically, each record holds the information pertaining to one item, such as an audio CD, a person, a purchase order, an automobile, and so on.

For example, the following shows a simple employee table.

empid	firstname	lastname	department	manager	phone
105	Peter	Tosh	2	45	555-5555
201	Bob	Marley	1	36	555-5551

This table holds six columns:

- **empid:** Holds the employee ID number. Relational databases make extensive use of ID numbers where the database manages the assignment of unique numbers so that each row can be referenced with these numbers to make each row unique (even if they have identical data). We can then refer to each employee by the ID number. The ID alone provides enough information to look up the employee.

- **firstname:** Holds the person's first name.

- **lastname:** Holds the person's last name.

- **department:** Holds the ID of the department in which the employee works. This would likely be a numeric ID of the department, where departments are defined in a separate table that has a unique ID for each department.

- **manager:** Holds the employee ID of the manager of the given employee. This is sort of self-referential, because in this example, a manager is actually an employee.

- **phone:** Holds the office phone number.

In real life, a company would likely store a lot more information about an employee, such as a taxation authority identification number (Social Security number in the U.S.), home address, and more, but not anything that's really different in principle to what you've already seen.

In this example, the column empid, the employee ID, would be used as the *primary key*. A primary key is a unique index for a table, where each element has to be unique because the database will use that element as the key to the given row and as the way to refer to the data in that row, in a manner similar to dictionary keys and values in Python. So, each employee needs to have a unique ID number, and once you have an ID number, you can look up any employee. So, the empid will act as the key into this table's contents.

The department column holds an ID of a department — that is, an ID of a row in another table. This ID could be considered a *foreign key*, because the ID acts as a key into another table. (In databases, a foreign key has a much more strict definition, so it's okay to think of it this way.)

For example, the following table shows a possible layout for the department table.

department id	name	manager
1	Development	47
2	QA	32

In these examples, the employee Peter Tosh works for department 2, the QA, or Quality Assurance, department in a dynamic world-class high-quality software development firm. Bob Marley works for department 1, the Development department.

In a large enterprise, there may be hundreds of tables in the database, with thousands or even millions of records in some tables.

Writing SQL Statements

The Structured Query Language, or SQL, defines a standard language for querying and modifying databases.

> *You can pronounce SQL as "sequel" or "s-q-l."*

SQL supports the basic operations listed in the following table.

Operation	Usage
Select	Perform a query to search the database for specific data.
Update	Modify a row or rows, usually based on a certain condition.
Insert	Create new rows in the database.
Delete	Remove a row or rows from the database.

In general, these basic operations are called QUID, short for Query, Update, Insert, and Delete, or CRUD, short for Create, Read, Update, and Delete. SQL offers more than these basic operations, but for the most part, these are the majority of what you're going to use to write applications.

> *If you are not familiar with SQL, look at a SQL book or search on the Internet. You will find a huge amount of tutorial material. You can also look at the website for this book for more references to SQL resources.*

SQL is important because when you access databases with the Python DB API, you must first create SQL statements and then execute these statements by having the database evaluate them. You then retrieve the results and use them. Thus, you will find yourself in the awkward position of using one language, Python, to create commands in another language, SQL.

The basic SQL syntax for the CRUD operations follows:

```
SELECT columns FROM tables WHERE condition ORDER BY columns ascending_or_
descending

UPDATE table SET new values WHERE condition

INSERT INTO table (columns) VALUES (values)

DELETE FROM table WHERE condition
```

In addition to this basic look at the available syntax, many more parameters and specifiers for each operation are optional. You can still use them with Python's DB API if you're familiar with SQL.

To insert a new row in the employee table, using the previous employee example, you can use a SQL query like the following (even though it's adding data and not getting data, the convention is that all SQL commands or statements can also be called queries):

```
insert into employee (empid, firstname, lastname, manager, dept, phone)
    values (3, 'Bunny', 'Wailer', 2, 2, '555-5553')
```

In this example, the first tuple (it's useful to think of these in Python terms, even though SQL will give these different names) holds the names of the columns in the order you are using for inserting your data. The second tuple, after the keyword `values`, holds the data items in the same order. Notice how SQL uses single quotes to delimit strings, and no quotes around numbers. (The phone number is different — it's actually a string because it has to be able to contain non-numbers, like dashes, periods, and plus signs, depending on how the data is entered.)

With queries, you can use shortcuts such as * to say that you want an operation to be performed using all of the columns in a table. For example, to query all of the rows in the department table, showing all of the columns for each row, you can use a query like the following:

```
select * from department
```

Note that SQL is not case-sensitive for its keywords, such as SELECT *and* FROM. *But, some databases require table and column names to be all uppercase. It is common, therefore, to see people use* SELECT *and* FROM *and other operations in all capital letters to make them easily distinguished from other parts of the query.*

This SQL statement omits the names of the columns to read and any conditions that would otherwise narrow down the data that would be returned. Thus the query will return all of the columns (from the *) and all of the rows (because there is no `where` clause).

You can perform a *join* with the `select` command, to query data from more than one table, but present it all in a single response. It's called a join because the data from both tables will be returned as though it was queried from a single table. For example, to extract the department name with each employee, you could perform a query like the following (all of which would need to be in one string to be a single query):

```
select employee.firstname, employee.lastname, department.name
from employee, department
where employee.dept =  department.departmentid
order by lastname desc
```

In this example, the `select` statement requests two columns from the employee table (the `firstname` and the `lastname`, but these are specified as coming from `employee` by the convention of specifying the table name and the column name in the table) and one from the department table (`department.name`). The `order by` section of the statement tells the database to order the results by the value in the `lastname` column, in descending order.

To simplify these queries, you can use *aliases* for the table names, which make them easier to type and to read (but don't change the logic or the syntax of your queries). For example, to use the alias *e* with the employee table, you can start a query as follows:

```
select e.firstname, e.lastname
from employee e
...
```

In this case, you must place the alias, *e*, after the table name in the `from` clause. You can also use the following format with the optional keyword `as`, which could be easier for you to read:

```
select e.firstname, e.lastname
from employee as e
...
```

To modify (or *update*) a row, use a SQL statement like the following:

```
update employee set manager=55 where empid=3
```

This example modifies the employee with an ID of 3 by setting that employee's manager to the employee with an ID of 55. As with other queries, numbers don't need to have quotes around them; however, strings would need to be quoted with single quotes.

To delete a row, use a SQL statement like the following:

```
delete employee where empid=42
```

This example deletes the employee with an ID of 42 but doesn't affect anything else in the database.

Defining Tables

When you first set up a database, you need to define the tables and the relations between them. To do this, you use the part of the SQL called the DDL, or Data Definition Language. (It defines the structure of your tables — get it?) DDL basics are pretty simple, where you use one operation to create tables, and another one to remove them:

```
CREATE TABLE tablename (column, type column type, ... )
DROP TABLE tablename
```

There is also an ALTER TABLE command to modify an existing table, but you won't need to do that for now. When you want to use this, a dedicated SQL book or web page will have more about this command.

Unfortunately, SQL is not an entirely standard language, and there are parts of it that each database handles differently. The DDL remains a part of SQL that has not been standardized. Thus, when defining tables you will find differences between the SQL dialects supported by the different databases, though the basics concepts are the same.

Setting Up a Database

In most cases when you're the programmer, you will already have a database that's up and running, perhaps even a database chosen by some other organization that you're going to have to use. For example, if you host your website with a website hosting company that provides bells and whistles, like a database, your hosting package may include access to the MySQL database. If you work for a large organization, your IT department may have already standardized on a particular database such as Oracle, DB/2, Sybase, or Informix. These latter packages are likely present in your workplace if you create enterprise applications with Python.

If you have no database at all, yet still want to work on the examples in this chapter, a good starting database is Sqlite. The main virtues of Sqlite are that it comes installed with Python, and it is simple and small, but functional. This makes it a great candidate for experimentation while you're learning, even if you have another database available to you. Just keep in mind that each database has its own quirks.

> *The examples in this chapter were written to work with Sqlite so that you can follow them without any external infrastructure being needed. You can easily modify these examples, though, to work with a different database. That's one of the great aspects of the Python DB API.*

Using Sqlite is as simple as importing the module. The following example shows you all you need to create a database.

If you are working with another database, such as SQL Server, chances are good that a database has already been created. If not, follow the instructions from your database vendor. (A lot of the time, you can get help on tasks like this from your Database Administrator, or DBA, who would really rather have you working on a test database instead of on a production database.)

With Sqlite, creating a database is rather easy.

Try It Out   Creating an Sqlite3 Database

Enter the following script and name the file createdb.py:

```
import os
import sqlite3
conn=sqlite3.connect('sample_database')
cursor=conn.cursor()
# Create tables.
cursor.execute("""
create table employee
```

```
        (empid integer,
        firstname varchar,
        lastname varchar,
        dept integer,
        manager integer,
        phone varchar)
        """)
    cursor.execute("""
    create table department
        (departmentid integer,
        name varchar,
        manager integer)
        """)
    cursor.execute("""
    create table user
        (userid integer,
        username varchar,
        employeeid integer)
        """)
    # Create indices.
    cursor.execute("""create index userid on user (userid)""")
    cursor.execute("""create index empid on employee (empid)""")
    cursor.execute("""create index deptid on department (departmentid)""")
    cursor.execute("""create index deptfk on employee (dept)""")
    cursor.execute("""create index mgr on employee (manager)""")
    cursor.execute("""create index emplid on user (employeeid)""")
    cursor.execute("""create index deptmgr on department (manager)""")
    conn.commit()
    cursor.close()
    conn.close()
```

When you run this script, you should see no output unless the script raised an error.

How It Works

Sqlite has its own API along with the standard Python DB API. This script uses the Sqlite API, but you'll notice that this API is very similar to the DB API covered in the following section, "Using the Python Database APIs." This section briefly describes the Sqlite specific code in the creatdb.py script.

Following is the code used to create a Connection object using the Sqlite module:

```
conn=sqlite3.connect('sample_database')
```

From there, the script gets a Cursor object, covered in the section "Working with Cursors." The Cursor object is used to create three tables and define indexes on these tables.

The script calls the commit method on the connection to save all the changes to disk.

Sqlite stores all of its data in the file sample_database. After running the createdb.py script, you should see the file in your Python30 directory.

You are now ready to start working with the Python database APIs.

Using the Python Database APIs

First, some history about Python and relational databases. Python's support for relational databases started out with ad hoc solutions, with one solution written to interface with each particular database, such as Oracle. Each database module created its own API, which was highly specific to that database because each database vendor evolved its own API based on its own needs. This is hard to support, because coding for one database and trying to move it to the other gives a programmer severe heartburn, as everything needs to be completely rewritten and retested.

Over the years, though, Python has matured to support a common database, or DB, API, that's called the DB API. Specific modules enable your Python scripts to communicate with different databases, such as DB/2, PostgreSQL, and so on. All of these modules, however, support the common API, making your job a lot easier when you write scripts to access databases. This section covers this common DB API.

The DB API provides a minimal standard for working with databases, using Python structures and syntax wherever possible. This API includes the following:

- ❑ Connections, which cover guidelines for how to connect to databases
- ❑ Executing statements and stored procedures to query, update, insert, and delete data with cursors
- ❑ Transactions, with support for committing or rolling back a transaction
- ❑ Examining metadata on the database module as well as on database and table structure
- ❑ Defining the types of errors

The following sections take you step by step through the Python database APIs.

Downloading Modules

You must download a separate DB API module for each database you need to access. For example, if you need to access an Oracle database as well as a MySQL database, you must download both the Oracle and the MySQL database modules.

> *See* `http://wiki.python.org/moin/DatabaseInterfaces` *for a listing of databases.*

Modules exist for most major databases with the notable exception of Microsoft's SQL Server. You can access SQL Server using an ODBC module, though. In fact, the mxODBC module can communicate with most databases using ODBC on Windows or an ODBC bridge on UNIX (including Mac OS X) or Linux. If you need to do this, you can search for more information on these terms online to find out how other people are doing it.

Download the modules you need. Follow the instructions that come with the modules to install them.

> *You may need a C compiler and build environment to install some of the database modules. If you do, this will be described in the module's own documentation, which you'll need to read.*

For some databases, such as Oracle, you can choose among a number of slightly different modules. You should choose the module that seems to best fit your needs or go to the website for this book and ask the authors for any recommendations if you're not sure.

Once you have verified that the necessary modules are installed, you can start working with Connections.

Creating Connections

A `Connection` object provides the means to communicate from your script to a database program. Note the major assumption here that the database is running in a separate process (or processes). The Python database modules connect to the database. They do not include the database application itself.

Each database module needs to provide a connect function that returns a `connection` object. The parameters that are passed to connect vary by the module and what is required to communicate with the database. The following table lists the most common parameters.

Parameter	Usage
Dsn	Data source name, from ODBC terminology. This usually includes the name of your database and the server where it's running.
Host	Host, or network system name, on which the database runs.
Database	Name of the database.
User	User name for connecting to the database.
Password	Password for the given user name.

For example, you can use the following code as a guide:

```
conn = dbmodule.connect(dsn='localhost:MYDB',user='tiger',password='scott')
```

Use your database module documentation to determine which parameters are needed.

With a `Connection` object, you can work with transactions, covered later in this chapter; close the connection to free system resources, especially on the database; and get a cursor.

Working with Cursors

A `cursor` is a Python object that enables you to work with the database. In database terms, the *cursor* is positioned at a particular location within a table or tables in the database, sort of like the cursor on your screen when you're editing a document, which is positioned at a pixel location.

To get a cursor, you need to call the `cursor` method on the `connection` object:

```
cursor = conn.cursor()
```

Once you have a cursor, you can perform operations on the database, such as inserting records.

Inserting Records

Enter the following script and name the file `insertdata.py`:

```
import os
import sqlite3

conn=sqlite3.connect('sample_database')
cursor = conn.cursor()

# Create employees.
cursor.execute("""
insert into employee (empid,firstname,lastname,manager,dept,phone)
values (1,'Eric','Foster-Johnson',1,1,'555-5555')""")

cursor.execute("""
insert into employee (empid,firstname,lastname,manager,dept,phone)
values (2,'Peter','Tosh',2,3,'555-5554')""")

cursor.execute("""
insert into employee (empid,firstname,lastname,manager,dept,phone)
values (3,'Bunny','Wailer',2,2,'555-5553')""")

# Create departments.
cursor.execute("""
insert into department (departmentid,name,manager)
values (1,'development',1)""")

cursor.execute("""
insert into department (departmentid,name,manager)
values (2,'qa',2)""")

cursor.execute("""
insert into department (departmentid,name,manager)
values (3,'operations',2)""")

# Create users.
cursor.execute("""
insert into user (userid,username,employeeid)
values (1,'ericfj',1)""")

cursor.execute("""
insert into user (userid,username,employeeid)
values (2,'tosh',2)""")

cursor.execute("""
insert into user (userid,username,employeeid)
values (3,'bunny',3)""")

conn.commit()

cursor.close()

conn.close()
```

When you run this script, you will see no output unless the script raises an error.

How It Works

The first few lines of this script set up the database connection and create a cursor object:

```
import os
import sqlite3
conn=sqlite3.connect('sample_database')
cursor = conn.cursor()
```

Note how we connect to an Sqlite database. To connect to a different database, replace this with your database-specific module, and modify the call to use the connect function from that database module, as needed.

The next several lines execute a number of SQL statements to insert rows into the three tables set up earlier: employee, department, and user. The execute method on the cursor object executes the SQL statement:

```
cursor.execute("""
insert into employee (empid,firstname,lastname,manager,dept,phone)
values (2,'Peter','Tosh',2,3,'555-5554')""")
```

This example uses a triple-quoted string to cross a number of lines as needed. You'll find that SQL commands, especially those embedded within Python scripts, are easier to understand if you can format the commands over a number of lines. This becomes more important with complex queries covered in examples later in this chapter.

To save your changes to the database, you must commit the transaction:

```
conn.commit()
```

Note that this method is called on the connection, not the cursor.

When you are done with the script, close the cursor and then the connection to free up resources. In short scripts like this, it may not seem important, but this helps the database program free its resources, as well as your Python script:

```
cursor.close()
```

```
conn.close()
```

You now have a very small amount of sample data to work with using other parts of the DB API, such as querying for data.

Try It Out   **Writing a Simple Query**

The following script implements a simple query that performs a join on the employee and department tables:

```
import os
import sqlite3
conn=sqlite3.connect('sample_database')
cursor = conn.cursor()
cursor.execute("""
select employee.firstname, employee.lastname, department.name
from employee, department
where employee.dept = department.departmentid
order by employee.lastname desc
""")
for row in cursor.fetchall():
    print(row)
cursor.close()
conn.close()
```

Save this script under the name `simplequery.py`. When you run this script, you will see output like the following:

```
('Bunny', 'Wailer', 'qa')
('Peter', 'Tosh', 'operations')
('Eric', 'Foster-Johnson', 'development')
```

How It Works

This script initializes the `connection` and `cursor` in the same manner as the previous script. This script, though, passes a simple join query to the `cursor execute` method. This query selects two columns from the employee table and one from the department table.

> *This is truly a simple query, but, even so, you'll want to format your queries so they are readable, similar to what is shown here.*

When working with user interfaces, you will often need to expand IDs stored in the database to human-readable values. In this case, for example, the query expands the department ID, querying for the department name. You simply cannot expect people to remember the meaning of strange numeric IDs.

The query also orders the results by the employees' last names, in descending order. (This means that it starts at the beginning of the alphabet, which is what you'd normally expect. However, you can reverse this and have them sorted in ascending order.)

After calling the `execute` method, the data, if any was found, is stored in the `cursor` object. You can use the `fetchall` method to extract the data.

> *You can also use the `fetchone` method to fetch one row at a time from the results.*

Note how the data appears as Python tuples:

```
('Bunny', 'Wailer', 'qa')
('Peter', 'Tosh', 'operations')
('Eric', 'Foster-Johnson', 'development')
```

You can use this example as a template to create other queries, such as the more complex join shown in the following Try It Out.

Try It Out   Writing a Complex Join

Enter this script and name the file finduser.py:

```
import sqlite3
conn=sqlite3.connect('sample_database')
cursor = conn.cursor()
username = 'bunny'
query = """
select u.username,e.firstname,e.lastname,m.firstname,m.lastname, d.name
from user u, employee e, employee m, department d where username=?
and u.employeeid = e.empid
and e.manager = m.empid
and e.dept = d.departmentid
"""
cursor.execute(query, (username,))
for row in cursor.fetchall():
    (username,firstname,lastname,mgr_firstname,mgr_lastname,dept) = row
    name=firstname + " " + lastname
    manager=mgr_firstname + " " + mgr_lastname
    print(username,":",name,"managed by",manager,"in",dept)
cursor.close()
conn.close()
```

When you run this script, you will see results like the following:

```
bunny : Bunny Wailer managed by Peter Tosh in qa
```

You need to pass the user name of a person to query from the database. This must be a valid user name of a person in the database. In this example, bunny is a user name previously inserted into the database.

How It Works

This script performs a join on all three example tables, using table-name aliases to create a shorter query. The purpose is to find a given user in the database by searching for that user name. This script also shows an example of expanding both the manager's ID to the manager's name and the department's ID to the department's name. All of this makes for more readable output.

This example also shows how you can extract data from each row into Python variables. For example:

```
(username,firstname,lastname,mgr_firstname,mgr_lastname,dept) = row
```

Note that this is really nothing new. See Chapter 3 for more on Python tuples, which is all `row` is.

An important new feature of this script, though, is the use of a question mark to enable you to build a query using dynamic data. When you call the `execute` method on the Cursor, you can pass a tuple of dynamic data, which the `execute` method will fill in for the question marks in the SQL statement. (This example uses a tuple of one element.) Each element in the tuple is used, in order, to replace the question marks. Thus, it is very important to have as many dynamic values as you do question marks in the SQL statement, as shown in the following example:

```
query = """
select u.username,e.firstname,e.lastname,m.firstname,m.lastname, d.name
from user u, employee e, employee m, department d where username=?
and u.employeeid = e.empid
and e.manager = m.empid
and e.dept = d.departmentid
"""

cursor.execute(query, (username,))
```

The query used in this example is very helpful when you want to start updating rows in the tables. That's because users will want to enter meaningful values. It is up to you, with your SQL statements, to translate the user input into the necessary IDs.

For example, the following script enables you to change the manager for an employee:

Personally, I'd like to make myself my own manager.

Try It Out   Updating an Employee's Manager

Enter the following script and name the file `updatemgr.py`:

```
import sqlite3
import sys
conn=sqlite3.connect('sample_database')
cursor = conn.cursor()
newmgr   = sys.argv[2]
employee = sys.argv[1]
# Query to find the employee ID.
query = """
select e.empid
from user u, employee e
where username=? and u.employeeid = e.empid
"""
cursor.execute(query, (newmgr,));
for row in cursor.fetchone():
    if (row != None):
        mgrid = row
# Note how we use the same query, but with a different name.
cursor.execute(query, (employee,));
for row in cursor.fetchone():
    if (row != None):
```

```
        empid = row
# Now, modify the employee.
cursor.execute("update employee set manager=? where empid=?", (mgrid,empid))
conn.commit()
cursor.close()
conn.close()
```

When you run this script, you need to pass the name of the user to update, as well as the name of the manager. Both names are user names from the user table. For example:

```
$ python finduser.py bunny
bunny : Bunny Wailer managed by Peter Tosh in qa
$ python updatemgr.py bunny ericfj
$ python finduser.py bunny
bunny : Bunny Wailer managed by Eric Foster-Johnson in qa
```

How It Works

The example output shows the before and after picture of the employee row, verifying that the updatemgr.py script worked.

The updatemgr.py script expects two values from the user: the user name of the employee to update and the user name of the new manager. Both of these names must be user names stored in the database. Both names are converted into IDs using a simple query. This is not very efficient, because it involves two extra round-trips to the database. A more efficient means would be to perform an inner select statement on the update statement. For simplicity, though, the separate queries are far easier to understand.

This example also shows the use of the fetchone method on the Cursor. The final SQL statement then updates the employee row for the given user to have a new manager.

The next example uses a similar technique to terminate an employee. You can really have fun with this one (terminate your friends, your enemies, and so on).

Try It Out   Removing Employees

Enter the following script and name the file terminate.py:

```
import sqlite3
import sys
conn=sqlite3.connect('sample_database')
cursor = conn.cursor()
employee=sys.argv[1]
# Query to find the employee ID.
query = """
select e.empid
from user u, employee e
where username=? and u.employeeid = e.empid
"""
```

```
cursor.execute(query,(employee,));
for row in cursor.fetchone():
    if (row != None):
        empid = row
# Now, modify the employee.
cursor.execute("delete from employee where empid=?", (empid,))
conn.commit()
cursor.close()
conn.close()
```

When you run this script, you need to pass the user name of the person to terminate. You should see no output unless the script raises an error:

```
$ python finduser.py bunny
bunny : Bunny Wailer managed by Eric Foster-Johnson in qa
$ python terminate.py bunny
$ python finduser.py bunny
```

How It Works

This script uses the same techniques as the updatemgr.py script by performing an initial query to get the employee ID for the given user name and then using this ID in a later SQL statement. With the final SQL statement, the script deletes the employee from the employee table.

Note that this script leaves the record in the user table. Question 3 of the exercises at the end of this chapter addresses this.

Working with Transactions and Committing the Results

Each connection, while it is engaged in an action, manages a *transaction*. With SQL, data is not modified unless you *commit* a transaction. The database then guarantees that it will perform all of the modifications in the transaction or none. Thus, you will not leave your database in an uncertain and potentially erroneous state.

To commit a transaction, call the commit method of a connection:

```
conn.commit()
```

Note that the transaction methods are part of the connection class, not the cursor class.

If something goes wrong, like an exception is thrown that you can handle, you should call the rollback method to undo the effects of the incomplete transaction; this will restore the database to the state it was in before you started the transaction, guaranteed:

```
conn.rollback()
```

The capability to roll back a transaction is very important, because you can handle errors by ensuring that the database does not get changed. In addition, rollbacks are very useful for testing. You can insert, modify, and delete a number of rows as part of a unit test and then roll back the transaction to undo the effects of all the changes. This enables your unit tests to run without making any permanent changes to the database. It also enables your unit tests to be run repeatedly, because each run resets the data.

See Chapter 12 for more on testing.

Examining Module Capabilities and Metadata

The DB API defines several globals that need to be defined at the module level. You can use these globals to determine information about the database module and the features it supports. The following table lists these globals.

Global	Holds
Apilevel	Should hold '2.0' for the DB API 2.0, or '1.0' for the 1.0 API.
Paramstyle	Defines how you can indicate the placeholders for dynamic data in your SQL statements. The values include the following: 'qmark' — Use question marks, as shown in the examples in this chapter. 'numeric' — Use a positional number style, with ':1', ':2', and so on. 'named' — Use a colon and a name for each parameter, such as :name. 'format' — Use the ANSI C sprintf format codes, such as %s for a string and %d for an integer. 'pyformat' — Use the Python extended format codes, such as %(name)s.

In addition, remember that pydoc is your friend. You can use pydoc to display information on modules, such as the database modules.

With a `cursor` object, you can check the definition attribute to see information about the data returned. This information should be a set of seven-element sequences, one for each column of result data. These sequences include the following items:

```
(name, type_code, display_size, internal_size, precision, scale, null_ok)
```

None can be used for all but the first two items, as shown in this example:

```
(('FIRSTNAME', None, None, None, None, None, None),
 ('LASTNAME', None, None, None, None, None, None),
 ('NAME', None, None, None, None, None, None))
```

Handling Errors

Errors happen. With databases, errors happen a lot. The DB API defines a number of errors that must exist in each database module. The following table lists these exceptions.

Exception	Usage
Warning	Used for non-fatal issues. Must subclass StandardError.
Error	Base class for errors. Must subclass StandardError.
InterfaceError	Used for errors in the database module, not the database itself. Must subclass Error.
DatabaseError	Used for errors in the database. Must subclass Error.
DataError	Subclass of DatabaseError that refers to errors in the data.
OperationalError	Subclass of DatabaseError that refers to errors such as the loss of a connection to the database. These errors are generally outside of the control of the Python scripter.
IntegrityError	Subclass of DatabaseError for situations that would damage the relational integrity, such as uniqueness constraints or foreign keys.
InternalError	Subclass of DatabaseError that refers to errors internal to the database module, such as a cursor no longer being active.
ProgrammingError	Subclass of DatabaseError that refers to errors such as a bad table name and other things that can safely be blamed on you.
NotSupportedError	Subclass of DatabaseError that refers to trying to call unsupported functionality.

Your Python scripts should handle these errors. You can get more information about them by reading the DB API specification. See `www.python.org/topics/database/` and `www.python.org/peps/pep-0249.html` for more information.

Summary

Databases provide a handy means for storing data. You can write Python scripts that can access all the popular databases using add-on modules. This chapter provided a whirlwind tour of SQL, the Structured Query Language, and covered Python's database APIs.

You also learned about the dbm modules that enable you to persist a dictionary using a variety of dbm libraries. These modules enable you to use dictionaries and transparently persist the data.

In addition, this chapter covered the Python database APIs, which define a standard set of methods and functions that you should expect from all database modules. This includes the following:

❑ A `connection` object encapsulates a connection to the database. Use the `connect` function on the database module to get a new connection. The parameters you pass to the `connect` function may differ for each module.

❑ A cursor provides the main object for interacting with a database. Use the `connection` object to get a cursor. The cursor enables you to execute SQL statements.

❑ You can pass dynamic data as a tuple of values to the cursor `execute` method. These values are placed into your SQL statements, enabling you to create reusable SQL statements.

❑ After performing a query operation, the `cursor` object holds the data. Use the `fetchone` or `fetchall` methods to extract the data.

❑ After modifying the database, call `commit` on the connection to commit the transaction and save the changes. Use the `rollback` method to undo the changes.

❑ Call `close` on each cursor when done. Call `close` on the connection when done.

❑ The DB APIs include a defined set of exceptions. Your Python scripts should check for these exceptions to handle the variety of problems that may arise.

Chapter 15 covers XML, HTML, and XSL style sheets, technologies frequently used for web development.

Exercises

1. Suppose you need to write a Python script to store the pizza preferences for the workers in your department. You need to store each person's name along with that person's favorite pizza toppings. Which technologies are most appropriate to implement this script?

   a. Set up a relational database such as MySQL or Sqlite.

   b. Use a dbm module such as dbm.

   c. Implement a web-service-backed rich web application to create a buzzword-compliant application.

2. Rewrite the following example query using table name aliases:

```
select employee.firstname, employee.lastname, department.name
from employee, department
where employee.dept = department.departmentid
order by employee.lastname desc
```

3. The `terminate.py` script, shown previously, removes an employee row from the employee table; but this script is not complete. There remains a row in the user table for the same person. Modify the `terminate.py` script to delete both the employee and the user table rows for that user.

Using Python for XML

XML has exploded in popularity over the past few years as a medium for storing and transmitting structured data. Python supports the wealth of standards that have sprung up around XML, either through standard libraries or a number of third-party libraries.

In this chapter you learn:

❑   Create and manipulate XML.

❑   Validate XML.

❑   Work with some of the standard libraries that come bundled with Python.

What Is XML?

The term XML is bandied around in corporate boardrooms and meetings around the world. Its flexibility and extensibility have encouraged people to think big, advocating XML for everything from a new, formatting-independent semantic code storage mechanism to a replacement for object serialization. But beyond the buzzwords and hype, what is it, really? Is it a panacea for the world's woes? Probably not. But it *is* a powerful, flexible, open-standards–based method of data storage. Its vocabulary is infinitely customizable to fit whatever kind of data you want to store. Its format makes it human readable, while remaining easy to parse for programs. It encourages semantic markup, rather than formatting-based markup, separating content and presentation from each other, so that a single piece of data can be repurposed many times and displayed in many ways.

A Hierarchical Markup Language

At the core of XML is a simple hierarchical markup language. Tags are used to mark off sections of content with different semantic meanings, and attributes are used to add metadata about the content.

Following is an example of a simple XML document that could be used to describe a library:

```
<?xml version="1.0"?>
<library>
  <book>
    <title>Sandman Volume 1: Preludes and Nocturnes</title>
    <author>Neil Gaiman</author>
  </book>
  <book>
    <title>Good Omens</title>
    <author>Neil Gamain</author>
    <author>Terry Pratchett</author>
  </book>
  <book>
    <title>"Repent, Harlequin!" Said the Tick-Tock Man</title>
    <author>Harlan Ellison</author>
  </book>
</library>
```

Notice that every piece of data is wrapped in a tag and that tags are nested in a hierarchy that contains further information about the data it wraps. Based on the previous document, you can surmise that `<author>` is a child piece of information for `<book>`, as is `<title>`, and that a library has an attribute called `owner`.

Unlike semantic markup languages like LaTeX, every piece of data in XML must be enclosed in tags. The top-level tag is known as the *document root*, which encloses everything in the document. An XML document can have only one document root.

Just before the document root is the XML declaration: `<?xml version="1.0"?>`. This mandatory element lets the processor know that this is an XML document. As of the writing of this book, there are two versions of XML—1.0 and 1.1. Because version 1.1 is not fully supported yet, for our examples we will be concentrating on version 1.0.

One problem with semantic markup is the possibility for confusion as data changes contexts. For instance, you might want to ship a list of book titles off to a database about authors. However, without a human to look at it, the database has no way of knowing that `<title>` means a book title, as opposed to an editor's business title or an author's honorific. This is where *namespaces* come in. A namespace is used to provide a frame of reference for tags and is given a unique ID in the form of a URL, plus a prefix to apply to tags from that namespace. For example, you might create a library namespace, with an identifier of `http://server.domain.tld/NameSpaces/Library` and with a prefix of `lib:` and use that to provide a frame of reference for the tags. With a namespace, the document would look like this:

```
<?xml version="1.0"?>
<lib:library
        xmlns:lib="http://server.domain.tld/NameSpaces/Library">
  <lib:book>
    <lib:title>Sandman Volume 1: Preludes and Nocturnes</lib:title>
    <lib:author>Neil Gaiman</lib:author>
  </lib:book>
  <lib:book>
    <lib:title>Good Omens</lib:title>
    <lib:author>Neil Gamain</lib:author>
```

```
        <lib:author>Terry Pratchett</lib:author>
    </lib:book>
    <lib:book>
        <lib:title>"Repent, Harlequin!" Said the Tick-Tock Man</lib:title>
        <lib:author>Harlan Ellison</lib:author>
    </lib:book>
</lib:library>
```

It's now explicit that the title element comes from a set of elements defined by a library namespace, and can be treated accordingly.

A namespace declaration can be added to any node in a document, and that namespace will be available to every descendant node of that node. In most documents, all namespace declarations are applied to the root element of the document, even if the namespace isn't used until deeper in the document. In this case, the namespace is applied to every tag in the document, so the namespace declaration must be on the root element.

A document can have and use multiple namespaces. For instance, the preceding example library might use one namespace for library information and a second one to add publisher information.

Notice the xmlns: prefix for the namespace declaration. Certain namespace prefixes are reserved for use by XML and its associated languages, such as xml:, xsl:, and xmlns:. A namespace declaration can be added to any node in a document, and that namespace will be available to every descendant node of that node.

This is a fairly simple document. A more complex document might contain CDATA sections for storing unprocessed data, comments, and processing instructions for storing information specific to a single XML processor. For more thorough coverage of the subject, you may want to visit http://w3cschools.org or pick up Wrox Press's *Beginning XML, 3rd Edition* (9780764570773) by David Hunter et al.

A Family of Standards

XML is more than just a way to store hierarchical data. If that were all there were to it, XML would quickly fall to more lightweight data storage methods that already exist. XML's big strength lies in its extensibility, and its companion standards, XSLT, XPath, Schema, and DTD languages, and a host of other standards for querying, linking, describing, displaying, and manipulating data. Schemas and DTDs provide a way for describing XML vocabularies and a way to validate documents. XSLT provides a powerful transformation engine to turn one XML vocabulary into another, or into HTML, plaintext, PDF, or a host of other formats. XPath is a query language for describing XML node sets. XSL-FO provides a way to create XML that describes the format and layout of a document for transformation to PDF or other visual formats.

Another good thing about XML is that most of the tools for working with XML are also written in XML, and can be manipulated using the same tools. XSLTs are written in XML, as are schemas. What this means in practical terms is that it's easy to use an XSLT to write another XSLT or a schema, or to validate XSLTs or schemas using schemas.

What Is a Schema/DTD?

Schemas and DTDs (Document Type Definitions) are both ways of implementing *document models*. A document model is a way of describing the vocabulary and structure of a document. It's somewhat akin to what a DBA does when creating a database. You define the data elements that will be present in your document, what relationship they have to one another, and how many of them you expect. In plain English, a document model for the previous XML example might read as follows: "A library is a collection of books with a single owner. Each book has a title and at least one author."

DTDs and schemas have different ways of expressing this document model, but they both describe the same basic formula for the document. Subtle differences exist between the two, as you see later, but they have roughly the same capabilities.

What Are Document Models For?

Document models are used when you want to be able to validate content against a standard before manipulating or processing it. They are useful whenever you will be interchanging data with an application that may change data models unexpectedly, or when you want to constrain what a user can enter, as in an XML-based documentation system where you will be working with hand-created XML rather than with something from an application.

Do You Need One?

In some applications, a document model might not be needed. If you control both ends of the data exchange and can predict what elements you are going to be receiving, a document model would be redundant.

Document Type Definitions

A *DTD* is a Document Type Definition. These were the original methods of expressing a document model and are ubiquitous throughout the Internet. DTDs were originally created for describing SGML, and the syntax has barely changed since that time, so DTDs have had quite a while to proliferate. The W3C (the World Wide Web Consortium, or one of the groups that brings standards to the Internet) continues to express document types using DTDs, so DTDs exist for each of the HTML standards, for Scalable Vector Graphics (SVG), MathML, and for many other useful XML vocabularies.

An Example DTD

If you were to translate the English description of the example library XML document into a DTD, it might look something like the following:

```
<?xml version="1.0"?>
<!ELEMENT library (book+)>
<!ATTLIST library
          owner CDATA #REQUIRED
>
<!ELEMENT book (title, author+)>
```

```
<!ELEMENT title (#PCDATA)>
<!ELEMENT author (#PCDATA)>
```

To add a reference to this DTD in the library file discussed before, you would insert a line at the top of the file after the XML declaration that read `<!DOCTYPE config SYSTEM "library.dtd">`, where `library.dtd` was the path to the DTD on your system.

Let's break this down, one step at a time. The first line, `<?xml version="1.0"?>`, tells you that this is going to be an XML document. Technically, this line is optional; DTDs don't behave like other XML documents, but we'll get to that later. The next line, `<!ELEMENT library (book+)>`, tells you that there is an element known as `library`, which can have one or more child elements of the `book` type. The syntax for element frequencies and grouping in DTDs is terse, but similar to that of regular expressions. The following table lists element frequency and element grouping operators in DTDs.

Operator	Definition
?	Specifies zero or one of the preceding elements. For instance, `editor?` would mean that a book could have an optional editor element.
+	Specifies one or more of the preceding elements. As in the previous example, `author+` means that a book has one or more authors.
,	Specifies a sequence of elements that must occur in that order. `(title, author+)` means that the book must have a title, followed by one or more authors, in that order.
(list)	Groups elements together. An operator applied after parentheses applies to all elements in the group. For instance, `(author, editor)+` would mean that a document could have one or more authors and one or more editors.
|	`Or` operator. This operator permits a choice between alternatives. As an example, `(author | editor)` would permit a book to have an author or an editor, but not both.
*	Specifies that zero or more of the preceding elements or group can appear. `(book, CD)*` would permit the library to have any number of books and CDs in it, or none at all.

The next bit is a little more complex:

```
<!ATTLIST library
        owner CDATA #REQUIRED
>
```

The first line specifies that the library element has a list of attributes. Notice that the attribute list is separate from the library element declaration itself and linked to it by the element name. If the element name changes, the attribute list must be updated to point to the new element name. Next is a list of attributes for the element. In this case, `library` has only one attribute, but the list can contain an unbounded number of attributes. The attribute declaration has three mandatory elements: an attribute name, an attribute type, and an attribute description. An attribute type can either be a data type, as specified by the DTD specification, or a list of allowed values. The attribute description is used to specify the behavior of the attribute. A default value can be described here, and whether the attribute is optional or required.

DTDs Aren't Exactly XML

As a holdover from SGML, DTDs are technically not exactly XML. Unlike schemas, they are difficult to manipulate and validate using the same tools as XML. If you apply a document type declaration at the beginning of a DTD, your parser will either ignore it or, more likely, generate a syntax error. Although there is a specification for creating DTDs, there is no document model in the form of a DTD for validating the structure of a DTD. Tools exist for validating DTDs, but they are distinct from the tools used to validate XML. On the other hand, there is a document model in the form of a schema against which schemas can be validated using standard XML tools.

Limitations of DTDs

DTDs have a number of limitations. Although it is possible to express complex structures in DTDs, it becomes very difficult to maintain. DTDs have difficulty cleanly expressing numeric bounds on a document model. If you wanted to specify that a library could contain no more than 100 books, you could write `<!ELEMENT library (book, book, book, book etc etc)>`, but that quickly becomes an unreadable morass of code. DTDs also make it hard to permit a number of elements in any order. If you have three elements that you could receive in any order, you have to write `<!ELEMENT book ( ( (author, ((title, publisher) | (publisher, title))) | (title, ((author, publisher) | (publisher, author))) | (publisher, ((author, title) | (title, publisher))))>`, which is beginning to look more like LISP (which is a language with a lot of parentheses) than XML and is far more complicated than it really should be. Finally, DTDs don't permit you to specify a pattern for data, so you can't express constructs such as "A telephone number should be composed of digits, dashes, and plus signs." Thankfully, the W3C has published a specification for a slightly more sophisticated language for describing documents, known as Schema.

Schemas

Schema was designed to address some of the limitations of DTDs and provide a more sophisticated XML-based language for describing document models. It enables you to cleanly specify numeric models for content, describe character data patterns using regular expressions, and express content models such as sequences, choices, and unrestricted models.

An Example Schema

If you wanted to translate the hypothetical library model into a schema with the same information contained in the DTD, you would wind up with something like the following:

```
<?xml version="1.0"?>
<xs:schema xmlns:xs="http://www.w3.org/2001/XMLSchema">

<xs:element name="library">
  <xs:complexType>
```

```
    <xs:sequence>
      <xs:element name="book" maxOccurs="unbounded">
        <xs:complexType>
          <xs:sequence>
            <xs:element name="title" type="xs:string"/>
            <xs:element name="author" type="xs:string" maxOccurs="unbounded"/>
          </xs:sequence>
        </xs:complexType>
      </xs:element>
    </xs:sequence>
    <xs:attribute name="owner" type="xs:string" use="required"/>
  </xs:complexType>

</xs:element>
</xs:schema>
```

This expresses exactly the same data model as the DTD, but some differences are immediately apparent.

Schemas Are Pure XML

To begin with, this document's top-level node contains a namespace declaration, specifying that all tags starting with xs: belong to the namespace identified by the URI "http://www.w3.org/2001/XMLSchema". For practical purposes, this means that you now have a document model that you can validate your schema against, using the same tools you would use to validate any other XML document.

Schemas Are Hierarchical

Next, notice that the preceding document has a hierarchy very similar to the document it is describing. Rather than create individual elements and link them together using references, the document model mimics the structure of the document as closely as possible. You can also create global elements and then reference them in a structure, but you are not required to use references; they are optional. This creates a more intuitive structure for visualizing the form of possible documents that can be created from this model.

Other Advantages of Schemas

Finally, schemas support attributes such as maxOccurs, which will take either a numeric value from 1 to infinity or the value unbounded, which expresses that any number of that element or grouping may occur. Although this schema doesn't illustrate it, schemas can express that an element matches a specific regular expression, using the pattern attribute, and schemas can express more flexible content models by mixing the choice and sequence content models.

XPath

XPath is a language for describing locations and node sets within an XML document. Entire books have been written on it. However, the basics are fairly simple. An XPath expression contains a description of a pattern that a node must match. If the node matches, it is selected; otherwise, it is ignored. Patterns are composed of a series of *steps*, either relative to a context node or absolutely defined from the document root. An absolute path begins with a slash, a relative one does not, and each step is separated by a slash.

A step contains three parts: an *axis* that describes the direction to travel, a *node test* to select nodes along that axis, and optional *predicates*, which are Boolean (true or false) tests that a node must meet. An example step might be `ancestor-or-self::book[1]`, where `ancestor-or-self` is the axis to move along, `book` is the node test, and `[1]` is a predicate specifying to select the first node that meets all the other conditions. If the axis is omitted, it is assumed to refer to the child axis for the current node, so `library/book[1]/author[1]` would select the first author of the first book in the library.

A node test can be a function as well as a node name. For instance, `book/node()` will return all nodes below the selected book node, regardless of whether they are text or elements.

The following table describes a handful of shortcuts for axes.

Shortcut	Meaning
@	Specifies the attribute axis. This is an abbreviation for `attribute::`.
*	Specifies all children of the current node.
//	Specifies any descendant of the current node. This is an abbreviation for `descendant-or-self::*//`. If used at the beginning of an XPath, it matches elements anywhere in the document.

For more thorough coverage of the subject, you may want to visit `http://w3schools.org` or pick up a book on XPath.

HTML as a Subset of XML

XML bears a striking resemblance to HTML. This isn't entirely by accident. XML and HTML both sprang from SGML and share a number of syntactic features. Earlier versions of HTML aren't directly compatible with XML, because XML requires that every tag be closed, and certain HTML tags don't require a closing tag, such as `<br>` and `<img>`. However, the W3C has declared the XHTML schema in an attempt to bring the two standards in line with each other. XHTML can be manipulated using the same sets of tools as pure XML. However, Python also comes with specialized libraries designed specifically for dealing with HTML.

The HTML DTDs

The current version of HTML is 4.01, which includes 4.01 Transitional, 4.01 Strict, and 4.01 Frameset, specifically for dealing with frames.

HTMLParser

The `HTMLParser` class, unlike the `htmllib` class, is not based on an SGML parser and can be used for both XHTML and earlier versions of HTML.

Try It Out   Using HTMLParser

1. Create a sample HTML file named `headings.html` that contains at least one `h1` tag. Save the file in your Python30 directory with the name "headings.html."

2. Cut and paste the following code from the wrox.com website into a file:

```
from html.parser import HTMLParser
class HeadingParser(HTMLParser):
  inHeading = False
  def handle_starttag(self, tag, attrs):
    if tag == "h1":
      self.inHeading = True
      print("Found a Heading 1")
  def handle_data(self, data):
    if self.inHeading:
      print(data)
  def handle_endtag(self, tag):
    if tag =="h1":
      self.inHeading = False
hParser = HeadingParser()
file = open("headings.html", "r")
html = file.read()
file.close()
hParser.feed(html)
```

3. Run the code.

How It Works

The `HTMLParser` class defines methods, which are called when the parser finds certain types of content, such as a beginning tag, an end tag, or a processing instruction. By default, these methods do nothing. To parse an HTML document, a class that inherits from `HTMLparser` and implements the necessary methods must be created. After a `parse` class has been created and instantiated, the parser is fed data using the `feed` method. Data can be fed to it one line at a time or all at once.

This example class only handles tags of type `<h1>`. When an `HTMLParser` encounters a tag, the `handle_starttag` method is called, and the tag name and any attached attributes are passed to it.

This `handle_starttag` method determines whether the tag is an `<h1>`. If so, it prints a message saying it has encountered an `h1` and sets a flag indicating that it is currently in an `<h1>`.

If text data is found, the `handle_data` function is called, which determines whether it is in an `<h1>`, based on the flag. If the flag is `true`, the method prints the text data.

If a closing tag is encountered, the `handle_endtag` method is called, which determines whether the tag that was just closed was an `<h1>`. If so, it prints a message, and then sets the flag to `false`.

XML Libraries Available for Python

Python comes standard with a number of libraries designed to help you work with XML. You have your choice of several DOM (Document Object Model) implementations, an interface to the nonvalidating Expat XML parser, and several libraries for using SAX (the Simple API for XML).

The available DOM implementations are as follows:

❑   `xml.dom`: A fully compliant DOM processor

❑   `Xml.dom.minidom`: A lightweight and much faster but not fully compliant implementation of the DOM specification

What Is SAX?

When parsing XML, you have your choice of two different types of parsers: SAX and DOM. SAX stands for the Simple API for XML. Originally only implemented for Java, it was added to Python as of version 2.0. It is a stream-based, event-driven parser. The events are known as *document events*, and a document event might be the start of an element, the end of an element, encountering a text node, or encountering a comment. For example, the following simple document:

```
<?xml version="1.0"?>
<author>
  <name>Ursula K. LeGuin</name>
</author>
```

might fire the following events:

```
start document
start element: author
start element: name
characters:  Ursula K. LeGuin
end element: name
end element: author
end document
```

Whenever a document event occurs, the parser fires an event for the calling application to handle. More precisely, it fires an event for the calling application's `Content Handler` object to handle. `Content Handlers` are objects that implement a known interface specified by the SAX API from which the parser can call methods. In the preceding example, the parser would call the `startDocument` method of the content handler, followed by two calls to the `startElement` method, and so on.

Stream-based

When parsing a document with SAX, the document is read and parsed in the order in which it appears. The parser opens the file or other datasource (such as a URL) as a stream of data (which means that it doesn't have to have it all at once) and then fires events whenever an element is encountered.

Because the parser does not wait for the whole document to load before beginning parsing, SAX can parse documents very soon after it starts reading the document. However, because SAX does not read the whole document, it may process a partial document before discovering that the document is badly formed. SAX-based applications should implement error-checking for such conditions.

Event-driven

When working with SAX, document events are handled by event handlers, similar to a GUI. You declare callback functions for specific types of document events, which are then passed to the parser and called when a document event occurs that matches the callback function.

What Is DOM?

At the heart of DOM lies the `Document` object. This is a tree-based representation of the XML document. Tree-based models are a natural fit for XML's hierarchical structure, making this a very intuitive way of working with XML. Each element in the tree is called a `Node` object, and it may have attributes, child nodes, text, and so on, all of which are also objects stored in the tree. DOM objects have a number of methods for creating and adding nodes, for finding nodes of a specific type or name, and for reordering or deleting nodes.

In-memory Access

The major difference between SAX and DOM is the latter's ability to store the entire document in memory and manipulate and search it as a tree, rather than force you to parse the document repeatedly, or force you to build your own in-memory representation of the document. The document is parsed once, and then nodes can be added, removed, or changed in memory and then written back out to a file when the program is finished.

Why Use SAX or DOM

Although either SAX or DOM can do almost anything you might want to do with XML, you might want to use one over the other for a given task for several reasons. For instance, if you are working on an application in which you will be modifying an XML document repeatedly based on user input, you might want the convenient random access capabilities of DOM. On the other hand, if you're building an application that needs to process a stream of XML quickly with minimal overhead, SAX might be a better choice for you. Following are some of the advantages and disadvantages you might want to be aware of when architecting your application to use XML.

Capability Trade-Offs

DOM is architected with random access in mind. It provides a tree that can be manipulated at runtime and needs to be loaded into memory only once. SAX is stream-based so data comes in as a stream one character after the next, but the document isn't seen in its entirety before it starts getting processed; therefore, if you want to randomly access data, you have to either build a partial tree of the document in memory based on document events, or reparse the document every time you want a different piece of data.

Most people find the object-oriented behavior of DOM very intuitive and easy to learn. The event-driven model of SAX is more similar to functional programming and can be more challenging to get up to speed on.

Memory Considerations

If you are working in a memory-limited environment, DOM is probably not the right choice. Even on a fairly high-end system, constructing a DOM tree for a 2 or 3 MB XML document can bring the computer grinding to a halt while it processes. Because SAX treats the document as a stream, it never loads the whole document into memory, so it is preferable if you are memory constrained or working with very large documents.

Speed Considerations

Using DOM requires a great deal of up-front processing time while the document tree is being built, but once the tree is built DOM allows for much faster searching and manipulation of nodes because the entire document is in memory. SAX is somewhat fast for searching documents, but not as efficient for their manipulation. However, for document transformations, SAX is considered to be the parser of choice because the event-driven model is fast and very compatible with how XSLT works.

SAX and DOM Parsers Available for Python

The following Python SAX and DOM parsers are available: `xml.sax` and `xml.dom.minidom`. They each behave a bit differently, so here is an overview of each of them.

xml.sax

`xml.sax` is the built-in SAX package that comes with Python. It uses the Expat nonvalidating parser by default but can be passed a list of parser instances that can change this behavior.

xml.dom.minidom

`xml.dom.minidom` is a lightweight DOM implementation, designed to be simpler and smaller than a full DOM implementation.

Try It Out   **Working with XML Using DOM**

1.   If you haven't already, save the example XML file from the beginning of this chapter in a file called `library.xml`.

2.   Either type in or get the following code from this book's website, and save it to a file called `xml_minidom.py`:

```
from xml.dom.minidom import parse
import xml.dom.minidom
def printLibrary(library):
  books = myLibrary.getElementsByTagName("book")
  for book in books:
    print("*****Book*****")
    print("Title: %s" % book.getElementsByTagName("title")[0].childNodes[0].data)
    for author in book.getElementsByTagName("author"):
      print("Author: %s" % author.childNodes[0].data)
# open an XML file and parse it into a DOM
myDoc = parse('library.xml')
myLibrary = myDoc.getElementsByTagName("lib:library")[0]
#Get all the book elements in the library
books = myLibrary.getElementsByTagName("book")
#Print each book's title and author(s)
printLibrary(myLibrary)
#Insert a new book in the library
newBook = myDoc.createElement("book")
newBookTitle = myDoc.createElement("title")
titleText = myDoc.createTextNode("Beginning Python")
newBookTitle.appendChild(titleText)
newBook.appendChild(newBookTitle)
newBookAuthor = myDoc.createElement("author")
authorName = myDoc.createTextNode("Peter Norton, et al")
newBookAuthor.appendChild(authorName)
newBook.appendChild(newBookAuthor)
myLibrary.appendChild(newBook)
print("Added a new book!")
printLibrary(myLibrary)
#Remove a book from the library
#Find ellison book
for book in myLibrary.getElementsByTagName("book"):
  for author in book.getElementsByTagName("author"):
    if author.childNodes[0].data.find("Ellison") != -1:
      removedBook= myLibrary.removeChild(book)
      removedBook.unlink()
print("Removed a book.")
```

```
    printLibrary(myLibrary)
    #Write back to the library file
    lib = open("library.xml", 'w')
    lib.write(myDoc.toprettyxml(" "))
    lib.close()
```

3. Run the file with `python xml_minidom.py`.

How It Works

To create a DOM, the document needs to be parsed into a document tree. This is accomplished by calling the `parse` method from `xml.dom.minidom`. This method returns a `Document` object, which contains methods for querying for child nodes, getting all nodes in the document of a certain name, and creating new nodes, among other things. The `getElementsByTagName` method returns a list of `Node` objects whose names match the argument, which is used to extract the root node of the document, the `<library>` node. The print method uses `getElementsByTagName` again, and then for each book node, prints the title and author. Nodes with text that follows them are considered to have a single child node, and the text is stored in the `data` attribute of that node, so `book.getElementsByTagName("title")[0].childNodes[0].data` simply retrieves the text node below the `<title>` element and returns its data as a string.

Constructing a new node in DOM requires creating a new node as a piece of the `Document` object, adding all necessary attributes and child nodes, and then attaching it to the correct node in the document tree. The `createElement(tagName)` method of the `Document` object creates a new node with a tag name set to whatever argument has been passed in. Adding text nodes is accomplished almost the same way, with a call to `createTextNode(string)`. When all the nodes have been created, the structure is created by calling the `appendChild` method of the node to which the newly created node will be attached. Node also has a method called `insertBefore(newChild, refChild)` for inserting nodes in an arbitrary location in the list of child nodes, and `replaceChild(newChild, oldChild)` to replace one node with another.

Removing nodes requires first getting a reference to the node being removed and then a call to `removeChild(childNode)`. After the child has been removed, it's advisable to call `unlink()` on it to force garbage collection for that node and any children that may still be attached. This method is specific to the `minidom` implementation and is not available in `xml.dom`.

Finally, having made all these changes to the document, it would be useful to be able to write the DOM back to the file from which it came. A utility method is included with `xml.dom.minidom` called `toprettyxml`, which takes two optional arguments: an indentation string and a newline character. If not specified, these default to a tabulator and \n, respectively. This utility prints a DOM as nicely indented XML and is just the thing for printing back to the file.

Working with XML Using SAX

This example shows you how you can explore a document with SAX.

```python
#!/usr/bin/python
from xml.sax          import make_parser
from xml.sax.handler import ContentHandler
#begin bookHandler
class bookHandler(ContentHandler):
  inAuthor = False
  inTitle = False
  def startElement(self, name, attributes):
    if name == "book":
      print( "*****Book*****")
    if name == "title":
      self.inTitle = True
      print("Title: ",)
    if name == "author":
      self.inAuthor = True
      print("Author: ",)
  def endElement(self, name):
    if name == "title":
      self.inTitle = False
    if name == "author":
      self.inAuthor = False
  def characters(self, content):
    if self.inTitle or self.inAuthor:
      print(content)
#end bookHandler
parser  = make_parser()
parser.setContentHandler(bookHandler())
parser.parse("library.xml")
```

How It Works

The xml.sax parser uses Handler objects to deal with events that occur during the parsing of a document. A handler may be a ContentHandler, a DTDHandler, an EntityResolver for handling entity references, or an ErrorHandler. A SAX application must implement handler classes, which conform to these interfaces and then set the handlers for the parser.

The ContentHandler interface contains methods that are triggered by document events, such as the start and end of elements and character data. When parsing character data, the parser has the option of returning it in one large block or several smaller whitespace-separated blocks, so the characters method may be called repeatedly for a single block of text.

The make_parser method creates a new parser object and returns it. The parser object created will be of the first parser type the system finds. The make_parser method can also take an optional argument consisting of a list of parsers to use, which must all implement the make_parser method. If a list is supplied, those parsers will be tried before the default list of parsers.

Intro to XSLT

XSLT stands for Extensible Stylesheet Language Transformations. Used for transforming XML into output formats such as HTML, it is a procedural, template-driven language.

XSLT Is XML

Like a Schema, XSLT is defined in terms of XML, and it's being used to supplement the capabilities of XML. The XSLT namespace is "`http://www.w3.org/1999/XSL/Transform`", which specifies the structure and syntax of the language. XSLT can be validated, like all other XML.

Transformation and Formatting Language

XSLT is used to transform one XML syntax into another or into any other text-based format. It is often used to transform XML into HTML in preparation for web presentation or a custom document model into XSL-FO for conversion into PDF.

Functional, Template-Driven

XSLT is a functional language, much like LISP. The XSLT programmer declares a series of *templates*, which are functions triggered when a node in the document matches an XPath expression. The programmer cannot guarantee the order of execution, so each function must stand on its own and make no assumptions about the results of other functions.

Python doesn't directly supply a way to create an XSLT, unfortunately. To transform XML documents, an XSLT must be created, and then it can be applied via Python to the XML.

In addition, Python's core libraries don't supply a method for transforming XML via XSLT, but a couple of different options are available from other libraries. Fourthought, Inc., offers an XSLT engine as part of its freely available 4Suite package, which unfortunately, at the time of this writing, does not support Python 3.0. However, there are also Python bindings for the widely popular libxslt C library, in particular lxml.

What Is lxml?

The following examples use the latest version of lxml, which, as of this writing, is 2.2. If you don't have it installed, please download it from `http://pypi.python.org/pypi/lxml/`. You will need it to complete the exercises later in this chapter.

lxml is a unique Python binding that utilizes the speed and rich features of the libxml2 and libxslt libraries alongside a simplistic API that allows you to work with both HTML and XML. The package uses the ElementTree API with a few twists, trying to make coding with libxml2 less error prone.

Importing lxml is fairly simple:

```
>>>import lxml
>>>from lxml import etree
```

Element Classes

Elements are the primary container objects for the ElementTree API, providing the core of your XML tree functionality. They behave like lists, and in fact, are technically lists. They are capable of having attributes and containing text, which we discuss in a bit. Let's first learn to create an element class. Type in the following:

```
>>>author = etree.Element("Horror")
>>>print(author.tag)
Horror
```

In this example, we created a new element class called `author`, and then assigned it a tag name: Horror. We then used the `print()` function and printed out the name via the element classes *tag* property. Element classes follow your standard XML tree hierarchy, and therefore support both parent and child elements.

Let's say that we wanted author to be the root element. We gave author the element tag name of "horror," and now we would like to add a group of horror writers to the `author` element class. These new elements will now become children of our horror element.

Try It Out   Creating Children Classes

```
>>>author=etree.Element("Horror")
>>>writer1=etree.SubElement(author,  "NeilGaiman")
>>>writer2=etree.SubElement(author,  "StephenKing")
>>>writer3=etree.SubElement(author,  "CliveBarker")
>>>print(etree.tostring(author))
 b'<Horror><NeilGaiman/><StephenKing/><CliveBarker/></Horror>'
>>>writer=author[0]
 >>>print(writer.tag)
 NeilGaiman
>>>writer=author[1]
 >>>print(writer.tag)
 StephenKing
>>>for writer in author:
         print(writer.tag)


NeilGaiman
StephenKing
CliveBarker
```

How It Works

A SubElement operates in much the same way as you would expect; that is, it is literally a subelement of an element, or in simpler terms, a child of a parent. When we wrote `etree.SubElement(author, "NeilGaiman")` we were telling Python to create a new child, writer1, whose element tag would be `"NeilGaiman"`, and whose parent would be `"author"`. This worked the same way for writer2 and writer3, as we saw when we printed out the subelements in "author" using the `etree.tostring` method.

Earlier I stated that element classes were lists, and as such, list functions work on them. Our statement writer=author[0] assigned the value of our first subelement to the variable writer. Likewise, using the for writer in author code lets us step through every subelement in the author class and print out their name tags.

In the beginning of this chapter we discussed attributes, and as stated before, elements can contain attributes, which help further describe the element.

```
>>>author=etree.Element("author", audience="Adult")
>>>print(author.get("audience"))
Adult
>>>author.etree.Element("author", type="fiction", bestseller="Yes")
>>>print(author.get("type"))
Fiction
>>>print(author.get("bestseller"))
Yes
>>>print(author.get("audience"))
None
```

We can add attributes to elements using etree.Element, as shown in the preceding code. You can add one attribute, or a thousand attributes, but it is important to note that you must declare them all at the same time. Take our example. We started off by giving our author an attribute called "audience", and assigned that value the descriptor, "Adult". When we used author.get to retrieve the value in our audience attribute (and display it with the print function), our program worked as it should, and printed out the word: Adult. However, we then tried to assign two more attributes to author (namely, type and bestseller), and then tried to print out audience, we got the result: None. This is because every time we assign a new attribute to an element, it overwrites the existing attributes.

There is a way of getting around this problem. Just as we use the get() method to retrieve data from an element, we can use the set() method to set an attribute, or add attributes:

```
>>>author.etree.Element("author", type="fiction", bestseller="Yes")
>>>etree.tostring(author)
b'<author type="fiction" bestseller="Yes"/>'
>>>author.set("audience", "Adult")
>>> etree.tostring(author)
b'<author type="fiction" bestseller="Yes" audience="Adult"/>'
```

Adding Text to Elements

In addition to attributes, we can also add text to our elements. When dealing with XML documents that are primarily data-driven, the only place you can place text is within the element. To do so is quite simple. In our next sample, we create a tree resembling a basic HTML document:

```
>>>html=etree.Element("html")
>>>body=etree.SubElement(html, "body")
>>>h1=etree.SubElement(body, "h1")
```

```
>>>h1.text="Introduction"
>>>paragraph=etree.SubElement(body, "p")
>>>paragraph.text="Here is some text representing our paragraph"
>>>etree.tostring(html)
b'<html><body><h1>Introduction</h1>
<p>Here is some text</p></body></html>'
>>>etree.tostring(paragraph)
b'<p>Here is some text</p>'
```

The preceding example is an excellent way to showcase parent-child relationships. Even though etree.tostring prints the results out on a single line, perhaps it would be better to view it as an actual tree structure:

```
<html>
        <body>
                <h1>Introduction</h1>
                <p>Here is some text</p>
        </body>
</html>
```

As you can see, <html> is the parent, <body> is the child of <html>, and <h1> and <p> are both siblings, whose parent is <body>.

In this scenario, the text property allows us to display content that the user could view, while any attributes we added would provide data about the elements themselves.

One last thing about the preceding code. You will notice that we use etree.tostring not only to print out the entire contents of HTML, but we also used it to hone in on the contents of paragraph specifically. This is a great method to see what a given element contains, but there are times when we do not wish to see the tags. What if we wanted to just see the text of an element, if there was any? For that, we could do the following:

```
>>>etree.tostring(paragraph, method="text")
b'Here is some text'
```

Parsing with lxml

Parsing with lxml is pretty straightforward. There are three parser functions to choose from, each with its own benefits and pitfalls. Each supports the parsing of a particular type of object, such as files, strings, and URLs (both the HTTP and FTP variety), with the simplest being our string parser: fromstring().

Of all the parser functions lxml has to offer, fromstring() is the easiest to use:

```
>>>sentence="<info>Here is a sentence</info>"
>>>info=etree.fromstring(sentence)
>>>print(info.tag)
info
>>>print(info.text)
Here is a sentence
```

In this code, we begin by assigning our variable sentence with an open and closed <info> tag, with some text nested in-between. We then create another variable, info, and use the etree.fromstring() function to parse the data in the sentence.

Another method of parsing is to use the XML() function, which is similar to fromstring(), but differs by writing XML literals straight to the source, like so:

```
>>>info=etree.XML("<info>Here is a sentence</info>")
>>>print(info.tag)
info
>>>print(info.text)
Here is a sentence
>>>etree.tostring(info)
b'<info>Here is a sentence</info>'
```

Here, we've skipped the initial step of creating and assigning data to the sentence variable, and instead used the XML() function to assign the data straight to info, saving us a step. When we print the tag and text from info, we get the same result as before.

Parsing Files

So far you have learned to parse simple strings. To truly understand the power of lxml parsing however, you need to learn to work with files and file-like objects, including URLs, objects with a .read method, and file name strings.

Unlike our other two parser functions, the parse() function returns an ElementTree object, instead of an Element object. This allows us to parse entire documents, and not just simple XML fragments:

```
>>>import io
>>>newsentence=io.StringIO("<info>This is another sentence</info>")
>>>somesentence=etree.parse(newsentence)
>>>etree.tostring(somesentence)
b'<info>This is another sentence</info>'
```

If you want to access the value in somesentence with a print() function, you can do so in the following manner:

```
>>>printit=somesentence.getroot()
>>> print(printit.tag)
info
>>> print(printit.text)
This is another sentence
```

This only scrapes the surface of what you can achieve with lxml. A complete coverage of the subject would easily encompass two books, which, unfortunately, we do not have space for here. For more information, you can visit the documentation for the module here: http://codespeak.net/lxml/index.html.

Summary

The key things to take away from this chapter are:

❑ How to parse XML using both SAX and DOM

❑ How to validate XML using xmlproc

❑ How to parse HTML using HTMLParser

❑ How to work with lxml

In Chapter 16, you learn more about network programming and e-mail. Before proceeding, however, try the exercises that follow to test your understanding of the material covered in this chapter. You can find the solutions to these exercises in Appendix A.

Exercises

1. Given the following configuration file for a Python application, write some code to extract the configuration information using a DOM parser:

```xml
<?xml version="1.0"?>
<!DOCTYPE config SYSTEM "configfile.dtd">
<config>
  <utilitydirectory>/usr/bin</utilitydirectory>
  <utility>grep</utility>
  <mode>recursive</mode>
</config>
```

2. Given the following DTD, named `configfile.dtd`, write a Python script to validate the previous configuration file:

```
<!ELEMENT config  (utilitydirectory, utility, mode)>
<!ELEMENT utilitydirectory    (#PCDATA)*>
<!ELEMENT utility    (#PCDATA)*>
<!ELEMENT mode   (#PCDATA)*>
```

3. Use SAX to extract configuration information from the preceding `config` file instead of DOM.

Network Programming

For more than a decade at the time this book is being written, one of the main reasons driving the purchase of personal computers is the desire to get online: to connect in various ways to other computers throughout the world. Network connectivity — specifically, Internet connectivity — is the "killer app" for personal computing, the feature that got a computer-illiterate general population to start learning about and buying personal computers *en masse*.

Without networking, you can do amazing things with a computer, but your audience is limited to the people who can come over to look at your screen or who can read the printouts or load the CDs and DVDs you distribute. Connect the same computer to the Internet and you can communicate across town or across the world.

The Internet's architecture supports an unlimited number of applications, but it boasts two killer apps of its own — two applications that people get online just to use. One is, of course, the incredibly popular World Wide Web, which is covered in Chapter 20, "Web Applications and Web Services."

The Internet's other killer app is e-mail, which is covered in depth in this chapter.

In this chapter you learn:

- ❏ To use standard libraries to write applications that compose, send, and receive e-mail
- ❏ To create programs that send and receive data in custom formats.
- ❏ The basics of socket programming

Try It Out   Sending Some E-mail

Jamie Zawinski, one of the original Netscape programmers, has famously remarked, "Every program attempts to expand until it can read mail." This may be true (it certainly was of the Netscape browser even early on when he worked on it), but long before your program becomes a mail reader, you'll probably find that you need to make it *send* some mail. Mail readers are typically end-user applications, but nearly any kind of application can have a reason to send mail: monitoring software, automation scripts, web applications, even games. E-mail is the time-honored way of sending automatic notifications, and automatic notifications can happen in a wide variety of contexts.

Python provides a sophisticated set of classes for constructing e-mail messages, which are covered a bit later. Actually, an e-mail message is just a string in a predefined format. All you need to send an e-mail message is a string in that format, an address to send the mail to, and Python's `smtplib` module. Here's a very simple Python session that sends out a bare-bones e-mail message:

```
>>> fromAddress = 'sender@example.com'
>>> toAddress = 'me@my.domain'
>>> msg = "Subject: Hello\n\nThis is the body of the message."
>>> import smtplib
>>> server = smtplib.SMTP("localhost", 25)
>>> server.sendmail(fromAddress, toAddress, msg)
{}
```

`smtplib` *takes its name from SMTP, the Simple Mail Transport Protocol. That's the protocol, or standard, defined for sending Internet mail. As you see, Python comes packaged with modules that help you speak many Internet protocols, and the module is always named after the protocol:* `imaplib`, `poplib`, `httplib`, `ftplib`, *and so on.*

Put your own e-mail address in `me@mydomain`, and if you've got a mail server running on your machine, you should be able to send mail to yourself, as shown in Figure 16-1.

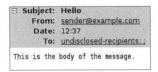

Figure 16-1

However, you probably don't have a mail server running on your machine. (You might have one if you're running these scripts on a shared computer, or if you set the mail server up yourself, in which case you probably already know a bit about networking and are impatiently waiting for the more advanced parts of this chapter.) If there's no mail server on the machine where you run this script, you'll get an exception when you try to instantiate the remote SMTP mail `server` object, something similar to this:

```
Traceback (most recent call last):
  File "<pyshell#9>", line 1, in <module>
    server=smtplib.SMTP("localhost",25)
  File "C:\Python31\lib\smtplib.py", line 239, in __init__
```

```
     (code, msg) = self.connect(host, port)
   File "C:\Python31\lib\smtplib.py", line 295, in connect
     self.sock = self._get_socket(host, port, self.timeout)
   File "C:\Python31\lib\smtplib.py", line 273, in _get_socket
     return socket.create_connection((host, port), timeout)
   File "C:\Python31\lib\socket.py", line 307, in create_connection
     raise error(msg)
socket.error: [Errno 10061] No connection could be made because the target
machine actively refused it)
```

What's going on here? Look at the line that caused the exception:

```
>>> server = smtplib.SMTP("localhost", 25)
```

The constructor for the `smtplib` class is trying to start up a network connection using IP, the Internet Protocol. The string `"localhost"` and the number 25 identify the Internet location of the putative mail server. Because you're not running a mail server, there's nothing at the other end of the connection, and when Python discovers this fact, it can't continue.

To understand the mystical meanings of `"localhost"` and 25, it helps to know a little about protocols, and the Internet Protocol in particular.

Understanding Protocols

A *protocol* is a convention for structuring the data sent between two or more parties on a network. It's analogous to the role of protocol or etiquette in relationships between humans. For instance, suppose that you wanted to go out with friends to dinner or get married to someone. Each culture has defined conventions describing the legal and socially condoned behavior in such situations. When you go out for dinner, there are conventions about how to behave in a restaurant, how to use the eating utensils, and how to pay. Marriages are carried out according to conventions regarding rituals and contracts, conventions that can be very elaborate.

These two activities are very different, but the same lower-level social protocols underlie both of them. These protocols set standards for things such as politeness and the use of a mutually understood language. On the lowest level, you may be vibrating your vocal cords in a certain pattern, but on a higher level you're finalizing your marriage by saying "I do." Violate a lower-level protocol (say, by acting rudely in the restaurant) and your chances of carrying out your high-level goal can be compromised. All of these aspects of protocols for human behavior have their correspondence in protocols for computer networking.

Comparing Protocols and Programming Languages

Thousands of network protocols for every imaginable purpose have been invented over the past few decades; it might be said that the history of networking is the history of protocol design. Why so many protocols? To answer this question, consider another analogy to the world of network protocols: Why so many programming languages? Network protocols have the same types of interrelation as programming languages, and people create new protocols for the same reasons they create programming languages.

Different programming languages have been designed for different purposes. It would be madness to write a word processor in the FORTRAN language, not because FORTRAN is objectively "bad," but because it was designed for mathematical and scientific research, not end-user GUI applications.

Similarly, different protocols are intended for different purposes. SMTP, the protocol you just got a brief look at, could be used for all sorts of things besides sending mail. No one does this because it makes more sense to use SMTP for the purpose for which it was designed, and use other protocols for other purposes.

A programming language may be created to compete with others in the same niche. The creators of a new language may see technical or aesthetic flaws in existing languages and want to make their own tasks easier. A language author may covet the riches and fame that come with being the creator of a popular language. A person may invent a new protocol because he's come up with a new type of application that requires one.

Some programming languages are designed specifically for teaching students how to program, or, at the other end of programming literacy, how to write compilers. Some languages are designed to explore new ideas, not for real use, and other languages are created as a competitive tool by one company for use against another company.

These factors also come into play in protocol design. Companies sometimes invent new, incompatible protocols to try to take business from a competitor. Some protocols are intended only for pedagogical purposes. For instance, this chapter, under the guise of teaching network programming, also teaches designing protocols for things like online chat rooms. Perfectly good protocols for this already exist, but they're too complex to be given a proper treatment in the available space.

The ADA programming language was defined by the U.S. Department of Defense to act as a common language across all military programming projects. The Internet Protocol was created to enable multiple previously incompatible networks to communicate with one another (hence the name "Internet").

Nowadays, even internal networks (intranets) usually run atop the Internet Protocol, but the old motives (the solving of new problems, competition, and so on) remain in play at higher and lower levels, which brings us to the most interesting reason for the proliferation of programming languages and protocols.

The Internet Protocol Stack

Different programming languages operate at different levels of abstraction. Python is a very high-level language capable of all kinds of tasks, but the Python interpreter itself isn't written in Python: It's written in C, a lower-level language. C, in turn, is compiled into a machine language specific to your computer architecture. Whenever you type a statement into a Python interpreter, there is a chain of abstraction reaching down to the machine code, and even lower to the operation of the digital circuits that actually drive the computer.

> There's a Python interpreter written in Java (Jython), but Java is written in C. PyPy is a project that aims to implement a Python interpreter in Python, but PyPy runs on top of the C or Java implementation. You can't escape C!

In one sense, when you type a statement into the Python interpreter, the computer simply "does what you told it to." In another, it runs the Python statement you typed. In a third sense, it runs a longer series of C statements, written by the authors of Python and merely activated by your Python statement. In a fourth sense, the computer runs a very long, nearly incomprehensible series of machine code statements. In a fifth, it doesn't "run" any program at all: You just cause a series of timed electrical impulses to be sent through the hardware. The reason we have high-level programming languages is because they're easier to use than the lower-level ones. That doesn't make lower-level languages superfluous, though.

English is a very high-level human language capable of all kinds of tasks, but one can't speak English just by "speaking English." To speak English, one must actually make some noises, but a speaker can't just "make some noises" either: We have to send electrical impulses from our brains that force air out of the lungs and constantly reposition the tongues and lips. It's a very complicated process, but we don't even think about the lower levels — only the words we're saying and the concepts we're trying to convey.

The soup of network protocols can be grouped into a similar hierarchical structure based on levels of abstraction, or *layers*. On the physical layer, the lowest level, it's all just electrical impulses and EM radiation. Just above the physical layer, every type of network hardware needs its own protocol, implemented in software (for instance, the Ethernet protocol for networks that run over LAN wires). The electromagnetic phenomena of the physical layer can now be seen as the sending and receiving of bits from one device to another. This is called the *data link layer*. As you go up the protocol stack, these raw bits take on meaning: They become routing instructions, commands, responses, images, web pages, and so on.

Because different pieces of hardware communicate in different ways, connecting (for example) an Ethernet network to a wireless network requires a protocol that works on a higher level than the data link layer. As mentioned earlier, the *common denominator* for most networks nowadays is the Internet Protocol (IP), which implements the network layer and connects all those networks together. IP works on the *network layer*.

Directly atop the network layer is the *transport layer*, which makes sure the information sent over IP gets to its destination reliably, in the right order, and without errors. IP doesn't care about reliability or error-checking: It just takes some data and a destination address, sends it across the network, and assumes it gets to that address intact.

TCP, the Transmission Control Protocol, does care about these things. TCP implements the transport layer of the protocol stack, making reliable, orderly communication possible between two points on the network. It's so common to stack TCP on top of IP that the two protocols are often treated as one and given a unified name, TCP/IP.

All of the network protocols you study and design in this chapter are based on top of TCP/IP. These protocols are at the *application layer* and are designed to solve specific user problems. Some of these protocols are known by name even to nonprogrammers: You may have heard of HTTP, FTP, BitTorrent, and so on.

When people think of designing protocols, they usually think of the application layer, the one best suited to Python implementations. The other current field of interest is at the other end in the data link layer: embedded systems programming for connecting new types of devices to the Internet. Thanks to the overwhelming popularity of the Internet, TCP/IP has more or less taken over the middle of the protocol stack.

A Little Bit About the Internet Protocol

Now that you understand where the Internet Protocol fits into the protocol stack your computer uses, there are only two things you really need to know about it: addresses and ports.

Internet Addresses

Each computer on the Internet (or on a private TCP/IP network) has one or more IP addresses, usually represented as a dotted series of four numbers, like "208.215.179.178." That same computer may also have one or more hostnames, which look like "wrox.com."

To connect to a service running on a computer, you need to know its IP address or one of its hostnames. (Hostnames are managed by DNS, a protocol that runs on top of TCP/IP and silently turns hostnames into IP addresses.) Recall the script at the beginning of this chapter that sent out mail. When it tried to connect to a mail server, it mentioned the seemingly magic string "localhost":

```
>>> server = smtplib.SMTP("localhost", 25)
```

"localhost" is a special hostname that always refers to the computer you're using when you mention it (each computer also has a special IP address that does the same thing: 127.0.0.1). The hostname is how you tell Python where on the Internet to find your mail server.

It's generally better to use hostnames instead of IP addresses, even though the former immediately gets turned into the latter. Hostnames tend to be more stable over time than IP addresses. Another example of the protocol stack in action: The DNS protocol serves to hide the low-level details of IP's addressing scheme.

Of course, if you don't run a mail server on your computer, "localhost" won't work. The organization that gives you Internet access should be letting you use its mail server, possibly located at mail.[your ISP].com or smtp.[your ISP].com. Whatever mail client you use, it probably has the hostname of a mail server somewhere in its configuration, so that you can use it to send out mail. Substitute that for "localhost" in the example code listed previously and you should be able to send mail from Python:

```
>>> fromAddress = 'sender@example.com'
>>> toAddress = '[your e-mail address]'
>>> msg = "Subject: Hello\n\nThis is the body of the message."
>>> import smtplib
>>> server = smtplib.SMTP("mail.[your ISP].com", 25)
>>> server.sendmail(fromAddress, toAddress, msg)
{}
```

Unfortunately, you still might not be able to send mail, for any number of reasons. Your SMTP server might demand authentication, which this sample session doesn't provide. It might not accept mail from the machine on which you're running your script (try the same machine you normally use to send mail). It might be running on a nonstandard port (see the following section). The server might not like the format of this bare-bones message, and expect something more like a "real" e-mail message; if so, the e-mail module described in the following section might help. If all else fails, ask your system administrator for help.

Internet Ports

The string "localhost" has been explained as a DNS hostname that masks an IP address. That leaves the mysterious number 25. What does it mean? Well, consider the fact that a single computer may host more than one service. A single machine with one IP address may have a web server, a mail server, a database server, and a dozen other servers. How should clients distinguish between an attempt to connect to the web server and an attempt to connect to the database server?

A computer that implements the Internet Protocol can expose up to 65,536 numbered *ports*. When you start an Internet server (say, a web server), the server process "binds" itself to one or more of the ports on your computer (say, port 80, the conventional port for a web server) and begins listening for outside connections to that port. If you've ever seen a website address that looked like "http://www.example .com:8000/", that number is the port number for the web server — in this case, a port number that violates convention. The enforcer of convention in this case is the Internet Assigned Numbers Authority.

> *The IANA list of protocols and conventional port numbers is published at* www.iana.org/ assignments/port-numbers.

According to the IANA, the conventional port number for SMTP is 25. That's why the constructor to the SMTP object in the above example received 25 as its second argument (if you don't specify a port number at all, the SMTP constructor will assume 25):

```
>>> server = smtplib.SMTP("localhost", 25)
```

The IANA divides the port numbers into "well-known ports" (ports from 0 to 1023), "registered ports" (from 1024 to 49151), and "dynamic ports" (from 49152 to 65535). On most operating systems, you must have administrator privileges to bind a server to a well-known port, because processes that bind to those ports are often themselves given administrator privileges. Anyone can bind servers to ports in the registered range, and that's what you'll do for the custom servers written in this chapter. The dynamic range is used by *clients*, not servers; we cover that later when talking about sockets.

Sending Internet E-mail

With a basic understanding of how TCP/IP works, the Python session from the beginning of this chapter should now make more sense:

```
>>> fromAddress = 'sender@example.com'
>>> toAddress = 'recipient@example.com'
>>> msg = "Subject: Hello\n\nThis is the body of the message."
>>> import smtplib
>>> server = smtplib.SMTP("localhost", 25)
>>> server.sendmail(fromAddress, toAddress, msg)
{}
```

If you don't have an SMTP server running on your machine, you should now be able to find out a hostname and port number that will work for you. The only aspect of the code I haven't explained is why the e-mail message looks the way it does.

The E-mail File Format

In addition to the large number of e-mail–related protocols that have been created, Internet engineers have designed a couple of file formats for packaging the parts of an e-mail message. Both of these protocols and file formats have been published in numbered documents called *RFCs*.

Throughout this chapter, until you start writing your own protocols, you'll be working with protocols and formats designed by others and specified in RFCs. These documents often contain formal language specifications and other not-quite-light reading, but for the most part they're pretty readable.

The current standard defining the format of e-mail messages is RFC 2822. Published in 2001, it updated the venerable RFC 822, which dates from 1982 (maybe RFC 2822 would have been published earlier if they hadn't had to wait for the numbers to match up). You may still see references to "RFC 822" as shorthand for "the format of e-mail messages," such as in Python's now deprecated rfc822 module.

> *To find a particular RFC, you can just search the web for "RFC x", or look on the official site at* www.ietf
> .org/rfc.html. *RFC 2822 is hosted at (among other places)* www.ietf.org/rfc/rfc2822.txt.

An e-mail message consists of a set of *headers* (metadata describing the message) and a *body* (the message itself). The headers are actually sent in a form like key-value pairs in which a colon and a space separate the key and the value (for instance, "Subject: Hello"). The body is just that: the text of the message.

You can create RFC 2822–compliant messages with Python using the Message class in Python's e-mail module. The Message object acts like a dictionary that maps message header names to their values. It also has a "payload," which is the body text:

```
>>>import os
>>>import sys
>>>import smtplib
>>>import mimetypes
>>>from optparse import OptionParser
>>>from e-mail import encoders
>>>from e-mail.message import Message
>>>message=Message()
>>>message['Subject']='Hello'
>>>message.set_payload('This is the body of the message')
>>>print(str(message))

Subject: Hello
This is the body of the message
```

That's more code than just specifying the e-mail string, but it's less error-prone, especially for a complex message. Also, you'll notice that you got back information that you didn't put into the message. This is because the smtplib adds some required headers onto your message when you send it.

RFC 2822 defines some standard message headers, described in the following table. It also defines data representation standards for some of the header values (for instance, it defines a way of representing e-mail addresses and dates). The standard also gives you space to define custom headers for use in your own programs that send and receive e-mail.

Header	Example	Purpose
To	To: Leonard Richardson <leonardr @example.com>	Addresses of people who should receive the message
From	From: Peter C. Norton <peter@example. com>	The e-mail address of the person who (allegedly) sent the message
Date	Date: Wed, 16 Mar 2009 14:36:07 - 0500 (EST)	The date the message was sent
Subject	Subject: Python book	A summary or title of the message, intended for human consumption
Cc	Cc: michael@example.com, Jason Diamond <jason@example.com>	Addresses of people who should receive the message, even though it's not addressed to them

Note a few restrictions on the content of the body. RFC 2822 requests that there be fewer than 1000 characters in each line of the body. A more onerous restriction is that your headers and body can only contain U.S. ASCII characters (that is, the first 127 characters of ASCII): no "international" or binary characters are allowed. By itself this doesn't make sense because you've probably already seen e-mail messages in other languages. How that happens is explained next.

MIME Messages

If RFC 2822 requires that your e-mail message contain only U.S. ASCII characters, how is it possible that people routinely send e-mail with graphics and other binary files attached? This is achieved with an extension to the RFC 2822 standard called MIME, the Multi-purpose Internet Mail Extension.

MIME is a series of standards designed around fitting non-U.S.-ASCII data into the 127 7-bit characters that make up U.S. ASCII. Thanks to MIME, you can attach binary files to e-mail messages, write messages and even headers (such as your name) using non-English characters, and have it all come out right on the other end (assuming the other end understands MIME, which almost everyone does nowadays).

The main MIME standard is RFC 1521, which describes how to fit binary data into the body of e-mail messages. RFC 1522 describes how to do the same thing for the headers of e-mail messages.

MIME Encodings: Quoted-printable and Base64

The most important parts of MIME are its encodings, which provide ways of encoding 8-bit characters into 7 bits. MIME defines two encodings: quoted-printable encoding and Base64 encoding. Python provides a module for moving strings into and out of each encoding,

The quoted-printable encoding is intended for text that contains only a few 8-bit characters, with the majority of characters being U.S. ASCII. The advantage of the quoted-printable encoding is that the text remains mostly legible once encoded, making it ideal for text written in or borrowing words from Western European languages (languages that can be represented in U.S. ASCII except for a few characters that use diacritical marks). Even if the recipient of your message can't decode the quoted-printable message, they should still be able to read it. They'll just see some odd-looking equal signs and hexadecimal numbers in the middle of words.

The Python module for encoding and decoding is quopri:

```
>>> import quopri

>>> encoded = quopri.encodestring(bytes("I will have just a
soupçon of soup.",'utf-8'))
>>> print(encoded)
I will have just a soup=E7on of soup.
>>> print(quopri.decodestring(encoded))
I will have just a soup\xe7on of soup.
```

Depending on your terminal settings, you might see the actual "ç" character in the last line, or you might see "\xe7." "\xe7" is the Python string representation of the "ç" character, just as "\E7" is the quoted-printable representation. In the session reproduced in the preceding code, that string was decoded into a Python string, and then re-encoded in a Python-specific form for display! (Note, the str object is wrapped in a bytes object because the encodestring method requires a string or buffer object. A str is really a list of characters, which is different from a list of bytes.)

The Base64 encoding, on the other hand, is intended for binary data. It should not be used for human-readable text, because it totally obscures the text:

```
>>> import base64

>>> encoded = base64.encodestring(bytes("I will have just a
soupçon of soup.",'utf-8'))
>>> print(encoded)
SSB3aWxsIGhhdmUganVzdCBhIHNvdXBvbiBvZiBzb3VwLg==
>>> print(base64.decodestring(encoded))
I will have just a soupçon of soup.
```

Why bother with Base64 when quoted-printable works on anything and doesn't mangle human-readable text? Apart from the fact that it would be kind of misleading to encode something as "quoted-printable" when it's not "printable" in the first place, Base64 encoding is much more efficient at representing binary data than quoted-printable encoding. Here's a comparison of the two encodings against a long string of random binary characters:

```
>>> import random
>>> import quopri
>>> import base64
>>> length = 10000
>>> randomBinary = ''.join([chr(random.randint(0,255)) for x in range(0,
length)])
>>> len(quopri.encodestring(bytes(randomBinary, 'utf-8'))) / float(length)
2.0663999999999998
>>> len(base64.encodestring(randomBinary)) / float(length)
1.3512
```

Those numbers will vary slightly across runs because the strings are randomly generated, but if you try this experiment you should get similar results to these every time. A binary string encoded as quoted-printable encoding is safe to send in an e-mail, but it's (on average) about twice as long as the original, unsendable string. The same binary string, encoded with Base64 encoding, is just as safe, but only about 1.35 times as long as the original. Using Base64 to encode mostly binary data saves space and bandwidth.

At the same time, it would be overkill to encode an ASCII string with Base64 just because it contains a few characters outside of the U.S. ASCII range. Here's the same comparison done with a long random string that's almost entirely composed of U.S. ASCII characters:

```
>>> import random
>>> import quopri
>>> import base64
>>> length = 10000
>>> randomBinary = ''.join([chr(random.randint(0,128)) for x in range(0,
length)])
>>> len(quopri.encodestring(bytes(randomBinary,'utf-8'))) / float(length)
1.0661
>>> len(base64.encodestring(bytes(randomBinary,'utf-8'))) / float(length)
1.3512
```

Here, the quoted-printable representation is barely larger than the original text (it's almost the same as the original text), but the Base64 representation is 1.35 times as long as the original, just as before. This demonstrates why MIME supports two different encodings: to quote RFC1521, "a 'readable' encoding [quoted-printable] and a 'dense' encoding [Base64]."

MIME is more "multi-purpose" than its name implies. Many features of MIME have been picked up for use outside of e-mail applications. The idea of using Base64 or quoted-printable to turn non-ASCII characters into ASCII shows up in other domains. Base64 encoding is also sometimes used to obscure text from human readability without actually encrypting it.

MIME Content Types

The other important part of MIME is its idea of a content type. Suppose you send your friend an e-mail message: "Here's that picture I took of you." and attach an image. Thanks to Base64 encoding, the recipient will get the encoded data as you sent it, but how is her mail reader supposed to know that it's an image and not some other form of binary data?

MIME solves this problem by defining a custom RFC 2822–format header called *Content-Type*. This header describes what kind of file the body is, so that the recipient's mail client can figure out how to display it. Content types include *text/plain* (what you'd get if you put a normal e-mail message into a MIME envelope), *text/html*, *image/jpeg*, *video/mpeg*, *audio/mp3*, and so on. Each content type has a "major type" and a "minor type," separated by a slash. The major types are very general and there are only seven of them, defined in the MIME standard itself. The minor types usually designate particular file formats.

The idea of a string having a "Content-Type," which tells the recipient what to do with it, is another invention of MIME used outside of the e-mail world. The most common use is in HTTP, the protocol used by the World Wide Web and covered in Chapter 20. Every HTTP response is supposed to have a "Content-Type" header (just like a MIME e-mail message), which tells the web browser how to display the response.

Creating a MIME Message with an Attachment

So far, so good. Python provides many submodules of the e-mail module for constructing MIME messages, including a module for each of the major content types. It's simple to use these to craft a MIME message containing an encoded image file.

```
import smtplib
from e-mail.mime.multipart import MIMEMultipart
from e-mail.mime.image import MIMEImage
msg=MIMEMultipart()
filename=('C:\Python30\photos.jpg')
msg['To']='jamesrobertpayne@yahoo.com'
msg['From']='james@developershed.com'
msg['Subject']='Some picture'
pic = open('C:\Python30\photos.jpg', 'rb')
img = MIMEImage(pic.read())
pic.close()
print(str(msg))
msg.attach(img)
sendit = smtplib.SMTP()
sendit.connect()
sendit.sendmail(me, family, msg.as_string())
sendit.close()
```

Of course, for `'photos.jpg'`, *you should substitute the file name of any other image file you have handy. Just put the file into the directory from which you invoke the Python session.*

Because you told the `MIMEImage` constructor that the picture was called `photo.jpg`, the mail client on the other end will be able to save it under that file name.

MIME Multipart Messages

There's just one problem. This isn't quite the e-mail message described earlier. That message was a short piece of text (`"Here's that picture I took of you."`) and an attached image. This message is just the image. There's no space for the text portion in the body of the message; putting it there would compromise the image file. The Content-Type header of a mail message can be `text/plain` or `image/jpeg`; it can't be both. So how do mail clients create messages with attachments?

In addition to classifying the file formats defined by other standards (for instance, *image* for image file formats), MIME defines a special major type called *multipart*. A message with a major content type of multipart can contain other MIME messages in its body, each with its own set of headers and its own content type.

The best way to see how this works is to create a multipart message using the `e-mail.mime.multipart` module, in conjunction with the `e-mail.mime*` modules for the files you want to attach. Here is a script called `FormatMimeMultipartMessage.py`, a slightly more complicated version of the previous example:

```
#!/usr/bin/python
from e-mail.mime.multipart import MIMEMultipart
import os
import sys
filename='C:\Python30\photos.jpg'
msg = MIMEMultipart()
msg['From'] = 'Me <me@example.com>'
msg['To'] = 'You <you@example.com>'
msg['Subject'] = 'Your picture'
from e-mail.mime.text import MIMEText
text = MIMEText("Here's that picture I took of you.")
msg.attach(text)
from e-mail.mime.image import MIMEImage
image = MIMEImage(open(filename, 'rb').read(), name=os.path.
split(filename)[1])
msg.attach(image)
```

Run this script, passing in the path to an image file, and you'll see a MIME multipart e-mail message that includes a brief text message and the image file, encoded in Base64:

```
# python FormatMimeMultipartMessage.py ./photo.jpg
From nobody Sun June 20 15:41:23 2009
Content-Type: multipart/mixed; boundary="===============1011273258=="
MIME-Version: 1.0
From: Me <me@example.com>
To: You <you@example.com>
Subject: Your picture


--===============1011273258==
Content-Type: text/plain; charset="us-ascii"
MIME-Version: 1.0
Content-Transfer-Encoding: 7bit

Here's that picture I took of you.
--===============1011273258==
Content-Type: image/jpeg; name="photo.jpg"
MIME-Version: 1.0
Content-Transfer-Encoding: base64

/4AAQSkZJRgABAQEASABIAAD//gAXQ3J1YXRlZCB3aXRoIFRoZSBHSU1Q//sAQwAIBgYHBgUI
...
[As before, much base64 encoded text omitted.]
...
3f7kklh4dg+UTZ1TsAAv1F69UklmZ9hrzogZibOqSSA8gZySSSJI/9k=
--===============1011273258==
```

When you send this message, it will show up at the other end looking more like you'd expect a message with an attachment to look. This is the kind of e-mail your e-mail client creates when you send a message with attachments.

Several features of this e-mail bear mentioning:

❏ The content type (`multipart/mixed`) isn't enough, by itself, to make sense of the message body. MIME also requires the definition of a "boundary," a string generated semi-randomly by Python and used in the body of the message to note where one part stops and another begins.

❏ The message as a whole has all the headers you associate with e-mail messages: `Subject`, `From`, `To`, and the MIME-specific `Content-Type` header. In addition to this, each part of the message has a separate set of headers. These are not message headers, although they're in the RFC 2822 header format; and some headers (MIME-Version and `Content-Type`) show up in both the message headers and the body. These are MIME message body headers, interpreted by the MIME parser. As far as RFC 2822 is concerned, they're part of the message body, just like the files they describe, the boundaries that separate MIME parts, and the text `"Here's that picture I took of you."`

❏ The MIME part containing the body of the message has an encoding of `7bit`. This just means that the part is not encoded at all. Every character in the part body was U.S. ASCII, so there was no need to encode it.

Python's mail classes are very useful once you know what kind of mail you want to construct: for text-only messages, use the simple `e-mail.message` class. To attach a file to a message, use one of the `e-mail.mime*` classes. To send multiple files, or a combination of text and files, use `e-mail.mime.multipart` in conjunction with the other `e-mail.mime*` classes.

A problem arises when you're not sure ahead of time which class to use to represent your e-mail message. Here's a class called `SmartMessage` for building e-mail messages that starts out keeping body text in a simple `Message` representation, but which will switch to `MimeMultipart` if you add an attachment. This strategy will generate the same range of e-mail message bodies as a typical end-user mail application: simple RFC 2822 bodies for simple messages, and complex MIME bodies for messages with attachments. Put this class in a file called `SendMail.py`:

```
from e-mail import encoders as Encoders
from e-mail.message import Message
from e-mail.mime.text import MIMEText
from e-mail.mime.multipart import MIMEMultipart
from e-mail.mime.nonmultipart import MIMENonMultipart
import mimetypes
class SmartMessage:
    """A simplified interface to Python's library for creating e-mail
    messages, with and without MIME attachments."""
    def __init__(self, fromAddr, toAddrs, subject, body):
        """Start off on the assumption that the message will be a simple RFC
        2822 message with no MIME."""
        self.msg = Message()
        self.msg.set_payload(body)
        self['Subject'] = subject
        self.setFrom(fromAddr)
        self.setTo(toAddrs)
        self.hasAttachments = False
```

```
def setFrom(self, fromAddr):
    "Sets the address of the sender of the message."
    if not fromAddr or not type(fromAddr)==type(''):
        raise Exception ('A message must have one and only one sender.')
    self['From'] = fromAddr
def setTo(self, to):
    "Sets the address or addresses that will receive this message."
    if not to:
        raise Exception ('A message must have at least one recipient.')
    self._addresses(to, 'To')
    #Also store the addresses as a list, for the benefit of future
    #code that will actually send this message.
    self.to = to
def setCc(self, cc):
    """Sets the address or addresses that should receive this message,
    even though it's not addressed directly to them ("carbon-copy")."""
    self._addresses(cc, 'Cc')
def addAttachment(self, attachment, filename, mimetype=None):
    "Attaches the given file to this message."
    #Figure out the major and minor MIME type of this attachment,
    #given its filename.
    if not mimetype:
        mimetype = mimetypes.guess_type(filename)[0]
    if not mimetype:
        raise Exception ("Couldn't determine MIME type for ", filename)
    if '/' in mimetype:
        major, minor = mimetype.split('/')
    else:
        major = mimetype
        minor = None
    #The message was constructed under the assumption that it was
    #a single-part message. Now that we know there's to be at
    #least one attachment, we need to change it into a multi-part
    #message, with the first part being the body of the message.
    if not self.hasAttachments:
        body = self.msg.get_payload()
        newMsg = MIMEMultipart()
        newMsg.attach(MIMEText(body))
        #Copy over the old headers to the new object.
        for header, value in self.msg.items():
            newMsg[header] = value
        self.msg = newMsg
        self.hasAttachments = True
    subMessage = MIMENonMultipart(major, minor, name=filename)
    subMessage.set_payload(attachment)
    #Encode text attachments as quoted-printable, and all other
    #types as base64.
    if major == 'text':
        encoder = Encoders.encode_quopri
    else:
        encoder = Encoders.encode_base64
    encoder(subMessage)
```

(continued)

(continued)

```
            #Link the MIME message part with its parent message.
            self.msg.attach(subMessage)
        def _addresses(self, addresses, key):
            """Sets the given header to a string representation of the given
            list of addresses."""
            if hasattr(addresses, '__iter__'):
                addresses = ', '.join(addresses)
            self[key] = addresses
        #A few methods to let scripts treat this object more or less like
        #a Message or MultipartMessage, by delegating to the real Message
        #or MultipartMessage this object holds.
        def __getitem__(self, key):
            "Return a header of the underlying message."
            return self.msg[key]
        def __setitem__(self, key, value):
            "Set a header of the underlying message."
            self.msg[key] = value
        def __getattr__(self, key):
            return getattr(self.msg, key)
        def __str__(self):
            "Returns a string representation of this message."
            return self.msg.as_string()
```

Try It Out   Building E-mail Messages with SmartMessage

To test out SmartMessage, put it into a file called SendMail.py and run a Python session like this one:

```
>>> from SendMail import SmartMessage
>>> msg = SmartMessage("Me <me@example.com>", "You <you@example.com>", "Your picture",
"Here's that picture I took of you.")
>>> print (str(msg))
Subject: Your picture
From: Me <me@example.com>
To: You <you@example.com>

Here's that picture I took of you.
>>> msg.addAttachment(open("photo.jpg").read(), "photo.jpg")
>>> print (str(msg))

Content-Type: multipart/mixed; boundary="===============1077328303=="
MIME-Version: 1.0
Subject: Your picture
From: Me <me@example.com>
To: You <you@example.com>

--===============1077328303==
Content-Type: text/plain; charset="us-ascii"
MIME-Version: 1.0
```

```
Content-Transfer-Encoding: 7bit

Here's that picture I took of you.
--===============1077328303==
Content-Type: image/jpeg
MIME-Version: 1.0
Content-Transfer-Encoding: base64

/9j/4AAQSkZJRgABAQEASABIAAD//gAXQ3J1YXRlZCB3aXRoIFRoZSBHSU1Q/9sAQwAIBgYHBgUI
...
[Once again, much base64 text omitted.]
...
3f7kklh4dg+UTZ1TsAAv1F69UklmZ9hrzogZibOqSSA8gZySSSJI/9k=
--===============0855656444==--
```

How It Works

SmartMessage wraps the classes in Python's e-mail module. When the SmartMessage object is first created, it keeps its internal representation in a Message object. This message has a simple string representation.

When a file is attached to the SmartMessage, though, a Message object won't do the job anymore. Message objects know only about RFC 2822, nothing about the MIME extensions. At this point, SmartMessage transparently swaps out the Message object for a MimeMultipart object with the same headers and payload.

This transparent swap avoids forcing the user to decide ahead of time whether or not a message should be MIME-encoded. It also avoids a lowest-common-denominator strategy of MIME-encoding each and every message, which is a wasteful operation for messages that are just one text part.

Sending Mail with SMTP and smtplib

Now that you know how to construct e-mail messages, it's appropriate to revisit in a little more detail the protocol used to send them. This is SMTP, another TCP/IP-based protocol, defined in RFC 2821.

Look at the original example one more time:

```
>>> fromAddress = 'sender@example.com'
>>> toAddress = [your e-mail address]
>>> msg = "Subject: Hello\n\nThis is the body of the message."
>>> import smtplib
>>> server = smtplib.SMTP("localhost", 25)
>>> server.sendmail(fromAddress, toAddress, msg)
{}
```

You connect to an SMTP server (at port 25 on localhost) and send a string message from one address to another. Of course, the location of the SMTP server shouldn't be hard-coded, and because some servers require authentication, it would be nice to be able to accept authentication information when creating the

SMTP object. Here's a class that works with the SmartMessage class defined in the previous section to make it easier to send mail. Because the two classes go together, add this class to SendMail.py, the file that also contains the SmartMessage class:

```python
from smtplib import SMTP
class MailServer(SMTP):

  "A more user-friendly interface to the default SMTP class."

    def __init__(self, server, serverUser=None, serverPassword=None, port=25):
        "Connect to the given SMTP server."
        SMTP.__init__(self, server, port)
        self.user = serverUser
        self.password = serverPassword
        #Uncomment this line to see the SMTP exchange in detail.
        #self.set_debuglevel(True)

    def sendMessage(self, message):
        "Sends the given message through the SMTP server."
        #Some SMTP servers require authentication.
        if self.user:
            self.login(self.user, self.password)

        #The message contains a list of destination addresses that
        #might have names associated with them. For instance,
        #"J. Random Hacker <jhacker@example.com>".  Some mail servers
        #will only accept bare e-mail addresses, so we need to create a
        #version of this list that doesn't have any names associated
        #with it.
        destinations = message.to
        if hasattr(destinations, '__iter__'):
            destinations = map(self._cleanAddress, destinations)
        else:
            destinations = self._cleanAddress(destinations)
        self.sendmail(message['From'], destinations, str(message))

    def _cleanAddress(self, address):
        "Transforms 'Name <e-mail@domain>' into 'e-mail@domain'."
        parts = address.split('<', 1)
        if len(parts) > 1:
            #This address is actually a real name plus an address:
            newAddress = parts[1]
            endAddress = newAddress.find('>')
            if endAddress != -1:
                address = newAddress[:endAddress]
        return address
```

Sending Mail with MailServer

This chapter's initial example constructed a message as a string and sent it through SMTPlib. With the SmartMessage and MailServer classes, you can send a much more complex message, using simpler Python code:

```
>>> from SendMail import SmartMessage, MailServer
>>> msg = SmartMessage("Me <me@example.com>",
                        "You <you@example.com>",
                        "Your picture",
                        "Here's that picture I took of you.")
>>> msg.addAttachment(open("photo.jpg").read(), "photo.jpg")
>>> MailServer("localhost").sendMessage(msg)
>>>
```

Run this code (substituting the appropriate e-mail addresses and server hostname), and you'll be able to send mail with MIME attachments to anyone.

How It Works

SmartMessage wraps the classes in Python's e-mail module. As before, the underlying representation starts out as a simple Message object but becomes a MimeMultipart object once photo.jpg is attached.

This time, the message is actually sent through an SMTP server. The MailServer class hides the fact that smtplilb expects you to specify the "To" and "From" headers twice: once in the call to the sendmail method and again in the body of the mail message. It also takes care of sanitizing the destination addresses, putting them into a form that all SMTP servers can deal with. Between the two wrapper classes, you can send complex e-mail messages from a Python script almost as easily as from a mail client.

Retrieving Internet E-mail

Now that you've seen how to send mail, it's time to go all the way toward fulfilling Jamie Zawinski's prophecy and expand your programs so that they can read mail. There are three main ways to do this, and the choice is probably not up to you. How you retrieve mail depends on your relationship with the organization that provides your Internet access.

Parsing a Local Mail Spool with mailbox

If you have a UNIX shell account on your mail server (because, for instance, you run a mail server on your own computer), mail for you is appended to a file (probably /var/spool/mail/[your username]) as it comes in. If this is how your mail setup works, your existing mail client is probably set up to parse that file. It may also be set up to move messages out of the spool file and into your home directory as they come in.

The incoming mailbox in /var/spool/mail/ is kept in a particular format called "mbox format." You can parse these files (as well as mailboxes in other formats such as MH or Maildir) by using the classes in the mailbox module.

Here's a simple script, MailboxSubjectLister.py, that iterates the messages in a mailbox file, printing out the subject of each one:

```
#!/usr/bin/python
import e-mail
import mailbox
import sys
if len(sys.argv) <2:
print("Usage: %s [path to mailbox file]" % sys.argv[0])
sys.exit([1])
path = sys.argv[1]
fp = open(path, 'rb')
subjects = []
for message in mailbox.PortableUnixMailbox(fp, e-mail.message_from_file):
    subjects.append(message['Subject'])
print('s message(s) in mailbox "%s":' % (len(subjects), path))
for subject in subjects:
    print('', subject)
```

UnixMailbox (and the other Mailbox classes in the mailbox module) take as their constructor a file object (the mailbox file), and a function that reads the next message from the file-type object. In this case, the function is the e-mail module's message_from_file. The output of this useful function is a Message object, or one of its MIME* subclasses, such as MIMEMultipart. This and the e-mail. message_from_string function are the most common ways of creating Python representations of messages you receive.

You can work on these Message objects just as you could with the Message objects created from scratch in earlier examples, where the point was to *send* e-mail messages. Python uses the same classes to represent incoming and outgoing messages.

Try It Out   **Printing a Summary of Your Mailbox**

If you have a UNIX account on your e-mail server, you can run the mailbox subject lister against your mail spool file, and get a list of subjects. If you don't have a UNIX account on your e-mail server, or if you use a web-based mail service, you won't be able to get your mail this way:

```
$ python MailboxSubjectLister.py /var/spool/mail/leonardr
4 message(s) in mailbox "/var/spool/mail/leonardr":
 DON'T DELETE THIS MESSAGE -- FOLDER INTERNAL DATA
 This is a test message #1
 This is a test message #2
 This is a test message #3
```

The first message isn't a real message; it's a dummy message sometimes created when you use a mail client to read your spool file. If your application works on spool files that are sometimes accessed through other means, you'll need to recognize and deal with that kind of message.

Fetching Mail from a POP3 Server with poplib

Parsing a local mail spool didn't require going over the network, because you ran the script on the same machine that had the mail spool. There was no need to involve a network protocol, only a file format (the format of UNIX mailboxes, derived mainly from RFC 2822).

However, most people don't have a UNIX shell account on their mail server (or if they do, they want to read mail on their own machine instead of on the server). To fetch mail from your mail server, you need to go over a network, which means you must use a protocol. There are two popular protocols for doing this. The first, which was once near-universal though now it's waning in popularity, is POP3, the third revision of the Post Office Protocol.

POP3 is defined in RFC 1939, but as with most popular Internet protocols, you don't need to delve very deeply into the details, because Python includes a module that wraps the protocol around a Python interface.

Here's POP3SubjectLister, a POP3-based implementation of the same idea as the mailbox parser script. This script prints the subject line of each message on the server:

```python
#!/usr/bin/python
from poplib import POP3
import e-mail
class SubjectLister(PpOP3):
    """Connect to a POP3 mailbox and list the subject of every message
    in the mailbox."""
    def __init__(self, server, username, password):
        "Connect to the POP3 server."
        POP3.__init__(self, server, 110)
        #Uncomment this line to see the details of the POP3 protocol.
        #self.set_debuglevel(2)
        self.user(username)
        response = self.pass_(password)
        if response[:3] != '+OK':
            #There was a problem connecting to the server.
            raise Exception (response)
    def summarize(self):
        "Retrieve each message, parse it, and print the subject."
        numMessages = self.stat()[0]
        print('%d message(s) in this mailbox.' % numMessages)
        parser = e-mail.Parser.Parser()
        for messageNum in range(1, numMessages+1):
            messageString = '\n'.join(self.top(messageNum, 0)[1])
            message = parser.parsestr(messageString)
            #message = parser.parsestr(messageString, True)
            print('', message['Subject'])
```

After the data is on this side of the network, there's no fundamental difference between the way it's handled with this script and the one based on the `UnixMailbox` class. As with the `UnixMailbox` script, you use the e-mail module to parse each message into a Python data structure (although here, you use the `Parser` class, defined in the `e-mail.Parser` module, instead of the `message_from_file` convenience function).

The downside of using POP3 for this purpose is that the `POP3.retr` method has side effects. When you call `retr` on a message on the server, the server marks that message as having been read. If you use a mail client or a program like `fetchmail` to retrieve new mail from the POP3 server, then running this script might confuse the other program. The message will still be on the server, but your client might not download it if it thinks the message has already been read.

POP3 also defines a command called `top`, which doesn't mark a message as having been read and which only retrieves the headers of a message. Both of these — `top` and `retr` — are ideal for the purposes of this script; you'll save bandwidth (not having to retrieve the whole message just to get the subject) and your script won't interfere with the operation of other programs that use the same POP3 mailbox. Unfortunately, not all POP3 servers implement the `top` command correctly. Because it's so useful when implemented correctly, though, here's a subclass of the `SubjectLister` class that uses the `top` command to get message headers instead of retrieving the whole message. If you know your server supports `top` correctly, this is a better implementation:

```
class TopBasedSubjectLister(SubjectLister):

    def summarize(self):
        """Retrieve the first part of the message and find the 'Subject:'
        header."""
        numMessages = self.stat()[0]
        print('%d message(s) in this mailbox.' % numMessages)
        for messageNum in range(1, numMessages+1):
            #Just get the headers of each message. Scan the headers
            #looking for the subject.
            for header in self.top(messageNum, 0)[1]:
                if header.find('Subject:') == 0:
                    print(header[len('Subject:'):])
                    break
```

Both `SubjectLister` and `TopBasedSubjectLister` will yield the same output, but you'll find that `TopBasedSubjectLister` runs a lot faster (assuming your POP3 server implements `top` correctly).

Finally, you'll create a simple command-line interface to the POP3-based `SubjectLister` class, just as you did for the `MailboxSubjectLister.py`. This time, however, you need to provide a POP3 server and credentials on the command line, instead of the path to a file on disk:

```
if __name__ == '__main__':
    import sys
    if len(sys.argv) < 4:
        print('Usage: %s [POP3 hostname] [POP3 user] [POP3 password]' % sys.
argv[0])
        sys.exit(0)
    lister = TopBasedSubjectLister(sys.argv[1], sys.argv[2], sys.argv[3])
    lister.summarize()
```

| Try It Out | **Printing a Summary of Your POP3 Mailbox** |

Run `POP3SubjectLister.py` with the credentials for a POP server, and you'll get a list of subjects:

```
$ python POP3SubjectLister.py pop.example.com [username] [password]
3 message(s) in this mailbox.
 This is a test message #1
 This is a test message #2
 This is a test message #3
```

When you go through the POP3 server, you won't get the dummy message you might get when parsing a raw UNIX mailbox file, as shown previously. Mail servers know that that message isn't really a message; the UNIX mailbox parser treats it as one.

How It Works

The `SubjectLister` object (or its `TopBasedSubjectLister` subclass) connects to the POP3 server and sends a "stat" command to get the number of messages in the mailbox. A call to `stat` returns a tuple containing the number of messages in the mailbox, and the total size of the mailbox in bytes. The lister then iterates up to this number, retrieving every message (or just the headers of every message) as it goes.

If `SubjectLister` is in use, the message is parsed with the `e-mail` module's Parser utility class, and the Subject header is extracted from the resulting `Message` or `MIMEMultipart` object. If `TopBasedSubjectLister` is in use, no parsing is done: The headers are retrieved from the server as a list and scanned for a "Subject" header.

Fetching Mail from an IMAP Server with imaplib

The other protocol for accessing a mailbox on a remote server is IMAP, the Internet Message Access Protocol. The most recent revision of IMAP is defined in RFC 3501, and it has significantly more features than POP3. It's also gaining in popularity over POP3.

The main difference between POP3 and IMAP is that POP3 is designed to act like a mailbox: It just holds your mail for a while until you collect it. IMAP is designed to keep your mail permanently stored on the server. Among other things, you can create folders on the server, sort mail into them, and search them. These are more complex features that are typically associated with end-user mail clients. With IMAP, a mail client only needs to expose these features of IMAP; it doesn't need to implement them on its own.

Keeping your mail on the server makes it easier to keep the same mail setup while moving from computer to computer. Of course, you can still download mail to your computer and then delete it from the server, as with POP3.

Here's `IMAPSubjectLister.py`, an IMAP version of the script you've already written twice, which prints out the subject lines of all mail on the server. IMAP has more features than POP3, so this script exercises proportionally fewer of them. However, even for the same functionality, it's a great improvement over the POP3 version of the script. IMAP saves bandwidth by retrieving the message subjects and nothing else: a single subject header per message. Even when POP3's `top` command is implemented correctly, it can't do better than fetching all of the headers as a group.

What's the catch? As the `imaplib` module says of itself, "to use this module, you must read the RFCs pertaining to the IMAP4 protocol." The `imaplib` module provides a function corresponding to each of the IMAP commands, but it doesn't do many transformations between the Python data structures you're used to creating and the formatted strings used by the IMAP protocol. You'll need to keep a copy of RFC 3501 on hand or you won't know what to pass into the `imaplib` methods.

For instance, to pass a list of message IDs into `imaplib`, you need to pass in a string like 1,2,3, — not the Python list (1,2,3). To make sure only the subject is pulled from the server, `IMAPSubjectLister.py` passes the string `"(BODY[HEADER.FIELDS (SUBJECT)])"` as an argument to an `imaplib` method. The result of that command is a nested list of formatted strings, only some of which are actually useful to the script.

This is not exactly the kind of intuitiveness one comes to expect from Python. `imaplib` is certainly useful, but it doesn't do a very good job of hiding the details of IMAP from the programmer:

```python
#!/usr/bin/python
from imaplib import IMAP4
class SubjectLister(IMAP4):
    """Connect to an IMAP4 mailbox and list the subject of every message
    in the mailbox."""
    def __init__(self, server, username, password):
        "Connect to the IMAP server."
        IMAP4.__init__(self, server)
        #Uncomment this line to see the details of the IMAP4 protocol.
        #self.debug = 4
        self.login(username, password)
    def summarize(self, mailbox='Inbox'):
        "Retrieve the subject of each message in the given mailbox."
        #The SELECT command makes the given mailbox the 'current' one,
        #and returns the number of messages in that mailbox. Each message
        #is accessible via its message number. If there are 10 messages
        #in the mailbox, the messages are numbered from 1 to 10.
        numberOfMessages = int(self._result(self.select(mailbox)))

        print('%s message(s) in mailbox "%s":' % (numberOfMessages, mailbox))
        #The FETCH command takes a comma-separated list of message
        #numbers, and a string designating what parts of the
        #message you want. In this case, we want only the
        #'Subject' header of the message, so we'll use an argument
        #string of '(BODY[HEADER.FIELDS (SUBJECT)])'.
        #
        #See section 6.4.5 of RFC3501 for more information on the
        #format of the string used to designate which part of the
        #message you want. To get the entire message, in a form
        #acceptable to the e-mail parser, ask for '(RFC822)'.
        subjects = self._result(self.fetch('1:%d' % numberOfMessages,
                                 '(BODY[HEADER.FIELDS (SUBJECT)])'))
        for subject in subjects:
            if hasattr(subject, '__iter__'):
```

```
                    subject = subject[1]
                    print('', subject[:subject.find('\n')])
        def _result(self, result):
            """Every method of imaplib returns a list containing a status
            code and a set of the actual result data. This convenience
            method throws an exception if the status code is other than
    "OK", and returns the result data if everything went all
            right."""
            status, result = result
            if status != 'OK':
                raise status (result)
            if len(result) == 1:
                result = result[0]
            return result
    if __name__ == '__main__':
        import sys
        if len(sys.argv) < 4:
            print('Usage: %s [IMAP hostname] [IMAP user] [IMAP password]' % sys.
    argv[0])
            sys.exit(0)
        lister = SubjectLister(sys.argv[1], sys.argv[2], sys.argv[3])
        lister.summarize()
```

Try It Out   Printing a Summary of Your IMAP Mailbox

Just execute IMAPSubjectLister.py with your IMAP credentials (just as with
POP3SubjectLister), and you'll get a summary similar to the two shown earlier in this chapter:

```
$ python IMAPSubjectLister.py imap.example.com [username] [password]
3 message(s) in mailbox "Inbox":
 This is a test message #1
 This is a test message #2
 This is a test message #3
```

How It Works

As with the POP3 example, the first thing to do is connect to the server. POP3 servers provide only
one mailbox per user, but IMAP allows one user any number of mailboxes, so the next step is to select
a mailbox.

The default mailbox is called "Inbox," and selecting a mailbox yields the number of messages in that
mailbox (some POP3 servers, but not all, return the number of messages in the mailbox when you
connect to the server).

Unlike with POP3, IMAP lets you retrieve more than one message at once. It also gives you a lot of
flexibility in defining which parts of a message you want. The IMAP-based SubjectLister makes
just one IMAP call to retrieve the subjects (and only the subjects) of every message in the mailbox.
Then it's just a matter of iterating over the list and printing out each subject. The real trick is knowing
what arguments to pass into imaplib and how to interpret the results.

IMAP's Unique Message IDs

Complaints about `imaplib`'s user-friendliness aside, you might have problems writing IMAP scripts if you assume that the message numbers don't change over time. If another IMAP client deletes messages from a mailbox while this script is running against it (suppose you have your mail client running, and you use it to delete some spam while this script is running), the message numbers will be out of sync from that point on.

The IMAP-based `SubjectLister` class minimizes this risk by getting the subject of every message in one operation, immediately after selecting the mailbox:

```
self.fetch('1:%d' % numberOfMessages, '(BODY[HEADER.FIELDS (SUBJECT)])')
```

If there are 10 messages in the inbox, the first argument to `fetch` will be 1:10. This is a slice of the mailbox, similar to a slice of a Python list, which returns all of the messages: message 1 through message 10 (IMAP and POP3 messages are numbered starting from 1).

Getting the data you need as soon as you connect to the server minimizes the risk that you'll pass a no-longer-valid message number onto the server, but you can't always do that. You may write a script that deletes a mailbox's messages, or that files them in a second mailbox. After you change a mailbox, you may not be able to trust the message numbers you originally got.

Try It Out   Fetching a Message by Unique ID

To help you avoid this problem, IMAP keeps a unique ID (UID) for every message under its control. You can fetch the unique IDs from the server and use them in subsequent calls using `imaplib`'s `uid` method. Unfortunately, this brings you even closer to the details of the IMAP protocol. The `IMAP4` class defines a separate method for each IMAP command (for example, `IMAP4.fetch`, `IMAP4.search`, and so on), but when you're dealing with IDs, you can't use those methods. You can use only the `IMAP4.uid` method, and you must pass the IMAP command you want as the first argument. For instance, instead of calling `IMAP4.fetch([arguments])`, you must call `IMAP4.uid('FETCH', [arguments])`.

```
>>> import imaplib
>>> import e-mail
>>> imap = imaplib.IMAP4('imap.example.com')
>>> imap.login('[username]', '[password]')
('OK', ['Logged in.'])
>>> imap.select('Inbox')[1][0]
'3'
>>>
>>> #Get the unique IDs for the messages in this folder.
... uids = imap.uid('SEARCH', 'ALL')
>>> print(uids)
('OK', ['49532 49541 49563'])
>>>
>>> #Get the first message.
... uids = uids[1][0].split(' ')
>>> messageText = imap.uid('FETCH', uids[0], "(RFC822)")[1][0][1]
>>> message = e-mail.message_from_string(messageText)
>>> print(message['Subject'])
This is a test message #1
```

How It Works

Getting a message by unique ID requires four IMAP commands. First and second, the client must connect to the server and select a mailbox, just as in the previous IMAP example. Third, the client needs to run a SEARCH command that returns a list of message UIDs. Finally, the client can pass in one of the UIDs to a FETCH command and get the actual message.

The last two steps both go through the IMAP4.uid method; if UIDs weren't involved, they would use the search and fetch methods, respectively.

Using imaplib to interact with an IMAP server can be a pain, but it's not as bad as communicating directly with the server.

POP3 servers also support UIDs, though it's less common for multiple clients to access a single POP3 mailbox simultaneously. A POP3 object's uidl method will retrieve the UIDs of the messages in its mailbox. You can then pass a UID into any POP3 object's other methods that take message IDs: for instance, retr and top. IMAP's UIDs are numeric; POP3's are the "message digests": hexadecimal signatures derived from the contents of each message.

Secure POP3 and IMAP

Both the POP3 or IMAP examples covered earlier in this section have a security problem: They send your username and password over the network without encrypting it. That's why both POP and IMAP are often run atop the Secure Socket Layer (SSL). This is a generic encryption layer also used to secure HTTP connections on the World Wide Web. POP and IMAP servers that support SSL run on different ports from the ones that don't: The standard port number for POP over SSL is 995 instead of 23, and IMAP over SSL uses port 993 instead of port 143.

If your POP3 or IMAP server supports SSL, you can get an encrypted connection to it by just swapping out the POP3 or IMAP4 class for the POP3_SSL or IMAP4_SSL class. Each SSL class is in the same module and has the same interface as its insecure counterpart but encrypts all data before sending it over the network.

Webmail Applications Are Not E-mail Applications

If you use a webmail system such as Yahoo! Mail or Gmail, you're not technically using a mail application at all: You're using a web application that happens to have a mail application on the other side. The scripts in this section won't help you fetch mail from or send mail through these services, because they implement HTTP, not any of the e-mail protocols (however, Yahoo! Mail offers POP3 access for a fee). Instead, you should look at Chapter 20 for information on how web applications work.

The libgmail project aims to create a Python interface to Gmail, one that can treat Gmail as an SMTP, POP3, or IMAP server. The libgmail homepage is at http://libgmail.sourceforge.net/.

Socket Programming

So far, you've concerned yourself with the protocols and file formats surrounding a single Internet application: e-mail. E-mail is certainly a versatile and useful application, but e-mail–related protocols account for only a few of the hundreds implemented atop the Internet Protocol. Python makes it easier to use the e-mail–related protocols (and a few other protocols not covered in this chapter) by providing wrapper libraries, but Python doesn't come with a library for every single Internet protocol. It certainly won't have one for any new protocols you decide to create for your own Internet applications.

To write your own protocols, or to implement your own Python libraries along the lines of `imaplib` or `poplib`, you'll need to go down a level and learn how programming interfaces to IP-based protocols actually works. Fortunately, it's not hard to write such code: `smtplib`, `poplib`, and others do it without becoming too complicated. The secret is the *socket library*, which makes reading and writing to a network interface look a lot like reading and writing to files on disk.

Introduction to Sockets

In many of the previous examples, you connected to a server on a particular port of a particular machine (for instance, port 25 of localhost for a local SMTP server). When you tell `imaplib` or `smtplib` to connect to a port on a certain host, behind the scenes Python is opening a connection to that host and port. Once the connection is made, the server opens a reciprocal connection to your computer. A single Python "socket" object hides the outgoing and incoming connections under a single interface. A socket is like a file you can read to and write from at the same time.

To implement a client for a TCP/IP-based protocol, you open a socket to an appropriate server. You write data to the socket to send it to the server, and read from the socket the data the server sends you. To implement a server, it's just the opposite: You *bind* a socket to a hostname and a port and wait for a client to connect to it. Once you have a client on the line, you read from your socket to get data from the client, and write to the socket to send data back.

It takes an enormous amount of work to send a single byte over the network, but between TCP/IP and the socket library, you get to skip almost all of it. You don't have to figure out how to get your data halfway across the world to its destination, because TCP/IP handles that for you. Nor need you worry about turning your data into TCP/IP packets, because the socket library handles that for you.

> *Just as e-mail and the Web are the killer apps for the use of the Internet, sockets might be considered the killer app for the adoption of TCP/IP. Sockets were introduced in an early version of BSD UNIX, but since then just about every TCP/IP implementation has used sockets as its metaphor for how to write network programs. Sockets make it easy to use TCP/IP (at least, easier than any alternative), and this has been a major driver of TCP/IP's popularity.*

As a first socket example, here's a super-simple socket server, `SuperSimpleSocketServer.py`:

```
#!/usr/bin/python
import socket
import sys
if len(sys.argv) < 3:
    print('Usage: %s [hostname] [port number]' % sys.argv[0])
    sys.exit(1)
```

```
hostname = sys.argv[1]
port = int(sys.argv[2])
#Set up a standard Internet socket. The setsockopt call lets this
#server use the given port even if it was recently used by another
#server (for instance, an earlier incarnation of
#SuperSimpleSocketServer).
sock = socket.socket(socket.AF_INET, socket.SOCK_STREAM)
sock.setsockopt(socket.SOL_SOCKET, socket.SO_REUSEADDR, 1)
#Bind the socket to a port, and bid it listen for connections.
sock.bind((hostname, port))
sock.listen(1)
print("Waiting for a request.")
#Handle a single request.
request, clientAddress = sock.accept()
print("Received request from", clientAddress)
request.send(bytes('-=SuperSimpleSocketServer 3000=-\n', 'utf-8'))
request.send(bytes('Go away!\n', 'utf-8'))
request.shutdown(2) #Stop the client from reading or writing anything.
print("Have handled request, stopping server.")
sock.close()
```

This server will serve only a single request. As soon as any client connects to the port to which it's bound, it will tell the client to go away, close the connection, stop serving requests, and exit.

Try It Out   Connecting to the SuperSimpleSocketServer with Telnet

The telnet program is a very simple client for TCP/IP applications. You invoke it with a hostname and a port; it connects you to that port; and then you're on your own. Anything you type is sent over a socket to the server, and anything the server sends over the socket is printed to your terminal. Telnet is included as a command-line program in Windows, Mac OS X, and UNIX installations, so you shouldn't have trouble getting it.

Because the example socket server doesn't really do anything, there's little point in writing a custom client for it. To test it out, just start up the server:

```
$ python SuperSimpleSocketServer.py localhost 2000
Waiting for a request.
```

Then, in a separate terminal, telnet into the server:

```
$ telnet localhost 2000
Trying 127.0.0.1...
Connected to rubberfish.
Escape character is '^]'.
-=SuperSimpleSocketServer 3000=-
Go away!
Connection closed by foreign host.
```

Go back to the terminal on which you ran the server and you should see output similar to this:

```
Received request from ('127.0.0.1', 32958)
Have handled request, stopping server.
```

How It Works

When you started the `SuperSimpleSocketServer`, you bound the process to port 2000 of the "localhost" hostname. When that script called `socket.accept`, it stopped running and began to "block" on socket input, waiting for someone to connect to the server.

When your telnet command opens up a TCP/IP connection to the `SuperSimpleSocketServer`, the `socket.accept` method call returns from its wait. At last, someone has connected to the server! The return values of `socket.accept` give the server the tools it needs to communicate with this client: a socket object and a tuple describing the network address of the client. The server sends some data to the client through the socket and then shuts down. No further socket connections will be accepted.

The only obscure thing here is that client address tuple: (`'127.0.0.1'`, `32958`). You've seen 127.0.0.1 already; it is a special IP address that refers to "this computer": it's the IP address equivalent of "localhost." A connection to the server from 127.0.0.1 means that the client is coming from the same computer that's running the server. If you'd telnetted in from another machine, that machine's IP address would have shown up instead.

The port number 32958 is a temporary or "ephemeral" port number for the client. Recall that what looks like a single, bidirectional "socket" object actually contains two unidirectional connections: one from the client to the server and one from the server to the client. Port 2000 on `localhost`, the port to which the server was bound when you started it up, is the destination for all client data (not that this client got a chance to send any data). The data sent by the server must also have a destination hostname and port, but not a predefined one. Whereas a server port is usually selected by the human in charge of the server, ephemeral ports are selected by the client's operating system. Run this exercise again and you'll see that each individual TCP/IP connection is given a different ephemeral port number.

Binding to an External Hostname

If you tried to telnet into the `SuperSimpleSocketServer` from another machine, as suggested previously, you might have noticed that you weren't able to connect to the server. If so, it may be because you started the server by binding it to `localhost`. The special `"localhost"` hostname is an internal hostname, one that can't be accessed from another machine. After all, from someone else's perspective, `"localhost"` means *their* computer, not yours.

This is actually very useful because it enables you to test out the servers from this chapter (and Chapter 20) without running the risk of exposing your computer to connections from the Internet at large (of course, if you are running these servers on a multiuser machine, you might have to worry about the other users on the same machine, so try to run these on a system that you have to yourself). However, when it comes time to host a server for real, and external connections are what you want, you need to bind your server to an external hostname.

If you can log in to your computer remotely via SSH, or you already run a web server, or you ever make a reference to your computer from another one, you already know an external hostname for your computer. On the other hand, if you have a dial-up or broadband connection, you're probably assigned a hostname along with an IP address whenever you connect to your ISP. Find your computer's IP address and do a DNS lookup on it to find an external hostname for your computer. If all else fails, you can bind servers directly to your external IP address (not 127.0.0.1, because that will have the same problem as binding to "localhost").

If you bind a server to an external hostname and still can't connect to it from the outside, there may be a firewall in the way. Fixing that is beyond what this book can cover. You should ask your local computer guru to help you with this.

The Mirror Server

Here's a server that's a little more complex (though not more useful) and that shows how Python enables you to treat socket connections like files. This server accepts lines of text from a socket, just as a script might on standard input. It reverses the text and writes the reversed version back through the socket, just as a script might on standard output. When it receives a blank line, it terminates the connection:

```python
#!/usr/bin/python
import socket

class MirrorServer:
    """Receives text on a line-by-line basis and sends back a reversed
    version of the same text."""

    def __init__(self, port):
        "Binds the server to the given port."
        self.socket = socket.socket(socket.AF_INET, socket.SOCK_STREAM)
        self.socket.setsockopt(socket.SOL_SOCKET, socket.SO_REUSEADDR, 1)
        self.socket.bind(port)
        #Queue up to five requests before turning clients away.
        self.socket.listen(5)

    def run(self):
        "Handles incoming requests forever."
        while True:
            request, client_address = self.socket.accept()
            #Turn the incoming and outgoing connections into files.
            input = request.makefile('rb', 0)
            output = request.makefile('wb', 0)
            l = True
            try:
                while l:
                    l = input.readline().strip()
                    if l:
                        output.write(l[::-1] + bytes('\r\n','utf-8'))
                    else:
                        #A blank line indicates a desire to terminate the
                        #connection.
                        request.shutdown(2) #Shut down both reads and writes.
            except socket.error:
                #Most likely the client disconnected.
                pass
```

(continued)

(continued)

```python
if __name__ == '__main__':
    import sys
    if len(sys.argv) < 3:
        print('Usage: %s [hostname] [port number]' % sys.argv[0])
        sys.exit(1)
    hostname = sys.argv[1]
    port = int(sys.argv[2])
    MirrorServer((hostname, port)).run()
```

Try It Out   **Mirroring Text with the MirrorServer**

As with the `SuperSimpleSocketServer`, you can use this without writing a specialized client. You can just telnet into the `MirrorServer` and enter some text. Enter a blank line and the server will disconnect you. In one terminal, start the server:

```
$ python MirrorServer.py localhost 2000
```

In another, telnet into the server as a client:

```
$ telnet localhost 2000
Trying 127.0.0.1...
Connected to rubberfish.
Escape character is '^]'.
Hello.
.olleH
Mirror this text!
!txet siht rorriM

Connection closed by foreign host.
$
```

The Mirror Client

Though you've just seen that the mirror server is perfectly usable through telnet, not everyone is comfortable using telnet. What you need is a flashy mirror server client with bells and whistles, so that even networking novices can feel the thrill of typing in text and seeing it printed out backward. Here's a simple client that takes command-line arguments for the server destination and the text to reverse. It connects to the server, sends the data, and prints the reversed text:

```python
#!/usr/bin/python
import socket

class MirrorClient:
    "A client for the mirror server."
```

```
def __init__(self, server, port):
    "Connect to the given mirror server."
    self.socket = socket.socket(socket.AF_INET, socket.SOCK_STREAM)
    self.socket.connect((server, port))

def mirror(self, s):
    "Sends the given string to the server, and prints the response."
    if s[-1] != '\n':
        s += '\r\n'
    self.socket.send(bytes(s, 'utf-8'))

    #Read server response in chunks until we get a newline; that
    #indicates the end of the response.
    buf = []
    input = ''
    while not '\n' in input:
        try:
            input = self.socket.recv(1024)
            buf.append(input)
        except socket.error:
            break
    return ''.join(buf)[:-1]

def close(self):
    self.socket.send(bytes('\r\n', 'utf-8')) #We don't want to mirror
    anything else.
    self.socket.close()

if __name__ == '__main__':
    import sys
    if len(sys.argv) < 4:
        print('Usage: %s [host] [port] [text to be mirrored]' % sys.argv[0])
        sys.exit(1)
    hostname = sys.argv[1]
    port = int(sys.argv[2])
    toMirror = sys.argv[3]

    m = MirrorClient(hostname, port)
    print (m.mirror(toMirror))
    m.close()
```

The mirror server turns its socket connection into a pair of files, but this client reads from and writes to the socket directly. There's no compelling reason for this; I just felt this chapter should include at least one example that used the lower-level socket API. Note how the server response is read in chunks, and each chunk is scanned for the newline character that indicates the end of the response. If this example had created a file for the incoming socket connection, that code would have been as simple as calling `input.readline`.

It's important to know when the response has ended, because calling `socket.recv` (or `input.readline`) will block your process until the server sends some more data. If the server is waiting for more data from the client, your process will block forever.

SocketServer

Sockets are very useful, but Python isn't satisfied with providing the same C-based socket interface you can get with most languages on most operating systems. Python goes one step further and provides `socketserver`, a module full of classes that let you write sophisticated socket-based servers with very little code.

Most of the work in building a `socketserver` is defining a request handler class. This is a subclass of the `socketserver` module's `BaseRequestHandler` class, and the purpose of each request handler object is to handle a single client request for as long as the client is connected to the server. This is implemented in the handler's `handle` method. The handler may also define per-request setup and tear-down code by overriding `setup` and `finish`.

The methods of a `BaseRequestHandler` subclass have access to the following three members:

❑ **request**: A socket object representing the client request: the same object obtained from `socket.accept` in the `MirrorServer` example.

❑ **client_address**: A 2-tuple containing the hostname and port to which any data the server outputs will be sent. The other object obtained from `socket.accept` in the `MirrorServer` example.

❑ **server**: A reference to the `socketserver` that created the request handler object.

By subclassing `StreamRequestHandler` instead of `BaseRequestHandler`, you also get access to the file-like objects that let you read from and write to the socket connection. `BaseRequestHandler` gives you access to two other members:

❑ **rfile**: The file corresponding to the data that comes in over the socket (from the client if you're writing a server, from the server if you're writing a client). Equivalent to what you get when you call `request.makefile('rb')`.

❑ **wfile**: The file corresponding to the data that you send over the socket (to the client if you're writing a server, to the server if you're writing a client). Equivalent to what you get when you call `request.makefile('wb')`.

By rewriting the `MirrorServer` as a `socketserver` server (specifically, a `TCPServer`), you can eliminate a lot of code to do with socket setup and teardown, and focus on the arduous task of reversing text. Here's `MirrorSocketServer.py`:

```python
#!/usr/bin/python
import socketserver

class RequestHandler(socketserver.StreamRequestHandler):
    "Handles one request to mirror some text."

    def handle(self):
        """Read from StreamRequestHandler's provided rfile member,
        which contains the input from the client. Mirror the text
        and write it to the wfile member, which contains the output
        to be sent to the client."""
        l = True
        while l:
            l = self.rfile.readline().strip()
            if l:
                self.wfile.write(l[::-1] + bytes('\n', 'utf-8'))

if __name__ == '__main__':
    import sys
    if len(sys.argv) < 3:
        print('Usage: %s [hostname] [port number]' % sys.argv[0])
        sys.exit(1)
    hostname = sys.argv[1]
    port = int(sys.argv[2])

    socketserver.TCPServer((hostname, port), RequestHandler).serve_forever()
```

Almost all of the socket-specific code is gone. Whenever anyone connects to this server, the TCPServer class will create a new RequestHandler with the appropriate members and call its handle method to handle the request.

The MirrorClient you wrote earlier will work equally well with this server, because across the network both servers take the same input and yield the same output. The same principle applies as when you change the implementation of a function in a module to get rid of redundant code but leave the interface the same.

Multithreaded Servers

One problem with both of these implementations of the mirror server is that only one client at a time can connect to a running server. If you open two telnet sessions to a running server, the second session won't finish connecting until you close the first one. If real servers worked this way, nothing would ever get done. That's why most real servers spawn threads or subprocesses to handle multiple connections.

The SocketServer module defines two useful classes for handling multiple connections at once: ThreadingMixIn and ForkingMixIn. A SocketServer class that subclasses ThreadingMixIn will automatically spawn a new thread to handle each incoming request. A subclass of ForkingMixIn will automatically fork a new subprocess to handle each incoming request. I prefer ThreadingMixIn because threads are more efficient and more portable than subprocesses. It's also much easier to write code for a thread to communicate with its parent than for a subprocess to communicate with its parent.

See Chapter 9 for an introduction to threads and subprocesses.

Here's `MultithreadedMirrorServer.py`, a multithreaded version of the `MirrorSocketServer`. Note that it uses the exact same `RequestHandler` definition as `MirrorSocketServer.py`. The difference here is that instead of running a `TCPServer`, you run a `ThreadingTCPServer`, a standard class that inherits both from `ThreadingMixIn` and `TCPServer`:

```python
#!/usr/bin/python
import socketserver

class RequestHandler(SocketServer.StreamRequestHandler):
    "Handles one request to mirror some text."

    def handle(self):
        """Read from StreamRequestHandler's provided rfile member,
        which contains the input from the client. Mirror the text
        and write it to the wfile member, which contains the output
        to be sent to the client."""
        l = True
        while l:
            l = self.rfile.readline().strip()
            if l:
                self.wfile.write(l[::-1] + bytes('\n', 'utf-8'))

if __name__ == '__main__':
    import sys
    if len(sys.argv) < 3:
        print('Usage: %s [hostname] [port number]' % sys.argv[0])
        sys.exit(1)
    hostname = sys.argv[1]
    port = int(sys.argv[2])
    server = socketserver.ThreadingTCPServer((hostname, port),
RequestHandler)
    server.serve_forever()
```

With this server running, you can run a large number of telnet sessions and `MirrorClient` sessions in parallel. `ThreadingMixIn` hides the details of spawning threads, just as `TCPServer` hides the details of sockets. The goal of all these helper classes is to keep your focus on what you send and receive over the network.

The Python Chat Server

For the mirror server, the capability to support multiple simultaneous connections is useful but it doesn't change what the server actually does. Each client interacts only with the server, and not even indirectly with the other clients. This model is a popular one; web servers and mail servers use it, among others.

There is another type of server, though, that exists to connect clients to each other. For many applications, it's not the server that's interesting: it's who else is connected to it. The most popular applications of this sort are online chat rooms and games. In this section, you design and build a simple chat server and client.

Perhaps the original chat room was the (non-networked) UNIX wall command, which enables you to broadcast a message to everyone logged in on a UNIX system. Internet Relay Chat, invented in 1988 and described in RFC 1459, is the most popular TCP/IP-based chat room software. The chat software you write here will have some of the same features as IRC, although it won't be compatible with IRC.

Design of the Python Chat Server

In IRC, a client that connects to a server must provide a *nickname*: a short string identifying the person who wants to chat. A nickname must be unique across a server so that users can't impersonate one another. Your server will carry on this tradition.

An IRC server provides an unlimited number of named *channels*, or *rooms*, and each user can join any number of rooms. Your server will provide only a single, unnamed room, which all connected users will inhabit.

Entering a line of text in an IRC client broadcasts it to the rest of your current room, unless it starts with the slash character. A line starting with the slash character is treated as a command to the server. Your server will act the same way.

IRC implements a wide variety of server commands: For instance, you can use a server command to change your nickname, join another room, send a private message to another user, or try to send a file to another user.

For example, if you issue the command /nick leonardr to an IRC server, you're attempting to change your nickname from its current value to leonardr. Your attempt might or might not succeed, depending on whether or not there's already a leonardr on the IRC server.

Your server will support the following three commands, taken from IRC and simplified:

❑   **/nick [nickname]**: As described earlier, this attempts to change your nickname. If the nickname is valid and not already taken, your nickname will be changed and the change will be announced to the room. Otherwise, you'll get a private error message.

❑   **/quit [farewell message]**: This command disconnects the user from the chat server. Your farewell message, if any, will be broadcast to the room.

❑   **/names**: This retrieves the nicknames of the users in the chat room as a space-separated string.

The Python Chat Server Protocol

Having decided on a feature set and a design, you must now define an application-specific protocol for your Python Chat Server. This protocol will be similar to SMTP, HTTP, and the IRC protocol in that it will run atop TCP/IP to provide the structure for a specific type of application. However, it will be much simpler than any of those protocols.

The mirror server also defined a protocol, though it was so simple it may have escaped notice. The mirror server protocol consists of three simple rules:

1. Send lines of text to the server.

2. Every time you send a newline, the server will send you back that line of text, reversed, with a newline at the end.

3. Send a blank line to terminate the connection.

The protocol for the Python Chat Server will be a little more complex than that, but by the standards of protocol design it's still a fairly simple protocol. The following description is more or less the information that would go into an RFC for this protocol. If you were actually writing an RFC, you would go into a lot more detail and provide a formal definition of the protocol; that's not as necessary here, because the protocol definition will be immediately followed by an implementation in Python.

Of course, if you did write an RFC for this, it wouldn't be accepted. The IRC protocol already has an RFC, and it's a much more useful protocol than this example.

Your Hypothetical Protocol in Action

One good way to figure out the problems involved in defining a protocol is to write a sample session to see what the client and server need to say to each other. Here's a sample session of the Python Chat Server. In the following transcript, a user nicknamed jamesp connects to a chat room in which a shady character nicknamed nrini is already lurking. The diagram shows what jamesp might send to the server, what the server would send to him in response, and what it would send to the other client (nrini) as a result of jamesp's input.

Me to the Server	The Server to Me	The Server to nrini
	Who are you?	
jamesp		
	Hello, jamesp, welcome to the Python Chat Server.	jamesp has joined the chat.
/names		
	nrini jamesp	
Hello!		
	<jamesp> Hello!	<jamesp> Hello!
/nick nrini		
	There's already a user named nrini here.	
/nick james		

Me to the Server	The Server to Me	The Server to nrini
	jamesp is now known as james	jamesp is now known as james
Hello again!		
	<james> Hello again!	<james> Hello again!
/quit Goodbye		
		james has quit: Goodbye

Initial Connection

After establishing a connection between the client and server, the first stage of the protocol is to get a nickname for the client. A client can't be allowed into a chat room without a nickname because that would be confusing to the other users. Therefore, the server will ask each new client: "Who are you?" and expect a nickname in response, terminated by a newline. If what's sent is an invalid nickname or the nickname of a user already in the chat room, the server will send an error message and terminate the connection. Otherwise, the server will welcome the client to the chat room and broadcast an announcement to all other users that someone has joined the chat.

Chat Text

After a client is admitted into the chat room, any line of text he sends will be broadcast to every user in the room, unless it's a server command. When a line of chat is broadcast, it will be prefaced with the nickname of the user who sent it, enclosed in angle brackets (for example, `"<jamesp> Hello, all."`). This will prevent confusion about who said what, and visually distinguish chat messages from system messages.

Server Commands

If the client sends a recognized server command, the command is executed and a private system message may be sent to that client. If the execution of the command changes the state of the chat room (for instance, a user changes his nickname or quits), all users will receive a system message notifying them of the change (for example, `"jamesp is now known as james"`). An unrecognized server command will result in an error message for the user who sent it.

General Guidelines

For the sake of convenience and readability, the chat protocol is designed to have a line-based and human-readable format. This makes the chat application usable even without a special client (although you will write a special client to make chatting a little easier). Many TCP/IP protocols work in similar ways, but it's not a requirement. Some protocols send only binary data, to save bandwidth or because they encrypt data before transmitting it.

Here's the server code, in PythonChatServer.py. Like MultithreadedMirrorServer, its actual server class is a ThreadingTCPServer. It keeps a persistent map of users' nicknames that point to the wfile members. That lets the server send those users' data. This is how one user's input can be broadcast to everyone in the chat room:

```python
#!/usr/bin/python
import socketserver
import re
import socket

class ClientError(Exception):
    "An exception thrown because the client gave bad input to the server."
    pass

class PythonChatServer(socketserver.ThreadingTCPServer):
    "The server class."

    def __init__(self, server_address, RequestHandlerClass):
        """Set up an initially empty mapping between a user's nickname
        and the file-like object used to send data to that user."""
        SocketServer.ThreadingTCPServer.__init__(self, server_address,
                                                 RequestHandlerClass)
        self.users = {}

class RequestHandler(SocketServer.StreamRequestHandler):
    """Handles the life cycle of a user's connection to the chat
    server: connecting, chatting, running server commands, and
    disconnecting."""

    NICKNAME = re.compile('^[A-Za-z0-9_-]+$') #Regex for a valid nickname

    def handle(self):
        """Handles a connection: gets the user's nickname, then
        processes input from the user until they quit or drop the
        connection."""
        self.nickname = None

        self.privateMessage('Who are you?')
        nickname = self._readline()
        done = False
        try:
            self.nickCommand(nickname)
            self.privateMessage('Hello %s, welcome to the Python Chat
Server.'\
                                % nickname)
            self.broadcast('%s has joined the chat.' % nickname, False)
        except ClientError (error):
            self.privateMessage(error.args[0])
            done = True
        except socket.error:
            done = True

        #Now they're logged in; let them chat.
        while not done:
            try:
```

```
                done = self.processInput()
            except ClientError (error):
                self.privateMessage(str(error))
            except socket.error (e):
                done = True

    def finish(self):
        "Automatically called when handle() is done."
        if self.nickname:
            #The user successfully connected before disconnecting.
            #Broadcast that they're quitting to everyone else.
            message = '%s has quit.' % self.nickname
            if hasattr(self, 'partingWords'):
                message = '%s has quit: %s' % (self.nickname,
                                                self.partingWords)
            self.broadcast(message, False)

            #Remove the user from the list so we don't keep trying to
            #send them messages.
            if self.server.users.get(self.nickname):
                del(self.server.users[self.nickname])
        self.request.shutdown(2)
        self.request.close()

    def processInput(self):
        """Reads a line from the socket input and either runs it as a
        command, or broadcasts it as chat text."""
        done = False
        l = self._readline()
        command, arg = self._parseCommand(l)
        if command:
            done = command(arg)
        else:
            l = '<%s> %s\n' % (self.nickname, l)
            self.broadcast(l)
        return done
```

Each server command is implemented as a method. The _parseCommand method, defined later, takes a line that looks like /nick and calls the corresponding method (in this case, nickCommand):

```
        #Below are implementations of the server commands.

    def nickCommand(self, nickname):
        "Attempts to change a user's nickname."
        if not nickname:
            raise ClientError ('No nickname provided.')
        if not self.NICKNAME.match(nickname):
            raise ClientError (Invalid nickname: %s' % nickname)
        if nickname == self.nickname:
            raise ClientError ('You are already known as %s.' % nickname)
        if self.server.users.get(nickname, None):
            raise ClientError ('There\'s already a user named "%s" here.' %
nickname)
        oldNickname = None
```

(continued)

(continued)

```
            if self.nickname:
                oldNickname = self.nickname
                del(self.server.users[self.nickname])
            self.server.users[nickname] = self.wfile
            self.nickname = nickname
            if oldNickname:
                self.broadcast('%s is now known as %s' % (oldNickname, self.
nickname))

    def quitCommand(self, partingWords):
        """Tells the other users that this user has quit, then makes
        sure the handler will close this connection."""
        if partingWords:
            self.partingWords = partingWords
        #Returning True makes sure the user will be disconnected.
        return True

    def namesCommand(self, ignored):
        "Returns a list of the users in this chat room."
        self.privateMessage(', '.join(self.server.users.keys()))

    # Below are helper methods.

    def broadcast(self, message, includeThisUser=True):
        """Send a message to every connected user, possibly exempting the
        user who's the cause of the message."""
        message = self._ensureNewline(message)
        for user, output in self.server.users.items():
            if includeThisUser or user != self.nickname:
                output.write(message)

    def privateMessage(self, message):
        "Send a private message to this user."
        self.wfile.write(self._ensureNewline(message))

    def _readline(self):
        "Reads a line, removing any whitespace."
        return self.rfile.readline().strip()

    def _ensureNewline(self, s):
        "Makes sure a string ends in a newline."
        if s and s[-1] != '\n':
            s += '\r\n'
        return s

    def _parseCommand(self, input):
        """Try to parse a string as a command to the server. If it's an
        implemented command, run the corresponding method."""
        commandMethod, arg = None, None
        if input and input[0] == '/':
            if len(input) < 2:
                raise ClientError, 'Invalid command: "%s"' % input
            commandAndArg = input[1:].split(' ', 1)
            if len(commandAndArg) == 2:
```

```
                command, arg = commandAndArg
            else:
                command, = commandAndArg
            commandMethod = getattr(self, command + 'Command', None)
            if not commandMethod:
                raise ClientError, 'No such command: "%s"' % command
        return commandMethod, arg

if __name__ == '__main__':
    import sys
    if len(sys.argv) < 3:
        print('Usage: %s [hostname] [port number]' % sys.argv[0])
        sys.exit(1)
    hostname = sys.argv[1]
    port = int(sys.argv[2])
    PythonChatServer((hostname, port), RequestHandler).serve_forever()
```

The Python Chat Client

As with the mirror server, this chat server defines a simple, human-readable protocol. It's possible to use the chat server through telnet, but most people would prefer to use a custom client.

Here's PythonChatClient.py, a simple text-based client for the Python Chat Server. It has a few niceties that are missing when you connect with telnet. First, it handles the authentication stage on its own: If you run it on a UNIX-like system, you won't even have to specify a nickname, because it will use your account name as a default. Immediately after connecting, the Python Chat Client runs the /names command and presents the user with a list of everyone in the chat room.

After connecting, this client acts more or less like a telnet client would. It spawns a separate thread to handle user input from the keyboard even as it reads the server's output from the network:

```
#!/usr/bin/python
import socket
import select
import sys
import os
from threading import Thread

class ChatClient:

    def __init__(self, host, port, nickname):
        self.socket = socket.socket(socket.AF_INET, socket.SOCK_STREAM)
        self.socket.connect((host, port))
        self.input = self.socket.makefile('rb', 0)
        self.output = self.socket.makefile('wb', 0)

        #Send the given nickname to the server.
        authenticationDemand = self.input.readline()
        if not authenticationDemand.startswith("Who are you?"):
            raise Exception ("This doesn't seem to be a Python Chat Server.")
        self.output.write(nickname + '\r\n')
        response = self.input.readline().strip()
```

(continued)

329

(continued)

```
        if not response.startswith("Hello"):
            raise Exception (response)
        print(response)

        #Start out by printing out the list of members.
        self.output.write('/names\r\n')
        print("Currently in the chat room:", self.input.readline().strip())

        self.run()

    def run(self):
        """Start a separate thread to gather the input from the
        keyboard even as we wait for messages to come over the
        network. This makes it possible for the user to simultaneously
        send and receive chat text."""

        propagateStandardInput = self.PropagateStandardInput(self.output)
        propagateStandardInput.start()

        #Read from the network and print everything received to standard
        #output. Once data stops coming in from the network, it means
        #we've disconnected.
        inputText = True
        while inputText:
            inputText = self.input.readline()
            if inputText:
                print inputText.strip()
        propagateStandardInput.done = True

    class PropagateStandardInput(Thread):
        """A class that mirrors standard input to the chat server
        until it's told to stop."""

        def __init__(self, output):
            """Make this thread a daemon thread, so that if the Python
            interpreter needs to quit it won't be held up waiting for this
            thread to die."""
            Thread.__init__(self)
            self.setDaemon(True)
            self.output = output
            self.done = False

        def run(self):
            "Echo standard input to the chat server until told to stop."
            while not self.done:
                inputText = sys.stdin.readline().strip()
                if inputText:
                    self.output.write(inputText + '\r\n')

if __name__ == '__main__':
    import sys
    #See if the user has an OS-provided 'username' we can use as a default
    #chat nickname. If not, they have to specify a nickname.
    try:
```

```
        import pwd
        defaultNickname = pwd.getpwuid(os.getuid())[0]
    except ImportError:
        defaultNickname = None

    if len(sys.argv) < 3 or not defaultNickname and len(sys.argv) < 4:
        print('Usage: %s [hostname] [port number] [username]' % sys.argv[0])
        sys.exit(1)

    hostname = sys.argv[1]
    port = int(sys.argv[2])

    if len(sys.argv) > 3:
        nickname = sys.argv[3]
    else:
        #We must be on a system with usernames, or we would have
        #exited earlier.
        nickname = defaultNickname

    ChatClient(hostname, port, nickname)
```

A more advanced chat client might have a GUI that put incoming text in a separate window from the text the user types, to keep input from being visually confused with output. As it is, in a busy chat room, you might be interrupted by an incoming message while you're typing, and lose your place.

Single-Threaded Multitasking with select

The reason PythonChatClient spawns a separate thread to gather user input is that a call to sys.stdin.readline won't return until the user enters a chat message or server command. A naïve chat client might call sys.stdin.readline and wait for the user to type something in, but while it was waiting the other users would keep chatting and the socket connection from the server would fill up with a large backlog of chat. No chat messages would be displayed until the user pressed the Enter key (causing sys.stdin.readline to return), at which time the whole backlog would come pouring onto the screen. Trying to read from the socket connection would cause the opposite problem: The user would be unable to enter any chat text until someone else in the chat room said something. Using two threads avoids these problems: One thread can keep an eye on standard input while the other keeps an eye on the socket connection.

However, it's possible to implement the chat client without using threads. (After all, telnet works more or less the same way as PythonChatClient, and the telnet program is older than the idea of threads.) The secret is to just peek at standard input and the socket connection — not trying to read from them, just seeing if there's anything to read. You do this by using the select function, provided by Python's select module.

select takes three lists of lists, and each second-level list contains file-type objects: one for objects you read (like sys.stdin), one for objects to which you write (like sys.stdout), and one for objects to which you write errors (like sys.stdout). By default, a call to select will block (wait for input), but only until at least *one* of the file-type objects you passed in is ready to be used. It will then return three lists of lists, which contain a subset of the objects you passed in: only the ones that are ready and have some data for the program to pay attention to. You might think of select as acting sort of like Python's built-in `filter` function, filtering out the objects that aren't ready for use. By using `select`, you can avoid the trap of calling `read` on a file-type object that doesn't have any data to read.

Here's a subclass of `ChatClient` that uses a loop over `select` to check whether standard input or the server input have unread data:

```
class SelectBasedChatClient(ChatClient):

    def run(self):
        """In a tight loop, see whether the user has entered any input
        or whether there's any from the network. Keep doing this until
        the network connection returns EOF."""
        socketClosed = False
        while not socketClosed:
            toRead, ignore, ignore = select.select([self.input, sys.stdin],
                                                     [], [])
            #We're not disconnected yet.
            for input in toRead:
                if input == self.input:
                    inputText = self.input.readline()
                    if inputText:
                        print(inputText.strip())
                    else:
                        #The attempt to read failed. The socket is closed.
                        socketClosed = True
                elif input == sys.stdin:
                    input = sys.stdin.readline().strip()
                    if input:
                        self.output.write(input + '\r\n')
```

You must pass in three lists to `select`, but you pass in empty lists of output files and error files. All you care about are the two sources of input (from the keyboard and the network), because those are the ones that might block and cause problems when you try to read them.

In one sense, this code is more difficult to understand than the original `ChatClient`, because it uses a trick to rapidly switch between doing two things, instead of just doing both things at once. In another sense, it's less complex than the original `ChatClient` because it's less code and it doesn't involve multithreading, which can be difficult to debug.

It's possible to use `select` to write servers without forking or threading, but I don't recommend writing such code yourself.

Other Topics

Many aspects of network programming are not covered in this chapter. The most obvious omission (the technologies and philosophies that drive the World Wide Web) are taken up Chapter 20. The following sections outline some other topics in networking that are especially interesting or important from the perspective of a Python programmer.

Miscellaneous Considerations for Protocol Design

The best way to learn about protocol design is to study existing, successful protocols. Protocols are usually well documented, and you can learn a lot by using them and reading RFCs. Here are some common design considerations for protocol design not covered earlier in this chapter.

Trusted Servers

The Python Chat Server is used by one client to broadcast information to all other clients. Sometimes, however, the role of a server is to mediate between its clients. To this end, the clients are willing to trust the server with information they wouldn't trust to another client.

This happens often on websites that bring people together, such as auction sites and online payment systems. It's also implemented at the protocol level in many online games, in which the server acts as referee.

Consider a game in which players chase each other around a map. If one player knew another's location on the map, that player would gain an unfair advantage. At the same time, if players were allowed to keep their locations secret, they could cheat by teleporting to another part of the map whenever a pursuer got too close. Players give up the ability to cheat in exchange for a promise that other players won't be allowed to cheat either. A trusted server creates a level playing field.

Terse Protocols

Information that can be pieced together by a client is typically not put into the protocol. It would be wasteful for a server that ran chess games to transfer a representation of the entire board to both players after every successful move. It would suffice to send "Your move was accepted." to the player who made the move, and describe the move to the other player. State-based protocols usually transmit the changes in state, rather than send the whole state every time it changes.

The protocol for the Python Chat Server sends status messages in complete English sentences. This makes the code easier to understand and the application easier to use through telnet. The client behavior depends on those status messages: For instance, `PythonChatClient` expects the string "Who are you?" as soon as it connects to the server. Doing a protocol this way makes it difficult for the server to customize the status messages, or for the client to translate them into other languages. Many protocols define numeric codes or short abbreviations for status messages and commands, and explain their meanings in the protocols' RFC or other definition document.

The Peer-to-Peer Architecture

All of the protocols developed in this chapter were designed according to the client-server architecture. This architecture divides the work of networking between two different pieces of software: the clients, who request data or services, and the servers, which provide the data or carry out the services. This architecture assumes a few powerful computers will act as servers, and a large number of computers will act as clients. Information tends to be centralized on the server: to allow for central control, to ensure fairness (for instance, in a game with hidden information), to make it unnecessary for clients to trust each other, or just to make information easier to find.

The other popular architecture is the *peer-to-peer architecture*. In this architecture, every client is also a server. A peer-to-peer protocol may define "client" actions and "server" actions, but every process that makes requests is also capable of serving them.

Though most of the protocols implemented on top of it use the client-server architecture, TCP/IP is a peer-to-peer protocol. Recall that a socket connection actually covers two unidirectional TCP/IP connections: one from you to your destination and one going the other way. You can't be a TCP/IP client without also being a TCP/IP server: you'd be sending data without any way of receiving a response.

At the application level, the most popular peer-to-peer protocol is BitTorrent. BitTorrent makes it easy to distribute a large file by sharing the cost of the bandwidth across all of the people who download it. Under the client-server architecture, someone who wanted to host a file would put it on her server and bear the full cost of the bandwidth for every download. The original BitTorrent implementation is written in Python, and the first release was in 2002. BitTorrent is proof positive that there's still room for clever new TCP/IP protocols, and that it's possible to implement high-performance protocols in Python.

Summary

Python provides high-level tools for using existing TCP/IP-based protocols, making it easy to write custom clients. It also comes packaged with tools that help you design your own networked applications. Whether you just want to send mail from a script, or you have an idea for the Internet's next killer app, Python can do what you need.

The key points to take away from this chapter are:

- ❑ The smtplib module takes its name from SMTP, the Simple Mail Transport Protocol. That's the protocol, or standard, defined for sending Internet mail.

- ❑ Protocols are a convention for structuring the data sent between two or more parties on a network.

- ❑ Localhost is a special hostname that always refers to the computer you're using when you mention it. The hostname is how you tell Python where on the Internet to find your mail server.

- ❑ MIME is a series of standards designed around fitting non-U.S.-ASCII data into the 127 7-bit characters that make up U.S. ASCII.

- ❑ You can use the mailbox module to parse files of the mbox type.

- ❑ PoP3 stands for Post Office Protocol. The 3 stands for the version.

- ❑ IMAP stands for Internet Message Access Protocol.

Exercises

1. Distinguish between the following e-mail-related standards: RFC 2822, SMTP, IMAP, MIME, and POP.

2. Write a script that connects to a POP server, downloads all of the messages, and sorts the messages into files named after the sender of the message. (For instance, if you get two e-mails from user@example.com, they should both go into a file called "user@example.com").

   What would be the corresponding behavior if you had an IMAP server instead? Write that script, too (use RFC 3501 as a reference).

3. Suppose that you were designing an IRC-style protocol for low-bandwidth embedded devices such as cell phones. What changes to the Python Chat Server protocol would it be useful to make?

4. A feature of IRC not cloned in the Python Chat Server is the /msg command, which enables one user to send a private message to another instead of broadcasting it to the whole room. How could the /msg command be implemented in the Python Chat Server?

5. When does it make sense to design a protocol using a peer-to-peer architecture?

Extension Programming with C

Don't let anybody mislead you: well-written code in C will always execute faster than code written in Python. Having said that, don't be misled: Developing code in Python will always be faster than developing code in C.

This may seem like a dilemma at first. You want to have fast code, and you want to produce it quickly. Balancing these, and the problem it creates, is actually easily solved. Develop your code in Python. After all, developer's time is much more expensive than the computer's time. Plus, humans have a miserable track record of predicting where a bottleneck is going to occur in a system. Spending time optimizing code up front by doing things like taking a lot of time to write a new program in C is usually wasted time. This is what led the esteemed computer scientist, C. A. R. Hoare, to say, "Premature optimization is the root of all evil." Of course, he was only talking about computer programs, but the point is there.

If you've written your code, optimized your algorithms, and still find performance is unacceptable, you should profile your application by finding out where it's spending its time, determine where the bottlenecks are, and reimplement those small parts in C as a Python extension module. That's part of what this chapter is about.

Or if you already have an existing body of code written in C and you want to leverage that from within Python, you can create a small Python extension module exposing that C code to your Python code so it can be called as though it were written in Python. This is probably the more common reason for implementing an extension module (a module written in a language other than Python).

In this chapter you learn:

❑   How to create an extension module in C for the standard Python interpreter (but you have to promise that you'll do so only if you have absolutely no other option.) This chapter assumes you are already familiar with C. If you're not, you need to rope someone who is familiar with C into helping you out.

❑ Basic and real-world, practical examples in which you define, in C, a class that can encode raw audio data into MP3-encoded data. Your class will be usable from Python and will make method calls on pure Python objects, demonstrating how you can communicate both ways.

❑ How to work with the Python API from C.

This chapter is just an introduction to using the Python API from C and is no way a substitute for the API documentation found at http://docs.python.org/. You should look up the function definitions you'll be using because they're mentioned throughout the examples.

Extension Module Outline

First of all, a Python extension module is nothing more than a normal C library. On UNIX machines, these libraries usually end in .so (for shared object). On Windows machines, you typically see .dll (for dynamically linked library).

Before you get started, you're going to need the Python header files. On UNIX machines, this usually requires installing a developer-specific package. Windows users get these headers as part of the package when they use the binary Python installer.

For your first look at a Python extension module, you'll be grouping your code into three parts: the C functions you want to expose as the interface from your module; a table mapping the names of your functions as Python developers will see them to C functions inside the extension module; and an initialization function.

Most extension modules can be contained in a single C source file, sometimes called the *glue*. Start the file out including Python.h, which will give you access to the internal Python API used to hook your module into the interpreter. Be sure to include Python.h *before* any other headers you might need. You'll follow the includes with the functions you want to call from Python.

Interestingly, the signatures of the C implementations of your functions will always take one of the following three forms:

```
PyObject *MyFunction(PyObject *self, PyObject *args);

PyObject *MyFunctionWithKeywords(PyObject *self,
                                 PyObject *args,
                                 PyObject *kw);

PyObject *MyFunctionWithNoArgs(PyObject *self);
```

Typically, your C functions will look like the first of the preceding three declarations. The arguments passed into your functions are packed into a tuple that you'll have to break apart in order to use, which explains how you can implement a function in C that takes only two arguments but can accept any number of arguments as called from Python.

Notice how each one of the preceding declarations returns a Python object. There's no such thing as a "void" function in Python as there is in C. If you don't want your functions to return a value, return the C equivalent of Python's None value instead. The Python headers define a macro, Py_RETURN_NONE, that does this for you.

Seeing these declarations should make it obvious how object-oriented Python is. *Everything* is an object. In C, you'll be using the Python API to work with these objects, but the concepts you know from Python still hold.

The names of your C functions can be whatever you like because they'll never be seen outside of the extension module. In fact, the functions are usually declared with the static keyword (which in C means they're not visible outside of the current source file). In the example code, functions usually are named by combining the Python module and function names together, as shown here:

```
static PyObject *foo_bar(PyObject *self, PyObject *args) {
    /* Do something interesting here. */
    Py_RETURN_NONE;
}
```

This would be a Python function called bar inside of the module foo. You'll be putting pointers to your C functions into the method table for the module that usually comes next in your source code.

This method table is a simple array of PyMethodDef structures. That structure looks something like this:

```
struct PyMethodDef {
    char         *ml_name;
    PyCFunction  ml_meth;
    int          ml_flags;
    char         *ml_doc;
};
```

That first member, ml_name, is the name of the function as the Python interpreter will present it when it's used in Python programs. The PyCFunction member must be the address to a function that has any one of the signatures described previously. ml_flags tells the interpreter which of the three signatures ml_meth is using. ml_flags will usually have a value of METH_VARARGS. This value can be bitwise or'ed with METH_KEYWORDS if you want to allow keyword arguments into your function. It can also have a value of METH_NOARGS that indicates you don't want to accept any arguments. Finally, the last member in the PyMethodDef structure, ml_doc, is the docstring for the function, which can be NULL if you don't feel like writing one — shame on you.

This table needs to be terminated with a sentinel that consists of NULL and 0 values for the appropriate members.

This is what a table containing an entry for your foo_bar function would look like:

```
static PyMethodDef foo_methods[] = {
    { "bar", (PyCFunction)foo_bar, METH_NOARGS, "My first function."
    },
        { NULL, NULL, 0, NULL }
};
```

Casting the address of foo_bar to a PyCFunction is necessary to get the compiler to *not* warn you about incompatible pointer types. This is safe because of the METH_NOARGS flag for the ml_flags member, which indicates to the Python interpreter that it should call your C function with only one PyObject * as an argument (and not two as would be the case if you used METH_VARARGS, or three if you used METH_VARARGS|METH_KEYWORDS).

The last part of your extension module is the initialization function. This function is called by the Python interpreter when the module is loaded. It's required that the function be named initfoo, where foo is the name of the module.

The initialization function needs to be exported from the library you'll be building. The Python headers define PyMODINIT_FUNC to include the appropriate incantations for that to happen for the particular environment in which you're compiling. All you have to do is use it when defining the function.

Putting this all together looks like the following:

```
#include <Python.h>

static PyObject *foo_bar(PyObject *self, PyObject *args) {
    /* Do something interesting here. */
    Py_RETURN_NONE;
}

static PyMethodDef foo_methods[] = {
    { "bar", (PyCFunction)foo_bar, METH_NOARGS, NULL },
    { NULL, NULL, 0, NULL }
};

PyMODINIT_FUNC initfoo() {
    Py_InitModule3("foo", foo_methods, "My first extension module.");
}
```

The Py_InitModule3 function is typically what you use to define a module because it lets you define a docstring for a module, which is always a nice thing to do.

Building and Installing Extension Modules

You can build the extension module in a couple of different ways. The obvious way is to build it the way you build all of the libraries on your platform. Save the previous example as foo.c. Then, to compile your module on Linux, you could do something like this:

```
gcc -shared -I/usr/include/python3.1 foo.c -o foo.so
```

Building the extension module on Windows would look something like this:

```
cl /LD /IC:\Python31\include foo.c C:\Python31\libs\python31.lib
```

For either of these commands to work, you'll need to have a C compiler installed and have it available in your path (if you're reading this chapter, you probably do). The Python headers need to be installed and accessible to the compiler. In both of these examples, the directory containing the Python headers is specified on the command line (as is the path to the Python library for the

Windows compiler). If your headers and libraries are located in a different location, the commands will have to be modified accordingly.

The name of the actual shared object (or DLL on Windows) needs to be the same as the string passed in to Py_InitModule3 (minus the .so or .dll extension). Optionally, you can suffix the base name of the library with module. So your foo extension module could be called foo.so or foomodule.so.

This works, but it's not the only way to do it. The new and improved way of building extension modules is to use distutils, which is included in all recent versions of Python.

The distutils package makes it possible to distribute Python modules, both pure Python and extension modules, in a standard way. Modules are distributed in source form and built and installed via a setup script (usually called setup.py). As long as your users have the required compiler packages and Python headers installed, this usually works.

The setup script is surprisingly succinct:

```
from distutils.core import setup, Extension
setup(name='foo', version='1.0', ext_modules=[Extension('foo',
['foo.c'])])
```

Running this script through the Python interpreter demonstrates that you're getting quite a bit more than initially expected with just two lines of code:

```
$ python setup.py
usage: setup.py [global_opts] cmd1 [cmd1_opts] [cmd2 [cmd2_opts] ...]
   or: setup.py --help [cmd1 cmd2 ...]
   or: setup.py --help-commands
   or: setup.py cmd --help

error: no commands supplied
```

Trying again with the --help-commands argument displays all of the commands your setup script can respond to:

```
$ python setup.py --help-commands
Standard commands:
  build           build everything needed to install
  build_py        "build" pure Python modules (copy to build
directory)
  build_ext       build C/C++ extensions (compile/link to build
directory)
  build_clib      build C/C++ libraries used by Python extensions
  build_scripts   "build" scripts (copy and fixup #! line)
  clean           clean up output of 'build' command
  install         install everything from build directory
  install_lib     install all Python modules (extensions and pure
Python)
  install_headers install C/C++ header files
  install_scripts install scripts (Python or otherwise)
  install_data    install data files
```

(continued)

(continued)

```
     sdist              create a source distribution (tarball, zip file,
   etc.)
     register           register the distribution with the Python package
   index
     bdist              create a built (binary) distribution
     bdist_dumb         create a "dumb" built distribution
     bdist_rpm          create an RPM distribution
     bdist_wininst      create an executable installer for MS Windows

   usage: setup.py [global_opts] cmd1 [cmd1_opts] [cmd2 [cmd2_opts] ...]
      or: setup.py --help [cmd1 cmd2 ...]
      or: setup.py --help-commands
      or: setup.py cmd --help
```

There's a lot going on here, but all you need for now is the `build` command. Executing that will compile `foo.c` into `foo.so` (on Linux) or `foo.dll` (on Windows). This file will end up in a subdirectory of the `build` directory in your current directory unless you change that with more command-line options.

For the module to be importable by the Python interpreter, it needs to be in the current directory or in a directory listed in the PYTHONPATH environmental variable or in a directory listed in the `sys.path` list, which you can modify at runtime, although I wouldn't recommend it.

The easiest way to get this to happen is to use another one of the setup script commands:

```
$ python setup.py install
```

If you hadn't already built the module, this would have done that for you because building is a prerequisite for installing (much like a `make` file). The `install` command also copies the module to the site-packages directory for your Python installation. This site-packages directory is listed in `sys.path`, so after this is done, you can start using the module.

On UNIX-based systems, you'll most likely need to run this command as root in order to have permissions to write to the site-packages directory. This usually isn't a problem on Windows. It's also possible to install modules in alternative locations using the `--home` or `--prefix` command-line options, but doing this leaves you responsible for ensuring they're put in a directory the Python interpreter knows about when it's run.

Passing Parameters from Python to C

After you have everything built and installed, importing your new extension module and invoking its one function is easy:

```
>>> import foo
>>> dir(foo)
['__doc__', '__file__', '__name__', 'bar']
>>> foo.bar()
```

If you tried to pass in any arguments to your function, the interpreter will rightfully complain:

```
>>> foo.bar(1)
Traceback (most recent call last):
  File "<stdin>", line 1, in ?
TypeError: bar() takes no arguments (1 given)
```

Because you'll most likely want to define functions that do accept arguments, you can use one of the other signatures for your C functions. For example, a "normal" function (one that accepts some number of parameters) would be defined like this:

```
static PyObject *foo_baz(PyObject *self, PyObject *args) {
    /* Parse args and do something interesting here. */
    Py_RETURN_NONE;
}
```

The method table containing an entry for the new function would look like this:

```
static PyMethodDef foo_methods[] = {
    { "bar",  (PyCFunction)foo_bar, METH_NOARGS, NULL },
    { "baz",  foo_baz, METH_VARARGS, NULL },
    { NULL, NULL, 0, NULL }
};
```

After making those changes to foo.c and saving them, you're going to want to close any open Python interpreters that imported the old version of the extension module so that you can recompile the source, start a new interpreter, and import the new version of the extension module. It's easy to forget to do this if you're compiling in one window and invoking Python in another.

Compiling the new version of your module and importing it will enable you to invoke the new function with any number of arguments of any type:

```
>>> foo.baz()
>>> foo.baz(1)
>>> foo.baz(1, 2.0)
>>> foo.baz(1, 2.0, "three")
```

The reason why anything goes is that you haven't written the C code to enforce a certain number and type of arguments.

The Python API gives you the PyArg_ParseTuple function to extract the arguments from the one PyObject pointer passed into your C function. This is a variadic function much like the standard sscanf function with which you might be familiar.

The first argument to PyArg_ParseTuple is the args argument. This is the object you'll be "parsing." The second argument is a format string describing the arguments as you expect them to appear. Each argument is represented by one or more characters in the format string. An i indicates that you expect the argument to be an integer-like object, which PyArg_ParseTuple will convert into a int as known in C. Specifying a d in the format string will give you a double, and s will give you a string (char *). For example, if you expected the baz function to be passed one integer, one double, and one string, your format string would be "ids". You can find the full list of indicators that you can include in a format string at http://docs.python.org/api/arg-parsing.html.

The remaining arguments to `PyArg_ParseTuple` are pointers to storage space of the appropriate type for your arguments, just like `sscanf`. Knowing this, you might rewrite `baz` to look like the following:

```
static PyObject *foo_baz(PyObject *self, PyObject *args) {
    int     i;
    double  d;
    char    *s;
    if (!PyArg_ParseTuple(args, "ids", &i, &d, &s)) {
        return NULL;
    }
    /* Do something interesting here. */
    Py_RETURN_NONE;
}
```

`PyArg_ParseTuple` will return 0 if it fails to extract exactly what was specified in the format string. It's important that you return `NULL` from your function when this happens so that the interpreter can generate an exception for your caller.

What about optional arguments? If you include a | (the vertical bar) character in your format string, the indicators to the left of the | will be required, but the indicators to the right will be optional. You're going to want to give your local storage for the optional arguments a default value because `PyArg_ParseTuple` won't write anything to those variables if the caller didn't specify the necessary arguments.

For example, if `baz` required one int, one double, and one string but also allowed an optional int, double, and then a string, you might rewrite it to look like this:

```
static PyObject *foo_baz(PyObject *self, PyObject *args) {
    int     i;
    double  d;
    char    *s;
    int     i2 = 4;
    double  d2 = 5.0;
    char    *s2 = "six";
    if (!PyArg_ParseTuple(args, "ids|ids", &i, &d, &s, &i2, &d2,
&s2)) {
        return NULL;
    }
    /* Do something interesting here. */
    Py_RETURN_NONE;
}
```

Lastly, this next and final form your C functions might take will only be necessary when your functions accept keyword arguments. In this case, you'll use the signature that accepts three `PyObject *` arguments and set the `ml_flags` member in your method table entry to `METH_VARARGS|METH_KEYWORDS`. Instead of using the `PyArg_ParseTuple` function to extract your arguments, you'll use `PyArg_ParseTupleAndKeywords`.

This is what the function might look like:

```
static PyObject *foo_quux(PyObject *self, PyObject *args, PyObject
*kw) {
    char *kwlist[] = { "i", "d", "s", NULL };
    int    i;
    double  d = 2.0;
    char    *s = "three";
    if (!PyArg_ParseTupleAndKeywords(args, kw, "i|ds", kwlist, &i,
&d, &s)) {
        return NULL;
    }
    /* Do something interesting here. */
    Py_RETURN_NONE;
}
```

This would be its entry in the method table right after the entry for the baz function but before the sentinel entry:

```
{ "quux", (PyCFunction)foo_quux, METH_VARARGS|METH_KEYWORDS, NULL },
```

PyArg_ParseTupleAndKeywords works just like PyArg_ParseTuple with the exception of two extra arguments. First, you need to pass in the pointer to the Python object containing the keyword arguments. Second, you need to indicate what keywords you're interested in. You do that with a NULL-terminated list of strings. In the preceding example, you're saying that your keywords are "i", "d", and "s".

Each keyword needs to correspond with one indicator in the format string even if you don't ever intend to have your callers use a keyword for certain arguments. Notice how the preceding example includes three indicators in the format string. The first, "i", is required whereas the other two, "d" and "s", are optional. You could call this function (from Python) in any of the following ways:

```
>>> foo.quux(1)
>>> foo.quux(i=1)
>>> foo.quux(1, 2.0)
>>> foo.quux(1, 2.0, "three")
>>> foo.quux(1, 2.0, s="three")
>>> foo.quux(1, d=2.0)
>>> foo.quux(1, s="three")
>>> foo.quux(1, d=2.0, s="three")
>>> foo.quux(1, s="three", d=2.0)
>>> foo.quux(i=1, d=2.0, s="three")
>>> foo.quux(s="three", d=2.0, i=1)
```

You can probably come up with even more variations.

Returning Values from C to Python

PyArg_ParseTuple and PyArg_ParseTupleAndKeywords convert from Python objects into C values but what about going the other way? How would you return a value from a function implemented in C back into Python?

All of the function signatures you saw previously return a `PyObject *`, so you need to use whatever the opposite of `PyArg_ParseTuple` is in order to turn a C value into a Python object. That function is called `Py_BuildValue`.

`Py_BuildValue` takes in a format string much like `PyArg_ParseTuple` does. Instead of passing in the addresses of the values you're building, you pass in the actual values. Here's an example showing how to implement an add function:

```
static PyObject *foo_add(PyObject *self, PyObject *args) {
    int a;
    int b;
    if (!PyArg_ParseTuple(args, "ii", &a, &b)) {
        return NULL;
    }
    return Py_BuildValue("i", a + b);
}
```

The Python equivalent of this function would look like this:

```
def add(a, b):
    return a + b
```

What if you want to return more than one value from your function? In Python, you do that by returning a tuple. In C, you do that by building a tuple with `Py_BuildValue`. If your format string has more than one indicator, you'll get a tuple. You can also be explicit and surround your indicators with parentheses:

```
static PyObject *foo_add_and_subtract(PyObject *self, PyObject *args)
{
    int a;
    int b;
    if (!PyArg_ParseTuple(args, "ii", &a, &b)) {
        return NULL;
    }
    return Py_BuildValue("(ii)", a + b, a - b);
}
```

To help visualize what this function is doing, this is what it would look like if implemented in Python:

```
def add_and_subtract(a, b):
    return (a + b, a - b)
```

Now, armed with just this knowledge, it's possible for you to create a wide variety of extension modules. Let's put this to good use and work on a real example.

The LAME Project

LAME is (or was) an acronym that originally stood for "LAME Ain't an MP3 Encoder." Whether or not it's officially considered an MP3 encoder isn't important to you, because it functions as a (most excellent) free and open-source library that *is* capable of encoding MP3s.

Dozens of software projects use LAME but not many are implemented in Python, which is why you'll be using it as an example to demonstrate just how easy it is to create extension modules for Python that leverage an existing C code base, even when the C code wasn't written to be interfaced with Python.

This example is also a very practical one. Consider how many years went into developing the LAME code base, which in case you don't know is many, many, *many* years. Would you really want to duplicate that work by reimplementing it in Python? Now consider what your answer would be if you were told how unbelievably slow it would run if you had a Python-only encoder! This isn't anything against Python, by the way. This would old true of any language that is higher-level than C. Languages such as Java, Perl, and so on would have the same limitation. This is a perfect example of code that you would *not* want to use Python to develop (there are very few examples where this is true).

Before creating an extension module that wraps the LAME library, you need to learn how to use the API exposed by that library. The core of the LAME API is small enough to create a quick demonstration with only a page or so of C code.

You need the LAME headers and libraries installed on your machine before you can write any code that uses its API, of course. The LAME Project's website is located on SourceForge at `http://lame .sourceforge.net/`. You can download the source code from there. Though you can download and compile and install the libraries for any part of the LAME package from there, you won't find any pre-built binaries on this site (presumably to avoid the potential legal issues of distributing an MP3 encoder). However, you *can* find links to sites that do provide downloadable binaries by looking for them on the LAME Project's website (if you'd rather not build from source).

You can find packages on the Web for most Linux distributions. Some names these packages may be listed under are lame, liblame, or the liblame-dev package. If you can't find a package or would rather build from source, `./configure`, make, and `make install` will work to build a complete working installation of LAME, just as they do with almost every other project you build from source on Linux.

Windows users can use any of the pre-built binaries but those don't usually come with the headers, so you'll have to download those from the main site. If you're doing that, you might as well build the libraries yourself. The LAME source code includes a Visual Studio workspace that can build everything you need to get through the rest of this chapter. There will be errors (there were for the author), but the build process makes it far enough to finish building just what you need, so you can ignore those errors and be OK.

The general overview of creating an MP3 file with LAME is described here:

1. Initialize the library.
2. Set up the encoding parameters.
3. Feed the library one buffer of audio data at a time (returning another buffer of MP3-encoded bytes of that data).
4. Flush the encoder (possibly returning more MP3 data).
5. Close the library.

That's it!

Here's an example written in C that uses the LAME API. It can encode any raw audio file into an MP3-encoded audio file. If you want to compile it to make sure it works, save it in a file called `clame.c`:

```c
#include <stdio.h>
#include <stdlib.h>

#include <lame.h>

#define INBUFSIZE 4096
#define MP3BUFSIZE (int)(1.25 * INBUFSIZE) + 7200

int encode(char *inpath, char *outpath) {
    int status = 0;
    lame_global_flags *gfp;
    int ret_code;
    FILE *infp;
    FILE *outfp;
    short *input_buffer;
    int input_samples;
    char *mp3_buffer;
    int mp3_bytes;

    /* Initialize the library. */
    gfp = lame_init();
    if (gfp == NULL) {
        printf("lame_init returned NULL\n");
        status = -1;
        goto exit;
    }

    /* Set the encoding parameters. */
    ret_code = lame_init_params(gfp);
    if (ret_code < 0) {
        printf("lame_init_params returned %d\n", ret_code);
        status = -1;
        goto close_lame;
    }

    /* Open our input and output files. */
    infp = fopen(inpath, "rb");
    outfp = fopen(outpath, "wb");

    /* Allocate some buffers. */
    input_buffer = (short*)malloc(INBUFSIZE*2);
    mp3_buffer = (char*)malloc(MP3BUFSIZE);

    /* Read from the input file, encode, and write to the output
file. */
    do {
        input_samples = fread(input_buffer, 2, INBUFSIZE, infp);
        if (input_samples > 0) {
            mp3_bytes = lame_encode_buffer_interleaved(
                gfp,
                input_buffer,
```

```
                    input_samples / 2,
                    mp3_buffer,
                    MP3BUFSIZE
            );
            if (mp3_bytes < 0) {
                printf("lame_encode_buffer_interleaved returned
    %d\n", mp3_bytes);
                    status = -1;
                    goto free_buffers;
            } else if (mp3_bytes > 0) {
                    fwrite(mp3_buffer, 1, mp3_bytes, outfp);
            }
        }
    } while (input_samples == INBUFSIZE);

    /* Flush the encoder of any remaining bytes. */
    mp3_bytes = lame_encode_flush(gfp, mp3_buffer,
sizeof(mp3_buffer));
    if (mp3_bytes > 0) {
        printf("writing %d mp3 bytes\n", mp3_bytes);
        fwrite(mp3_buffer, 1, mp3_bytes, outfp);
    }

    /* Clean up. */

free_buffers:
    free(mp3_buffer);
    free(input_buffer);

    fclose(outfp);
    fclose(infp);

close_lame:
    lame_close(gfp);

exit:
    return status;
}

int main(int argc, char *argv[]) {
    if (argc < 3) {
        printf("usage: clame rawinfile mp3outfile\n");
        exit(1);
    }
    encode(argv[1], argv[2]);
    return 0;
}
```

To compile the file on Linux, this command should work (assuming you installed a package like liblame-dev or that the lame development components have installed the appropriate header files in /usr/include/lame):

```
gcc -I/usr/include/lame clame.c -lmp3lame -o clame
```

On Windows, you'll probably have to use a command like this (assuming you built from source):

```
cl /IC:\lame-3.98.2\include clame.c \
   C:\lame-3.98.2\libmp3lame\Release\libmp3lame.lib \
   C:\lame-3.98.2\mpglib\Release\mpglib.lib
```

Those command-line parameters are telling the compiler where to find the LAME headers and necessary libraries. You'll probably have to adjust them to point to the correct directories.

That wasn't too bad, was it? Of course, this code doesn't know how to extract data out of a WAV or any other sort of audio file. It is assumed here that the input file contains nothing but raw, 16-bit, signed samples at 44.1 kHz. Turning a WAV file into one of these raw files is a simple command on most UNIX-based machines (assuming you have the sox program, which should also be available as a package):

```
sox test.wav -t raw test.raw
```

The LAME Extension Module

To create an extension module that enables you to encode a raw audio file into an MP3 could be as simple as creating a simple function that invokes the encode function you defined in the preceding example:

```
#include <Python.h>

#include <lame.h>

/* defined in clame.c */
int encode(char *, char *);

static PyObject *pylame1_encode(PyObject *self, PyObject *args) {
    int status;
    char *inpath;
    char *outpath;
    if (!PyArg_ParseTuple(args, "ss", &inpath, &outpath)) {
        return NULL;
    }
    status = encode(inpath, outpath);
    return Py_BuildValue("i", status);
}

static PyMethodDef pylame1_methods[] = {
    { "encode", pylame1_encode, METH_VARARGS, NULL },
    { NULL, NULL, 0, NULL }
};

PyMODINIT_FUNC initpylame1() {
    Py_InitModule3("pylame1", pylame1_methods, "My first LAME
module.");
}
```

Here the `encode` function accepts two string arguments — the input path and the output path.

Try saving the preceding code in a file called `pylame1.c` and compiling it with this command:

```
gcc -shared -I/usr/include/python3.1 -I/usr/include/lame \
  pylame1.c clame.c \
  -lmp3lame -o pylame1.so
```

On Windows, you'll need something like this:

```
cl /LD /IC:\Python31\include /IC:\lame-3.96.1\include \
  pylame1.c clame.c \
  C:\Python31\libs\python31.lib \
  C:\lame-3.98.2\libmp3lame\Release\libmp3lame.lib \
  C:\lamexs-3.98.2\mpglib\Release\mpglib.lib
```

Note that you're compiling the same `clame.c` example you used in the previous section into this DLL by including it on the command line.

This works, but it's not ideal; you have no way of influencing how the `encode` function works other than by passing in two strings. What if you wanted to encode something other than a raw audio file? How about a WAV file or perhaps some audio data you're streaming off the network? There's no reason why you couldn't implement that functionality in Python, where it would be much easier to do.

You have two options: You can have the Python code pass the audio data into the `encode` function, one chunk at a time, just like you do in the C function. Or, you can pass some object with a `read` method in to `encode`, which would then read its data from that object.

Although the second option might sound more object oriented, the first is the better choice because it provides more flexibility. You could always define some sort of object that reads from some source and passes it on to the encoder, but it would be a lot harder to go the other way around.

Using this design is going to require that you make some changes in the extension module. Right now, there's just one function, and that's fine because that function is doing all of the work for you. With the new approach, however, you'll be making multiple calls to the function that you'll be using to encode the audio data as MP3 data. You can't have the function re-open the file every time it's called, so you're going to need to maintain some state information about where you are in the file somewhere. You can have the caller maintain that state, or you can encapsulate it inside some object defined by your module, which is the approach you'll be taking here.

The new version of your extension module needs to expose a class so that your clients can create instances of this class and invoke methods on them. You'll be hiding a small amount of state in those instances so they can remember which file they're writing to between method calls.

As you learn what you need to do for this new module, you'll see the snippets of code relevant to what is being explained. The entire source for `pylame2.c` is shown later so you can see the snippets together in all of their glory.

The C language syntax doesn't directly support defining a new class, but it does have structures; and in C structures can contain function pointers, which is good enough for what you're trying to do right now. When the Python interpreter creates a new instance of your class, it will actually be allocating enough space to store a new instance of your structure. It's that structure that will contain all of your state for each object.

The Python interpreter needs to store some information in your objects as well. Every object has a reference count and a type, so the first part of your structure has to contain these in order for the Python interpreter to find them:

```
typedef struct {
    PyObject_HEAD
    /* State goes here. */
} pylame2_EncoderObject;
```

The `PyObject_HEAD` macro will add the appropriate members to the structure — you just have to make sure that it's the first thing you add.

You need to provide a function to create the new instances of this structure:

```
static PyObject *Encoder_new(PyTypeObject *type, PyObject *args,
PyObject *kw) {
    pylame2_EncoderObject *self = (pylame2_EncoderObject *)
type->tp_alloc(type, 0);
    /* Initialize object here. */
    return (PyObject *)self;
}
```

Think of this as equivalent to Python's __new__ method. This function will be called by the interpreter when it needs to create a new instance of your type. Notice how you're not calling `malloc` directly but are instead invoking some other function as indicated by the `tp_alloc` member of the `PyTypeObject` that was passed in to your function. You see what function that is in a bit.

You also need a function to free your instances:

```
static  void Encoder_dealloc(PyObject *self) {
    self->ob_type->tp_free(self);
}
```

Think of this function as equivalent to Python's __del__ method and being a counterpart to `Encoder_new`. Because you're calling `tp_free` on your object's type object here, you're probably assuming that the `tp_free` function is the counterpart to the `tp_alloc` function and you're right.

What about the other methods your object is supposed to support? Do you add function pointers to your structure to represent those? If you did, each instance would be eating up memory with the exact same set of pointers, which would be a waste. Instead, you're going to store the function pointers for your methods in a separate structure and your objects will refer to that structure.

Remember that each object knows its type — there's a pointer to a type object hiding inside the `PyObject_HEAD` macro. Therefore, you need another structure to represent that:

```
static PyTypeObject pylame2_EncoderType = {
    PyObject_HEAD_INIT(NULL)
    0,                                  /* ob_size */
    "pylame2.Encoder",                  /* tp_name */
    sizeof(pylame2_EncoderObject),      /* tp_basicsize */
    0,                                  /* tp_itemsize */
    Encoder_dealloc,                    /* tp_dealloc */
    0,                                  /* tp_print */
    0,                                  /* tp_getattr */
    0,                                  /* tp_setattr */
    0,                                  /* tp_compare */
    0,                                  /* tp_repr */
    0,                                  /* tp_as_number */
    0,                                  /* tp_as_sequence */
    0,                                  /* tp_as_mapping */
    0,                                  /* tp_hash */
    0,                                  /* tp_call */
    0,                                  /* tp_str */
    0,                                  /* tp_getattro */
    0,                                  /* tp_setattro */
    0,                                  /* tp_as_buffer */
    Py_TPFLAGS_DEFAULT,                 /* tp_flags */
    "My first encoder object.",         /* tp_doc */
    0,                                  /* tp_traverse */
    0,                                  /* tp_clear */
    0,                                  /* tp_richcompare */
    0,                                  /* tp_weaklistoffset */
    0,                                  /* tp_iter */
    0,                                  /* tp_iternext */
    0,                                  /* tp_methods */
    0,                                  /* tp_members */
    0,                                  /* tp_getset */
    0,                                  /* tp_base */
    0,                                  /* tp_dict */
    0,                                  /* tp_descr_get */
    0,                                  /* tp_descr_set */
    0,                                  /* tp_dictoffset */
    0,                                  /* tp_init */
    0,                                  /* tp_alloc */
    Encoder_new,                        /* tp_new */
    0,                                  /* tp_free */
};
```

This is going to be the structure for what you're going to get a pointer to when your Encoder_new function is called. There's a lot to that structure (and even more that you can't see yet), but you're letting most of the members default to NULL for now. You'll go over the important bits before moving on.

The PyObject_HEAD_INIT macro adds the members that are common to all types. It must be the first member in the structure. It's like PyObject_HEAD except that it initializes the type pointer to whatever you pass in as an argument.

Remember: In Python, types are objects, too, so they also have types. You could call a type's type a "type type." The Python API calls it PyType_Type. It's the type of type objects. You really want to be able to pass &PyType_Type into this macro but some compilers won't let you statically initialize a structure member with a symbol defined in some other module, so you'll have to fill that in later.

The next member, ob_size, might look important but it's a remnant from an older version of the Python API and should be ignored. The member after the name of your type, tp_basicsize, represents the size of all your object instances. When the interpreter needs to allocate storage space for a new instance, it will request tp_basicsize bytes.

Most of the rest of the members are currently NULL, but you'll be filling them in later. They'll hold function pointers for some of the more common operations that many objects support.

The tp_flags member specifies some default flags for the type object, which all type objects need; and the tp_doc member holds a pointer to the docstring for the type, which you always want to provide because you're a good Python citizen.

Notice the tp_alloc and tp_free members, which are set to NULL. Aren't those the members you're calling from Encoder_new and Encoder_dealloc? Yes, they are, but you're going to use a Python API function to fill them in with the appropriate addresses later on because some platforms don't like it when you statically initialize structure members with addresses of functions in other libraries.

At this point, you've defined two structures. To actually make them available via your extension module, you need to add some code to your module's initialization function:

```
PyMODINIT_FUNC initpylame2() {
    PyObject *m;
    if (PyType_Ready(&pylame2_EncoderType) < 0) {
        return;
    }
    m = Py_InitModule3("pylame2", pylame2_methods, "My second LAME
module.");
    Py_INCREF(&pylame2_EncoderType);
    PyModule_AddObject(m, "Encoder", (PyObject *)
&pylame2_EncoderType);
}
```

PyType_Ready gets a type object "ready" for use by the interpreter. It sets the type of the object to PyType_Type and sets a number of the function pointer members that you had previously left NULL, along with a number of other bookkeeping tasks necessary in order to hook everything up properly, including setting your tp_alloc and tp_free members to suitable functions.

After you get your type object ready, you create your module as usual, but this time you're saving the return value (a pointer to a module object) so you can add your new type object to the module. Previously, you had been ignoring the return value and letting the method table define all of the members of the module. Because there's no way to fit a PyObject pointer into a method table, you need to use the PyModule_AddObject function to add your type object to the module. This function takes in the pointer to the module returned from Py_InitModule3, the name of your new object as it should be known in the module, and the pointer to the new object itself.

If you were to compile what you had so far, you'd be able to create new Encoder instances:

```
>>> import pylame2
>>> e = pylame2.Encoder()
```

That object doesn't do you much good, however, because it doesn't have any useful behavior yet.

To make these objects useful, you have to allow for some information to be passed into their initialization functions. That information could simply be the path to the file to which you want to write. Your initialization function could use that path to open a file handle that would enable you to write to it, but there'll be no writing until somebody invokes the encode method on your object. Therefore, your object needs to retain the handle for the file it opened.

You're also going to be invoking functions defined in the LAME library, so your objects will also need to remember the pointer to the lame_global_flags structure returned by lame_init.

Here's your structure with state and a modified Encoder_new function to initialize it:

```
typedef struct {
    PyObject_HEAD
    FILE *outfp;
    lame_global_flags *gfp;
} pylame2_EncoderObject;

static PyObject *Encoder_new(PyTypeObject *type, PyObject *args,
PyObject *kw) {
    pylame2_EncoderObject *self = (pylame2_EncoderObject *)
type->tp_alloc(type, 0);
    self->outfp = NULL;
    self->gfp = NULL;
    return (PyObject *)self;
}
```

You're not checking args and kw here, because this is the equivalent of Python's __new__ method, not __init__. It's in your C implementation of __init__ that you'll be opening the file and initializing the LAME library:

```
static int Encoder_init(pylame2_EncoderObject *self,
                        PyObject *args, PyObject *kw) {
    char *outpath;
    if (!PyArg_ParseTuple(args, "s", &outpath)) {
        return -1;
    }
    if (self->outfp || self->gfp) {
        PyErr_SetString(PyExc_Exception, "__init__ already called");
        return -1;
    }
    self->outfp = fopen(outpath, "wb");
    self->gfp = lame_init();
    lame_init_params(self->gfp);
    return 0;
}
```

Your __init__ implementation is checking two things. The first you've already seen. You're using PyArg_ParseTuple to ensure that you were passed in one string parameter. The second check is ensuring that the outfp and gfp members of your instance are NULL. If they're not, this function must already have been called for this object, so return the appropriate error code for this function after using the PyErr_SetString function to "set" an exception. After you return into the Python interpreter, an exception will be raised and your caller is going to have to catch it or suffer the consequences. You need to do this because it's always possible to call __init__ twice on an object. With this code in place, calling __init__ twice on your objects might look like this:

```
>>> import pylame2
>>> e = pylame2.Encoder("foo.mp3")
>>> e.__init__("bar.mp3")
Traceback (most recent call last):
  File "<stdin>", line 1, in ?
Exception: __init__ already called
```

Of course, you could be nice and reinitialize the object, but that's not necessary for what you want to get done today. You should also be checking for errors, of course.

To indicate that you want this initialization function to be called for each new instance of your class, you need to add the address that this function needs to your type object:

```
(initproc)Encoder_init,             /* tp_init */
```

You're casting it here because you cheated and declared that Encoder_init accepted a pylame2_EncoderObject * as its first argument instead of the more generic PyObject *. You can get away with this type of stuff in C, but you have to be absolutely certain that you know what you're doing.

Because your instances now contain state that reference resources, you need to ensure that those resources are properly disposed of when the object is released. To do this, update your Encoder_dealloc function:

```
static void Encoder_dealloc(pylame2_EncoderObject *self) {
    if (self->gfp) {
        lame_close(self->gfp);
    }
    if (self->outfp) {
        fclose(self->outfp);
    }
    self->ob_type->tp_free(self);
}
```

If you were to build your module with the code you have so far, import it, create an encoder object, and then delete it (using the del keyword or rebinding the variable referencing your object to None or some other object), you would end up with an empty file in the current directory because all you did was open and then close it without writing anything to it. You're getting closer!

You now need to add support for the encode and close methods to your type. Previously, you had created what was called a method table, but that was really defining module-level functions. Defining methods for classes is just as easy but different. You define the methods just like the module-level functions and then create a table listing them:

```
static PyObject *Encoder_encode(PyObject *self, PyObject *args) {
    Py_RETURN_NONE;
}

static PyObject *Encoder_close(PyObject *self) {
    Py_RETURN_NONE;
}

static PyMethodDef Encoder_methods[] = {
    { "encode", Encoder_encode, METH_VARARGS,
          "Encodes and writes data to the output file." },
    { "close", (PyCFunction)Encoder_close, METH_NOARGS,
          "Closes the output file." },
    { NULL, NULL, 0, NULL }
};
```

Then the address of the table is used to initialize the tp_methods member of your type object:

```
Encoder_methods,                    /* tp_methods */
```

With those stubs in place, you could build the module and see the methods and even call them on your objects:

```
>>> import pylame2
>>> e = pylame2.Encoder('foo.mp3')
>>> dir(e)
['__class__', '__delattr__', '__doc__', '__getattribute__',
'__hash__','__init__', '__new__', '__reduce__', '__reduce_ex__', '__repr__',
'__setattr__', '__str__', 'close', 'encode']
>>> e.encode()
>>> e.close()
```

All you have to do now is implement the functions. Here's Encoder_encode (sans complete error-checking):

```
static PyObject *Encoder_encode(pylame2_EncoderObject *self,
PyObject *args) {
    char *in_buffer;
    int in_length;
    int mp3_length;
    char *mp3_buffer;
    int mp3_bytes;
    if (!(self->outfp && self->gfp)) {
        PyErr_SetString(PyExc_Exception, "encoder not open");
        return NULL;
    }
    if (!PyArg_ParseTuple(args, "s#", &in_buffer, &in_length)) {
        return NULL;
    }
    in_length /= 2;
    mp3_length = (int)(1.25 * in_length) + 7200;
    mp3_buffer = (char *)malloc(mp3_length);
    if (in_length > 0) {
```

(continued)

(continued)

```
            mp3_bytes = lame_encode_buffer_interleaved(
                self->gfp,
                (short *)in_buffer,
                in_length / 2,
                mp3_buffer,
                mp3_length
            );
            if (mp3_bytes > 0) {
                fwrite(mp3_buffer, 1, mp3_bytes, self->outfp);
            }
        }
        free(mp3_buffer);
        Py_RETURN_NONE;
    }
```

You expect this argument to be passed a string. Unlike strings in C, which are simple NULL-terminated arrays of characters, you expect that this string will contain embedded NULL characters (the NULL character, which is simple the end-of-string indication in C has the value of '\0' in C. Note the single quotes — in C remember that the different quotes have different meanings. NULL can also be shown as " " in C.) Therefore, instead of using the "s" indicator when parsing the arguments, you use "s#", which allows for embedded NULL characters. `PyArg_ParseTuple` will return both the bytes in a buffer and the length of the buffer instead of tacking a NULL character on the end. Other than that, this function is pretty straightforward.

Here's `Encoder_close`:

```
    static PyObject *Encoder_close(pylame2_EncoderObject *self) {
        int mp3_length;
        char *mp3_buffer;
        int mp3_bytes;
        if (!(self->outfp && self->gfp)) {
            PyErr_SetString(PyExc_Exception, "encoder not open");
            return NULL;
        }
        mp3_length = 7200;
        mp3_buffer = (char *)malloc(mp3_length);
        mp3_bytes = lame_encode_flush(self->gfp, mp3_buffer,
    sizeof(mp3_buffer));
        if (mp3_bytes > 0) {
            fwrite(mp3_buffer, 1, mp3_bytes, self->outfp);
        }
        free(mp3_buffer);
        lame_close(self->gfp);
        self->gfp = NULL;
        fclose(self->outfp);
        self->outfp = NULL;
        Py_RETURN_NONE;
    }
```

You need to make sure you set `outfp` and `gfp` to `NULL` here to prevent `Encoder_dealloc` from trying to close them again.

For both `Encoder_encode` and `Encoder_close`, you're checking to make sure your object is in a valid state for encoding and closing. Somebody could always call `close` and then follow that up with another call to `close` or even a call to `encode`. It's better to raise an exception than to bring down the process hosting your extension module.

You've gone over a lot to get to this point, so it would probably help if you could see the entire extension module in one large example:

```c
#include <Python.h>

#include <lame.h>

typedef struct {
    PyObject_HEAD
    FILE *outfp;
    lame_global_flags *gfp;
} pylame2_EncoderObject;

static PyObject *Encoder_new(PyTypeObject *type, PyObject *args,
PyObject *kw) {
    pylame2_EncoderObject *self = (pylame2_EncoderObject *)
type->tp_alloc(type, 0);
    self->outfp = NULL;
    self->gfp = NULL;
    return (PyObject *)self;
}

static void Encoder_dealloc(pylame2_EncoderObject *self) {
    if (self->gfp) {
        lame_close(self->gfp);
    }
    if (self->outfp) {
        fclose(self->outfp);
    }
    self->ob_type->tp_free(self);
}

static int Encoder_init(pylame2_EncoderObject *self, PyObject *args,
PyObject *kw) {
    char *outpath;
    if (!PyArg_ParseTuple(args, "s", &outpath)) {
        return -1;
    }
    if (self->outfp || self->gfp) {
        PyErr_SetString(PyExc_Exception, "__init__ already called");
        return -1;
    }
    self->outfp = fopen(outpath, "wb");
    self->gfp = lame_init();
    lame_init_params(self->gfp);
    return 0;
}
```

(continued)

(continued)

```c
static PyObject *Encoder_encode(pylame2_EncoderObject *self,
PyObject *args) {
    char *in_buffer;
    int in_length;
    int mp3_length;
    char *mp3_buffer;
    int mp3_bytes;
    if (!(self->outfp && self->gfp)) {
        PyErr_SetString(PyExc_Exception, "encoder not open");
        return NULL;
    }
    if (!PyArg_ParseTuple(args, "s#", &in_buffer, &in_length)) {
        return NULL;
    }
    in_length /= 2;
    mp3_length = (int)(1.25 * in_length) + 7200;
    mp3_buffer = (char *)malloc(mp3_length);
    if (in_length > 0) {
        mp3_bytes = lame_encode_buffer_interleaved(
            self->gfp,
            (short *)in_buffer,
            in_length / 2,
            mp3_buffer,
            mp3_length
        );
        if (mp3_bytes > 0) {
            fwrite(mp3_buffer, 1, mp3_bytes, self->outfp);
        }
    }
    free(mp3_buffer);
    Py_RETURN_NONE;
}

static PyObject *Encoder_close(pylame2_EncoderObject *self) {
    int mp3_length;
    char *mp3_buffer;
    int mp3_bytes;
    if (!(self->outfp && self->gfp)) {
        PyErr_SetString(PyExc_Exception, "encoder not open");
        return NULL;
    }
    mp3_length = 7200;
    mp3_buffer = (char *)malloc(mp3_length);
    mp3_bytes = lame_encode_flush(self->gfp, mp3_buffer,
sizeof(mp3_buffer));
    if (mp3_bytes > 0) {
        fwrite(mp3_buffer, 1, mp3_bytes, self->outfp);
    }
    free(mp3_buffer);
    lame_close(self->gfp);
    self->gfp = NULL;
    fclose(self->outfp);
    self->outfp = NULL;
    Py_RETURN_NONE;
```

```
    }

static PyMethodDef Encoder_methods[] = {
    { "encode", (PyCFunction)Encoder_encode, METH_VARARGS,
          "Encodes and writes data to the output file." },
    { "close", (PyCFunction)Encoder_close, METH_NOARGS,
          "Closes the output file." },
    { NULL, NULL, 0, NULL }
};

static PyTypeObject pylame2_EncoderType = {
    PyObject_HEAD_INIT(NULL)
    0,                              /* ob_size */
    "pylame2.Encoder",              /* tp_name */
    sizeof(pylame2_EncoderObject),  /* tp_basicsize */
    0,                              /* tp_itemsize */
    (destructor)Encoder_dealloc,    /* tp_dealloc */
    0,                              /* tp_print */
    0,                              /* tp_getattr */
    0,                              /* tp_setattr */
    0,                              /* tp_compare */
    0,                              /* tp_repr */
    0,                              /* tp_as_number */
    0,                              /* tp_as_sequence */
    0,                              /* tp_as_mapping */
    0,                              /* tp_hash */
    0,                              /* tp_call */
    0,                              /* tp_str */
    0,                              /* tp_getattro */
    0,                              /* tp_setattro */
    0,                              /* tp_as_buffer */
    Py_TPFLAGS_DEFAULT,             /* tp_flags */
    "My first encoder object.",     /* tp_doc */
    0,                              /* tp_traverse */
    0,                              /* tp_clear */
    0,                              /* tp_richcompare */
    0,                              /* tp_weaklistoffset */
    0,                              /* tp_iter */
    0,                              /* tp_iternext */
    Encoder_methods,                /* tp_methods */
    0,                              /* tp_members */
    0,                              /* tp_getset */
    0,                              /* tp_base */
    0,                              /* tp_dict */
    0,                              /* tp_descr_get */
    0,                              /* tp_descr_set */
    0,                              /* tp_dictoffset */
    (initproc)Encoder_init,         /* tp_init */
    0,                              /* tp_alloc */
    Encoder_new,                    /* tp_new */
    0,                              /* tp_free */
};
```

(continued)

(continued)

```c
static PyMethodDef pylame2_methods[] = {
    { NULL, NULL, 0, NULL }
};

PyMODINIT_FUNC initpylame2() {
    PyObject *m;
    if (PyType_Ready(&pylame2_EncoderType) < 0) {
        return;
    }
    m = Py_InitModule3("pylame2", pylame2_methods, "My second LAME
module.");
    Py_INCREF(&pylame2_EncoderType);
    PyModule_AddObject(m, "Encoder", (PyObject *)
&pylame2_EncoderType);
}
```

You can now save this file as `pylame2.c` and compile it.

On Linux:

```
gcc -shared -I/usr/include/python3.1 -I/usr/include/lame pylame2.c \
  -lmp3lame -o pylame2.so
```

On Windows:

```
cl /LD /IC:\Python31\include /IC:\lame-3.98.2\include pylame2.c \
  C:\Python31\libs\python31.lib \
  C:\lame-3.98.2\libmp3lame\Release\libmp3lame.lib \
  C:\lame-3.98.2\mpglib\Release\mpglib.lib
```

Once that's done, you can exercise your new extension module with a simple driver script written entirely in Python:

```python
import pylame2

INBUFSIZE = 4096

encoder = pylame2.Encoder('test.mp3')
input = file('test.raw', 'rb')
data = input.read(INBUFSIZE)

while data != '':
    encoder.encode(data)
    data = input.read(INBUFSIZE)

input.close()
encoder.close()
```

That completes version 2 of your extension module. You're able to read data from anywhere. Your sample driver is still reading from the raw input file you created earlier, but there's nothing stopping it from extracting that information out of a WAV file or reading it from a socket.

The only deficiency with this version of the module is that you can't customize how the encoded data is written. You're going to fix that in the next revision of the module by "writing" to an object and not directly to the file system. Intrigued? Read on.

Using Python Objects from C Code

Python's a dynamically typed language, so it doesn't have a formal concept of interfaces even though we use them all the time. The most common interface is the "file" interface. Terms like "file-like object" describe this interface. It's really nothing more than an object that "looks like" a file object. Usually, it can get by with only either a read or write method and nothing more.

For the next version of your extension module, you're going to allow your users to pass in any file-like object (supporting a write method) when constructing new encoder objects. Your encoder object will simply call the write method with the MP3-encoded bytes. You don't have to be concerned about whether it's a real file object or a socket or anything else your users can dream up. This is polymorphism at its finest.

In the last version of the module, your object held a FILE *. You need to change this by adding a reference to a PyObject and removing the FILE *:

```
typedef struct {
    PyObject_HEAD
    PyObject *outfp;
    lame_global_flags *gfp;
} pylame3_EncoderObject;
```

Encoder_new can stay the same because all it does is set outfp to NULL. Encoder_dealloc, however, needs to be modified:

```
static void Encoder_dealloc(pylame3_EncoderObject *self) {
    if (self->gfp) {
        lame_close(self->gfp);
    }
    Py_XDECREF(self->outfp);
    self->ob_type->tp_free(self);
}
```

Instead of calling fclose, you use the Py_XDECREF macro to decrement the reference count by one. You can't delete the object, because there might be other references to it. In fact, other references to this object are likely because the object came from outside of this module. You didn't create it, but somebody else did and passed it in to you. They probably still have a variable bound to that object.

If you're decrementing the reference count here in Encoder_dealloc, you must be incrementing it someplace else. You're doing that in Encoder_init:

```
static int Encoder_init(pylame3_EncoderObject *self,
                        PyObject *args, PyObjecti*kw) {
    PyObject *outfp;
    if (!PyArg_ParseTuple(args, "O", &outfp)) {
```

(continued)

(continued)

```
            return -1;
        }
        if (self->outfp || self->gfp) {
            PyErr_SetString(PyExc_Exception, "__init__ already called");
            return -1;
        }
        self->outfp = outfp;
        Py_INCREF(self->outfp);
        self->gfp = lame_init();
        lame_init_params(self->gfp);
        return 0;
    }
```

You've modified the format string for `PyArg_ParseTuple` to contain "0" instead of "s". "O" indicates that you want an object pointer. You don't care what type of object it is; you just don't want `PyArg_ParseTuple` to do any kind of conversion from the object to some primitive C data type.

After you're sure you were passed the correct number of arguments and __init__ hasn't been called before, you can store the object argument for later use. Here you're using the `Py_INCREF` macro to increment the reference count. This will keep the object alive until you decrement the count.

Why did the previous macro, `Py_XDECREF`, have an X in it, whereas this one did not? There are actually two forms of these macros. The "X" versions check to ensure that the pointer isn't NULL before adjusting the reference count. The non-"X" versions don't do that check. They're faster, but you have to know what you're doing in order to use them correctly. The documentation for `PyArg_ParseTuple` tells us that if it succeeds, the output pointer will be valid, so you were safe using `Py_INCREF` here, but you might not have been that safe using `Encoder_dealloc`.

Making sure that you perfectly balance your increments with your decrements is the trickiest part of implementing extension modules, so be careful. If you don't, you could leak memory, or you might access an object that's already been deleted, which is never a good thing.

It's also very important to pay attention to the documentation for the different API functions you use in terms of references. Some functions will increase the reference count before returning it. Others won't. The documentation for `PyArg_ParseTuple` states that the reference count is not increased, which is why you have to increment it if you expect it to stick around for as long as you need it.

Now that you have an object (that hopefully has a `write` method), you need to use it. Instead of calling `fwrite` in `Encoder_encode` and `Encoder_close`, you want to call the `write` method on your object. The Python API has a function called `PyObject_CallMethod` that will do exactly what you need it to do. Here's the snippet of code you would use in both `Encoder_encode` and `Encoder_close` to call the `write` method on your object:

```
    PyObject* write_result = PyObject_CallMethod(
                                 self->outfp, "write", "(s#)",
    mp3_buffer, mp3_bytes);
    if (!write_result) {
        free(mp3_buffer);
        return NULL;
    }
    Py_DECREF(write_result);
```

`PyObject_CallMethod` requires three parameters. The first is the object on which you're invoking the method. This object will be the first argument into the method, usually called `self`. The second argument to `PyObject_CallMethod` is the name of the method. The third argument is a format string describing the arguments. This can be `NULL` if there are no arguments. When it's not `NULL`, it looks very similar to a `PyArg_ParseTuple` format string except it's always surrounded with parentheses. `PyObject_CallMethod` is basically calling `Py_BuildValue` for you with these parameters, and the tuple that results is being passed in to your method.

`PyObject_CallMethod` returns a `PyObject *`. All `write` method implementations probably return `None`, but you're still responsible for decrementing the reference count.

Because most of `pylame3.c` hasn't changed from `pylame2.c`, I won't include the entire file here. It shouldn't be too difficult to insert the changes described in this section.

Once the new version of the module is compiled, you can use any file-like object you want as a parameter to the `Encoder` object. Here's an example that demonstrates this:

```python
import pylame3

INBUFSIZE = 4096

class MyFile(file):

    def __init__(self, path, mode):
        file.__init__(self, path, mode)
        self.n = 0

    def write(self, s):
        file.write(self, s)
        self.n += 1

output = MyFile('test3.mp3', 'wb')
encoder = pylame3.Encoder(output)
input = file('test.raw', 'rb')

data = input.read(INBUFSIZE)
while data != '':
    encoder.encode(data)
    data = input.read(INBUFSIZE)

input.close()
encoder.close()
output.close()

print('output.write was called %d times' % output.n)
```

This example includes a class derived from the built-in file object to show off some of the stuff you can do. OK, it's not that impressive, but it at least shows how flexible your new extension module can be. As long as you pass in an object that has a `write` method, your extension module is happy.

Summary

In this chapter, you learned how to expose simple functions implemented in C to Python developers by creating an extension module and defining a method table. Converting Python objects to C values is done using `PyArg_ParseTuple`. Going the opposite way, turning a C value into a Python object is done using `Py_BuildValue`.

You also looked at how to define new types in an extension module by defining the object and type structures. You set up the type object so that it could create new instances of your type and later destroy them. Making sure that you correctly increment and decrement the reference counts of objects that you use requires careful consideration.

There's a lot more to writing extension modules, of course, but not enough room in one chapter to cover it all. Be sure to consult the documentation at `http://docs.python.org/ext/ext.html` and `http://docs.python.org/api/api.html`.

The key points to take away from this chapter are:

❑ While code that is written in C may run faster than code written in Python, it is important to note that writing code in Python is much faster than writing it in C.

❑ Python extension modules are normal C libraries. On UNIX machines, these libraries usually end in `.so` (for shared object). On Windows machines, you typically see `.dll` (for dynamically linked library).

❑ The distutils package makes it possible to distribute Python modules in a standard way.

❑ The --help-commands argument displays all of the commands that a setup script is capable of responding to.

❑ You can use PyArg_ParseTuple and PyArg_ParseTupleAndKeywords to convert from Python objects into C values. To do the reverse, use Py_BuildValue.

Exercises

1. Add a new module-level function to the `foo` module you created earlier in the chapter. Call the function `reverse_tuple` and implement it so that it accepts one tuple as an argument and returns a similarly sized tuple with the elements in reverse order. Completing this exercise is going to require research on your part because you need to know how to "unpack" a tuple. You already know one way to create a tuple (using `Py_BuildValue`), but that's not going to work for this exercise, because you want your function to work with tuples of arbitrary size. The Python/C API documentation for tuples (at `http://docs.python.org/api/tupleObjects.html`) lists all of the functions you need to accomplish this. Be careful with your reference counting!

2. `List` and `dictionary` objects are an extremely important part of nearly all Python applications so it would be useful to learn how to manipulate those objects from C. Add another function to the `foo` module called `dict2list` that accepts a dictionary as a parameter and returns a list. The members of the list should alternate between the keys and the values in the dictionary. The order isn't important as long as each key is followed by its value. You'll have to look up how to iterate over the items in the dictionary (*hint:* look up `PyDict_Next`) and how to create a list and append items to it (*hint:* look up `PyList_New` and `PyList_Append`).

Numerical Programming

In this chapter, you learn how to use Python to work with numbers. You've already seen some arithmetic examples, but after reading this chapter, you'll have a better understanding of the different ways you can represent numbers in Python, of how to perform mathematical computations, and of efficient ways of working with large numerical data sets.

Numerical code lies at the heart of technical software, and is used widely in science, engineering, finance, and related fields. Almost any substantial program does some nontrivial numerical computation, so it pays to be familiar with some of the contents of this chapter even if you are not working in one of these fields. For instance, if you are writing a script to analyze web logs, you might want to compute statistics on the rate of hits on your web server; if you are writing a program with a graphical user interface, you might need math functions to compute the coordinates of the graphics in your GUI.

Parts of this chapter require some understanding of math beyond simple arithmetic. Feel free to skip over these if you have forgotten the math being used. The last section of this chapter, which discusses numerical arrays, is technically more advanced than most of the material in this book, but it's important reading if you plan to use Python for handling large sets of numbers.

Designing software that performs complex numerical computation, known as *numerical analysis*, is both a science and an art. There are often many ways of doing a computation, and numerical analysis tells you which of these will produce an answer closest to the correct result. Things can get tricky, especially when working with floating-point numbers, because, as you will see, a floating-point number is merely an approximation of a real number. This chapter mentions numerical precision but doesn't go into the finer points, so if you are embarking on writing software that performs extensive floating-point computations, consider flipping through a book on numerical analysis to get a sense of the kind of problems you might run into.

In this chapter you learn:

❑   The different data types that relate to numbers.

❑   Some basic (and advanced) math operators.

- ❏ How to perform mathematical equations on arrays.
- ❏ How to work with the math and array modules.

Numbers in Python

A number, like any object in Python, has a type. Python has three basic numerical types. One of these, int, represents integers, and float represents floating-point numbers. The third numeric type, which is covered later in this chapter, represents complex floating-point numbers.

Integers

You've already seen the integer type, int. If you write an ordinary number in your program like 42, called a *literal* number, Python creates an int object for it:

```
>>> x = 42
>>> type(x)
<class 'int'>
```

You didn't have to construct the int explicitly, but you could if you want, like this:

```
>>> x = int(42)
```

You can also use the int constructor to convert other types, such as strings or other numerical types, to integers:

```
>>> x = int("17")
>>> y = int(4.8)
>>> print(x, y, x - y)
17 4 13
```

In the first line, Python converts a string representing a number to the number itself; you can't do math with "17" (a string), but you can with 17 (an integer). In the second line, Python converted the floating-point value 4.8 to the integer 4 by *truncating* it—chopping off the part after the decimal point to make it an integer.

When you convert a string to an int, Python assumes the number is represented in base 10. You can specify another base as the second argument. For instance, if you pass 16, the number is assumed to be hexadecimal:

```
>>> hex_number = "a1"
>>> print(int(hex_number, 16))
161
```

You can specify hexadecimal literals by prefixing the number with 0x. For example, hexadecimal 0xa1 is equivalent to decimal 161. Similarly, literals starting with just a 0 are assumed to be octal (base 8), so octal 0105 is equivalent to decimal 69. These conventions are used in many other programming languages, too.

Long Integers

What's the largest number Python can store in an `int`? Prior to Python 3.0, Python used at least 32 bits to represent integers, which meant that you could store numbers at least as large as $2^{31}-1$ and negative numbers as small as -2^{31}. If you needed to store a larger number, Python provided the `long` type, which represented arbitrarily large integers.

For example, long before the search engine Google existed, mathematicians defined a *googol*, a one followed by 100 zeros. To represent this number in Python, you used to type out the hundred zeros, or you could have saved yourself the trouble by using the exponentiation operator, `**`:

```
>>> googol = 10 ** 100
>>> print(googol)
10000000000000000000000000000000000000000000000000000000000000
0000000000000000000000000000000000000000
```

The preceding was an example of a long integer. Starting in Python 3.0, the long type no longer exists; instead, `int` has been extended so that there is no limit to the size of an integer.

Floating-point Numbers

In Python, a floating-point number is represented by a `float` object. A floating-point number is only an approximation to a real number, so you may sometimes see results that look strange. For example:

```
>>> x = 1.1
>>> x
1.1000000000000001
>>> print(x)
1.1
```

What's going on here? You assigned to x the floating-point *approximation* to the number 1.1. The floating-point number that Python can represent that is closest to 1.1 is actually a tiny bit different, and Python is honest with you and shows this number when you ask for the full representation of x. When you print x, however, Python provides you with a "nice" depiction of the number, which doesn't show enough decimal places to illustrate the floating-point approximation.

Simply entering x at the command prompt prints what you would get by calling `repr(x)`. *Entering* `print x` *prints what you would get by calling* `str(x)`.

As with integers, you can use the `float` constructor to covert strings to numbers (but only in base 10). For example:

```
>>> x = float("16.4")
```

Very large and very small floating-point numbers are represented with *exponential notation*, which separates out the power of ten. A googol as a floating-point number would be `1e+100`, which means the number 1 times ten raised to the power 100. The U.S. national debt at the time this was written, according to the Treasury Department website, was:

```
>>> debt = 11322188570453.51
```

Python prefers exponential notation to print a number this large:

```
>>> print(debt)
1.13221885705e+13
```

You can also enter literals with exponential notation.

Floating-point Precision

A floating-point number is an approximation. As you have seen, it can carry only a limited number of digits of precision.

Formally, Python does not make any promises about the number of digits of precision retained in `float` variables. However, internally Python uses the C type `double` to store the contents of `float` objects, so if you know the precision of a C `double` variable on a platform, you'll know the precision of a Python `float` when running on that platform.

Most systems store a `double` in 64 bits and provide about 16 digits of precision.

Formatting Numbers

You can convert any Python number to a string using the `str` constructor. This produces the text that would be printed by the `print` statement, as a string object. For simple applications, this is adequate.

For better control of the output format, use Python's built-in string formatting operator, `%`.

Note that this has nothing to do with the remainder operator. If you use `%` after a string, that's the string formatting operator. If you use `%` between two numbers, you get the remainder operator.

Following are some details on formatting numbers. If you are familiar with the `printf` function in C, you already know much of the syntax for formatting numbers in Python.

To format an integer, use the `%d` conversion in the format string. For a floating-point number, use `%f`. If you use `%d` with a floating-point number or `%f` with an integer, Python will convert the number to the type indicated by the conversion. For example:

```
>>> print("%d" % 100)
100
>>> print("%d" % 101.6)
101
```

You probably didn't really notice, because it's so obvious, that Python formatted these integers in base 10. For some applications, you might prefer your output in hexadecimal. Use the %x conversion to produce this. If you use %#x, Python puts 0x before the output to make it look just like a hexadecimal literal value, like so:

```
>>> print("%#x" % 100)
0x64
```

Similarly, %o (that's the letter "o," not a zero) produces output in octal, and %#o produces octal output preceded by a 0.

For integers, you can specify the width (number of digits) of the output by placing a number after the % in the format string. If the number starts with 0, the output will be left-padded with zeros; otherwise, it will be padded with spaces. In the examples that follow, the output is surrounded with parentheses so you can see exactly what Python generates for the %d conversions:

```
>>> print("z is (%6d)" % 175)
z is (   175)
>>> print("z is (%06d)" % 175)
z is (000175)
```

When you format floating-point numbers, you can specify the total width of the output, and/or the number of digits displayed after the decimal place. If you want the output to have total width w and to display p decimal places, use the conversion %w.pf in the format string. The total width includes the decimal point and digits after the decimal point. Unlike converting a float to an integer value, Python *rounds to the nearest digit* in last decimal place:

```
>>> x = 20.0 / 3
>>> print("(%6.2f)" % x)
(  6.67)
```

If you omit the number before the decimal point, Python uses as much room as necessary to print the integer part and the decimal places you asked for:

```
>>> print("(%.4f)" % x)
(6.6667)
```

You can demand as many digits as you want, but remember that a float carries a limited precision and, therefore, contains information for only 16 digits or so. Python will add zero digits to fill out the rest:

```
>>> two_thirds = 2.0 / 3
>>> print("%.40f" % two_thirds)
0.6666666666666666630000000000000000000000
```

The number you see may be slightly different, because architectures handle the details of floating-point computations differently.

If you omit the number after the decimal point (or specify zero decimal places), Python doesn't show any decimal places and omits the decimal point, too:

```
>>> print("(%4.f)" % x)
(   7)
```

For example, the following function formats the ratio of its arguments, num and den, as a percentage, showing one digit after the decimal point:

```
>>> def as_percent(num, den):
...     if den == 0:
...         ratio = 0
...     else:
...         ratio = float(num) / den
...     return "%5.1f%%" % (100 * ratio)
...
>>> print("ratio = " + as_percent(6839, 13895))
ratio =  49.2%
```

One nice thing about this function is that it confirms that the denominator is not zero, to avoid division-by-zero errors. Moreover, look closely at the format string. The first % goes with the f as part of the floating-point conversion. The %% at the end is converted to a single % in the output: Because the percent symbol is used to indicate a conversion, Python requires you to use *two* of them in a format string if you want one in your output.

You don't have to hard-code the width or number of decimal places in the format string. If you use an asterisk instead of a number in the conversion, Python takes the value from an extra integer argument in the argument tuple (positioned before the number that's being formatted). Using this feature, you can write a function that formats U.S. dollars. Its arguments are an amount of money and the number of digits to use for the dollars part, not including the two digits for cents:

```
>>> def format_dollars(dollars, places):
...     return "$%*.2f" % (places + 3, dollars)
...
>>> print(format_dollars(499.98, 5))
$  499.98
```

In the format string, you use * instead of the total width in the floating-point conversion. Python looks at the argument tuple and uses the first value as the total width of the conversion. In this case, you specify three more than the desired number of digits for dollars, to leave room for the decimal point and the two digits for cents.

Even more options are available for controlling the output of numbers with the string formatting operator. Consult the Python documentation for details, under the section on sequence types (because strings are sequences) in the *Python Library Reference*.

Characters as Numbers

What about characters? C and C++ programmers are used to manipulating characters as numbers, because C's char type is just another integer numeric type. Python doesn't work like this, though. In Python, a character is just a string of length one, and cannot be used as a number.

Occasionally, you might need to convert between characters and their numeric values. Python provides the built-in function ord to convert a single character to its numeric code and the function asc to convert back from a numeric code to a character. The numeric code must be between 0 and 255.

> *Strictly speaking, this code is not ASCII, because ASCII only goes up to 127. However, the first 127 values converted by* ord *and* asc *are ASCII code values.*

If you are a Usenet regular, you are probably familiar with the *rot13* cipher. It's not particularly secure; all it does is rotate letters of the alphabet 13 positions forward, wrapping around from "z" to "a." Using chr and ord functions, it's not hard to implement in Python:

```python
def rot13_character(character):
    # Look up codes for ends of the alphabet.
    a = ord('a')
    z = ord('z')
    A = ord('A')
    Z = ord('Z')

    code = ord(character)
    # Rotate lower-case characters.
    if a <= code <= z:
        code = a + (code - a + 13) % 26
    # Rotate upper-case characters.
    elif A <= code <= Z:
        code = A + (code - A + 13) % 26
    # Leave other characters alone.
    else:
        pass
    return chr(code)


def rot13(plaintext):
    # Loop over letters in the text.
    ciphertext = ""
    for character in plaintext:
        ciphertext += rot13_character(character)
    return ciphertext
```

The program is composed of two functions. The first, rot13_character, applies rot13 to a single character. If it's an uppercase or lowercase letter, it is rotated 13 places; otherwise, it is left alone. (In case you are not familiar with the remainder operator, %, it is described in the next section.) The main function, rot13, takes the message to be coded (the "plaintext") and creates the encoded message (the "ciphertext") by rotating each letter.

Type the preceding code into a module file named `rot13.py`. In Python, import the module and try it out:

```
>>> import rot13
>>> message = rot13.rot13("This is a TOP-SECRET encoded message.")
>>> print(message)
Guvf vf n GBC-FRPERG rapbqrq zrffntr.
```

`rot13` has the nice property that it is its own inverse: To decode a rot13-encoded message, you just apply `rot13` to it again:

```
>>> print(rot13.rot13(message))
This is a TOP-SECRET encoded message.
```

Mathematics

In addition to the usual complement of arithmetic operations, Python includes some handy built-in math functions, and a `math` module that provides other commonly used functions. Coverage of arithmetic operators may seem obvious, but you should also understand some subtle points about how Python handles certain numeric types.

Arithmetic

Python provides the normal arithmetic operators + (addition), − (subtraction), * (multiplication), and / (division) for numerical types. You can mix numerical types when using these operators; Python automatically chooses the more flexible type for the result:

```
>>> i = 10
>>> f = 6.54
>>> print(i + f)
16.54
```

When adding an integer, `i`, and a floating-point number `f`, Python chose a `float` for the result.

These operators all have special forms for updating the values of variables, written by adding an equals sign right after the operator. Instead of writing

```
>>> total = total + 6
>>> coefficient = coefficient / 2
```

you can simply write:

```
>>> total += 6
>>> coefficient /= 2
```

and so forth.

When dividing two integers, Python always uses an `integer` type for the result, unless the result is fractional, as is the case in the following example:

```
>>> print 10 / 3
3.33333333333
```

> ### Floor Division
>
> Python provides another division operator, called *floor division*, which explicitly rounds down the quotient to an integer. Floor division is represented by `//`. You can use it with `float` objects as well: for instance, `6.6//3.0` evaluates to `2.0`.

The exponentiation operator `**` is used previously in examples. It, too, works for integer and floating-point values. The function that follows uses it to compute compounded interest. The function returns the amount of money you would have if you put `starting_balance` in a bank account with APR `annual_rate` and waited for `years`:

```
>>> def compound(starting_balance, annual_rate, years):
...     return starting_balance * ((1 + annual_rate) ** years)
...
```

Ten grand in the bank at 4 percent APR for a century yields:

```
>>> print(compound(10000, 0.04, 100))
505049.481843
```

That's half a million bucks. Start saving now.

Also useful is the remainder operator `%`. It's like floor division, but instead of returning the quotient, it returns the remainder. Using it, you can format a number of months into whole years and remaining months:

```
>>> def format_months(months):
...     print("%d years, %d months" % (months // 12, months % 12))
...
>>> format_months(100)
8 years, 4 months
```

Built-in Math Functions

A few very common mathematical functions are available as built-in functions. The simplest is `abs`, which returns the absolute value of a number. The number that `abs` returns is the same type as the number you pass it:

```
>>> print(abs(-6.5))
6.5
```

Also useful are `min` and `max`, which return the smallest or largest of several values. You can call them either with several numeric arguments or with a single argument that is a sequence (such as a list or tuple) of numbers. The values needn't all be the same type:

```
>>> print(min(6, 7, 2, 8, 5))
2
>>> print(max([0, 43.5, 19, 5, -6]))
43.5
```

The `round` function rounds a floating-point value to a specified number of digits. This is similar to the behavior you saw before in the `%f` conversions, except the result is not a string but rather another floating-point number with which you can perform further computations. Specify the number to round, and the number of decimal places you want to keep:

```
>>> print(round(1234.56789, 2))
1234.57
```

You can even specify a negative number of decimal places, which rounds to that multiple of 10:

```
>>> print(round(1234.56789, -2))
1200.0
```

Lastly, the `sum` function adds numbers in a sequence. Together with `range`, you can compute the sum of the first 100 positive integers:

```
>>> print(sum(range(1, 101)))
5050
```

Suppose in your Python programming class you got a 96 percent and 90 percent on the two homework assignments, a perfect score on the final project, and an 88 percent on the final exam. What's your average for the class? Of course, you would write a Python function to compute it. The function uses `sum` and computes the mean, or average, value of a sequence of numbers:

```
>>> def mean(numbers):
...     if numbers:
...         return float(sum(numbers)) / len(numbers)
...     else:
...         raise ValueError("no numbers specified")
...
>>> print(mean([96, 90, 100, 88]))
93.5
```

It's a good idea to make sure that the sequence of numbers isn't empty, to avoid dividing by zero. In this case, the function raises an exception if the sequence is empty.

The `math` module contains the standard transcendental functions listed here. All these functions take `float` arguments and return `float` values:

- ❑ Square root: `sqrt`
- ❑ Exponentiation: `exp`
- ❑ Logarithms: `log` (natural logarithm), `log10` (base 10 logarithm)
- ❑ Trigonometric functions: `sin`, `cos`, and `tan`; arguments are in radians
- ❑ Inverse trigonometric functions: `asin`, `acos`, and `atan`; results are in radians
- ❑ Hyperbolic functions: `sinh`, `cosh`, and `tanh`

A few other useful math functions are included:

- ❑ `hypot(x, y)` is equivalent to `sqrt(x ** 2 + y ** 2)`
- ❑ `atan2(x, y)` is like `atan(x / y)` but gets the quadrant right and handles a zero denominator
- ❑ `floor` and `ceil` are the standard floor and ceiling functions; their results are integers but represented as `float` values

The `math` package also contains the constants `pi` and `e`.

Here's some sample code that uses the `math` module. It will give you flashbacks to your freshman physics class. It's a function that computes the time of flight and range of a projectile launched into the air (such as a cannonball), neglecting friction. Examine it at least long enough to understand how the Python code works. Pay attention to how `sin`, `cos`, and `pi` are imported from `math`, which saves you from having to refer to them as `math.sin` and so on. It's a handy technique for commonly used functions. Note also how carefully the units used in the arguments and results are documented. Many failed rocket launches attest to the importance of this practice.

```
from math import sin, cos, pi

def trajectory(velocity, angle):
    """Compute time of flight and range of a projectile.

    For a projectile with initial 'velocity' in meters/sec launched at
    'angle' from horizontal in degrees, returns time of flight in sec
    and range in meters, neglecting friction."""

    # Gravitational acceleration in meters/sec^2.
    g = 9.8
    # Convert 'angle' to radians.
    angle = angle * pi / 180
    # Compute horizontal and vertical components of velocity.
    v_h = velocity * cos(angle)
    v_v = velocity * sin(angle)
    # Compute the time of flight and range.
    tof = 2 * v_v / g
    range = tof * v_h
    return tof, range
```

Suppose you throw a ball into the air at 40 m/sec (about 90 mph) at a 45° angle. How long will it stay in the air, and how far away will it land? Save the preceding code into a file named `ballistic.py`, and then call the function like this:

```
>>> from ballistic import trajectory
>>> tof, range = trajectory(40, 45)
>>> print("time of flight: %.1f sec, range: %.0f meters" % (tof, range))
time of flight: 5.8 sec, range: 163 meters
```

Complex Numbers

A *complex number* is the sum of a real number and an imaginary number. In case you need a refresher, an imaginary number is a multiple of the *imaginary unit*, which is the square root of –1. Mathematicians (and math teachers) usually use the symbol *i* for the imaginary unit, whereas engineers often use *j*.

In Python, an imaginary number is written as a number followed by j (with no intervening spaces):

```
>>> imaginary_number = 16j
```

To create a complex number, add (or take the difference of) a real number and an imaginary number:

```
>>> complex_number = 6 + 4j
```

Python stores the complex number as a single object, whose type is `complex`:

```
>>> print(complex_number)
(6+4j)
>>> print(type(complex_number))
<class 'complex'>
```

If you prefer, you can use the `complex` constructor to construct complex number objects. This assignment is equivalent to the preceding one:

```
>>> complex_number = complex(6, 4)
```

Let's make sure that 1j is really the imaginary unit:

```
>>> print(1j ** 2)
(-1+0j)
```

This verifies that j^2 is in fact –1, and also demonstrates that the result of an arithmetic operation involving `complex` values is itself a `complex`, even if the result happens to be a real number (that is, has a zero imaginary part).

> You can't write j by itself to represent the imaginary unit. You must write 1j. By itself, j represents the variable named "j."

Both the real and imaginary parts of a `complex` object are stored as floating-point values, even if you specified them as integers. Remember that 1/3 in Python returns zero? Not so for complex numbers:

```
>>> print((1+0j)/3)
(0.333333333333+0j)
```

Arithmetic works for complex numbers as you would expect, and you can mix `int`, `float`, and `complex` in the same expression:

```
>>> print(2 * (10 + 3j) * (6.5 - 4j) / (1 - 1j) + 30)
(127.5+56.5j)
```

A few other operations round out Python's handling of complex numbers. First, the mathematical operations *Re* and *Im* return the real and imaginary parts of a complex number, respectively. These are provided in Python by attributes named `real` and `imag` that every `complex` object has. The value of each is a `float`:

```
>>> x = 5 - 6j
>>> print(x.real)
5.0
>>> print(x.imag)
-6.0
```

You saw before that the built-in `abs` function returns the absolute value of an `int`, `long`, or `double` object. For `complex` numbers, it returns the magnitude, which is the square root of the sum of the squares of the real and imaginary parts. You can verify this by using the `hypot` function discussed previously:

```
>>> print(abs(x))
7.81024967591
>>> import math
>>> print(math.hypot(x.real, x.imag))
7.81024967591
```

Finally, every `complex` object has a method `conjugate`, which returns the complex conjugate. This is the complex number with the same real part and negated imaginary part. Keep in mind that whereas `real` and `imag` are attributes (you don't call them), `conjugate` is a method (you must call it):

```
>>> print(x.conjugate())
(5+6j)
```

The transcendental functions in the `math` package work only on and return `float` values. For instance, you can't actually take the square root of –1 to obtain 1j:

```
>>> print(math.sqrt(-1))
Traceback (most recent call last):
  File "<interactive input>", line 1, in ?
ValueError: math domain error
```

That's a shame, because square roots and most of the other functions in `math` can be defined on complex numbers, too. Fortunately, Python provides a parallel module named `cmath`, which contains versions of the same functions that operate on and return `complex` objects. Its version of the square root function can handle –1:

```
>>> import cmath
>>> print(cmath.sqrt(-1))
1j
```

Precision of Complex Numbers

Let's verify the famous and very fundamental mathematical identity $e^{i\pi} + 1 = 0$:

```
>>> print(cmath.exp(1j * cmath.pi) + 1)
1.22460635382e-016j
```

What's this? It's a complex number with real part of zero and imaginary part approximately 1.225×10^{-16}. That's close, but not quite equal to zero.

Python stores both the real part and the complex part with the same precision as a float value, about 16 digits on most systems. That means Python's representation of $e^{i\pi}$ is equal to –1 only to about 16 digits. Therefore, you shouldn't be surprised if the result after adding +1 is off by about 10^{-16}.

Arrays

You've learned how to perform computations with individual numbers, be they integers, floating-point numbers, or even complex numbers. What if you want to perform computations on many numbers? A group of numbers is typically arranged into an *array*. In this section, you learn different ways of implementing arrays in Python.

Keep in mind that arrays may be multidimensional. If you arrange numbers in a row, you have a one-dimensional array. A vector in linear algebra is an example; another is a list of daily closing prices of your favorite stock. You can also arrange your numbers on a rectangular grid, to produce a two-dimensional array. A grayscale image is often represented as a two-dimensional array, where each value is the lightness of one pixel in the image. In some applications, you may want to arrange your numbers into higher-dimensional arrays as well.

You've already seen one technique for constructing arrays in Python, when you wrote the `mean` function earlier. That function takes a sequence of numbers (of arbitrary length) and computes the numbers' mean. You can think of this sequence of numbers as an array and can think of `mean` as a function that acts on an array. You can invoke the function with a list of numbers, but it works with any sequence type, including tuples. These built-in types are the simplest way of building arrays.

> ### Lists or Tuples?
>
> Which should you use for arrays: lists or tuples? Remember that lists can be modified, whereas tuples cannot. Therefore, if you need to add to, remove from, or change the array, use a list. Though you can perform these operations on a tuple by creating a new tuple with numbers added, removed, or changed, this is more difficult to code and often runs more slowly. For fixed sequences of numbers, you can use tuples.

Let's take another example of a function that operates on an array. You already wrote a function that computes the mean of an array of numbers. Now write a function that computes the standard deviation. To remind you, the standard deviation is an indication of how much the numbers vary among themselves. If they're all almost the same, the standard deviation will be small, whereas if they are all over the place, the standard deviation will be large. The formula for the standard deviation that you will use is shown in Figure 18-1.

$$\sigma = \sqrt{\frac{1}{N}\sum_{i=1}^{N} x_i^2 - \mu^2}$$

Figure 18-1

Here $x_1, \ldots, x_N$ are the numbers in the array, μ is their mean, and N is the length of the array.

You could implement a standard deviation function several different ways. Here's one of them:

```
from math import sqrt

def stddev(numbers):
    n = len(numbers)
    sum = 0
    sum_of_squares = 0
    for number in numbers:
        sum += number
        sum_of_squares += number * number
    return sqrt(sum_of_squares / n - (sum / n) ** 2)
```

This function loops over the numbers to compute their sum of squares. Simultaneously, it computes their sum, because it needs that to compute the mean. The last line computes the standard deviation according to the preceding formula. You might have noticed that the function uses `number * number` when computing the sum of squares instead of `number ** 2`; that's because squaring a number by multiplying it by itself is faster than using the general exponentiation operator.

Watch `stddev` in action. Remember that it takes one argument, a sequence of numbers (not several numerical arguments):

```
>>> print(stddev((5.6, 3.2, -1.0, 0.7)))
2.50137462208
```

Think for a moment about some advantages and drawbacks of using lists of numbers for arrays:

❏ The elements of a Python list need not be of the same type. You can create a list for which some elements are int, float, long, and double, or other objects like strings or even other sequences. For some applications, this is very handy. For instance, you may want to store None in a sequence to indicate that a value is not known. For other applications, it's important to make sure that all of the values in an array are of the same type. In that case, you'll have to write extra code to ensure this.

❏ Lists are single-dimensional, which makes them natural for expressing one-dimensional arrays. You can create two-dimensional arrays as lists of lists and higher-dimensional arrays analogously, but this can get complicated.

❏ Lists are a standard part of Python. They're always available (you don't even have to import a module), and you already know how to use them.

❏ Lists can be pickled. That makes it easy to store your list in a file for later use.

❏ Internally, Python represents each element in a list as a separate object. Therefore, if you have a list of a million numbers (not at all unusual in many fields), you force Python to keep track of 1,000,001 objects: the list itself and all of its elements. This both wastes a lot of memory and makes Python work pretty hard whenever you access or modify the array.

This last point is a major limitation in many types of numerical work. To address it, you can use one of two other array implementations that store numbers more efficiently.

The Array Module

The Python standard library has just the ticket: a module array for one-dimensional arrays of numbers. The array type in this module stores numbers all together in memory as one object subject to the constraint that all of them must be of the same type. The numerical types supported by array are not the same as Python's numeric types. (In fact, they correspond to the numerical types in the C language.) An array can store numbers equivalent to Python's int and float, as well as integers of other sizes, and floating-point numbers of other precisions. (An array can store long values, but not arbitrarily large ones, and cannot store complex values at all.)

When you create an array, you have to specify the numerical type to store in the array. The type is specified by a single character. To store numbers as Python int objects, use "l"; for float use "d". (Other options are available; see the documentation for the array module for a list of them.) If you don't specify anything else, you'll get an empty array:

```
>>> import array
>>> a = array.array("l")
>>> print(a)
array('l')
```

Generally, you can use an array object just as you would an ordinary list. You can insert, append, or delete elements, and the indexing syntax is the same. (Note that in versions of Python earlier than 2.4, an array object is somewhat more limited than a list object.) For example:

```
>>> a.append(15)
>>> a.extend([20, 17, 0])
>>> print(a)
array('l', [15, 20, 17, 0])
>>> a[1] = 42
>>> print(a)
array('l', [15, 42, 17, 0])
>>> del a[2]
>>> print(a)
array('l', [15, 42, 0])
```

You can also convert a list or tuple to an array object by passing it to the constructor:

```
>>> t = (5.6, 3.2, -1.0, 0.7)
>>> a = array.array("d", t)
>>> print(a)
array('d', [5.5999999999999996, 3.2000000000000002, -1.0, 0.69999999999999996])
```

Here again you see the approximate nature of floating-point values.

In fact, because an array object behaves very much like a list, you can pass it to the same stddev function you wrote previously, and it works just fine:

```
>>> print(stddev(a))
2.50137462208
```

If you ever need to convert back to an ordinary tuple or list, just pass the array to the tuple or list constructor:

```
>>> back_again = tuple(a)
>>> print(back_again)
(5.5999999999999996, 3.2000000000000002, -1.0, 0.69999999999999996)
```

Compared to lists, array objects have the following advantages and disadvantages:

❑   All elements of an array are the same type.

❑   Like a list, an array is one-dimensional.

❑   The array module is part of Python's standard library (but don't forget to import it).

❑   An array object cannot automatically be pickled.

❑   An array object stores its values much more efficiently than a list of numbers does. However, computations on the numbers are generally not much faster, because computations are performed using Python's normal number objects.

Summary

In this chapter, you learned how to perform many kinds of numerical computations in Python. You experimented first with Python's built-in integer and floating-point number types and saw how to use Python's built-in arithmetic operations. Then you moved on to higher mathematics, using the special functions in the `math` module and Python's complex number type.

Finally, you learned two different ways of representing arrays of numbers: The simplest method is to use a list or tuple of numbers. For more efficient storage, use the `array` module included with Python.

The key things to take away from this chapter are:

❑ A number, like any object in Python, has a type. Python has three basic numerical types. One of these, int, represents integers, and float represents floating-point numbers. The third numeric type represents complex floating-point numbers.

❑ You can convert any Python number to a string using the `str` constructor. This produces the text that would be printed by the `print` statement, as a string object.

❑ To format an integer, use the `%d` conversion in the format string. For a floating-point number, use `%f`. If you use `%d` with a floating-point number or `%f` with an integer.

❑ Python provides the normal arithmetic operators + (addition), – (subtraction), * (multiplication), and / (division) for numerical types.

❑ The array type in the array module stores numbers all together in memory as one object. (Note that they must all be the same type.)

❑ The math module contains the functions: `sqrt` (square root), `exp` (exponentiation), `log`/`log10` (natural logarithm and base 10 logarithm), `sin`, `cos`, and `tan` (trigonometric functions), `asin`, `acos`, and `atan` (inverse trigonometric functions), and the hyperbolic functions: `sinh`, `cosh`, and `tanh`.

Exercises

1. Write a function that expresses a number of bytes as the sum of gigabytes, megabytes, kilobytes, and bytes. Remember that a kilobyte is 1024 bytes, a megabyte is 1024 kilobytes, and so on. The number of each should not exceed 1023. The output should look something like this:

```
>>> print(format_bytes(9876543210))
9 GB + 203 MB + 5 KB + 746 bytes
```

2. Write a function that formats an RGB color in the color syntax of HTML. The function should take three numerical arguments: the red, green, and blue color components, each between zero and one. The output is a string of the form #RRGGBB, where RR is the red component as a value between 0 and 255, expressed as a two-digit hexadecimal number, and GG and BB likewise for the green and blue components.

For example:

```
>>> print(rgb_to_html(0.0, 0.0, 0.0)  # black)
#000000
>>> print(rgb_to_html(1.0, 1.0, 1.0)  # white)
#ffffff
>>> print(rgb_to_html(0.8, 0.5, 0.9)  # purple)
#cc80e6
```

3. Write a function named `normalize` that takes an array of `float` numbers and returns a copy of the array in which the elements have been scaled such that the square root of the sum of their squares is one. This is an important operation in linear algebra and other fields.

Here's a test case:

```
>>> for n in normalize((2.2, 5.6, 4.3, 3.0, 0.5)):
...     print("%.5f" % n,)
...
0.27513 0.70033 0.53775 0.37518 0.06253
```

An Introduction to Django

If you have ever developed web applications, you are probably aware that it can oftentimes be a tedious task. To help ease this problem, some languages have turned to web application frameworks such as Ruby on Rails or Java's Spring Framework to handle some of the basic building blocks common to all web applications, leaving the programmer to concentrate on the more interesting aspects.

Nearly every language has at least one — and in many instances quite a few — frameworks, and Python is no exception. Built upon the Python language, Django is the standard web application framework used by Python developers who want to build for the Web on the fly.

You do not need to know web development to read this chapter, but it will certainly make things easier. At the bare minimum you should have a solid understanding of procedural programming, and be comfortable working with decision making (if statements and loops), as well as data storage through lists and hashes. If not, it might be worth going back and reviewing the previous chapters in this book.

In this chapter you learn:

- ❏ To define what a framework is and explain why you would use one
- ❏ To install the latest version of Django
- ❏ To explain what the MVC/MTV Architecture is
- ❏ To create views and templates in Django
- ❏ To incorporate databases into your Django web applications

What Are Frameworks and Why Would I Use One?

Earlier I bandied about the term *web application framework* without really explaining what one was. To fully understand not only the what, but also the why of frameworks, it is essential to understand some of the core fundamentals that pretty much every web application/database-centric website must have as a foundation.

The first of the foundations is database connectivity. This is a vital part of any web application. It contains many records you may not even think about. Here is where you will store information like user name, permissions, settings, comments, profiles — the list goes on and on. Django supports quite a few databases (covered later in the chapter), some of which do and do not use SQL.

The second foundation is the administrative panel. An administrative panel gives the admin, and others, the ability to work with anything stored in the database. For instance, if you want to change a user's permissions from a registered user to a super administrator, you will need an admin panel.

Next up is the ability to leave comments. Despite the seemingly endless amount of useless comments that eat up acres of landscape on the Web, they are still a vital aspect of any well-designed website. They allow users to feel as though they are part of a community and not a lone voice whispering into the wind.

Another important feature of this type of site is user authentication. This controls how the users sign in, ensures secure logins, decides who has permission to do what on the site, and so forth.

You are not even halfway through the list of the tenants that dictate a well-thought-out web application, and as you can see, it is a lot to think about, and program. And let's face it — it's not very interesting. You have not even touched upon user-interfaces and design, which really should be the main focus of the site.

In the days before frameworks, a programmer would have to code all of the above and more by hand, eating up oodles of time, which in turn increases production costs. Fortunately for us, though, frameworks take care of the mundane aspects. All of the above, and more, can instantly be set up thanks to Django.

Other Features of Web Frameworks

In addition to what is listed in the preceding section, frameworks offer the following:

URL Mapping, Frameworks, and Django (in particular) — Interpret URLs so they are more friendly (and intuitive) to both the user, and more importantly, search engines and indexing. A good example of this is the URL: `/mypage.cgi?cat=comic&topic=superman`. The URL mapping feature would change this to a simpler address, such as `/mypage/comic/superman`. Visitors to your site are more likely to remember this URL if they want to automatically come to this page again, and it makes it easier for search engines to understand the underlying structure of your website.

Caching — Web caching is the process of storing a copy of a document. When this page is revisited, if certain criteria are met, the page is loaded from memory, instead of a new page being requested. This, in turn, increases the speed by which the page loads and the overall usability of the site.

Templating — A template gives a uniform look to a website, and serves many purposes. For one, it looks professional. Secondly, it ensures that users do not become confused and think that they have left your site. Next, it creates a seamless feel, so that every part of the site behaves in the manner you expect it to. For example, if clicking a print button on one page prints a document, the print button on every page will do the same thing, and will also appear in the same spot. Perhaps more importantly, templating can reduce the number of pages within a website. By having a "flat page," your site can access the database and grab certain data, displaying it in the page. A good way to think of this is to consider a website that lists author bios. If your site features 10,000 authors, in the old days you may have had to write 10,000 pages — one for each author. With templating, however, you have one "flat page" that reaches into the database and fills in the data for one of the 10,000 authors in the database. So essentially you now have one page that can dynamically act as many.

A full run-down of web frameworks and their features is beyond the scope of this book, but with the preceding information, you should have a pretty steady handle on the possibilities. It is certainly enough information to get you started using frameworks.

Django — How It All Began

Django, pronounced with a silent "d" and rhyming with Bang-o, was named after the gypsy jazz guitarist Django Reinhardt. It was created by a group of programmers at a little place called World Online, which at the time was the department responsible for web design for the *Lawrence Journal-World* newspaper in Kansas, among other properties.

Often forced to scramble to meet last-minute deadlines and asked to write new web apps on the fly, two men by the names of Adrian Holovaty and Simon Willison developed a new web framework to handle the demands of the editorial staff. Two years later, in 2005, the team joined up with Jacob Kaplan-Moss and released the framework to the open source community under the name of Django.

Because Django was originally built to handle the needs of several online newspapers, it has earned both the prestige and the stigma of being a "content" framework, good for publishers but little else. This, of course, is simply not true. Django is just as powerful and flexible as any other framework, as you will soon see.

For more information on the history and purpose behind Django, feel free to visit `http://www.djangoproject.com/`.

Installing Django

At the time of this writing, the current version of Django is 1.1. As with many libraries and components, it has not been upgraded to work with Python version 3.1. However, it does work with Python 2.6, and as such, you will be working with that version for the remainder of this chapter. If you do not have a copy of Python 2.6 installed, please install it at this time. It installs the same as version 3.1. You can find it at `http://www.python.org/download/`.

To install Django, go to `http://www.djangoproject.com/download/`. I suggest that you download the official version and steer clear of the latest development version. If you do decide to go with the development version, you probably do not need instructions on how to install it, so for the purposes of this chapter, you will use the latest version.

For Windows users, installation is fairly simple. Download the `.tar.gz` file and extract it to your `Python26` folder (this is typically located at `C:/Python26`). Once the file has been unzipped, open up your command prompt (Start Menu ⇨ All Programs ⇨ Accessories ⇨ Command Prompt) and change the directory to your `Python26` folder by typing in the following at the prompt:

```
cd  C:\Python26\Django-1.1
```

Next, type in:

```
setup.py install
```

You will see the program installing and configuring a bunch of packages. Finally, it will finish, and Django will be officially installed. The install location, for the record, will be something along the lines of `C:\Python26\Lib\site-packages`.

To test your installation, all you need to do is open up IDLE and type the following:

```
>>>import django
>>>django.VERSION
(1, 1, 0, 'final', 0)
```

To install Django on non-Windows computers, such as Linux, Mac OS X, or other UNIX-based systems, download the `tar.gz` file and untar it with:

```
tar xzvf Django-1.0.0-final.tar.gz
```

Note that you will have to change the 1.0.0 to whatever version you have downloaded. Next, change the directory to the directory in which the file was untarred:

```
cd Django-1.0.0
```

where 1.0.0 is the version number. Finally, enter **sudo python setup.py install** in your command prompt, and wait for the magic to happen. To test that it is working, use the same method described earlier.

Understanding Django's Architecture

Before you begin developing your first Django project, let's touch upon one final aspect of web frameworks — namely, architecture. Most frameworks operate under the MVC architecture, or Model-View-Controller. Django is no different, though at times you will hear that it runs under an MTV, or Model-Template-View architecture, which, for me at least, is simply a matter of semantics.

For web application purposes, MVC architecture is best described by the following breakdown:

- ❑ **Model** — The actual data or content that is displayed in the page and is stored in a database, XML node, or other area.

- ❑ **View** — The web page, be it HTML, XHTML, or markup language.

- ❑ **Controller** — The portion of code that collects the data from the model (database/xml) and passes it to the view (web page).

Though this may be a simplistic view, for your purposes, it is more than sufficient.

Initial Project Setup

Because this is your first time doing a Django project, you must do some things first. Note that a project in Django terms doesn't follow the typical sense of the word project. In Django, a project refers to the settings of an instance of Django, which is comprised of Django and application-specific settings as well as database options.

To start with, create a new directory. To do this, navigate to the location where a file called django-admin.py resides, which is usually in your site-packages\django\bin directory. Here is what you type into your command prompt to change to that directory:

```
cd C:\Python26\Lib\site-packages\django\bin
```

Next, you need to run the django-admin.py file and tell it to create a new directory where your project and code will be stored. For the purposes here, call this new directory newsite. Type the following in your command prompt:

```
django-admin.py startproject newsite
```

Note that in the future you can change newsite to whatever you would like to call your directory.

Startproject is a command that creates not only a new directory, but stores four important files inside of it. They are:

- ❑ __init__.py — This empty file allows Python to treat your directory (in this case newsite) as a package. You may remember that packages are nothing more than groups of Python modules.

- ❑ manage.py — This is a command-line utility for interacting with Django projects.

- ❑ settings.py — This file allows you to change the settings and general configuration of your project. Following is the code you will see if you open it in IDLE:

```
# Django settings for newsite project.
DEBUG = True
TEMPLATE_DEBUG = DEBUG
ADMINS = (
    # ('Your Name', 'your_email@domain.com'),
)
MANAGERS = ADMINS
```

```
DATABASE_ENGINE = ''                # 'postgresql_psycopg2', 'postgresql',
'mysql', 'sqlite3' or 'oracle'.
DATABASE_NAME = ''                  # Or path to database file if using sqlite3.
DATABASE_USER = ''                  # Not used with sqlite3.
DATABASE_PASSWORD = ''              # Not used with sqlite3.
DATABASE_HOST = ''                  # Set to empty string for localhost. Not used
with sqlite3.
DATABASE_PORT = ''                  # Set to empty string for default. Not used
with sqlite3.

# Local time zone for this installation. Choices can be found here:

# http://en.wikipedia.org/wiki/List_of_tz_zones_by_name

# although not all choices may be available on all operating systems.

# If running in a Windows environment this must be set to the same as your

# system time zone.

TIME_ZONE = 'America/Chicago'

# Language code for this installation. All choices can be found here:

# http://www.i18nguy.com/unicode/language-identifiers.html

LANGUAGE_CODE = 'en-us'

SITE_ID = 1

# If you set this to False, Django will make some optimizations so as not

# to load the internationalization machinery.
USE_I18N = True

# Absolute path to the directory that holds media.

# Example: "/home/media/media.lawrence.com/"
MEDIA_ROOT = ''

# URL that handles the media served from MEDIA_ROOT. Make sure to use a
# trailing slash if there is a path component (optional in other cases).
# Examples: "http://media.lawrence.com", "http://example.com/media/"
MEDIA_URL = ''

# URL prefix for admin media -- CSS, JavaScript and images. Make sure to use a
# trailing slash.
# Examples: "http://foo.com/media/", "/media/".
ADMIN_MEDIA_PREFIX = '/media/'

# Make this unique, and don't share it with anybody.
```

```
SECRET_KEY = 'ms159e^bu=@m&grk106cl4kq&b058)*b4#01p69z@xop1y4zas'

# List of callables that know how to import templates from various sources.
TEMPLATE_LOADERS = (
    'django.template.loaders.filesystem.load_template_source',
    'django.template.loaders.app_directories.load_template_source',
#     'django.template.loaders.eggs.load_template_source',
)
MIDDLEWARE_CLASSES = (
    'django.middleware.common.CommonMiddleware',
    'django.contrib.sessions.middleware.SessionMiddleware',
    'django.contrib.auth.middleware.AuthenticationMiddleware',
)

ROOT_URLCONF = 'newsite.urls'
TEMPLATE_DIRS = (
    # Put strings here, like "/home/html/django_templates" or "C:/www/django/
templates".
    # Always use forward slashes, even on Windows.
    # Don't forget to use absolute paths, not relative paths.
)

INSTALLED_APPS = (
    'django.contrib.auth',
    'django.contrib.contenttypes',
    'django.contrib.sessions',
    'django.contrib.sites',
)
```

I discuss how to modify this file later on.

❑   `urls.py` — This is where all of the URLs for your current Django project will be stored.

The final step to take before you can begin working with your first project is to set up the development server. The development server allows you to test your site and see its progress without having to set up your actual web server (you'll eventually need to do this when you are ready to have your site go live to the public.)

The first step to set up the server is to change your directory to the `newsite`:

```
cd C:\Python26\Lib\site-packages\django\bin\newsite
```

Next, you will need run the `manage.py` file and give it the `runserver` command:

```
manage.py runserver
```

After a few seconds your command prompt will display the following:

```
Django version 1.1, using settings 'newsite.settings'
Development server is running at http"//127.0.0.1:8000/
Quit the server with CTRL-BREAK.
...
```

Your server is now set up to run locally. You can view the result by typing the following into your web browser's address bar: http://127.0.0.1:8000/. Note that this will only be visible from your computer, so do not expect outsiders to be able to view your page.

And that is all there is to it. Now you are finally ready to get your hands dirty!

Creating a View

You read about views earlier in the discussion on the Model-View-Controller architecture. As you will recall, in simple terms, the view is nothing more than an HTML or XHTML page. For the first few examples in this chapter, you are going to create the HTML inside of your Python code. This is purely for demonstrational purposes; in reality, your HTML would be inside of a templated page. But don't worry — I will cover that soon enough.

Try It Out   **Making a View**

For this example, you are going to create a very simple view to display some text in your user's browser. Start off by opening up a text file or new window in IDLE and enter the following code, being sure to save the file as myfirstview.py in the newsite directory:

```
from django.http import HTTPResponse
def sometext(request):
    mypage= "<html><body><H1>Welcome to My First Page!</H1></body></html>"
    return HttpResponse(mypage)
```

Now, open up a browser window and type in the address http://127.0.0.1:8000/sometext/. Note that you will need to have your web development server running. If you closed it, just follow the steps from the previous sections to restart it.

Not quite what you were expecting, right? Don't worry, you didn't do anything wrong. Creating your myfirstview.py file is just the first step. All it does is create a function (in this case, sometext) that holds the makeup of a simple web page with a header that reads: Welcome to My First Page!

To actually have the page display in a web browser, you need to tell Django to activate the page. You do this in the __urls.py__ file that was automatically generated when you ran the startproject function earlier.

If you open up the __urls.py__ file in a text editor or IDLE, you will see the following code:

```
from django.conf.urls.defaults import *

# Uncomment the next two lines to enable the admin:
# from django.contrib import admin
# admin.autodiscover()

urlpatterns = patterns('',
    # Example:
    # (r'^mysite/', include('mysite.foo.urls')),

    # Uncomment the admin/doc line below and add 'django.contrib.admindocs'
    # to INSTALLED_APPS to enable admin documentation:
    # (r'^admin/doc/', include('django.contrib.admindocs.urls')),
```

```
# Uncomment the next line to enable the admin:
# (r'^admin/', include(admin.site.urls)),
)
```

As it stands, this code does nothing. When you are finished with it, however, it will act as the catalyst to display your `myfirstview.py` file.

Try It Out   **Creating a URLconf**

URLconfs are a simple way to tell Django which code it should use for which URL. For instance, if you have a URL such as `www.mysite.com/purple`, your URLconf might tell Django explicitly to use the file `purple.py`. If your URL is `www.mysite.com/spaghetti`, your URLconf might tell Django to use the code found in the file `spaghettiview.py`.

Before you get ahead of yourself, however, delete all of the text in your __urls.py__ file and replace it with the following:

```
from django.conf.urls.defaults import *
from newsite.myfirstview import sometext

urlpatterns = patterns('',
                        ('^sometext/$', sometext),

)
```

Now when you refresh your browser (or if you closed it, simply go to `http://127.0.0.1:8000/sometext/`) your result should be a blank page with an `<H1>` header that reads simply: Welcome to My First Page!

Congratulations, you have created your first view!

How It Works

Let's start by explaining how your view works. First, for consistency's sake, you will want to identify any view file by using the word "view" in the title, such as `myfirstview.py`. This makes it easier to spot which files are views in your directory and which are not.

The first step was to import the `django.http` module, and one of its classes, `HttpResponse`. Next, you created an instance of the `HttpResponse` class by creating a view function named `sometext`. This view function takes the parameter `request`, which must always be the first parameter of any view function.

Finally, you used `return` to return your `HttpResponse`, which you have filled with a bit of HTML code.

The __urls.py__ file, meanwhile, starts off by importing everything from the `django.conf.urls .defaults` module. Within this module is a function known as `patterns`, whose purpose is to save its value into the `urlpatterns` variable.

Next, you imported the function `sometext` from your module `myfirstview` (from `newsite .myfirstview import sometext`). After that, you added the value of patterns to `urlpatterns`, which, as stated earlier, is a tuple. This tuple uses a regular expression as its first element, and the `sometext` view function as its second element.

If you remember, earlier I said that URLconfs told Django which code to use for which URL. The way this translates in the previous example is that the code:

```
urlpatterns = patterns('',
                       ('^sometext/$', sometext),

)
```

tells Django that when it sees the URL `/sometext`, it should use the `sometext` view function found within your module `myfirstview`.

Although this barely scrapes the surface of what you can do with views and URLconfs, it should be enough to get you started; a full explanation of views is beyond the scope of this book.

Working with Templates

Now that you understand the ways that views and URLconfs work, you can begin to work with templates. As stated previously, embedding HTML in your Python is not the best way to go about creating views. In this section, you learn to use templates instead.

Templates, in their simplest form, are a way to ensure consistency across a site. Using a template also saves time; you may recall the discussion about the 10,000 author bios?

Like an HTML document, templates are made up of many different tags — too numerous to cover here — as well as filters. As you continue through this section, I will try to cover the most important ones. These filters and tags control how the page looks, regardless of the data that is displayed in them. Think of them the way you would a school uniform; different students with different attributes all wear the same clothes, and therefore have a level of uniformity.

To see a template in action, open up your Command Prompt and navigate to the `newsite` folder (if you are not already there):

```
cd C:\Python26\Lib\site-packages\django\bin\newsite
```

Next, run the following command:

```
manage.py shell
```

This command opens up the interactive interpreter. At this point you are probably wondering why you don't just use the IDLE editor, and it is a valid question. The reason you use the interactive interpreter, at least for now, is because it automatically sets your Django settings file for you. If you try to run the code in the next section in IDLE, it simply won't work. Later in the chapter, you learn how to edit your Django settings so that you can code wherever you like. For now, though, you are going to let the `manage.py` shell do all of your work for you.

For your first step, you need to import the template system. You do this like so:

```
>>>from django import template
```

Now you are going to create a template object. In this case, you want to create an object that will eventually hold a book title:

```
>>>btitle = template.Template('Your book is titled {{ book }}.')
```

The next bit of code will actually fill or give context to your template object:

```
>>> a = template.Context({'book': 'American Gods'})
```

Within the template object is a method called `render()`, which returns the rendered template as a string, evaluating every variable and template tag in the proper context. Here is how you use it:

```
>>>print btitle.render(a)
Your book is titled American Gods.
```

Try It Out   Creating a Template

Now that you have learned the fundamentals of the template system, you can put it to work. Type the following code into the interactive interpreter:

```
>>>from django.template import Template, Context
>>>myfirsttemplate = """<H1>Welcome to {{owner}}'s Library</H1>
...<p>Below you will find a list of {{owner}}'s favorite books</p>
...<br />
...<H3> Book Title: {{books}} Author: {{author}} </H3>"""
>>>a=Template(myfirsttemplate)
>>>b=Context({'owner': 'James Payne', 'books': 'American Gods', 'author':
'Neil Gaimen'})
>>>print a.render(b)
<H1>Welcome to James Payne's Library</H1>
<p>Below you will find a list of James Payne's favorite books. </p>
<br />
<H3>Book Title: American Gods Author: Neil Gaimen </H3>
```

There you have it: a simple template.

How It Works

Even though there is very little code, there is a lot going on. That, of course, is part of the beauty that is Django. To explain the process, let's go through each bit of code a line at a time.

First, you imported the `Template` and `Context` classes from the `django.template` module. Next, you created a variable named `myfirsttemplate`, which holds the text of your template. Note that this variable holds all of the data from your first `<H1>` tag all the way through to the closing `</H3>` tag.

You then created your template object, with the simple name of a, by assigning it the value of myfirsttemplate. This is followed by the creation of a context object, which you used to map the variable names to their respective values (that is, owner is mapped to James Payne). Lastly, you printed the rendering, which shows what happens when the tags in the template are executed.

Using Templates and Views

Now that you know how to use views, modify your URLconfs, and create templates, you can use your view and template together, instead of embedding the HTML directly in your code.

Before you do, however, I just want to make a quick note: Django templates are not a mandatory part of the system. Python provides its own set of templates. However, Django's built-in templating system is pretty flexible and powerful, so you might want to strongly consider using it instead.

Try It Out   Using Templates and Views

You need to take several steps in order to ensure that your template works with your view. For starters, you will need to create your template. If you have not done so yet, create a new folder in your newsite directory and name it templates (note that it is not mandatory that you place your template directory here. I am simply doing it now for demonstration purposes).

Next, open a new text file and type in the following code, being sure to save the file as myfirsttemplate.html:

```
<H1>Welcome to {{owner}}'s Library</H1><p>Below you will find a list of
{{owner}}'s favorite books</p>
<br />
<H3> Book Title: {{books}} Author: {{author}} </H3>
```

You will note that you have not defined your variables (in Django, anything wrapped in double brackets [{{}}] is a variable). Don't fear; you'll be doing that shortly.

Now that your template is defined and saved to the newsite/templates folder, the next step is to create a new view (if you still have the myfirstview.py view, you can simply modify it so that it has the code in the following example). Name the view myfirstview.py and enter in the following code:

```
from django.shortcuts import render_to_response
def sometext(request):
    return render_to_response('myfirsttemplate.html',{'owner': 'James Payne',
                                        'books': 'American Gods',
                                        'author': 'Neil Gaimen'})
```

This is the first time you have seen a lot of the code in this file. For starters, 90 percent of the time, this is the method you will use to view a template. Other methods exist, but they are not as efficient.

This code starts off by importing the method render_to_response from the django.shortcuts module. Render_to_response is a nifty method that essentially handles the creation of template objects, the contexting (adding values to the template object), and the rendering, saving you from typing out a bunch of code as you did in previous examples.

After your importing, you define a new function and give it the required request parameter. You then return the `render_to_response` method, telling it the name of your template (`myfirsttemplate.html`). Your second argument acts as the context, allowing you to give values to `owner`, `books`, and `author`. This second argument is not mandatory; however, if you leave it empty, your page will not display those variables.

Now that you have created your template and your view, only one step remains. You must now modify your `__settings.py__` file. If you recall, this is located in your `newsite` folder. Open up this file in IDLE or Notepad. You should see something along the following lines:

```
# Django settings for newsite project.

DEBUG = True
TEMPLATE_DEBUG = DEBUG

ADMINS = (
    # ('Your Name', 'your_email@domain.com'),
)

MANAGERS = ADMINS

DATABASE_ENGINE = ''             # 'postgresql_psycopg2', 'postgresql',
'mysql', 'sqlite3' or 'oracle'.
DATABASE_NAME = ''               # Or path to database file if using sqlite3.
DATABASE_USER = ''               # Not used with sqlite3.
DATABASE_PASSWORD = ''           # Not used with sqlite3.
DATABASE_HOST = ''               # Set to empty string for localhost. Not used
with sqlite3.
DATABASE_PORT = ''               # Set to empty string for default. Not used
with sqlite3.

# Local time zone for this installation. Choices can be found here:
# http://en.wikipedia.org/wiki/List_of_tz_zones_by_name
# although not all choices may be available on all operating systems.
# If running in a Windows environment this must be set to the same as your
# system time zone.
TIME_ZONE = 'America/Chicago'

# Language code for this installation. All choices can be found here:
# http://www.i18nguy.com/unicode/language-identifiers.html
LANGUAGE_CODE = 'en-us'

SITE_ID = 1

# If you set this to False, Django will make some optimizations so as not
# to load the internationalization machinery.
USE_I18N = True

# Absolute path to the directory that holds media.
# Example: "/home/media/media.lawrence.com/"
MEDIA_ROOT = ''
```

```
# URL that handles the media served from MEDIA_ROOT. Make sure to use a
# trailing slash if there is a path component (optional in other cases).
# Examples: "http://media.lawrence.com", "http://example.com/media/"
MEDIA_URL = ''

# URL prefix for admin media -- CSS, JavaScript and images. Make sure to use a
# trailing slash.
# Examples: "http://foo.com/media/", "/media/".
ADMIN_MEDIA_PREFIX = '/media/'

# Make this unique, and don't share it with anybody.
SECRET_KEY = 'ms159e^bu=@m&grk106cl4kq&b058)*b4#01p69z@xop1y4zas'

# List of callables that know how to import templates from various sources.
TEMPLATE_LOADERS = (
    'django.template.loaders.filesystem.load_template_source',
    'django.template.loaders.app_directories.load_template_source',
#     'django.template.loaders.eggs.load_template_source',
)

MIDDLEWARE_CLASSES = (
    'django.middleware.common.CommonMiddleware',
    'django.contrib.sessions.middleware.SessionMiddleware',
    'django.contrib.auth.middleware.AuthenticationMiddleware',
)

ROOT_URLCONF = 'newsite.urls'

TEMPLATE_DIRS = (
    # Put strings here, like "/home/html/django_templates" or
"C:/www/django/templates".
    # Always use forward slashes, even on Windows.
    # Don't forget to use absolute paths, not relative paths.
)

INSTALLED_APPS = (
    'django.contrib.auth',
    'django.contrib.contenttypes',
    'django.contrib.sessions',
    'django.contrib.sites',
)
```

For now, you only need to concern yourself with one small section:

```
TEMPLATE_DIRS = (
    # Put strings here, like "/home/html/django_templates" or
"C:/www/django/templates".
    # Always use forward slashes, even on Windows.
    # Don't forget to use absolute paths, not relative paths.
)
```

This portion of the __settings.py__ code is where you tell Django to find your templates. Add the following code to the file, being sure to include the comma (,) at the end of the inserted line, and save it:

```
TEMPLATE_DIRS = (
    'C:/Python26/Lib/site-packages/django/bin/newsite/templates',
    # Put strings here, like "/home/html/django_templates" or
"C:/www/django/templates".
    # Always use forward slashes, even on Windows.
    # Don't forget to use absolute paths, not relative paths.
)
```

Basically, what you are doing here is telling Django that your template is located in the `newsite/templates` directory.

And that is all there is to it. To view your web page, restart the Django development server again (if you do not have it running already) by typing `manage.py runserver` into your interactive interpreter. Then, open up a new web browser and enter the following address: http://127.0.0.1:8000/sometext/. You should now see the results of your handiwork.

This is the tip of the iceberg when it comes to working with Django templates. Many tags have not been touched upon, and the list is growing all the time. However, this should give you a good starting place as you delve further into templating.

Models

You may recall the conversation about Django having an MVC (Model-View-Controller) architecture. As stated, sometimes Django's architecture is referred to as MTV (Model-Template-View). Most people in the Django community will agree that both are correct. In either case, so far you have viewed both the View and Template portion of Django's architecture, leaving you with only one further aspect: the Model.

Simply put, a model in Django describes the data that is held in your database. This description gives you information on how to access the data, the various relationships in the database, and how to validate your data. Another way to look at it is to think of it as an SQL Create Statement, only a little more defined. This added definition comes courtesy of the way Django creates tables; it does so through Python code instead of SQL (note that Django does use SQL code, but the data structures that it returns are all Python).

An example of this extra definition would be how most databases that work on SQL handle URLs. There is no special data type to handle them. In Django, however, there is. This type of higher definition capability gives you more control over your data types.

Creating a Model: First Steps — Configure the Database Settings

Because you used sqlite3 for the examples in chapter 14, it only makes sense to use it here as well. Fortunately, because you are using Python 2.6 for this chapter, there are no additional components to install.

You will recall from the discussion on templates that you needed to change some settings in a file — appropriately named __settings.py__. For databases, you will need to use this file as well. If you closed the folder, never fear; you can find it by navigating to your `newsite` directory.

Open the file with Notepad or IDLE, and scan through the file until you see some code near the top, similar to the following:

```
DATABASE_ENGINE = ''              # 'postgresql_psycopg2', 'postgresql',
'mysql', 'sqlite3' or 'oracle'.
DATABASE_NAME = ''                # Or path to database file if using sqlite3.
DATABASE_USER = ''                # Not used with sqlite3.
DATABASE_PASSWORD = ''            # Not used with sqlite3.
DATABASE_HOST = ''                # Set to empty string for localhost. Not used
with sqlite3.
DATABASE_PORT = ''                # Set to empty string for default. Not used
with sqlite3.
```

This is the portion of the __settings.py__ file where you configure your database. If you look at the comments for each option, you will notice that most of them require you to do nothing if you are using sqlite3 — yet another reason why it is a good idea to use it.

Still, although you only have to use two of these options, it is useful to understand what the rest do, in the event that you need to use a separate database program.

First in the list is Database Engine. This setting is where you tell Django which database engine you will be using. You can choose from four options, and each has a separate engine you will need to install if you want to use them with Django (again, if you are using SQLite3, you do not need to worry about downloading an engine). The four options are PostgreSQL (version 1.x and 2.x), MySQL, SQLite3, and Oracle. Whichever database you choose to use, you must place its name within the single quotes, like so:

```
DATABASE_ENGINE = 'sqlite3'
```

The preceding code tells Django to use SQLite3 as its database engine. If you wanted to use MySQL, you would change 'sqlite3' to 'mysql' If you wanted to use PostgreSQL version 1.x, you would replace it with 'postgresql' and so forth (note that version 2.x of PostgreSQL would use 'postgresql_psycopg2').

The next option is Database Name, which does exactly what might you might expect it to do — it allows you to specify to Django the name of the database you are going to be using. Because you are using SQLite3, you have to include a path to the database file you are using, such as the one shown here:

```
DATABASE_NAME = 'C:/Python26/Lib/site-packages/django/bin/newsite/sample_
database.db'
```

If you are not using SQLite3, you simply enter the name of the database file you want to use, and not the path:

```
DATABASE_NAME = 'sample_database'
```

Next up is the setting DATABASE_USER. This tells Django which user to connect to the database as. This is important because different database users can have different privileges. For SQLite3 users, this field is left blank. For any other systems, use something along these lines:

```
DATABASE_USER = 'chew_bacca'
```

And of course if you are signing in with a user name, you will likely have a password, so your next setting is DATABASE_PASSWORD. If you are using SQLite3, this is left blank. Likewise, if you do not use a password, it is also left blank. Otherwise, use the following convention:

```
DATABASE_PASSWORD = 'chewie'
```

Your last setting is DATABASE_HOST, which tells Django the host that it should use to connect to your database. As with most of the examples, if you are using SQLite3, this setting will be left blank. Likewise, if you are hosting the database on your own computer, you can leave this blank. Otherwise, enter the host name you are using.

That is all there is to configuring your database. If you want to make sure that it works, open up the Interactive Interpreter (as mentioned in the previous sections) by running manage.py shell. Then type in the following code:

```
>>>from django.db import connection
>>>cursor=connection.cursor()
```

If nothing happens when you type this, don't worry — your file is configured properly. If you get an error message, however, that means that something is not set properly in your file. Just read the error message you receive and go back through your file to ensure everything is set properly.

Creating a Model: Creating an Application

Applications — or Django Apps — are a Python package that consists of models, views, and a variety of other code. They differ from Django projects, in that Django projects consist of one or more applications and the settings for those applications.

Another difference between an application and a project is that you do not always need to create an application. In fact, the only instance where you really need to create an application (that is, where it is a requirement) is when you are using models or database-driven sites.

Now that you understand what an application is, how it differs from a project, and when it is a requirement, you can create your first one. The code is pretty simple. Just type the following into your command prompt (making sure you are in the newsite directory):

```
manage.py startapp employees
```

If nothing happens, you are in luck — you created an application. If you get an error it is likely because you are not in the appropriate directory or there was a typo. To see the results of what you just created, open up your newsite folder and take a gander. You should see a new directory called employees.

Click inside of that directory and you will see four files: __init.py__, __models.py__, __tests.py__, and __views.py__.

Conveniently, Django creates a blank model and view file for you — thoughtful, right? These are the files that you will be working with for the upcoming example.

For starters, open up the __models.py__ file and modify it so it looks like the following code:

```
from django.db import models

class Employer(models.Model):
    name = models.CharField(max_length=50)
    website = models.URLField()
    industry =models.CharField(max_length=50)

class Employee(models.Model):
    first_name = models.CharField(max_length=50)
    last_name = models.CharField(max_length=50)
    address = models.CharField(max_length=50)
    hire_date = models.DateField()
    email = models.EmailField()
```

You start off this code by importing models from django.db. You then create your first class, Employer, which is a subclass of the models class. Next, you begin creating the fields that will be contained within the Employer class and defining their respective data type. It is important to know from here that the Employer class is now acting as the equivalent of a table in a database.

The first field in the Employer class is name, which you define as a CharField. The max_length=50 portion is where you set the parameter, which basically tells Django that the field contains characters, and no more than 50 of them.

You continue creating your second class, Employee, which will hold information about — you guessed it — the employees. Once all of the fields are done, you are finished creating your model.

Working with Models: Installation

Earlier, you created a model, which, as the name implies, is literally a model of what your data is going to look like and what type of data it will hold. Up to this point you haven't actually created the tables yet. To do that, you must install them.

To do this, you have to go back once in your newsite directory and open up the __settings.py__ file again. Scroll down until you see the section for Installed_Apps. You will notice that four files are already listed in here. Leave those alone for now, because they are default files. Simply modify the section so it looks like this:

```
INSTALLED_APPS = (
        'newsite.employees',
)
```

Next, modify the `Middle_Ware Classes` section by deleting the classes that are in there by default (the Installed Apps that you deleted rely on these and will cause errors when you try to create your database):

```
MIDDLEWARE_CLASSES = (

)
```

Now save the file and run the following command in your Interactive Interpreter:

```
manage.py validate
```

As is probably obvious from the command, this code validates your model and ensures that everything is defined properly. If you get a message saying 0 errors found, all is right in the world. If not, something was not defined properly in your model.

Now you are going to have Django create your tables by executing some SQL code for you. Type in the following:

```
manage.py syncdb employees
```

This code creates the tables in your database (assuming that they do not yet exist). You will see the following when you execute the command:

```
Creating table employees_employer
Creating table employees_employee
```

This means that it created the tables `employer` and `employee` in the `employees.db`. And that is all there is to installing your model!

Summary

You've really only touched the surface of what Django is capable of in this chapter. Alongside having the ability to create powerful and interactive websites in a snap, Django's true power lies in its database-driven capabilities. Though this chapter was not a comprehensive study (it would require a book about the same size as this one to accomplish that), it should be more than enough to get you started down the right path.

You started off learning Django's background and history, which is important to understand because it gives you some key insights as to why you may want to use Django, and what some of its strengths — and weaknesses — are. You also got an overview of frameworks in general, and took a rudimentary glance at the MVC and MTV architectures — the basic building blocks of a lot of frameworks.

After that, you dove into installing Django and worked on configuring your setup files. Then it was straight into creating URLConfs, views, templates, and — where you finally left off — models.

The key things to take away from this chapter are:

❑　Django is a powerful tool in the online publication industry, but has potential for virtually every type of web application.

❑　Django runs under the MVC architecture, or Model-Template-Controller, and is commonly said to truly be MTV or Model- Template-View.

❑　Model is the actual data or content that is displayed in the page and is stored in a database, XML node, or other area.

❑　View is the webpage, be it HTML, XHTML, or markup language.

❑　Controller is the portion of code that collects the data from the model (database/xml) and passes it to the view (web page).

❑　The __settings.py__ file is where you configure your Django settings. Here you can define which databases are being used, which applications, and much, much more.

❑　Applications — or Django Apps — are a Python package that consists of models, views, and a variety of other code. They are different from Django projects, in that Django projects consist of one or more applications and the settings for those applications.

Exercises

1.　Configure the __settings.py file to work with each type of database that Django supports.

2.　Explain the MVC and MTV architectures and elaborate on the differences between the two.

3.　Create a template that shows the menu from a restaurant and have it display.

4.　Working with the same data fields you used in exercise 3, create a model that shows a menu from a restaurant and have Django create the database.

Web Applications and Web Services

If you've ever surfed the Web, you've probably used web applications: to do research, to pay your bills, to send e-mail, or to buy from an online store. As a programmer, you may even have written web applications in other languages. If you have, you'll find the experience of doing so in Python comfortingly familiar, and probably easier. If you're just starting out, rest assured that there's no better way to enter this field than with Python.

When the World Wide Web was invented in the early 1990s, the Internet was used mainly by university students, researchers, and employees of technology companies. Within a few years, the Web had brought the Internet into popular use and culture, co-opting proprietary online services or driving them into bankruptcy. Its triumph is so complete that for many people, the Web is synonymous with the Internet, a technology that predates it by more than 20 years.

Our culture became dependent on the Web so quickly that it hardly seems necessary to evangelize the benefits for the user of web applications over traditional client-server or standalone applications. Web applications are accessible from almost anywhere in the world. Installing one piece of software on your computer — a web browser — gives you access to all of them. Web applications present a simple user interface using a limited set of widgets. They are (usually) platform independent, usable from any web browser on any operating system — including ones not yet created when the application was written.

If you haven't yet written your own web applications, however, you might not know about the benefits of developing for the web platform. In many respects, the benefits for the developer are the flip side of the benefits for the user. A web application doesn't need to be distributed; its users come to it. Updates don't have to be distributed either: When you upgrade the copy of the program on your server, all of your users start using the new version. Web applications are by convention easy to pick up and use, and because others can link to a web application from their own web sites, driving traffic there, buzz and word-of-mouth spread much more quickly. As the developer, you also have more freedom to experiment and more control over the environment in which your software runs.

The virtues of the Web are the virtues of Python: its flexibility, its simplicity, and its inclusive spirit. Python applications are written on Internet time; a hobbyist's idea can be explored in an evening and become a Web fad the next day.

Python also comes packaged with simple, useful modules for interacting with web clients and servers: `urllib.parse`, `urllib`, `urllib.request`, `urllib.error`, `cgi`, even `http.server`. Many (some would say too many) open-source frameworks are also available that make it easy to build a complex Python web application. Frameworks such as Django — covered in Chapter 19 — Zope, and others, provide templating, authentication, access control, and more, freeing you up to work on the code that makes your application special.

It's a huge field, perhaps the most active in the Python community, but this chapter gets you started. You learn how to use basic, standard Python modules to make web applications people will find useful. You also learn how to make them even more useful by creating "web service" interfaces that make it possible for your users to use your applications as elements in their own programs. In addition, you learn how to write scripts of your own to consume popular web services and turn the knowledge gained to your advantage.

If you're reading this chapter, you've probably used web applications before and perhaps have written a web page or two, but you probably don't know how the Web is designed or how web applications work behind the scenes. If your experience is greater, feel free to skip ahead, although you may find the next section interesting. If you've been writing web applications, you might not have realized that the Web actually implements a specific architecture, and that keeping the architecture in mind leads to better, simpler applications.

In this chapter you learn:

❑ All about the web's architecture, including what REST is and the important concepts behind it.

❑ How to create and run your own simple web server.

❑ How to work with HTTP Request's and Responses.

❑ How to utilize other web services.

❑ The proper "web service etiquette."

REST: The Architecture of the Web

It might seem strange to think of the Web as having an architecture at all, especially for anyone who started programming as or after the Web became popular. Because it's so tightly integrated into your daily life, the assumptions that drive the Web might seem invisible or have the flavor of defaults. They are out there, though, differing from what came before and arranged into a coherent architecture. The architecture of the Web was formally defined in 2000 by Roy Fielding, one of its founders. He calls the web architecture Representational State Transfer, or REST. This section briefly summarizes the most important concepts behind REST, while connecting them to the workings of HTTP (the protocol that implements REST) and providing examples of architectures that made the same decisions differently.

> **REST Resources**
>
> Fielding's dissertation on architectural styles and REST is available at www.ics
> .uci.edu/~fielding/pubs/dissertation/top.htm. Chapter 5 describes
> REST. Introductions that are more informal are available at the REST Wiki, at
> http://rest.blueoxen.net/, and at the Wikipedia entry for REST, at
> http://en.wikipedia.org/wiki/REST.

Characteristics of REST

Much of this chapter is dedicated to writing applications that use the features of the REST architecture to best advantage. As a first step toward learning about those features, here's a brief look at some of the main aspects of REST.

A Distributed Network of Interlinked Documents

The most fundamental characteristic of an architecture is the purpose it serves. Without this to use as a guideline, there would be no way to distinguish good architectures from bad ones. Therefore, the first characteristic of REST is the problem it solves: the creation of a "distributed hypermedia system," to quote the Fielding dissertation. REST drives the Web: a network of documents that link to one another, dispersed over a large number of geographically scattered computers under varied ownership. All of REST's other characteristics must be evaluated against this one.

A Client-Server Architecture

The second characteristic of REST is the nature of the actors in a REST architecture. REST defines a client-server relationship between actors, as opposed to, say, the peer-to-peer relationship defined by BitTorrent or other file-sharing programs. A document on the Web is stored on (or generated by) a particular server and delivered upon request to a client who asks for it. A client talks only to servers, and a server only to its clients. In HTTP, the server is a web server, and the client is typically a web browser.

Servers Are Stateless

The third characteristic of REST is that no session state is kept on the server. Every request made by a client must contain all of the information necessary to carry out that request. The web server need not know anything about previous requests the client may have made. This requirement is why web browsers pass cookies and authentication credentials to a site with every single request, rather than only once at the beginning of a long session.

An HTTP session lasts only as long as one back-and-forth transaction between client and server: The client requests a document from the server, and the server delivers the response, which either contains the requested document or explains why the server couldn't deliver it. Protocols like FTP and SSH, in which the client and server communicate more than once per session, must keep state on the server side so that each communication can be understood in the context of the previous one. REST puts this burden on the client instead.

Many frameworks and applications build sessions on top of HTTP by using cookies, special URLs, or some other trick. There's nothing wrong with this — it's not illegal or immoral, and it has its benefits — but by doing this, the application forfeits the benefits of the stateless server. A user might find it impossible to come back to a particular document or might get stuck in a bad state and be unable to do anything about it because the problem is on the server.

Resources

Because the problem REST solves is that of managing a distributed network of documents, its unit of storage is the document, or in REST terms, the *resource*. A static web page is a resource according to REST, but so is one that's dynamically generated by a web application. On the Web, anything interesting you can get with your web browser is a resource.

Each resource has at least one unique identifier, a string that names it and no other resource. In the world of HTTP, this is the resource's URL. The resource identifier `http://www.python.org/` identifies a well-known resource that talks about Python. `http://python.org/` is another identifier for the same resource. `http://www.google.com/search?q5Python` is an identifier denoting a dynamic resource: one created upon request by a web application. This custom-made resource is an index full of references to other resources; all of which should pertain in some way to Python (the language or the snake). It didn't have to be this way: WAIS, one of the technologies subsumed by the Web, treated searches and search results as first-class objects. In the REST architecture, these things exist only within resources and their identifiers.

A web object that can't be reached by typing an address is not technically a REST resource, because it has no identifier. If you can only get to a web page by submitting a form in your web browser, that page is not a resource; it's a side effect of your form submission. It's generally a good idea to make your web pages real resources. A resource is more useful than a nonresource that contains the same information: It can be bookmarked, passed around to others, accessed automatically, and used as input to scripts that manipulate resources.

Representations

When you request a resource with your web browser, what you actually get back is a *representation* of that resource. In the most common case, a resource has only one representation: The resource is a file on the disk of the web server, and its representation is byte-for-byte the same as that file. However, a single resource may have multiple representations. A news site may make each of its stories available in an HTML file, a stripped-down printer-friendly HTML file, a plaintext file, a PDF file, and so on.

A web client may choose a representation for a resource by choosing between that resource's identifiers (for instance, `story.html` or `story.html?printable`), or it may simply tell the server which format it prefers and let the server decide which representation is most appropriate.

REST Operations

We normally think of web pages as things we read, but we act on the Web as well, creating and changing pages through the same tool we use to retrieve them. If you have a weblog, you're familiar with creating new web resources by using your web browser, but it also happens in other contexts. When you send e-mail through a webmail application, an archive page is created that contains the message you sent. When you buy something from an online store, a receipt page is made available, and other pages on the site change to show the outstanding order.

The action of retrieving a resource should be idempotent: The fact that you made the request should not change the contents of the resource. Resource modification is a different operation altogether. In addition to retrieving a resource, REST also enables a client to create, modify, and delete a server's resources (given the proper authorization, of course). A client creates a new resource by specifying, in some format, a representation for the resource, and modifies an existing resource by specifying the desired new representation. It's up to the web application to render to the exact format of the representation it wants.

In HTTP, the four basic operations are implemented by four commands, or *verbs*, as described in the following table.

HTTP Verb	Purpose
GET	Retrieves a resource's representation
POST	Modifies a resource to bring it in line with the provided new representation
PUT	Creates a new resource from the provided representation
DELETE	Deletes an existing resource

These four commands are often compared to the basic file system operations (read, write, create, and delete) and to the four basic SQL commands (SELECT, UPDATE, INSERT, and DELETE). Unfortunately, as you see in a bit, web browsers support only the first two commands.

HTTP: Real-World REST

Although REST's principles are generally applicable, it's realized primarily in HTTP, the protocol that drives the Web. The best way to understand HTTP is to see it in action. To that end, you're going to write a web server.

No, really. It's easy to write a web server in Python. In fact, the simplest one takes just a few lines of code, because Python is packaged with a web server, and all you have to do is activate it.

Try it Out   **Python's Three-Line Web Server**

Enter this script into a file called EasyWebServer.py:

```python
#!/usr/bin/python
import http.server
from http.server import HTTPServer
from http.server import BaseHTTPRequestHandler

def run(server_class=HTTPServer, handler_class=BaseHTTPRequestHandler):
  server_address=('',8000)
  httpd=server_class(server_address, handler_class)
  httpd.serve_forever()
if __name__ == '__main__':
  run()
```

Run the script and you'll be able to access your new web server by visiting the URL
`http://localhost:8000/`.

If another server is already running on port 8000 on your machine, just change the port number in the script and in the URL when you check it and voila!

How It Works

The script drives an `HTTPServer` object, which listens on port 8000 for HTTP requests. Every time you hit the web server with a web browser, an object will be spawned to handle your request. The server will serve pages forever until you interrupt it by killing the script.

When you run this script, the directory in which you ran it becomes a REST-accessible resource, as do all of its files and subdirectories. When you use your web browser to make an HTTP request for one of those resources, the server looks on disk for a file corresponding to the resource you requested and serves it to you as part of the HTTP response.

Binding the web server to the special hostname `localhost` prevents people on the Internet at large, or elsewhere on your local network, from using your web server (see Chapter 16 for more details). However, anyone else on the computer you're using can visit `http://localhost:8000/` and see everything you're serving. If you're running this script on a shared machine, make sure you run it from a directory that doesn't contain documents you don't want to share.

When you're ready to start serving web pages and applications to everyone on the Internet, you'll need to bind the web server to an external-facing hostname or IP address. Again, Chapter 16 has more information on this.

The Visible Web Server

Because you're already programming your own web servers, it's not difficult to write one that enables you to see your own sample HTTP request and response. Here's a script called `VisibleWebServer.py`. It includes a subclass of `SimpleHTTPRequestHandler` that does everything `SimpleHTTPRequestHandler` does, but that also captures the text of the HTTP request and response and prints them to standard output. When you make a request, it just prints out a little log message to the server's standard output. When you hit the Visible Web Server, you get everything:

```python
#!/usr/bin/python
import http.server
from http.server import SimpleHTTPRequestHandler
from http.server import HTTPServer

#The port of your local machine on which you want to run this web
#server.  You'll access the web server by visiting,
#e.g. "http://localhost:8000/"

PORT = 8000

class VisibleHTTPRequestHandler(SimpleHTTPRequestHandler):
    """This class acts just like SimpleHTTPRequestHandler, but instead
    of logging only a summary of each hit to standard output, it logs
```

```
the full HTTP request and response."""

def log_request(self, code='-', size='-'):
    """Logs a request in great detail. This method is called by
    SimpleHTTPRequestHandler.do_GET()."""
    print(self._heading("HTTP Request"))
    #First, print the resource identifier and desired operation.
    print(self.raw_requestline,)
    #Second, print the request metadata
    for header, value in self.headers.items():
        print(header + ":", value)

def do_GET(self, method='GET'):
    """Handles a GET request the same way as
    SimpleHTTPRequestHandler, but also prints the full text of the
    response to standard output."""
    #Replace the file object being used to output response with a
    #shim that copies all outgoing data into a place we can see
    #later. Then, give the actual work of handling the request to
    #SimpleHTTPRequestHandler.
    self.wfile = FileWrapper(self.wfile)
    SimpleHTTPRequestHandler.do_GET(self)
    #By this time, the shim file object we created previously is
    #full of the response data, and is ready to be displayed. The
    #request has also been displayed, since it was logged by
    #log_request() (called by SimpleHTTPRequestHandler's do_GET)
    print("")
    print(self._heading("HTTP Response"))
    print(self.wfile)

def _heading(self, s):
    """This helper method formats a header string so it stands out
    from the data beneath it."""
    line = '=' * len(s)
    return line + '\n' + s + '\n' + line

class FileWrapper:
    """This class wraps a file object, such that everything written to
    the file is also silently appended to a buffer that can be printed
    out later."""

    def __init__(self, wfile):
        """wfile is the file object to which the response is being
        written, and which this class silently replaces."""
        self.wfile = wfile
        self.contents = []

    def __getattr__(self, key):
        """If someone tries and fails to get an attribute of this
        object, they're probably trying to use it as the file object
        it replaces. Delegate to that object."""
        return getattr(self.wfile, key)

    def write(self, s):
```

(continued)

(continued)

```
            """Write a string to the 'real' file and also append it to the
            list of strings intended for later viewing."""
            self.contents.append(s)
            self.wfile.write(s)

        def __str__(self):
            """Returns the output so far as a string."""
            return ''.join(self.contents)

    if __name__ == '__main__':
        httpd = HTTPServer(('localhost', PORT), VisibleHTTPRequestHandler)
        httpd.serve_forever()
```

Note how even though `SimpleHTTPRequestHandler` wasn't designed for its output to be intercepted, it wasn't terribly difficult to replace its output file with an impostor that does what you need. Python's operator overloading makes it easy for one object to impersonate another. In the following exercise, you actually use this script and consider a sample request and response.

<hr>

Try It Out   **Seeing an HTTP Request and Response**

Create a file called `hello.html` in the directory in which you put `VisibleWebServer.py`. Put the following HTML code into the file:

```
<html>
 <body>Hello, world!</body>
</html>
```

Start up `VisibleWebServer.py` and, using a web browser, visit the URL `http://localhost:8000/hello.html`. In the standard output of the `VisibleWebServer.py` process, you should see output much like the following:

```
============
HTTP Request
============
b'GET /testpage.html HTTP/1.1\r\n'
Accept: image/gif, image/x-xbitmap, image/jpeg, image/pjpeg, application/x-
ms-application, application/vnd.ms-xpsdocument, application/xaml+xml,
application/x-ms-xbap, application/msword, application/vnd.ms-excel,
application/vnd.ms-powerpoint, application/x-shockwave-flash, */*
Accept-Language: en-us
UA-CPU: x86
Accept-Encoding: gzip, deflate
User-Agent: Mozilla (compatible; MSIE 7.0; Windows NT 6.0; GTB6; SLCC1; .NET
CLR 2.0.50727; Media Center PC 5.0; InfoPath.1; InfoPath.2; .NET CLR
3.5.30729; .NET CLR 3.0.30618)
Host: localhost:8000
Connection: Keep-Alive

============
HTTP Response
============
HTTP/1.0 200 OK
Server: SimpleHTTP/0.6 Python/3.1.1
```

```
Date: Thu, 24 Sep 2009 00:47:25 GMT
Content-type: text/html
Content-Length: 42

<html>
 <body>Hello, world!</body>
</html>
```

How It Works

When you request `hello.html`, the `HTTPServer` object created by `VisibleWebServer.py` spawns a `VisibleHTTPRequestHandler` object to handle your request. This does everything that a `SimpleHTTPRequestHandler` spawned by `EasyWebServer.py` would do, but it also makes sure the full text of the HTTP request and response are printed to standard output. `SimpleHTTPRequestHandler` would have just printed a summary of the request.

> If you use the FireFox or Mozilla web browser, you can install an extension that will let you see portions of every HTTP request you make and every response you get. The extension is called LiveHTTPHeaders, and it's available from `http://livehttpheaders.mozdev.org/`. This can be very useful in debugging web applications, but you can see only the headers, not the actual request or response data.

> Several web applications also exist that will make an HTTP request on your behalf and show you the request and response. The most full-featured application of this sort is Web-Sniffer, at `http://web-sniffer.net/`.

The HTTP Request

An HTTP request has two parts. The first line of the request is the command; it contains an HTTP verb, a resource identifier, and (optionally) the version of HTTP being used:

```
GET /hello.html HTTP/1.1
```

Here the verb is GET and the resource identifier is `/hello.html`.

The second part of the HTTP request is a series of headers: key-value pairs describing the client and providing additional information about the request:

```
host: localhost:8000
accept-language: en
accept-encoding: gzip, compress
accept: text/*, */*;q=0.01
```

In the REST architecture, all information necessary to identify the resource should be kept in the identifier. Because `SimpleHTTPServer` serves only static files, you'll use `/foo.html` to uniquely identify one file on disk. Another web server might be able to dynamically generate a representation of `/foo.html` instead of just looking for a file on disk, but `/foo.html` would still identify one particular resource.

Though the identifier should completely identify the resource, the key-value pairs can be used to make smaller-scale decisions about which representation of the resource to show — for instance, to send a localized version of a document in response to the Accept-Language header. HTTP headers are also used to regulate caching and to transmit persistent client state (that is, cookies) and authentication information.

> *Web browsers generally send HTTP headers with capitalized names like "User-Agent," and that's how this chapter refers to particular headers. A quirk of the* `SimpleHTTPRequestHandler` *class means that the Visible Web Server prints out header names in lowercase even if that's not how they were received, but it doesn't matter much: HTTP headers are not case-sensitive. "User-Agent" and "user-agent" are the same header.*

The HTTP Response

The HTTP response tells the story of how the web server tried to fulfill the corresponding request. It begins with a status code, which summarizes the response:

```
HTTP/1.1 200 OK
```

In this case, the response code was 200 (OK), which means everything went fine and your resource is enclosed. Less desirable status codes you may have seen in your web browsing include the following:

❑ 403 (Forbidden), which means the resource might or might not exist but you're not allowed to receive it anyway

❑ 404 (File Not Found) The most famous HTTP status code that you'll actually see in your browser, this means the resource is just gone and has left no forwarding address, or was never there

❑ 500 (Internal Server Error), which is often caused by a bug in a web application

> *All forty standard error codes are defined and categorized in RFC 2616, available at* www.w3.org/ Protocols/rfc2616/rfc2616-sec10.html. *Some of them are obscure, but it pays to know them. For instance, the 204 response code, "No Content," can be used in a web application to take action when the user clicks a link, without making the user's web browser load another page.*

Following the status code are a number of headers, in the same key-value format as HTTP request headers:

```
Server: SimpleHTTP/0.6 Python/3.1.0
Date: Thu, 24 Sep 2009 00:47:25 GMT
Content-type: text/html
Content-Length: 42
```

Just as request headers contain information potentially useful to the web server, response headers contain information potentially useful to the web browser. By far the most important HTTP response header is "Content-Type." Without this header, the web browser wouldn't know how to display the document being sent. The content type of /foo.html is text/html, which tells the web browser to render the representation it receives as HTML. If the client had requested /foo.jpg instead, the content type would have been image/jpeg, and the browser would have known to render the document as a graphic instead.

A blank line follows the response headers, and the rest of the response consists of the document being delivered (if any). For a successful GET request, the document is the resource that was requested. For a successful POST, PUT, or DELETE request, the result document is often the new version of the resource that was changed, or a status message talking about the success of the operation. An unsuccessful operation often results in an HTTP response containing a document describing the error and possibly offering help.

Web applications are considered more or less "RESTful" depending on how well they employ the features of HTTP. There are no hard-and-fast rules for this, and sometimes convenience wins out over RESTfulness, but HTTP has conventions, and you might as well use them to your advantage instead of reinventing them unnecessarily. Some rules of thumb for designing RESTful interfaces follow:

Keep resource identifiers transparent. A user should be able to figure out what kind of resource is on the other end of a resource identifier just by looking at it. The biggest challenge to achieving this is designing the resource identifier so that it holds all of the information necessary to uniquely identify the resource.

On the other hand, don't put something into the resource identifier if it doesn't help identify a resource. Ask the user to provide that information in an HTTP header instead, or in the data of a POST, DELETE, or PUT request.

Don't put something into the data of a POST, DELETE, or PUT request if it makes sense to put it into one of the standard HTTP headers. For instance, authentication information can be submitted through HTTP authentication. If you make a resource available in multiple formats, you can have clients use the HTTP header "Accept" to specify which one they want.

Don't return a status code of 200 ("OK") on an error, unless there's really no HTTP error that conveys the problem. 500 (problem on the server end) and 400 (problem on the user end) are good general-purpose errors. One problem with this rule is that browsers such as Internet Explorer may show their own generic error screen if they receive an error code other than 200, blocking a document you might have generated to help the user with her specific problem.

CGI: Turning Scripts into Web Applications

Using different web browsers and resources, experiment with the Visual Web Server until it becomes boring. Unless you find this whole topic boring, this encroaching ennui probably means you're pushing the limits of what's to be learned from examining HTTP requests and responses. Fortunately, it gets much more interesting very quickly: The next phase is the dynamic world of web applications.

REST is easy to implement when you're just serving files off of a hard disk, but that only covers the part of REST whereby you request resources. Representations, the means by which you create, modify, and delete resources, don't come into the picture at all. Although a set of static HTML files is technically a web application, it's not a very interesting one.

You can handle the transfer of representations and the creation of dynamic applications in a number of ways (remember the chapter on Django?), but the venerable standard is the Common Gateway Interface (CGI). CGI was developed in the early 1990s and has remained more or less the same since its creation. The goal of CGI is to enable someone to write a script that can be invoked from an HTTP request, without having to know anything about web server programming. A web server that supports CGI is capable of transforming certain HTTP requests into script invocations.

> *The CGI standard is hosted at* `http://hoohoo.ncsa.uiuc.edu/cgi/`. *The page hasn't changed since 1996, but neither has CGI.*

Because CGI is implemented inside the web server, it must be enabled through web server configuration. The setup of CGI is highly dependent on the brand of web server and on your system administrator's idea of how a system should be administrated. Even different Linux distributions have different out-of-the-box setups for CGI. Rather than give comprehensive instructions for all contingencies, or evade the issue altogether and assume you can get it working, following are a few lines of Python that implement a simple CGI server; save this under the name of `EasyCGIServer.py`. This server can be used for all of the CGI examples in this chapter. Once again, a built-in Python module makes it easy.

```python
#!/usr/bin/python
import http.server
from http.server import HTTPServer
from http.server import CGIHTTPRequestHandler

def run(server_class=HTTPServer, handler_class=CGIHTTPRequestHandler):
    server_address=('',8001)
    httpd=server_class(server_address, handler_class)
    httpd.serve_forever()
if __name__ == '__main__':
    run()
```

The code is as simple as that for `EasyWebServer`; in fact, it's nearly identical. The only new feature `EasyCGIServer` supports is special treatment of the `cgi-bin` directory, which is where CGI scripts are kept.

Try it Out   Running a CGI Script

Create a directory called `cgi-bin` beneath the directory in which you keep `EasyWebServer.py` and `EasyCGIServer.py`. Put the following code in the file `cgi-bin/hello.cgi`:

```python
#!/usr/bin/python
Print("Content-type: text/plain\n")
Print("Hello, world!")
```

> *The filenames of all the CGI scripts in this chapter will have the* `.cgi` *extension. This visually distinguishes the CGI scripts from the regular Python scripts, and makes it possible to run them on web servers that will only execute a CGI script if it has a* `.cgi` *extension.*

If you're on a UNIX-based system, you'll also need to make `hello.cgi` editable with the `chmod` command:

```
# chmod u+x ./cgi-bin/hello.cgi
```

Run `hello.cgi` from the command line to make sure the script works:

```
# ./cgi-bin/hello.cgi
Content-type: text/plain

Hello, world!
```

Start `EasyWebServer.py` and use a web browser to visit `http://localhost:8001/cgi-bin/hello.cgi`. Either your web browser will invite you to download `hello.cgi` as a Python script, or you will see the source code to `hello.cgi` as plaintext in your web browser:

```
#!/usr/bin/python
print "Content-type: text/plain\n"
print "Hello, world!"
```

Kill `EasyWebServer.py` and start up `EasyCGIServer.py` instead. In your web browser, reload `http://localhost:8001/cgi-bin/hello.cgi`. You should see the string "Hello, world!" as plaintext in your web browser:

```
Hello, world!
```

How It Works

When you requested `/cgi-bin/hello.cgi` through `EasyWebServer`, the server interpreted it the way `EasyWebServer` interprets every request: as a request for a static file to be found on disk. What you received was the contents of the static file `/cgi-bin/hello.cgi`.

When you requested the same resource through `EasyCGIServer`, the server interpreted it differently. Instead of treating `hello.cgi` as a file to be read, `EasyCGIServer` treated it as a script to be run. The script was executed as from the command line, and its output was used to create the HTTP response. What you saw in your web browser was the content part of the HTTP response, rendered according to the Content-Type header provided by the script. Any executable `.py` or `.cgi` script you put into `cgi-bin/` will be run by `EasyWebServer` when requested, and its output will be used to create an HTTP response.

The Web Server Makes a Deal with the CGI Script

The CGI standard specifies a deal that a CGI-enabled web server makes with any file it chooses to interpret as a CGI script. The web server is responsible for receiving and parsing the HTTP request, for routing the request to the correct script, and for executing that script just as you might execute a Python script from the command line. It's also responsible for modifying the script's runtime environment to include CGI-specific variables, whose values correspond to information about the runtime environment, and information found in the HTTP request. For instance, the User-Agent header becomes the environment variable `HTTP_USER_AGENT`, and the HTTP verb invoked by the request becomes the environment variable `HTTP_METHOD`. As with any other environment variables, these special variables can be accessed through the `os.environ` dictionary, and the script can use them to evaluate the HTTP request.

In return for this service, the CGI script is expected to take over the duties of the web server for the duration of that HTTP session. Anything the script writes to standard output is output as part of the HTTP response. This means that in addition to producing a document of some kind, the script needs to output any necessary HTTP headers as a preface to the document. At the very least, every CGI script must output the Content-Type HTTP header.

If you're having trouble getting a script to work through the web browser, you can try setting the appropriate CGI environment variables manually and executing the script from the command line.

CGI's Special Environment Variables

Your script might find more than 20 special CGI variables in its environment. The important ones are covered a bit later, but first look at a very simple CGI script that gives you the tools you need to explore the variables yourself. It's called `PrintEnvironment.cgi`:

```
#!/usr/bin/python

import os
import cgitb
cgitb.enable()
```

The `cgitb` module will give you exception reporting and stack tracebacks in your web browser, similar to what you see when a command-line Python script throws an exception. It'll save you from getting mysterious 500 error codes, and from having to look through web server logs to find the actual error message:

```
#Following is a list of the environment variables defined by the CGI
#standard. In addition to these 17 predefined variables, each HTTP
#header in the request has a corresponding variable whose name begins
#with "HTTP_". For instance, the value of the "User-Agent" header is
#kept in "HTTP_USER_AGENT".
CGI_ENVIRONMENT_KEYS = [ 'SERVER_SOFTWARE',
                         'SERVER_NAME',
                         'GATEWAY_INTERFACE',
                         'SERVER_PROTOCOL',
                         'SERVER_PORT',
                         'REQUEST_METHOD',
                         'PATH_INFO',
                         'PATH_TRANSLATED',
                         'SCRIPT_NAME',
                         'QUERY_STRING',
                         'REMOTE_HOST',
                         'REMOTE_ADDR',
                         'AUTH_TYPE',
                         'REMOTE_USER',
                         'REMOTE_IDENT',
                         'CONTENT_TYPE',
                         'CONTENT_LENGTH' ]

#First print the response headers. The only one we need is Content-type.
print("Content-type: text/plain\n")

#Next, print the environment variables and their values.
print("Here are the headers for the request you just made:")
```

```
for key, value in os.environ.items():
    if key.find('HTTP_') == 0 or key in CGI_ENVIRONMENT_KEYS:
        print(key, "=", value)
```

Put this file in your `cgi-bin/` directory, make it executable, and visit `http://localhost:8000/cgi-bin/PrintEnvironment.cgi`. You should see something like the following:

```
Here are the headers for the request you just made:
SERVER_SOFTWARE => SimpleHTTP/0.6 Python/3.1.0
REQUEST_METHOD => GET
PATH_INFO =>
SERVER_PROTOCOL => HTTP/1.1
QUERY_STRING =>
CONTENT_LENGTH =>
SERVER_NAME => rubberfish
PATH_TRANSLATED => /home/jamesp/LearningPython/listings
SERVER_PORT => 8001
CONTENT_TYPE => text/plain
HTTP_USER_AGENT =>
HTTP_ACCEPT =>  text/html, text/plain, text/rtf, text/*, */*;q=0.01

GATEWAY_INTERFACE => CGI/1.1
SCRIPT_NAME => /cgi-bin/PrintEnvironment.py
REMOTE_ADDR => 127.0.0.1
REMOTE_HOST => rubberfish
```

With the `PrintEnvironment.py` file in place, you're defining a resource with the identifier `http://localhost:8000/cgi-bin/PrintEnvironment.cgi`. When you run `EasyCGIServer`, this resource is defined by the output you get when you run the Python code in `PrintEnvironment.cgi`; and, depending on the content of your request, it can be different every time you hit that URL.

`PrintEnvironment.cgi` contains an enumeration of the defined CGI environment variables and only prints the values of those variables. The purpose of this is twofold: to put that information where you'll see it and to avoid leaking information that might be contained in other irrelevant environment variables.

`EasyCGIServer` inherits the environment of the shell you used to run it; this means that if you run `EasyCGIServer` instead of Apache or another web server, a version of `PrintEnvironment.cgi` that printed the whole environment would print `PATH` and all the other environment variables in your shell. This information would swamp the legitimate CGI variables and possibly disclose sensitive information about your user account. Remember that any web servers you set up on your computer can be accessed by anyone else on the same machine, and possibly by the Internet at large. Don't expose information about yourself unnecessarily.

A few of the CGI-specific environment variables deserve further scrutiny here:

❑ REQUEST_METHOD is the HTTP verb corresponding to the REST method you used against this resource. Because you were just trying to retrieve a representation of the resource, you used the GET HTTP verb.

❑ QUERY_STRING and PATH_INFO are the two main ways in which a resource identifier makes it into a CGI script. You can experiment with these two variables by accessing PrintEnvironment.cgi in different ways. For instance, GETting the resource identifier /cgi-bin/PrintEnvironment.cgi/pathInfo/?queryString will set PATH_INFO to pathInfo/ and QUERY_STRING to queryString. The strange-looking, hard-to-understand URLs you often see when using web applications are usually long QUERY_STRINGs.

❑ HTTP_USER_AGENT is a string provided by the web browser you used to access the page, which corresponds to the "User-Agent" HTTP header and which is supposed to identify the web browser you're using. It's interesting as an example of an HTTP header being transformed into a CGI environment variable. Another such variable is HTTP_REFERER, derived from the "Referer" HTTP header. The "Referer" header is provided whenever you click a link from one page to another, so that the second page knows how you accessed it.

Accepting User Input through HTML Forms

It's possible to manipulate the output of PrintEnvironment.cgi enough to prove that it serves dynamic resources, but the interface to it isn't that good. To get different text back, you have to use different web browsers, hack the URL (that is, request different resources), or do even weirder things. Most web applications eschew this type of interface in favor of one based on HTML forms. You can make a lot of useful web applications just by writing simple CGIs that print HTML forms and read the QUERY_STRING and PATH_INFO variables.

A brief recap of HTML forms seems appropriate here, because the forms are relevant only to web applications. Even if you already know HTML, it's useful to place HTML forms in the context of the REST architecture.

An HTML form is enclosed within <FORM> tags. The opening <FORM> tag has two main attributes: action, which contains the identifier of the CGI script to call or the resource to be operated upon, and method, which contains the HTTP verb to be used when submitting the form.

HTML Forms' Limited Vocabulary

The only HTTP verbs supported by HTML forms are GET, for reading a resource, and POST, for writing to a resource. A form action of PUT or DELETE is invalid HTML, and most web browsers will submit a POST request instead. As you'll see, this puts a bit of a kink in the implementation of REST-based web applications, but it's not too bad.

Between the opening <FORM> tag and the closing </FORM> tag, special HTML tags can be used, which a web browser renders as GUI controls. The GUI controls available include text boxes, checkboxes, radio button groups, buttons that activate form submission (all achieved with the INPUT tag), large text entry fields (the TEXTAREA tag), and drop-down selection boxes (the SELECT tag).

If you put that HTML in a file called `SimpleHTMLForm.html` in the root directory of your `EasyCGIServer` installation, you can retrieve it via the URL `http://localhost:8001/SimpleHTMLForm.html`. Because it's not a CGI script, `EasyCGIServer` will serve it as a static file, just as `EasyWebServer` would. If you then click the Submit button, the form data will be encoded by the web browser into a GET request, and submitted to a resource with a long identifier beginning with `/cgi-bin/PrintFormSubmission.cgi`. Unfortunately, there's nothing on disk — no file and no script — corresponding to that resource identifier, so instead of doing anything useful, the web server is going to return a "page not found" error document (status code: the famous 404). With Python's `cgi` module, though, it's easy to put a script in place that will take the form submission and do something with it.

The cgi Module: Parsing HTML Forms

When you click one of the Submit buttons on `SimpleHTMLForm.html`, notice that you're not exactly GETting the resource `/cgi-bin/PrintFormSubmission.cgi`, the resource specified in the `action` attribute of the `<FORM>` tag. You're GETting a slightly different resource, something with the long, unwieldy identifier of `/cgi-bin/PrintFormSubmission.cgi?textField=Some+text&radioButton=2&button=Submit`.

This is how a GET form submission works: The web browser gathers the values of the fields in the form you submitted and encodes them so they don't contain any characters not valid in a URL (for instance, spaces are replaced by plus signs). It then appends the field values to the form destination, to get the actual resource to be retrieved. Assuming there's a CGI at the other end to intercept the request, the CGI will see that encoded form information in its `QUERY_STRING` environment variable. A similar encoding happens when you submit a form using the POST verb, but in that case the form data is sent as part of the data, not as part of the resource identifier. Instead of being made available to the script in environment variables, POSTed data is made available on standard input.

The `cgi` module knows how to decode the form data present in HTTP requests, whether the request uses GET or POST. The `cgi` module can obtain the data from environment variables (GET) or standard input (POST), and use it to create a reconstruction of the original HTML form in a class called `FieldStorage`.

`FieldStorage` can be accessed just like a dictionary, but the safest way to use it is to call its `getfirst()` method, passing in the name of the field whose value you want.

Safety When Accessing Form Values

Why is `form.getfirst('fieldName')` safer than `form['fieldName']`? The root of the problem is that sometimes a single form submission can legitimately provide two or more values for the same field (for instance, this happens when a user selects more than one value of a selection box that allows multiple selections). If this happens, `form['fieldName']` will return a list of values (for example, all the selected values in the multiple-selection box) instead of a single value. This is fine as long as your script is expecting it to happen, but because users have complete control of the data they submit to your CGI script, a malicious user could easily submit multiple values for a field in which you were only expecting one.

If someone pulls that trick on you and your script is using `form['fieldName']`, you'll get a list where you were expecting a single object. If you treat a list as though it were a single object your script will surely crash. That's why it's safer to use `getfirst`: It is always guaranteed to return only the first submitted value, even if a user is trying to crash your script with bad data.

In older versions of Python prior to 2.2, the `getfirst` method is not available. Instead, to be safe you need to simulate `getfirst` with code like the following:

```
fieldVal = form.getValue("field")
if isinstance(fieldVal, list): #More than one "field" was submitted.
    fieldVal = fieldVal[0]
```

When you're actually expecting multiple values for a single CGI variable, use the _getlist_ method instead of `getfirst` to get all the set values.

Now that you know about the `FieldStorage` object, it's easy to write the other half of `SimpleHTMLForm.html`: `PrintFormSubmission.cgi`, a CGI script that prints the values it finds in the form's fields:

```
#!/usr/bin/python
import cgi
import cgitb
cgitb.enable()

form = cgi.FieldStorage()
textField = form.getfirst("textField")
radioButton = form.getfirst("radioButton")
submitButton = form.getfirst("button")

print('Content-type: text/html\n')
print('<html>')
print('<body>')
print('<p>Here are the values of your form submission:</p>')
print('<ul>')
print('<li>In the text field, you entered "%s".</li>' % textField)
print('<li>Of the radio buttons, you selected "%s".' % radioButton)
print('<li>The name of the submit button you clicked is "%s".' %
submitButton)
print('</ul>')
print('</body>')
print('</html>')
```

Now, when you click the submit button on `SimpleHTMLForm.html`, instead of getting a 404 Not Found error, you'll see something similar to what is shown in Figure 20-1.

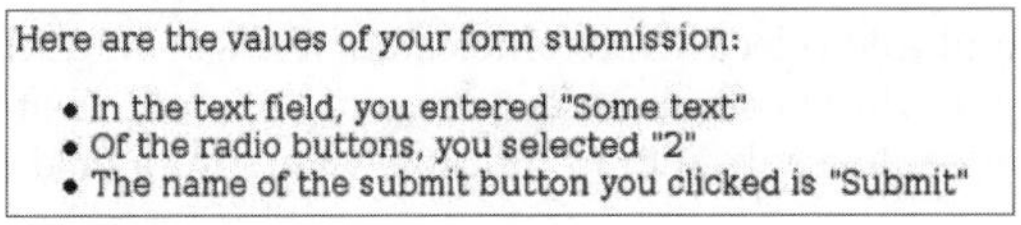

Here are the values of your form submission:

- In the text field, you entered "Some text"
- Of the radio buttons, you selected "2"
- The name of the submit button you clicked is "Submit"

Figure 20-1

So far so good. You can go a little further, though, and create a script capable of printing out any form submission at all. That way, you can experiment with HTML forms of different types. To get started, have the new script print out a fairly complex HTML form when you hit it without submitting a form to it. The script that follows deserves to be called `PrintAnyFormSubmission.cgi`:

```python
#!/usr/bin/python
import cgi
import cgitb
import os

cgitb.enable()
form = cgi.FieldStorage()

print('Content-type: text/html\n')
print('<html>')
print('<body>')
if form.keys():
    verb = os.environ['REQUEST_METHOD']
    print('<p>Here are the values of your %s form submission:' % verb)
    print('<ul>')
    for field in form.keys():
        valueObject = form[field]
        if isinstance(valueObject, list):
            #More than one value was submitted. We therefore have a
            #whole list of ValueObjects. getlist() would have given us
            #the string values directly.
            values = [v.value for v in valueObject]
            if len(values) == 2:
                connector = '" and "' #'"Foo" and "bar"'
            else:
                connector = '", and "' #'"Foo", "bar", and "baz"'
            value = '", "'.join(values[:-1]) + connector + values[-1]
        else:
            #Only one value was submitted. We therefore have only one
            #ValueObject. getfirst() would have given us the string
            #value directly.
            value = valueObject.value
        print('<li>For <var>%s</var>, I got "%s"</li>' % (field, value))
else:
    print('''<form method="GET" action="%s">

<p>Here's a sample HTML form.</p>

<p><input type="text" name="textField" value="Some text" /><br />
<input type="password" name="passwordField" value="A password" />
<input type="hidden" name="hiddenField" value="A hidden field" /></p>

<p>Checkboxes:
<input type="checkbox" name="checkboxField1" checked="checked" /> 1
<input type="checkbox" name="checkboxField2" selected="selected" /> 2
</p>

<p>Choose one:<br />
<input type="radio" name="radioButton" value="1" /> 1<br />
```

(continued)

(continued)

```
<input type="radio" name="radioButtons" value="2" checked="checked" /> 2<br />
<input type="radio" name="radioButtons" value="3" /> 3<br /></p>

<textarea name="largeTextEntry">A lot of text</textarea>

<p>Choose one or more: <select name="selection" size="4" multiple="multiple">
<option value="Option 1">Option 1</option>
<option value="Option 2" selected="selected">Option 2</option>
<option value="Option 3" selected="selected">Option 3</option>
<option value="Option 4" selected="selected">Option 4</option>
</select></p>

<p><input type="Submit" name="button" value="Submit this form" />
<p><input type="Submit" name="button" value="Submit this form (Button #2)" />

</form>''' % os.environ['SCRIPT_NAME'])

print('</body>')
print('</html>')
```

Try It Out   Printing Any HTML Form Submission

Put `PrintAnyFormSubmission.cgi` in your `cgi-bin/` directory and start up `EasyCGIServer`. Visit `http://localhost:8001/cgi-bin/PrintAnyFormSubmission.cgi`. You'll be given an HTML form that looks something like what is shown in Figure 20-2.

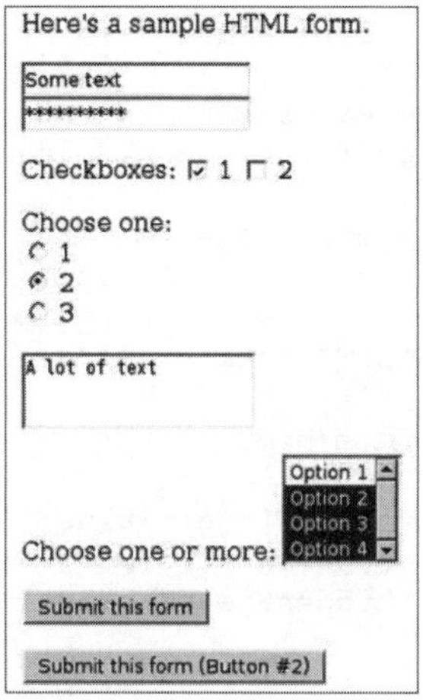

Figure 20-2

Change any of the form data you want and click one of the Submit buttons. You'll be taken to a screen that looks like the one shown in Figure 20-3.

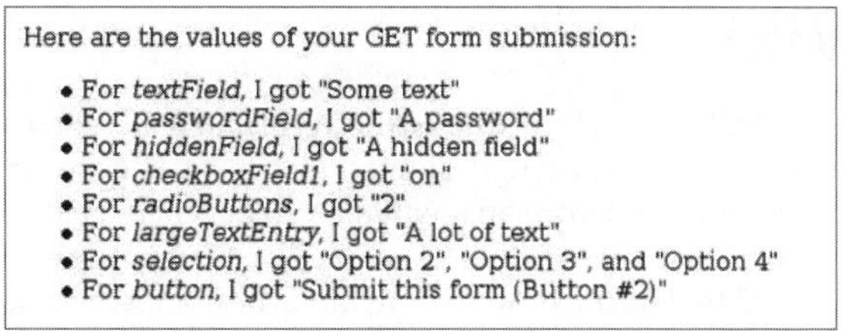

Here are the values of your GET form submission:

- For *textField*, I got "Some text"
- For *passwordField*, I got "A password"
- For *hiddenField*, I got "A hidden field"
- For *checkboxField1*, I got "on"
- For *radioButtons*, I got "2"
- For *largeTextEntry*, I got "A lot of text"
- For *selection*, I got "Option 2", "Option 3", and "Option 4"
- For *button*, I got "Submit this form (Button #2)"

Figure 20-3

How It Works

When you first request the resource identified by `/cgi-bin/PrintAnyFormSubmission.cgi`, the script uses the `cgi` module to look for a form submission. Because there are no form variables, it assumes you didn't submit a form at all and presents the default resource: a fairly complex HTML form for you to play with.

When you click one of the Submit buttons, you request a very different resource: something like `/cgi-bin/PrintAnyFormSubmission.cgi?textField=Some+text&passwordField=A+password &hiddenField=A+hidden+field&checkboxField1=on&radioButtons=2&largeTextEntry=A+lo t+of+text&selection=Option+2&selection=Option+3&selection=Option+4&button=Submit +this+form+%28Button+%232%29`. This time, the `cgi` module picks up a lot of form variables and outputs a dynamically generated resource that iterates over the submitted form variables to describe the form you submitted. If you submit the form again with different values, you're requesting a slightly different resource and the HTML output by the script will be different in corresponding ways.

If you're new to web programming, note especially that even though there was a `checkboxField2` *field in the form submitted, there's no mention of it in the description of the form submission. Web browsers don't encode unchecked checkboxes into the form submission, so they don't show up at all in the* `FieldStorage` *object. This can be a little annoying.*

You can use `SimpleHTMLForm.html` against this script as well as against `PrintFormSubmission.cgi`. In fact, you can use any form at all against this script, including forms designed for other web applications, as long as you change the form's `action` attribute to point to `/cgi-bin/ PrintFormSubmission.cgi`. However, if you don't provide any inputs at all (that is, you GET the base resource `/cgi-bin/PrintFormSubmission.cgi`), you'll be given the default HTML form. This pattern — a CGI script that, when invoked with no arguments, prints its own form — is a powerful tool for building self-contained applications. Note also how the script uses the special CGI-provided environment variable `SCRIPT_NAME` to refer to itself. Even if you name this script something else or put it in another directory, the form it generates will still refer to itself.

Like the `EasyHTTPServer`, `PrintAnyFormSubmission.cgi` is a good way to experiment with a new concept, but it gets boring quickly. It's time to move on to something more interesting: a real web application.

Building a Wiki

With a basic knowledge of REST, the architecture of the Web; and CGI, the main way of hooking up programs to that architecture, you're ready to design and build a basic application. The next few pages detail the construction of a simple content management system called a *wiki*.

The wiki was invented in 1995 by Ward Cunningham and is best known today as the base for Wikipedia (www.wikipedia.org), a free online encyclopedia (see Figure 20-4). Cunningham's original wiki (http://c2.com/cgi/wiki/) is still popular among programmers, containing information on and discussion of technical and professional best practices. Of course, there's also the REST wiki mentioned earlier.

Figure 20-4

The most distinctive features of wikis are as follows:

❑ **Open, web-based editing** — Some content management systems require special software or a user account to use, but wiki pages are editable through any web browser. On most wikis, every page is open to editing by anyone at all. Because of problems with spam and vandalism, some wikis have begun to require user accounts. Even with wikis that distinguish between members and nonmembers, though, the norm is that any member can edit any page. This gives wikis an informal feel, and the near lack of barriers to entry encourages people to contribute.

❑ **A flat namespace of pages** — Each page in a wiki has a unique name. Page names are often *WikiWords*, strings formed by capitalizing several words (the title of the page) and pushing them together. That is, WikiPageNames OftenLookLikeThis. There is no directory structure in a wiki; all pages are served from the top level. Pages are organized through the creation of additional pages to serve as indexes and portals.

❑ **Linking through citing** — One wiki page can link to another simply by mentioning its WikiWord name in its own body. When a page is rendered, all WikiWords cited therein are linked to the corresponding pages. A page may reference a WikiWord for which no page yet exists: At rendering time, such a reference is linked to a form for creating the nonexistent page. Wikis that don't name their pages with WikiWords must define some other convention for linking to another page in the same wiki.

❑ **Simple, text-based markup** — Rather than require the user to input HTML, wikis employ a few simple rules for transforming ASCII text into the HTML displayed when a page is rendered. Sample rules include the use of a blank line to signify a new paragraph, and the use of *asterisks* to bold a selection. Unfortunately, these conventions are only informal, and there are no hard-and-fast rules. So, the specific rules differ widely across the various wiki implementations.

See `http://c2.com/cgi/wiki?WikiDesignPrinciples` *for Cunningham's original wiki design principles.*

Sample applications often lack important features necessary to make the application fit for actual use. An online store application presented within the context of this chapter would be too complex to be easily understood, yet not complete enough to actually use to run an online store. Because the defining features of a wiki are so few and simple, it's possible to design, build, and explain a fully fledged wiki in just a few pages. BittyWiki, the application designed and built in this chapter according to the principles just described, weighs in at under 10 kilobytes, but it's not the shortest wiki written in Python.

See `http://infomesh.net/2003/wypy/wypy.txt` *for a wiki written in only 814 characters and 11 lines of Python. It's acutely painful to behold.*

The BittyWiki Core Library

Before writing any code, you need to make a couple of design decisions about the nature of the wiki you want to create. In the following examples, the design decisions made are the ones that lead to the simplest wiki back end: after all, for the purposes of this discussion, the important part of BittyWiki is the interface it presents to the Web, not the back end.

Back-end Storage

Wiki implementations store their pages in a variety of ways. Some keep their files on disk, some in a database, and some in a version-controlled repository so that users can easily repel vandalism. For simplicity's sake, a BittyWiki installation will keep a page on a disk file named after that page. All of a given wiki's pages will be kept in the same directory. Because the wiki namespace is flat, no subdirectories are needed.

WikiWords

Each wiki implementation that uses WikiWords must decide which strings are valid names of wiki pages, so that it can automatically link citations of those pages. BittyWiki uses one of the simplest WikiWord definitions: It treats as a WikiWord any string of letters and numbers that begins with a capital letter and contains at least two capitals. "WikiWord" is itself a WikiWord, as are "WikiWord2," "WikiworD," "WWW," and "AI."

Any wiki page can be retrieved by name, but you also need a default page for when no name is specified. The default page will be the one called "HomePage."

Writing the BittyWiki Core

On the basis of those design decisions, it's now possible to write the core of BittyWiki: the code that reads from and writes to the back end, and that processes the WikiWord links. Put this code into BittyWiki.py, in your cgi-bin/ directory or somewhere in your PYTHON_PATH:

```python
"""This module implements the BittyWiki core code: that which is not
bound to any particular interface."""

import re
import os

class Wiki:
    "A class representing a wiki as a whole."
    HOME_PAGE_NAME = "HomePage"

    def __init__(self, base):
        "Initializes a wiki that uses the provided base directory."
        self.base = base

        if not os.path.exists(self.base):
            os.makedirs(self.base)
        elif not os.path.isdir(self.base):
            raise IOError('Wiki base "%s" is not a directory!' % self.base)

    def getPage(self, name=None):
        """Retrieves the given page for this wiki, which may or may not
        currently exist."""
        if not name:
            name = self.HOME_PAGE_NAME
        return Page(self, name)

class Page:
    """A class representing one page of a wiki, containing all the
    logic necessary to manipulate that page and to determine which other
    pages it references."""

    #We consider a WikiWord any word beginning with a capital letter,
    #containing at least one other capital letter, and containing only
    #alphanumerics.
    WIKI_WORD_MATCH = "((([A-Z][a-z0-9]*){2,})"
```

```
        WIKI_WORD = re.compile(WIKI_WORD_MATCH)
        WIKI_WORD_ALONE = re.compile('^%s$' % WIKI_WORD_MATCH)

        def __init__(self, wiki, name):
            """Initializes the page for the given wiki with the given
            name, making sure the name is valid. The page may or may not
            actually exist right now in the wiki."""

            #WIKI_WORD matches a WikiWord anywhere in the string. We want to make
            #sure the page is a WikiWord and nothing else.
            if not self.WIKI_WORD_ALONE.match(name):
                raise(NotWikiWord, name)
            self.wiki = wiki
            self.name = name
            self.path = os.path.join(self.wiki.base, name)

        def exists(self):
            "Returns true if there's a page for the wiki with this name."
            return os.path.isfile(self.path)

        def load(self):
            "Loads this page from disk, if it exists."
            if not hasattr(self, 'text'):
                self.text = ''
                if self.exists():
                    self.text = open(self.path, 'r').read()

        def save(self):
            "Saves this page. If it didn't exist before, it does now."
            if not hasattr(self, 'text'):
                self.text = ''
            out = open(self.path, 'w')
            out.write(self.text)
            out.close()

        def delete(self):
            "Deletes this page, assuming it currently exists."
            if self.exists():
                os.remove(self.path)

        def getText(self):
            "Returns the raw text of this page."
            self.load()
            return self.text

class NotWikiWord(Exception):
    """Exception thrown when someone tries to pass off a non-WikiWord
     as a WikiWord."""
    Pass
```

Try it Out	Creating Wiki Pages from an Interactive Python Session

In just a bit, you're going to give BittyWiki a web interface, and spend much of the rest of the chapter accessing it via HTTP. The easiest way to get used to the basic API, however, is to play with BittyWiki from an interactive Python session — no web interface needed:

```
>>> from BittyWiki import Wiki
>>> wiki = Wiki("localwiki")
>>> homePage = wiki.getPage()
>>> homePage.text = "Here's the home page.\n\nIt links to PageTwo and
PageThree."
>>> homePage.save()
```

The `localwiki` directory now contains your wiki's files:

```
>>> #The "localwiki" directory now contains your wiki's files.
>>> import os
>>> open(os.path.join("localwiki","HomePage")).read()
"Here's the home page.\n\nIt links to PageTwo and PageThree."
```

`HomePage` references other pages in the wiki, but none of them exist yet:

```
>>> page2 = wiki.getPage("PageTwo")
>>> page2.exists()
False
```

Of course, you can create one of those pages:

```
>>> page2.text = "Here's page 2.\n\nIt links back to HomePage."
>>> page2.save()
>>> page2.exists()
True
```

Finally, a look at the `NotWikiWord` exception:

```
>>> wiki.getPage("Wiki")
Traceback (most recent call last):
  File "<stdin>", line 1, in ?
  File "BittyWiki.py", line 25, in getPage
    return Page(self, name)
  File "BittyWiki.py", line 47, in __init__
    raise NotWikiWord, name
BittyWiki.NotWikiWord: Wiki
```

The BittyWiki Web Interface

The BittyWiki library provides a way to manipulate the wiki, but it has no user interface. You can write standalone scripts to manipulate the repository, or create pages from an interactive prompt, but wikis were intended to be used over the Web. Another set of design decisions awaits, related to how BittyWiki should expose the wiki pages and operations as REST resources.

Resources

Because REST is based on resources, the first thing to consider when designing a web application is the nature of the resources to provide. A wiki provides only one type of resource: pages out of a flat namespace. Information in the URL path is easier to read than keeping it in the string, so a wiki page should be retrieved by sending a GET request to the CGI, appending the page name to the CGI path. The resulting resource identifier looks like /bittywiki.cgi/PageName. To modify a page, a POST request should be sent to its resource identifier.

The allowable operations on a wiki page are as follows: creating one, reading one, updating one, and deleting one. These four operations are so common to different types of resources that they have their own acronym (CRUD), used to describe the many applications designed for performing those operations. A wiki is a web-based CRUD application for named pages of text kept in a flat namespace.

Most wikis either implement page delete as a special administrator command, or don't implement it at all; this is because a page delete command makes vandalism very easy. BittyWiki's naïveté with respect to the delete command is perhaps its least realistic feature.

Request Structure

Not by coincidence, the CRUD operations correspond to the four main HTTP verbs: Recall that the same four operations show up repeatedly, whether the subject is databases, file system access, or web resources. Ideally, one CRUD operation would map to one HTTP verb.

When users request a page for reading, the only information they must provide is the page name. Therefore, for the read operation, no additional information must be tacked on to the resource identifier defined in the previous section. A simple GET to the resource identifier will suffice.

When modifying a page, it's necessary to send not only the name of the page but its desired new contents. POSTing the data to the resource identifier should suffice to do that.

Now you run into a problem: You have two more operations (create and delete), but only one HTTP method (POST) is both suitable for those operations and also supported by the HTML forms that will make up your interface. These operations must be consolidated somehow.

It makes no sense to "create" a page that already exists or to "edit" a nonexistent page, so those two operations could be combined into a single write operation. There are still two actions (write and delete) to go through POST, so the problem remains.

The solution is to have users put a marker in their POST data to indicate which operation they want to perform, rather than just post the data they want to use in the operation. The key for this marker is operation, and the allowable values are write and delete.

But Wait — There's More (Resources)

So far, the design assumes that the write and delete actions are triggered in response to HTML form submissions. Where are those HTML forms going to come from? Because the forms need to be dynamically generated based on the name of the page they're modifying, they must be generated by the wiki program. This makes them a new type of resource. Contrary to what was stated earlier, BittyWiki actually serves two types of resources. Its primary job is to serve pages, but it must also serve HTML forms for manipulating those pages.

Unlike pages, forms can't be created, updated, or deleted by the user: they can only be read. (After they're read, however, they can be used to create, update, or delete pages.) The forms should therefore be accessible through GET URLs.

Because the user will be requesting a form to write or delete a particular page, it makes sense to base the resource identifier for the form on that of the page. You have two ways of doing this. The first is to continue to append to the PATH_INFO of the identifier, so that the form to delete the page at `/bittywiki.cgi/MyPage` is located at `/wiki.cgi/MyPage/delete`. The other way is to use the QUERY_STRING, so that that form is located at `/wiki.cgi/MyPage?operation=delete`.

There's no right or wrong solution. However, because the operation keyword is already in use for the POST form submissions, and because the pages (not the forms) are the real point of a wiki, BittyWiki implements the second strategy. The possible values are the same as for the POST commands: write and delete.

To summarize: Each wiki page in BittyWiki boasts three associated resources. Each resource might behave differently in response to a GET and a POST, as shown in the following table.

Resource	What GET does	What POST does
`/bittywiki.cgi/PageName`	Displays the page if it exists; displays create form if not	Nothing
`/bittywiki.cgi/PageName?operation=write`	Displays edit form	Writes page, provides status
`/bittywiki.cgi/PageName?operation=delete`	Displays delete form	Deletes page, provides status

If no page name is specified (that is, someone GETs the bare resource `/bittywiki.cgi/`), the CGI will ask the core wiki code to retrieve the default page.

There are tradeoffs to consider when you're designing your resource identifiers and weighing PATH_INFO against QUERY_STRING. Both "/foo.cgi/clients/MegaCorp" and "/foo.cgi?client=MegaCorp" are legitimate REST identifiers for the same resource. The advantage of the first one is that it looks a lot nicer, more like a "real" resource. If you want to give the appearance of hierarchy in your data structure, nothing does it as well as a PATH_INFO-based identifier scheme.

The problem is that you can't use that scheme in conjunction with an HTML form that lets you, for example, select MegaCorp from a list of clients. The destination of an HTML form needs to be defined at the time the form is printed, so the best you can do ahead of time would be /foo.cgi/, letting the web browser tack on "?client=MegaCorp" when the user submits the form. If your application has this problem, you might consider defining two resource identifiers for each of your resources: an identifier that uses PATH_INFO, and one that uses QUERY_STRING.

Wiki Markup

The final question is to consider how to transform the plaintext typed by writers into the HTML displayed to readers. Some wikis are extravagant and let writers do things like draw tables and upload images. BittyWiki supports only a few very basic types of text-to-HTML markup:

❑ To ensure valid HTML, all pages are placed within paragraph (<p>) tags.

❑ Two consecutive newlines are treated as a paragraph break.

❑ Any HTML manually typed into a wiki page is escaped, so that it's displayed to the viewer instead of being interpreted by the web browser.

Because there are so few markup rules, BittyWiki pages will look a little bland, but prohibiting raw HTML will limit the capabilities of any vandals that happen along.

With these design decisions made, it's now possible to create the CGI web interface to BittyWiki. This code should go into bittywiki.cgi, in the same cgi-bin/ directory where you put BittyWiki.py:

```python
#!/usr/bin/python
import cgi
import cgitb
import os
import re
from BittyWiki import Wiki, Page, NotWikiWord
cgitb.enable()

#First, some HTML templates.
MAIN_TEMPLATE = '''<html>
<head><title>%(title)s</title>
<body>%(body)s<hr />%(navLinks)s</body>
</html>'''

VIEW_TEMPLATE = '''%(banner)s
<h1>%(name)s</h1>
%(processedText)s'''

WRITE_TEMPLATE = '''%(banner)s
<h1>%(title)s</h1>
<form method="POST" action="%(pageURL)s">
 <input type="hidden" name="operation" value="write">
 <textarea rows="15" cols="80" name="data">%(text)s</textarea><br />
 <input type="submit" value="Save">
</form>'''

DELETE_TEMPLATE = '''<h1>%(title)s</h1>
<p>Are you sure %(name)s is the page you want to delete?</p>

<form method="POST" action="%(pageURL)s">
 <input type="hidden" name="operation" value="delete">
```

(continued)

(continued)

```
      <input type="submit" value="Delete %(name)s!">
    </form>'''

    ERROR_TEMPLATE = '<h1>Error: %(error)s</h1>'
    BANNER_TEMPLATE = '<p style="color:red;">%s</p><hr />'

    #A snippet for linking a WikiWord to the corresponding wiki page.
    VIEW_LINK = '<a href="%s">%%(wikiword)s</a>'

    #A snippet for linking a WikiWord with not corresponding page to a
    #form for creating that page.
    ADD_LINK = '%%(wikiword)s<a href="%s">?</a>'
```

Rather than print out HTML pages from inside the CGI script, it's often useful to define HTML templates as strings ahead of time and use Python's string interpolation to fill them with dynamic values. This helps to separate presentation and content, making it much easier to customize the HTML. Separating the HTML out from the Python code makes it possible to hand the templates over to a web designer who doesn't know Python.

One feature of Python that deserves wider recognition is its capability to do string interpolation with a map instead of a tuple. If you have a string `"A %(foo)s string"`, and a map containing an item keyed to `foo`, interpolating the string with the map will replace `"%(foo)s"` with the string value of the item keyed to `foo`:

```
class WikiCGI:

    #The possible operations on a wiki page.
    VIEW = ''
    WRITE = 'write'
    DELETE = "delete"

    def __init__(self, wikiRoot):
        self.wiki = Wiki(wikiRoot)

    def run(self):
        toDisplay = None
        try:
            #Retrieve the wiki page the user wants.
            page = os.environ.get('PATH_INFO', '')
            if page:
                page = page[1:]
            page = self.wiki.getPage(page)
        except NotWikiWord, badName:
            page = None
            error = '"%s" is not a valid wiki page name.' % badName
            toDisplay = self.makeError(error)

        if page:
            #Determine what the user wants to do with the page they
            #requested.
```

```
makeChange = os.environ['REQUEST_METHOD'] == 'POST'
if makeChange:
    defaultOperation = self.WRITE
else:
    defaultOperation = ''
form = cgi.FieldStorage()
operation = form.getfirst('operation', defaultOperation)

#We now know which resource the user was trying to access
#("page" in conjunction with "operation"), and "form"
#contains any representation they were submitting.  Now we
#delegate to the appropriate method to handle the operation
#they requested.
operationMethod = self.OPERATION_METHODS.get(operation)
if not operationMethod:
    error = '"%s" is not a valid operation.' % operation
    toDisplay = self.makeError(error)

if not page.exists() and operation and not \
    (makeChange and operation == self.WRITE):
    #It's okay to request a resource based on a page that
    #doesn't exist, but only if you're asking for the form to
    #create it, or actually trying to create it.
    toDisplay = self.makeError('No such page: "%s"' % page.name)

if operationMethod:
    toDisplay = operationMethod(self, page, makeChange, form)

#All the operation methods, as well as makeError, are expected
#to return a set of values that can be used to render the HTML
#response: the title of the page, the body template to use, a
#map of variables to interpolate into the body template, and a
#set of navigation links to put at the bottom of the page.
title, bodyTemplate, bodyArgs, navLinks = toDisplay
if page and page.name != Wiki.HOME_PAGE_NAME:
    backLink = '<a href="%s">Back to wiki homepage</a>'
    navLinks.append(backLink % self.makeURL())
print("Content-type: text/html\n")
print(MAIN_TEMPLATE % {'title' : title,
                       'body' : bodyTemplate % bodyArgs,
                       'navLinks' : ' | '.join(navLinks)})
```

When the `WikiCGI` class is instantiated, it finds out which resource is being requested, and what the user wants to do with that resource. It delegates to one of a number of methods (yet to be defined) that handle the various possible operations.

Each of these methods is expected to return the skeleton of a web page: the title, a template string (one of the templates defined earlier: `VIEW_TEMPLATE`, `WRITE_TEMPLATE`, and so on), a map of variables to use when interpolating that template, and a set of links to help the user navigate the wiki.

The last act of `WikiCGI` instantiation is to fill out this skeleton: to interpolate the provided variable map into the page-specific template string and then to interpolate *that* into the overarching main template. The result, a complete HTML page, is simply printed to standard output.

The next part of the CGI defines the three operation-specific methods, which take a page and (possibly) a resource representation stored in form data; make any appropriate changes; and return the raw materials for a document:

```python
    def viewOperation(self, page, makeChange, form=None, banner=None):
        """Renders a page as HTML, either as the result of a request
        for it as a resource, or as a side effect of some other
        operation."""
        if banner:
            banner = BANNER_TEMPLATE % banner
        else:
            banner = ''
        if not page.exists():
            title = 'Creating %s' % page.name
            toDisplay = (title, WRITE_TEMPLATE,
                           {'title' : title,
                            'banner' : banner,
                            'pageURL' : self.makeURL(page),
                            'text' : ''},
                           [])
        else:
            writeLink = '<a href="%s">Edit this page</a>' \
                           % self.makeURL(page, self.WRITE)
            deleteLink = '<a href="%s">Delete this page</a>' \
                           % self.makeURL(page, self.DELETE)
            toDisplay = (page.name, VIEW_TEMPLATE,
                           {'name' : page.name,
                            'banner' : banner,
                            'processedText' : self.renderPage(page)},
                           [writeLink, deleteLink])
        return toDisplay

    def writeOperation(self, page, makeChange, form):
        "Saves a page, or displays its create or edit form."
        if makeChange:
            data = form.getfirst('data')
            page.text = data
            page.save()
            #The operation is done, but we still need a document to
            #return to the user. Display the new version of this page,
            #with a banner.
            toDisplay = self.viewOperation(page, 0, banner='Page saved.')
        else:
            navLinks = []
            pageURL = self.makeURL(page)
            if page.exists():
                title = 'Editing ' + page.name
                navLinks.append('<a href="%s">Back to %s</a>' % (pageURL,
                                                                 page.name))
            else:
                title = 'Creating ' + page.name
```

```
            toDisplay = (title, WRITE_TEMPLATE, {'title' : title,
                                                 'banner' : '',
                                                 'pageURL' : pageURL,
                                                 'text' : page.getText()},
                    navLinks)
        return toDisplay

    def deleteOperation(self, page, makeChange, form=None):
        "Deletes a page, or displays its delete form."
        if makeChange:
            page.delete()
            banner = 'Page "%s" deleted.' % page.name
            #The page is deleted, but we still need a document to
            #return to the user. Display the wiki homepage, with a banner.
            toDisplay = self.viewOperation(self.wiki.getPage(), 0,
                                           banner=banner)
        else:
            if page.exists():
                title = 'Deleting ' + page.name
                pageURL = self.makeURL(page)
                backLink = '<a href="%s">Back to %s</a>'
                toDisplay = (title, DELETE_TEMPLATE, {'title' : title,
                                                     'name' : page.name,
                                                     'pageURL' : pageURL},
                            [backLink % (pageURL, page.name)])
            else:
                error = "You can't delete a page that doesn't exist."
                toDisplay = self.makeError(error)
        return toDisplay

    #A registry mapping 'operation' keys to methods that perform the
operations.
    OPERATION_METHODS = { VIEW : viewOperation,
                         WRITE: writeOperation,
                         DELETE: deleteOperation }

    def makeError(self, errorMessage):
        "Creates a set of return values indicating an error."
        return (ERROR_TEMPLATE, "Error", {'error' : errorMessage,
                                          'mainURL' : self.makeURL("")}, [])

    def makeURL(self, page="", operation=None):
        "Creates a URL to the resource defined by the given page and resource."
        if hasattr(page, 'name'):
            #A Page object was passed in, instead of a page name.
            page = page.name
        url = os.environ['SCRIPT_NAME'] + '/' + page
        if operation:
            url += '?operation=' + operation
        return url
```

The last main section of this CGI is the code that transforms the raw wiki text into HTML, linking WikiWords to BittyWiki resources and creating paragraph breaks:

```
#A regular expression for use in turning multiple newlines
#into paragraph breaks.
MULTIPLE_NEWLINES = re.compile("(\r?\n){2,}")

def renderPage(self, page):
    """Returns the text of the given page, with transforms applied
    to turn BittyWiki markup into HTML: WikiWords linked to the
    appropriate page or add form, and double newlines turned into
    paragraph breaks."""

    #First, escape any HTML present in the bare text so that it is
    #shown instead of interpreted.
    text = page.getText()
    for find, replace in (('<', '&lt;'), ('>', '&gt;'), ('&', '&amp;')):
        text = text.replace(find, replace)

    #Link all WikiWords in the text to their view or add resources.
    html = '<p>' + page.WIKI_WORD.sub(self._linkWikiWord, text) \
            + '</p>'

    #Turn multiple newlines into paragraph breaks.
    html = self.MULTIPLE_NEWLINES.sub('</p>\n<p>', html)
    return html

def _linkWikiWord(self, match):
    """A helper method used to replace a WikiWord with a link to view
    the corresponding page (if it exists), or a link to create the
    corresponding page (if it doesn't)."""
    linkedPage = self.wiki.getPage(match.group(0))
    link = ADD_LINK
    if linkedPage.exists():
        link = VIEW_LINK
    link = link % self.makeURL("%(wikiword)s")
    #The link now looks something like:
    # <a href="/cgi-bin/bittywiki.cgi/%(wikiword)s">%(wikiword)s</a>
    #We'll interpolate 'wikiword' to fill in the actual page name.
    return link % {'wikiword' : linkedPage.name}
```

Finally, here is the code that invokes `WikiCGI` against a particular wiki when this file is run as a script:

```
if __name__ == '__main__':
    WikiCGI("wiki/").run()
```

Once you're underway, you'll be able to start editing pages of your own.

Make this code executable and try it out in conjunction with `EasyCGIServer` or with your web host's CGI setup. Hitting `http://localhost:8001/cgi-bin/bittywiki.cgi` (or the equivalent on your web host) sends you to the form for creating the wiki's homepage. You can write a homepage, making references to other pages that don't exist yet, and then click the question marks near their names to create them. You can build your wiki starting from there; this is how real wikis grow. A wiki is an excellent tool for managing collaboration with other members of a development team, or just for keeping track of your own notes. They're also easy and fun to build, which is why so many implementations exist.

BittyWiki is a simple but fully functional wiki with a simple but flexible design. The presentation HTML is separated from the logic, and the job of identifying the resource is done by a method that then dispatches to one of several handler methods. The handler methods identify the provided representation (if any), take appropriate action, and return the resource representation or other document to be rendered. The resources and operations were designed by considering the problem according to the principles of REST. This type of design and architecture are a very useful way of building standalone web applications.

Web Services

So far, the web applications developed in this chapter share one unstated underlying assumption: their intended audience is human. The same is true of most applications available on the Web. The resource representations served by the typical web application (the wiki you just wrote being no exception) are a conglomeration of data, response messages, layout code, and navigation, all bundled together in an HTML file intended to be rendered by a web browser in a form pleasing to humans. When interaction is needed, applications present GUI forms for you to fill out through a human-computer interface; and when you submit the forms, you get more pretty HTML pages. In short, web applications are generally written by humans for humans.

Yet web applications, even the most human centric, have always had nonhuman users: software clients not directly under the direction of a human — to give them a catchy name, robots. From search engine spiders to automatic auction bidding scripts to real-time weather display clients, all sorts of scripted clients consume web applications, often without the knowledge of the people who originally wrote those applications. If a web application proves useful, someone will eventually write a robot that uses it.

In the old days, robots had no choice but to impersonate web browsers with humans driving them. They would make HTTP requests just like a web browser would, and parse the resulting HTML to find the interesting parts. Though this is still a common technique, more and more web applications are exposing special interfaces solely for the benefit of robots. Doing so makes it easier to write robots, and frees the server from using its bandwidth to send data that won't be used. These interfaces are called *web services*. Big-name companies like Google, Yahoo!, Amazon, and eBay have exposed web service APIs to their web applications, as have many lesser-known players.

Many fancy standards have been created around web services, some of which are covered later in this chapter, but the basic fact is that *web services are just web applications for robots*. A web service usually corresponds to a web application, and makes some of the functionality of that application available in robot-friendly form. The only reason these fancy standards exist is to make it easier to write robots or to expose your application to robots.

Robots have different needs than humans. Humans can glance at an HTML rendering of a page and separate the important page-specific data from the navigation, logos, and clutter. A robot has no such ability: It must be programmed to parse out the data it needs. If a redesign changes the HTML a site produces, any robot that reads and parses that HTML must be reprogrammed. A human can recall or make up the input when a web application requires it; a robot must be programmed ahead of time to provide the right input. Because of this, it's no surprise that web services tend to have better usage documentation than their corresponding web applications, nor that they serve more structured resource representations.

Web services and the scripts that use them can exist in symbiotic relationships. If you provide web services that people want to use, you form a community around your product and get favorable publicity from what they create. You can give your users the freedom to base new applications on yours, instead of having to implement their feature requests yourself. Remember that if your application is truly useful, people are going to write robots that use it no matter what you do. You might as well bless this use, monitor it, and track it.

The benefits of consuming others' web services are more obvious: You gain access to data sets and algorithms you'd otherwise have to implement yourself. You don't need to get permission to use these data sets, because web services are prepackaged permission.

Even if you control both the producers and the consumers of data, advantages exist to bridging the gap with web services. Web services enable you to share code across machines and programming languages, just as web applications can be accessed from any browser or operating system.

Python is well suited to using and providing web services. Its loose typing is a good match for the various web service standards, which provide limited or nonexistent typing. Because Python lets you overload a class's method call operator, it's possible to make a web service call look exactly like an ordinary method call. Finally, Python's standard library provides good basic web support. If a high-level protocol won't meet your needs or its library has a bug, you can drop to the next lowest level and still get the job done.

How Web Services Work

Web services are just web applications for robots, so it's natural that they should operate just like normal web applications: You send an HTTP request and you get some structured data back in the response. A web service is supposed to be used by a script, though, so the request that goes in and the response that comes out need to be more formally defined. Whereas a web application usually returns a full-page image that is rendered by a browser and parsed by the human brain, a web service returns just the "important" data in some easily parseable format, usually XML. There's also usually a human-readable or machine-parseable description of the methods being exposed by the web service, to make it easier for users to write a script that does what they want.

Three main standards for web services exist: REST, XML-RPC, and SOAP. For each standard, this chapter shows you how to use an existing public web service to do something useful, how to expose the BittyWiki API as a web service, and how to make a robot manipulate the wiki through that web service.

REST Web Services

If REST is so great for the Web that humans use, why shouldn't it also work for robots? The answer is that it works just fine. The hypertext links and HTML forms you designed for your human users are access points into a REST API that can just as easily be used by a properly programmed robot. All you need to add is a way to provide robot-friendly representations of your resources, and a way for robots to get at those representations.

If you're designing a web application from scratch, keep in mind the needs of both humans and robots. You should end up able to expose similar APIs to your HTML forms and to external scripts. It's unlikely you'll expose the exact same features to humans and to robots, but you'll be able to reuse a lot of architecture and code.

In some situations you might want to create a new, simpler API and expose that as your web service instead. This might happen if you're working on an application with an ugly API that was never meant to be seen by outsiders, if your web application is very complex, or if the people writing robots only want to use part of the full API.

REST Quick Start: Finding Bargains on Amazon.com

Amazon.com, the popular online store, makes much of its data available through a REST web service called Amazon Web Services. Perhaps the most interesting feature of this web service is the capability it offers to search for books or other items and then retrieve metadata, pictures, and reviews for an item. Amazon effectively gives you programmatic access to its product database, something that would be difficult to duplicate or obtain by other means.

> *The Amazon Web Services homepage is at* `http://aws.amazon.com/`.

To use Amazon Web Services you need a *subscription ID*. This is a 13-character string that identifies your account. You can get one for free by signing up at `www.amazon.com/gp/aws/registration/registration-form.html/`. After you have an API key, you can use it to query Amazon Web Services. Because the AWS interface is RESTful, you invoke it by sending a `GET` request to a particular resource: The results are returned within an XML document. It's the web service equivalent of Amazon's search

The Amazon Web Services are actually something of a REST heretic. Though most of AWS's design is RESTful, it defines a few operations that make changes on the server side when you `GET` them. For instance, the AWS `CartModify` operation enables you to add or remove items from your Amazon shopping cart just by making a `GET` request. Recall that `GET` requests shouldn't change any resources on the server side; you should use `POST`, `PUT`, or `DELETE` for such operations. Presumably, the AWS designers chose consistency (using `GET` for everything) over RESTfulness.

Because the AWS API isn't purely RESTful, it's not necessarily safe to pass around the resource identifiers AWS gives you. Someone else might end up adding books to your shopping cart by mistake! This is exactly the sort of thing to avoid when designing your own REST API.

engine web application. Instead of a user interface based on HTML forms, AWS has rules for constructing resources. Instead of a pretty HTML document containing your search results, it gives you a structured XML representation of them.

Peeking at an Amazon Web Services Response

You can invoke Amazon Web Services using the same `urllib` module you'd use to download a web page. Here's an interactive Python session that searches for books by James Joyce (slightly reformatted and edited for brevity):

```
>>> import urllib
>>> author = "Joyce, James"
>>> subscriptionID = [your subscription id]
>>> url = "http://xml.amazon.com/onca/xml3?f=xml&t=webservices-20&dev-t=%s&ty
pe=lite&mode=books&AuthorSearch=%s" % (subscriptionID, urllib.quote(author))
>>> print(urllib.urlopen(url).read())
<?xml version="1.1" encoding="UTF-8"?>
<ProductInfo xmlns:xsi="http://www.w3.org/2001/XMLSchema-instance" xsi:noName
spaceSchemaLocation="http://xml.amazon.com/schemas3/dev-lite.xsd">
...
<Details url="http://www.amazon.com/exec/obidos/ASIN/0142437344/webservices-
20?dev-t=D8O1OTR1OIMN7%26camp=2025%26link_code=xm2">
        <Asin>0142437344</Asin>
        <ProductName>A Portrait of the Artist As a Young Man (Penguin Classics)
</ProductName>
        <Catalog>Book</Catalog>
        <Authors>
            <Author>James Joyce</Author>
        </Authors>
        <ReleaseDate>25 March, 2003</ReleaseDate>
        <Manufacturer>Penguin Books</Manufacturer>

<ImageUrlSmall>http://images.amazon.com/images/P/0142437344.01.THUMBZZZ.jpg</
ImageUrlSmall>

<ImageUrlMedium>http://images.amazon.com/images/P/0142437344.01.MZZZZZZZ.
jpg</ImageUrlMedium>

<ImageUrlLarge>http://images.amazon.com/images/P/0142437344.01.LZZZZZZZ.jpg</
ImageUrlLarge>
        <Availability>Usually ships in 24 hours</Availability>
        <ListPrice>$9.00</ListPrice>
        <OurPrice>$8.10</OurPrice>
        <UsedPrice>$1.95</UsedPrice>
    </Details>
...
</ProductInfo>
```

How It Works

All we did there was open a URL and read it. You can visit the same URL in a web browser (treating the web service as a web application) and get the exact same data we did from the interactive Python session. The differences between web applications and web services have nothing to do with architecture; both use the architecture of the Web. The only differences are related to the format of the requests and responses.

Two problems exist with just opening that resource and reading it, however (whether from a script or from a web browser), and they should be obvious from that session log. The AWS URL to do a search is really long and difficult to remember. Even with a reference guide, it's hard to keep all the URL parameters straight. Second, the response is a lot of XML data. It'll take some work to parse it or transform it into a more human-friendly form. Fortunately, that work has already been done for us.

A popular web service will eventually sprout clients written in every major programming language. For Amazon Web Services, the standard Python client is PyAmazon, originally written by Mark Pilgrim and now maintained by Michael Josephson. This module abstracts the details of the Amazon Web Services REST API. It enables you to request one of those complex resources just by making a method call, and retrieve a list of Python objects instead of a mass of XML. Behind the scenes, it uses urllib to retrieve a resource (just like we did), and then parses the XML response into a Python data structure. Thanks to PyAmazon, it's easy to have Pythonic fun with Amazon Web Services.

> Download PyAmazon from www.josephson.org/projects/pyamazon/ and install it into your PYTHON_PATH or into the directory in which you plan to write your scripts that use AWS. While you're at it, also download OnDemandAmazonList, a class that lets you iterate over paginated lists of AWS search results as though they were normal Python lists. The sample application that follows uses OnDemandAmazonList to make the code more natural.

Introducing WishListBargainFinder

Amazon lets individuals and booksellers advertise their used copies of books on its site, and Amazon presents the lowest used price for a book alongside its own price for a new book. If you look back at that XML search result for James Joyce, you'll see that *A Portrait of the Artist as a Young Man* is available new from Amazon for $8.10 ("OurPrice"), but people are also selling used copies for as low as $1.95 ("UsedPrice"). That's a pretty good price, even when you factor in shipping. Many of the books listed on Amazon are available used for as little as one cent. Amazon will show you the lowest used price for any individual book, but it's not so easy to scan a whole list looking for bargains.

Amazon users can keep "wish lists" of things they'd like to own. If you keep one yourself, you've selected out of the millions of items on Amazon a few that you'd be especially interested in buying for a bargain. Amazon Web Services provides a wish list search, so it's possible to write a script that uses AWS to go through a wish list and identify the bargains. If you don't mind buying used, this could save you a lot of money.

Here's a class, BargainFinder, that accepts a list obtained from an AWS query and scans it for second-hand bargains. Bargains can be defined as costing less than a certain amount (say, $3), or as costing a certain amount less than the corresponding items new from Amazon (say, 75% less). It, and the code fragments that follow it, are part of a file I call WishListBargainFinder.py:

```python
import copy
import re
import amazon

class BargainFinder:
    """A class that, given a list of Amazon items, finds out which
    items in the list are available used at a bargain price."""

    def __init__(self, bargainCoefficient=.25, bargainCutoff=3.00):
        """The bargainCoefficient is how little an item must cost
        used, versus its new price, to be considered a bargain. The
        default bargain coefficient is .25, meaning that an item
        available used for less than 25% of its Amazon price is
        considered a bargain.

        The bargainCutoff is for finding bargains among items that are
        cheap to begin with. The default bargainCutoff is 5, meaning
        that any item available used for less than $3.00 is considered
        a bargain, even if it's available new for only a little more
        than $3.00."""
        if bargainCoefficient >= 1:
            raise Exception, 'It makes no sense to look for "bargains" that ' \
                + 'cost more used than new!'
        self.coefficient = bargainCoefficient
        self.cutoff = bargainCutoff

    def printBargains(self, items):
        """Find the bargains in the given list and present them in a
        textual list."""
        bargains = self.getBargains(items)
        printedHeader = 0
        if bargains:
            print ('Here are items available used for less than $%.2f, ' + \
                    'or for less than %.2d%% of their Amazon price:') \
                % (self.cutoff, self.coefficient*100))
            prices = bargains.keys()
            prices.sort()
            for usedPrice in prices:
                for bargain, amazonPrice in bargains[usedPrice]:
                    savings = ''
                    if amazonPrice:
                        percentageSavings = (1-(usedPrice/amazonPrice)) * 100
                        savings = '(Save %.2d%% off $%.2f) ' \
                                    % (percentageSavings, amazonPrice)
                    Print(' $%.2f %s%s' % (usedPrice, savings,
                                            bargain.ProductName))
        else:
            print("Sorry, I couldn't find any bargains in that list.")

    def getBargains(self, items):
        "Scan the given list, looking for bargains."
        bargains = {}
        for item in items:
```

```
            bargain = False
            amazonPrice = self.getPrice(item, "OurPrice")
            usedPrice = self.getPrice(item, "UsedPrice")
            if usedPrice:
                if usedPrice < self.cutoff:
                    bargain = True
                if amazonPrice:
                    if (amazonPrice * self.coefficient) > usedPrice:
                        bargain = True
            if bargain:
                #We sort the bargains by the used price, so the
                #cheapest items are displayed first.
                bargainsForPrice = bargains.get(usedPrice, None)
                if not bargainsForPrice:
                    bargainsForPrice = []
                    bargains[usedPrice] = bargainsForPrice
                bargainsForPrice.append((item, amazonPrice))
        return bargains

    def getPrice(self, item, priceField):
        """Retrieves the named price field (eg. "OurPrice",
        "UsedPrice", and attempts to parse its currency string into a
        number."""
        price = getattr(item, priceField, None)
        if price:
            price = self._parseCurrency(price)
        return price

    def _parseCurrency(self, currency):
        """A cheap attempt to parse an amount of currency into a
        floating-point number: Strip out everything but numbers,
        decimal point, and negative sign."""
        return float(self.IRRELEVANT_CURRENCY_CHARACTERS.sub('', currency))
    IRRELEVANT_CURRENCY_CHARACTERS = re.compile("[^0-9.-]")
```

This class won't quite work as is, because it assumes that a list of query results obtained from PyAmazon (the items argument to getBargains) works just like a Python list. Actually, AWS query results are delivered in pages of 10. Making a single AWS query returns only the single page you request, and you'll need extra logic to iterate from the last item on the first page to the first item of the second.

That's why OnDemandAmazonList was invented. This class, available from the same website as PyAmazon itself, hides the complexity of retrieving successive AWS result pages behind an interface that looks just like a Python list. You iterate over an OnDemandAmazonList as you would any other list, and behind the scenes it makes the necessary web service calls to get the data you want. This is another example of why Python excels at web services: It makes it easy to hide this kind of inconvenient detail.

With OnDemandAmazonList, it's a simple matter to put an interface on the BargainFinder class with code that retrieves a wish list as an OnDemandAmazonList, and runs it through the BargainFinder to find the items on the wish list that are available used for a bargain price. You could just as easily use the BargainFinder to find bargains in the result set of any other AWS query, so long as you made sure to wrap the query in an OnDemandAmazonList:

```
from OnDemandAmazonList import OnDemandAmazonList
def getWishList(subscriptionID, wishListID):
    "Returns an iterable version of the given wish list."
    kwds = {'license_key' : subscriptionID,
 'wishlistID' : wishListID,
            'type' : 'lite'}
    return OnDemandAmazonList(amazon.searchByWishlist, kwds)

if __name__ == '__main__':
    import sys
    if len(sys.argv) != 3:
        print 'Usage: %s [AWS subscription ID] [wish list id]' % sys.argv[0]
        sys.exit(1)
    subscriptionID, wishListID = sys.argv[1:]
    wishList = getWishList(subscriptionID, wishListID)
    BargainFinder().printBargains(wishList)
```

Here's the `WishListBargainFinder` running against my mother's wish list:

```
# python WishListBargainFinder.py [My subscription ID] 1KT0ATF9MM4FT
Here are items available used for less than $3.00, or for less than 25% of
their Amazon price:
$0.29 (Save 94% off $4.99) Clockwork : Or All Wound Up
$1.99 (Save 68% off $6.29) The Fifth Elephant: A Novel of Discworld
$2.95 (Save 57% off $6.99) Interesting Times (Discworld Novels (Paperback))
$2.96 (Save 52% off $6.29) Jingo: A Novel of Discworld
```

A quick word about Amazon wish list IDs: The `WishListBargainFinder` *takes a wish list ID as command-line input, but wish list IDs are a little bit hidden in the Amazon web application. To find a person's wish list ID, you need to go to his or her wish list and then look at the* id *field of the URL. The wish list ID is a twelve-character series of letters and numbers that looks like* BUWBWH9K2H77.

You can programmatically search for a user's wish list by making an AWS call (using the ListSearch *operation), but because that method is not yet supported by* PyAmazon, *you'll have to construct the URL and parse the XML yourself. For guidance, look at the examples on Amazon's site:* http://aws .amazon.com/resources/.

Giving BittyWiki a REST API

Let's revisit BittyWiki, the simple wiki application you created in the previous section as a sample web application. By design, BittyWiki already exposes a very simple REST API. Recall that in addition to the name of the page, which is always part of the resource identifier, there are only two variables to consider: operation and data. operation tells BittyWiki what you want to do to the page you named, and data contains the data you want to shove into the page. Now consider this API from a robot's point of view.

The first thing to consider is how to even determine whether a given request comes from a human (more accurately, a web browser) or a robot. You might think this is easy; after all, the User-Agent HTTP header you saw earlier is supposed to identify the software that's making the request. The problem is that there's no definitive list of web browsers. New browsers and robots are being created all the time, and some use the same underlying libraries (a web browser and a robot written in Python might both claim to be urllib). The User-Agent string isn't reliable enough to be used as a basis for this decision.

Most web services solve this problem by creating a second set of resource identifiers that mirror the resource identifiers used by the web application but serve up robot-friendly resource representations. The "robot's entrance" for your application might be an entirely separate script (`app-api.cgi` instead of `app.cgi`) or a standard string prepended to the `PATH_INFO` of a resource identifier (`app.cgi/api/foo` instead of `app.cgi/foo`). The `PATH_INFO` solution yields nicer-looking resource identifiers, but BittyWiki's REST web service will be implemented as a separate CGI, just because it's easier to present.

One final note with respect to `PUT` and `DELETE`. Web services are free from dependence on HTML forms. Though the `PUT` and `DELETE` HTTP verbs aren't supported by web browsers, they are supported by many (but not all) programmable clients. You could simplify the preexisting BittyWiki interface a little by bringing in `PUT` and `DELETE`. Doing this would let you get rid of the `operation` argument, which is only used to distinguish a `PUT`- or `POST`-style `POST` request from a `DELETE`-style `POST` request. However, for the sake of correspondence with the web application, and because not all programmable clients support `PUT` and `DELETE`, the BittyWiki REST web service won't take this route.

The second thing to consider is which features of the web application it makes sense to expose through an external API. Why would someone want programmatic access to the contents of a wiki? A wiki's users might create two types of robot:

❑   A robot that modifies or creates wiki pages — for instance, an automated test system that posts a daily status report to a particular wiki page

❑   A robot that retrieves wiki pages — to archive or mirror a wiki or to render wiki pages to an end user in some format besides HTML

The first type of robot might need to create, edit, and delete a wiki page. That functionality can remain more or less intact, but unlike in a web application, there's no need to present a nice-looking document after taking a requested action. All the robot needs to know is whether or not its request was carried out. The document returned for a `POST` operation need only contain a status message.

Both types of robots need to retrieve pages from the wiki. What they actually need, though, is not the HTML rendering of the page (the thing you get when you `GET /bittywiki.cgi/PageName`), but the raw page data (the thing that shows up in the edit box when you `GET /bittywiki.cgi/PageName? operation=write`). The first type of robot needs the data in this format because it's going to do its own rendering, and it's easier to render from the raw data than from HTML. The second type of robot needs it in this format for a similar reason; it's because that's what shows up in the edit box because that's how it's stored on the back end.

BittyWiki's REST API for robots is therefore basically similar to the REST API for web browsers. The only difference is the format of the responses: Instead of human-readable HTML documents, the REST web service outputs plaintext documents. A more complicated REST web service, like Amazon's, would probably output documents formatted in XML or sparse HTML, expecting the client to parse them. Here's the plaintext result of GETting `http://localhost:8001/cgi-bin/bittywiki-rest.cgi`; compare it to the HTML output when you GET `http://localhost:8001/cgi-bin/bittiwiki.cgi`:

```
This is the home page for my BittyWiki installation.

Here you can learn about the philosophy and technologies that drive web
applications: REST, CGI, and the PythonLanguage.
```

The structure of `bittywiki-rest.cgi` is also similar to `bittywiki.cgi`:

```python
#!/usr/bin/python
import cgi
import cgitb
cgitb.enable()
import os
import re
from BittyWiki import Wiki, Page, NotWikiWord

class WikiRestApiCGI:

    #The possible operations on a wiki page.
    VIEW = ''
    WRITE = 'write'
    DELETE = 'delete'

    #The possible response codes this application might return.
    RESPONSE_codeS = { 200 : 'OK',
                       400 : 'Bad Request',
                       404 : 'Not Found'}

    def __init__(self, wikiBase):
        "Initialize with the given wiki."
        self.wiki = Wiki(wikiBase)

    def run(self):
        """Determine the command, dispatch to the appropriate handler,
        and print the results as an XML document."""
        toDisplay = None
        try:
            page = os.environ.get('PATH_INFO', '')
            if page:
                page = page[1:]
            page = self.wiki.getPage(page)
        except NotWikiWord, badName:
            toDisplay = 400, '"%s" is not a valid wiki page name.' % badName

        if not toDisplay:
            form = cgi.FieldStorage()
            operation = form.getfirst('operation', self.VIEW)
            operationMethod = self.OPERATION_METHODS.get(operation)
            if operationMethod:
                if not page.exists() and operation != self.WRITE:
                    toDisplay = 404, 'No such page: "%s"' % page.name
                else:
                    toDisplay = operationMethod(self, page, form)
            else:
                toDisplay = 400, '"%s" is not a valid operation.' % operation
```

```
#Print the response.
responseCode, payload = toDisplay
print('Status: %s %s' % (responseCode,
                       self.RESPONSE_codeS.get(responseCode)))
print('Content-type: text/plain\n')
print(payload)
```

The main code figures out the resource and the desired operation and hands this off (along with any provided representation) to a handler method. The result is then rendered — but this time as plaintext:

```
def viewOperation(self, page, form=None):
    "Returns the raw text of the given wiki page."
    return 200, page.getText()

def writeOperation(self, page, form):
    "Writes the specified page."
    page.text = form.getfirst('data')
    page.save()
    return 200, "Page saved."

def deleteOperation(self, page, format, form=None):
    "Deletes the specified page."
    if not page.exists():
        toDisplay = 404, "You can't delete a page that doesn't exist."
    else:
        page.delete()
        toDisplay = 200, "Page deleted."
    return toDisplay

#A registry mapping 'operation' keys to methods that perform the
operations.
OPERATION_METHODS = { VIEW : viewOperation,
                      WRITE: writeOperation,
                      DELETE: deleteOperation }
```

The three operation handler methods are also similar to their counterparts in `bittywiki.cgi`, though simpler because they produce less data.

Wiki Search-and-Replace Using the REST Web Service

What good is this web service for BittyWiki? Well, here's an only slightly contrived example: Suppose that you get someone to host a BittyWiki installation for an open-source project you're working on, called Foo. You create a lot of wiki pages that mention the name of the project in their text ("Foo is a triphasic degausser for semantic defribulation") and in the titles of the pages (BenefitsOfFoo, FooDesign, and so on). All is going well until one day when you decide to change the name of your project to Bar. It would take a long time to manually change those wiki pages (including renaming many of them), and you don't have access to the server on which the wiki is actually hosted, so you can't write a script to crawl the file system. What do you do?

Here's a Python script, `WikiSpiderREST.py`, which acts as a wiki search-and-replace spider. Starting at the HomePage of the wiki (which is a WikiWord), it crawls the wiki by following WikiWord links, and replaces all of the instances of one string (for example, "Foo") with another string (for example, "Bar").

A page whose name contains the old string (for example, "FooDesign") is deleted and re-created under a different name (for example, "BarDesign"). `WikiSpiderREST.py` keeps track of the pages it has processed so as not to waste time or get stuck in a loop:

```python
#!/usr/bin/python
import re
import urllib

class WikiReplaceSpider:
    "A class for running search-and-replace against a web of wiki pages."

    WIKI_WORD = re.compile('(([A-Z][a-z0-9]*){2,})')

    def __init__(self, restURL):
        "Accepts a URL to a BittyWiki REST API."
        self.api = BittyWikiRestAPI(restURL)

    def replace(self, find, replace):
        """Spider wiki pages starting at the front page, accessing them
        and changing them via the provided API."""

        processed = {} #Keep track of the pages already processed.
        todo = ['HomePage'] #Start at the front page of the wiki.
        while todo:
            for pageName in todo:
                print('Checking "%s"; % pageName)
                try:
                    pageText = self.api.getPage(pageName)
                except RemoteApplicationException, message:
                    if str(message).find("No such page") == 0:
                        #Some page mentioned a WikiWord that doesn't exist
                        #yet; not a big deal.
                        pass
                    else:
                        #Some other problem; pass it on up.
                        raise RemoteApplicationException, message
                else:
                    #This page actually exists; process it.
                    #First, find any WikiWords in this page: they may
                    #reference other existing pages.
                    for wikiWord in self.WIKI_WORD.findall(pageText):
                        linkPage = wikiWord[0]
                        if not processed.get(linkPage) and linkPage not in todo:
                            #We haven't processed this page yet: put it on
                            #the to-do list.
                            todo.append(linkPage)

                    #Run the search-and-replace on the page text to get the
                    #new text of the page.
                    newText = pageText.replace(find, replace)

                    #Check to see if this page name matches
                    #search and replace. If it does, delete it and
                    #recreate it with the new text; otherwise, just
```

```
                              #save the new text.
                              newPageName = pageName.replace(find, replace)
                              if newPageName != pageName:
                                  print(' Deleting "%s", will recreate as "%s"' \
                                          % (pageName, newPageName))
                                  self.api.delete(pageName)
                              if newPageName != pageName or newText != pageText:
                                  print(' Saving "%s"' % newPageName
                                  self.api.save(newPageName, newText))
                              #Mark the new page as processed so we don't go through
                              #it a second time.
                              if newPageName != pageName:
                                  processed[newPageName] = True
                          processed[pageName] = True
                          todo.remove(pageName)
```

So far, there's been nothing REST-specific except the reference to a BittyWikiRestAPI class. That's about to change as you go ahead and define that class, as well as others that implement a general Python interface to the BittyWiki REST API:

```
    class BittyWikiRestAPI:

        "A Python interface to the BittyWiki REST API."

        def __init__(self, restURL):
            "Do all the work starting from the base URL of the REST interface."
            self.base = restURL

        def getPage(self, pageName):
            "Returns the raw markup of the named wiki page."
            return self._doGet(pageName)

        def save(self, pageName, data):
            "Saves the given data to the named wiki page."
            return self._doPost(pageName, { 'operation' : 'write',
                                            'data' : data })

        def delete(self, pageName):
            "Deletes the named wiki page."
            return self._doPost(pageName, { 'operation' : 'delete' })

        def _doGet(self, pageName):
            """Does a generic HTTP GET. Returns the response body, or
            throws an exception if the response code indicates an error."""
            url = self._makeURL(pageName)
            return self.Response(urllib.urlopen(url)).body

        def _doPost(self, pageName, data):
            """Does a generic HTTP POST. Returns the response body, or
            throws an exception if the response code indicates an error."""
            url = self._makeURL(pageName)
            return self.Response(urllib.urlopen(url, urllib.urlencode(data))).body
```

(continued)

(continued)

```
        def _makeURL(self, pageName):
    "Returns the URL to the named wiki page."
            url = self.base
            if url[-1] != '/':
                url += '/'
            return url + pageName

        class Response:
            """This class handles the HTTP response returned by the REST
            web service."""

            def __init__(self, inHandle):
                self.body = None
                statusCode = None

                info = inHandle.info()
                #The status has automatically been read into an object
                #that also contains all the HTTP headers. The status
                #string looks like '200 OK'
                statusHeader = info['status']
                statusCode = int(statusHeader.split(' ')[0])

                #The remaining data is the plain-text response. In a more
                #complex application, this might be structured text or
                #XML, and at this point it would need to be parsed.
                self.body = inHandle.read()

                #The response codes in the 2xx range are the only good
                #ones. Getting any other response code should result in
                #an exception.
                if statusCode / 100 != 2:
                    raise RemoteApplicationException, self.body

    class RemoteApplicationException(Exception):
        """A simple exception class for use when the REST API returns an
        error condition."""
        pass
```

The BittyWikiRestAPI class uses the urllib library to GET and POST things to BittyWiki's REST interface CGI. It interprets the response as a status message, an exception message, or the text of a requested page. This class could be distributed in a standalone module to encourage developers to write BittyWiki add-ons in Python.

Note that the Response class is defined *within* the BittyWikiRestAPI class: No one else is going to use it, and putting it here makes it invisible outside the class. This is completely optional, but it makes the top-level view neater.

Finally, some code that implements a command-line interface to the spider:

```
if __name__ == '__main__':
    import sys
    if len(sys.argv) == 4:
        restURL, find, replace = sys.argv[1:]
    else:
        print('Usage: %s [URL to BittyWiki REST API] [find] [replace]' \
            % sys.argv[0])
        sys.exit(1)
    WikiReplaceSpider(restURL).replace(find, replace)
```

Try It Out   **Wiki Searching and Replacing**

Use your BittyWiki installation to create a few wiki pages around a particular topic. In the example, a few pages have been created for the mythical Foo project.

Run the `WikiSpiderREST.py` command to change your topic to another one. You should see output similar to this:

```
$ python WikiSpiderREST.py http://localhost:8001/cgi-bin/bittywiki-rest.cgi
Foo Bar
Checking "HomePage"
 Saving "HomePage"
Checking "FooCaseStudies"
 Deleting "FooCaseStudies", will recreate as "BarCaseStudies"
 Saving "BarCaseStudies"
Checking "CVSRepository"
 Saving "CVSRepository"
Checking "CaseStudy2"
Checking "BenefitsOfFoo"
 Deleting "BenefitsOfFoo", will recreate as "BenefitsOfBar"
 Saving "BenefitsOfBar"
Checking "CaseStudy1"
 Saving "CaseStudy1"
Checking "FooDesign"
 Deleting "FooDesign", will recreate as "BarDesign"
 Saving "BarDesign"
```

Lo and behold: The wiki pages have been changed and, where necessary, renamed.

How It Works

`WikiSpiderREST.py` keeps a list of WikiWords to check and possibly subject to search-and-replace. To process one of the WikiWords, it retrieves the corresponding page through the BittyWiki web service API. If the page actually exists, its text is scanned, and all of its WikiWords are put on the list of items to check later. The page then has its text modified using string search-and-replace, and is saved through the web service API. If the page name contains the string to be replaced, it's deleted and a new page with the same content is created — again, through the web service API. The next WikiWord in the list is then checked, and so on.

Because `WikiSpiderREST.py` *has no knowledge of wiki pages that are inaccessible from the HomePage, it's not guaranteed to get all of the pages on the wiki. It only gets the ones human users would see if they started at the HomePage and clicked all of the links.*

XML-RPC

XML-RPC is a protocol that does the same job as REST: It makes it easy to write a robot that accesses and/or modifies some remote application just by making HTTP requests. Some important differences exist, though. Whereas a REST call looks like manipulation of a document repository, an XML-RPC looks like a function call (in fact, in Python implementations, the call to the web service is disguised as a function call). Instead of sending a GET or POST to the resource you want to retrieve or modify, as with REST, XML-RPC traditionally has you do all your calls by POSTing to one special "server" resource. The data you POST contains an XML representation of a function you'd like to call, and any arguments to that function. As with REST, the response to your call is a document containing any information you requested, any status messages, and so on.

BittyWiki is simple enough that everything you pass in or get out is a mere string. We're fortunate in this regard because strings are the only data type supported by REST. If you need to pass an integer into a REST application, you need to encode it as a string and trust that the resource handler will know to turn it back into an integer. If you need to pass in an ordered list, you need to learn the server's preferred way of representing an ordered list as a string. One REST application might represent lists as "item1,item2,item3"; another might represent them as "item1 | item2 | item3 |"; a third might represent them as a custom-defined XML data structure. The major shortcoming of REST is that there's no standard way of marshalling different data types into strings, or of unmarshalling a string into typed data. You need to relearn the request and response format for every REST web service you use.

Here's the canonical sample XML-RPC client application. The public XML-RPC server `betty.userland.com` provides some example methods, including one that returns the name of a U.S. state, given an index, into an alphabetical list:

```
>>> import xmlrpc.client
>>> from xmlrpc.client import ServerProxy
>>> server=xmlrpc.client.ServerProxy("http://bettey.userland.com")
>>> server.examples.getStateName(41)
'South Dakota'
```

If this were a REST web service, the forty-first state in the list would be accessible as a distinct resource, perhaps `http://betty.userland.com/StateNames/41`. You'd get the name of a state by GETting the appropriate resource. You might have access to a Python library that handles the request and response details (the way the PyAmazon library handles the details of Amazon Web Services), but such libraries need to be written anew for each REST web service, because there's no REST standard for data structure representation.

XML-RPC's main advantage over REST is that it provides a standard way of encoding simple data structures into request and response data. XML-RPC specifies different XML strings for encoding the integer 4, the floating-point value 4.0, the string "4", and a list containing only the string "4". What you get back from an XML-RPC call is not a document that you have to parse, but a description of a data structure that can be automatically created for you by xmlrpc.client, the XML-RPC library that comes with Python. It's possible to make any kind of XML-RPC call using just one library (xmlrpc.client).

By now, you'll have noticed that Python is not very fastidious about types, and it will work with you on transforming one type to another. That said, its built-in types cover just about everything for which XML-RPC defines a representation: Booleans, integers, floating-point numbers, strings, arrays, and dictionaries. For binary data and dates, `xmlrpc.client` provides wrapper classes.

The XML-RPC spec, at www.xml-rpc.com/spec/, *is short and sweet.*

The XML-RPC Request

The XML-RPC request body is the body of an HTTP POST request. It's an XML document containing a `methodCall` element. The `methodCall` element contains two elements of its own: `methodName`, which designates the method to be called; and `params`, which contains a list of the parameters to be passed as arguments into the method.

Here's a sample XML-RPC request for a hypothetical method that sorts a list of numbers in either ascending or descending order:

```
<?xml version="1.1"?>
<methodCall>
 <methodName>searchsort.sortList</methodName>
 <params>
  <param>
   <value>
    <array>
     <data>
       <value><i4>10</i4></value>
       <value><i4>2</i4></value>
     </data>
    </array>
   </param>
   <param><value><boolean>1</boolean></param>
   </params>
</methodCall>
```

This is the XML-RPC equivalent of invoking a hypothetical local method with the following code:

```
import searchsort
searchsort.sortList([10, 2], True)
```

Given what you know about `xmlrpc.client`, it's no surprise that this method request would be generated and POSTed when you ran code like this:

```
import xmlrpc.client
xmlrpc.client.ServerProxy("http://sortserver/RPC").searchsort.sortList([10,
2], True)
```

Representation of Data in XML-RPC

The XML-RPC `methodName` can be any string, but XML-RPC methods are traditionally grouped into named packages, such as `searchsort` in the preceding example. In a Python implementation, this makes it look like a module called `searchsort` that contains the functions to expose, like `sortList`.

XML-RPC parameters can be any of the following types:

Data Type	Sample XML-RPC Representation
Boolean True or False	`<boolean>1</boolean>`
A string	`<string>James Joyce</string>`
An integer	`<i4>10</i4>`
A floating-point number	`<double>5.1</double>`

An array (items can be of any type, or a mixed type)	`<array>`
	  `<data>`
	    `<value><i4>10</i4></value>`
	    `<value><i4>2</i4></value>`
	  `</data>`
	`</array>`

A dictionary (keys must be strings; values can be any type)	`<struct>`
	  `<member>`
	    `<name>search</name>`
	`<value><string>James Joyce</string></value>`
	  `</member>`
	  `<member>`
	    `<name>channels</name>`
	    `<value><boolean>1</boolean></value>`
	  `</member>`
	`</struct>`

A date and time	`<dateTime.iso8601>20090914T19:11:20 </dateTime.iso8601>` (Use `xmlrpc.client`'s `DateTime` wrapper class, which can be instantiated from a time tuple, seconds since epoch, and so on.)
Binary data	`<base64>AVRoaXMgaXMgYmluYXJ5IGRhdGEu</base64>`

Strongly typed languages can have problems with some of these: mixed-type arrays, for example. Dynamic languages like Python handle these in stride.

The XML-RPC Response

The body of the XML-RPC response is an XML document describing the return value of the function invoked by the request.

Assuming the hypothetical `searchsort.sortList` method does what it says, when invoked with the sample body given earlier it'll return a response that looks like this:

```
<?xml version="1.1"?>
<methodResponse>
 <params>
  <param>
   <value>
    <array>
     <data>
       <value><i4>2</i4></value>
       <value><i4>10</i4></value>
     </data>
    </array>
   </value>
  </param>
 </params>
</methodResponse>
```

The response has the same basic structure as the request, but it's sparser. It's missing a `methodName` element because it's assumed you know which method you just called. It has a `params` element, just like the request; but whereas the request's `params` element could contain any number of `param children` (the arguments to the method), the response list is only allowed to contain a single `param child`: the return value.

If Something Goes Wrong

A REST web service is expected to flag error conditions using HTTP status codes, in conjunction with error documents that describe the problem. As you might expect, XML-RPC does a similar thing in a more structured way.

If an XML-RPC server can't complete a request for any reason, it returns a response containing a `fault`, instead of one containing a return value in `params`. A sample fault response is as follows:

```
<?xml version="1.1"?>
<methodResponse>
 <fault>
  <value>
   <struct>
    <member>
     <name>faultCode</name>
     <value><int>4</int></value>
    </member>
    <member>
     <name>faultString</name>
```

(continued)

459

(continued)

```
        <value><string>No such method: "searchSort.sortList".</string></value>
      </member>
    </struct>
  </value>
 </fault>
</methodResponse>
```

The `fault` element describes an XML-RPC struct (that is, a Python dictionary) with two members: `faultString`, which contains a human-readable description of what went wrong, and `faultCode`, the equivalent to the HTTP status code used to signify failure in REST contexts (even an XML-RPC call that results in a fault response will have an HTTP status code of 200). The advantage of `faultCode`s is that you can define them as you please for whatever problems are specific to your application. The disadvantage is that, unlike with HTTP status codes, there's no consensus as to what `faultCode`s mean. You'll need to reach an understanding with your users about the meanings of your service's `faultCode`s.

Within Python, a response with a `fault` corresponds to an `xmlrpc.client.Fault` object, a subclass of `Error`. If you're using Python's XML-RPC libraries, you can just raise and catch exceptions normally, instead of having to worry about creating or parsing XML-RPC faults.

Exposing the BittyWiki API through XML-RPC

If you doubt that Python programmers are spoiled, consider this: Not only does the language come bundled with a library that makes it easy to write XML-RPC clients; it also comes bundled with an XML-RPC server. As with the other `server` classes, `xmlrpc.server` runs as a standalone web server on its own port. However, the XML-RPC functionality is also available as a CGI program that accepts HTTP POSTs in XML-RPC format. This is implemented in another class, `CGIXMLRPCRequestHandler`, the name of which probably has more consecutive capital letters than any other class name in the Python standard library.

Here's a script, `bittywiki-xmlrpc.cgi`, that exposes the BittyWiki API either through an XML-RPC CGI (if you invoke it without command-line arguments, the way a CGI-enabled web server would) or through a standalone XML-RPC server (if you pass it through the port to use on the command line):

If you're using the `EasyCGIServer` presented earlier, or another server based on Python's `CGI-HTTPServer`, using this script as a CGI may not work for you. If you run into problems with the CGI, try using another web server, such as Apache, or running a standalone XML-RPC server instead of going through a CGI.

```python
import sys
import xmlrpc.server
from BittyWiki import Wiki

class BittyWikiAPI:
    """A simple wrapper around the basic BittyWiki functionality we
    want to expose to the API."""

    def __init__(self, wikiBase):
        "Initialize a wiki located in the given directory."
```

```
        self.wiki = Wiki(wikiBase)

    def getPage(self, pageName):
        "Returns the text of the given page."
        page = self.wiki.getPage(pageName)
        if not page.exists():
            raise NoSuchPage, page.name
        return page.getText()

    def save(self, pageName, newText):
        "Saves a page of the wiki."
        page = self.wiki.getPage(pageName)
        page.text = newText
        page.save()
        return "Page saved."

    def delete(self, pageName):
        "Deletes a page of the wiki."
        page = self.wiki.getPage(pageName)
        if not page.exists():
            raise NoSuchPage, pageName
        page.delete()
        return "Page deleted."

class NoSuchPage(Exception):
    pass
```

So far, nothing XML-RPC specific — just a nicely packaged interface to the three basic functions of the BittyWiki API. Next, you write a function that exposes those three functions to XML-RPC. You have two ways of doing this: You can register functions one at a time or register an object instance, which registers all that object's methods at once. This example provides code for both ways of registering the methods, but the instance registration is commented out, because in earlier versions of Python it exposed a security vulnerability:

```
def handlerSetup(handler, api):
    """This function registers the methods of the BittyWiki API
    as functions of an XML-RPC handler."""

    #Register the standard functions used by XML-RPC to advertise which methods
    #are available on a given server.
    handler.register_introspection_functions()

    #Register the BittyWiki API methods as XML-RPC functions in the
    #'bittywiki' namespace.
    handler.register_function(api.getPage, 'bittywiki.getPage')
    handler.register_function(api.save, 'bittywiki.save')
    handler.register_function(api.delete, 'bittywiki.delete')
```

Finally, the script portion, which starts up either a standalone XML-RPC server that can serve any number of requests, or a CGI-based XML-RPC script, which serves only the current request:

```
if __name__ == '__main__':
    WIKI_BASE = 'wiki/'
    api = BittyWikiAPI(WIKI_BASE)
    standalonePort = None
    if len(sys.argv) > 1:
        #The user provided a port number; that means they want to
        #run a standalone server.
        standalonePort = sys.argv[1]
        try:
            standalonePort = int(standalonePort)
        except ValueError:
            #Oops, that wasn't a port number. Chide the user and exit.
            scriptName = sys.argv[0]
            print('Usage:')
            print(' "%s [port number]" to start a standalone server.' \
                    % scriptName)
            print(' "%s" to invoke as a CGI.' % scriptName)
            sys.exit(1)
        isStandalone = 1
        print("Starting up standalone XML-RPC server on port %s." \
                % standalonePort)
        handler = xmlrpc.server.SimpleXMLRPCServer\
                (('localhost', standalonePort))
    else:
        #No port number specified; this is a CGI invocation.
        handler = xmlrpc.server.CGIXMLRPCRequestHandler()

    handlerSetup(handler, api)

    if standalonePort:
        handler.serve_forever()
    else:
        handler.handle_request()
```

| Try It Out | Manipulating BittyWiki through XML-RPC |

It's now possible to make XML-RPC calls against BittyWiki from other machines and even other programming languages, just as you were earlier making XML-RPC calls against Meerkat (which is written in PHP).

In one window, start the standalone XML-RPC server (alternatively, make sure the web server that serves the XML-RPC CGI is running):

```
# python BittyWiki-XMLRPC.py 8001
Starting up standalone XML-RPC server on port 8001.
```

In another, start an interactive Python session:

```
>>> import xmlrpc.server
>>> server = xmlrpc.server.ServerProxy("http://localhost:8001/")
```

```
>>> bittywiki = server.bittywiki
>>> bittywiki.getPage("CreatedByXMLRPC")
Traceback (most recent call last):
  File "<stdin>", line 1, in ?
  ...
    raise Fault(**self._stack[0])
xmlrpc.server.Fault: <Fault 1: 'No such page:CreatedByXMLRPC'>
>>> bittywiki.save("CreatedByXMLRPC", "This page was created through the XML-
RPC interface.")
'Page saved.'
>>> bittywiki.getPage("CreatedByXMLRPC")
'This page was created through the XML-RPC interface.'
```

You're using web services, but you didn't have to write special client code or (except at the beginning, when you connected to the server) even be aware that you're using web services. Of course, the changes you make to the wiki through this interface will also show up for people using the web application or BittyWiki's REST-based web service.

Wiki Search-and-Replace Using the XML-RPC Web Service

Remember `WikiSpiderREST.py`, the script that crawled BittyWiki pages using its REST API to perform search-and-replace operations? You had to write a custom class (`BittyWikiRESTAPI`) to construct the right URLs to use against the REST interface, and a custom XML parser to process the response documents you got in return. Of course, once you have written that stuff, it can be reused in any application that uses BittyWiki's REST API, but the main selling point of XML-RPC is that such classes aren't necessary: `xmlrpc.client` handles everything. Put that to the test by rewriting `WikiSpiderREST.py` as `WikiSpiderXMLRPC.py`:

```python
#!/usr/bin/python
import re
import xmlrpc.client

class WikiReplaceSpider:
    "A class for running search-and-replace against a web of wiki pages."

    WIKI_WORD = re.compile('(([A-Z][a-z0-9]*){2,})')

    def __init__(self, rpcURL):
        "Accepts a URL to a BittyWiki XML-RPC API."
        server = xmlrpc.client.ServerProxy(rpcURL)
        self.api = server.bittywiki

    def replace(self, find, replace):
        """Spider wiki pages starting at the front page, accessing them
        and changing them via the XML-RPC API."""

        processed = {} #Keep track of the pages already processed.
        todo = ['HomePage'] #Start at the front page of the wiki.
        while todo:
```

(continued)

(continued)

```
            for pageName in todo:
                print('Checking "%s"' % pageName)
                try:
                    pageText = self.api.getPage(pageName)
                except xmlrpc.client.Fault, fault:
                    if fault.faultString.find("No such page") == 0:
                        #We tried to access a page that doesn't exist;
                        #not a big deal.
                        pass
                    else:
                        #Some other problem; pass it on up.
                        raise xmlrpc.client.Fault, fault
                else:
                    #This page actually exists; process it.

                    #First, find any WikiWords in this page: they may
                    #reference other pages.
                    for wikiWord in self.WIKI_WORD.findall(pageText):
                        linkPage = wikiWord[0]
                      if not processed.get(linkPage) and linkPage not in todo:
                            #We haven't processed this page yet: put it on
                            #the to-do list.
                            todo.append(linkPage)

                    #Run the search-and-replace on the page text to get the
                    #new text of the page.
                    newText = pageText.replace(find, replace)

                    #Check to see if this page name matches the search
                    #string. If it does, delete it and recreate it
                    #with the new text; otherwise, just save the new
                    #text in the existing page.
                    newPageName = pageName.replace(find, replace)
                    if newPageName != pageName:
                        print(' Deleting "%s", will recreate as "%s"' \
                                % (pageName, newPageName))
                        self.api.delete(pageName)
                    if newPageName != pageName or newText != pageText:
                        print(' Saving "%s"' % newPageName)
                        saveResponse = self.api.save(newPageName, newText)
                    #Mark the new page as processed so we don't go through
                    #it a second time.
                    if newPageName != pageName:
                        processed[newPageName] = True
                processed[pageName] = True
                todo.remove(pageName)
```

The `WikiReplaceSpider` class looks almost exactly the same as before. The only big difference is that, whereas before a method call like `api.getPage` moved into custom REST code you had to write, it now moves into preexisting `xmlrpclib` code. Without those API-specific classes to implement, the `WikiReplaceSpider` class is pretty much *all* the code:

```
if __name__ == '__main__':
    import sys
    if len(sys.argv) == 4:
        rpcURL, find, replace = sys.argv[1:]
    else:
        print('Usage: %s [URL to BittyWiki XML-RPC API] [find] [replace]' \
            % sys.argv[0])
        sys.exit(1)
    WikiReplaceSpider(rpcURL).replace(find, replace)
```

That's it. This spider works just like the REST version, but it takes less code because there's no one-off code to deal with the specifics of the REST API. This script is run just like the REST version, but the URL passed in is the URL to the XML-RPC interface, instead of the URL to the REST interface:

```
$ python WikiSpiderXMLRPC.py http://localhost:8000/cgi-bin/bittywiki-xmlrpc.
cgi Foo Bar
Checking "HomePage"
 Saving "HomePage"
Checking "FooCaseStudies"
 ...
```

SOAP

XML-RPC solves REST's main problem by defining a standard way to represent data types such as integers, dates, and lists. However, while XML-RPC was being defined, the W3C's XML working group was working on its own representation of those data types and many others. After XML-RPC became popular, the W3C turned its attention to it, and started redesigning it to use WC3's preexisting standards. Along the way, ambition broadened the scope of the project to include any kind of message exchange, not just procedure calls and their return values. The result was SOAP. The acronym originally stood for Simple Object Access Protocol, but because the standard's scope has been expanded so far beyond simple remote procedure calls, the acronym itself is no longer applicable.

SOAP may still be simple compared to COM or CORBA, but it's a lot more complicated than XML-RPC. Fortunately, you don't need all of SOAP just to expose a web application as a web service. The part you do need looks basically like XML-RPC with a more general XML encoding scheme. SOAP gives you access to a broader range of data types than XML-RPC, and even lets you define your own.

Unfortunately, at the time of this writing, Python 3.1 does not widely support SOAP and useful third-party modules such as `SOAPpy` have not yet been updated to work with the current version (or even Python version 2.6 for that matter). Because there is every reason to anticipate that this will be corrected in the (hopefully) near future, this section demonstrates how to use SOAP (and specifically the `SOAPpy` module) in Python version 2.4. If you want to try out the examples, I recommend downloading and installing Python 2.4 on your computer. Otherwise, just follow along; the examples closely mirror those of the previous XML-RPC examples, so it should not be too difficult.

Note that writing any of the following code in Python 2.6 and above will not work.

SOAP Quick Start

Just as with REST and XML-RPC, a SOAP message is typically sent as the data portion of an HTTP POST request. Just as with those other protocols, then, it's technically possible to use a SOAP web service without any SOAP-specific tools: Just construct the message by hand, send it off with urllib, and parse the response with the xml.sax module. Realistically, though, you need a SOAP library to use SOAP with Python. A SOAP library will deal with transforming Python data structures to SOAP's XML representations and back, just as xmlrpc.client does for XML-RPC.

Unfortunately, there's no "soaplib" bundled with Python, but you can download one. There are two SOAP libraries for Python. The one library used in this chapter is SOAPpy, which provides an xmlrpc .client-like version of a SOAP client and a SOAP server.

> If you're running Debian GNU/Linux, you can just install the "soappy" package; if not, you can download the distribution from http://pywebsvcs.sourceforge.net/. ZSI, the other Python SOAP package, is also available from that site. Be warned that SOAPpy requires two other packages: fpconst, a floating-point library, and PyXML, a set of XML utilities. More information and links to the packages are available in the SOAPpy README file.

The SOAP Request

Here's a transcript of a hypothetical SOAP RPC call that tries to sort a list in ascending order; compare it to the XML-RPC transcript earlier that called an XML-RPC version of the same method:

```
<?xml version="1.1" encoding="UTF-8"?>
<SOAP-ENV:Envelope SOAP-ENV:encodingStyle="http://schemas.xmlsoap.org/soap/
encoding/"
  xmlns:SOAP-ENV="http://schemas.xmlsoap.org/soap/envelope/"
  xmlns:SOAP-ENC="http://schemas.xmlsoap.org/soap/encoding/"
  xmlns:xsi="http://www.w3.org/1999/XMLSchema-instance"
  xmlns:xsd="http://www.w3.org/1999/XMLSchema">
<SOAP-ENV:Body>
 <ns1:sortList xmlns:ns1="urn:SearchSort" SOAP-ENC:root="1">
  <v1 SOAP-ENC:arrayType="xsd:int[2]" xsi:type="SOAP-ENC:Array">
   <item>10</item>
   <item>2</item>
  </v1>
  <v2 xsi:type="xsd:boolean">True</v2>
 </ns1:sortList>
</SOAP-ENV:Envelope>
```

The first thing to notice is all those xmlns declarations. SOAP is very particular about XML namespaces, whereas XML-RPC is much more informal and serves standalone XML documents. SOAP uses XML namespaces to define the format of the SOAP message itself (SOAP-ENV), the data types (such as xsd: boolean and the SOAP-specific SOAP-ENC:Array), and the very *concept* of a data type (xsi:type). This gives SOAP a lot more flexibility in how its data is encoded, but between XML Schema (xsd) and the SOAP data encoding schema (SOAP-ENC), most of the basic data types are already defined for you. Only in more complicated cases will you need to define custom data types.

The other namespace mentioned in this message is urn:SearchSort. That's the namespace of the method you're trying to call. As mentioned before, this is like the way the XML-RPC version of this request named its method searchsort.sortList, instead of just sortList. SOAP has formalized the

XML-RPC convention, and uses XML namespaces to distinguish between different methods with the same name. Your SOAP call must be executed in a particular XML namespace. If you use a Python SOAP library to make SOAP calls, this is probably the only namespace you'll actually have to worry about.

If you ignore the namespaces, this message looks a lot like the XML-RPC message you saw earlier. There's a method call tag that contains a list of tags for the arguments to be passed into the method. Instead of the method call tag containing a child tag with the method name, here the tag is simply named after the method to be called. In XML-RPC, the arguments were listed inside a separate `params` tag. Here, they're direct children of the method call tag. The SOAP message is a little more concise, but (again, disregarding the namespace declarations) just as easy to read.

Compare the XML-RPC representation of the array to be sorted, which you saw earlier, to the SOAP representation of the same array:

```
<array>
 <data>
  <value><i4>2</i4></value>
  <value><i4>10</i4></value>
 </data>
</array>
<v1 SOAP-ENC:arrayType="xsd:int[2]" xsi:type="SOAP-ENC:Array">
 <item>10</item>
 <item>2</item>
</v1>
```

This difference between the two protocols is typical. There's more up-front definition in SOAP and more references to external documents that formally define the data types. The upside of that is that once the definition is done, it takes fewer bytes to actually define a data structure. It doesn't make much difference with a small array like this, but consider an array with thousands or millions of elements. SOAP is more efficient than XML-RPC at representing large data structures.

The SOAP Response

Here's a possible response you might get from a SOAP server after sending it the `sortList` request:

```
<?xml version="1.1" encoding="UTF-8"?>
<SOAP-ENV:Envelope SOAP-ENV:encodingStyle="http://schemas.xmlsoap.org/soap/
encoding/"
xmlsn:SOAP-ENV="http://schemas.xmlsoap.org/soap/envelope/"
  xmlns:SOAP-ENC="http://schemas.xmlsoap.org/soap/encoding/"
  xmlns:xsi="http://www.w3.org/1999/XMLSchema-instance"
  xmlns:xsd="http://www.w3.org/1999/XMLSchema">
<SOAP-ENV:Body>
 <ns1:sortList xmlns:ns1="urn:SearchSort" SOAP-ENC:root="1">
  <return SOAP-ENC:arrayType="xsd:int[2]" xsi:type="SOAP-ENC:Array">
   <item>2</item>
   <item>10</item>
  </return>
 </ns1:sortList>
</SOAP-ENV:Envelope>
```

Just as with XML-RPC, a SOAP response has the same basic structure as a SOAP request. Where the SOAP request had a list of arguments, the SOAP response has a single return value. This, too, is similar to XML-RPC: Recall that an XML-RPC response contained a *params* list, which was only allowed to contain one param — the return value. SOAP makes this convention more natural by eliminating the params tag and just returning the return value.

If Something Goes Wrong

If you make a SOAP request that makes the server code throw an exception, the Body of the response you get back will contain a Fault element. It might look something like this:

```
</SOAP-ENV:Body>
 <SOAP-ENV:Fault SOAP-ENC:root="1">
  <faultcode>SOAP-ENV:Client</faultcode>
  <faultstring>No method urn:SearchSort:sortList found</faultstring>
  <detail xsi:type="xsd:string">
   There's no method "sortList" in the urn:SearchSort namespace.
  </detail>
 </SOAP-ENV:Fault>
</SOAP-ENV:Body>
```

The faultstring and detail sub-elements of Fault are for human-readable descriptions, and the faultcode element describes the type of error. Whereas XML-RPC says nothing about the fault code except that it must be an integer, SOAP defines four standard strings to serve as fault codes. Two of them (mustUnderstand and VersionMismatch) you probably won't encounter in basic SOAP use. The other two fault codes serve, appropriately enough, to identify who caused the fault. If you're writing a SOAP client and you get a faultcode of Client, that means you caused the error (for instance, in the preceding, by calling a method that doesn't exist in the namespace you specified). If the faultcode is Server, that means there's nothing wrong with your request but the server can't fulfill it at the moment — perhaps the server code can't access a database or some other necessary resource.

Within a Python interface, the details of a response with a Fault are hidden from you, pretty much as in XML-RPC. If a Python method you've exposed through SOAP throws an exception, the SOAP server automatically transforms the exception into a SOAP response with a Fault element. If you're using SOAPpy and you call a remote method that responds with a Fault, it is transformed into a subclass of Error: SOAPpy.Types.faultType.

Exposing a SOAP Interface to BittyWiki

In principle, there's no reason why you shouldn't be able to run a SOAP server from a CGI script: Remember that despite all the additional complexity and mystique of SOAP, it's just like REST and XML-RPC in that it's just a document being POSTed to a URL and another document being sent in return. Unfortunately, SOAPpy doesn't provide a CGI script that serves SOAP requests, only a standalone server, SOAPServer.

> *ZSI, the other SOAP implementation for Python, does offer a CGI-based server.*

The following sample script, BittyWiki-SOAPServer.py, exposes the BittyWiki interface to SOAP using a standalone server. This file should go into the same directory as the file BittyWiki.py, so that you can use the core BittyWiki engine. Alternatively, you can put `BittyWiki.py` into one of the directories in your PYTHON_PATH so you can use it from anywhere:

```python
#!/usr/bin/python
import sys
import SOAPpy
from BittyWiki import Wiki

class BittyWikiAPI:
    """A simple wrapper around the basic BittyWiki functionality we
    want to expose to the API."""

    def __init__(self, wikiBase):
        "Initialize a wiki located in the given directory."
        self.wiki = Wiki(wikiBase)

    def getPage(self, pageName):
        "Returns the text of the given page."
        page = self.wiki.getPage(pageName)
        if not page.exists():
            raise NoSuchPage, page.name
        return page.getText()

    def save(self, pageName, newText):
        "Saves a page of the wiki."
        page = self.wiki.getPage(pageName)
        page.text = newText
        page.save()
        return "Page saved."

    def delete(self, pageName):
        "Deletes a page of the wiki."
        page = self.wiki.getPage(pageName)
        if not page.exists():
            raise NoSuchPage, page.name
        page.delete()
        return "Page deleted."

class NoSuchPage(Exception):
    """An exception thrown when a caller tries to access a page that
    doesn't exist."""
    pass
```

The actual API code is exactly the same as for the XML-RPC server; it could even be moved into a common library. The only difference is that now you register it with a SOAPServer instead of a SimpleXMLRPCServer:

```python
DEFAULT_PORT = 8002
NAMESPACE = 'urn:BittyWiki'
WIKI_BASE = 'wiki/'
if __name__ == '__main__':
    api = BittyWikiAPI(WIKI_BASE)
    port = DEFAULT_PORT
    if len(sys.argv) > 1:
```

(continued)

(continued)

```
            port = sys.argv[1]
            try:
                port = int(port)
            except ValueError:
                #Oops, that wasn't a port number. Chide the user and exit.
                print 'Usage: "%s [optional port number]"' % sys.argv[0]
                sys.exit(1)
        print "Starting up standalone SOAP server on port %s." % port
        handler = SOAPpy.SOAPServer(('localhost', port))
        handler.registerObject(api, NAMESPACE)
        handler.serve_forever()
```

Try It Out   **Manipulating BittyWiki through SOAP**

In one window, start the standalone SOAP server:

```
$ python BittyWiki-SOAPServer.py 8002
Starting up standalone XML-RPC server on port 8002.
```

In another, start an interactive Python session:

```
>>> import SOAPpy
>>> bittywiki = SOAPpy.SOAPProxy("http://localhost:8002/", "urn:BittyWiki")
>>> bittywiki.getPage("CreatedBySOAP")
<Fault SOAP-ENV:Server: Method urn:BittyWiki:getPage failed.: __main__.
NoSuchPage CreatedBySOAP>
Traceback (most recent call last):
  File "<stdin>", line 1, in ?
  ...
SOAPpy.Types.faultType: <Fault SOAP-ENV:Server: Method urn:BittyWiki:getPage
failed.: __main__.NoSuchPage CreatedBySOAP>
>>> bittywiki.save("CreatedBySOAP", "This page was created through the SOAP
interface.")
'Page saved.'
>>> bittywiki.getPage("CreatedBySOAP")
'This page was created through the SOAP interface.'
```

The experience of using SOAP, hidden behind SOAPpy, is similar to the experience of using XML-RPC, hidden behind xmlrpclib. You can make method calls, passing in standard Python objects, and let the library take care of all the details.

Wiki Search-and-Replace Using the SOAP Web Service

Here's WikiSpiderSOAP.py, another wiki search-and-replace client similar to the ones described earlier for BittyWiki's REST and XML-RPC interfaces. By now, this code should be familiar. The pattern is always the same: Set up some reference to the basic BittyWiki API and run the basic search-and-replace spider algorithm using it. The only major difference between this version and the XML-RPC version is the exception handling: xmlrpclib and SOAPpy act differently when something goes wrong on the server side, so the exception handling code must be different. Other than that, the SOAP-based search-and-replace spider looks more or less the same as the XML-RPC one:

```
#!/usr/bin/python
import re
import SOAPpy

class WikiReplaceSpider:
    "A class for running search-and-replace against a web of wiki pages."

    WIKI_WORD = re.compile('(([A-Z][a-z0-9]*){2,})')

    def __init__(self, rpcURL):
        "Accepts a URL to a BittyWiki SOAP API."
        self.api = SOAPpy.SOAPProxy(rpcURL, "urn:BittyWiki")
        self.api.config.dumpSOAPIn=1

    def replace(self, find, replace):
        """Spider wiki pages starting at the front page, accessing them
        and changing them via the XML-RPC API."""

        processed = {} #Keep track of the pages already processed.
        todo = ['HomePage'] #Start at the front page of the wiki.
        while todo:
            for pageName in todo:
                print 'Checking "%s"' % pageName
                try:
                    pageText = self.api.getPage(pageName)
                except SOAPpy.Types.faultType, fault:
                    if fault.detail.find("NoSuchPage") != -1:
                        #Some page mentioned a WikiWord that doesn't exist
                        #yet; not a big deal.
                        pass
                    else:
                        #Some other problem; pass it on up.
                        raise SOAPpy.Types.faultType, fault
                else:
                    #This page actually exists; process it.
                    #First, find any WikiWords in this page: they may
                    #reference other existing pages.
                    for wikiWord in self.WIKI_WORD.findall(pageText):
                        linkPage = wikiWord[0]
                        if not processed.get(linkPage) and linkPage not in todo:
                            #We haven't processed this page yet: put it on
                            #the to-do list.
                            todo.append(linkPage)

                    #Run the search-and-replace on the page text to get the
                    #new text of the page.
                    newText = pageText.replace(find, replace)

                    #Check to see if this page name matches the search
                    #string. If it does, delete it and recreate it
                    #with the new text; otherwise, just save the new
                    #text in the existing page.
```

(continued)

(continued)

```
                    newPageName = pageName.replace(find, replace)
                    if newPageName != pageName:
                        print ' Deleting "%s", will recreate as "%s"' \
                            % (pageName, newPageName)
                        self.api.delete(pageName)
                    if newPageName != pageName or newText != pageText:
                        print ' Saving "%s"' % newPageName
                        self.api.save(newPageName, newText)
                    #Mark the new page as processed so we don't go through
                    #it a second time.
                    if newPageName != pageName:
                        processed[newPageName] = True
                processed[pageName] = True
                todo.remove(pageName)

    if __name__ == '__main__':
        import sys
        if len(sys.argv) == 4:
            rpcURL, find, replace = sys.argv[1:]
        else:
            print 'Usage: %s [URL to BittyWiki SOAP API] [find] [replace]' \
                % sys.argv[0]
            sys.exit(1)
        WikiReplaceSpider(rpcURL).replace(find, replace)
```

This spider works just like the REST and the XML-RPC versions described earlier in this chapter:

```
$ python WikiSpiderSOAP.py http://localhost:8002/ Foo Bar
Checking "HomePage"
 Saving "HomePage"
Checking "FooCaseStudies"
. . .
```

Note that because `BittyWiki-SOAPServer.py` runs its own web server, there's no need to point to a script somewhere on the web server that handles the SOAP interface. The entire web server is the SOAP interface.

That concludes the use of Python version 2.4 for now; we return to it in the section on WSDL later on.

Documenting Your Web Service API

Exposing a web service API won't do any good unless the people who want to write robots can figure out how to use it. If you were to distribute a Python module with inadequate documentation (shame on you), a determined user could try to figure out the API by looking at the source code and, if necessary, making experimental changes, learning through trial and error. That isn't possible when you expose a web service, so it's especially important that you have a real way of getting the API information to your users.

Human-Readable API Documentation

In my opinion, no matter which web service protocol you're using, nothing beats an up-to-date human-readable description of an API. This can be written manually or generated through introspection and the use of Python docstrings. Up next are three sample documents that describe the three web service APIs for the BittyWiki application created in this chapter. They're all extremely short, but they contain all the information a user needs to write an application using any of them.

The BittyWiki REST API Document

To get the raw wiki markup for the page "WikiPage", GET the URL http://localhost:8000/cgi-bin/bittywiki-rest.cgi/WikiPage. You'll get an XML data structure in which the <data> tag contains the wiki markup of the WikiPage page. If the WikiPage page doesn't exist, you'll get an error.

To modify the contents of the page "WikiPage", POST to the URL http://localhost:8000/cgi-bin/bittywiki-rest.cgi/WikiPage. Set data equal to the wiki markup you want to write to the page, and operation to the string write. You'll receive an XML data structure in which the <message> tag contains a status message. If the WikiPage page doesn't exist, it will be automatically created.

To delete the page "WikiPage", POST to the URL http://localhost:8000/cgi-bin/bitty wiki-rest.cgi/WikiPage. Set "operation" to the string delete. You'll receive an XML data structure in which the <message> tag contains a status message. If the WikiPage page doesn't exist, you'll get an error.

The BittyWiki XML-RPC API Document

The BittyWiki API server is located at http://localhost:8001/. It exposes three methods:

❑ **bittywiki.getPage(string pageName)** — Returns the text of the named page. Passing an empty string designates the wiki homepage. This throws a fault if you request a page that doesn't exist.

❑ **bittywiki.save(string pageName, string text)** — Sets the text of the named page. If the page doesn't already exist, it is automatically created.

❑ **bittywiki.delete(string pageName)** — Deletes the named page. This throws a fault if you try to delete a page that doesn't exist.

The BittyWiki SOAP API Document

The BittyWiki SOAP server is located at http://localhost:8002/. It exposes three methods in the namespace "urn:BittyWiki":

❑ **getPage(string pageName)** — Returns the text of the named page. Passing an empty string designates the wiki homepage. This throws a fault if you request a page that doesn't exist.

❑ **save(string pageName, string text)** — Sets the text of the named page. If the page doesn't already exist, it is automatically created.

❑ **delete(string pageName)** — Deletes the named page. This throws a fault if you try to delete a page that doesn't exist.

The XML-RPC Introspection API

An unofficial addendum to the XML-RPC specification defines three special functions in the "system" namespace, as a convenience to users who might not know which functions an XML-RPC server supports, or what those functions might do. These special functions are the web service equivalent of Python's ever-useful `dir` and `help` commands. Both `xmlrpc.server` and `CGIXMLRPCRequestHandler` support two of the three introspection functions, assuming you call the `register_introspection_functions` method on the server or handler object after instantiating it:

```
handler=xmlrpc.server.SimpleXMLRPCServer((host,port))
handler.register_introspection_functions()
```

Method Name	What It Does
`System.listMethods()`	Returns the names of all the functions the server makes available.
`System.methodHelp(string funcName)`	Returns a string with documentation for the named function. Implemented in Python by returning the function's Python docstring.
`System.methodSignature(string funcName)`	Returns the signature and return type of the named function. Not automatically supported by the Python implementation because Python function definitions don't include type information.

Try It Out   Using the XML-RPC Introspection API

Start up and connect to the BittyWiki XML-RPC server (or CGI) as before. In addition to the BittyWiki methods shown earlier, you can use the XML-RPC introspection methods:

```
>>> import xmlrpc.client
>>> server=xmlrpc.client.ServerProxy("http://localhost:8001/")
>>> server.system.listMethods()
['bittywiki.delete', 'bittywiki.getPage', 'bittywiki.save', 'system.
listMethods', 'system.methodHelp', 'system.methodSignature']
>>> server.system.methodHelp("bittywiki.save")
'Saves a page of the wiki.'
>>> server.system.methodSignature("bittywiki.save")
'signatures not supported'
```

XML-RPC introspection isn't meant as a substitute for a human-readable API document. For one thing, it's hard to get people excited about using your API if they must use XML-RPC method calls to even see what it is. However, the introspection API does make it a lot easier to experiment with an XML-RPC web service from an interactive Python shell.

WSDL

Many SOAP-based web services define their interface in a WSDL file. WSDL is basically a machine-parseable version of the human-readable API document shown earlier in this section.

Recall that XML-RPC defines a set of rules for transforming a few basic data structures into XML documents and back into data structures. WSDL allows such rules to be constructed on the fly. It's more or less a programming language-agnostic schema for describing functions: their names, the data types of their arguments, and the data types of their return values. Although WSDL is associated with SOAP, it's possible to use SOAP without using WSDL (in fact, you did just that throughout this chapter's section on SOAP).

A WSDL file is an XML document (of course!), which defines the following aspects of your web service inside its `definitions` element:

❏ Any custom data types defined by your web service. These go into `complexType` elements of a `types` list.

❏ The formats of the messages sent and received by your web service; that is, the signatures and return values of the functions your web service defines. These are defined in a series of `message` elements, and may make reference to any custom data types you defined earlier.

❏ The names of the functions your web service provides, along with the input and output messages expected by each. This is in the `portType` element, which contains an `operation` element for each of the web service's functions.

❏ A binding of your web service's functions to a specific protocol — that is, HTTP. For simple SOAP applications, this section is an exercise in redundancy: You end up just listing all of your functions again. It exists because SOAP is protocol-independent; you need to explicitly state that you're exposing your methods over HTTP. This goes in the `binding` element.

❏ Finally, the URL to your web service. This is defined in the `service` element.

Note that because you are once again working with SOAP, and the SOAP libraries have not been updated (at the time of this writing) to work with Python version 2.6 or 3.0, you will once more rely on Python version 2.4 for the following examples. Here's `BittyWiki.wsdl`, a WSDL file for the SOAP API exposed by BittyWiki:

```
<?xml version="1.1"?>
<definitions name="BittyWiki"
             targetNamespace="urn:BittyWiki"
             xmlns:xsd="http://www.w3.org/2001/XMLSchema"
             xmlns:soap="http://schemas.xmlsoap.org/wsdl/soap/"
         xmlns="http://schemas.xmlsoap.org/wsdl/">

<!--Descriptions of the functions exposed by the BittyWiki API.  The
definitions of the functions reference message elements which will be
defined afterwards.-->
<portType name="BittyWikiPortType">
  <operation name="getPage">
      <input message="sendPageName"/>
      <output message="getPageText"/>
  </operation>

  <operation name="save">
```

(continued)

(continued)

```
            <input message="sendPageNameAndText"/>
            <output message="getStatusMessage"/>
    </operation>

    <operation name="delete">
        <input message="sendPageName"/>
        <output message="getStatusMessage"/>
    </operation>
</portType>
```

The WSDL parser now knows which functions are exposed by BittyWiki, but nothing about the signatures or return types of those functions. Those come next:

```
<!--Descriptions of the method signatures used by the BittyWiki API.
For instance, this first one is for a method where you send in a page name.
This method signature is common to getPage() and delete().-->
<message name="sendPageName">
  <part name="pageName" type="xsd:string"/>
</message>

<message name="sendPageNameAndText">
    <part name="pageName" type="xsd:string"/>
    <part name="pageText" type="xsd:string"/>
</message>

<!--Descriptions of the possible return values obtained from the
BittyWiki API. The first one is for a return value that contains
a wiki page's markup: that is, the return value of getPage().-->
<message name="getPageText">
    <part name="pageText" type="xsd:string"/>
</message>

<message name="getStatusMessage">
    <part name="message" type="xsd:string"/>
</message>
```

A rather redundant section follows, as the four SOAP functions are bound to SOAP-over-HTTP:

```
<!--A binding of the BittyWiki API functions (previously defined only
in the abstract) to the specific "SOAP-over-HTTP" protocol.-->
<binding type="BittyWikiPortType" name="BittyWikiSOAPBinding">
<soap:binding style="rpc" transport="http://schemas.xmlsoap.org/soap/http" />
  <operation name="getPage">
   <input><soap:body use="literal" namespace="urn:BittyWiki" /></input>
   <output><soap:body use="literal" namespace="urn:BittyWiki" /></output>
  </operation>

  <operation name="save">
   <input><soap:body use="literal" namespace="urn:BittyWiki" /></input>
   <output><soap:body use="literal" namespace="urn:BittyWiki" /></output>
  </operation>

  <operation name="delete">
   <input><soap:body use="literal" namespace="urn:BittyWiki" /></input>
   <output><soap:body use="literal" namespace="urn:BittyWiki" /></output>
```

```
  </operation>
 </binding>
```

Finally, the code to let WSDL know where to find the BittyWiki web service:

```
<!--A link to the BittyWiki web service on the web. It uses the
BittyWiki API defined in BittyWikiPortType, as realized by its
SOAP-over-HTTP binding, BittyWikiSOAPBinding.-->
<service name="BittyWiki">
 <port name="BittyWikiPort" binding="BittyWikiSOAPBinding">
  <soap:address location="http://localhost:8002/"/>
 </port>
</service>
</definitions>
```

The BittyWiki API doesn't define any custom data types, *so there's no types element in its WSDL file.
If you want to see a* types *element that has some* complexTypes, *look at the WSDL file for the
Google Web APIs.*

WSDL is pretty complicated: That WSDL file is bigger than the Python script implementing the web
service it describes. WSDL files are usually generated from the corresponding web service source code,
so that humans don't have to specify them. It's not possible to do this from Python code because a big
part of WSDL is defining the data types, and Python functions don't have predefined data types. Both
the SOAPpy and ZSI libraries can parse WSDL (in fact, they share a WSDL library: wstools), but there's
not much in the way of Python-specific resources for generating WSDL.

Try It Out   Manipulating BittyWiki through a WSDL Proxy

The following looks more or less like the previous example of BittyWiki manipulation through direct
SOAP calls:

```
>>> import SOAPpy
>>> proxy = SOAPpy.WSDL.Proxy(open("BittyWiki.wsdl"))
>>> proxy.getPage("SOAPViaWSDL")
<Fault SOAP-ENV:Server: Method urn:BittyWiki:getPage failed.: __main__.
NoSuchPage SOAPViaWSDL>
Traceback (most recent call last):
  ...
SOAPpy.Types.faultType: <Fault SOAP-ENV:Server: Method urn:BittyWiki:getPage
failed.: __main__.NoSuchPage SOAPViaWSDL>
>>> proxy.save("SOAPViaWSDL", "This page created through SOAP via WSDL.")
'Page saved.'
>>> proxy.getPage("SOAPViaWSDL")
'This page created through SOAP via WSDL.'
```

The main difference here is that going through WSDL will stop you from calling web service methods
that don't exist:

```
>>> proxy.noSuchMethod()
Traceback (most recent call last):
  ...
AttributeError: noSuchMethod
```

```
>>>
>>> server = SOAPpy.SOAPProxy("http://localhost:8002/", "urn:BittyWiki")
>>> server.noSuchMethod()
<Fault SOAP-ENV:Client: No method urn:BittyWiki:noSuchMethod found:
exceptions.AttributeError BittyWikiAPI instance has no attribute
'noSuchMethod'>
Traceback (most recent call last):
  ...
SOAPpy.Types.faultType: <Fault SOAP-ENV:Client: No method urn:BittyWiki:
noSuchMethod found: exceptions.AttributeError BittyWikiAPI instance has no
attribute 'noSuchMethod'>
```

Both attempts to call noSuchMethod raised an exception, but going through WSDL meant the problem was caught on the local machine instead of the server. This ability is a lot more interesting to a compiled language: WSDL makes it possible to apply the same compile-time checks to web service calls as to local function calls.

And once more, that rounds out the usage of Python version 2.4 for this chapter.

Choosing a Web Service Standard

This chapter described three standards for web services, each with a different philosophy, each with advantages and drawbacks. REST aims to get the most out of the facilities provided by HTTP, but it lacks a standard encoding for even simple data types. XML-RPC provides that encoding, but it's verbose and *only* deals with simple data types and compositions of simple data types. SOAP offers the structured data types of XML-RPC with the flexibility of REST, but its added complexity makes hard cases more difficult to understand than if they'd just been implemented with REST.

Industry trends favor REST and SOAP over XML-RPC. SOAP has the backing of large software companies such as IBM and Microsoft; REST has the backing of independent web service users and developers. That's because APIs based around REST and XML-RPC are generally easier to learn and use. Whenever web services expose the same API through different protocols, the simplest one generally wins. For instance, Amazon exposes a SOAP API in addition to the REST API covered in this chapter, but about 80 percent of its users choose REST over SOAP.

Which should you choose? Well, if you were a big fan of large software companies like IBM and Microsoft, you probably wouldn't be using Python in the first place. You would be using Java or .NET: two strongly typed languages with good SOAP tool support. In most cases, the extra functionality of SOAP isn't needed, and Python's support for SOAP isn't consummate with the added complexity, so why choose it unnecessarily?

You should start off by planning to expose a well-designed REST or XML-RPC API. If, during the design or implementation stage, you start running into problems with your choice, look into using SOAP (once the libraries have been updated). Unless you're doing heavy-duty automatic business process software, or interfacing with a statically typed language like Java or .NET, you'll probably be able to see the REST or XML-RPC API through to the end. Your users will thank you for the simpler interface.

My ideal web service would have a RESTful interface in which each resource could accept POST data in the format defined by XML-RPC (or some simple subset of SOAP). The web service could then be designed along REST principles, but some variant of `xmlrpc.client` or `SOAPpy` could be used to marshal and unmarshal the data without requiring the creation of custom parsers.

Whatever you choose, please try to keep web services in mind from the moment you begin the design: *A web service is just a web application for robots.* If you want your application to inspire creativity and not just meet a predefined need, you must give up some of the control to your users.

Web Service Etiquette

A web service may have users who skirt the rules, or administrators who feel the users are ungrateful for the service they're being provided. In the interests of harmony, here are a few basic pieces of advice for managing the social aspect of web services.

For Consumers of Web Services

If you write a robot to consume someone else's web services, it's important to play by the rules. In particular, don't try to evade any limitations such as license keys or daily limits on your access to the API. Access to a web service is a privilege, not a right. It's better to run out of API calls and have to complete a task later than you planned than to have your access taken away altogether.

For Producers of Web Services

If you're planning to expose your web application through a web service, you need to consider the flip side of these issues. If your audience is already scripting your application, you've got a leg up because you don't have to guess what people might do with it. Before you design your web services, poll your robot-writing users to see what parts of your application they're using. Make your web services available on terms that allow users to move over to the new system, or they'll have no incentive to switch.

As producer of a public web service, you might feel like the burden of etiquette falls completely on your users. After all, you're providing a service to them and not expecting anything in return. Nonetheless, it's important to make your terms of use palatable because the people writing the robots have the final advantage: So long as you provide a web application with the same functionality as the web service, determined users can always write a robot to use the web application however they want. There's no foolproof way you can distinguish between a robot that uses your site and the web browser a human might use to use your site. They're both pieces of software running on someone's computer, making an HTTP request. All the HTTP headers, including the User-Agent and the authentication headers, can be forged by a robot.

That said, if a particular robot is causing you trouble, you can solve the problem with the same tools you'd use against a troublesome human user.

Using Web Applications as Web Services

It's possible to write scripts that consume web applications as though they were web services. After all, that's how the idea of web services got started in the first place. Some sites still haven't gotten the web services religion, or might have web services that don't expose the functionality you need. To write the robot you have in mind, you'd have to go through the application.

This chapter doesn't cover how to write such scripts, but the general principles are similar to web services; and if this topic interests you, you'll eventually find yourself doing it. When you do, don't do anything that violates the site's terms of service. In addition, don't access the site more than a human user would. If you can, run your script in off hours so you don't add to the load on the system. Finally, ask the site administrators for a web service interface so you can work against a more stable interface that uses less bandwidth.

Summary

Web applications are powerful and popular; with Python, they're also easy to write. The REST architecture made the Web usable and successful: Employing it when designing your application gives you a head start. Web applications are designed for humans; a web service is just a web application designed for use by software scripts instead. Expose REST and XML-RPC web services for simplicity and easy adoption; SOAP for heavy-duty tasks or when interfacing with Java or .NET applications. Make use of the web services provided by others: They're opening up their data sets and algorithms for your benefit.

Exercises

1. What's a RESTful way to change BittyWiki so that it supports hosting more than one Wiki?

2. Write a web application interface to `WishListBargainFinder.py`. (That is, a web application that delegates to the Amazon Web Services.)

3. The wiki search-and-replace spider looks up every new WikiWord it encounters to see whether it corresponds to a page of the wiki. If it finds a page by that name, that page is processed. Otherwise, nothing happens and the spider has wasted a web service request. How could the web service API be changed so that the spider could avoid those extra web service requests for non-existent pages?

4. Suppose that, to prevent vandalism, you change BittyWiki so that pages can't be deleted. Unfortunately, this breaks the wiki search-and-replace spider, which sometimes deletes a page before re-creating it with a new name. What's a solution that meets both your needs and the needs of the spider's users?

Integrating Java with Python

Java is an object-oriented programming language. Java programs are compiled from source code into byte codes. The Java runtime engine, called a *Java virtual machine*, or *JVM*, runs the compiled byte codes. Sound familiar? At an abstract level at least, Java and Python are very similar. Like Java, Python programs are compiled into byte codes, although this can be done at runtime.

Despite these similarities, some differences between the languages exist:

❑ With Python, you can run scripts directly from the source code. Compiling is optional. If you don't compile your Python code in advance, the `python` command will take care of this for you.

❑ Java syntax is based on C and C++, two very popular programming languages. This makes it easy for developers using C++ to migrate to Java. Consequently, Java is considered a more serious and businesslike language than Python.

❑ Python syntax is very simple and easy to learn, but the syntax has diverged far from C.

❑ With its simple syntax and built-in support for lists, dictionaries, and tuples, you'll find Python code much easier to write than Java code. Generally, Python programs require a lot less code than the corresponding Java code.

❑ Java has an advantage over Python in terms of standard APIs, though. The base Java language includes a mature database API, an API for parsing XML documents, an API for remote communication, and even an API to access LDAP directory servers. You can do all of this in Python, but Python lacks the richness, and standardization, of the many Java APIs. This becomes more apparent when you write enterprise applications in Python. Java's enterprise APIs, called Java EE, enable Java to be a player in the enterprise market. Python, unfortunately, has been relegated to a minimal role in the enterprise market.

When writing enterprise applications, you'll likely need to write them in Java. Even though Python can work well in this space, Java controls the mind share for the enterprise. Luckily, you can get the best of both worlds with Jython, an implementation of Python in Java.

Jython enables you to execute Python code from within a Java virtual machine — that is, from within any Java application.

In this chapter you learn:

❏   Reasons for scripting within Java applications

❏   Comparing Jython with the regular C-based Python implementations

❏   Installing Jython

❏   Running Python scripts from Jython

❏   Calling Java code from Python scripts

❏   Extending Java classes with Python classes

❏   Writing Java EE servlets in Python

❏   Embedding the Jython interpreter in your Java applications

Note that you'll want to have some familiarity with both Java and Python to be able to integrate Python and Java.

Scripting within Java Applications

Most software developers consider Java to be a large systems programming language, a serious language for serious tasks. Python, in this way of thinking, comes from the realm of scripting languages such as Perl and Tcl. As such, many developers typically don't respect Python because scripting languages are, of course, created for people who cannot program. You know this isn't true, but the split between programming and scripting languages remains, even though Python gracefully bridges this gap.

Despite this lack of respect, scripting languages have proven to be very productive and are widely deployed as critical parts of companies small and large (and huge and gigantic, too). You can generally accomplish a lot more in less time with less code using a scripting language than you can with a system programming language like Java.

With Java applications, scripting comes in handy for a number of reasons, including the following:

❏   The scripting language can act as a macro extension language. Much like Visual Basic for Applications (VBA) enables you to script extensions to Microsoft Office; you can enable users to extend your own Java applications using Jython. Complex text editors such as jEdit (www.jedit.org) enable you to write scripts in this fashion.

❏   Use Jython to speed the development of Java applications. As a high-level scripting language, you can take advantage of the productivity features of Python when compared to the complexity of Java.

❏   Explore and debug running systems. Using the interactive capabilities of Jython, you can explore a running Java application. You can execute code as needed, all interactively. You already take this for granted in Python, but it's something that Java just doesn't have.

❏ You can script unit tests much faster than writing them in Java. Many organizations feel uncomfortable about introducing scripting languages, especially open-source ones. Using scripts for testing provides the advantages of scripting without shipping the scripting packages in your application or using the scripting packages in production.

❏ In addition to unit testing, scripting works well for full system testing. A system-testing package called the Grinder uses Jython to create test scripts. See `http://grinder.sourceforge.net/` for more on the Grinder.

❏ You can create one-off scripts for tasks such as data migration. If you just need to update a particular row in a database table, or fix a particular setting, you can do this a lot quicker using a script.

❏ You can extend enterprise applications without having to redeploy the application. This is very handy if you need to keep your system running all the time. In addition, developers can extend the functionality of the system without requiring the security permissions to redeploy the application.

Jython, being based on the very popular Python language, enables you to do all of this, and more.

Comparing Python Implementations

The traditional Python implementation, often called C-Python, compiles and runs on a huge number of platforms, including Windows, Linux, and Mac OS X. C-Python is written in the C programming language. The Java-based Jython compiles and runs on any platform that supports the Java virtual machine. This includes Windows, Linux, and Mac OS X. In this respect, the two Python implementations are very similar in how cross-platform they are.

However, Jython isn't up to date compared to the traditional C-Python implementation. The C-Python implementation sports new features that have not yet been written in the Java implementation. That's understandable, because C-Python is where the first development happens, and the Jython developers have to re-implement every Python feature in Java.

Which foundation you use for Python scripting, C-Python or Jython, doesn't really matter, because both support the Python language. In general, you'll want to use C-Python unless you have a specific need to work within the Java platform. In that case, obviously, use Jython!

The rest of this chapter shows you how to do just that.

Installing Jython

As an open-source project, Jython doesn't follow a set release cycle. Your best bet is to download the latest release from `www.jython.org`. Then, follow the instructions on the website for installing Jython.

Older versions of Jython, such as 2.1, are packaged as a Java `.class` file of the installation program. When you run the file, the program will install Jython on your hard disk. Newer pre-release versions come packaged as a Zip file. Unzip the file to install Jython.

After installing Jython, you should have two executable scripts in the Jython installation directory: `jython` and `jythonc`, similar in purpose to `python` and `pythonc`. The `jythonc` script, though, is intended to compile Python code into Java `.class` files. You need to have the `jython` script in your path, or available so you can call it.

On Windows, you will get DOS batch files `jython.bat` and `jythonc.bat`.

Running Jython

The `jython` script runs the Jython interpreter. The `jythonc` script runs the Jython compiler, which compiles Jython code to Java `.class` files. In most cases, you'll want to use the `jython` script to run Jython.

Running Jython Interactively

Like Python with the `python` command, Jython supports an interactive mode. In this mode, you can enter Jython expressions, as you'd expect. Jython expressions are for the most part the same as Python expressions, except you can call upon the Java integration as well.

To run the Jython interpreter, run the `jython` script (`jython.bat` on Windows).

Try It Out	Running the Jython Interpreter

Run the interpreter and then enter in the following expressions:

```
>>> 44 / 11
4
>>> 324 / 101
3
>>> 324.0 / 101.0
3.207920792079208
>>> 324.0 / 101
3.207920792079208
>>> import sys
>>> sys.executable
'C:\\jython2.5.0\\jython.bat'
>>> sys.platform
'java1.6.0_03'
>>> sys.version_info
(2, 5, 0, 'final', 0)
>>>
```

How It Works

As shown in this example, the Jython interpreter appears and acts like the Python interpreter. This is just what you'd expect, because Jython is supposed to be an implementation of the Python language on top of the Java platform.

Math operations should work mostly the same as with Python. ("Mostly the same" means that some floating-point operations will create slightly different results.) Also note that this example is using Jython 2.5.

On the same platform, you can see the differences when you run the same expressions with the python command, the C-Python interpreter. For example:

```
>>> 44 / 11
4
>>> 324 / 101
3
>>> 324.0 /101.0
3.2079207920792081
>>> 324.0 / 101
3.2079207920792081
>>> import sys
>>> sys.executable
'C:\\Python31\\pythonw.exe'
>>> sys.platform
win32
>>> sys.version_info
(3, 1, 0, 'final', 0)
>>>
```

Running Jython Scripts

As with the python command, jython can also run your scripts, as shown in the following example.

Try It Out   Running a Python Script

Enter the following simple script and name the file jysys.py:

```
import sys

print('Python sys.path:')
print(sys.path)

print('Script arguments are:')
print(sys.argv)
```

When you run this script with jython, you should see output like the following:

```
Python sys.path:
['', ' C:\\jython2.5.0\\LIB','__classpath__', '__pyclasspath__/',
'C:\\jython2.5.0\\LIB\\site-packages']
Script arguments are:
['']
```

The file paths will differ depending on where you installed Jython.

How It Works

The `sys.path` property holds a very small number of directories, especially when compared to the standard C-Python distribution. For example, you can run the same script with the `python` interpreter as shown here:

```
Python sys.path:
['C:\\Python31\\Lib\\idlelib', C:\\Windows\\system32\\python31.zip',
 'C:\\Python31\\DLLs', 'C:\\Python31\\lib', 'C:\\Python31\\lib\\plat-win',
 'C:\\Python31', 'C:\\Python31\\lib\\site-packages']
```

In this case, note the larger number of directories in the `sys.path` property.

These examples were run on Windows Vista. The paths will differ on other operating systems.

You'll notice that the startup time for `jython`-run scripts is a lot longer than that for `python`-run scripts. That's because of the longer time required to start the `java` command and load the entire Java environment.

Controlling the jython Script

The `jython` script itself merely acts as a simple wrapper over the `java` command. The `jython` script sets up the Java classpath and the `python.home` property. You can also pass arguments to the `jython` script to control how Jython runs, as well as arguments to your own scripts. The basic format of the `jython` command line follows:

```
jython jython_arguments what_to_run arguments_for_your_script
```

The *jython_arguments* can be `-S` to not imply an import site when Jython starts and `-i` to run Jython in interactive mode. You can also pass Java system properties, which will be passed in turn to your Jython scripts. The format for this is `-Dproperty=value`, which is a standard Java format for passing property settings on the command line.

You'll normally pass the name of a Jython script file as the *what_to_run* section of the command. The `jython` script offers more options, though, as shown in the following table.

Option	Specifies
`filename.py`	Runs the given Jython script file.
`-c command`	Runs the command string passed on the command line.
`-jar jarfile`	Runs the Jython script __run__.py in the given jar file.
`-`	Reads the commands to run from stdin. This allows you to pipe Jython commands to the Jython interpreter.

You can choose any one of the methods listed in the table.

In addition, the *arguments_for_your_script* are whatever arguments you want to pass to your script. These will be set into `sys.argv[1:]` as you'd expect.

Making Executable Commands

Note that because `jython` is a script, you cannot use the traditional shebang comment line to run Jython scripts. (On UNIX and Linux systems, that's the line that starts with the hash, or sharp, symbol and then has the exclamation point, or "bang," so you get "sh(arp)-bang." This tells the system that this command is how the program you're running should be invoked.) For example, with a Python script, you can add the following line as the first line of your script:

```
#! /usr/bin/python
```

If your script has this line as the first line, and if the script is marked with execute permissions, the operating system can run your Python scripts as commands.

> *Note that Windows is the lone exception. Windows uses a different means to associate files ending in* `.py` *with the Python interpreter.*

With Jython scripts, though, you cannot use this mechanism. That's because many operating systems require that the program that runs a script be a binary executable program, not a script itself. That is, you have a script you wrote that you want run by the `jython` script.

To get around this problem, use the `env` command. For example, change the shebang line to the following:

```
#! /usr/bin/env jython
```

For this line to work, the `jython` script must be in your path.

Try It Out **Making an Executable Script**

Insert the following lines into the previous `jysys.py` script. The new line is marked in bold.

```
#! /usr/bin/env jython

import sys

print('Python sys.path:')
print(sys.path)

print('Script arguments are:')
print(sys.argv)
```

Save this new file under the name `jysys`, with no extension. Use the `chmod` command to add execute permissions, as shown in the following example:

```
$ chmod a+x jysys
```

You can then run this new command:

```
$ ./jysys 1 2 3 4
Python sys.path:
['', ' C:\\jython2.5.0\\LIB','__classpath__', '__pyclasspath__/',
'C:\\jython2.5.0\\LIB\\site-packages']
Script arguments are:
['./jysys', '1', '2', '3', '4']
```

How It Works

The shebang comment works the same for Jython as it does for all other scripting languages. The only quirk with Jython is that the `jython` command itself is a script that calls the `java` command.

In the next section, you learn more about how the `java` command runs Jython scripts.

Running Jython on Your Own

You don't have to use the `jython` script to execute Jython scripts. You can call the Jython interpreter just like any other Java application.

The `jython` script itself is fairly short. Most of the action occurs by calling the `java` command with a large set of arguments, split up here for clarity:

```
java -Dpython.home="C:\\jython2.5.0\" \
    -classpath C:\\jython2.5.0\\jython.jar:$CLASSPATH" \
    "org.python.util.jython" "$@"
```

The paths will differ depending on where you installed Jython. The `jython` script, though, does nothing more than run the class `org.python.util.jython` from the jar file `jython.jar` (which the script adds to the Java classpath). The script also sets the `python.home` system property, necessary for Jython to find support files.

To run Jython on your own, you just need to ensure that `jython.jar` is in the classpath. Execute an interpreter class, such as `org.python.util.jython`. In addition, you need to set the `python.home` system property.

You also need to ensure that Jython is properly installed on every system that will run your Jython scripts.

Packaging Jython-Based Applications

Jython isn't a standalone system. It requires a large number of Python scripts that form the Jython library. Thus, you need to include the `jython.jar` file as well as the Jython library files. At a bare minimum, you need the `Lib` and `cachedir` directories that come with the Jython distribution.

Jython needs to be able to write to the `cachedir` *directory.*

Java applications, especially Java EE enterprise applications, usually don't require a set of files stored in a known location on the file system. If you include Jython, though, you'll need to package the files, too.

Up to now, you can see that Jython really is Python, albeit an older version of Python. The real advantage of Jython lies in the capability to integrate Python with Java, offering you the best of both worlds.

Integrating Java and Jython

The advantage of Jython comes into play when you integrate the Jython interpreter into your Java applications. With this combination, you can get the best of both the scripting world and the rich set of Java APIs. Jython enables you to instantiate objects from Java classes and treat these objects as Python objects. You can even extend Java classes within Jython scripts.

Jython actively tries to map Java data types to Python types and vice versa. This mapping isn't always complete because the feature is under active development. For the most part, however, you'll find that Jython does the right thing when converting to and from Python types.

Using Java Classes in Jython

In general, treat Java classes as Python classes in your scripts. Jython uses the Python syntax for importing Java classes. Just think of Java packages as a combination of Python modules and classes. For example, to import `java.util.Map` into a Jython script, use the following code:

```
from java.util import Map
```

Note how this looks just like a Python import. You can try this out in your own scripts, as shown in the following example.

Try It Out   **Calling on Java Classes**

Enter the following script and name the file `jystring.py`:

```
import sys
from java.lang import StringBuffer, System


sb = StringBuffer(100)    # Preallocate StringBuffer size for performance.

sb.append('The platform is: ')
sb.append(sys.platform)  # Python property
sb.append(' time for an omelette.')

sb.append('\n')      # Newline
sb.append('Home directory: ')
sb.append( System.getProperty('user.home') )
```

```
sb.append('\n')        # Newline
sb.append('Some numbers: ')
sb.append(44.1)
sb.append(', ')
sb.append(42)
sb.append(' ')

# Try appending a tuple.
tup=( 'Red', 'Green', 'Blue', 255, 204, 127 )
sb.append(tup)

print(sb.toString())


# Treat java.util.Properties as Python dictionary.
props = System.getProperties()

print('User home directory:', props['user.home'])
```

When you run this script, you should see the following output:

```
$ jython jystring.py
The platform is: java1.6.0_03 time for an omelette.
Home directory: /Users/James
Some numbers: 44.1, 42 ('Red', 'Green', 'Blue', 255, 204, 127)
User home directory: /Users/James
```

Note that your output will depend on where your home directory is located and which version of Java you have installed.

How It Works

This script imports the Java `StringBuffer` class and then calls a specific constructor for the class:

```
from java.lang import StringBuffer


sb = StringBuffer(100)
```

The Jython interpreter converts the value `100` from a Python number to a Java number.

In Java programs, you do not need to import classes from the `java.lang` *package. In Jython, import every Java class you use.*

You can pass literal text strings as well as Python properties to the `StringBuffer` append method:

```
sb.append('The platform is: ')
sb.append(sys.platform)   # Python property
```

This example shows that Jython will correctly convert Python properties into Java strings for use in a Java object. You can also pass the data returned by a Java method:

```
sb.append( System.getProperty('user.home') )
```

In this case, the `System.getProperty` method returns an object of the Java type `Object`. Again, Jython properly handles this case, as Jython does with numbers:

```
sb.append(44.1)
```

```
sb.append(42)
```

You can even append a Python tuple:

```
tup=( 'Red', 'Green', 'Blue', 255, 204, 127 )
sb.append(tup)
```

The preceding example shows that Jython does the right thing when converting the tuple to a Java text string.

In addition to converting Python types to Java types, Jython works the other way as well. You can pass a Java `String` object, returned by the `toString` method, to the Python `print` function:

```
print sb.toString()
```

This shows how you can treat Java strings as Python strings. You can also treat Java hash maps and hash tables as Python dictionaries, as shown in the following example:

```
props = System.getProperties()
```

```
print('User home directory:', props['user.home'])
```

The Java `System.getProperties` method returns an object of type `java.util.Properties`, which Jython automatically converts into a Python dictionary.

Data type conversions as shown by this example are just what you'd expect when you integrate Java and Python. Jython does a lot of work under the covers, though. Java has a class hierarchy, as does Python. A large part of Jython is an attempt to merge these two large hierarchies together. Ultimately, you tend to get the best of both worlds.

For example, Python has the ability to pass named properties to a constructor. This proves especially useful when you work with APIs such as Swing for user interfaces. The Swing API has many, many classes. Each class supports a large number of properties on objects. Working with Java alone, you can call only the constructors that have been defined, and the parameters must be placed in a particular order. With Python, though, you can pass named properties to the object's constructor and set as many properties as needed within one call.

The following example shows this technique.

Try It Out   Creating a User Interface from Jython

Enter the following script and name the file jyswing.py:

```
from java.lang import System
from javax.swing import JFrame, JButton, JLabel
from java.awt import BorderLayout

# Exit application
def exitApp(event):
    System.exit(0)

# Use a tuple for size
frame = JFrame(size=(500,100))

# Use a tuple for RGB color values.
frame.background = 127,255,127


button = JButton(label='Push to Exit', actionPerformed=exitApp)
label = JLabel(text='A Pythonic Swing Application',
    horizontalAlignment=JLabel.CENTER)

frame.contentPane.add(label, BorderLayout.CENTER)
frame.contentPane.add(button, BorderLayout.WEST)

frame.setVisible(1)
```

When you run this script, you should see a window like the one shown in Figure 21-1.

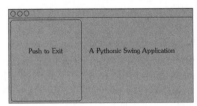

Figure 21-1

Click the button to exit the application.

How It Works

This script shows how you can use Jython with the complex Swing APIs. Although this example is almost all calls to Java APIs, it is much shorter than the corresponding Java program would be. That's because of the handy built-in features that come with Python, such as support for tuples and setting properties.

The script starts by importing several classes in the AWT and Swing APIs. The JFrame class acts as a top-level window in an application. You can create a JFrame widget with the following statements:

```
frame = JFrame(size=(500,100))
```

The `size` property on a `JFrame` widget is an instance of another Java class, `java.awt.Dimension`. In this example, you can make a `Dimension` object from a tuple and then pass this object to set the size property of the `JFrame`.

This shows how Jython can make working with the Swing APIs palatable. Creating a user interface with Swing usually involves a lot of tedious coding. Jython greatly reduces this effort.

You can use the Python support for tuples and the Jython-provided integration with Java APIs to set colors as well:

```
frame.background = 127,255,127
```

This sets the background color to a light green.

This example uses an 8-bit color definition, with values of zero to 255 for each of the red, green, and blue components of the color. Therefore, 255 means that the green value is set to all on, and the red and blue values are set to half on.

Jython makes it easy to create interactive widgets on the screen. For example, the following code creates a `JButton` widget and sets the widget to call the function `exitApp` when the user clicks the button:

```
def exitApp(event):
    System.exit(0)

button = JButton(label='Push to Exit', actionPerformed=exitApp)
```

In this case, the `exitApp` function calls the Java method `System.exit` to exit the Java engine and therefore quit the application. Jython enables you to set Java properties to Python functions, such as `exitApp` in this example. In Java, you would need to make a class that implements the methods in the `java.awt.event.ActionListener` interface and then pass in an instance of this class as the action listener for the `JButton`. The Jython approach makes this much easier.

The example also creates a `JLabel` widget, which displays a text message, an image, or both. The `jyswing.py` script sets the horizontal alignment so that the text displays in the center of the widget's bounds:

```
label = JLabel(text='A Pythonic Swing Application',
    horizontalAlignment=JLabel.CENTER)
```

In this example, the value `JLabel.CENTER` is a constant on the `JLabel` class.

In Java terms, `JLabel.CENTER` is a public static final value on the class.

Once created, you need to place the widgets within a container. In the example script, you need to place the `JButton` and `JLabel` widgets in the enclosing `JFrame` widget, as shown by the following code:

```
frame.contentPane.add(label, BorderLayout.CENTER)
frame.contentPane.add(button, BorderLayout.WEST)
```

In Swing applications, you add widgets to the content pane of the `JFrame`, not directly to the JFrame itself.

Finally, the script makes the `JFrame` widget visible:

```
frame.setVisible(1)
```

Note that the Java `setVisible` method expects a Java Boolean value, but using the Python True would be flagged as a syntax error because the Java `boolean` objects aren't 0 and 1, as they are in Python; they're a class that gets used sometimes, whereas 0 and 1 get used at other times in Java. This is one area where Python data types and constants are not yet mapped to their Java equivalents.

Accessing Databases from Jython

JDBC, or Java Database Connectivity, provides a set of APIs to access databases in a consistent manner. Most, but not all, differences between databases can be ignored when working with JDBC.

Python has a set of database APIs as well, as described in Chapter 14. A large difference between the Python APIs and the Java APIs is that the Java JDBC drivers are almost all written entirely in Java. Furthermore, almost all JDBC drivers are written by the database vendors. Most Python DB drivers, such as the ones for Oracle, are written in C with a Python layer on top. Most are written by third parties, and not by the database vendors. The Java JDBC drivers, then, can be used on any platform that supports Java. The Python DB drivers, though, must be recompiled on each platform and may not work on all systems that support Python.

With Jython, the `zxJDBC` package provides a Python DB-compliant driver that works with any JDBC driver. That is, `zxJDBC` bridges between the Python and Java database APIs, enabling your Jython scripts to take advantage of the many available JDBC drivers and to use the simpler Python DB APIs.

When working with JDBC drivers, you need the value of four properties to describe the connection to the database, shown in the following table.

Property	Holds
JDBC URL	Description of the connection to the database in a format defined by the driver.
User name	Name of a user who has access rights to the database.
Password	Password of the user. This is the password to the database, not to an operating system.
Driver	Name of the Java class that provides the JDBC driver.

You need to gather these four values for any database connection you need to set up using JDBC. The `zxJDBC` module requires these same values. To connect to a database using the `zxJDBC` driver, you can use code like the following:

```
from com.ziclix.python.sql import zxJDBC

url='jdbc:hsqldb:hsql://localhost/xdb'
user='sa'
pw=''
```

```
driver='org.hsqldb.jdbcDriver'

db = zxJDBC.connect(url, user, pw, driver)
```

The values shown here for the JDBC connection come from the default values for the HSqlDB database, covered in the section "Setting Up a Database," later in the chapter.

Working with the Python DB API

Once you have a connection, you can use the same techniques shown in Chapter 14. The zxJDBC module provides a DB 2.0 API-compliant driver. (Well, mostly compliant.) For example, you can create a database table using the following code:

```
cursor = db.cursor()

cursor.execute("""
create table user
    (userid integer,
    username varchar,
    firstname varchar,
    lastname varchar,
    phone varchar)
""")

cursor.execute("""create index userid on user (userid)""")
```

After creating a table, you can insert rows using code like the following:

```
cursor.execute("""
insert into user (userid,username,firstname,lastname,phone)
values (4,'scientist','Hopeton','Brown','555-5552')
""")
```

Be sure to commit any modifications to the database:

```
db.commit()
```

You can query data using code like the following:

```
cursor.execute("select * from user")
for row in cursor.fetchall():
    print(row)

cursor.close()
```

See Chapter 14 for more on the Python DB APIs.

Setting Up a Database

If you already have a database that includes a JDBC driver, you can use that database. For example, Oracle, SQL Server, Informix, and DB2 all provide JDBC drivers for the respective databases.

If you have a database set up, try to use it. If you have no database, a handy choice is HSqlDB. HSqlDB provides a small, fast database. A primary advantage of HSqlDB is that because it is written in Java, you can run it on any platform that runs Java.

> *See* https://sourceforge.net/projects/hsqldb/files/hsqldb/hsqldb_1_8_1/ *for more on the* HSqlDB *database. You can download this open-source free package from this site.*

You'll find installing HSqlDB quite simple. Just unzip the file you download and then change to the new hsqldb directory. To run the database in server mode, with the default parameters, use a command like the following:

```
$ java -cp ./lib/hsqldb.jar org.hsqldb.Server -database.0 mydb -dbname.0 xdb
[Server@922804]: [Thread[main,5,main]]: checkRunning(false) entered
[Server@922804]: [Thread[main,5,main]]: checkRunning(false) exited
[Server@922804]: Startup sequence initiated from main() method
[Server@922804]: Loaded properties from
[/Users/James/writing/python/chap22/server.properties]
[Server@922804]: Initiating startup sequence...
[Server@922804]: Server socket opened successfully in 160 ms.
[Server@922804]: Database [index=0, id=0, db=file:mydb, alias=xdb]
opened successfully in 1168 ms.
[Server@922804]: Startup sequence completed in 1444 ms.
[Server@922804]: 2009-08-22 20:09:33.417 HSQLDB server 1.8.1 is online
[Server@922804]: To close normally, connect and execute SHUTDOWN SQL
[Server@922804]: From command line, use [Ctrl]+[C] to abort abruptly
```

You can stop this database by typing Ctrl+C in the shell window where you started HSqlDB. You now have a database that you can connect to using the default properties shown in the following table.

Property	Value
JDBC URL	driver.jdbc:hsqldb:hsql://localhost/xdb
User name	sa
Password	' ' (two single quotes, an *empty string*)
Driver	org.hsqldb.jdbcDriver

Working with JDBC drivers requires that you add the JDBC jar or jars to the Java classpath. The `jython` script doesn't handle this case, so you need to modify the script. For example, to use the HSqlDB database, modify the script to add the `hsqldb.jar` file:

```
#!/bin/sh
################################################################################
# This file generated by Jython installer

java -Dpython.home=" C:\\jython2.5.0" \
    -classpath \
    "C:\\jython2.5.0jython.jar:$CLASSPATH:./hsqldb.jar" \
    "org.python.util.jython" "$@"
```

The bold text shows the additional jar file. This example assumes that the file `hsqldb.jar` will be located in the current directory. That may not be true. You may need to enter the full path to this jar file.

To pull all this together, try the following example, built using the HSqlDB database.

Try It Out   Create Tables

Enter the following script and name the file `jyjdbc.py`:

```python
from com.ziclix.python.sql import zxJDBC


# Modify as needed for your database.
url='jdbc:hsqldb:hsql://localhost/xdb'
user='sa'
pw=''
driver='org.hsqldb.jdbcDriver'


db = zxJDBC.connect(url, user, pw, driver)

cursor = db.cursor()

cursor.execute("""
create table user
    (userid integer,
    username varchar,
    firstname varchar,
    lastname varchar,
    phone varchar)
""")

cursor.execute("""create index userid on user (userid)""")
```

```
cursor.execute("""
insert into user (userid,username,firstname,lastname,phone)
values (1,'ericfj','Eric','Foster-Johnson','555-5555')
""")

cursor.execute("""
insert into user (userid,username,firstname,lastname,phone)
values (2,'tosh','Peter','Tosh','555-5554')
""")

cursor.execute("""
insert into user (userid,username,firstname,lastname,phone)
values (3,'bob','Bob','Marley','555-5553')
""")

cursor.execute("""
insert into user (userid,username,firstname,lastname,phone)
values (4,'scientist','Hopeton','Brown','555-5552')
""")

db.commit()


cursor.execute("select * from user")
for row in cursor.fetchall():
    print(row)


cursor.close()
db.close()
```

When you run this script, you will see output like the following:

```
$ jython jyjdbc.py
(1, 'ericfj', 'Eric', 'Foster-Johnson', '555-5555')
(2, 'tosh', 'Peter', 'Tosh', '555-5554')
(3, 'bob', 'Bob', 'Marley', '555-5553')
(4, 'scientist', 'Hopeton', 'Brown', '555-5552')
```

How It Works

This script is almost the same as the `createtable.py` script from Chapter 14. This shows the freedom the Python DB API gives you, because you are not tied to any one database vendor. Other than the code to establish the connection to the database, you'll find your database code can work with multiple databases.

To establish a connection to HSqlDB, you can use code like the following:

```
from com.ziclix.python.sql import zxJDBC

# Modify as needed for your database.
url='jdbc:hsqldb:hsql://localhost/xdb'
user='sa'
```

```
pw=''
driver='org.hsqldb.jdbcDriver'

db = zxJDBC.connect(url, user, pw, driver)
```

This code uses the default connection properties for HSqlDB for simplicity. In a real-world scenario, you never want to use the default user name and password. Always change the database administrator user and password. Furthermore, HSqlDB defaults to having no password for the administration user, sa (short for system administrator). This, of course, provides a large hole in security.

The following code, taken from Chapter 14, creates a new database table:

```
cursor = db.cursor()

cursor.execute("""
create table user
    (userid integer,
    username varchar,
    firstname varchar,
    lastname varchar,
    phone varchar)
""")

cursor.execute("""create index userid on user (userid)""")
```

Though SQL does not standardize the commands necessary to create databases and database tables, this table sports a rather simple layout, so you should be able to use these commands with most SQL databases.

The code to insert rows also comes from Chapter 14, as does the query code. In this, it is Python, with the DB 2.0 API, that provides this commonality. The Jython zxJDBC module follows this API. For example, the code to query all the rows from the user table follows:

```
cursor = db.cursor()

cursor.execute("select * from user")
for row in cursor.fetchall():
    print(row)

cursor.close()
```

The zxJDBC module, though, extends the Python DB API with the concept of static and dynamic cursors. (This ties to the concepts in the java.sql.ResultSet API.) In the Python standard API, you should be able to access the rowcount attribute of the Cursor object. In Java, a ResultSet may not know the full row count for a given query, which may have returned potentially millions of rows. Instead, the JDBC standard allows the ResultSet to fetch data as needed, buffering in the manner determined by the database vendor or JDBC driver vendor. Most Java code that reads database data will then iterate over each row provided by the ResultSet.

To support the Python standard, the zxJDBC module needs to read in all the rows to properly determine the rowcount value. This could use a huge amount of memory for the results of a query on a large table. This is what the zxJDBC documentation calls a *static* database cursor.

To avoid the problem of using too much memory, you have the option of getting a dynamic cursor. A *dynamic* cursor does not set the rowcount value. Instead, a dynamic cursor fetches data as needed. If you request a dynamic cursor, you cannot access the rowcount value, but, you can iterate through the cursor to process all the rows returned by the query. To request a dynamic cursor, pass a 1 to the cursor method:

```
cursor = db.cursor(1)
```

Dynamic cursors are not part of the Python DB API, so code using this technique will not work with any DB driver except for the Jython zxJDBC driver.

Database access is essential if you are writing enterprise applications. You also need it to be able to create robust web applications.

Writing Java EE Servlets in Jython

Most Java development revolves around enterprise applications. To help (or hinder, depending on your view), Java defines a set of standards called Java EE, or Java Platform Enterprise Edition. The Java EE standards define an application server and the APIs such a server must support. Organizations can then choose application servers from different vendors, such as WebSphere from IBM, WebLogic from Bea, JBoss from the JBoss Group, and Tomcat from the Apache Jakarta project. Java developers write enterprise applications that are hosted on one of these application servers.

A *servlet* is defined as a small server-based application. The term servlet is a play on applet, which describes a small application. Because in the Java arena applets always run on the client, the server equivalent needed a new name, hence servlet. Each servlet provides a small piece of the overall application, although the term small may be defined differently than you are used to, because most enterprise applications are *huge*.

Within a Java EE application server, servlets are passive request-response applications. The client, typically a web browser such as Internet Explorer or Firefox, sends a request to the application server. The application server passes the request to a servlet. The servlet then generates the response, usually an HTML document that the server sends back to the client. In virtually all cases, the HTML document sent back to the client is created dynamically. For example, in a web ordering system, the HTML document sent back may be the results of a search or the current prices for a set of products.

The benefit of writing servlets is that Java EE provides a well-defined API for writing your servlets, and multiple vendors support this API. Contrast this situation with the Python situation where you can choose from many Python Web APIs, but you won't find anywhere near the vendor support you find in the Java EE arena.

With Jython, you can write Java servlets in Python, simplifying your work immensely. To do so, though, you need an application server that supports servlets.

Setting Up an Application Server

If you already have a Java EE application server, use that. If not, try Tomcat. Tomcat, from the Apache Jakarta project, provides a free open-source servlet engine (called a *servlet container* in Java EE-speak).

Download Tomcat from `http://jakarta.apache.org/tomcat/`. To install, unzip the file you downloaded in a directory. You should see a Tomcat directory based on the version you downloaded, such as `jakarta-tomcat-6.0.20`. Change to this directory. In this directory, you will see a number of files and subdirectories. The two most important subdirectories are `bin`, which contains scripts for starting and stopping Tomcat, and `webapps`, which is where you need to place any Jython scripts you create (in a special subdirectory covered in the next section).

To run Tomcat, change to the `bin` subdirectory and run the `startup.sh` script (`startup.bat` on Windows). For example:

```
$ ./startup.sh
Using CATALINA_BASE:    /Users/jamesp/servers/jakarta-tomcat-5.0.28
Using CATALINA_HOME:    /Users/jamesp/servers/jakarta-tomcat-5.0.28
Using CATALINA_TMPDIR:  /Users/jamesp/servers/jakarta-tomcat-5.0.28/temp
Using JAVA_HOME:        /Library/Java/Home
```

You must ensure that the JAVA_HOME environment variable is set, or Tomcat will not start. To verify Tomcat is running, enter the following URL into a web browser: `http://localhost:8080/`. You should see a document like the one shown in Figure 21-2.

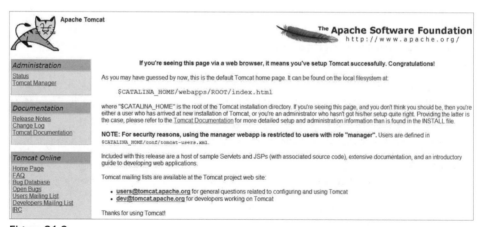

Figure 21-2

Once you have an application server such as Tomcat running, the next step is to deploy an application — in this case, a special Python servlet called `PyServlet`.

Adding the PyServlet to an Application Server

Jython includes a class called `org.python.util.PyServlet` that acts as a front end for Python scripts. The `PyServlet` class will load Python scripts, compile these scripts, and then execute the scripts as if they were Java servlets (which, in fact, they are, as shown in the following section "Extending HttpServlet").

To make all this magic work, though, you need to create a bona fide Java EE web application. Luckily, this isn't that hard. Change to the directory in which you installed Tomcat and run the following commands, which create directories:

```
$ cd webapps
$ mkdir jython
```

This command creates a directory under webapps with the name of jython. This means the name of your web application will be jython:

```
$ mkdir webapps/jython/WEB-INF
```

This command creates a WEB-INF directory. The name and case of this directory are very important. In Java EE, the WEB-INF directory contains the libraries and deployment information about your web application:

```
$ mkdir webapps/jython/WEB-INF/lib
```

The lib subdirectory holds any jar files needed by your web application. You need one jar file, jython. jar, from the Jython installation. Copy this file into the webapps/jython/WEB-INF/lib directory that you just created.

Next, you need to modify a file named web.xml in the tomcat 6.0/conf directory. Enter the following text into web.xml:

```
<web-app>
  <servlet>
    <servlet-name>PyServlet</servlet-name>
    <servlet-class>
      org.python.util.PyServlet
    </servlet-class>
    <load-on-startup>1</load-on-startup>
    <init-param>
      <param-name>python.home</param-name>
      <param-value>c:\jython-2.5</param-value>
    </init-param>
    <init-param>
      <param-name>python.path</param-name>
      <param-value>
        c:\jython-2.5\lib\site-packages
      </param-value>
    </init-param>
  </servlet>
  <servlet-mapping>
    <servlet-name>PyServlet</servlet-name>
    <url-pattern>*.py</url-pattern>
  </servlet-mapping>
</web-app>
```

Change the path in bold to the full path to the directory in which you installed Jython.

Next, you need to create some Python scripts within the new web application.

This chapter presents a whirlwind introduction to Java EE, a frightfully complicated subject. If you're not familiar with Java EE, you can look up more information in a Java EE tutorial, or visit http://java.sun.com/javaee/.

Extending HttpServlet

The `javax.servlet.http.HttpServlet` class provides the main hook for Java EE developers to create servlets. Java EE developers extend `HttpServlet` with their own classes to create servlets. With the `PyServlet` class, you can do the same with Jython. With Jython, however, this task becomes a lot easier than writing everything in Java.

Use the following code as a template for creating your servlet classes in Jython:

```
from javax.servlet.http import HttpServlet

class verify(HttpServlet):
  def doGet(self, request, response):
    self.handleRequest(request, response)

  def doPost(self, request, response):
    self.handleRequest(request, response)

  def handleRequest(self, request, response):
    response.setContentType('text/html');
    out = response.getOutputStream()
    print >>out, "YOUR OUTPUT HERE"
    out.close()
    return
```

Your classes must inherit from `HttpServlet`. In addition, you need to create two methods, `doGet` and `doPost`, as described in the following table.

Method	Usage
DoGet	Handles GET requests, which place all the parameters on the URL
DoPost	Handles POST requests, usually with data from a form

In virtually all cases, you want both methods to perform the same task. Any differences in these methods only serve to make your web applications harder to debug. Therefore, write another method that both can call, such as the `handleRequest` method shown in the previous template.

In your `handleRequest` method, you must perform a number of tasks. All must be correct, or you will see an error or no output. These tasks include the following:

❑ Set the proper content type on the response object. In most cases, this will be text/html.

❑ Get an output stream from the response object.

503

❑   Write all output to this stream.

❑   Close the stream.

The following example shows how to create a real servlet from this code template.

Try It Out   **Writing a Python Servlet**

Enter the following and save the file as `webapps/jython/verify.py`:

```
import sys
from javax.servlet.http import HttpServlet

class verify(HttpServlet):
  def doGet(self, request, response):
    self.handleRequest(request, response)

  def doPost(self, request, response):
    self.handleRequest(request, response)

  def handleRequest(self, request, response):
    response.setContentType("text/html");

    out = response.getOutputStream()
    print >>out, "<html><head><title>"
    print >>out, "Jython Is Running</title></head>"
    print >>out, "<body>"
    print >>out, "<h2>Jython is running</h2>"
    print >>out, "<p>"
    print >>out, "Version:", sys.version, " verified."
    print >>out, "</p>"
    print >>out, "</body></html>"
    out.close()
    return
```

You must place this file within your web application in the `webapps/jython` directory. After saving the file, stop and then restart Tomcat to ensure that your changes are recognized.

Test your new servlet by entering the following URL in your web browser: `http://localhost:8080/jython/verify.py`. Figure 21-3 shows the results you should see.

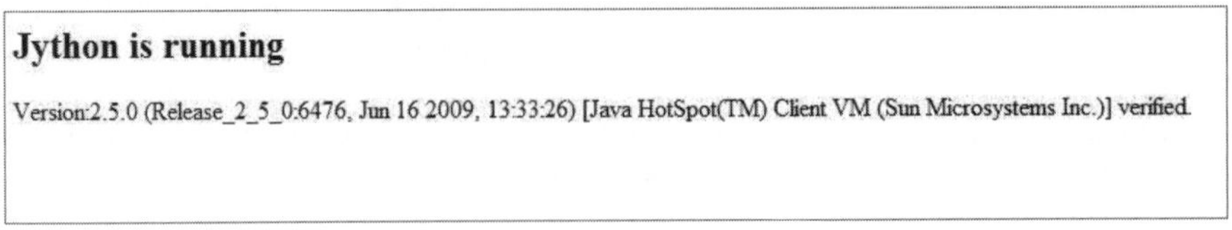

Jython is running

Version:2.5.0 (Release_2_5_0:6476, Jun 16 2009, 13:33:26) [Java HotSpot(TM) Client VM (Sun Microsystems Inc.)] verified.

Figure 21-3

How It Works

Three crucial parts make this servlet work:

❑ Tomcat must be running.

❑ You must have the correct directory structure and contents for your web application.

❑ The URL must name a Python script in your web application. The script must have a `.py` file name extension.

In the `web.xml` file modified previously, you registered the servlet `PyServlet` for all files ending with a `.py` extension. Thus, with a URL of `http://localhost:8080/jython/verify.py`, Tomcat will direct the servlet `PyServlet` to handle the request. The following table splits this URL into its important components.

Component	Usage
`http://`	Defines the protocol used, HTTP in this case.
`jython`	This is the name of your web application (it could be any name you wanted). With Tomcat, there must be a `webapps/jython` directory.
`verify.py`	Name of a file within the web application. The .py extension signals that the `PyServlet` should handle the request.

The actual servlet class itself is rather small and follows the code template shown previously. The main action of this servlet occurs in the `handleRequest` method:

```
def handleRequest(self, request, response):
    response.setContentType("text/html");

    out = response.getOutputStream()
    print >>out, "<html><head><title>"
    print >>out, "Jython Is Running</title></head>"
    print >>out, "<body>"
    print >>out, "<h2>Jython is running</h2>"
    print >>out, "<p>"
    print >>out, "Version:", sys.version, " verified."
    print >>out, "</p>"
    print >>out, "</body></html>"
    out.close()
    return
```

Most of this method is a number of `print` statements, sending HTML-formatted text to the output stream. Compare this method for creating web applications with the technologies introduced in Chapter 20.

As you can see, you really need to know both Python and Java, at least a bit, to be able to work with Jython. That's why choosing the right tools is important.

Choosing Tools for Jython

Because Jython focuses on working with Java as well as Python, the best choice for Jython tools comes from the Java arena. The following tools can help with your Jython work:

❑ The jEdit text editor (www.jedit.org/) includes a number of plugins for working with Python. The editor highlights Python syntax, whether you are working with Python or Jython. In addition, the JythonInterpreter plugin includes an embedded Jython interpreter. See http://plugins.jedit.org/ for more on jEdit plugins.

❑ The Eclipse Integrated Development Environment, or IDE, provides excellent support for Java development. In addition, one Eclipse plugins stand out for Jython usage: PyDev, for working with Python, at http://sourceforge.net/projects/pydev/; download Eclipse itself from www.eclipse.org.

Whichever tools you choose, all you really need is a text editor and a command-line shell. Furthermore, the tools you choose can help with testing, especially testing Java applications.

Testing from Jython

Because Jython provides an interactive environment on top of the Java platform, Jython makes an excellent tool for interactive testing. The following examples show how you can use Jython's interactive mode to explore your Java environment.

Try It Out　　Exploring Your Environment with Jython

Enter the following commands to see information on the Java `Map` interface:

```
$ jython
Jython 2.1 on java1.4.2_05 (JIT: null)
Type "copyright", "credits" or "license" for more information.
>>> from java.util import Map
>>> print(dir(Map))
['__Entry__','__class__','__contains__','__delattr__','__delitem__','__doc__',
'__eq__','__getattribute__','__getitem__','__hash__','__init__','__iter__',
'__len__','__ne__','__new__','__reduce__','__reduce_ex__','__repr__',
'__setattr__','__setitem__','__str__','class','clear','containsKey',
'containsValue','empty','entrySet','equals','get','getClass','hashCode',
'isEmpty','keySet','notify','notifyAll','put','putAll','remove','size',
'toString','values','wait']
>>>
```

How It Works

This example uses the Python `dir` function to display information about the `java.util.Map` interface in Java. You can list information on any Java class or interface.

As another example, you can examine the JNDI, or Java Naming and Directory Interface, classes such as InitialContext, as shown here:

```
$ jython
Jython 2.1 on java1.4.2_05 (JIT: null)
Type "copyright", "credits" or "license" for more information.
>>> from  javax.naming import InitialContext
>>> print(dir(InitialContext))
['APPLET', 'AUTHORITATIVE', 'BATCHSIZE', 'DNS_URL', 'INITIAL_CONTEXT_
FACTORY', '
LANGUAGE', 'OBJECT_FACTORIES', 'PROVIDER_URL', 'REFERRAL', 'SECURITY_
AUTHENTICAT
ION', 'SECURITY_CREDENTIALS', 'SECURITY_PRINCIPAL', 'SECURITY_PROTOCOL',
'STATE_
FACTORIES', 'URL_PKG_PREFIXES', '__class__', '__delattr__', '__doc__', '__eq__',
 '__getattribute__', '__hash__', '__init__', '__ne__', '__new__', '__reduce__',
'__reduce_ex__', '__repr__', '__setattr__', '__str__', 'addToEnvironment', 'bind
', 'class', 'close', 'composeName', 'createSubcontext', 'destroySubcontext', 'do
Lookup', 'environment', 'equals', 'getClass', 'getEnvironment', 'getNameInNamesp
ace', 'getNameParser', 'hashCode', 'list', 'listBindings', 'lookup', 'lookupLink
', 'nameInNamespace', 'notify', 'notifyAll', 'rebind', 'removeFromEnvironment',
'rename', 'toString', 'unbind', 'wait']
>>>
```

Combine this technique with an embedded Jython interpreter to examine a running application. See the following section, "Embedding the Jython Interpreter," for more information on embedding the Jython interpreter.

In addition to using Jython's interactive mode, you can also write tests in Jython.

Many organizations shy away from open-source software such as Jython. You may find it much easier to introduce Jython just for writing tests, something that will not go into production. Once your organization gains some experience with Jython, people may be more receptive to using Jython in more areas.

The examples so far have all used the jython script to run Jython scripts, except for the PyServlet servlet example. With the PyServlet class, you have a Java class with the Jython interpreter. You can add the Jython interpreter to your own classes as well.

Embedding the Jython Interpreter

By embedding the Jython interpreter in your own Java classes, you can run scripts from within your application, gaining control over the complete environment. That's important because few Java applications run from the command line.

You can find the Jython interpreter in the class `org.python.util.PythonInterpreter`.

You can use code like the following to initialize the Jython interpreter:

```
Properties props = new Properties();

props.put("python.home", pythonHome);

PythonInterpreter.initialize(
    System.getProperties(),
    props,
    new String[0]);

interp = new PythonInterpreter(null, new PySystemState());
```

Note that this is Java code, not Python code.

You must set the `python.home` system property.

Calling Jython Scripts from Java

After initializing the interpreter, you can execute a Jython script with a call to the `execfile` method. For example:

```
interp.execfile(fileName);
```

You need to pass the full name of the file to execute. You can see this in action with the following example.

Try It Out   **Embedding Jython**

Enter the following Java program and name the file `JyScriptRunner.java`:

```java
package jython;


import java.util.Properties;

import org.python.util.PythonInterpreter;
import org.python.core.PySystemState;


/**
 * Runs Jython scripts.
 */
public class JyScriptRunner {

    private PythonInterpreter interp;
```

```java
    /**
     * Initializes the Jython interpreter.
     */
    public void initialize(String pythonHome) {
        Properties props = new Properties();

        props.put("python.home", pythonHome);

        PythonInterpreter.initialize(
            System.getProperties(),
            props,
            new String[0]);

        interp = new PythonInterpreter(null, new PySystemState());

    }

    /**
     * Runs the given script.
     */
    public void run(String fileName) {
        interp.execfile(fileName);
    }


    public static void main(String[] args) {
        String fileName = args[0];

        JyScriptRunner runner = new JyScriptRunner();

        String pythonHome = System.getProperty("python.home");

        runner.initialize(pythonHome);

        runner.run(fileName);
    }
}
```

Because this is a Java program, you will need to compile the program with a command like the following:

```
$ javac -classpath ./jython.jar JyScriptRunner.java
```

When you run this Java program, you will see output like the following:

```
$ java -cp ./jython.jar:. \
    -Dpython.home="c:/jython2.5" \
    jython.JyScriptRunner jystring.py
The platform is: java1.6.0_03 time for an omelette.
Home directory: c:/jython2.5
Some numbers: 44.1, 42 ('Red', 'Green', 'Blue', 255, 204, 127)
User home directory: /Users/jamesp
```

This example runs the `jystring.py` example script. You will need to change the `-Dpython.home` setting to the location where you have installed Jython. Also change the `./jython.jar` to the location where you have the file `jython.jar`.

How It Works

The program expects the caller to pass two values: the setting for the `python.home` system property and the name of a script to execute. You must have the `jython.jar` located in the current directory (or change the command line to refer to the location of your `jython.jar` file).

The `JyScriptRunner` class includes a `main` method, called when you run the program. The `main` method extracts the system property `python.home` as well as the file name from the command line (held in the `args` array). The `main` method then instantiates a `JyScriptRunner` object.

The `main` method initializes the `JyScriptRunner` object and then calls the `run` method to execute the script. Any errors encountered in the Jython script will result in exceptions that stop the program.

This is probably about the simplest Jython interpreter you can create. In your applications, you'll likely want to control the location of the Python home directory, perhaps placing this under an application directory.

Handling Differences between C-Python and Jython

The C-Python platform creates a complete environment based on Python standards and conventions. Jython, on the other hand, tries to create a complete Python environment based on the Java platform. Because of this, there are bound to be differences between the two implementations. These differences are compounded when you mix Java code into your Jython scripts.

The Jython interpreter will attempt to convert Python types into the necessary Java types to call methods on Java classes. Wherever possible, the Jython interpreter tries to do the right thing, so in most cases you don't have to pay much attention to these type conversions. If you are unsure which Python types are needed to call a particular Java method, look at the types listed in the following table.

Python Type	Java Type
None	Null
Integer (any non-zero value is true)	Boolean
Integer	short, int, long, byte
String	byte[], char[], java.lang.String
String of length 1	Char
Float	float, double

Python Type	Java Type
String	java.lang.Object, converted to java.lang.String
Any	java.lang.Object
Class or JavaClass	java.lang.Class
Array (must contain objects of a given type or subclasses of the given type)	Array of a particular type

For example, if a Java method expects a type of `java.lang.Object` and you pass a Python `String`, Jython will convert the Python `String` to a `java.langString` object. Jython will pass any other Python object type unchanged.

You can do many more things with Jython beyond the introduction provided in this chapter. For example, you can create classes in Jython and then call those classes from Java. (Look in the source code for the `PyServlet` class to see an example of this.)

Summary

Jython provides the capability to combine the scripting power of Python with the enterprise infrastructure of Java. Using Jython can make you a much more productive Java developer, especially in organizations where Python is not accepted but Java is.

Jython allows you to do the following:

❑ Run Python scripts from the Java platform. Because these scripts differ from Python, they are usually called *Jython* scripts.

❑ Call on Java code and classes from within your scripts. This enables you to take advantage of the rich set of Java libraries from Jython scripts.

❑ Create user interfaces with the Java Swing API. Jython scripts can use Python's tuple and property support to dramatically reduce the code required to create Swing-based user interfaces.

❑ Access any database that provides a JDBC driver. The `zxJDBC` driver bridges from the Python DB API to the Java JDBC API.

❑ Run Jython scripts as Java servlets by using the handy `PyServlet` class from your Java EE web applications.

❑ Interactively gather information on Java classes and execute methods on those classes. This is very useful for testing.

❑ Embed the Jython interpreter in your own Java classes, enabling you to execute Jython scripts and expressions from your Java code.

This chapter wraps up this tutorial on Python. The appendixes provide answers to the chapter exercises and links to Python resources.

Exercises

1. If Python is so cool, why in the world would anyone ever use another programming language such as Java, C++, C#, Basic, or Perl?

2. The Jython interpreter is written in what programming language? The `python` command is written in what programming language?

3. When you package a Jython-based application for running on another system, what do you need to include?

4. Can you use the Python DB driver modules, such as those described in Chapter 14, in your Jython scripts?

5. Write a Jython script that creates a window with a red background using the Swing API.

Part IV
Appendices

Answers to the Exercises

Chapter 1

1. In the Python shell, type the string, `"Rock a by baby,\n\ton the tree top,\t\` `when the wind blows\n\t\t\t the cradle will drop."` Feel free to experiment with the number of `\n` and `\t` escape sequences to see how this affects what gets displayed on your screen. You can even try changing their placement. What do you think you are likely to see?

2. In the Python shell, use the same string indicated in Exercise 1, but this time, display it using the `print()` function. Once more, try differing the number of `\n` and `\t` escape sequences. How do you think it will differ?

Exercise 1 Solution

```
'Rock a by baby,\n\ton the tree top,\t\twhen the wind blows\n\t\t\t the
cradle will drop.'
```

Because this is not being printed, the special characters (those preceded with a backslash) are not translated into a form that will be displayed differently from how you typed them.

Exercise 2 Solution

```
Rock a by baby,
        on the tree top,                    when the wind blows
                        the cradle will drop.
```

When they are printed, "\n" and "\t" produce a newline and a tab character, respectively. When the `print()` function is used, it will render them into special characters that don't appear on your keyboard, and your screen will display them.

Chapter 2

Do the following first three exercises in Notepad and save the results in a file called `ch2_exercises.py`. You can run it from within Python by opening the file and choosing Run Module.

1. In the Python shell, multiply 5 and 10. Try this with other numbers as well.

2. Print every number from 6 through 14 in base 8.

3. Print every number from 9 through 19 in base 16.

4. Try to elicit other errors from the Python interpreter — for instance, by deliberately misspelling `print` as `pinrt`. Notice how as you work on a file in the Python shell, it will display `print` differently than it does `pinrt`.

Exercise 1 Solution

```
>>> 5 * 10
50
```

Exercise 2 Solution

```
>>> print("%o" % 6)
6
>>> print("%o" % 7)
7
>>> print("%o" % 8)
10
>>> print("%o" % 9)
11
>>> print("%o" % 10)
12
>>> print("%o" % 11)
13
>>> print("%o" % 12)
14
>>> print("%o" % 13)
15
>>> print("%o" % 14)
16
```

Exercise 3 Solution

```
>>> print("%x" % 9)
9
>>> print("%x" % 10)
a
>>> print("%x" % 11)
b
>>> print("%x" % 12)
c
```

```
>>> print("%x" % 13)
d
>>> print("%x" % 14)
e
>>> print("%x" % 15)
f
>>> print("%x" % 16)
10
>>> print("%x" % 17)
11
>>> print("%x" % 18)
12
>>> print("%x" % 19)
13
```

Exercise 4 Solution

When an unknown function is called, Python doesn't know that the name that's been typed in is necessarily a function at all, so it just flags a general syntax error:

```
>>> pintr("%x" & x)
  File "<input>", line 1
    Pintr("%x" & x)

SyntaxError: invalid syntax
```

You'll notice, however, that Python Shell will display print in bold when you type it. This is because print is a special word to Python, and Python Shell knows this. You can help yourself catch errors by paying attention to how the editor reacts to what you've typed.

Chapter 3

Perform all of the following in the Python shell:

1. Create a list called `dairy_section` with four elements from the dairy section of a supermarket.

2. Print a string with the first and last elements of the `dairy_section` list.

3. Create a tuple called `milk_expiration` with three elements: the month, day, and year of the expiration date on the nearest carton of milk.

4. Print the values in the `milk_expiration` tuple in a string that reads "This milk carton will expire on 12/10/2005."

5. Create an empty dictionary called `milk_carton`. Add the following key/value pairs. You can make up the values or use a real milk carton:

   ❑   `expiration_date`: Set it to the `milk_expiration` tuple.

   ❑   `fl_oz`: Set it to the size of the milk carton on which you are basing this.

❑   `Cost`: Set this to the cost of the carton of milk.

❑   `brand_name`: Set this to the name of the brand of milk you're using.

6.   Print out the values of all of the elements of the `milk_carton` using the values in the dictionary, and not, for instance, using the data in the `milk_expiration` tuple.

7.   Show how to calculate the cost of six cartons of milk based on the cost of `milk_carton`.

8.   Create a list called cheeses. List all of the cheeses you can think of. Append this list to the `dairy_section` list, and look at the contents of `dairy_section`. Then remove the list of cheeses from the array.

9.   How do you count the number of cheeses in the cheese list?

10.   Print out the first five letters of the name of your first cheese.

Exercise 1 Solution

```
>>> dairy_section = ["milk", "cottage cheese", "butter", "yogurt"]
```

Exercise 2 Solution

```
>>> print("First: %s and Last %s" % (dairy_section[0], dairy_section[1]))
First: milk and Last cottage cheese
```

Exercise 3 Solution

```
>>> milk_expiration = (10, 10, 2009)
```

Exercise 4 Solution

```
>>> print("This milk will expire on %d/%d/%d" % (milk_expiration[0],
milk_expiration[1], milk_expiration[2]))
This milk will expire in 10/10/2009
```

Exercise 5 Solution

```
>>> milk_carton = {}
>>> milk_carton["expiration_date"] = milk_expiration
>>> milk_carton["fl_oz"] = 32
>>> milk_carton["cost"] = 1.50
>>> milk_carton["brand_name"] = "Milk"
```

Exercise 6 Solution

```
>>> print("The expiration date is %d/%d/%d" %
(milk_carton["expiration_date"][0], milk_carton["expiration_date"][1],
milk_carton["expiration_date"][2]))
The expiration date is 10/10/2009
```

Exercise 7 Solution

```
>>> print("The cost for 6 cartons of milk is %.02f" % (6*
milk_carton["cost"]))
The cost for 6 cartons of milk is 9.00
```

Exercise 8 Solution

```
>>> cheeses = ["cheddar", "american", "mozzarella"]
>>> dairy_section.append(cheeses)
>>> dairy_section
['milk', 'cottage cheese', 'butter', 'yogurt', ['cheddar', 'american',
'mozzarella']]
>>> dairy_section.pop()
['cheddar', 'american', 'mozzarella']
```

Exercise 9 Solution

```
>>> len(dairy_section)
4
```

Exercise 10 Solution

```
>>> print("Part of some cheese is %s" % cheeses[0][0:5])
Part of some cheese is chedd
```

Chapter 4

Perform all of the following in the codeEditor Python shell:

1. Using a series of `if ... :` statements, evaluate whether the numbers from 0 through 4 are True or False by creating five separate tests.

2. Create a test using a single `if ... :` statement that will tell you whether a value is between 0 and 9 inclusively (that is, the number can be 0 or 9 as well as all of the numbers in between, not just 1–8) and print a message if it's a success. Test it.

3. Using `if ... :`,`elif ,...:` and `else:`, create a test for whether a value referred to by a name is in the first two elements of a sequence. Use the `if ... :` to test for the first element of the list; use `elif ... :` to test the second value referenced in the sequence; and use the `else:` clause to print a message indicating whether the element being searched for is not in the list.

4. Create a dictionary containing foods in an imaginary refrigerator, using the name `fridge`. The name of the food will be the key, and the corresponding value of each food item should be a string that describes the food. Then create a name that refers to a string containing the name of a food. Call the name `food_sought`. Modify the test from Exercise 3 to be a simple `if ... :` test (no `elif ... :` or `else:` will be needed here) for each key and value in the refrigerator using a `for ... in ... :` loop to test every key contained in the fridge. If a match is found, print a message that contains the key and the value and then use break to leave the loop. Use an

else ... : statement at the end of the for loop to print a message for cases in which the element wasn't found.

5. Modify Exercise 3 to use a `while` ... : loop by creating a separate list called `fridge_list` that will contain the values given by `fridge.keys`. As well, use a variable named, `current_key` that will refer to the value of the current element in the loop that will be obtained by the method `fridge_list.pop`. Remember to place `fridge_list.pop` as the last line of the `while` ... : loop so that the repetition will end normally. Use the same `else:` statement at the end of the while loop as the one used at the end of Exercise 3.

6. Query the fridge dictionary created in Exercise 3 for a key that is not present, and elicit an error. In cases like this, the `KeyError` can be used as a shortcut to determining whether or not the value you want is in the list. Modify the solution to Exercise 3 so that instead of using a `for ... in ... :` a `try:` block is used.

Exercise 1 Solution

The key theme here is that 0 is `False`, and everything else is considered not `False`, which is the same as `True`:

```
>>> if 0:
...     print("0 is True")
...
>>> if 1:
...     print("1 is True")
...
1 is True
>>> if 2:
...     print("2 is True")
...
2 is True
>>> if 3:
...     print("3 is True")
...
3 is True
>>> if 4:
...     print("4 is True")
...
4 is True
>>> if 5:
...     print("5 is True")
...
5 is True
```

Exercise 2 Solution

```
>>> number = 3
>>> if number >= 0 and number <= 9:
...     print("The number is between 0 and 9: %d" % number)
...
The number is between 0 and 9: 3
```

Exercise 3 Solution

```
>>> test_tuple = ("this", "little", "piggie", "went", "to", "market")
>>> search_string = "toes"
>>> if test_tuple[0] == search_string:
...     print("The first element matches")
... elif test_tuple[1] == search_string:
...     print("the second element matches")
... else:
...     print("%s wasn't found in the first two elements" % search_string)
...
toes wasn't found in the first two elements
```

Exercise 4 Solution

```
>>> fridge = {"butter":"Dairy spread", "peanut butter":"non-dairy spread",
"cola":"fizzy water"}
>>> food_sought = "chicken"
>>> for food_key in fridge.keys():
...     if food_key == food_sought:
...         print("Found what I was looking for: %s is %s" % (food_sought,
fridge[food_key]))
...         break
... else:
...     print("%s wasn't found in the fridge" % food_sought)
...
chicken wasn't found in the fridge
```

Exercise 5 Solution

```
>>> fridge = {"butter":"Dairy spread", "peanut butter":"non-dairy spread",
"cola":"fizzy water"}
>>> fridge_list = fridge.keys()
>>> current_key = fridge_list.pop()
>>> food_sought = "cola"
>>> while len(fridge_list) > 0:
...     if current_key == food_sought:
...         print("Found what I was looking for: %s is %s" % (food_sought,
fridge[current_key]))
...         break
...     current_key = fridge_list.pop()
... else:
...     print("%s wasn't found in the fridge" % food_sought)
...
Found what I was looking for: cola is fizzy water
```

Exercise 6 Solution

```
>>> fridge = {"butter":"Dairy spread", "peanut butter":"non-dairy spread",
"cola":"fizzy water"}
>>> food_sought = "chocolate milk"
>>> try:
```

```
...          fridge[food_sought]
... except KeyError:
...          print("%s wasn't found in the fridge" % food_sought)
... else:
...          print("Found what I was looking for: %s is %s" % (food_sought,
fridge[food_key]))
...
chocolate milk wasn't found in the fridge
```

Chapter 5

1. Write a function called `do_plus` that accepts two parameters and adds them together with the "+" operation.

2. Add *type checking* to confirm that the type of the parameters is either an integer or a string. If the parameters aren't good, `raise` a TypeError.

3. This one is a lot of work, so feel free to take it in pieces. In Chapter 4, a loop was written to make an omelet. It did everything from looking up ingredients to removing them from the fridge and making the omelet. Using this loop as a model, alter the `make_omelet` function by making a function called `make_omelet_q3`. It should change `make_omelet` in the following ways to get it to more closely resemble a real kitchen:

    a. The fridge should be passed into the new `make_omelet` as its first parameter. The fridge's type should be checked to ensure it is a dictionary.

    b. Add a function to check the fridge and subtract the ingredients to be used. Call this function `remove_from_fridge`. This function should first check to see if enough ingredients are in the fridge to make the omelet, and only after it has checked that should it remove those items to make the omelet. Use the error type LookupError as the type of error to raise.

    c. The items removed from the fridge should be placed into a dictionary and returned by the `remove_from_fridge` function to be assigned to a name that will be passed to `make_food`. After all, you don't want to remove food if it's not going to be used.

    d. Rather than a cheese omelet, choose a different default omelet to make. Add the ingredients for this omelet to the `get_omelet_ingredients` function.

4. Alter `make_omelet` to raise a TypeError error in the `get_omelet_ingredients` function if a salmonella omelet is ordered. Try ordering a salmonella omelet and follow the resulting stack trace.

Exercise 1 Solution

```
def do_plus(first, second):
    return first + second
```

Exercise 2 Solution

```
def do_plus(first, second):
    for param in (first, second):
```

```
        if (type(param) != type("")) and (type(param) != type(1)):
            raise TypeError("This function needs a string or an integer")
    return first + second
```

Exercise 3 Solution

```
# Part 1 - fridge has to go before the omelet_type.  omelet_type is an
# optional parameter with a default parameter, so it has to go at the end.
# This can be used with a fridge such as:
# f = {'eggs':12, 'mozzarella cheese':6,
#      'milk':20, 'roast red pepper':4, 'mushrooms':3}
# or other ingredients, as you like.
def make_omelet_q3(fridge, omelet_type = "mozzarella"):
    """This will make an omelet.  You can either pass in a dictionary
    that contains all of the ingredients for your omelet, or provide
    a string to select a type of omelet this function already knows
    about
    The default omelet is a mozzarella omelet"""

    def get_omelet_ingredients(omelet_name):
        """This contains a dictionary of omelet names that can be produced,
and their ingredients"""
        # All of our omelets need eggs and milk
        ingredients = {"eggs":2, "milk":1}
        if omelet_name == "cheese":
            ingredients["cheddar"] = 2
        elif omelet_name == "western":
            ingredients["jack_cheese"] = 2
            ingredients["ham"]         = 1
            ingredients["pepper"]      = 1
            ingredients["onion"]       = 1
        elif omelet_name == "greek":
            ingredients["feta_cheese"] = 2
            ingredients["spinach"]     = 2
        # Part 5
        elif omelet_name == "mozzarella":
            ingredients["mozzarella cheese"] = 2
            ingredients["roast red pepper"] = 2
            ingredients["mushrooms"] = 1
        else:
            print("That's not on the menu, sorry!")
            return None
        return ingredients
    # part 2 - this version will use the fridge that is available
    # to the make_omelet function.
    def remove_from_fridge(needed):
        recipe_ingredients = {}
        # First check to ensure we have enough
        for ingredient in needed.keys():
            if needed[ingredient] > fridge[ingredient]:
                raise LookupError("not enough %s to continue" % ingredient)
        # Then transfer the ingredients.
        for ingredient in needed.keys():
            # Remove it from the fridge
```

```
                fridge[ingredient] = fridge[ingredient] - needed[ingredient]
                # and add it to the dictionary that will be returned
                recipe_ingredients[ingredient] = needed[ingredient]
            # Part 3 - recipe_ingredients now has all the needed ingredients
            return recipe_ingredients

    # Part 1, continued - check the type of the fridge
    if type(fridge) != type({}):
        raise TypeError("The fridge isn't a dictionary!")

    if type(omelet_type) == type({}):
        print("omelet_type is a dictionary with ingredients")
        return make_food(omelet_type, "omelet")
    elif type(omelet_type) == type(""):
        needed_ingredients = get_omelet_ingredients(omelet_type)
        omelet_ingredients = remove_from_fridge(needed_ingredients)
        return make_food(omelet_ingredients, omelet_type)
    else:
        print("I don't think I can make this kind of omelet: %s" %
        omelet_type)
```

Exercise 4 Solution

The get_omelet_ingredient from make_omelet_q3 could be changed to look like the following:

```
def get_omelet_ingredients(omelet_name):
    """This contains a dictionary of omelet names that can be produced,
and their ingredients"""
    # All of our omelets need eggs and milk
    ingredients = {"eggs":2, "milk":1}
    if omelet_name == "cheese":
        ingredients["cheddar"] = 2
    elif omelet_name == "western":
        ingredients["jack_cheese"] = 2
        ingredients["ham"]         = 1
        ingredients["pepper"]      = 1
        ingredients["onion"]       = 1
    elif omelet_name == "greek":
        ingredients["feta_cheese"] = 2
        ingredients["spinach"]     = 2
    # Part 5
    elif omelet_name == "mozzarella ":
        ingredients["mozzarella  cheese"] = 2
        ingredients["roast red pepper"] = 2
        ingredients["mushrooms"] = 1
    # Question 4 - we don' want anyone hurt in our kitchen!
    elif omelet_name == "salmonella":
        raise TypeError("We run a clean kitchen, you won't get this
        here")
    else:
        print("That's not on the menu, sorry!")
        return None
    return ingredients
```

When run, the error raised by trying to get the salmonella omelet will result in the following error:

```
>>> make_omelet_q3({'mozzarella cheese':5, 'eggs':5, 'milk':4, 'roast red
pepper':6, 'mushrooms':4}, "salmonella")
Traceback (most recent call last):
  File "<stdin>", line 1, in ?
  File "ch5.py", line 209, in make_omelet_q3
    omelet_ingredients = get_omelet_ingredients(omelet_type)
  File "ch5.py", line 179, in get_omelet_ingredients
    raise TypeError, "We run a clean kitchen, you won't get this here"
TypeError: We run a clean kitchen, you won't get this here
>>>
```

Note that depending on the contents of your ch5.py file, the exact line numbers shown in your stack trace will be different from those shown here.

Next, you can see that line 179 is where get_omelet_ingredients raised the error (though it may be at a different line in your own file).

If you called this from within another function, the stack would be one layer deeper, and you would see the information relating to that extra layer as well.

Chapter 6

Each of the following exercises builds on the exercises that preceded it:

1. Add an option to the Omelet class's mix method to turn off the creation messages by adding a parameter that defaults to True, indicating that the "mixing . . ." messages should be printed.

2. Create a method in class Omelet that uses the new mix method from Exercise 1. Called quick_cook, it should take three parameters: the kind of omelet, the quantity wanted, and the Fridge that they'll come from. The quick_cook method should do everything required instead of requiring three method calls, but it should use all of the existing methods to accomplish this, including the modified mix method with the mix messages turned off.

3. For each of the methods in the Omelet class that do not have a docstring, create one. In each docstring, make sure you include the name of the method, the parameters that the method takes, what the method does, what value or values it returns upon success, and what it returns when it encounters an error (or what exceptions it raises, if any).

4. View the docstrings that you've created by creating an Omelet object.

5. Create a Recipe class that can be called by the Omelet class to get ingredients. The Recipe class should have the ingredient lists of the same omelets that are already included in the Omelet class. You can include other foods if you like. The Recipe class should include methods to retrieve a recipe, get(recipe_name), a method to add a recipe as well as name it, and create (recipe_name, ingredients), where the ingredients are a dictionary with the same format as the one already used in the Fridge and Omelet classes.

6. Alter the __init__ method of Omelet so that it accepts a Recipe class. To do this, you can do the following:

   a. Create a name, self.recipe, that each Omelet object will have.

   b. The only part of the Omelet class that stores recipes is the internal method __known_kinds. Alter __known_kinds to use the recipes by calling self.recipe.get() with the kind of omelet that's desired.

   c. Alter the set_new_kind method so that it places the new recipe into self.recipe and then calls set_kind to set the current omelet to the kind just added to the recipe.

   d. In addition, modify __known_kinds to use the recipe method's get method to find out the ingredients of an omelet.

7. Try using all of the new classes and methods to determine whether you understand them.

Exercise 1 Solution

```
def mix(self, display_progress = True):
    """
    mix(display_progress = True) - Once the ingredients have been
obtained from a fridge call this
    to prepare the ingredients.  If display_progress is False do not print
messages.
    """
    for ingredient in self.from_fridge.keys():
        if display_progress == True:
            print("Mixing %d %s for the %s omelet" %
(self.from_fridge[ingredient], ingredient, self.kind))
        self.mixed = True
```

Exercise 2 Solution

Note that you could go one step further and make the quiet setting of the mix function an option, too. As it is, this doesn't give you much feedback about what's going on, so when you test it, it may look a bit strange.

```
def quick_cook(self, fridge, kind = "cheese", quantity = 1):
    """
    quick_cook(fridge, kind = "cheese", quantity = 1) -
        performs all the cooking steps needed.  Turns out an omelet fast.
    """

    self.set_kind(kind)
    self.get_ingredients(fridge)
    self.mix(False)
    self.make()
```

Exercise 3 Solution

Just the documentation, not the functions, would look something like this. However, you should find a format that suits you.

Note that only undocumented functions will have their docstrings described here.

```
class Omelet:
    """This class creates an omelet object.  An omelet can be in one of
    two states: ingredients, or cooked.
    An omelet object has the following interfaces:
    get_kind() - returns a string with the type of omelet
    set_kind(kind) - sets the omelet to be the type named
    set_new_kind(kind, ingredients) - lets you create an omelet
    mix() - gets called after all the ingredients are gathered from the
fridge
    cook() - cooks the omelet
    """
    def __init__(self, kind="cheese"):
        """__init__(self, kind="cheese")
        This initializes the Omelet class to default to a cheese omelet.
        Other methods
        """
        self.set_kind(kind)
        return

    def set_kind(self, kind):
        """
        set_kind(self, kind) - changes the kind of omelet that will be
created
            if the type of omelet requested is not known then return False
        """
    def get_kind(self):
        """
        get_kind() - returns the kind of omelet that this object is making
        """

    def set_kind(self, kind):
        """
        set_kind(self, kind) - changes the kind of omelet that will be created
            if the type of omelet requested is not known then return False
        """

    def set_new_kind(self, name, ingredients):
        """
        set_new_kind(name, ingredients) - create a new type of omelet that is
            called "name" and that has the ingredients listed in "ingredients"
        """
    def __known_kinds(self, kind):
        """
        __known_kinds(kind) - checks for the ingredients of "kind" and returns
them
```

```
                    returns False if the omelet is unknown.
          """

    def get_ingredients(self, fridge):
        """
        get_ingredients(fridge) - takes food out of the fridge provided
        """

    def mix(self):
        """
        mix() - Once the ingredients have been obtained from a fridge call this
        to prepare the ingredients.
        """
    def make(self):
        """
        make() - once the ingredients are mixed, this cooks them
        """
```

Exercise 4 Solution

```
>>> print("%s" % o.__doc__)
This class creates an omelet object.  An omelet can be in one of
    two states: ingredients, or cooked.
    An omelet object has the following interfaces:
    get_kind() - returns a string with the type of omelet
    set_kind(kind) - sets the omelet to be the type named
    set_new_kind(kind, ingredients) - lets you create an omelet
    mix() - gets called after all the ingredients are gathered from the fridge
    cook() - cooks the omelet

>>> print("%s" % o.set_new_kind.__doc__)

        set_new_kind(name, ingredients) - create a new type of omelet that is
            called "name" and that has the ingredients listed in "ingredients"
```

You can display the remaining docstrings in the same way.

Exercise 5 Solution

```
    class Recipe:
        """
        This class houses recipes for use by the Omelet class
        """

        def __init__(self):
            self.set_default_recipes()
            return

        def set_default_recipes(self):
            self.recipes = {"cheese" : {"eggs":2, "milk":1, "cheese":1},
                            "mushroom" : {"eggs":2, "milk":1, "cheese":1,
"mushroom":2},

                            "onion" : {"eggs":2, "milk":1, "cheese":1, "onion":1}}
```

```
    def get(self, name):
        """
        get(name) - returns a dictionary that contains the ingredients needed
to
        make the omelet in name.
        When name isn't known, returns False
        """
        try:
            recipe = self.recipes[name]
            return recipe
        except KeyError:
            return False

    def create(self, name, ingredients):
        """
        create(name, ingredients) - adds the omelet named "name" with the
ingredients
        "ingredients" which is a dictionary.
        """

        self.recipes[name] = ingredients
```

Exercise 6 Solution

Note that the order of parameters in the interface for the class has now been changed, because you can't place a required argument after a parameter that has an optional default value.

When you test this, remember that you now create an omelet with a recipe as its mandatory parameter.

```
    def __init__(self, recipes, kind="cheese"):
        """__init__(self, recipes, kind="cheese")
        This initializes the omelet class to default to a cheese omelet.

        """
        self.recipes = recipes
        self.set_kind(kind)

        return

    def set_new_kind(self, name, ingredients):
        """
        set_new_kind(name, ingredients) - create a new type of omelet that is
            called "name" and that has the ingredients listed in "ingredients"
        """
        self.recipes.create(name, ingredients)
        self.set_kind(name)
        return
    def __known_kinds(self, kind):
        """
        __known_kinds(kind) - checks for the ingredients of "kind" and returns
them
            returns False if the omelet is unknown.
        """
        return self.recipes.get(kind)
```

Chapter 7

Moving code to modules and packages is straightforward and doesn't necessarily require any changes to the code to work, which is part of the ease of using Python.

In these exercises, the focus is on testing your modules, because testing is essentially writing small programs for an automated task.

1. Write a test for the Foods.Recipe module that creates a recipe object with a list of foods, and then verifies that the keys and values provided are all present and match up. Write the test so that it is run only when Recipe.py is called directly, and not when it is imported.

2. Write a test for the Foods.Fridge module that will add items to the Fridge, and exercise all of its interfaces except get_ingredients, which requires an Omelet object.

3. Experiment with these tests. Run them directly from the command line. If you've typed them correctly, no errors should come up. Try introducing errors to elicit error messages from your tests.

Exercise 1 Solution

Remember that you're not a regular user of your class when you write tests. You should feel free to access internal names if you need to!

```
if __name__ == '__main__':
    r = Recipe()
    if r.recipes != {"cheese" : {"eggs":2, "milk":1, "cheese":1},
                     "mushroom" : {"eggs":2, "milk":1, "cheese":1,
"mushroom":2},
                     "onion" : {"eggs":2, "milk":1, "cheese":1, "onion":1}}:
        Print("Failed: the default recipes is not the correct list")
    cheese_omelet = r.get("cheese")
    if cheese_omelet != {"eggs":2, "milk":1, "cheese":1}:
        print("Failed: the ingredients for a cheese omelet are wrong")
    western_ingredients = {"eggs":2, "milk":1, "cheese":1, "ham":1,
    "peppers":1, "onion":1}
    r.create("western", western_ingredients)
    if r.get("western") != western_ingredients:
        print("Failed to set the ingredients for the western")
    else:
        print("Succeeded in getting the ingredients for the western.")
```

Exercise 2 Solution

At the end of the Fridge module, insert the following code. Note the comment about changing the add_many function to return True. If you don't do that, add_many will return None, and this test will always fail!

```
if __name__ == '__main__':
    f = Fridge({"eggs":10, "soda":9, "nutella":2})
    if f.has("eggs") != True:
```

```
        print("Failed test f.has('eggs')")
    else:
        print("Passed test f.has('eggs')")
    if f.has("eggs", 5) != True:
        print("Failed test f.has('eggs', 5)")
    else:
        print("Passed test f.has('eggs', 5)")
    if f.has_various({"eggs":4, "soda":2, "nutella":1}) != True:
        print('Failed test f.has_various({"eggs":4, "soda":2, "nutella"1})')
    else:
        print('Passed test f.has_various({"eggs":4, "soda":2, "nutella"1})')
    # Check to see that when we add items, that the number of items in the
fridge
    # is increased!
    item_count = f.items["eggs"]
    if f.add_one("eggs") != True:
        print('Failed test f.add_one("eggs")')
    else:
        print('Passed test f.add_one("eggs")')
    if f.items["eggs"] != (item_count + 1):
        print('Failed f.add_one() did not add one')
    else:
        print('Passed f.add_one() added one')
    item_count = {}
    item_count["eggs"] = f.items["eggs"]
    item_count["soda"] = f.items["soda"]
    # Note that the following means you have to change add_many to return True!
    if f.add_many({"eggs":3,"soda":3}) != True:
        print('Failed test f.add_many({"eggs":3,"soda":3})')
    else:
        print('Passed test f.add_many({"eggs":3,"soda":3})')
    if f.items["eggs"] != (item_count["eggs"] + 3):
        print("Failed f.add_many did not add eggs")
    else:
        print("Passed f.add_many added eggs")
    if f.items["soda"] != (item_count["soda"] + 3):
        print("Failed f.add_many did not add soda")
    else:
        print("Passed f.add_many added soda")

    item_count = f.items["eggs"]
    if f.get_one("eggs") != True:
        print('Failed test f.get_one("eggs")')
    else:
        print('Passed test f.get_one("eggs")')
    if f.items["eggs"] != (item_count - 1):
        print("Failed get_one did not remove an eggs")
    else:
        print("Passed get_one removed an eggs")

    item_count = {}
    item_count["eggs"] = f.items["eggs"]
    item_count["soda"] = f.items["soda"]
    eats = f.get_many({"eggs":3, "soda":3})
    if eats["eggs"] != 3 or eats["soda"] != 3:
```

```
        print('Failed test f.get_many({"eggs":3, "soda":3})')
    else:
        print('Passed test f.get_many({"eggs":3, "soda":3})')

    if f.items["eggs"] != (item_count["eggs"] - 3):
        print("Failed get many didn't remove eggs")
    else:
        print("Passed get many removed eggs")

    if f.items["soda"] != (item_count["soda"] - 3):
        print("Failed get many didn't remove soda")
    else:
        print("Passed get many removed soda")
```

Exercise 3 Solution

You can try to generate errors by mistyping the name of a key in one place in the module, and confirming that this results in your tests warning you. If you find situations that these tests don't catch, you should try to code a test for that situation so it can't ever catch you.

Chapter 8

   1.   Create another version of the (nonrecursive) `print_dir` function that lists all subdirectory names first, followed by names of files in the directory. Names of subdirectories should be alphabetized, as should file names. (For extra credit, write your function in such a way that it calls `os.listdir` only one time. Python can manipulate strings faster than it can execute `os.listdir`.)

   2.   Modify the `rotate` function to keep only a fixed number of old versions of the file. The number of versions should be specified in an additional parameter. Excess old versions above this number should be deleted.

Exercise 1 Solution

Here's a simple but inefficient way to solve the problem:

```
import os

def print_dir(dir_path):
    # Loop through directory entries, and print directory names.
    for name in sorted(os.listdir(dir_path)):
        full_path = os.path.join(dir_path, name)
        if os.path.isdir(full_path):
            print(full_path)

    # Loop again, this time printing files.
    for name in sorted(os.listdir(dir_path)):
        full_path = os.path.join(dir_path, name)
```

```
        if os.path.isfile(full_path):
            print(full_path)
```

Here's the extra-credit solution, which only scans and sorts the directory once:

```
import os

def print_dir(dir_path):
    # Loop through directory entries.  Since we sort the combined
    # directory entries first, the subdirectory names and file names
    # will each be sorted, too.
    file_names = []
    for name in sorted(os.listdir(dir_path)):
        full_path = os.path.join(dir_path, name)
        if os.path.isdir(full_path):
            # Print subdirectory names now.
            print(full_path)
        elif os.path.isfile(full_path):
            # Store file names for later.
            file_names.append(full_path)

    # Now print the file names.
    for name in file_names:
        print(name)
```

Exercise 2 Solution

```
import os
import shutil

def make_version_path(path, version):
    if version == 0:
        return path
    else:
        return path + "." + str(version)


def rotate(path, max_keep, version=0):
    """Rotate old versions of file 'path'.

    Keep up to 'max_keep' old versions with suffixes .1, .2, etc.
    Larger numbers indicate older versions."""

    src_path = make_version_path(path, version)
    if not os.path.exists(src_path):
        # The file doesn't exist, so there's nothing to do.
        return

    dst_path = make_version_path(path, version + 1)
    if os.path.exists(dst_path):
        # There already is an old version with this number.  What to do?
```

```
        if version < max_keep - 1:
            # Renumber the old version.
            rotate(path, max_keep, version + 1)
        else:
            # Too many old versions, so remove it.
            os.remove(dst_path)

    shutil.move(src_path, dst_path)
```

Chapter 9

Chapter 9 is a grab-bag of different features. At this point, the best exercise is to test all of the sample code, looking at the output produced and trying to picture how the various ideas introduced here could be used to solve problems that you'd like to solve or would have liked to solve in the past.

Chapter 10

1. How can you get access to the functionality provided by a module?

2. How can you control which items from your modules are considered public? (Public items are available to other Python scripts.)

3. How can you view documentation on a module?

4. How can you find out what modules are installed on a system?

5. What kind of Python commands can you place in a module?

Exercise 1 Solution

You get access to the functionality with a module by importing the module or items from the module.

Exercise 2 Solution

If you define the variable __all__, you can list the items that make up the public API for the module. For example:

```
__all__ = ['Meal','AngryChefException', 'makeBreakfast',
    'makeLunch', 'makeDinner', 'Breakfast', 'Lunch', 'Dinner']
```

If you do not define the __all__ variable (although you should), the Python interpreter looks for all items with names that do not begin with an underscore.

Exercise 3 Solution

The help function displays help on any module you have imported. The basic syntax follows:

```
help(module)
```

Exercise 4 Solution

Look in the directories listed in the variable sys.path for the locations of modules on your system. You need to import the sys module first.

Exercise 5 Solution

Any Python commands can be placed in a module. Your modules can have Python commands, Python functions, Python variables, Python classes, and so on. In most cases, though, you want to avoid running commands in your modules. Instead, the module should define functions and classes and let the caller decide what to invoke.

Chapter 11

1. Modify the scan_pdf.py script to start at the root, or topmost, directory. On Windows, this should be the topmost directory of the current disk (C:, D:, and so on). Doing this on a network share can be slow, so don't be surprised if your G: drive takes a lot more time when it comes from a file server). On UNIX and Linux, this should be the topmost directory (the root directory, /).

2. Modify the scan_pdy.py script to match only PDF files with the text *boobah* in the file name.

3. Modify the scan_pdf.py script to exclude all files with the text *boobah* in the file name.

Exercise 1 Solution

```
import os, os.path
import re

def print_pdf (arg, dir, files):
    for file in files:
        path = os.path.join (dir, file)
        path = os.path.normcase (path)
        if not re.search (r".*\.pdf", path): continue
        if re.search (r" ", path): continue

        print(path)

os.path.walk ('/', print_pdf, 0)
```

Note how this example just changes the name of the directory to start processing with the os.path.walk function.

Exercise 2 Solution

```
import os, os.path
import re
```

```
def print_pdf (arg, dir, files):
    for file in files:
        path = os.path.join (dir, file)
        path = os.path.normcase (path)
        if not re.search (r".*\.pdf", path): continue
        if not re.search (r"boobah", path): continue

        print(path)

os.path.walk ('.', print_pdf, 0)
```

This example just includes an additional test in the `print_pdf` function.

Exercise 3 Solution

```
import os, os.path
import re

def print_pdf (arg, dir, files):
    for file in files:
        path = os.path.join (dir, file)
        path = os.path.normcase (path)
        if not re.search (r".*\.pdf", path): continue
        if re.search (r"boobah", path): continue

        print(path)

os.path.walk ('.', print_pdf, 0)
```

Note how this example simply removes the `not` from the second test.

Chapter 13

1. Experiment with different layouts using different pack orders.

2. Practice modifying the look of your widgets by changing every property.

Chapter 14

1. Suppose you need to write a Python script to store the pizza preferences for the workers in your department. You need to store each person's name along with that person's favorite pizza toppings. Which technologies are most appropriate to implement this script?

   a. Set up a relational database such as MySQL or Sqlite.

   b. Use a dbm module such as dbm.

   c. Implement a web-service-backed rich web application to create a buzzword-compliant application.

2. Rewrite the following example query using table name aliases:

```
select employee.firstname, employee.lastname, department.name
from employee, department
where employee.dept =  department.departmentid
order by employee.lastname desc
```

3. The `terminate.py` script, shown previously, removes an employee row from the employee table; but this script is not complete. There remains a row in the user table for the same person. Modify the `terminate.py` script to delete both the employee and the user table rows for that user.

Exercise 1 Solution

The choice is c, of course. Just joking. The most appropriate choice is b, with the keys being the person's name and the values holding the pizza ingredients, perhaps using commas to separate the different ingredients.

Exercise 2 Solution

You can use any alias you like. Here is one example:

```
select e.firstname, e.lastname, d.name
from employee e, department d
where e.dept =  d.departmentid
order by e.lastname desc
```

Exercise 3 Solution

You don't have to change much. The changes are in **bold:**

```
import sys
import sqlite3

conn=sqlite3.connect('sample_database')
cursor = connection.cursor()

employee = sys.argv[1]

# Query to find the employee ID.
query = """
select e.empid
from user u, employee e
where username=? and u.employeeid = e.empid
"""
cursor.execute(query,(employee,));
for row in cursor.fetchone():
    if (row != None):
        empid = row

# Now, modify the employee.
```

```
cursor.execute("delete from employee where empid=?", (empid,))
cursor.execute("delete from user where employeeid=?", (empid,))

connection.commit()
cursor.close()
connection.close()
```

Chapter 15

1. Given the following configuration file for a Python application, write some code to extract the configuration information using a DOM parser:

```
<?xml version="1.0"?>
<!DOCTYPE config SYSTEM "configfile.dtd">
<config>
  <utilitydirectory>/usr/bin</utilitydirectory>
  <utility>grep</utility>
  <mode>recursive</mode>
</config>
```

2. Given the following DTD, named `configfile.dtd`, write a Python script to validate the previous configuration file:

```
<!ELEMENT config  (utilitydirectory, utility, mode)>
<!ELEMENT utilitydirectory     (#PCDATA)*>
<!ELEMENT utility     (#PCDATA)*>
<!ELEMENT mode (#PCDATA)*>
```

3. Use SAX to extract configuration information from the preceding `config` file instead of DOM.

Exercise 1 Solution

```
from xml.dom.minidom import parse
import xml.dom.minidom

# open an XML file and parse it into a DOM
myDoc = parse('config.xml')
myConfig = myDoc.getElementsByTagName("config")[0]

#Get utility directory
myConfig.getElementsByTagName("utilitydirectory")[0].childNodes[0].data

#Get utility
myConfig.getElementsByTagName("utility")[0].childNodes[0].data

#get mode
myConfig.getElementsByTagName("mode")[0].childNodes[0].data

#.....Do something with data.....
```

Exercise 2 Solution

```python
#!/usr/bin/python

from xml.parsers.xmlproc import xmlval

class docErrorHandler(xmlval.ErrorHandler):
  def warning(self, message):
    print(message)
  def error(self, message):
    print(message)
  def fatal(self, message):
    print(message)

parser=xmlval.XMLValidator()
parser.set_error_handler(docErrorHandler(parser))
parser.parse_resource("configfile.xml")
```

Exercise 3 Solution

```python
#!/usr/bin/python

from xml.sax         import make_parser
from xml.sax.handler import ContentHandler

#begin configHandler
class configHandler(ContentHandler):
  inUtildir = False
  utildir = ''
  inUtil = False
  util = ''
  inMode = False
  mode = ''

  def startElement(self, name, attributes):

    if name == "utilitydirectory":
      self.inUtildir = True

    elif name == "utility":
      self.inUtil = True

    elif name == "mode":
      self.inMode = True

  def endElement(self, name):
    if name == "utilitydirectory":
      self.inTitle = False

    elif name == "utility":
      self.inUtil = False

    elif name == "mode":
      self.inMode = False
```

```
    def characters(self, content):
      if self.inUtildir:
        utildir = utildir + content
      elif self.inUtil:
        util = util + content
      elif self.inMode:
        mode = mode + content
#end configHandler

parser  = make_parser()
parser.setContentHandler(configHandler())
parser.parse("configfile.xml")

#....Do stuff with config information here
```

Chapter 16

1. Distinguish between the following e-mail-related standards: RFC 2822, SMTP, IMAP, MIME, and POP.

2. Write a script that connects to a POP server, downloads all of the messages, and sorts the messages into files named after the sender of the message. (For instance, if you get two e-mails from user@example.com, they should both go into a file "user@example.com").

    What would be the corresponding behavior if you had an IMAP server instead? Write that script, too (use RFC 3501 as a reference).

3. Suppose that you were designing an IRC-style protocol for low-bandwidth embedded devices such as cell phones. What changes to the Python Chat Server protocol would it be useful to make?

4. A feature of IRC not cloned in the Python Chat Server is the /msg command, which enables one user to send a private message to another instead of broadcasting it to the whole room. How could the /msg command be implemented in the Python Chat Server?

5. When does it make sense to design a protocol using a peer-to-peer architecture?

Exercise 1 Solution

RFC 2822 is a file format standard that describes what e-mail messages should look like.

MIME is a file format standard that describes how to create e-mail messages that contain binary data and multiple parts, while still conforming to RFC 2822.

SMTP is a protocol used to deliver an e-mail message to someone else.

POP is a protocol used to pick up your e-mail from your mail server.

IMAP is a newer protocol that does the same job as POP. It's intended to keep the e-mail on the server permanently, instead of just keeping it until you pick it up.

Exercise 2 Solution

Here's a script that uses POP:

```
#!/usr/bin/python
from poplib import POP3
from email import parser

#Connect to the server and parse the response to see how many messages there
#are, as in this chapter's previous POP example.
server = POP3("pop.example.com")
server.user("[user]")
response = server.pass_("[password]")
numMessages = response[response.rfind(', ')+2:]
numMessages = int(numMessages[:numMessages.find(' ')])

#Parse each email and put it in a file named after the From: header of
#the mail.
parser = parser()
openFiles = {}
for messageNum in range(1, numMessages+1):
    messageString = '\n'.join(server.retr(messageNum)[1])
    message = email.parsestr(messageString, True)
    fromHeader = message['From']
    mailFile = openFiles.get(fromHeader)
    if not mailFile:
        mailFile = open(fromHeader, 'w')
        openFiles[fromHeader] = mailFile
    mailFile.write(messageString)
    mailFile.write('\n')
#Close all the files to which we wrote mail.
for openFile in openFiles.values():
    openFile.close()
```

Because IMAP enables you to sort messages into folders on the server, an IMAP version of this script can simply create new mailboxes and move messages into them. Here's a script that does just that:

```
#!/usr/bin/python
from imaplib import IMAP4
import email
import re

#Used to parse the IMAP responses.
FROM_HEADER = 'From: '
IMAP_UID = re.compile('UID ([0-9]+)')

#Connect to the server.
server = IMAP4('imap.example.com')
server.login('[username]', '[password]')
server.select('Inbox')

#Get the unique IDs for every message.
uids = server.uid('SEARCH', 'ALL')[1][0].split(' ')
uidString = ','.join(uids)
```

```
#Get the From: header for each message
headers = server.uid('FETCH', '%s' % uidString,
                      '(BODY[HEADER.FIELDS (FROM)])')
for header in headers[1]:
    if len(header) > 1:
        uid, header = header
        #Parse the IMAP response into a real UID and the value of the
        #'From' header.
        match = IMAP_UID.search(uid)
        uid = match.groups(1)[0]

        fromHeader = header[len(FROM_HEADER):].strip()

        #Create the mailbox corresponding to the person who sent this
        #message. If it already exists the server will throw an error,
        #but we'll just ignore it.
        server.create(fromHeader)

        #Copy this message into the mailbox.
        server.uid('COPY', uid, fromHeader)

#Delete the messages from the inbox now that they've been filed.
server.uid('STORE', uidString, '+FLAGS.SILENT', '(\\Deleted)')
server.expunge()
```

Exercise 3 Solution

In general, move as much text as possible out of the protocol and into the client software, which needs to be downloaded only once. Some specific suggestions:

❑   Send short status codes instead of English sentences: for instance, send "HELLO" instead of "Hello [nickname], welcome to the Python Chat Server!".

❑   Assign a number to every user in the chat room, and send the number instead of their nickname whenever they do something — for instance, broadcast '4 Hello' instead of '<user> Hello' whenever a user sends a message.

❑   Use a compression technique to make the chat text itself take up less bandwidth.

Exercise 4 Solution

The easiest way is to simply define a method 'msgCommand' and let the _parseCommand dispatch it. Here's a simple implementation of msgCommand:

```
def msgCommand(self, nicknameAndMsg):
    "Send a private message to another user."
    if not ' ' in nicknameAndMsg:
        raise ClientError('No message specified.')
    nickname, msg = nicknameAndMsg.split(' ', 1)
    if nickname == self.nickname:
        raise ClientError('What, send a private message to yourself?')
    user = self.server.users.get(nickname)
    if not user:
```

```
        raise ClientError('No such user: %s' % nickname)
    msg = '[Private from %s] %s' % (self.nickname, msg)
    user.write(self._ensureNewline(msg))
```

Exercise 5 Solution

❑   The peer-to-peer architecture is more general than the client-server architecture. The peer-to-peer design of TCP/IP makes it a flexible general-purpose protocol. It's easier to implement a client-server protocol atop TCP/IP than it is to implement a peer-to-peer design on top of a client-server protocol. If you want a general-purpose protocol, try to preserve the peer-to-peer nature of TCP/IP.

❑   Consider using peer-to-peer when it makes sense for a client to download some data from a server and then immediately start serving it to other clients. A peer-to-peer architecture for the distribution of e-mail doesn't make sense, because most e-mail is addressed to one person only. Once that person has downloaded the e-mail, it shouldn't be automatically distributed further. A peer-to-peer architecture for the distribution of newsletters makes more sense.

❑   Peer-to-peer is most useful when you have some way of searching the network. When a network resource doesn't have a single, unambiguous location (the way a file hosted on a web server does), it's more difficult to find what you want, and search facilities are more important.

Chapter 17

1.   Add a new module-level function to the foo module you created earlier in the chapter. Call the function reverse_tuple and implement it so that it accepts one tuple as an argument and returns a similarly sized tuple with the elements in reverse order. Completing this exercise is going to require research on your part because you need to know how to "unpack" a tuple. You already know one way to create a tuple (using Py_BuildValue), but that's not going to work for this exercise, because you want your function to work with tuples of arbitrary size. The Python/C API documentation for tuples (at http://docs.python.org/api/tupleObjects.html) lists all of the functions you need to accomplish this. Be careful with your reference counting!

2.   List and dictionary objects are an extremely important part of nearly all Python applications so it would be useful to learn how to manipulate those objects from C. Add another function to the foo module called dict2list that accepts a dictionary as a parameter and returns a list. The members of the list should alternate between the keys and the values in the dictionary. The order isn't important as long as each key is followed by its value. You'll have to look up how to iterate over the items in the dictionary (hint: look up PyDict_Next) and how to create a list and append items to it (hint: look up PyList_New and PyList_Append).

Chapter 18

1.   Write a function that expresses a number of bytes as the sum of gigabytes, megabytes, kilobytes, and bytes. Remember that a kilobyte is 1024 bytes, a megabyte is 1024 kilobytes, and so on. The number of each should not exceed 1023. The output should look something like this:

```
>>> print(format_bytes(9876543210))
9 GB + 203 MB + 5 KB + 746 bytes
```

2. Write a function that formats an RGB color in the color syntax of HTML. The function should take three numerical arguments: the red, green, and blue color components, each between zero and one. The output is a string of the form #RRGGBB, where RR is the red component as a value between 0 and 255, expressed as a two-digit hexadecimal number, and GG and BB likewise for the green and blue components.

    For example:

    ```
    >>> print(rgb_to_html(0.0, 0.0, 0.0)  # black)
    #000000
    >>> print(rgb_to_html(1.0, 1.0, 1.0)  # white)
    #ffffff
    >>> print(rgb_to_html(0.8, 0.5, 0.9)  # purple)
    #cc80e6
    ```

3. Write a function named `normalize` that takes an array of `float` numbers and returns a copy of the array in which the elements have been scaled such that the square root of the sum of their squares is one. This is an important operation in linear algebra and other fields.

    Here's a test case:

    ```
    >>> for n in normalize((2.2, 5.6, 4.3, 3.0, 0.5)):
    ...     print("%.5f" % n,)
    ...
    0.27513 0.70033 0.53775 0.37518 0.06253
    ```

Exercise 1 Solution

```
def format_bytes(bytes):
    units = (
        ("GB", 1024 ** 3),
        ("MB", 1024 ** 2),
        ("KB", 1024 ** 1),
        ("bytes", 1),
        )
    terms = []
    for name, scale in units:
        if scale > bytes:
            continue
        # Show how many of this unit.
        count = bytes // scale
        terms.append("%d %s" % (count, name))
        # Compute the leftover bytes.
        bytes = bytes % scale
    # Construct the full output from the terms.
    return " + ".join(terms)
```

Exercise 2 Solution

```
def rgb_to_html(red, green, blue):
    # Convert floats between zero and one to ints between 0 and 255.
    red = int(round(red * 255))
    green = int(round(green * 255))
```

```
    blue = int(round(blue * 255))
    # Write out HTML color syntax.
    return "#%02x%02x%02x" % (red, green, blue)
```

Exercise 3 Solution

Solution using a list of numbers:

```
from math import sqrt

def normalize(numbers):
    # Compute the sum of squares of the numbers.
    sum_of_squares = 0
    for number in numbers:
        sum_of_squares += number * number
    # Copy the list of numbers.
    result = list(numbers)
    # Scale each element in the list.
    scale = 1 / sqrt(sum_of_squares)
    for i in xrange(len(result)):
        result[i] *= scale
    return result
```

This very concise `numarray` version works only when called with a `numarray.array` object. You can convert a different array type with `numbers = numarray.array(numbers)`:

```
from math import sqrt
import numarray

def normalize(numbers):
    return numbers / sqrt(numarray.sum(numbers * numbers))
```

Chapter 19

1. Configure the __settings.py file to work with each type of database that Django supports.

2. Explain the MVC and MTV architectures and elaborate on the difference between the two.

3. Create a template that shows the menu from a restaurant and have it display.

4. Working with the same data fields you used in exercise 3, create a model that shows a menu from a restaurant and have Django create the database.

Chapter 20

1. What's a RESTful way to change BittyWiki so that it supports hosting more than one Wiki?

2. Write a web application interface to `WishListBargainFinder.py`. (That is, a web application that delegates to the Amazon Web Services.)

3. The wiki search-and-replace spider looks up every new WikiWord it encounters to see whether it corresponds to a page of the wiki. If it finds a page by that name, that page is processed. Otherwise, nothing happens and the spider has wasted a web service request. How could the web service API be changed so that the spider could avoid those extra web service requests for nonexistent pages?

4. Suppose that, to prevent vandalism, you change BittyWiki so that pages can't be deleted. Unfortunately, this breaks the wiki search-and-replace spider, which sometimes deletes a page before re-creating it with a new name. What's a solution that meets both your needs and the needs of the spider's users?

Exercise 1 Solution

Put the name of the wiki in the resource identifier, before the page name: Instead of "/PageName", it would be "/Wikiname/PageName". This is RESTful because it puts data in the resource identifier, keeping it transparent. Not surprising, this identifier scheme also corresponds to the way the wiki files would be stored on disk.

Exercise 2 Solution

```python
#!/usr/bin/python
import cgi
import cgitb
import os
from WishListBargainFinder import BargainFinder, getWishList
cgitb.enable()

SUBSCRIPTION_ID = '[Insert your subscription ID here.]'
SUBSCRIPTION_ID = 'D8O1OTR1OIMN7'

form = cgi.FieldStorage()
wishListID = form.getfirst('wishlist', '')

args = {'title' : 'Amazon Wish List Bargain Finder',
        'action' : os.environ['SCRIPT_NAME'],
        'wishListID' : wishListID}

print('Content-type: text/html\n')
print('''<html><head><title>%(title)s</title></head>
<form method="get" action="%(action)s">
<h1>%(title)s</h1>
Enter an Amazon wish list ID:
<input name="wishlist" length="13" maxlength="13" value="%(wishListID)s" />
<input type="submit" value="Find bargains"/>
</form>''' % args

if wishListID:
    print('<pre>')
    BargainFinder().printBargains(getWishList(SUBSCRIPTION_ID, wishListID))
    Print('</pre>')

print('</body></html>')
```

Note that this points to an improvement in `BargainFinder`: creating a method that returns the bargain information in a data structure, which can be formatted in plaintext, HTML, or any other way, instead of just printing the plaintext of the bargains.

Exercise 3 Solution

For REST: The BittyWiki web application already outputs rendered HTML because that's what web browsers know how to parse. However, a BittyWiki page served by the web application includes navigation links and other elements besides just a rendering of the page text. If web service users aren't happy scraping away that extraneous HTML to get to the actual page text, or if you want to save bandwidth by not sending that HTML in the first place, there are two other solutions. The first is to have web service clients provide the HTTP Accept header in `GET` requests to convey whether they want the "text/plain" or "text/html" flavor of the resource. The second is to provide different flavors of the same document through different resources. For instance, `/bittywiki-rest.py/PageName.txt` could provide the plaintext version of a page, and `/bittywiki-rest.py/PageName.html` could provide the rendered HTML version of the same page.

For XML-RPC and SOAP, the decision is simpler. Just have clients pass in an argument to `getPage` specifying which flavor of a page they want.

Exercise 4 Solution

This could be fixed by changing the `GET` resource or `getPage` API call to return not only the raw text of the page, but a representation of which WikiWords on the page correspond to existing pages. This could be a list of WikiWords that have associated pages, or a dictionary that maps all of the page's referenced WikiWords to `True` (if the word has an associated page) or `False` (if not). The advantage of the second solution is that it could save the robot side from having to keep its own definition of what constitutes a WikiWord.

Exercise 5 Solution

Create a new API call specifically for renaming a page. In XML-RPC or SOAP, this would be as simple as creating a `rename` function and removing the `delete` function. For a REST API, you might add a capability to the `POST` request that creates a new wiki page: Instead of providing the data, let it name another page of the wiki to use as the data source, with the understanding that the other page will be deleted afterward.

Chapter 21

1. If Python is so cool, why in the world would anyone ever use another programming language such as Java, C++, C#, Basic, or Perl?

2. The Jython interpreter is written in what programming language? The `python` command is written in what programming language?

3. When you package a Jython-based application for running on another system, what do you need to include?

4. Can you use the Python DB driver modules, such as those described in Chapter 14, in your Jython scripts?

5. Write a Jython script that creates a window with a red background using the Swing API.

Exercise 1 Solution

Many organizations have an investment in another programming language. Jython, though, enables you to use Python in a Java environment.

Exercise 2 Solution

Jython is written in Java. The `python` interpreter is written in C.

Exercise 3 Solution

You need to include your Jython scripts, of course, but also the following:

❑ The `jython.jar` Java library

❑ The Jython `Lib` directory

❑ The Jython `cachedir` directory. This directory must be writeable.

Exercise 4 Solution

No, unless the DB drivers are written in Python or Java. Most Python DB drivers are written in C and Python, and so cannot run from Jython (without a lot of work with the Java Native Interface, or JNI). Luckily, the Jython `zxJDBC` module enables you to call on any JDBC driver from your Jython scripts. This opens up your options to allow you to access more databases than those for which you can get Python DB drivers.

Exercise 5 Solution

This is probably the simplest way to create such a window:

```
from javax.swing import JFrame

frame = JFrame(size=(500,100))

# Use a tuple for RGB color values.
frame.background = 255,0,0

frame.setVisible(1)
```

You can get fancy and add widgets such as buttons and labels, if desired.

Online Resources

Python is software available from the Internet, and Python's best day-to-day resources can all be found there. This appendix describes the software that is used in this book and how to install it.

Most Python-related software can be downloaded for free, and much of it can be downloaded as source code and compiled — for those of you interested in doing that for yourself. For those readers who begin with the second part of the book, this may be the challenge you're looking for. However, the broader audience for this book will be glad to know that everything you need to follow along with the book's examples can be installed as packages for the operating systems on which they are supported.

Software

The examples in this book require that your computer have additional software installed, as well as an appropriate and functioning operating system such as Windows 2000, XP, XP Pro, 2003, or Vista; Linux (Red Hat's Fedora RC3 or newer; Debian testing or unstable; or a similarly current distribution), Ubuntu, or Mac OSX.

Following is a brief list of the required software, with a description and the URL from which the software can be downloaded:

❑   **Python:** www.python.org/ is the home page for the Python language. You can find out about all things Python there, including additional online tutorials, introductions to the language, and mailing lists to help you out. The people who write, maintain, change, and use Python are there. You can find a complete, if terse, set of documentation available there as well. The version of software used in this book is Python 3.1.1, and to download it you can click the Download link at the top of the Python home page, or go directly to www.python.org/download/. If you're lucky, maybe you'll find a more recent version of Python there that you can use! At the time of publication, Python 3.1.1 has been released.

For Windows, use the Windows `.msi` installer of the most recent Python 3.1.1 installations.

For Linux systems, install the package provided for your distribution by the maintainer of the distribution (for example, the `.deb` packages from `debian.org` or the `.rpm` packages from `redhat.com`, such as the information at `www.python.org/download/releases/3.1.1/`). For other Linux distributions, see the home page for this book for comments from other readers that the authors will be compiling.

For Mac users, you can find information about Python 3.1.1 on the Mac at `www.python .org/download/mac/`.

❏ **Tkinter:** The GUI programming chapter in this book is written using the `tkinter` interface, which gives you access to the Tcl/TK graphical user interface toolkit from within Python. It is cross-platform and is portable across every system.

For more information, visit `http://wiki.python.org/moin/TkInter`.

❏ **PyUnit:** The unit testing framework for Python. This module provides a systematic way of writing tests within your own source code so that you can verify that your code works as you expect. PyUnit now comes as part of the standard Python library, and is better known as unittest.

PyUnit's home page is at `http://pyunit.sourceforge.net/`.

❏ **MySQL:** A popular and fast open-source relational database system. Python has robust MySQL support:

    ❏ `www.mysql.com/` — This is the home page for mysql.com, the company that maintains the MySQL database.

    ❏ `http://sourceforge.net/projects/mysql-python` — This is the home page of the `mysql-python` module, but there is a minimum amount of documentation online.

❏ **Jython:** An implementation of the Python language in pure Java, Jython provides access to all of the tools available in the commercial Java product space, but it enables you to program using Python as your language. Visit `www.jython.org/`.

❏ **Sqlite3:** For our database section, we used Sqlite3 to create simple database structures. It is a lightweight library written in C that is compliant with the DB-API 2.0. You can find more information at `http://docs.python.org/library/sqlite3.html`.

❏ **Django:** A higher-level web framework for Python, Django is a great tool to get a site up and running in no time. Perfect for database driven sites and web applications, it helps save time by setting up a basic "framework" for the developer. To download and read more about it, visit `http://www.djangoproject.com/`.

For More Information

You can find a lot of Python-related information on the Internet. In addition, you can find information related to the specific components that appear in this book. As a result of the constantly changing nature of Python and its modules, please look at this book's web page at www.wrox.com, and follow the instructions in the introduction to find the specific page for this book. That's the place to go for help with installing software, to download samples and provide feedback to the authors, and to receive help with anything in the book. In addition, you can find more packages and information about the ones that have been mentioned here online at the website for this book.

What's New in Python 3.1

Python is constantly changing in little ways. Python 3.1 has evolved from version 2.6, but it contains important changes. This appendix introduces you to the changes relevant to the topics covered in this book. This means that this is not an exhaustive treatment by any means but only a selection of topics touched on in the book — topics that you may want to know as someone new to Python.

You can find the official list of changes to Python 3.1 at `http://docs.python.org/3.1/whatsnew/3.1.html`. If a newer version of Python is available by the time you read this, you can find the list of changes for that version on the Python website as well.

Print Is Now a Function

In the olden days of yore, print was a statement. With version 3.1, it has reached the major leagues and is now a bonafide function — specifically, `print()`.

Certain APIs Return Views and Iterators

The following no longer return lists, but instead return views and iterators:

❑   The dict methods — `dict.keys()`, `dict.items()`, and `dict.values`. You will also note that `dict.iterkeys()`, `dict.iteritems()`, and `dict.itervalues()` are no longer supported methods in Python.

❑   Both `map()` and `filter()` return iterators instead of lists.

❑   The `range()` method has replaced `xrange()` and is used in the same manner.

❑   The `zip()` method is now used to return an iterator.

Integers

The long data type has been renamed to int (basically the only integral type is now int). It works in roughly the same manner as the long type did. Integers no longer have a limit, and as such, `sys.maxint` has been deprecated. In addition, when dividing numbers such as 2/4, you will be given a float. If you want to have the results truncated, you can still use 2//4.

Unicode and 8-bit

Unicode and 8-bit strings have been replaced with text and binary data. All text is considered to be Unicode, but the encoded Unicode is now presented as strictly binary data. Hence, text is stored in str, whereas data is stored in bytes. If you should ever try to mix these two data types, it will result in the raising of a TypeError. If you want to mix str and bytes, you must convert them. If you wanted to, for instance, convert a byte to a str, you would use `bytes.decode()`. To go from a str to a byte, you would likewise use `str.encode()`.

Another change is how you work with literals. The use of u"..." literals for Unicode text has been removed entirely, while the use of b"..." literals for binary data is still usable.

There are many changes to Unicode and 8-bit — far more than I could cover here. See the section on Unicode and 8-bit at the What's New page here: `http://docs.python.org/dev/py3k/whatsnew/3.1.html`.

Exceptions

The use of raise exception has been replaced. You no longer write it as `raise Exception, "I take exception to that!"` Instead you would use the following:

```
exception("I take exception to that!")
```

Similarly, if you wish to catch an exception, you write it in the following manner:

```
try:
a=int("hotdog")
except ValueError as oops:
print("ValueError has occurred ", oops)
```

This would return the result:

```
ValueError has occurred  invalid literal for int() with base 10: 'hotdog'
```

Other changes to exceptions exist as well. For instance, all exception objects use the __traceback__ attribute to store the value of the traceback. Additionally, the StandardError was removed.

Classes

Old-style classes have been removed entirely from Python 3.1. This leaves us with a simple, single object model based on new-style classes. Definitions for these classes are similar to their previous versions, however, object is now implicitly a superclass.

Comparisons, Operators, and Methods

There are several changes that have been made to the way comparison operators work in Python 3.1. For starters, comparisons have to make logical sense now. For example, you cannot use 0>none. In past versions this would have returned False, but since you cannot compare zero to nothing, it now returns an error.

The function cmp() and the method __cmp__() have both been removed.

As for Operators, they have experienced the following changes:

❑ Unbound methods have been removed.

❑ The operator !=now returns the complete opposite of ==.

❑ Next() has been renamed and is now __next()__

❑ The following have all been removed: __delitem__(), __getslice__(), __hex__(), __members__, __methods__, __oct__(), and __setslice__().

Syntactical Changes

There are many syntax changes in Python 3.1. Again, this list is too much to cover in the limited space we have here, but the following changes are some of the more important ones.

The keywords as, with, True, False, and None have become reserved words.

When working with Metaclasses, it is important to note that the old method

```
Class Example:
    __metaclass__ = Apple
...
```

is no longer valid. Instead you would write:

```
Class Example(metaclass=Apple):
...
```

In addition, the module-global __metaclass__ variable has been removed.

The old method for writing list comprehensions was to use:

```
[for var in example1, example2, example 3]
```

This has now changed to:

```
[for var in (example1, example2, example3)]
```

The old standby <> has been removed and replaced with != .

Both string literals and integer literals have been changed. String literals no longer accept the leading u and U, while integer literals no longer accept the leading l or L.

The keyword exec() has been removed, though it still functions as a function.

Packages and Modules

The following modules have been removed from Python 3.1. Note that this is not a complete list:

- ❑ cfmfile
- ❑ cl
- ❑ md5 and sha (replaced with hashlib)
- ❑ mimetools, MimeWriter, mimify, multifile, and rfc822 (replaced with the e-mail package)
- ❑ posixfile
- ❑ sv
- ❑ timing (use time.clock instead)
- ❑ Canvas
- ❑ commands and popen2 (replaced with subprocess)
- ❑ compiler
- ❑ dircache
- ❑ dl
- ❑ fpformat
- ❑ htmllib (replaced with HTMLParser)
- ❑ mhlib (replaced with mailbox)
- ❑ stat (changed to os.stat)
- ❑ urllib (replaced with urllib2)

In addition, the following modules have been renamed:

- ❑ _winreg is now winreg
- ❑ ConfigParser is now configparser
- ❑ copy_reg is now copyreg
- ❑ Queue is now queue
- ❑ SocketServer is now socketserver
- ❑ markupbase is now _markupbase
- ❑ repr is now reprlib
- ❑ test.test_support is now test.support

To make things simpler, Python 3.1 has also gathered some similar modules and grouped them into a single package. They are listed below:

- ❑ dbm now contains: anydbm, dbhash, dbm, dumbdbm, gdbm, and whichdb.
- ❑ html now contains: HTMLParser andhtmlentitydefs.
- ❑ http now contains: httplib, BaseHTTPServer, CGIHTTPServer, SimpleHTTPServer, Cookie, and cookielib.
- ❑ tkinter now contains every Tkinter-related module with the sole exception of turtle.
- ❑ urllib now contains urllib, urllib2, urlparse, and robotparse.
- ❑ xmlrpc now contains xmlrpclib, DocXMLRPCServer, and SimpleXMLRPCServer.

Builtins

The following builtins were removed:

- ❑ `apply()`
- ❑ `callable()`
- ❑ `coerce()`
- ❑ `execfile()`
- ❑ `the file type`
- ❑ `reduce()`
- ❑ `reload()`
- ❑ `dict.has_key()`

In addition, `raw_input()` has been changed to input().

The 2to3 Tool

While not an end all be all to converting your Python 2x code to 3x, the 2to3 tool can certainly help in many areas. Basically, what the program does is take your existing code and apply a set of fixers to it, transforming old code into new. For instance, if you were to run 2to3 on the following code:

```
print "Hi, my name is James and I am a Pythonaholic"

It would convert it to:
print("Hi, my name is James and I am a Pythonaholic")
```

Pretty nifty right? There are, of course, many caveats for using the tool. First and foremost, the code you run it against must work properly, so you will want to rigorously test your Python 2x code to ensure there are no errors. Next, you must note that 2to3 will not fix everything; there are some things it has not been programmed to convert. For these things, 2to3 will print a warning, which you will need to manually change.

For more information on using 2to3 and documentation on its fixers, visit the Python documentation at http://docs.python.org/dev/py3k/library/2to3.html#to3-reference.

Glossary

The following terms are used in the book and are presented here for your convenience.

127.0.0.1 A special IP address used to denote "this computer." See also localhost.

Anonymous Anonymous functions and variables are not bound to names. Examples of this are the functions created by the lambda function, a list, or a tuple created but never associated with a name.

Base64 An encoding strategy defined by MIME that escapes an entire string as a whole. More efficient than quoted-printable for binary data.

BitTorrent A peer-to-peer protocol that distributes the cost of hosting a file among all the parties downloading it.

Call stack When code is executing, the call stack is the list of functions that your code has executed to reach that point in the program. As functions or methods are entered, the location in the file is noted along with the parameters that the function was called with, and the entry point is marked in the call stack. When a function is exited, its entry in the call stack is removed. When an exception occurs, a stack trace is printed that indicates where in the program the problem occurred.

CGI The Common Gateway Interface: A standard for web servers that makes it easy to expose web interfaces to scripts.

Class (1) A class is a definition that can be used to create objects. A particular class definition contains the declarations of the data and the methods that objects that are instances of that particular class will have available to them. In Python, functions that appear within the context of a class are considered to be methods. (2) An object holds data as well as the methods that operate on that data. A class defines what data is stored and what methods are available. Python is a little looser than most programming languages, such as Java, C++, or C#, in that Python lets you break rules enforced in other languages. For example, Python, by default, lets you access data inside a class. This does violate some of the concepts of object-oriented programming but with good reason: Python aims first and foremost to be practical.

Client-server Describes an architecture in which one actor (the server) is a repository for information requested and acted upon by other actors (the clients).

Comment Comments are text in a program that Python does not pay attention to. At any point outside of a string where a hash mark (#) appears, from that point until the end of the line, the Python interpreter ignores all text.

Content type A MIME concept used to indicate the type of a file being sent encoded inside an e-mail message. Also used by web servers to indicate the type of file being served.

DB API A Python API for accessing databases. The neat thing about this API is that you can use the same Python code to work with any database for which there is a DB-compliant driver. This includes Oracle, DB2, and so on. The only differences in your code will likely be the code to connect to the database, which differs by vendor.

DBM Short for database manager, DBM libraries provide a means to persist Python dictionaries.

Dictionary A data type in Python that is indexed by an arbitrary value that is set by the programmer. The value can be any kind of Python object. The index is called the "key" and the object that a key references is referred to as its "value."

DNS Domain Name System. A service that runs on top of TCP and resolves hostnames (wrox.com) to IP addresses (208.215.179.178).

Document Model A way of describing the vocabulary and structure of a document. Defines the data elements that will be present in a document, what relationship they have to one another, and how many of them are expected.

DOM The Document Object Model, a tree-based API recommendation from the W3C for working with XML documents.

DTD Document Type Definition. A specification for producing a Document Model.

Dynamic port See Ephemeral port.

Encapsulation Encapsulation is the idea that a class can hide the internal details and data necessary to perform a certain task. A class holds the necessary data, and you are not supposed to see that data under normal circumstances. Furthermore, a class provides a number of methods to operate on that data. These methods can hide the internal details, such as network protocols, disk access, and so on. Encapsulation is a technique to simplify your programs. At each step in creating your program, you can write code that concentrates on a single task. Encapsulation hides the complexity.

Encryption The act of hiding information so that it is difficult or impossible to recover without a secret password. Data is encrypted when it is recoverable. Data that is scrambled and unrecoverable should be thought of as lost instead.

Ephemeral port   High-numbered IP ports are often created to receive data over TCP/IP as part of a particular socket connection. Ephemeral ports are administered by the operating system, and have a lifetime of a single socket connection.

Escape sequences   Special characters that begin with the backslash, such as \n for a newline.

Fault   A term used in web services to denote an error condition. Similar to Python's exceptions, and generally implemented the same way as exceptions in Python are.

Float   A floating-point number is a number with a fractional or decimal component. Fractions can be represented as decimal values using a float value. When arithmetic is done with a float and an integer, the integer will be promoted to being a float.

Function   A function is a collection of code defined using a name, and which is invoked through that name.

Header   An item of metadata found both in e-mail messages and in HTTP requests and responses. A header line consists of a key and value separated by a colon and a space. For instance: "Subject: Hello".

Hexadecimal   Base 16 notation, where the numbers are from 0 through 15, and are represented by the numbers 0–9. Once single digits are exhausted, the letters A–F are used. So the number 11 in hex is B.

hostname   A human-readable identifier for a computer on an IP network, for instance: wrox.com. Hostnames are administered through DNS.

HTTP body   The data portion of an HTTP request or response.

HTTP headers   The metadata portion of an HTTP request or response: a series of key-value pairs. HTTP defines some standard headers, and CGI defines some more: applications can define their own.

HTTP   HyperText Transfer Protocol, the protocol devised to let web browsers and web servers communicate.

HTTP request   The string sent by an HTTP client to the server, requesting some operation on some resource.

HTTP response   The string sent by an HTTP server to a client, in response to an HTTP request. In REST terminology, it contains either a representation of a resource or a document describing action taken on a resource.

HTTP status code   A numeric code used in an HTTP response to denote the status of the corresponding request. Forty of these are defined in the HTTP standard.

HTTP verb   A string used in an HTTP request to describe what the client wants to do to a resource (for instance, retrieve a representation of it or modify it).

Idempotent   An idempotent action has no side effects. A term taken from mathematics: Multiplying a number by 1 is an idempotent action. So should be calling an object's accessor method or (in REST) making an HTTP GET request.

Imaginary number   A special number that acts like a float but cannot be mixed freely with floats or integers. If they are mixed, a complex number is the result, not an imaginary number.

IMAP   The Internet Message Access Protocol. Also known as IMAP4. A protocol for retrieving and managing mail. IMAP4 intends for you to store your mail on the server. See also POP.

Infinite loop   A loop that has no termination clause, such as "while True:". Often, infinite loops are an accidental situation, but they can be useful as long as there are actions that will happen, and there is code being executed. One example is a server waiting for connections.

Inheritance   Inheritance means that a class can inherit, or gain access to, data and methods defined in a parent class. This just follows common sense in classifying a problem domain. For example, a rectangle and a circle are both shapes. In this case, the base class would be Shape. The Rectangle class would then inherit from Shape, as would the Circle class. Inheritance allows you to treat objects of both the Rectangle and Circle classes as Shapes, meaning you can write more generic code. For the most part, the base class should be general and the subclasses specialized. Oftentimes inheritance is called specialization.

Input/Output   An umbrella term that covers any kind of operation that reads or writes data. Writing to screen, inputting from the keyboard, and network connections are all examples of Input/Output.

Integer   Whole numbers, without a fractional or decimal component.

I/O   See Input/Output.

IP address   The location of a computer on an IP network. For instance, 208.215.179.178.

IP   The Internet Protocol. Connects networks based on different technologies (for instance, Ethernet and wireless) into a single network.

IRC   Internet Relay Chat. A protocol for online chat rooms.

Iterator   Iterators are objects that you can use in certain contexts that generate a sequence of outputs. Unlike sequence objects, an iterator like xrange doesn't have to return a finite list. The object can continue to create return values when its next method is invoked. Iterators can be used with `for` loops.

J2EE   Java 2 Enterprise Edition, a set of standards for writing enterprise-worthy Java applications. There are no real corresponding Python standards, but the Twisted framework and others provide enterprise-worthy features for Python.

JVM   Java Virtual Machine, the runtime engine of the Java platform. The `java` command runs Java applications similar to the way the `Python` command runs Python applications.

Jython   An implementation of Python written in the Java language that runs on top of the Java platform.

List   A list is a type of sequence, as well as being an iterator. It is similar to a tuple, except that it can be modified after it is created. A list is created by using the square brackets ([]).

localhost   A special hostname used to denote "this computer." See also 127.0.0.1.

Loop   A loop is a form of repetition where a set of operations is performed, and the operations are repeated until a set of conditions are set.

Method   A method is a function inside the context of an object (it is also called a method when you write it inside of a class). It has automatic access to all of the data within the object that it was invoked from.

MIME   Multipurpose Internet Mail Encoding. A set of standards that make it possible to send multiple files and international and binary data through e-mail, while still complying with RFC 2822.

Module   A module is a collection of code within a file. Modules can contain functions, named variables, and classes. When a module is used in a program, it is made available using the import built-in word, and it lives within a scope named after the module. So in a module named `"mymodule"` the function `"myfunction"` would be called by calling "`mymodule.myfunction()`". This can be modified by the way the module is imported; importing the modifiers `"from"` and `"as"` can modify the behavior of import so that the module is seen as having a different name. The current module can be found by looking at the variable name "`__name__`", which is created locally in each module's scope. If `__name__` is "`__main__`" then the scope is currently the top-level module — that is, the program being run.

Module   A module is just a Python source file. A module can contain variables, classes, functions, and any other element available in your Python scripts.

Multipart message   A MIME message that contains more than one "document" (for instance, a text message and an image).

Object   An object is an instance of a class. Objects contain data and methods that are defined in the class. Multiple objects of the same class may exist in the same program at the same time, using different names. Each object has data that will be different from other objects of the same type. Objects are bound to a name when they are created.

Octal   Base 8 notation, where the numbers range from 0–7.

Package   A package is a grouping of modules in a directory that contains a file called `__init__.py`. Together, all the files in the directory can act together to implement a combined package that appears, when it's used, to act like a single module. The module can contain subdirectories that can also contain modules. The package offers an organizational structure for distributing more complex program structures, and it also allows for the conditional inclusion of code that may only work on one platform (for instance, if one file could not work except on a Mac OS X system, it could be put into its own file and called only after the correct platform had been verified).

Peer-to-peer   Describes an architecture in which all actors have equal standing.

Polymorphism   Polymorphism means that subclasses can override methods for more specialized behavior. For example, a Rectangle and a Circle are both Shapes. You may define a set of common operations, such as move and draw, that should apply to all shapes. But the draw method for a Circle will obviously be different from the draw method for a Rectangle. Polymorphism allows you to name both methods draw and then call these methods as if the Circle and the Rectangle were both Shapes (which they are, at least in this example).

POP   The Post Office Protocol. Also known as POP3. A protocol for downloading e-mail from a server. POP intends that you delete the mail from the server after downloading it. See also IMAP.

Port   Along with an IP address, a port number identifies a particular service on an Internet network.

Protocol   A convention for structuring the data sent between parties on a network. HTTP and TCP/IP are examples of protocols.

Protocol stack   A suite of protocols in which the higher-level protocols delegate to the lower-level ones.

Quoted-printable   An encoding strategy defined by MIME that escapes each non-US ASCII character individually. More efficient than Base64 for text that contains mostly U.S. ASCII characters.

Quotes   In Python, strings are defined by being text within quotes. Quotes can be either single ('), double ("), or triple (" " " or ' ' '). If a string is started with a single quote, it must be ended with a single quote. A string begun with a double quote must be terminated with a double quote. A string begun with a triple quote must be terminated with a triple quote of the same kind (' ' ' must be matched by ' ' ', and " " " must be matched by " " "). Single and double quotes function in exactly the same way. Triple quotes are special because they can enclose multi-line strings (strings that contain newlines).

Range   Range generates a list of numbers, by default from zero to the number it is given as a parameter, by one. It can also be instructed to start at a number other than zero and to increment in steps rather than by one.

RDBMS   Relational Database Management System. See Relational database.

Relational database   In a relational database, data is stored in tables — two-dimensional data structures. Each table is made up of rows, also called records. Each row in turn is made up of columns. Typically, each record holds the information pertaining to one item, such as an audio CD, a person, a purchase order, an automobile, and so on.

Representation   In REST terminology, a depiction of a resource. When you request a resource, what you get back is a representation. One resource may have multiple representations. For instance, a single document resource may have HTML, PostScript, and plain-text representations.

Resource   In REST terminology, an object that can be accessed and/or manipulated from the Web. Can take a number of forms: For instance, it may be a document located on the server, a row in a database, or even a physical object (such as an item you order in an online store).

Resource identifier   A string that uniquely identifies a resource. Generally equivalent to a URL. One resource may have multiple identifiers.

REST   REpresentational State Transfer, a name for the architecture of the World Wide Web.

RESTfulness   An informal metric of how well a web application conforms to the design.

RFC 2822   The standard format for Internet e-mail messages. Requires that e-mail messages be formatted in U.S. ASCII.

Robot   A script that makes HTTP requests while not under the direct control of a human.

RSS   Rich Site Summary, or RDF Site Summary. An XML-based format for syndicating content.

SAX   The Simple API for XML. A stream-based XML parser.

Scope   Names of data and code; variable names, class names, function names, and so on, which have different levels of visibility. Names that are visible within a function or method are either in their scope or come from a scope that is at a level above the scope of the operation accessing it.

Sequence   A sequence is a category of data types. A sequence can refer to any type of object that contains an ordered numerical index, starting from zero, which contains references to values. Each value referenced from an index number can be any Python object that could normally be referenced by a variable name. Elements in a sequence are de-referenced by using the square brackets after the name of the sequence. So for a sequence named "seq," the fourth element is de-referenced when you see "seq[3]". It is 3 instead of 4 because the first index number of the sequence is 0.

SMTP   Simple Mail Transport Protocol. The standard protocol for sending Internet e-mail.

SOAP   Originally stood for Simple Object Access Protocol. A standard for making web service calls, similar to XML-RPC but more formally defined.

Socket   A two-way connection over an IP network. Sockets allow programmers to treat network connections like files.

Spider   Robot that, given a starting web page, follows links to find other web pages to operate on. Most search engines have implemented spiders.

SQL   Structured query language, pronounced either sequel or S-Q-L. Language used to access relational databases.

SSL   Secure Socket Layer. A protocol that runs between TCP/IP and some other protocol (such as SMTP or HTTP), providing end-to-end encryption.

Stack trace   See Call stack.

String   Any combination of letters or numbers enclosed in quotation marks (either single, double, or a series of three single or double quotes together). Strings are made up of multiple instances of characters (a character is a data type that holds a single letter or number enclosed in quotation marks). In Python 3.1 there are two types of strings: str and bytes. The str type holds text, while the bytes type holds data. If you wish to blend the two types together, you must explicitly convert between the two. If you want to convert a string to a byte you would use str.encode(); to go from a byte to a string you would use bytes. decode().

TCP/IP   A term used to describe a very common protocol stack: TCP running on top of IP.

TCP   Transport Control Protocol: Makes reliable, orderly communication possible between two points on an IP network.

Tuple   A tuple is a type of sequence as well as an iterator. A tuple is similar to a list, except that once a tuple has been defined, the number of elements, and the references to elements in it, cannot be changed (however, if it references an object whose data you can change, such as a list or a dictionary, the data within that other type can still be changed). Tuples are created with the parentheses "()". When you create a tuple that has only one element, you must put a comma after that single element. Failing to do this will create a string.

UID   Unique ID. Used in a variety of contexts to denote an ID that is unique and stable over time.

Unicode   Unicode is a system for encoding strings so that the original letters can be determined, even if someone using a different character encoding, by default, reads that string later. (Think of someone using a computer localized for Russia trying to read a document written in Hebrew — internally, characters can be thought of as numbers in a lookup table, and with different languages and character sets, character #100 in either character set is likely to be different.)

User agent   A web browser or HTTP-enabled script.

Variable   A variable is what data bound to a name is called. The name "variable" usually refers to the basic types and not more complex objects. This is true even though integers, floats, imaginary numbers, and strings are all objects in Python. This way of thinking is a convention that carries over from other languages where the distinction is made.

Web application   A program that exposes its interface through HTTP instead of through a command-line or GUI interface.

Web service   A web application designed for use by HTTP-enabled scripts instead of human beings with web browsers.

Well-known port   IP port numbers between 0 and 1023 are well-known ports. Popular services like web servers tend to run on well-known ports, and services running on well-known ports often run with administrator privileges.

Whitespace   Whitespace refers to the names of the characters that you can't see when you are typing or reading. Newlines, spaces, and tab characters are all whitespace. Python pays attention to whitespaces at the beginnings of lines, and it is aware of newlines at the ends of lines, except inside list or tuple definitions, and except inside triple-quoted strings.

wiki   A web application that allows its users to create and edit web pages through a web interface.

WSDL   Web Services Description Language, a way of representing method calls in XML.

XML   eXtensible Markup Language. A specification for creating structured markup languages with customized vocabularies.

XML-RPC   The RPC stands for Remote Procedure Call. XML-RPC is a standard for making web service calls. It defines a way of representing simple data structures in XML, sending data structures over HTTP as arguments to a function call, and getting another data structure back as a return value.

XML schema   A specification for producing a Document Model.

XML validation   The process of checking that an XML document is well formed and conforms to its document model.

XML wellformedness   The process of checking that an XML document conforms to the XML specification.

Xrange   Xrange generates an xrange object, which is an iterable object that behaves similarly to a list, but because a list is not created there is no additional memory used when larger ranges of numbers are required.

XSL-FO   Extensible Style Language Formatting Objects. Markup language for graphical display. Commonly used for producing documents for final presentation.

XSLT   Extensible Style Language for Transformations. A programming language for transforming XML.

Index